DICTIONARY
OF TELELITERACY

DICTIONARY OF

TELELITERACY

. . . .

Television's 500 Biggest
Hits, Misses, and Events

DAVID
BIANCULLI

CONTINUUM · NEW YORK

1996
The Continuum Publishing Company
370 Lexington Avenue, New York, NY 10017

Printed in the United States of America

Library of Congress Cataloging-in-Publication Data

Bianculli, David.
Dictionary of teleliteracy: television's 500 biggest hits,
misses, and events / David Bianculli,
p.   cm.
Includes bibliographical references and index.
ISBN 0-8264-0577-0 (hardcover)
1. Television programs—United States—Encyclopedias. I. Title.
PN1992.3.U5B5 1996
791.45'75'0973—dc20   95–52615
CIP

To Virgil
and Reba Bianculli,
with love

CONTENTS

· ·

D

E

F

G

M

N

O

P

Q

R

S

T

U

V

W

INTRODUCTION

. . . .

Perhaps the best way to introduce this book is to begin by discussing two others: *Bartlett's Familiar Quotations*, edited by Justin Kaplan, and *The Dictionary of Cultural Literacy*, written by E. D. Hirsch, Jr., Joseph F. Kett, and James Trefil.

In the current (sixteenth) edition of *Bartlett's Familiar Quotations*, only two television programs are considered significant and familiar enough to justify inclusion in the same compendium as selected quotations from Geoffrey Chaucer and William Shakespeare. One is *Sesame Street*, with two citations; the other is *Monty Python's Flying Circus*, with three. The Cookie Monster's "Me want cookie!," Kermit the Frog's "It's not easy bein' green," and the Python troupe's parrot sketch, lumberjack song, and "stuck-up stickybeaks" line—according to *Bartlett* general editor Kaplan, that's it for TV.

In *The Dictionary of Cultural Literacy*, the current (second) edition of which was published in 1995, the authors define cultural literacy as "the names, phrases, events, and other items that are familiar to most literate Americans." Yet television programs and personalities rarely make the cut, and when they do, the reasons for their inclusion seem arbitrary or downright puzzling. In the first, more telling *Dictionary of Cultural Literacy* edition from 1988, Bob Hope makes the list, but Johnny Carson doesn't. *Roots* does, but *Holocaust* doesn't. Perhaps these can be explained away by the fact that Hope's road-movie career and radio stardom make his subsequent TV popularity "acceptable," and that *Roots* is included because it is based on a book—but the story dramatized in *Holocaust* is a made-for-TV original.

But that doesn't explain why there's an entry in *The Dictionary of Cultural Literacy* for *Star Trek*. Once you make room for *Star Trek*, how do you ignore *The Honeymooners?* Yet that book does—and, to add insult to injury, its authors peruse the entire fifty-year history of television and come up with only one TV character important enough to cite as an individual reference. Look for it under "Bunker, Archie."

Well, I hate to be the deBunker of such efforts, but I believe television deserves better treatment—and much, much more of it.

Here, then, is my own attempt to compile an admittedly subjective, hardly exhaustive *Dictionary of Teleliteracy*. In this book's predecessor, 1992's *Teleliteracy: Taking Television Seriously,* I made the case for TV in general, and defined teleliteracy as an awareness and appreciation of the medium's most popular or meaningful offerings. In this book, my goal is to get down to specifics, and to annotate and analyze the five hundred most memorable events and programs from the first fifty years of postwar television history: 1945 to 1995. Memorable doesn't necessarily mean good; if it did, this volume would be a lot thinner. Conversely, as with any other art form, excellence by itself is no guarantee of mass acceptance or awareness. It kills me, for example, to look at my own list of programs that just missed the cutoff point, and to see such potent television "castoffs" as variety specials by Fred Astaire and Barbra Streisand, and Bette Midler in *Gypsy,* and *Frank's Place,* and the collapse of the Berlin Wall (great event, not-so-great TV coverage). It makes me angry that there's no room in this book for *My So-Called Life* or *The Trials of Life,* but that's life. And if it makes you angry, too—if you become incensed that I could include *The A-Team* yet exclude *Absolutely Fabulous*— that is an argument, and a debate, it is my pleasure, as well as my intention, to instigate.

A few final notes. One, I have omitted commercials and music videos and other short-form TV from consideration here. Separate books could be written about the five hundred most memorable videos or TV ads, and I'd love to read those books; I just wouldn't want to write them. The same goes for sporting events, except for the attention-demanding World Series and Super Bowls. Two, this book is intended to complement, rather than replace, the more encyclopedic TV collections. Three, think of the following five hundred entries as a compendium of our shared television memories—programs and events that have stood, or are likely to stand, the test of time. In my argument for teleliteracy, consider this Exhibit A. And B, and C. . . .

···

ABC News Nightline. See *Nightline*.

ABC World News Tonight. *1978–   , ABC*. The early history of ABC News is complicated but undistinguished. ABC-TV got into the news business in August 1948, two years after both NBC and CBS, with a fifteen-minute nightly combination of news and commentary called, fittingly, *News and Views*. H. R. Baukhage and Jim Gibbons anchored on weeknights, and Pauline Frederick did solo duty on Sunday—making her the almost forgotten first female news anchor in TV history. In 1952, much more ambitiously, ABC presented four newscasters in an expanded prime-time program called *All Star News*. With Frederick as the biggest name, it should have been called "No Star News," but, with its leisurely combination of news, analysis, and features, it deserves credit as a low-tech forerunner of both *Nightline* and *The MacNeil/Lehrer NewsHour*. ABC scheduled *All Star News* on various nights, at various lengths, and in various time slots, but wherever the show wound up, it wound up as a massive ratings failure. Why? Because the network kept sending *All Star News* on kamikaze missions, scheduling it directly opposite some of the most popular shows on television. There was an hour of *All Star News* against *The Ed Sullivan Show* and *The Colgate Comedy Hour* on Sundays, for example, and an hour opposite *Arthur Godfrey and His Friends* on Wednesdays, and a half-hour opposite *You Bet Your Life* and *The George Burns and Gracie Allen Show* on Thursdays. By the fall of 1953, *All Star News* was history, replaced by a fifteen-minute nightly newscast, *John Daly and the News*, hosted by the man who had just landed a job at rival network CBS, moderating a new TV game show called *What's My Line?* Daly held both jobs simultaneously until 1960, at which time a procession of news anchors came and went, beginning with John Cameron Swayze, a news pioneer for NBC back with *Camel News Caravan* in the forties. The most famous of the short-timers in the sixties were Peter Jennings, solo anchor of the ABC evening newscast from 1963–65, and Frank Reynolds, solo anchor in 1968 and coanchor, with Howard K. Smith, in 1969. In 1970, Smith and Harry Reasoner teamed up for five years, at which time Reasoner went solo for a season before being paired, in an infamously uncomfortable TV news "marriage," with Barbara Walters in October 1976. Two years later, ABC News President Roone Arledge renamed the newscast *World News Tonight*, and teamed Walters with three other anchors, each reporting from a different national bureau; Walters soon stepped down to concentrate on interviews and specials, establishing a basic "troika" design for the evening newscast, with duties divided among Reynolds in Washington, Jennings in London, and Max Robinson in Chicago. It was during this period that Reynolds, chief among equals, anchored ABC's coverage of the March 1981 attempted assassination of President Ronald Reagan and made a memorable—and understandable—outburst after getting conflicting information that White House press secretary James Brady was (a) dead and (b) alive. In a rare show of on-air emotion, Reynolds shouted, "Let's get it nailed down, somebody!" In 1983, after Reynolds died, the "troika" format was abandoned and Jennings took over; the newscast was retitled *ABC World News Tonight with Peter Jennings*. By the end of the decade, thanks largely to the smooth professionalism of Jennings and his talented cadre of correspondents, ABC led the evening news ratings race for the first time in history. Halfway through the nineties, with such impressive offshoots as *Nightline* and *This Week with David Brinkley*, once-laughable ABC has established itself as the broadcast network with the most ambitious, talented, and popular news organization—at long last, a true "All Star News."

Academy Awards, The. *1953–60, NBC; 1961–70, ABC; 1971–75, NBC; 1976–   , ABC*. The first nationally televised Oscars were in 1953 (Los Angeles, understandably, covered the awards ceremony on local TV for years before that), with Bob Hope as host. The film community was rather disdainful of TV in those days, and the feeling often was mutual. When the show threatened to run overtime in 1954, NBC cut off Best Actor winner William Holden (for *Stalag 17)* in midspeech, and didn't even bother hanging around for the Best Picture Award, which went to *From Here to Eternity*. Since then, many Oscar telecasts have seemed to *last* an eternity. As for posterity, forget about the winners and losers (who remembers?)—and the acceptance speeches, too, except for Sally Field's "You like me, you really like me!" outburst after winning Best Actress for *Places in the Heart* at the 1985 ceremony. Even though *The Academy Awards* are the most popular of all awards shows on TV (and even *that's* relative, because only the 1970 show ranks among TV's all-time Top 40 programs), there are only three Oscar categories that seem to count, and stick, with viewers: Wildest Unscripted Stunt, Most Outrageous Designer Outfit, and Most Horrendous Production Number. In the first category, Wildest Unscripted Stunt, world-class honors would have to include the protest speech by Sacheen Littlefeather, who was dispatched by Marlon Brando in 1973 to accept his Best Actor Oscar for *The Godfather* (and, in the process, scold the Academy for its portrayals of Native Americans), and the fleeting but unforgettable appearance by Robert Opel the following year. He's the guy who, in celebration of the "streaking" craze popular at the time, ran onstage naked behind an unsuspecting (and fully clothed) David Niven. You had to be there—at least to see the complete display of theater in the raw, because the TV camera caught Opel only from the waist up. For the record, Niven's ad-libbed retort was as classy as his disapproving double take: "Isn't it fascinating," Niven asked, "that probably the only laugh this man will ever get in his life is by stripping off his clothes and showing his shortcomings?" For

Most Outrageous Designer Outfit, every Oscar viewer can fill in his or her own "Fashion Victim" list (although no list would be complete without at least one appearance by Cher). And for Most Horrendous Production Number, I'd like to put forth this nomination for the all-time worst: 1989's opening number, in which Snow White danced and sang with Rob Lowe. It was a Lowe point for the Oscars—and, for Lowe himself, the second most embarrassing thing he'd ever been caught doing on video. But out of something that bad came something really good: the following year, host Billy Crystal came up with a new way to open the Oscars, and provided a witty musical montage that, for four years, became a minitradition, and maxitreat, of each annual telecast. (Well, *almost* every telecast; the 1993 effort was, by Crystal's own high standards, way below par.) Whoopi Goldberg hosted in 1994, and was no improvement; David Letterman took over in 1994, and did so poorly, at least by his own standards, that he ridiculed himself for months afterward. The Academy, taking Letterman's self-abuse to heart, rehired Goldberg for 1996, leaving only one major winner during the post-Crystal Oscar era: Tom Hanks, who won consecutive Best Actor Academy Awards for *Philadelphia* and *Forrest Gump* and, on both occasions, delivered literate and passionate thank-yous that made Oscar acceptance speeches worthwhile again. I liked him, I really liked him.

Addams Family, The. *1964–66, ABC*. The theme song of this show has something in common with the theme of *The Twilight Zone:* in four brief notes, it conjures up an entire, eerie world. (And, in this case, almost requires listeners to snap their fingers twice in response.) Based on the Charles Addams cartoons in *The New Yorker, The Addams Family* was like a Halloween version of *The Beverly Hillbillies*. Both shows were about eccentric outsiders whose family values were wildly different from those of their neighbors—neighbors who invariably treated them with disdain. Yet these unwelcome oddballs always ended up enjoying the upper hand. In the case of TV's *The Addams Family,* one of those hands belonged to the disembodied Thing, whose digital derring-do was only one key element of the series. Others included the giant butler Lurch (Ted Cassidy) and his low-groan "You rang?" catch phrase; the hairy, high-pitched Cousin Itt; the aforementioned theme song by composer Vic Mizzy, who not only concocted the playful lyrics ("The house is a museum / When people come to see 'em / They really are a scre-am / The Addams Family"), but sang them as well; and, memorably, the excited sexual state of John Astin's Gomez whenever Carolyn Jones's Morticia spoke French. Few TV couples, then or since, exhibited as much happiness and mutual infatuation as the Addamses. *The Addams Family* was revived as one of the earliest TV reunion telemovies, 1977's *Halloween with the Addams Family,* and remade again in 1991, as a big-budget theatrical film starring Raul Julia as Gomez and Anjelica Huston as Morticia (both actors were wonderful, as was young Christina Ricci as morbid daughter Wednesday). The filmmakers claimed the movie relied more on the original Addams cartoons than the TV series for its inspiration, but few people familiar with both would buy that. The amorous heat of Gomez and Morticia—and, indeed, even the *names* of Gomez and

Morticia—are just a few of the things taken straight from the video version. (The characters in Addams's *New Yorker* cartoons were nameless; the cartoonist provided a list of suggested names at the TV producer's request.) *The Addams Family* movie did well enough at the boxoffice to generate a 1993 sequel called *Addams Family Values*. Both films were funny and clever, but both films also managed to mangle one of the most lovable aspects of the TV series. In the *Addams Family* movies, thanks to state-of-the-art special effects, Thing was shown moving freely around the set, letting its fingers do the walking. It's an example of the movies messing up a perfect TV concept, because part of the fun in the TV version was imagining what, if anything, the Thing's hand was attached to. You really have to hand it to Ted Cassidy, by the way: on the TV version, he did double duty as Lurch and Thing for the entire run of the series, unless both Lurch and Thing were on camera at the same time. In such cases, Thing was played by a hand-in.

Admiral Broadway Revue. See *Your Show of Shows.*

Adventures of Jonny Quest, The. *1964–65, ABC.* After bringing *The Flintstones* and *The Jetsons* to prime time, ABC animatedly placed another William Hanna-Joseph Barbera cartoon series on its schedule—and though *The Adventures of Jonny Quest,* like *The Jetsons,* lasted only a season, it, too, enjoyed a long afterlife, thanks to years of Saturday morning reruns as the retitled *Jonny Quest.* Jonny, the eleven-year-old globe-trotting son of a famous scientist, arguably was an early prototype for *Young Indiana Jones.* His best friend, unless you count his dog Bandit, was an Indian buddy named Hadji, usually employed as unenlightened comic relief. Such was the residual effect of this animated adventure series that, in 1993, The Cartoon Network presented a marathon of all thirty-five *Jonny Quest* episodes in what it called a special *Re-Quest Fest,* while The USA Network presented an all-new movie-length cartoon sequel, *Jonny's Golden Quest.* It was every bit as good as the original, which in no way should be misconstrued as a compliment. However, there is one memorable claim to fame for the original *Jonny Quest.* The voice of the title character was provided by a young actor named Tim Matthieson, who changed his last name to Matheson and grew up to star as Otter in *National Lampoon's Animal House.* The animated Jonny was growing up also: in 1995, TNT presented another new movie-length cartoon feature, *Jonny Quest vs. the Cyber Insects,* and announced plans to launch an all-new 1996 TV series, *The Real Adventures of Jonny Quest,* with Jonny now a teenager. Playing Jonny's father, Dr. Benton Quest, in this new TV *Quest:* George Segal.

Adventures of Ozzie & Harriet, The. *1952–66, ABC.* Ozzie and Harriet Nelson's comedic talents first flourished on radio's *The Red Skelton Show* in the early forties, after the birth of sons David and Ricky, and broadcasting's original "Married . . . With Children" family soon went solo with its own radio sitcom, *The Adventures of Ozzie & Harriet,* in 1944. It wasn't until 1949, though, that Ozzie allowed his sons to portray themselves on the show (replacing child actors Tommy Bernard and Henry Blair). That was in plenty of time, though, for the whole Nelson family to be showcased in the 1952 film *Here Come the Nelsons,* which was the blueprint for the TV version premiering later that same year—beginning a fourteen-year run that presented a blissful picture of suburbia, and, as a sidelight, launched Ricky Nelson as a fifties teen musical idol. Ozzie Nelson controlled his show carefully and effectively, kept the focus small, and, once Ricky came of teen-idol age, used the series to showcase his son's pop songs—sometimes as part of the plot, sometimes as stand-alone encores that could be thought of as prototypes of music videos. The effect of these *Ozzie & Harriet* TV "spots" was substantial, and immediate: Ricky Nelson's first single, "Teenager's Romance" (backed with a cover of Fats Domino's "I'm Walking"), sold almost 60,000 copies in the first three days of release. Subsequent hits getting boosts from *Ozzie & Harriet* cross-promotion included "Poor Little Fool" and "Travelin' Man." In the nineties, TV's full-Nelson star treatment extended to a third generation, when the singer's twin sons became fleetingly familiar MTV fixtures as the lookalike rock duo known as Nelson; almost simultaneously, his daughter Tracy was visible on TV as the priest's sidekick on *Father Dowling Mysteries*—but was nun too good. Somewhere in between (specifically, in 1973), Ozzie and Harriet Nelson tried an ill-fated comeback in a syndicated series called *Ozzie's Girls,* but the show's premise was a big mistake. With Ricky (now Rick) out of the house, and brother David serving as off-camera producer, *Ozzie's Girls* had Ozzie and Harriet renting out their sons' room to two attractive young boarders. The result? Mass boardom. But the Nelsons' legacy lives on—in memories of Ozzie's sweaters, Rick's pop songs, the squeaky-clean image projected on the show by the whole Nelson family (the title *Ozzie & Harriet,* like *The Donna Reed Show* and *Father Knows Best,* today stands for a simpler, more nuclear type of family life), and in reruns and specials packaged and hosted by David Nelson for The Disney Channel.

Adventures of Superman, The. *1951–57, syndicated.* A truly multimedia kind of guy, Superman started as a comic-book hero in *Action Comics* in 1938, showed up as the star of his own radio series the same year (with Bud Collyer, later the host of *To Tell the Truth,* as Clark Kent and his costumed alter ego), became the first animated superhero (thanks to the Fleischer studio's 1941 cartoons), was featured in live-action movie serials, and, in 1951, finally got his own syndicated TV series, starring George Reeves as the Man of Steel, with Phyllis Coates (and, after one season, Noel Neill) as Lois Lane and Jack Larson as Jimmy Olson. "Look! Up in the sky! It's a bird! It's a plane! It's . . . Superman!" was a catch phrase that persists to this day, and the tacky flying effects and overall silliness are remembered almost as fondly. Comedian Robert Wuhl noted in an HBO standup special, quite accurately, that bad guys always fired their guns at Superman's chest, then tossed their empty guns at him . . . which Reeves, as Superman, always ducked to avoid. What Wuhl wanted to know is: why, if Superman can stand there and take a round of bullets without flinching, does he bother dodging the empty gun? Good question. *The Adventures of Superman* was stronger on action than logic, but did respond quite logically, and commendably, when parents and critics voiced concern that young children were emulating Superman's behavior by attempting to fly, sometimes off of dangerously high rooftops. Reeves instantly filmed a special message to his young fans, urging them not to try, and the furor died down as quickly as it had begun. Decades later, a big-budget 1978 *Superman* film, with Christopher Reeve in the title role, launched renewed interest in comic-book heroes on the large and small screens. Many *Superman* big-screen sequels followed, as did a flop film version of *Supergirl*, and unrelated comic-book movie versions of *Batman, Dick Tracy*, and others. In the late eighties, a TV series called *The Adventures of Superboy*, carried in syndication like the original *Adventures of Superman*, carried on the tradition. That effort was surpassed, though, by ABC's *Lois & Clark: The New Adventures of Superman*, which premiered in 1993, and was up, up, and away above all previous *Superman* TV series, with Dean Cain as a cool Clark and Teri Hatcher as a very alluring Lois. During the 1995–96 season, *Lois & Clark* abandoned the long-established romantic triangle of Lois, Clark, and Superman in order to advance the Super-stagnant story line, with Clark revealing his secret identity to Lois and proposing marriage. Eventually she accepted, setting the stage for new dramatic complications—and some super-sexy love scenes. Meanwhile, *Lois & Clark* acknowledged its TV predecessor by hiring Coates, the original Lois Lane, to play Lois's mother in one episode.

ALF. *1986–90, NBC.* ALF was short for Alien Life Form, and was short, period. He also was hairy, and looked like Cousin Itt from *The Addams Family*—crossed with the face of an anteater and the attitude of Don Rickles. Max Wright of *Buffalo Bill* (another sitcom co-created by Tom Patchett) played the human inventor who housed the world's most illegal alien, and puppeteer Paul Fusco provided ALF's voice, and was the man responsible for the creation of the ALF character and his wisecracking persona. But persona-lly, I was never that impressed with this sitcom (its humor was too broad, its laugh track too loud), even though *ALF* made enough of a dent with kids that it's sure to be remembered by the next generation of teleliterates. ABC, apparently, shares that opinion, and picked up the NBC concept (minus Wright) for a two-hour 1996 comedy telemovie, *Project: ALF*.

Alfred Hitchcock Presents. *1955–60, CBS; 1960–62, NBC; 1985–86, NBC; 1987–88, USA Network.* **Alfred Hitchcock Hour.** *1962–64, CBS; 1964–65, NBC.* What is there to say about this wonderful anthology series? This, for starters: Hitchcock got more respect and acclaim as a TV host of these suspense stories than he was getting at the time as a director, and it's worth noting that most of the crew for *Psycho* (including cameraman John L. Russell) came from his weekly TV series. Some individual stories, like 1958's "Lamb to the Slaughter"—written by Roald Dahl, directed by Hitchcock himself, and starring Barbara Bel Geddes, later Miss Ellie of *Dallas*, as a woman who uses a frozen leg of lamb as a murder weapon, then cooks it and serves it to the police investigating the crime—are individual classics, and Hitchcock's wry disdain for his advertisers, a more ghoulish variation of Arthur Godfrey's established technique, made him just as popular as the stories he presented.

(Hitchcock's droll closing remarks, in which he often blithely informed viewers that the killer in the story eventually was punished for his or her misdeeds, were his way of satisfying the network's morality-conscious censors with a "crime doesn't pay" coda while simultaneously protecting the impish integrity of the dramas as filmed.) Hitchcock directed seventeen of the episodes in *Alfred Hitchcock Presents* (and one of the episodes in its longer sister show, *The Alfred Hitchcock Hour*), and other directors included Robert Altman, Sydney Pollack, and William Friedkin. Actor Norman Lloyd, who occasionally directed or starred in episodes of the series, also served as one of its producers, helping to attract and present an impressive array of writers (Dahl, Robert Bloch, Ray Bradbury, John Cheever, Richard Levinson, William Link, and, somewhat surprisingly, A. A. Milne) and performers (Robert Redford, Robert Duvall, Bette Davis, Walter Matthau, Elizabeth Montgomery, Art Carney, Peter Falk, Vincent Price, Katharine Ross, Joanne Woodward, Dick Van Dyke, Ed Asner, and Rip Torn). In a typically Hitchcockian twist, Hitchcock's trademark hosting appearances were continued even after his death. Years later, NBC and the USA Network colorized old Hitchcock introductions and recycled them, pairing them with brand-new suspense stories for a modern TV remake. Also outliving the series are the enduring "Good eee-vening" catch phrase, the macabre theme music (Gounod's *Funeral March of a Marionette*), the way Hitchcock's silhouette filled out his own caricatured profile during the opening credits—and, of course, the many wonderfully entrancing episodes, from Peter Lorre and Steve McQueen as the finger-chopping bettors of 1960's Lloyd-directed "Man from the South" to Billy Mumy as the gun-toting child of 1961's "Bang! You're Dead!" Other highlights from *Alfred Hitchcock Presents* and *The Alfred Hitchcock Hour* included 1955's "Breakdown," with Joseph Cotton as a totally paralyzed car-crash victim, and 1957's "The Glass Eye," with Jessica Tandy and William Shatner in a spooky tale about a mysterious ventriloquist. Like well-crafted short stories, they will be remembered, and treasured, for generations.

All in the Family. *1971–79, CBS.* How venerable is *All in the Family?* Well, Carroll O'Connor's Archie Bunker is the only fictional TV character to rank an individual citation in *The Dictionary of Cultural Literacy* by E. D. Hirsch and company, and Archie's armchair rests comfortably, and quite popularly, in the Smithsonian. It's a case of an imitation outgrowing, and improving upon, the original. Producer Norman Lear's trend-setting, bigotry-confronting sitcom was based on a British series, *Till Death Us Do Part,* which starred Warren Mitchell as Alf. In this sitcom, Alf was no Alien Life Force, but instead was a boisterous working-class conservative with a deferential wife, flighty daughter, and liberal son-in-law. *Till Death* had been running in England, quite successfully, for seven years by the time Alf became Archie and made the transition to America—becoming, in the process, not just a comedy, but a controversy. Archie's abrasiveness and outrageousness set him apart from virtually every other character on American TV at the time, and *All in the Family* labored hard to tackle sensitive issues, rather than flee in the opposite direction. O'Connor's deft acting helped give Archie a lovable core, which defused, if not excused, a lot of the character's behavior. That, in turn, infuriated some viewers, who felt the sitcom was perpetuating, rather than ridiculing, racist and sexist attitudes. But with Jean Stapleton's Edith getting in her innocently delivered yet hilariously accurate rejoinders, she served as the Alice Kramden to Archie's Ralph: invariably, all of his bombast and anger proved no match for his wife's common sense and uncommon goodness. For much of its run, including five straight seasons as TV's most popular series, *All in the Family* set America talking like few other shows of its time, and spun off such successful series as *Maude, Good Times*, and *The Jeffersons*. (By the time *All in the Family* had devolved into *Archie Bunker's Place* in 1979, Archie Bunker's Place in current conversational circles was less secure.) Sally Struthers and Rob Reiner, as Gloria and her husband "Meathead," were the other members of this very nuclear and warring family (they weren't called Bunker for nothing), and the series itself was durable enough to be saluted in prime time with a twentieth anniversary special in 1990, then repeated on CBS—in prime time—the following summer. Notably, twenty-year-old *All in the Family* reruns proved more popular in prime time than Norman Lear's new series, *Sunday Dinner*, with which *Family* was paired. It's not surprising, because *Family*, especially in the early years, crackled with excitement and interest. It was a dangerous line *All in the Family* was tiptoeing, but the series painted a more knowing and accurate portrait of its particular time, locale, and social class than any previous sitcom since *The Honeymooners*. As for Archie's memorable catch phrases, he spouted too many to enumerate, so I'll stifle myself. But thanks to O'Connor's central performance and the contributions by the show's writers, directors, producers, and costars, Archie Bunker, along with Ralph Kramden, Ted Baxter, Columbo, and a few others, is one of the most widely and instantly identifiable icons in the television canon. *All in the Family* hasn't aged as well as other shows having the same impact; it was a true reflector of its times, and the times, they have a'changed. In 1994, the enormity of that change was driven home—to Archie's home—when the old Bunker household in Queens was used as the setting of a new Lear sitcom, *704 Hauser Street*. The new occupant and patriarch of that home, played by John Amos of Lear's *Good Times*, was Ernie Cumberpatch, an African-American liberal whose conservative son, with whom he argued constantly, was dating a white Jewish woman. Even with all those built-in culture clashes, *704* generated nothing but yawns, and the unfunny CBS semisequel folded after five weeks.

All My Children. *1970– , ABC*. Susan Lucci may never win a daytime Emmy for her long-standing role as Erica Kane, but she's parlayed it into a second career anyway, starring in (mostly awful) prime-time telemovies. *All My Children* is one of TV's "next-generation" soaps—the new serial by *One Life to Live* creator Agnes Nixon was launched the first week of 1970—and was one of the first to appeal to college students in significant numbers. By now, the list of now-famous *All My Children* alumni—on the performing side, that is—should be fuller than it is, given the show's longevity. Yet like the show itself, it's surprisingly thin. Lucci, who's been with *All My Children* since the beginning and has matured much more than the serial itself, is virtually the franchise. By the end of 1995, the year *All My Children* celebrated its twenty-fifth anniversary with a prime-time ABC special, Lucci's character had walked down the aisle enough times to qualify for frequent-walker miles. Her full name, at that point, was Erica Kane Martin Brent Cudahy Chandler Montgomery Montgomery Marick. And counting. . . .

Amahl and the Night Visitors. *1951, NBC*. Gian Carlo Menotti's holiday story, broadcast initially by NBC on Christmas Eve, 1951, was the very first TV offering fully sponsored by Hallmark, and was received so warmly that the card company, the very next year, embarked on a regular series of specials called *Hallmark Hall of Fame*. As for *Amahl*, it was such a hit that it was restaged or repeated annually for years afterward; the 1953 production, presented under the *Hallmark Hall of Fame* banner, was the first sponsored TV show to be presented in color. The story and songs in the opera told of a young boy named Amahl, a crippled shepherd—a sort of biblical Tiny Tim—who accompanied the Three Wise Men on their journey to Bethlehem for what became the first Christmas. *Amahl*, the first opera commissioned specifically for television, has since become an accepted operatic standard—and, more than four decades later, remains the most famous and popular opera ever written for TV. Not that it has much competition. And these days, if your kids say they want to check out *Amahl*, it probably means they want to go shopping.

Amazing Stories. *1985–87. NBC*. Steven Spielberg's *Amazing Stories* was a victim of too-high expectations, but it did what an anthology series should do: it encouraged and showcased new talent, took chances, and left behind a legacy. Part of what *Amazing Stories* did was reverse the direction of the flow of talent from TV's so-called "Golden Age," when Arthur Penn and other directors and writers abandoned television for the movies. Part of Spielberg's plan was to woo Hollywood talent back to TV for episodes of his anthology show, and it worked: Martin Scorsese directed Sam Waterston and Tim Robbins in "Mirror, Mirror," a 1986 episode about a haunted horror writer, and Clint Eastwood, Joe Dante, Paul Bartel, and Danny De Vito all directed shows. The other built-in plus for *Amazing Stories* was the way it encouraged young talent; Spielberg, after all, had gotten his start on a TV anthology series, directing a segment of the pilot for Rod Serling's *Night Gallery*, and was open to new ideas and fresh faces. Consequently, you had Tim Burton's animated creations delighting audiences in a 1987 episode called "The Family Dog" (which eventually spawned a shortlived, inferior CBS spinoff in 1993), and Kevin Costner and Kiefer Sutherland starring in an exciting 1985 episode about WWII pilots, and Forest Whitaker appearing in a 1986 episode, and so on. *Amazing Stories* should have been around longer, and promoted better. It also could have been written better, but many of the writers best suited to concocting truly "amazing stories" were already contributing to another anthology series, the revival of *The Twilight Zone*, just underway at CBS. Yet many good installments were generated, including "Fine Tuning," based on a story by Spielberg, which was a playful variation on *Close Encounters of the Third Kind* with television, not music, as the common link between two worlds. On this world, the legacy of *Amazing Stories* is tied largely to Spielberg's name, rather than with the inherent value of its cleverest shows. Years later, HBO's *Tales from the Crypt* would come closer to succeeding at the type of format Spielberg was proposing. When encountering repeats or collections of *Amazing Stories*, however, look in particular for "Mummy, Daddy," a giddy and clever story, starring Bronson Pinchot, about a horror-movie actor who is mistaken for a real mummy.

American Bandstand. *1957–87, ABC; 1987–89, syndicated; 1989–90, USA Network.* Rock 'n' roll, performed by black musicians as well as white singers covering black music, slipped into middle-class American households by way of this long-running music series, which began in Philadelphia in 1952 and went nationwide in 1957, with Dick Clark beginning a reign only slightly shorter than Queen Elizabeth's. England had *Ready! Steady! Go!*, America had *American Bandstand*, and both shows predated MTV by a generation. In terms of TV history, I give it a 78—it wasn't the greatest show on earth, but it had a good beat, and you could dance to it. Even so, I totally understand if, after all these years and all those dance numbers, you still candstand *Bandstand*.

American Playhouse. *1982–   , PBS.* This is one of those TV treasures that probably won't be fully appreciated until it's gone—but believe me, its overall batting average stacks up favorably against any Golden Age anthology series you'd care to compare it to. Certainly, the roster of talent *American Playhouse* has fostered over its lengthy run is little short of amazing, and how hard is it to demand respect for a TV series whose theatrical productions include such films as *Testament, Stand and Deliver, The Thin Blue Line*, and *Longtime Companion?* Not hard at all. Moreover, the 1984 *American Playhouse* production of Sam Shepard's *True West* introduced John Malkovich and Gary Sinise to a nationwide audience; the same year's production of Philip Roth's *The Ghost Writer* was one of the best treatments ever to dramatize the thinking process of a writer; the 1982 miniseries *Oppenheimer* (starring Sam Waterston as the father of the atomic bomb) and the 1984 miniseries *Concealed Enemies* (about the Alger Hiss case) were superb docudramas; and Jonathan Demme's lighthearted version of Kurt Vonnegut's *Who Am I This Time?*, starring Susan Sarandon and Christopher Walken, remains another personal favorite. *American Playhouse* has presented recent stage productions of *Into the Woods, The Grapes of Wrath*, and *Tru* to PBS viewers across the country, and, even with its funding slashed and its schedule and resources drastically reduced, basically does a better job of realizing the potential of TV, year in and year out, than the vast majority of series on television. The show's most recent artistic triumph: *Ethan Frome*, a haunting 1994 adaptation of the Edith Wharton novel, starring Liam Neeson and Patricia Arquette as ill-fated lovers.

America's Funniest Home Videos. *1990–95, ABC.* **America's Funniest Home Videos Hour.** *1995–   , ABC.* It's official: fifteen million people *can* be wrong.

This fluke-hit ABC series simultaneously taps (a) the increasing popularity of the home camcorder and (b) the basest parts of human nature. Uncontrolled babies and animals and accident-prone adults provide the vast majority of the "amateur footage" used in this series, which will be remembered in the future for eliminating the middleman and getting the *audience* to provide the subpar entertainment. Host Bob Saget conducts a competition among invited semi-finalists for the week's "best video," which often results in them enduring, and reliving, the largest doses of coast-to-coast humiliation since those poor contestants on *Queen for a Day*. The short-range legacy of *America's Funniest Home Videos* is, alas, painfully obvious. ABC paired it with an even stupider spinoff called *America's Funniest People*, while NBC launched *I Witness Video*—a tasteless series of "reality footage" from amateur and TV news photographers, and a show that could just as easily (and accurately) be called *America's Most Depressing Home Videos*. Actually, the whole *trend* is depressing. Though those spinoff and ripoff video shows were gone by the midnineties, ABC filled the void by doubling the length of Saget's series—and, in effect, filling one void with another.

America's Most Wanted. *1988–   , Fox*. In future years, this show will be recalled as the leading proponent of "bounty-hunter television," in which viewers are encouraged to phone in with anonymous tips and help capture bad guys. It's a little like an adult, high-tech expansion of the "Crimestoppers Club" on the animated *Dick Tracy* TV series, or like an interactive version of *The Fugitive*—except the villains it catches (more than forty per year, on average, since the series began) are real, and the presence of host John Walsh lends this Fox series some valuable credibility. (Walsh's involvement is due directly to an earlier TV legacy: the search for his abducted son was dramatized in a well-received 1983 docudrama called *Adam*.) The concept of *America's Most Wanted* is not at all new. A radio series called *Gangbusters*, which premiered in 1937 and was popular enough to last twenty years, presented a TV version in 1952, alternating with a new cop show called *Dragnet* on alternate Thursdays. Both series were as dominant for NBC on Thursday nights as *The Cosby Show* would be in the mideighties, or *ER* in the midnineties, yet *Gangbusters* was canceled within the year, as soon as Jack Webb could produce enough *Dragnet* episodes to run weekly. However, with its dramatic reenactments of crimes, its descriptions of criminals, and its requests that viewers with further information phone the FBI or the local police, *Gangbusters* was an obvious early template for *America's Most Wanted*. Another potential inspiration came at the conclusion of most episodes of the 1965–74 series *The F.B.I.*, when star and host Efrem Zimbalist Jr. would identify a "Most Wanted" fugitive and encourage viewers to be on the lookout. In other countries, TV producers and networks have been sparked by similar inspirations. West Germany's *Case XYZ: Unsolved*, which premiered in 1967, was the first crimestopping show to include reenactments; England has *Crimewatch: UK*, and Australia has *Australia's Most Wanted*, both of which predated *America's Most Wanted* on Fox. So, for that matter, did NBC's *Unsolved Mysteries*, but only as a series of specials beginning in January 1987, hosted first by Raymond Burr and then by Karl Malden. It was only after *America's Most Wanted* made audience inroads for the Fox network that NBC scheduled *Unsolved Mysteries* as a weekly series, trotting out Robert Stack (of the vintage crime-busting series *The Untouchables*) and showcasing him as the tough-talking host. In both *Unsolved Mysteries* and *America's Most Wanted*, the results are impressive, even though the dramatic reconstructions are suspiciously heavy-handed and some of the tactics are rather questionable. There's a little "Big Brother" mentality hovering around the edges of this show, and with its brutal and often lurid recreations, *America's Most Wanted* can have its violence and condemn it, too.

America 2-Night. See *Fernwood 2-Night.*

Amos 'n' Andy. *1951–1953, CBS.* The good news is, the National Association for the Advancement of Colored People's organized protest of this TV series awakened many people to the limited, and usually derogatory, portrayal of blacks on network television. The bad news is, *Amos 'n' Andy* was a truly funny show, and, though some characters were shiftless, conniving, and anything but role models, others were judges, lawyers, and other authority figures—and at least the TV series, unlike the hit radio show on which it was based, gave the starring roles to black actors, rather than to white actors imitating black dialects. The words *Amos 'n' Andy* today are largely associated with racist attitudes of an earlier time, and the show itself remains so sensitive a topic that it has yet to be revived for general syndication. However, interested viewers who seek out episodes of the TV series on videotape, or at an archival collection such as New York's Museum of Television & Radio, will encounter a sitcom superior, in its caliber of scripts and its ensemble acting, to most of today's TV comedies. Alvin Childress and Spencer Williams did a wonderful job embodying, and expanding upon, the characters created for radio by Freeman Gosden and Charles Correll, and Tim Moore's blustery Kingfish, in particular, is a brilliant comic portrayal. Episodes of *Amos 'n' Andy*, seen today, hold up quite well, employing sophisticated physical slapstick and familiar character comedy in the *I Love Lucy* vein. The problem with *Amos 'n' Andy*, back then, was that it wasn't part of a wider spectrum. Had, say, *F Troop* been the only TV series featuring whites, the broad caricatures on that series might have been seen as no less insulting to *that* race. Sadly, the lack of ethnic diversity continues to plague commercial network TV; happily, *Amos 'n' Andy* seems overdue for a reevaluation by TV and cultural historians.

Amy Fisher: My Story. *1992, NBC.* **The Amy Fisher Story.** *1993, ABC.* **Casualties of Love: The "Long Island Lolita" Story.** *1993, CBS.* Just in case there are any lingering doubts that this book will address only the most positive memorable events in TV history, the act of including this tacky telemovie troika ought to nip *that* idea in the Buttafuoco. Individually, none of these docudramas about teen Amy Fisher's assault on the wife of her alleged lover, Joey Buttafuoco, is worth noting; ABC's version, largely because of Drew Barrymore, was the least terrible, but that's hardly an endorsement.

Yet collectively, since there was such a race to cash in on this story and the results were so successful (at least in terms of attracting an audience), the initial ramifications were significant, and frightening. CBS, NBC, and ABC all presented their Fisher telemovies within a one-week period, and all three landed in the Top 15, despite their wildly conflicting points of view. NBC's *Amy Fisher: My Story*, with Noelle Parker and Ed Marinaro as Amy and Joey, took Amy's side and made Joey the manipulative villain; CBS's *Casualties of Love: The 'Long Island Lolita' Story*, with Alyssa Milano and Jack Scalia, took Joey's side and made Amy the manipulative vixen; and ABC's *The Amy Fisher Story*, with Barrymore and Anthony John Denison, took neither side, and basically portrayed them both as amoral idiots in heat. When all three versions did well, the networks happily jumped to the conclusion that they didn't have to be first with the story, nor did the story have to be told well, if audiences were familiar enough with the real-life event in advance. The success of the *Amy Fisher* telemovies sped up the process even more, making such sober crime docudramas as *In Cold Blood*, or even television's *Fatal Vision*, an apparently endangered species, in addition to generating a network feeding frenzy for similarly sensationalistic celebrity biographical dramas. In 1994, the heat generated by that greedy competitiveness resulted in dueling docudramas on the Menendez murder case (April's *Honor Thy Father and Mother: The True Story of the Menendez Brothers* telemovie on Fox, followed in May by the CBS miniseries *Menendez: A Killing in Beverly Hills*), and, in October, two different telemovies about, but not starring or condoned by, Roseanne (Fox's *Roseanne: An Unauthorized Biography* and NBC's *Roseanne and Tom: Behind the Scenes*). The *Roseanne* biographies, in particular, were so horrendous—and, what really mattered more, so relatively unsuccessful— the networks appeared to learn their lesson and retreat from the competitive, cynical cycle accellerated by the Amy Fisher sagas. If there's one thing TV history has taught us, though, it's that network executives have astoundingly short memories, especially when it comes to learning from prior mistakes and excesses.

Andy Griffith Show, The. *1960 68, CBS.* From Earle Hagen's whistling theme song at the beginning to the walk by the lake at the end, this sitcom is one of America's most durable and beloved shared memories; Charles Kuralt, in a 1992 *Andy Griffith Show* reunion special, tenderly and succinctly described the series in general, and that fishing-hole scene in particular, as a "rural Eden." (An earlier reunion special, 1986's *Return to Mayberry*, was that season's highest-rated telemovie.) Reruns of *The Andy Griffith Show* remain among the most popular programs on Ted Turner's TBS superstation, and the shows, even under repeated scrutiny, are surprisingly sophisticated. Don Knotts, as terminally hyper deputy Barney Fife, walked away with a lot of Emmys and most of the attention, but the core of the show, to me, is Andy Taylor's quiet, credible relationship with his son, Opie. Griffith played those scenes marvelously, and Ron Howard, as Opie, was one of the few child actors on television who never acted like he was acting. (Another is Jerry Mathers of *Leave It to Beaver.)* Watch for a repeat of the episode "Opie the Birdman," in which Opie kills a bird with his slingshot and is punished by his father in a very wise way (he opens the window and forces Opie to hear the cries of her hungry babies), to witness just one example of the quality stories, and quality acting, presented on *The Andy Griffith Show.* This durable sitcom, which itself was a spinoff of *The Danny Thomas Show,* eventually spun off *Gomer Pyle, U.S.M.C.* and *Mayberry, R.F.D.,* and *The Andy Griffith Show* also deserves partial credit for inspiring another successful comedy about unassuming rural folk. Media professor Robert J. Thompson of the S. I. Newhouse School of Public Communication at New York's Syracuse University is convinced that Paul Henning's 1961 *Andy Griffith Show* script for an episode called "Crime-Free Mayberry" helped inspire his next TV project, which premiered less than a year later—*The Beverly Hillbillies.* When *The Andy Griffith Show* called it quits in 1968, it went out on top, ceasing production while still ranked as America's most popular TV series. Only one other series in TV history has done that: *I Love Lucy,* in 1957. After *The Andy Griffith Show,* Ron Howard grew up to become an acclaimed film director *(Parenthood, Apollo 13),* and Griffith, beginning in 1986, had another lengthy TV run as the star of *Matlock,* playing a variation on the crafty Southern lawyer he had portrayed in the fact-based miniseries *Fatal Vision.* From 1988–90, Griffith and Knotts reunited when Knotts joined the *Matlock* cast as neighbor Les "Ace" Calhoun—but for *Andy Griffith Show* fans, the most resonant reminder of that classic sitcom came during the premiere of the 1995 CBS series *American Gothic,* which starred Gary Cole (of, coincidentally, *Fatal Vision* fame) as a small-town Southern sheriff. This particular sheriff was as evil as Griffith's Andy Taylor was good, but was endowed with a powerful sense of teleliteracy. While sauntering down the jailhouse corridor on his way to frighten a prisoner into committing suicide, this demonic sheriff amused himself—and me—by whistling the theme to *The Andy Griffith Show.*

Another World. *1964– , NBC.* Still soapy after all these years, *Another World* premiered on NBC in 1964, and was the first daytime soap to spin off *another* daytime soap—1970's *Somerset,* which set after six summers, but which nonetheless had the good taste to recognize Ann Wedgeworth as a major talent. *(Texas,* a 1980 daytime soap that tried to cash in on the success of *Dallas,* was yet another *Another World* spinoff.) Over the years, the *Another World* cast has included some noteworthy, and even talented, performers, such as Charles Durning and the aforementioned Wedgeworth, both of whom wound up on the CBS sitcom *Evening Shade;* Susan Sullivan and Ted Shackelford, later of the prime-time soaps *Falcon Crest* (her) and *Dallas* and *Knots Landing* (him); Rue McClanahan, later of *The Golden Girls;* Nancy Marchand, previously of *Marty* and later of *Lou Grant;* Christina Pickles, later of *St. Elsewhere;* Morgan Freeman, later of the film *Driving Miss Daisy;* Faith Ford, who moved on to *Murphy Brown;* and William Russ, who played Roger Lococco on *Wiseguy.* Of the cast members who stayed put, the most famous is Linda Dano as Felicia Gallant, whose more than decade of loyalty to her daytime showcase conceivably could be described as a Gallant gesture.

Apollo 11 Moon Landing. See *Moon Landing*.

Archie Show, The. *1968–69, CBS.* This Saturday morning cartoon series, "inspired" by the Archie Comics characters that have been kicking around in the same Riverdale High corridors since the forties, isn't remembered at all, thank goodness—but the same can't be said of its dreadfully famous, and famously dreadful, offshoot: the mammoth bubblegum pop-music hit "Sugar, Sugar," which hit the top of the charts in 1969—usurping, of all things, "Honky Tonk Women" by the Rolling Stones. In terms of TV history, maybe it's worth pointing out that The Archies managed to survive on Saturday morning TV, in some incarnation, for a frighteningly long ten years, in such offshoots as *The U.S. of Archie* and *The Bang-Shang Lalapalooza Show.* And that the guiding hand behind the musical TV incarnation of the original *Archies* was Don Kirshner, who had recently done the same thing for a slightly less animated group and series called *The Monkees,* and that the producer and cowriter of "Sugar, Sugar" was Jeff Barry, the same guy who had produced the Monkees' "I'm a Believer." Then again, maybe not; maybe a quiet descent into oblivion is the best revenge. Forget I said anything.

Army-McCarthy Hearings, The. *1954, various networks.* It was April 1954, one month after Edward R. Murrow took on the smear tactics of Wisconsin Senator Joseph McCarthy in a landmark *See It Now* broadcast on CBS. Mc-Carthy—aided by, among others, legal counsel Roy Cohn—was presiding over the most famous of his Senate subcommittee investigations into various branches of government. The Army hearings, thanks to Boston lawyer Joseph Welch's stirring defense of a young colleague, effectively ended McCarthy's paranoid reign of terror. Welch's emotional rebuke to McCarthy has gone down in TV as well as political history: "Have you no sense of decency, sir?" he asked the committee chairman. "At long last, have you left no sense of decency?" In a very real sense, it was the one-two punch of television—of *See It Now* followed by the hearings—that did McCarthy in. And though CBS threw the first punch, it was up to two struggling networks, ABC and the now-defunct DuMont (a brave but brief player during TV's early years), to deliver the knockout blow. CBS and NBC were reluctant to disrupt their profitable daytime schedules, and limited their coverage mostly to nightly digests; after the first two days, when NBC cut back its on-air commitment, only ABC and DuMont carried the hearings live. ABC, with more stations, got most of the credit, and gained stature nationwide even as McCarthy lost his.

Arsenio Hall Show, The. *1989–94, syndicated.* Before getting his own late-night showcase, Arsenio Hall apprenticed on two other TV talk shows: as an occasional performer on Alan Thicke's forgettably awful *Thicke of the Night,* and as a thirteen-week fill-in host of Fox's *The Late Show* in 1987, after the departure of Joan Rivers. Hall made *The Late Show* his own, but Fox executives already had decided to replace it with *The Wilton North Report*, and was committed to its two hosts, Phil Cowan and Paul Robins. Fox should have been committed for *hiring* those two hosts; *The Wilton North Report* lasted only one month, and was horrendous enough to earn honors, or dishonors, as the second-worst talk series in Fox history. (For the all-time worst, see *The Chevy Chase Show.*) Meanwhile, Hall was snapped up by Paramount for syndication and, once his *Arsenio Hall Show* premiered in 1989, became a major player in what soon were dubbed "the talk show wars"—a war Hall escalated, in 1992, by predicting he would "kick Jay's ass," referring to *Tonight Show* rival Jay Leno. Hall's strength, and considerable achievement, was that he built a strong black following without alienating whites. As both host and executive producer, his all-inclusive guest list ranged from rappers to crooners, from movie stars to star athletes, from Wesley Snipes to Sinead O'Connor—a range so wide that Hall almost qualified as a next-generation Ed Sullivan, but with a lot more stage presence. Many of Hall's trademark phrases quickly percolated into the culture (especially, but not exclusively, black culture): "Let's get busy," "Things that make you go Hmmmm!," the term "posse," and, courtesy of a wildly enthusiastic studio audience, the "Woof! Woof! Woof!" barking, accompanied by a raised, rolling fist, that served as a savvy substitute for applause. This last phenomenon, which Cleveland native Hall had co-opted after watching the exuberant "Dawg Pound" football fans at home Browns games, was immortalized by Julia Roberts in the race track scene of *Pretty Woman*, and exemplified the crossover strength of Hall's appeal. Mariah Carey made her national TV debut on Hall's show, Martin Lawrence and Ellen DeGeneres were among the young comics he championed, and usually elusive celebrity guests included Tom Cruise, Michael Jackson, Elizabeth Taylor, The Artist Formerly Known as Prince, and The Artist Still Known as Madonna. The very best installments of *The Arsenio Hall Show* were memorable indeed. There was presidential candidate Bill Clinton sporting shades and a saxophone in June 1992, performing "God Bless the Child" and "Heartbreak Hotel" and calculatedly demonstrating his sax appeal. (Six months later, Clinton checked out of "Heartbreak Hotel" and into the White House.) More somberly, there was the 1991 conversation with Hall's close friend, Earvin "Magic" Johnson, who had just revealed his diagnosis as being HIV positive, and the lengthy discussion with Ice-T, whom Hall prodded to explain and defend his artistic decisions in writing and recording the infamous "Cop Killer." Hall's very best show, though, was broadcast the day after the verdict was announced in the Rodney King case. From an otherwise closed Paramount Studios, Hall insisted upon going on the air live, as parts of Los Angeles burned around him, to discuss the angry reaction to the verdict and the apparently widening chasm between black and white perspectives, and to try to find ways to bridge that gulf. *The Arsenio Hall Show* was one such bridge, and it would have been valuable to have that same bridge still standing after the verdict was announced in the O.J. Simpson case, but Hall's series had folded the year before. "Only two more nights," Hall told his audience during his last week on the air in May 1994, "and then the talk shows go

Amos 'n' Andy with Alvin Childress, Spencer Williams, and Tim Moore's Kingfish.

The Andy Griffith Show, with Griffith's Andy Taylor and Ron Howard's Opie.

The Arsenio Hall Show, in which Hall, right, hosted the likes of rapper Ice-T.

back to the white guys." It's a shame to say he was right, but that's basically what happened.

Arthur Godfrey's Talent Scouts. *1948–58, CBS.* **Arthur Godfrey and His Friends.** *1949–59, CBS.* This entry may as well include *Arthur Godfrey and His Friends,* because the two shows ran on TV virtually simultaneously, were equally as durable (each show lasted ten years), and were almost equally popular; for the 1952–53 TV season, *I Love Lucy* was number one in the ratings, *Talent Scouts* number two, and *Friends* number three. Both shows borrowed their looseness and variety from vaudeville—and from radio, where 1945's *Arthur Godfrey Time* and 1946's *Arthur Godfrey's Talent Scouts* had provided the blueprints, and the core of talent, for Godfrey's TV ventures. Godfrey had a lot of charm and impishness; as Alfred Hitchcock would do later, he bit the hand that fed him by poking fun at his sponsors. Audiences loved Godfrey so much at first that he was able to sustain two hit series at once, with *Talent Scouts* running on Mondays and *Friends* on Wednesdays. But in 1953, an increasingly self-impressed Godfrey turned on one of his beloved *Friends,* singer Julius LaRosa, and fired him on live TV for allegedly wanting too much of the limelight. (LaRosa's replacement: Pat Boone.) Godfrey's show outlasted, but never outlived, that incident, and Godfrey's own popularity dimmed steadily. As with *Amos 'n' Andy,* Godfrey is now remembered at least as much for the on-air controversy he stirred as for the programs themselves.

Art Linkletter's House Party. *1952–69, CBS.* Through time, only one strong echo remains of this daytime fifties and sixties TV version of Linkletter's radio show: the title of his "Kids Say the Darndest Things" interview segment with children, which generated several best-sellers. Other than that, Linkletter today is best known for his late-night TV ads hawking Craftmatic adjustable beds. Fame does the darndest things—but Linkletter is astute and amiable enough to acknowledge that. In 1994, Linkletter was on national TV again, hosting a PBS special called *Art Linkletter on Positive Aging* and looking remarkably vibrant and at ease. He started the special by describing his recent surprise visit at a home for the aged. He had dropped in to cheer up some of the patients, but soon encountered one who showed no glimmer of recognition at being face to face with the once-famous host of *House Party* and *People Are Funny.* After an uncomfortable silence, Linkletter finally asked her, "Do you know who I am?" "No," she reportedly replied, "but if you go to the front desk, they'll tell you."

As the World Turns. *1956– , CBS.* This was the soap that championed the slow pace, and emphasis on lengthy conversations and closeups, that came to typify the genre in the years after its 1956 debut. *As the World Turns* is the second-oldest soap opera currently on television; only the *Guiding Light,* also created for TV by Irma Phillips, has a longer tenure. There's another connection between these two serial dinosaurs as well: Ruth Warrick, after playing a sexy nurse on *Guiding Light,* was cast by Phillips as Edith Hughes, the central seductress on *As the World Turns*—and crafted one of the most popular and controversial soap characters of the fifties. Warrick had played opposite Orson Welles, as his first wife, in *Citizen Kane,* and after leaving the *World* orbit would duplicate her soap-opera success in two other famous serials: *Peyton Place* and *All My Children.* Eileen Fulton, who joined *As the World Turns* in 1960 as Lisa Miller, played an equally famous, even more villainous villainess. For once, though, it was the "good woman" who triumphed on this soap, or at least outlasted the rest. Helen Wagner, who began portraying Edith's sister-in-law, Nancy Hughes, when *As the World Turns* premiered in April 1956, has begun her fifth decade of playing the same character (now known as Nancy Hughes McClosky) on the same series—an unprecedented feat in this or any other TV genre. As for those who have left *As the World Turns,* this particular daytime soap boasts a ton of very famous alumni, including James Earl Jones (as Dr. Jerry Turner, 1966), Swoosie Kurtz (Ellie Bradley, 1971), Dana Delany (Haley Wilson, 1981), Meg Ryan (Betsy Stewart, 1982–84), Marisa Tomei (Marcy Thompson, 1983–85), and Julianne Moore (as both Frannie Hughes and her half sister Sabrina, 1985–88).

Ascent of Man, The. *1975, PBS.* This 1974 documentary series from Time-Life Films and BBC-TV (imported for American viewers in 1975) explored the societal and scientific advances and artistic masterpieces of Western civilization. It also gave viewers credit for a sense of intelligence, as well as a sense of inquisitiveness. The host for this thirteen-part series, Jacob Bronowski from California's Salk Institute, was one of those rare experts who could speak, enthusiastically and seemingly extemporaneously, while guiding viewers through subjects and ideas both technical and challenging. In this genre, Brownowski's work is a clear link between Kenneth Clark's *Civilisation,* which preceded it, and such superb subsequent efforts as James Burke's *Connections,* Jonathan Miller's *The Body in Question,* and David Attenborough's *The Trials of Life.*

A-Team, The. *1983–87, NBC.* What, from this program, will survive in cultural memory? This and only this: the unique spectacle of Mr. T, who prefigured the "wrestling renaissance" of the late eighties and became the hottest TV character since Henry Winkler's Fonzie. George Peppard, as team leader Hannibal Smith ("I love it when a plan comes together"), was intended as the star of this inane action series, but pity the poor fool who had to costar with Mr. T, the man playing "B.A." Baracas. (The initials supposedly stood for Bad Attitude, not Bad Acting.) Festooned with gold chains and adorned with a mohawk haircut, Mr. T's *A-Team* character was as attention-getting—and complex—as his three-letter name. (Which reminds me of a nonapocryphal, true story from the *A-Team* era. While attending the annual TV critics' press tour in Los Angeles one summer, I happened to be entering the lobby of the Century Plaza Hotel just as Mr. T was exiting. Two grade-school boys were waiting by the door for his autograph, but the *A-Team* star brushed past them brusquely, claiming he had no time. As he left the building, one boy turned to the other and said, "How hard could it be? Three letters and a dot.") For series creator Stephen J. Cannell, *The A-Team* was a financial high point but creative low point; for posterity, he's much better represented by *The Rockford Files* and *Wiseguy*. Yet for NBC, this creative low point is what provided the network's only Top 10 hit during the early eighties, and provided the profits that allowed NBC to keep afloat such initial ratings "losers" as *St. Elsewhere* and *Cheers*.

Autobiography of Miss Jane Pittman, The. *1974, CBS.* Anyone who saw this 1974 CBS telemovie, based on the novel by Ernest Gaines, remembers its amazingly visual (and emotional) climax. Cicely Tyson, as the stooped, elderly, but proud "Miss Jane," caps a century's worth of experiences—stretching all the way back to pre-Civil War slavery—by defiantly and boldly making her way up the courthouse steps, leaning on her cane for support, to become the town's first black person to drink from the water fountain labeled "White Only." Tyson's performance was a major triumph: always credible, never showy. Her success in this role, and the critical and popular acceptance of the drama itself, certainly played a part in ABC's decision to reexamine the inherent drama of race relations by mounting a version of Alex Haley's *Roots* three years later. And, fittingly, Tyson played a part in that groundbreaking drama as well—portraying Binta, Kunta Kinte's mother, in the opening installment.

Avengers, The. *1966–69, ABC.* In the sixties, this was the wittiest, wildest, and kinkiest action series on the air, and I couldn't get enough of it. Patrick Macnee's secret agent John Steed was teamed, over the course of this series, with several lovely and notably self-reliant ladies. Before that, in England, *The Avengers* began with Steed paired with Ian Hendry's David Keel, a doctor pressed into service as a secret agent—but that first season's worth of shows, from 1961, was never shown in America. For that matter, the 1962–64 episodes costarring Honor Blackman, whose Cathy Gale was Steed's first leather-clad female cohort, weren't seen in America until A&E imported them in 1990. But Blackman, who left the series to play Pussy Galore in *Goldfinger,* and Linda Thorson's stylish Tara King, who was the final female in the original *Avengers* series, paled in comparison to Diana Rigg's Emma Peel, Steed's most acclaimed partner. The name "Emma Peel," it turns out, was a pun on the demographic function her role was meant to fulfill. With her sexy catsuits and aggressive independence, Steed's second female partner was designed for what the British TV insiders called "Male Appeal," or, in short, "M-Appeal." But the fiercely, proudly liberated Mrs. Peel had lots of F-appeal, too, and *The Avengers* became a sizable cult hit in America, as in England. A later series, *The New Avengers,* starring Macnee and two cohorts (Gareth Hunt as Mike Gambit and Joanna Lumley as Purdey), surfaced and sank in the midseventies. Like the original series, though, it drew on a bank of clever plots, good writers, and some of the best character actors in England—and though *The New Avengers* sank quickly, Lumley eventually resurfaced in the nineties, in a big way, as Patsy, the brazen blonde floozy on another cult

British import, *Absolutely Fabulous*. As for *The Avengers*, what episodes to watch for? From the Macnee-Rigg era, look for "Epic" (a broad spoof with *Sunset Boulevard* villains forcing Mrs. Peel to star in a movie about her own death), "Who's Who???" (two foreign agents "swap bodies" with Steed and Emma), and, for sheer outrageousness, "A Touch of Brimstone," an early episode in which Emma was costumed, against her will, as "the Queen of Sin." From the Macnee-Thorson era, look for John Cleese and others in a slapstick episode called "Look (Stop Me if You've Heard This One) but There Were These Two Fellows" and Thorson's Tara King being held hostage and brainwashed in "Pandora." Of all the *Avengers* alumni, Rigg has fared the best. She's never outdistanced her most famous role, but certainly has outdone it— as one of the stars (along with Laurence Olivier) of a brilliant 1984 TV production of Shakespeare's *King Lear*, and, most recently, as host of the PBS series *Mystery!* and the star of one of that anthology series' best miniseries, *Mother Love*.

Bang the Drum Slowly. *1956, CBS*. Paul Newman, playing a star major-league pitcher who befriends a catcher teammate with Hodgkin's disease, is the star of this ambitious live TV drama, the most famous installment of a largely forgotten Theatre Guild anthology series called *The U. S. Steel Hour* (1953–55, ABC; 1955–63, CBS). Albert Salmi played the catcher, and the story was based on a novel by Mark Harris, who wrote the teleplay adaptation himself. Surviving kinescopes of this baseball drama show that Newman, whose character sometimes moved the story along by talking directly to the camera, occasionally was nervous and sometimes mannered in the role. At other times, though, he was quite good, as were the costars, including Salmi and George Peppard. Seventeen years later, Harris adapted his novel again, this time for the movies, where Michael Moriarty played the pitcher and Robert De Niro the catcher. Although the live TV version has since been reappraised and recycled, on the *Golden Age of Television* series as well as on home video, it's the movie, and the title, people remember most.

Barbara Walters Specials, The. *1976–   , ABC*. The same year Barbara Walters went to ABC to co-anchor the network news with Harry Reasoner, she also embarked on a TV venture that proved much more durable and successful: her prime-time celebrity interview specials, now beginning their third decade as a TV institution. Walters, her manner of speech, and her intensely personal questioning style were satirized early, and often, by Gilda Radner in her "Baba Wawa" persona on *Saturday Night Live*, but the acerbic attention didn't seem to hurt. Before long, an edition of *The Barbara Walters Specials* was used as the annual opening act for ABC's telecast of the Academy Awards, and whenever anyone in show business attained superstar status—from Robin Williams and Farrah Fawcett in the seventies to Jim Carrey and Sharon Stone in the nineties—sitting for an interview on *The Barbara Walters Specials* was part of the expected rite of passage. And when she talked with established legends from film, TV, and even politics, Walters was similarly expected to make her interview subjects laugh, wince, and maybe even cry. Her most famous interview, perhaps, is her 1981 conversation with Katharine Hepburn, because of its widely repeated, and even more widely ridiculed, "If you were a tree . . . ?" question. It turns out, though, that the question from Walters was prompted by a previous answer from Hepburn, who was explaining how she came to accept her own mortality. Hepburn said she considered herself as a very strong "thing" that was destined to die, "sort of a tree or something." Walters's follow-up question: "What kind of a tree are you, if you think you're a tree?" Hepburn opted for an oak, but, in the long run, the oak was on Walters, who saw the "tree" query come back to haunt her—giving her the somewhat undeserved reputation of being a TV interviewer whose bite was less than her . . . bark.

Baretta. *1975–78, ABC.* Robert Blake has had a varied and fascinating career, from his days as a child star on some of the *Our Gang* and *Red Ryder* films (under his real name, Mickey Gubitosi) to his spellbinding role as a hot-headed killer in *In Cold Blood.* Yet some of Blake's best performances were as himself. Like Burt Reynolds, Blake parlayed his sense of humor, and his candor and self-deprecation, into a whole new career by joking around on *The Tonight Show* with host Johnny Carson. Carson liked Reynolds because Reynolds poked fun at his own TV flops; similarly, Carson liked Blake because he talked with equal honesty about his outrageous past and the silly demands of his corporate bosses at Universal Television—executives Blake dismissed disparagingly as "suits." The exposure Reynolds got led to his successful movie career, while Blake grafted his antiestablishment, tough-talking attitude onto the character of TV cop Baretta. Baretta was a chameleonic street detective who spoke in aphorisms ("Don't do the crime if you can't do the time"; "You can take that to the bank"), had a pet cockatoo, and helped and/or flirted with an endless succession of women, whom he invariably introduced as "cousins" to his old friend and neighbor, Billy—played by Tom Ewell, who costarred with Marilyn Monroe in *The Seven Year Itch.* One of Baretta's most unforgettable "cousins," a flashy undercover cop from England, was played by Joan Collins—pre-*Dynasty.* At the time, *Baretta,* despite the cockatoo, had a more realistic flavor than most cop shows, and Blake had a more natural style; he was to the midseventies what Bruce Willis was to the late eighties in *Moonlighting,* with more intensity and individuality than just about anyone else in prime time. There's another parallel, too. In terms of aggressively fighting for the type of quality show he wanted to present, Blake was to the seventies what Tom and Dick Smothers were to the sixties, what Bill Cosby was to the eighties, and what Roseanne was to the nineties. Universal Television had hired Blake to take over Tony Musante's role in the series *Toma,* which was about a loner cop who was partial to disguises, but by the time Blake was through, the studio gave in and gave the character and series a new name. The catchy *Baretta* theme song, "Keep Your Eye on the Sparrow," was written by Dave Grusin.

Barney & Friends. *1992– , PBS.* "I love you / you love me / we're a happy family." That's the unavoidable phrase Barney the purple dinosaur sings on each of these shows, which have become so popular since being distributed by PBS that *Barney & Friends* is an automatic candidate for future teleliteracy—even though its audience, at first exposure, is basically *pre*literate. When Barney started out on home video in 1988, as the star of *Barney and the Backyard Gang,* he didn't seem to be anything special. Come to think of it, he *still* doesn't, but sometimes the feverish craze surrounding certain children's shows just can't be evaluated or explained rationally. For further proof, and similar types of overbearing tie-in merchandising, see also: *Teenage Mutant Ninja Turtles.* The stunning, disturbing truth, though, is that *Barney* is in a league all his own, at least in terms of prepubescent profit margins. For the years 1993 and 1994, *Forbes* estimated Barney's combined earnings at a dino-mite $84 million—more than twice as much as Michael Jackson earned during the same period. In fact, the magazine ranks the fuzzy dinosaur third on its list of the richest Hollywood entertainers for those two years, ranked behind only Steven Spielberg and Oprah Winfrey. There's no word on how many of Barney's bucks trickle down to Baby Bop—but with our children, and our wallets, supporting this magenta monster so indiscriminately, it certainly gives us reason to be fearful of the fuscsia.

Barney Miller. *1975–82, ABC.* Producer Danny Arnold's midseventies sitcom began as a somewhat standard comedy focusing on a police captain's life at work and at home, but quickly evolved into a work-only format. For the remainder of its existence, the long-running series remained confined almost entirely to the precinct house in which Barney (Hal Linden) and his colleagues worked, waited, joked, and talked. Especially talked. The strength of the series was its focus on character, and its endless parade of eccentrics from the outside world—a format later copied by *Night Court* and many other shows. Today it's recalled fondly as a sort of comedic *Hill Street Blues*—but since this sitcom came first, perhaps *Hill Street Blues* should be remembered as a more dramatic *Barney Miller. Barney Miller* generated a 1977 spinoff, *Fish,* starring Abe Vigoda, but *Fish* flopped. (I could have avoided that joke, but decided to include it for the halibut.)

Batman. *1966–68, ABC.* This strongly tongue-in-cheek ABC series initially was presented twice weekly, with cliffhangers between the Wednesday and Thursday night episodes ("Tune in tomorrow—Same Bat-time, same Bat-channel!"), and caught on almost immediately: *Batman* premiered in January 1966, and ended the season a few months later with both the Wednesday and Thursday installments in the overall Top 10. The show's popularity as a sixties fad was brief, but the central character (who *wore* briefs) was much more durable and adaptable. Cartoonist Bob Kane's Batman character first appeared in *Detective Comics* in 1939, and, like *Superman*, was a multimedia costumed hero in the forties; in addition to his comic-book exploits, the caped crusader was showcased in a *Batman* serial in 1943 and a *Batman and Robin* serial in 1949, and even showed up as a guest star on the *Superman* radio series. It was not until the TV series of the sixties, though, when the character was played as camp, that Batman notched his first Hollywood success. Adam West's Batman, like Burt Ward's Robin, was hopelessly strait-laced and straight-faced, and the comic-book feel was accentuated by tilted camerawork (used whenever inside a villain's lair), by Robin's goofy, G-rated expletives (such as "Holy oleo!," "Holy red herring!," and my favorite, "Holy priceless collection of Etruscan snoods!"), and such action balloon words, superimposed during fistfights, as "Oooff!," "Thwapp!" and "Powie!" Neil Hefti's sassy "Batman" theme didn't hurt, either; his version, as well as a cover version by The Marketts, made the Top 40 that first summer. *Batman* became such a popular sixties fad that to guest-star on it, or make a cameo appearance, was all the rage, and it's the villains who are freshest in memory a generation later: Burgess Meredith's squawky Penguin, Frank Gorshin's giggling, googly-eyed Riddler, Cesar Romero's white-faced Joker, and Julie Newmar's purrfect Catwoman. A bigger-budget 1966 summer movie version featuring all four of those flashy villains (with Lee Meriwether substituting for Newmar) was intended to predate the series premiere, but ended up following its first season because ABC had rushed the weekly *Batman* series onto the schedule in January. By the time the *Batman* film hit theaters in August, the TV series already had peaked in the ratings, and would never be as popular again—but Batman himself would. Two decades later, another movie version of *Batman*, this one much darker, was presented in 1989, with Tim Burton directing, Michael Keaton in the title role, and Jack Nicholson as the Joker. This more somber and sexy *Batman* was the third most popular film of the decade, earning $150 million in box-office receipts. Holy windfall! Naturally, *Batman Returns*, also directed by Burton, was next, with Danny De Vito as the Penguin and Michelle Pfeiffer as Catwoman. The franchise switched hands for 1995's *Batman Forever*, with Val Kilmer as the new Batman, Joel Schumacher as the new director, and sidekick Robin making his first post-sixties screen appearance, courtesy of Chris O'Donnell. It was even more of a financial success than its predecessors, and, once again, there were two bad guys with which to contend: Jim Carrey as the Riddler and Tommy Lee Jones as Two-Face. As with the TV series, the villains in those films got, and deserved, most of the attention; from those three movies, the standout stars were Nicholson, Pfeiffer, and Carrey, respectively, who more than did justice—or, in this case, injustice—to the Joker, Catwoman, and the Riddler. For future additions to the cinematic rogues' gallery, I suggest tapping two other delightful characterizations from the TV series: Victor Buono's sneering, schizophrenic King Tut, and Joan Collins's Siren, whose singing voice could mesmerize any man within earshot. Meanwhile, back on the small screen, the Fox network in 1992 unveiled *Batman: The Animated Series* (subsequently renamed, following the addition of a cartoon costar, *The Adventures of Batman and Robin*), a new

The Avengers, with Diana Rigg and Patrick Macnee as a most stylish set of TV spies.

Batman, with Adam West and Burt Ward as the "Holy Original!" Dynamic Duo.

Baywatch, with the buoyant Pamela Anderson, Alexandra Paul, and Yasmine Bleeth.

version painting the Caped Crusader as square-jawed and bulked-up, with stylishly moody animation and plots. It was this animated series, not ABC's live-action *Batman* from the sixties, which marked the TV debut of Poison Ivy, the comic-book villainess pegged to bedevil Batman in the fourth modern *Batman* film.

Bat Masterson. *1959–61, NBC*. This Western series isn't syndicated or seen much any more, but the theme song ("Back when the west was very young / there lived a man named Masterson / He wore a cane and derby hat / They called him Bat / Bat Masterson") and Gene Barry's stylish getup—pearl-handled walking stick and all—are likely to strike familiar chords in anyone over thirty-five. In more ways than one, *Bat Masterson* was a dandy series.

Bay Area Earthquake. See *World Series, The*.

Baywatch. *1989–90, NBC; 1990–   , syndicated*. This nineties version of "jiggle television," starring David Hasselhoff (formerly of the equally inane *Knight Rider* series) as a Southern California lifeguard, was canceled by NBC after a single season—yet because of its phenomenal popularity in Europe and elsewhere, new episodes were produced for first-run syndication, and *Baywatch* not only survived, but thrived, drawing a weekly worldwide audience estimated at one billion viewers. (Apparently, the phrase "There's a sucker born every minute" may have been a lowball estimate.) The heroes and heroines of *Baywatch* take turns engaging in all manner of shoreside rescues, from heart attacks to shark attacks, while simultaneously showing off their sleek physiques. These action sequences, mixed in with various romantic entanglements and mandatory moralizing (Hasselhoff's lifeguard Mitch also happens to be single-handedly raising a teenage son), form the frothy center of most *Baywatch* episodes, which hardly explains this show's global popularity among viewers in so many different cultures. Why do they watch *Baywatch*? Basically, to ogle, an activity that knows no language barrier. Hasselhoff is the main attraction for buff buffs interested in males; on the female side, the primary anatomical draw is Pamela Anderson (also known, more recently, under her married name of Pamela Lee), who quit a simultaneous job as the "Tool Time" girl on ABC's hit *Home Improvement* to devote full time to *Baywatch*. In the nineties, this series is an instant laugh-inducer when mentioned by stand-up comics, much as *Charlie's Angels* was in the seventies—and *Baywatch* has spread to other corners of pop culture as well, including a ludicrous 1995 syndicated spinoff series called *Baywatch Nights* (in which Hasselhoff's Mitch, not at all weary from saving people all day, saves more of them at night as a partner in a detective agency) and a shameful dress-up doll called "Baywatch Barbie." It's easy, though, to tell the tiny *Baywatch* dolls from their life-sized counterparts: the smaller action figures are more expressive.

Beany and Cecil. *1962–67, ABC*. People's memories of this series and its characters may vary widely, and seem almost irreconcilable. For example: was

Cecil the Seasick Sea Serpent a cartoon dragon—or a hand puppet? Right on both counts. First came the local Los Angeles TV show in 1949–53 (kinescopes of which eventually were syndicated nationwide) called *Time for Beany*. That was Bob Clampett's clever series starring the puppet pals, with Stan Freberg supplying the voice of Cecil, and Daws Butler (who later provided the voices of Elroy on *The Jetsons*, Quick Draw McGraw, Yogi Bear, Huckleberry Hound, and others) as Beany. Another noteworthy contributor to the early *Beany* show—which was done live, five days a week—was scriptwriter Bill Scott, who later teamed with Jay Ward on *Rocky and His Friends*. Clampett revived the Beany and Cecil characters in cartoon form in the late fifties, and ABC gave them their own show, titled *Beany and Cecil*, in 1962.

Beatles Anthology, The. *1995, ABC*. In 1964, when the Beatles appeared for the first time on *The Ed Sullivan Show*, the group broke all existing audience records for a TV entertainment show, with six out of ten people watching television that evening tuned to the Fab Four. Thirty-one years later, a six-hour oral and aural history of the Beatles was presented on ABC, and another record was broken: *The Beatles Anthology 1*, the first of three double-album companion CDs (of outtakes and rarities) tied to the TV series, entered the *Billboard* charts at number one, selling an estimated, and unprecedented, 1.2 million copies in its first week of release. As a promotional tool for that two-record set, as well as for its 1996 successors and the subsequent home-video boxed set (a documentary more than twice as long as the ABC version), ABC's *The Beatles Anthology* was a total success. For the network itself, success was less than total; reviews were mixed, and the audience drawn to ABC over those three November nights was hardly of Sullivanesque proportions (earning a 13.8 rating and 23 percent audience share, compared to a 45.3 rating and 60 share for that career-making *Ed Sullivan Show* appearance). Yet among true Beatles fans, the major complaint about the network version of *The Beatles Anthology* was that it skimmed or skipped over so many fascinating points in the group's history—a defect the eventual home-video release, at more than twice the length (without commercials), was expected to rectify. Even so, ABC's *The Beatles Anthology* was, in and of itself, a magical history tour. One obvious highlight was the group's raucous 1965 Shea Stadium concert performance of "I'm Down," so vibrant both musically and visually; another was the much more sedate sight of the three surviving Beatles sitting together reminiscing about their visit to India, with George Harrison prodded by Ringo Starr into playing, on ukelele, one of his never-recorded songs from the period. What made *The Beatles Anthology* inarguably worthy of inclusion here, though, was that its first ABC installment concluded with the world premiere of the first new Beatles song since 1970: "Free As a Bird," a John Lennon composition, and home recording, to which the three surviving Beatles added additional lyrics and vocals. The video was especially satisfying, integrating old and new footage into a bird's-eye-view montage that soared and swooped above and around various Beatle allusions, from the office of a "Paperback Writer" to the grave of "Eleanor Rigby," from an egg man ("I Am the Walrus") to an English sheepdog (the inspiration for

"Martha My Dear"), from the pedestrian crosswalk at Abbey Road to the car-crash from "A Day in the Life" (or, perhaps, from the "Paul is dead" rumors of 1969). "Real Love," the other "new" Beatles song unveiled during *The Beatles Anthology*, was a less ambitious video production—and the entire televised anthology, though evocative and at times very impressive, turned out to be less nakedly honest, in terms of the group's internal dynamics and external influences, than Eric Idle's 1978 satirical documentary, *The Rutles—All You Need Is Cash*.

Beat the Clock. *1950–58, CBS; 1958–61, ABC.* This stunt game show, which had people do silly and often messy things while competing for prizes, began on radio in 1949, shifted quickly and effortlessly to TV in 1950, and ran successfully in prime time for most of the decade—while simultaneously offering a daytime version. Bud Collyer, who hosted both the radio and TV versions, was radio's original *Superman* (and, come to think of it, looked a *lot* like Clark Kent). Neil and Danny Simon were two of the writers concocting stunts during the show's infancy, and among the paycheck-hungry young actors hired to road-test the stunts during rehearsals was James Dean. Producers Mark Goodson and Bill Todman revived the series in syndication with new hosts from 1969–74, but after that, their *Clock* had run down. In the nineties, probably the most familiar element of *Beat the Clock* is its title—although its messy style lives on in many current game shows, specifically the ones made for and starring children on the Nickelodeon cable network.

Beavis and Butt-Head. *1993– , MTV. Beavis and Butt-Head*, the animated series by Mike Judge (who also provides the voices and patented slacker laughs of the program's not-so-dynamic duo), actually is two shows in one. One show, the one that initially got the series and MTV into trouble, involves the comic exploits of these pubescent delinquents as they cause trouble at school, out in the neighborhood, or while performing their fittingly brainless tasks as employees at Burger World. The other part of *Beavis and Butt-Head*, the part that is so refreshingly irreverent, is their primary after-hours recreational activity: watching videos on MTV and commenting on them, like a remedial rock-video version of *Mystery Science Theater 3000*. When *Beavis and Butt-Head* premiered as cartoon shorts on MTV's *Liquid Television* in 1992, the exploits of Butt-Head (dark hair, braces, says "huh-huh-huh" a lot) and Beavis (light hair, demonic expression, says "huh-huh-huh" a lot) were intended for mature audiences, even if they reveled in shocking immaturity. They were misogynist, homophobic, pyromaniac, sadistic misfits who played "frog baseball," started fires, tortured insects with firecrackers, sniffed paint thinner, and intentionally served deep-fried rodents to their unsuspecting fast-food customers. MTV almost instantly demanded full-length, only slightly tamer episodes, mistakenly placing early showings of *Beavis and Butt-Head* where younger viewers could see them; as a result, one Ohio woman blamed the series in 1993 for inspiring her five-year-old son to set the family's mobile home on fire, accidentally killing his younger sister. Though the facts failed to support the accusation, the controversy prompted MTV to move the series to a late-night slot, where it should have been all along. Even so, the show's genuinely imitated behavior—the boys' almost constant grunting laughter, and their infantile delight with mild obscenities and rude references—continued somehow to find and influence young viewers, even while amusing or infuriating older ones. But when it came to watching and analyzing rock videos, Beavis and Butt-Head were, and are, nothing less than idiot savants of teleliteracy, deconstructing images with a fascinating mixture of insights, insults, and hilarious misunderstandings (as when Beavis "recognizes" Paul Simon as "that dude from Africa that used to be in the Beatles"). Metallica, AC/DC, and the like are "cool," while most other video artists "suck"—the crude binary equivalent of Roger Ebert and Gene Siskel's thumbs-up, thumbs-down approach. As couch-potato slackers with simplistic opinions, the characters of Beavis and Butt-Head are dysfunctional descendants of the explosion-loving farmers of "Farm Film Report" and the beer-swilling goofballs of "The Great White North" (both duos courtesy of *Second City TV*), Wayne and Garth of "Wayne's World" on *Saturday Night Live*, and the genial protagonists of the film *Bill & Ted's Excellent Adventure*. In all those skits and movies, though, the humor was less subversive: the simple, daring brilliance behind *Beavis and Butt-Head* is that the TV-watching part of the show ridicules not only everything else on MTV, but most of the people who watch it. Kurt Loder, who anchors the network's news reports, confessed to *Playboy* in 1995 that Beavis and Butt-Head are "the greatest rock critics of all time," while, for a while, David Letterman mentioned them almost nightly on his show, so taken was he by what he called the purity of their stupidity. My own favorite example of their charming cluelessness came on one Christmas show, when a channel-surfing Beavis and Butt-Head stumbled upon one of those "Yule log" telecasts and mistook the unchanging image of a burning hearth for some kind of minimalist video—and, in the same telecast, encountered a Christmas carol sung by the host of *Max Headroom*, the duo's spiritual and attitudinal forebear, and were thoroughly baffled. Yet even as pure stupidity, *Beavis and Butt-Head* remains the smartest thing MTV has ever offered. Heh-heh-heh.

Ben Casey. *1961–66, ABC.* "Man . . . Woman . . . Birth . . . Death . . . Infinity." With those words, uttered by Sam Jaffe as the wise, grizzled Dr. Zorba, *Ben Casey* launched each week into its somber theme music—and into another drama exploring medical diseases, cures, ethics, and dilemmas. Today, the name "Ben Casey," like those of "Dr. Kildare" and "Marcus Welby, M.D.," carries the connotation of the perfect, caring physician—the Perry Mason of doctors. However, Casey, as played by Vince Edwards, was a lot more ruggedly handsome than Robert Young's paternal Dr. Welby. In 1988, twenty-two years after *Ben Casey* went off the air, a more paternal-looking Edwards starred in a telemovie called *The Return of Ben Casey*. By then, though, the image of the "perfect doctor" had long been pronounced dead by the fascinatingly flawed folks of *St. Elsewhere*.

Benny Hill Show, The. *1979–81, syndicated.* This long-running, consistently infantile British series of specials was exported to America, in series form, a decade after first appearing in England, but arrived at just the right time in TV history to get maximum attention: post-*Three's Company*, pre-*Hill Street Blues*. None of Hill's regular antics were seen then as blatantly "incorrect"—not his forays into blackface, not the scantily clad dancers, and certainly not his extended silent skits, which treated women as sex objects and old men as objects of ridicule. And here's something frightening: the half-hour shows syndicated in the States were the more *restrained* parts of his one-hour Thames Television specials, which featured lots more nudity and lots less taste. But to give the durable Hill his due, he came from, and was perpetuating, the English Music Hall tradition; he wrote his own skits and music, and *The Benny Hill Show* was the closest modern descendent of silent pictures. You could even mount an argument that the use of TV in *The Benny Hill Show* was somewhat in the tradition of *The Ernie Kovacs Show* and the "dirty old man" and "falling-tricycle" skits on *Rowan & Martin's Laugh-In*. You could, but I won't. Instead, I'll say that the best thing about *The Benny Hill Show* was this: it showed American viewers, once and for all, that not all British television was of the caliber, or tone, of the stuff presented on *Masterpiece Theatre*.

Beverly Hillbillies, The. *1962–71, CBS.* One statistic I unearthed about this show continues to amaze me. In the entire fifty-year-plus history of network television, *The Beverly Hillbillies* is the *only* series to wind up as the top-rated show on television in its first season on the air. *I Love Lucy* and *The Cosby Show* ended their freshman seasons in third place, and second place was snagged by a handful of shows, including *Bewitched, A Different World, Laverne & Shirley*, and *Roseanne*. (After its freshman season, in case you're wondering, *ER* was ranked fourth.) But first place in its first year? Only *The Beverly Hillbillies* has done that, ever. And here's another nugget I dug up that puts this show's popularity in depressingly clear perspective: when the Beatles broke all-time audience records by appearing on *The Ed Sullivan Show* that first time in 1964, the record that was broken belonged to a regular episode of *The Beverly Hillbillies* broadcast only the month before—the one in which Irene Ryan's Granny mistakes a kangaroo for a giant rabbit. Sociologists and media professors love to analyze why *The Beverly Hillbillies* struck such a nerve, but the fact that it was funny probably didn't hurt. Ryan's Granny and Buddy Ebsen's Jed Clampett were a big part of, and partial reason for, the rural population explosion that invaded CBS sitcoms throughout the sixties. Creator Paul Henning's *Beverly Hillbillies* hailed from the general vicinity of Hooterville, which became the setting of *Petticoat Junction*—which, in turn, was followed by the spinoff series *Green Acres*, which essentially inverted the *Beverly Hillbillies* formula by having city folks move to the country. The theme song, "The Ballad of Jed Clampett," written by Henning himself, was a hit for Lester Flatt and Earl Scruggs, and remains stubbornly ensconsed in popular memory. A 1981 telemovie, *The Return of the Beverly Hillbillies*, was made after Ebsen's post-*Hillbillies* series, *Barnaby Jones*, had come and gone, but time had taken its toll. The telemovie covered for the 1973 death of Irene Ryan by having Imogene Coca play "Granny's Maw," dealt with the 1980 death of Raymond Bailey by eliminating his role as greedy banker Milton Drysdale, and gave holdout Max Baer, Jr.'s, role of cousin Jethro Bodine to another actor, Ray Young. Donna Douglas and Nancy Kulp, as, respectively, Elly May Clampett and Jane Hathaway (Drysdale's prim assistant), were the only other series regulars to return, and thus shared top billing with Ebsen for the telemovie remake. (Further down that 1981 cast list, playing an attractive character named only "Heather," was a young actress named Heather Locklear.) Kulp then pursued a supporting role of a very different kind—as a member of the U. S. Congress. She was unsuccessful, and died in 1991. In 1993, CBS saluted the series, and reunited Ebsen, Baer, and Douglas, in a belated thirtieth-anniversary prime-time special called *The Legend of the Beverly Hillbillies*. That same year, not at all coincidentally, Hollywood presented a *Beverly Hillbillies* movie remake, featuring Jim Varney as Jed, Cloris Leachman as Granny, and Lily Tomlin as Jane Hathaway. It was a cinematic offering that counted on the sentiment in the friendly phrase ending each episode of the original series: "Y'all come back now, y'hear?" However, anyone who did come back, and sat through that big-screen remake, quickly realized the movie folk in Californee had botched it again. In the original *Beverly Hillbillies*, the only thing that was crude was the black gold— the Texas tea. And the original series was so beloved, it's one of only three situation comedies with episodes ranked among the all-time Top 40 of TV's highest-rated offerings. That rarefied listing includes the finales of *M*A*S*H* and *Cheers*—and two episodes of *The Beverly Hillbillies*.

Beverly Hills, 90210. *1990–* , *Fox*. Just when you thought it was safe to write off TV producer Aaron Spelling, he hit gold again with this widely imitated youth ensemble series. In the sixties, Spelling's production credits included *Burke's Law, Honey West*, and *The Mod Squad;* in the seventies, he ruled TV with a successful string of cartoonish action and anthology series, including *Charlie's Angels, The Love Boat, Hart to Hart*, and *Fantasy Island;* and in the eighties, before stumbling late in the decade with a series of flop sitcoms and serials, Spelling continued his success with the likes of *Dynasty, Hotel*, and *T. J. Hooker*. But in the nineties, working for the Fox network, his production company struck gold, giving teen (and preteen) viewers their first cult series of the decade: creator Darren Star's drama about the angst-filled days and nights of the largely privileged classmates of West Beverly High. The pilot focused on two transfers from the midwest, the brother-sister twins Brandon (Jason Priestley) and Brenda (Shannen Doherty), but the real scene-stealers were the beautiful and popular Kelly (Jennie Garth) and the surly and charismatic Dylan (Luke Perry). Luke's Dylan, like James Marshall's James Hurley on the much more adult *Twin Peaks*, was an intentional echo of the motorcycle-riding, quiet-talking James Dean persona—which had been left almost untouched on TV since the late sixties, when Michael Parks drove around the country on his motorcycle in *Then Came Bronson*. By its second season, *Beverly Hills, 90210* was a major hit, and Perry did more to popularize long sideburns than anyone since Elvis Presley. But by the third season, many of the show's formerly loyal fans began to tire of its repetitive plots and relatively shallow characters—especially Brenda. By the time *90210* devoted itself to a lengthy "love-triangle" story featuring Kelly, Brenda, and Luke, the show seemed frighteningly like a live-action version of *The Archies*, with Kelly as blonde Betty, Brenda as brunette Veronica, Dylan as their mutual boyfriend Archie, and Brandon as the affable Jughead. Brenda finally was written out of the show in 1994 after a series of headline-grabbing off-camera antics by Doherty, and with new cast members added to pick up the slack, the show didn't miss a beat. Not that the beat was that tough: *Degrassi High*, a Canadian series distributed by PBS, presented much more credible students and situations, but Star's soap-opera approach (he went on to create *Melrose Place* as a *90210* spinoff) proved much more popular and durable, even if it proved more laughable. Perry finally left the series in 1995, clocking five years portraying the kind of stifling teen-idol role that Johnny Depp (in another Fox series, *21 Jump Street*) jettisoned after three. *Beverly Hills, 90210* will survive in memory long after it wanes in popularity, if only because, like so many of Spelling's other inexplicably popular hits, it sparked so many instant imitators.

Bewitched. *1964–72, ABC*. Long before the term was coined to describe the way TV viewers use their remote controls to sample several channels in rapid succession, this series was famous for its "zapping." The premise of this show can be read two ways. Either it's a show quietly supporting equality and integration (love conquers all, no matter how strongly your genetic differences), or one that quietly subverts the then-burgeoning women's liberation movement (a woman, no matter how powerful, should accede to a man's wishes). Better to just let it remain a silly, funny fantasy show—one that was astoundingly similar to, though superior to, the contemporaneous *I Dream of Jeannie*. Like Barbara Eden on that series, Elizabeth Montgomery ended up playing two roles on *Bewitched:* Samantha the married witch and her impish, dark-haired cousin Serena. Dick York, as Samantha's husband Darrin, was replaced by Dick Sargent midway through the series' run, but without denting the show's popularity one bit. This was a women-driven sitcom all the way, thanks to the talent of Montgomery (who subsequently turned to more serious fare in a string of dramatic telemovies and miniseries) and Agnes Moorehead, who played Samantha's mother. Still a hit in syndication, as well as a key member of the Nick at Nite family, *Bewitched* is interesting to watch these days because it reveals how casually TV used to treat the social imbibing of alcohol—and also because the advertising-agency satire and comic hypocrisy is right on the money. David White's greedy ad-executive Larry Tate, in some ways, was the TV forefather of David Clennon's Miles Drentell on *thirtysomething:* the client was always right, and the employee, no matter how close a friend, was always expendable.

Bionic Woman, The. *1976–77, ABC; 1977–78, NBC*. To have poor Lindsay Wagner go from the impressive 1973 movie *The Paper Chase* to this distaff spinoff of *The Six Million Dollar Man* was unbelievable. To have her win

an Outstanding Lead Actress in a Drama Series Emmy Award for it was
. . . unforgettable.

Bob Hope Specials. *1950– , NBC*. How much clout, and audience loyalty,
did Bob Hope have at the top of his game on NBC? There's an easy way to
put it. No single entertainer has ever gathered more people in front of their
TV sets at one time than Bob Hope did for his *Bob Hope Christmas Show* in
1970. The only programs to draw a larger audience than that special, in the
entire history of TV, were the finale of *M*A*S*H*, the "Who shot J.R.?"
episode of *Dallas*, the final installment of *Roots*, five Super Bowls, one night
of Olympic Games, and the TV premiere of *Gone with the Wind*. To put it
in even better perspective, Hope's *next* most popular *Christmas Show*, in
1971, nestles on the all-time top-rated programs list just two notches below
a 1964 installment of *The Ed Sullivan Show*—the one featuring The Beatles.
Of course, taking nothing away from Hope, there was a clear reason why those
particular shows drew so many viewers. Those shows were Hope's annual
Christmas visits with American soldiers overseas (filmed for delayed broadcast), and were rare outpourings of support for the troops in Vietnam at a
time of ever-heightening protests against the war. This was nothing Hope had
concocted recently, or with an eye on the ratings, either. The very first TV
special Hope hosted, a local broadcast from Madison Square Garden in 1948
(the same summer Milton Berle first hosted *Texaco Star Theater*), was a salute
to the men and women of the U.S. Armed Forces, and his 1950 holiday NBC
special showed him visiting troops stationed in Japan and Korea. However,
Hope's other specials, then and later, came to rely on a lazily repetitive
formula ("Here's a really great gal," "How 'bout that kid?"), in which one
ingredient and guest star was exchanged the following year for another: this
year's Kim Novak was next year's Jayne Mansfield, this year's Joey Heatherton
was next year's Raquel Welch, this year's Tom Jones was next year's Engelbert
Humperdinck, and so on. In the eighties and nineties, as Hope entered his
own eighties and nineties, the editing on his monologues got heavier, and his
specials increasingly relied upon vintage clips and a less formal (and less
taxing) conversational format. In 1995, at age ninety-two, Hope hosted NBC-
TV network specials for the forty-fifth consecutive year, including an August
"personal scrapbook" called *Bob Hope: Memories of World War II*. Yet during
the winter holiday season of 1995, for the first time in many decades, no Bob
Hope special was scheduled by NBC. Quietly and unofficially, an amazing
era had come to an end, but Bob Hope long will be remembered, not only
for his sharp and still delightful radio and film work, but as one of the television medium's major institutions—the only one to become so established
and revered without the benefit of a weekly showcase for his talents. Thanks
for the memories, Bob.

Bob Newhart Show, The. *1972–78, CBS*. One of the classic, classy MTM
comedies of the seventies. Newhart's hound-dog reaction shots were priceless,
and he could time a joke, and a silence, better than any sitcom comedian but
Jack Benny. This sitcom, duly picked up as part of the Nick at Nite lineup in

1993, had the requisite goofy neighbor (Bill Daily, post-*I Dream of Jeannie*) and wacky work partners (Marcia Wallace and Peter Bonerz as, respectively, a receptionist and orthodontist), but the heart of the show was the relationship between Bob and Emily Hartley, played so perfectly by Newhart and the captivating, very funny Suzanne Pleshette. Also very memorable: Jack Riley's therapy-group sourpuss Elliott Carlin. Few TV series have been alluded to more fondly or frequently by other prime-time shows, or had their characters more actively "recycled" in sly cameo homages. For the best of them, see the entries under *Newhart* and *St. Elsewhere*. Thanks for the memories, Bob.

Bold Ones, The. *1969–73, NBC.* This rotating anthology series bridged, in both quality and spirit, the "Golden Age" dramas of the fifties with the issue dramas of the seventies and eighties. A handful of different series were broadcast under the *Bold Ones* umbrella title, including *The Doctors*, which starred E. G. Marshall as a senior physician (the type of role he'd still be playing, a quarter-century later, on *Chicago Hope*) and David Hartman as a dedicated young doctor. The best-known component of *The Bold Ones*, though, was *The Lawyers*, starring Burl Ives, Joseph Campanella, and James Farentino, as the legal firm of Nichols, Darrell, and Darrell (no relation to the Larry, Darryl, and Darryl of *Newhart* fame). As attorneys, each brought something else to the defense table: Ives's Walter Nichols was a wily legal veteran, Campanella's Brian Darrell a by-the-books scholar, and Farentino's Neil (Brian's younger brother) an impulsive, flamboyant, but effective advocate. Taken together, they were potent, charismatic and effective enough to be considered TV's original courtroom "Dream Team." The very best element of *The Bold Ones*, though, was *The Senator*, which starred Hal Holbrook as an idealistic junior senator up against the system, and tackling headline issues, in a big way. Unfortunately, *The Senator* premiered in 1970, and it was probably too soon after the 1968 murder of Robert F. Kennedy to have viewers embracing a fictional senator with charisma and idealism, fighting against the odds for what he believed was right. I would have voted for Holbrook's *Senator*, but I didn't have a Nielsen box. *The Senator* was sent packing after one season.

Bonanza. *1959–73, NBC.* This amazingly popular series premiered in 1959, as television's first Western to be televised in color. NBC's parent company, RCA, wanted to sell color TVs, and producing *Bonanza* in full color turned out to be a bonanza indeed. In addition to all the TV sales it sparked, *Bonanza* also was TV's highest-rated series in the midsixties, and held on long enough to avoid cancellation until 1973. Like *Gunsmoke*, *Bonanza* had a very moral center, lashing out against bigotry and even treating most Native American characters, and Mexicans and blacks, with a then-unusual sense of decency. The scripts were sometimes hokey, but the casting saved a lot of stories. Lorne Greene's patriarch, Pa Cartwright, was a TV icon, and his original "my three sons"—Pernell Roberts's brooding Adam, Dan Blocker's gentle-giant Hoss, and Michael Landon's Little Joe—accounted for the show's popularity and durability. (It certainly wasn't because of the way they sang the theme song in the pilot episode—the one that began "We got a right / to pick a little fight / Bonanza!"—although the theme song itself, as an instrumental, was a Top 20 hit in 1961.) With its stress on traditional values and respect for elders, and its love of the land, the sensibility of *Bonanza* was actually more Indian than Cowboy. The first seasons of the show were the best, and developed characters whose familiarity and charisma would carry *Bonanza* for fourteen years. Roberts left after six years on the Ponderosa—a very successful stretch compared to most TV series, but less than half of the eventual length of this particular Western's tenure. By riding off into the sunset when he did, Roberts inadvertently, and somewhat impatiently, established an "I'm Gonna Quit This Show and Become a Big Star" precedent later echoed, no less misguidedly, by McLean Stevenson on *M*A*S*H*, Patrick Duffy on *Dallas* (who wisely recanted), Shelley Long on *Cheers*, and David Caruso on *NYPD Blue*. Blocker died while *Bonanza* was still on the air, but the others all went on to star in other series: Greene in the absurdly bad *Battlestar: Galactica*, Roberts in the nearly as awful *Trapper John, M.D.*, and Landon in the very successful *Little House on the Prairie* and *Highway to Heaven*. A flop telemovie, *Bonanza: The Next Generation*, was launched in syndication in 1988, but the closest on-air ties it had to the original was in casting one of Landon's sons, Michael Landon, Jr., as the son of Little Joe, and Lorne Greene's daughter, Gillian, in a supporting role. Landon, Sr., was readying his fourth series, CBS's *Us*, when he developed, and died from, pancreatic cancer in 1991. Two years later, yet another attempt to revive *Bonanza* resulted in a one-hour syndicated action series called *Bonanza: The Legends of the Ponderosa*, which ran out of legends (and ideas) in less than a season. NBC also returned to the Ponderosa, presenting one telemovie, *Bonanza: The Return*, in 1993 (with Landon Jr. again, Blocker's son Dirk, and Ben Johnson as Bronc Evans, to whom Ben Cartwright willed the running of the ranch), and another with the same cast, *Bonanza: Under Attack*, in 1995. Posterity, though, will embrace originality—the original *Bonanza* series, the original *Bonanza* cast, and the original *Bonanza* theme song. Minus the lyrics, that is.

Bozo the Clown. *1956– , syndicated.* Until Ronald McDonald came along, the most famous clowns on TV—not counting politicians—were Clarabell from *Howdy Doody* and good old Bozo, a Capitol Records character "franchised" to local TV markets by entrepreneur Larry Harmon, with most stations providing their own hosts (the same trick was employed, beginning at about the same time in the fifties, by *Romper Room*.) In 1995, Harmon signed a five-year contract extension with Chicago superstation WGN, ostensibly carrying him and his current Bozo showcase, *Bozo Super Sunday*, to the year 2000. The most famous Bozo, undoubtedly, was Washington, D.C.'s Willard Scott, took his clowning around to the *Today* show. At one point in the sixties, there were approximately 250 local Bozos starring in children's TV shows around the world, and though the craze has peaked and flattened, the *Bozo the Clown* character certainly made his mark. No one insults anybody else, after all, by saying "You Ronald!" or "You Clarabell!"

Brady Bunch, The. *1969–74, ABC.* How I hated this show. I still do—only more fervently, because now my kids have discovered it in syndication and actually watch it (thankfully, at least they laugh as much at the fashions as at the alleged jokes). There have been so many incarnations and reincarnations of *The Brady Bunch*, everything from *The Brady Bunch Hour* variety show to *The Brady Brides* and the more recent *The Bradys*, that it's not worth mentioning them all. I'd be remiss, though, if I didn't note that *A Very Brady Christmas* was both the most popular telemovie of 1988, and the absolute worst. In fact, in my professional opinion, *A Very Brady Christmas* has surpassed both *Still the Beaver* and *The Harlem Globetrotters on Gilligan's Island* to become the worst telemovie in TV history. (Since producer Sherwood Schwartz created both *Gilligan's Island* and *The Brady Bunch*, he's basically the king of the bottom of the TV barrel.) For the record, the climax of *A Very Brady Christmas* has Robert Reed, as architect Mike Brady, trapped in a collapsed building. He's revived, and steered to safety, by the sounds of Christmas carols sung, like a musical beacon, by his anxious family members, who are huddled outside the police barricades. When Mike Brady emerges safely into the arms of the bunched-up Bradys (Florence Henderson's Carol, of course, had led the Carol-ing), the camera pans upward and focuses on the street sign at the corner where this Christmas miracle occurred—and, honest, it's 34th Street. The mind reels. The movie reeks. Yet *The Brady Bunch* refuses to die, and, in fact, manages to thrive. A Chicago theatrical company's stage production of *The Real Live Brady Bunch*—live re-creations of various *Brady Bunch* episodes, line for line—was so successful it was packed off to New York, where it was just as big a hit Off-Broadway. Melanie Hutsell, the actress parodying Eve Plumb's Jan in that stage show, parlayed her whiny "Marcia, Marcia, Marcia!" mantra into a job as a regular on *Saturday Night Live*, where she lasted three years (more than long enough to demonstrate she could do little else). Other examples of Bradymania? They happen almost annually, like rites of spring. In Douglas Coupland's 1991 *Generation X* novel, he defined his term "tele-parablizing" as "morals used in everyday life that derive from TV sitcom plots," using a *Brady Bunch* episode as the example: "That's just like the episode where Jan lost her glasses." In 1992, Barry Williams's *Growing Up Brady: I Was a Teenage Greg*, written with Chris Kreski, was published, selling about a bazillion more copies than my own *Teleliteracy: Taking Television Seriously* the same year (it's an appreciation of irony, rather than petty bitterness, that drives me to point that out). In 1993, ABC presented *Bradymania: A Very Brady Special*, hosted by Henderson herself. And in 1995, Bradymania hit its peak with *The Brady Bunch Movie*, a bigscreen treatment starring Gary Cole and Shelley Long as Mike and Carol Brady, with Christine Taylor as an uncanny lookalike for Maureen McCormick's Marcia. *The Brady Bunch Movie* not only sold more tickets than any other film during the first few weeks of its release, but it actually told its story, presented its characters, and alluded to the TV-episode *Brady Bunch* canon in ways that were witty. Cole, in particular, was devastatingly deadpan, and the whole cinematic venture was better than expected—and better, by an infinite margin, than the original, execrable *Brady Bunch* series. Despite the steady stream of Bradymania and the unprecedented appeal of the movie version, I remain of the opinion that, posterity or no posterity, *The Brady*

Bunch is entirely forgettable. Unfortunately, its theme song is not. "Here's the story / of a man named Brady. . . . " You know the rest. And you ought to be ashamed of yourself.

Branded. *1965–66, NBC.* This show, set in the post-Civil War era, starred Chuck Connors of *The Rifleman* as Jason McCord, an army officer unfairly courtmartialed for alleged cowardice at the Battle at Bitter Creek. He was the sole survivor of a bloody massacre, and claimed to have been knocked unconscious, waking up amid a field of corpses before leaving to seek help. His commanders thought otherwise, and charged McCord with desertion. After he was found guilty, McCord roamed the territories, searching for the fellow officer McCord believed framed him and was the real deserter. This made *Branded* an obvious variation of *The Fugitive*, which had premiered two seasons before, but the angst McCord felt here, and the level of acting Connors delivered, made this a much better series than his previous, more familiar *Rifleman* series. Unfortunately, *Branded*, unlike *The Fugitive*, never got a chance to wrap up its storyline. McCord never found his two-armed man, because, after a single season, NBC gave *Branded* a dishonorable discharge from its schedule. But those who saw it, then or in subsequent syndicated reruns, tend to remember two things quite clearly: the theme song ("Branded! / Scorned as the one who ran! / What do you do when you're branded / and you know you're a man?"), and the sight of McCord's stripes being ripped off his uniform—a graphic form of prime-time emasculation, military style.

Brian's Song. *1971, ABC.* This telemovie, which had a lot in common thematically with the "Golden Age" drama *Bang the Drum Slowly*, was a hit with critics as well as viewers, and brought so much respect to the telemovie form that it's one of the few one-shot offerings being listed here. James Caan and Billy Dee Williams play Chicago Bears players Brian Piccolo and Gale Sayers, respectively, in a story dramatizing their relationship as Piccolo fights a tough, ultimately unsuccessful battle with cancer. Michel Legrand's title theme has become a familiar instrumental standard, and *Brian's Song* was such an acclaimed TV drama that it subsequently was released theatrically—the first telemovie to earn that honor. *Brian's Song* holds up very well today, which can't be said of most TV dramas from that early era of made-for-TV movies. Most of them didn't hold up *then*.

Brideshead Revisited. *1982, PBS.* This 1981 British miniseries truly lived up to the title of *Great Performances*, the umbrella series presenting it to American audiences the following year. Jeremy Irons, Anthony Andrews, Laurence Olivier, John Gielgud, Claire Bloom, Stephane Audran—casts don't come much more talented than this, and every episode of *Brideshead* used its players, and its lush scenery, to maximum effect. This eleven-hour Granada TV adaptation of Evelyn Waugh's novel was the epitome of everything a miniseries could and *should* be: sumptuous, sprawling, intelligent, and completely addictive. The story of Charles Ryder (Irons), a young painter who becomes infatuated with the aristocratic Marchmain family and their ancestral home of Brideshead, remains one of the most acclaimed long-form dramas ever made. It was adapted by John Mortimer, author of the stories inspiring another acclaimed TV presentation, *Rumpole of the Bailey.*

Broadway Open House. *1950–51, NBC.* Eventually, this *Tonight Show* precursor, which ran in NBC's late-night slot beginning in 1950, will fade from memory completely. But even now, a lot of people who never saw this show from TV's early days have heard the name, or seen pictures, of Dagmar (actually, an actress named Jennie Lewis), the buxom sidekick who eventually overshadowed Jerry Lester, one of the show's two rotating hosts. It's sort of similar to what happened with Pat Sajak and Vanna White on *Wheel of Fortune,* only Sajak didn't get upset, as Lester did; he just smiled and got a bigger bank account. The other *Broadway Open House* host, veteran vaudevillian Morey Amsterdam, would make a more lasting mark later on *The Dick Van Dyke Show.*

Buffalo Bill. *1983–84, NBC.* In word-association tests a few years from now, the most likely response to the TV title *Buffalo Bill* will be limited to a vague recollection of it as a show whose central character, talk-show host "Buffalo Bill" Bittinger, was too abrasive to succeed on network TV. That's unfortunate, because this series, created by Tom Patchett and Jay Tarses, was a lot deeper and funnier than that—and there are more than a few similarities between the characters and situations of *Buffalo Bill* and those of the subsequent, instantly successful *The Larry Sanders Show,* which also was built around the onstage and backstage antics of an often abrasive TV talk-show host. Then again, given the talented cast and writers of *Buffalo Bill,* it might have thrived on cable as well, had it premiered there instead of on network TV. Dabney Coleman, as Bittinger, was great, and the supporting cast alone should warrant this series getting a more revered reputation as years go by. It included Geena Davis, Joanna Cassidy, Meshach Taylor of *Designing Women,* Charles Robinson of *Night Court,* and Max Wright of *ALF.* And for those who watched the series, there was an obvious nominee for most memorable episode: the one in which Bittinger hosted a studio full of Jerry Lewis imitators.

Bullwinkle Show, The. *1961–63, NBC.* **Rocky and His Friends.** *1959–61, ABC.* Sherman, set the Wayback Machine to 1959. That's when Jay Ward's *Rocky and His Friends* premiered on ABC, unveiling a cast of cartoon characters and features so delightful that any one of them could have sustained a series of its own. One of them, in fact, stole the show from his squirrelly partner: when the show moved to NBC in 1961, it was retitled *The Bullwinkle Show.* After that show's cancellation, repeats were presented by NBC, then ABC, until the early seventies. Today, the two shows, *Rocky and His Friends* and *The Bullwinkle Show,* are lumped together in memory, referred to under the generic term "Rocky and Bullwinkle." Whatever the name, it's a brilliantly written, cleverly performed, tackily drawn cartoon series, and I adore every frame of it. (I also spend way too much money every time I visit the Dudley

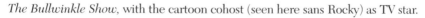

Bonanza, with the core Cartwrights: Dan Blocker as Hoss, Lorne Greene as Pa, Pernell Roberts as Adam, and Michael Landon as Little Joe.

The Bullwinkle Show, with the cartoon cohost (seen here sans Rocky) as TV star.

Do-Right Emporium in Los Angeles, so I'm hardly an objective analyst on this particular point.) Ward created *Rocky and His Friends* with Bill Scott, who was no silent partner; in fact, he provided the voices of Bullwinkle J. Moose, Mr. Peabody, and Dudley Do-Right. June Foray was both Rocket J. Squirrel and Natasha Fatale, Paul Frees was Boris Badenov (I was in my twenties before I got *that* pun), and Hans Conried was Do-Right's mustachioed nemesis, Snidely Whiplash. Edward Everett Horton was responsible for the nervous-sounding narration of "Fractured Fairy Tales," while William Conrad, who had played Matt Dillon on the radio version of *Gunsmoke* (and would later play a rotund detective in TV's *Cannon* series), narrated the moose's misadventures here before moving on to serve as a much more somber, and slowly paced, narrator on TV's *The Fugitive*. Every segment of Ward's cartoon series was a delight, from "Dudley Do-Right" and "Peabody's Improbable History" to "Aesop's Fables" and "Fractured Fairy Tales"—and, of course, the "Rocky and Bullwinkle" serials. There's so much worth treasuring, and remembering, that any list would be incomplete. All lists, however, would have to include Bullwinkle's magic tricks ("Nuthin' up muh sleeve!," "Watch me pull a rabbit outta muh hat!") and Rocky's weary rejoinders ("Again?," "That trick *never* works!"), and scheming spies Boris Badenov and Natasha Fatale, and Conrad's breathless "Rocky" narration, and Bullwinkle's college alma mater "Wassamotta U.," and Horton's distinctive readings of the "Fractured Fairy Tales," and Ward's bouncy music, and, of course, Mr. Peabody's time-tripping Wayback machine. My favorite joke from the whole series? Tough call. How do you choose between a jewel-encrusted toy boat called "The Ruby Yacht of Omar Khayyam" and an intelligence-increasing hat called the "Kirwood Derby"? (That latter joke was a pun on Durward Kirby, the sidekick on *The Garry Moore Show*, who was not at all amused by the reference.) Then again, maybe it's when Bullwinkle pushes a wheelbarrow full of box tops into a bank to inquire about opening an account. "What kind?" asks the bank officer. "Just checking?" "No," Bullwinkle replies. "I really mean it." Or, just maybe, it's the alternate title of a "Rocky and Bullwinkle" adventure about a landslide: "Avalanche is better than done." You get the idea: once you start enumerating, you wind up with an eighty-way tie for first place. My love of good comedy writing, and painfully bad puns, came from this series, and I know I'm not alone in treasuring the memory of this series. Matt Groening invoked its memory as his main inspiration when creating *The Simpsons*, Steven Spielberg cited it as his earliest TV influence, and the show continues to find enthusiastic audiences even now. A live-action 1992 movie called *Boris and Natasha*, with Dave Thomas and Sally Kellerman, was a disappointment both commercially and creatively, but other *Bullwinkle* ventures in the nineties were less Rocky. PBS took the show seriously enough to televise a 1991 documentary called *Of Moose and Men: The Rocky and Bullwinkle Story*. When six cassettes of collected "Rocky & Bullwinkle" adventures were released on the home-video market that same year, all six landed in the Top 10 videocassette sales chart. And when Nickelodeon added old *Rocky and His Friends* and *The Bullwinkle Show* reruns to its daytime schedule under the banner "Moose-o-Rama," a whole new generation of viewers started warming to the same good stories and bad puns. Ward's cartoon exploits continued with *George of the Jungle*, but the theme songs for the animated serials on that show (for "Super Chicken," "Tom Slick," and "George" himself) were much better than the jokes. It was a good series, no question, but the "Rocky and Bullwinkle" cartoons were great—and that's no Bullwinkle.

Burke's Law. *1963–65, ABC; 1994–95, CBS*. The original *Burke's Law* series, in the sixties, took Gene Barry, and his well-heeled, well-dressed persona from *Bat Masterson,* and made him even better-heeled and better-dressed. In the polar opposite of an undercover cop, Barry played a Los Angeles chief of detectives who was also a millionaire, solving crimes while driving around in a chauffeured Rolls-Royce—like Bruce Wayne would have done if he hadn't come up with all that Batman business. *Burke's Law* was crammed with familiar guest stars, a tactic relied on often in later series from the show's producer, Aaron Spelling. This show was silly but fun, though I preferred its spinoff, *Honey West* (starring Anne Francis)—and tired quickly of its renamed, spyseries revamped "sequel," the even more gimmicky 1965–66 *Amos Burke, Secret Agent*. In the nineties, the star and his series reappeared in a new *Burke's Law*, with Barry's Burke now serving as chief of homicide. Peter Barton played his son, and each week's episode was populated with such an eclectic guest roster (one typical installment featured Dom DeLuise, Frankie Avalon, Shadoe Stevens, and *Beverly Hills, 90210* regular Kathleen Robertson), it made you wonder how far away *The Love Boat* was docked.

Burning Bed, The. *1984, NBC*. This intense and often violent telemovie was a ratings hit, a stereotype shatterer, and a social harbinger, all in one. One of TV's most popular telemovies ever, *The Burning Bed* starred Farrah Fawcett in the fact-based tale of a battered wife who, after years of physical and mental abuse at the hands of her husband (Paul LeMat), retaliates by burning him alive in bed as he sleeps. The stereotype that was shattered was Fawcett's jiggly persona from her *Charlie's Angels* days. In acting terms, Fawcett already had done that a few years earlier, in the 1981 miniseries *Murder in Texas* (playing, coincidentally, another prisoner of an unfortunate marriage), but not enough viewers, critics, or casting agents had noticed to make a dent. With *The Burning Bed*, though, so many people took note of Fawcett's raw and powerful performance that she moved on to the likes of 1986's film version of *Extremities,* and helped make the title of this telemovie somewhat synonymous with the concept of a formerly lightweight actor or actress making, or trying to make, a "serious" image shift. Finally, as to the social harbinger idea, *The Burning Bed* concluded by dramatizing, in empathic fashion, the ensuing trial in which Fawcett's defendant was charged with murder and, because of her history of abuse, ultimately acquitted. It was one of the first televised accounts of the "victim defense," a legal approach which since has become much more common, and sometimes employed in cases a lot less sympathetic and credible than this one. (Does the name "Menendez" ring a bell?)

· ·

Caesar's Hour. See *Your Show of Shows.*

Cagney & Lacey. *1982–88, CBS.* One of the few TV series in history to be genuinely resurrected by fan mail and support, *Cagney & Lacey* was yanked by CBS—then reinstated. Sharon Gless, who won multiple Emmys, was actually the third actress to play Chris Cagney: Loretta Swit played the female cop in the original telemovie, and Meg Foster played her in the show's precancellation run. Tyne Daly, as Cagney's partner, was the one and only Mary Beth Lacey. It was a female "buddy picture" long before *Thelma and Louise,* and a rarity for TV, which at the time was much more likely to pair female leads for sitcoms than dramas. Because of that enlightened focus, *Cagney & Lacey* sometimes got more credit and praise than it deserved, although both actresses were quite good, and several episodes, such as Cagney's drunken binge, were genuine showcases. One playfully clever show, tweaking the *Police Woman* style of TV dramas from the decade before, featured Shannon Tweed as an actress visiting the police station to tag along with some "real" cops. And Daly's Lacey, with her working-class attitude, no-nonsense demeanor, and solid but stressful marriage, was TV's closest thing to *Roseanne* until *Roseanne* came along. In 1994, the duo reunited for *Cagney & Lacey: The Return,* the first of several CBS telemovies dramatizing the continued exploits of Chris and Mary Beth.

Camel News Caravan. *1949–56, NBC.* The earliest regularly scheduled network TV newscasts were anything but slick, even if they *were* sponsored by oil companies. In 1946, there was a CBS newscast sponsored by Gulf, and an NBC program titled *The Esso Newsreel,* but only for a few days each week. The first network news program to air each weekday was NBC's *Camel Newsreel Theater,* which premiered in February 1948 with John Cameron Swayze as the largely unseen narrator-host. A year later, the show was so successful it was expanded by fifty percent—from ten to a whopping fifteen minutes a night. Swayze, who in Kansas City had inaugurated the country's first regular newscast way back in the experimental days of 1937, was given a prominent on-camera role, and the show was given a new title, *Camel News Caravan.* Swayze rode the *Caravan* for its entire seven-year trip, but Swayze wasn't the "anchorman," for that term hadn't been coined yet; he was known as the show's "commentator." As older viewers may remember, Swayze opened each show with a standard salutation ("Ladies and gentlemen, a good evening to you!"), and closed each program with a friendly and casual, "That's the story, folks. Glad we could get together. This is John Cameron Swayze saying goodnight." And though Swayze wasn't Layze, he did rely strongly on correspondents from the field, especially, in later years, a young Washington reporter named David Brinkley. In 1956, NBC replaced *Camel News Caravan* with *The Huntley-Brinkley Report*—and Swayze went on to earn fame of a different kind, and for a new generation of viewers, as the trusted tester of Timex watches in a series of classic commercials ("takes a licking and keeps on ticking").

Candid Camera. *1948, ABC; 1949, NBC; 1949–50, CBS; 1951–1952, ABC; 1953, NBC; 1960–67, CBS; 1990, CBS.* "Smile, you're on *Candid Camera*," after all these years, still is a part of popular culture and language, and the perennial appeal of watching people caught in the act of acting naturally is the only plausible explanation for the instant success of *America's Funniest Home Videos*. Allen Funt had the field all to himself when he started out in the late forties, but advanced technology, ironically, eventually proved to be his undoing. His first shot with the format was in 1947, with radio's *Candid Microphone*—a show that, because portable tape recorders had yet to be invented, required Funt to lure victims into the studio "office" on some silly ruse. The following year, ABC beckoned, and *Candid Microphone* moved to TV and evolved into *Candid Camera*—enjoying a successful run for years, and boasting such on-air contributors as Woody Allen, whose trademark bit was to hire an unsuspecting temporary secretary and dictate the world's most formal love letters. After its initial run, *Candid Camera* kept popping up as syndicated specials, short-lived series spinoffs, and so on. There even was a sequel, *The New Candid Camera*, syndicated in the midseventies, as well as more "mature" *Candid Camera* films and TV series, both official (Funt's own 1970 *What Do You Say to a Naked Lady?*) and unofficial. The bald-faced ripoffs (like Fox's *Totally Hidden Video*) loosened Funt's hold on the franchise, but the crushing blow was the wide availability of home camcorders, which handed a candid camera to anyone who wanted and could afford one. The upshot: NBC's *I Witness Video*, which reversed the formula by having the subjects hold the cameras and send in their footage. But at the height of *Candid Camera*, the program showed an enthusiasm for sight gags and TV technology that was outdone only by Ernie Kovacs. Who can forget the car that split in half while driving, or the talking mailbox, or any number of goofy stunts? Not me. And not a lot of other people, either, because lots of us *still* react to incredible situations by laughing nervously, looking around suspiciously, and saying, "OK, where's the camera?"

Captain Kangaroo. *1955–84, CBS.* Bob Keeshan's Captain, like Fred Rogers's Mister Rogers, was a quiet, friendly, soothing video host and voice—one that made very young children, in several different generations of viewers, feel instantly comfortable with television. The good Captain presided over a bunch of friends and activities that, like his jangling key ring and the *Captain Kangaroo* theme music, have continued to chime long after the Treasure House itself was shut down. Mr. Green Jeans, Mr. Moose, Bunny Rabbit and his carrot fixation, Grandfather Clock, Dancing Bear, the notably nonviolent cartoon animated antics of Tom Terrific (and Mighty Manfred the Wonder Dog)—what a gentle, sweet show it was. And it was Keeshan's Captain Kangaroo, decades before the PBS series *Reading Rainbow,* who would pull out picture books and read, slowly and beautifully, from the likes of *Mike Mulligan and His Steam Shovel,* prompting an instant upsurge in the sales and library demand for that title across the country. (What MTV could do for records, *Captain Kangaroo* did for picture books.) It's somewhat ironic that, while most people have no problem identifying Keeshan as the Captain, naming the actor who played his sidekick, Mr. Green Jeans, generally is much tougher. It's ironic because when Keeshan himself was cast as the sidekick, playing Clarabell the silent clown on *Howdy Doody,* he was hungry for wider recognition, a motive that caused him to leave that show (along with several other supporting cast members) in 1952. Keeshan's first job after *Howdy Doody* was advising a local New York show called *Uncle Lumpy's Cabin,* which starred Hugh Brannum as Uncle Lumpy. Within two years, after two local shows of his own, Keeshan launched *Captain Kangaroo*—with Brannum, the former Uncle Lumpy, as Mr. Green Jeans. (The show's third major contributor, puppeteer Cosmo Allegretti, also toiled in relative anonymity, though he was seen on TV every day . . . as Dancing Bear.) *Captain Kangaroo* premiered on CBS as a one-hour show in 1955, and stayed pretty much the same for decades; it was reduced to a half-hour show in 1981, and canceled three years later. Its thirty-year run makes *Captain Kangaroo* the longest-running national children's program in the history of network television—a record soon to be surpassed, fittingly, by *Mister Rogers' Neighborhood.* To its eternal shame, CBS, which in the midnineties was mounting TV anniversary specials at the drop of a hat (or the drop of a ratings point), did nothing in 1995 to mark the fortieth anniversary of *Captain Kangaroo.* In any fair *Kangaroo* court, CBS would be judged guilty of neglect.

Captain Midnight. *1952, syndicated; 1953, ABC; 1954–56, CBS.* If the name *Captain Midnight* doesn't ring a bell, maybe his *ring* will—his Flight Commander Signet Ring, that is. Or his Secret Squadron Decoder Badge, or his Captain Midnight Hot Ovaltine Mug, or any of the other premiums viewers could get by joining Captain Midnight's "Secret Squadron"—for the price of a quarter, and a seal from a jar of Ovaltine. The *Captain Midnight* character had been a radio staple for some fifteen years before this half-hour TV version was launched, with Richard Webb inheriting the role of the crime-busting, Communist-chasing hero. When *Captain Midnight* was dropped by CBS, repeats of the show continued in syndication for years, with a new title—*Jet Jackson, Flying Commando*—and overdubbed dialogue to cover the hero's name change. If you had a Secret Squadron Decoder Badge and turned it to "B6" (the most common setting for deciphering the on-air clues), you might call that stunt, and the original series itself, 22–8–4–19–12. Don't bother scrambling for your descrambler: today's secret word is T-A-C-K-Y.

Captain Video and His Video Rangers. *1949–55, DuMont.* Got your decoder rings ready, Rangers at home? In the late forties and early fifties, *Captain Video* was to little kids what Uncle Miltie was to adults: an instant hit, and a one-man example of the possibilities of this new visual medium. Well, make that a two-man example, because two different actors played Captain Video (Richard Coogan started the role in 1949, and radio's Green Hornet, Al Hodge, took over in 1951). Young Don Hastings served as loyal sidekick, The Video Ranger, to them both. *Captain Video* was a cheaply made show, even by DuMont's standards, but the sci-fi gimmicks and at-home interaction (thanks to fan clubs and tie-in toys) kept *Captain Video* flying until DuMont itself crashed in 1955. Speaking of flying: like *The Lone Ranger* and *The Green Hornet, Captain Video* took its theme song from the annals of classical music: in its case, the overture to Wagner's *The Flying Dutchman*. For the bulk of its run, *Captain Video* led off DuMont's prime-time schedule five nights a week, broadcast live, an hour a night (in 1950 it went *six* hours a week). That's an awful lot of *Video* video—and awfully cheap, because the special-effects budget was twenty-five dollars per *week*. Because *Captain Video* was TV's first science-fiction show, and became so popular so quickly, it had plenty of instant imitators. Before *Captain Video*, children's TV was largely puppet shows and story time. Within a year, there were such spaced-out *Video* imitators as *Space Patrol* and *Tom Corbett, Space Cadet*. One final, funny measure of how popular *Captain Video* was at the time: it was the program Norton demanded to watch on the brand-new TV he "shared" with Ralph on the premiere half-hour episode of *The Honeymooners* in 1955—a teleliterate reference that, all by itself, has helped keep the *Captain Video* name alive.

Car 54, Where Are You? *1961–63, NBC.* Sing along *without* Mitch: "There's a holdup in the Bronx / Brooklyn's broken out in fights / There's a traffic jam in Harlem that's backed up to Jackson Heights. . . . " Nat Hiken, who created the Sergeant Bilko character immortalized by Phil Silvers on *The Phil Silvers Show,* went on to concoct this equally energetic sitcom, starring the Mutt-and-Jeff pair of Fred Gwynne as laid-back cop Francis Muldoon and Joe E. Ross as his hyperkinetic partner, Gunther Toody. Nickelodeon's Nick at Nite has revived this series, among many other classic TV sitcoms, to great effect; even without renewed exposure, however, the original series' rapid-fire, enter-tainingly antic theme song, and its cartoonish characters, and especially Toody's apelike exclamation of "Ooh! Ooh! Ooh!," would linger. Gwynne, of course, would go on to *The Munsters* (along with Al Lewis, a.k.a. Grandpa, who played Officer Leo Schnauzer on *Car 54*). Brown wouldn't. The memory of the original *Car 54* was tarnished, rather than burnished, by a movie remake in the nineties—a remake so bad that, though it was completed in 1991, it wasn't released until three years later. This new, unimproved *Car 54, Where Are You?* starred David Johansen as Toody, John C. McGinley as Mul-doon, and Rosie O'Donnell as Toody's wife, Lucille (played in the series by Beatrice Pons). Except for Fran Drescher as a redheaded temptress named Velma, every performer in the *Car 54* movie was horrendous. Even more horrendous: the drastically revamped title song (done as a rap tune, with almost all new lyrics), and the level of wit typified by the film's unseen radio dispatcher, who gets on the police band and asks, "Car 54, where the f——— are you?" This new *Car 54* is worthless, but the classic series definitely is worth another look. Today, perhaps the part of television's *Car 54* that has increased in value the most is its New York location footage. This show was getting great use out of the city—and its streets, buildings, and everyday faces—years before Woody Allen even *thought* of filming there.

Carol Burnett Show, The. *1967–78, CBS.* One of the best of the old-fashioned variety shows, this long-lasting series benefited from good writing, but mostly from some likable actors who were obviously enjoying themselves performing silly skits. Burnett's male costar, Harvey Korman, was just as adept as Burnett at adopting various outrageous guises and mannerisms, and, once Tim Conway joined the cast in 1975, a lot of the fun from *The Carol Burnett Show* came from watching Conway do all sorts of unscripted business merely to crack up his fellow cast members—especially Korman. Vicki Lawrence took her character of Mama from one set of skits and spun her off into a terrible series, *Mama's Family*, then went from that to an equally terrible daytime talk show named *Vicki!*; Lyle Waggoner went on to the no less wretched *The Adventures of Wonder Woman;* and Korman and Conway went on to a series of memorably forgettable disasters. Unlikely as it seems, though, Conway forged an unlikely yet lucrative subsequent career as Dorf, the sawed-off star of a series of tongue-in-cheek instructional videos. Burnett achieved success in dramatic telemovies *(Friendly Fire),* and relative failure in an attempt to recreate her old variety-show success (with *Carol & Company* and a new *Carol Burnett Show* in the early nineties). In 1993, a prime-time reunion show got everyone together, and demonstrated, with its generous sampling of skits from the series' lengthy run, just how much the old *Carol Burnett Show* had added to TV's vocabulary. Aside from Burnett tugging her ear lobe at the end of each show, the most famous image from the entire series has got to be Burnett, as the impoverished Scarlett O'Hara in a satire of *Gone with the Wind,* wearing a dress made out of draperies—with the curtain rods still attached. My favorite skits of all, though, were the ones with Conway as Mr. Tudball, an exasperated executive trying, but invariably failing, to gain the cooperation of his high-heeled, low-IQ secretary, Burnett's Mrs. Wiggins (or, as he called her, "Mrs. Huh-wiggins"). Those skits were like classic little comedy shorts, and, like much of the rest of *The Carol Burnett Show,* hold up flawlessly in syndication.

Cavalcade of Stars, The. *1949–52, DuMont.* You think the "late-night wars" of 1993 were high-stakes poker, with CBS wooing and stealing David Letterman from NBC after Jay Leno got (and kept) the *Tonight Show* job? Well, you're right, they were—but they weren't anything new, and they weren't any tougher than what *Cavalcade of Stars* had to endure in the early years of television. If the name *Cavalcade of Stars* doesn't mean much in the nineties, it's because DuMont's competition was so good at stealing talent from this particular show in the fifties. A large-scale variety show, DuMont's biggest and best, *Cavalcade* began with comedian Jack Carter as host; after one season, Carter was snatched by NBC, which gave Carter his own show with a good time slot: the lead-in to *Your Show of Shows.* That first hit was no big loss. DuMont recovered by replacing Carter with Jerry Lester—but four months later, NBC stole him too, and almost immediately handed Lester hosting chores on *Broadway Open House,* the late-night precursor to NBC's *The Tonight Show.* Without Lester, DuMont turned to a comic named Jackie Gleason, who hired some impressive talent (most notably Art Carney), worked with his writers to develop some resonant characters (including Ralph Kramden, Reginald Van Gleason III, Joe the Bartender, and the Poor Soul), and basically did some great work. So great that, after two years on DuMont, Gleason was offered tons of money to jump ship to CBS—and took it, bringing most of his characters, and even Carney, with him. Larry Storch took over as the final *Cavalcade of Stars* host, but three direct hits were all the show, and the network, could sustain. *Stars* came tumbling down, and DuMont itself followed a few years later.

CBS Evening News. *1962– , CBS.* This is the newscast with the longest, most direct network lineage. Instead of the frequent and sometimes frantic alterations in title, tone, and personnel at the other networks' newscasts, the nightly newscast at CBS has been a study in relative steadiness—the Dan Rather-Connie Chung "anchor divorce" notwithstanding. Douglas Edwards was in the saddle as *The CBS-TV News* launched its fifteen-minute nightly newscast in 1948, and he remained the steady voice and journalistic star of the show, soon retitled *Douglas Edwards with the News,* until 1962. That's when *The CBS Evening News with Walter Cronkite* took over, and "Uncle Walter" held court until 1981, when the passing of the baton was noted in the show's new title, *The CBS Evening News with Dan Rather.* Rather has been there ever since, either as a solo anchor or (from June 1, 1993, to May 18, 1995) as coanchor of *The CBS Evening News with Dan Rather and Connie Chung*—the most unsuccessful and awkward coanchor teaming since ABC paired Harry Reasoner with Barbara Walters two decades earlier. Even given that brief, failed Rather-Chung experiment, *The CBS Evening News* has been a virtual model of network news stability. Chung enjoyed anchor status for only two years, but Edwards was at the helm for fourteen years, Cronkite for nineteen, and Rather for fifteen and counting. Amazingly, that's a total of only four regular anchors in the entire forty-eight-year history of the CBS nightly newscasts. Of the four, Cronkite made the largest mark on TV history—and, in terms of the John F. Kennedy assassination and the 1969 moon landing, served as a central figure in two of the most momentous news stories of the century, making Cronkite as much a TV icon as such fictional figures as Archie Bunker and Ralph Kramden. Cronkite's vaunted objectivity, as well as his longevity at *The CBS Evening News,* eventually earned him a place in national polls as "the most trusted man in America." Ironically, though, what we recall most about Cronkite, as with Frank Reynolds and even Rather, are the *subjective* moments, the times when emotion leaked through the anchorman façade. With Cronkite, there were three such moments, each of which has enough residual impact to demand greater mention in individual *Teleliteracy* entries: the death of John F. Kennedy, the Apollo 11 moon shot and landing, and Cronkite's "thugs" remark at the 1968 Democratic convention. Cronkite's news judgment and clout were such that he could, on rare but well-timed occasions, advance or affect a story merely by reporting or commenting on it at length. His important, atypically subjective remarks during a 1968 CBS special, *Walter Cronkite in Vietnam*, were credited by then-President Lyndon Baines Johnson as persuading him that America no longer supported the war. "It is increasingly clear to this reporter," Cronkite concluded on that special, "that the only rational way out then will be to negotiate, not as victors, but as an honorable people who lived up to their pledge to defend democracy and did the best they could." David Halberstam, in *The Powers That Be*, wryly yet accurately noted that "it was the first time in American history a war had been declared over by an anchorman." Cronkite also demonstrated his media muscle during the first year of Watergate, by devoting fourteen minutes of his network's October 27, 1972, newscast to a detailed look at the Watergate burglary attempt and its possible political ramifications. *The Washington Post* had been advancing the story almost daily, but when *The CBS Evening News with Walter Cronkite* deemed it worthy of such prominent attention, other media outlets kicked coverage of the story into a higher gear. These momentous moments aside, Cronkite's most widely remembered contribution is not any single news report, but his nightly, reassuring signoff: "And that's the way it is. . . . " His continued place in broadcast news history is evidenced by the fact that CBS and cable's Discovery Channel agreed to collaborate in 1996 on a proudly intimate TV offering called *Walter Cronkite Remembers*. Speaking of remembering: in the entire history of *The CBS Evening News*, the most memorable, if not significant, news report probably was Morley Safer's 1965 "Zippo lighter" story from Vietnam, which showed American marines setting fire to villagers' huts in Cam Ne. On the softer side, *The CBS Evening News* deserves lots of credit for its "On the Road" features with Charles Kuralt, which were pure poetry—and for its commentaries by Eric Sevareid, which began the night *The CBS Evening News* expanded in 1963, and lasted until Sevareid reached CBS's then-mandatory retirement age in 1977. Sevareid's commentaries, too, were poetry, pure and simple. (Well, maybe not so simple.) Since Rather's reign began in 1981, *The CBS Evening News* has had its share of both triumph and tumult. Rather always seems energized, and at his very best, when reporting from the scene of earthquakes, floods, hurricanes, and other disasters; failing those, he sometimes manages to be caught up in storms or disasters of a less literal kind. In 1987, angry that CBS Sports was allowing coverage of a semifinal U.S. Open women's tennis match to eat into his scheduled newscast time, Rather walked off the set—just before the sports department returned the network signal back to news, leaving viewers of that particular newscast with nothing to watch but blank, black air. Seven minutes later, Rather returned, but for those seven minutes, no news was not good news, and the show may as well have been called *The CBS Evening News Without Dan Rather*. By the nineties, though, Rather had become Rather statesmanlike when compared to Chung, whose *Evening News* duties were overshadowed, and eventually undercut, by the celebrity interviews she did with the likes of (eventually disgraced) Olympics skater Tonya Harding and Speaker of the House Newt Gingrich's mother,

Kathleen, who stage-whispered to Chung, in an infamous quote that ended up getting Chung lots of bad (and unfair) press for "sneakily" eliciting it, that Newt had called First Lady Hillary Clinton "a bitch." After a few more infamous moments, such as behind-the-scenes chafing about who covered what after the Oklahoma City bombing of 1995, CBS had little choice but to play musical chairs with its two leading anchors, and Chung was the one left without a chair when the music stopped. Rather has taken to his new solo career very enthusiastically, even going so far—in a literal as well as figurative sense—as to fly to Bosnia (as did NBC's Tom Brokaw) to anchor from there as American troops arrived in December 1995. A few years earlier, pre-Chung, Rather had reported just as aggressively from Tiananmen Square in 1989, and Kuwait City at the end of the Persian Gulf War in 1991. Yet Rather's all-time most famous *CBS Evening News* moment to date was his 1988 live interview with then vice-president George Bush, which—despite Rather's understandable determination to get Bush to reveal, in detail, his role in the Iran-Contra affair—is remembered more for the temperature, rather than the content, of the verbal exchanges. Sorry, but that's the way it is.

Challenger Disaster. *1986, various networks.* It's one of the most indelible, emotional TV images ever: the twin plumes of smoke, signaling that something had gone tragically wrong with the January 28, 1986, launch of the Challenger space shuttle. Only CNN (and, on the West Coast, NBC) televised the launch live, but as soon as disaster struck, the other networks joined in and provided replays and coverage for hours. One particularly raw and unfortunate picture captured by network cameras was a close-up of the parents of Christa McAuliffe, one of the astronauts aboard, as it slowly dawned on them what was happening in the sky above them. Peter Jennings, watching that tape for the first time along with the rest of his ABC audience, said coldly he didn't think we'd be seeing *that* again—a message to his control room as well as his viewers, and a commendable show of both restraint and good taste. As much impact as the disaster had on adult viewers, it probably meant even more to children, many of whom were watching CNN's live launch coverage in their classrooms because McAuliffe was the first schoolteacher to be sent into space. (CNN, in fact, had cameras in place to relay reactions of students from McAuliffe's own school.) I've visited a lot of colleges and high schools in recent years, and one thing that always comes up is that the Challenger explosion, to the younger generation, appears to carry as much emotional resonance as the John F. Kennedy assassination did to those of a generation earlier. In both cases, TV brought tragedy, sudden death, and grief into the lives of young viewers, perhaps for the first time. In 1990, ABC presented a monumentally bad docudrama version of the tragedy, with Karen Allen as McAuliffe; titled *Challenger,* the telemovie had all the depth and verisimilitude of an Irwin Allen disaster movie.

Charlie Brown Christmas, A. *1965, CBS.* The first *Peanuts* special still draws viewers whenever CBS shows it, and the Vince Guaraldi music hasn't aged any more than Charlie Brown, Snoopy, and the rest of the gang from this delightful 1965 holiday cartoon. Like the annual showing of *The Wizard of Oz*, it continues to be a TV tradition—and deserves to be, because it's thoroughly delightful. The lecture by Linus on "the true meaning of Christmas" ought to be required viewing for every family in America; the nice thing is, it doesn't *have* to be required viewing, because most people want to see it anyway. The only bad aspect of the network's treatment of this true Christmas classic is that, to make room for the additional commercial time allotted in the years since *A Charlie Brown Christmas* first was produced and presented more than thirty years ago, the cartoon has been trimmed in some spots and, in all the rest, slightly sped up by computer (a process called time compression). In some places, it's so bad it almost sounds like a *Chipmunks* special instead, and the only true way to enjoy the special and its music as intended is to rent or buy the home-video version, which hasn't been artificially accelerated, or purchase Guaraldi's charming soundtrack album. A 1992 "sequel," *It's Christmas Time Again, Charlie Brown*, proved just how good, and rare, the original version was. Coproduced by CBS and Shell Oil as a home-video "special offer" for local gas stations ($4.99 with a fill up), *It's Christmas Time Again* was broadcast that year by CBS the day after Thanksgiving, and was a real Shell-out.

Charlie's Angels. *1976–81, ABC.* What is there to say? The apex of what was called "jiggle television" helped push ABC to the top in the midseventies, thanks in no small part to Farrah Fawcett's hair (among other attributes). Costars Jaclyn Smith and (later) Cheryl Ladd have carved out small-screen, small-ambition careers in telemovies and miniseries since then, Kate Jackson (after starring in *Scarecrow and Mrs. King* in the mideighties) has been less visible, and late arrivals Shelley Hack and Tanya Roberts actually have *weakened* their résumés since then. Hack was the worst *Angels* actress of them all—and with Roberts as part of the mix, that's quite an insult. Amazingly, it's Farrah Fawcett, a truly bad actress when she starred on this series, who developed over time into the best and most popular performer, starring in *The Burning Bed* and the miniseries *Murder in Texas* and *Small Sacrifices*. At the time, *Charlie's Angels* never disappointed: it was always as horrendous and inept as you could hope to expect, and was the kind of guilty pleasure that was no less enjoyable with the sound off. Oh, I forgot to mention David Doyle as Bosley, and John Forsythe as the voice of good old unseen Charlie. Sorry, Charlie, but it's just as well. These days, *Charlie's Angels* is little more than an artifact of a time when TV's exploitation of women was shameless—and shockingly effective. (Those arguments about *Charlie's Angels* being a feminist showcase, with three women out there solving crimes and catching bad guys, would be a lot more persuasive if they didn't treat Charlie like a long-distance pimp, or if clothes and hair styles weren't given more attention than the scripts.) Little more than a decade after the ABC series first premiered, the Fox network had plans on the drawing board to launch a revival, *Angels '88*, but the project died on the drawing board because of the writers' strike that year. Too bad, because one of the new angels cast for *Angels '88* was Téa Leoni, who later proved so charming in Fox's *Flying Blind* and ABC's

The Naked Truth. Because there were no completed scripts, the network's plans for *Angels '88* were 86'ed. As a direct result, though, Fox went out to find a TV show that didn't *need* scripts, and developed low-cost "reality programming" as a result. Instead of a new set of *Angels,* Fox settled on a new *video verité* showcase called *COPS.*

"Checkers" Speech. *1952, CBS and NBC.* Quick: Name another televised speech by a vice-president that's as famous as Richard Nixon's 1952 shaggy-dog monologue, which kept him on the bottom half of the Republican ticket that year. There isn't one, unless you count Spiro Agnew's "nattering nabobs of negativism" one-liner or Dan Quayle's attack on *Murphy Brown* as an unfit, unwed mother—and I don't. Only CBS and NBC carried Nixon's speech live, but the reach, and the impact, was more than enough to do the trick; Nixon used television wisely and effectively here (if more than a bit cynically), in sharp contrast to his dismal appearance during the presidential debates eight years later. In 1952, charged with impropriety for maintaining a "slush" fund collected from political supporters (a clear harbinger of similar Watergate abuses), Nixon opted to deliver a live televised address in his defense. He maintained his innocence, talked about his wife's cloth coat, and, most famously of all, defiantly said that even if forced to return everything sent to him by supporters, he would refuse to give back a cocker spaniel named Checkers, sent to the Nixons by someone in Texas. "The kids, like all kids, love that dog," Nixon told the TV audience, "and I just want to say this, right now: that regardless of what they say, we're going to keep it." It's not too much of a stretch to say it was Nixon's dogged determination that saved his political career that night—a career that, from that point on, could quite accurately be described as Checkered.

Cheers. *1982–93, NBC.* A generation from now, *Cheers* will be regarded with the same reverent affection we now feel for such classic sitcoms as *The Honeymooners, The Dick Van Dyke Show,* and *M*A*S*H.* It is to the eighties what those shows were, respectively, to the fifties, sixties, and seventies—a class act from start to finish. Speaking of finish, the heavily promoted ninety-minute final episode of *Cheers,* broadcast in May 1993, was expected by NBC to draw huge audiences, and did: it earned a 45.4 Nielsen rating and 64 percent audience share, tying it for twentieth place on TV's all-time Top 20. That made it the second most popular sitcom episode in television history, topped only by the finale of *M*A*S*H.* That's a far cry from the first season of *Cheers,* when it wound up ranked seventy-fourth out of ninety-nine prime-time series, but *Cheers* was a great comedy from first to last; like any new tavern setting up shop, it merely took a while to draw a substantial crowd. Brilliantly written and directed, and skillfully (and playfully) performed, *Cheers* was a wonderful weekly peek at a neighborhood bar where, in the words of the show's well-known theme song, "everybody knows your name." In *Teleliteracy,* this book's companion predecessor, Kurt Vonnegut said of this series, "I would say that television has produced one comic masterpiece, which is *Cheers.* I wish I'd written that instead of everything I *had* written."

Hyperbole, undeniably, but *Cheers* really *is* a brilliant comedy. Every cast member added to the series' magic, from the late Nicholas Colasanto as Coach to Bebe Neuwirth as the brittle yet beguiling Lilith. Ted Danson never got enough credit for the different levels of humor he explored as Sam Malone, the recovering alcoholic and former pro baseball player who tended bar, and *Cheers* got terrific work out of the likes of Shelley Long, Kirstie Alley, Rhea Perlman, Kelsey Grammer, and Woody Harrelson. Put it this way: if you combined three good episodes of *Cheers*, and performed them on Broadway with the original cast, you'd have a better and funnier show than most of the comedies in New York these days. One of the many secrets of the show's success was that every viewer could identify with someone. My own favorite characters were the perennial patrons Norm and Cliff, played to scene-stealing perfection by George Wendt and John Ratzenberger. They took beer-loving lethargy and know-nothing authority, respectively, to almost mythic levels. In the inspired final episode, written by Glen and Les Charles and directed by James Burrows (the series' three co-creators), Danson's Sam reunited with Long's Diane, who returned for this farewell episode, and decided to quit his job and follow her to California. When Cliff, Norm, and the other barflies protested, Sam lashed out at them for resenting his desire to move on. "All you fellas do is just sit there and watch the world go by," Sam tells them, adding, "I need more than this. *You* should need more than this." (At least one person took his advice. Grammer's Frasier divorced Lilith, flew to Seattle, and became a radio talk-show therapist there, thus getting his own show in more ways than one. NBC's *Frasier*, which began the season after *Cheers* ended, carried on the tradition superbly.) By the end of the *Cheers* finale episode, Sam had changed his mind, said farewell to Diane, and returned to the bar for a reunion with his forgiving buddies. After everyone else said good bye, Sam locked up, and was turning out the lights (a sly tribute to the ending of *The Mary Tyler Moore Show*) as an unidentified, shadowy customer showed up at the door, peered through the glass, and knocked. "Sorry, we're closed," Sam said, uttering the words that turned away an eager customer and ended the series. *Cheers* was great while it lasted, right to the very last scene—but, sadly, *we* were that customer.

Chevy Chase Show, The. *1993, Fox.* The most famous flop in the late-night talk-show wars of the early nineties, *The Chevy Chase Show* made its much-publicized debut on September 7, 1993, and was canceled less than six weeks later—so suddenly that Chase was denied the opportunity for an official farewell program. (He did what was to be his final show on Friday, October 15, and Fox executives pulled the plug on the series over the weekend.) On paper, *The Chevy Chase Show* wasn't that horrendous an idea. Chase, with his *Saturday Night Live* background and following, could do comedy and go with the live-TV flow. Also, with his musical interests, he could stress that aspect as well, and even had a keyboard built into his desk so he could do some playful jazz with his house band. In those respects, Chevy Chase was closest in style to Steve Allen. The key and ultimately disastrous difference, though, is that Allen was interested in his guests and a good interviewer,

LEFT: *Cagney & Lacey,* with Sharon Gless and Tyne Daly out on some rare undercover work.
RIGHT: *Captain Kangaroo,* with Bob Keeshan and, for once, a real bunny rabbit.

LEFT: *Captain Video and His Video Rangers,* with Al Hodge as one of two Video Rangers.
RIGHT: *Cheers,* with Ted Danson's Sam and Nicholas Colasanto's Coach behind the bar.

whereas Chase seemed to prepare little and care less, except when he knew the guest and could reminisce about old times. At their best, such exchanges were cloying; at their worst, they were unwatchable, a conclusion quickly reached by late-night viewers. One final, notoriously stupid aspect of *The Chevy Chase Show* was its set design, which incorporated a giant fish tank as part of the prominent background. The problem was, whatever was swimming in the tank usually was more interesting than the conversation taking place in front of it. Chase himself, making a very funny cameo appearance on *The Larry Sanders Show* two years later, poked fun at *The Chevy Chase Show* in general, and that aquarium concept in particular. "I should never have done that show," he confided to Garry Shandling's Larry. "I had *fish* behind my head." Too bad Chase didn't get to do a finale episode: he could have sung "Tanks For the Memories." Or, perhaps, "The Age of Aquariums."

China Beach. *1988–91, ABC.* The first attempt to mount a dramatic series about the Vietnam War came in 1980, when Gary David Goldberg, a *Lou Grant* producer who had yet to create either *Family Ties* or *Brooklyn Bridge*, developed a one-hour series pilot called *Bureau* for MTM Productions. It was about war correspondents, and Goldberg's plan was to dramatize one year of the Vietnam War each season, starting with 1967 and culminating, eight years later, with a final episode about the fall of Saigon. The show was quite good (Goldberg eventually showed me the pilot), but CBS refused to air it; TV executive and MTM founder Grant Tinker said later that "the network, however well we had done it, probably didn't want a show about Vietnam." So instead, another MTM project, *Hill Street Blues*, stepped forward the following season and got credit for some of the TV innovations featured in the unseen *Bureau,* including hand-held camera sequences, gritty realism offset by adult humor, and a large ensemble of talented but little-known actors (Richard Dysart, later of *L. A. Law,* and Peter Jurasik, later of *Hill Street,* were among the stars). That same year, 1981, writer-producer Stirling Silliphant proposed a similar Vietnam-era series to ABC, but that network wasn't interested, either—although that project's telemovie pilot, *Fly Away Home,* was televised to help offset production costs. It wasn't until 1987, with the premiere of the CBS series *Tour of Duty,* that the Vietnam War was considered dramatically "suitable" for a weekly TV series. That show, which starred Terence Knox as a veteran sergeant, was pretty much an updated version of *Combat* (which isn't an insult, by the way), and was scheduled by CBS largely—make that totally—because Oliver Stone's *Platoon* movie had paved the way the year before. The next Vietnam drama on TV was *China Beach,* which did for Vietnam what *M*A*S*H* had done for the Korean War: looked at it through the eyes of the medical personnel stationed there. (The two series also had an antiwar sensibility in common, and shared the same morbid sight and sounds of medical helicopters forever arriving with incoming wounded.) Dana Delany, as nurse Colleen McMurphy, started off strong and got even stronger, and *China Beach* went through *its* tour of duty with some of the most dramatic story lines of its day. For its swan song, the series presented seven episodes jumping back and forth in time, following the various characters from childhood to Vietnam, and then stateside to the eighties, where the war wounds, physical and psychological, still ran deep. Its climax, bringing some of the surviving characters to an impromptu reunion at the Vietnam Memorial, was an eloquent ending to creator John Sacret Young's intelligent, stirringly emotional series. *China Beach* never attained mass popularity, but many of its viewers were fiercely loyal, and, until and unless something better comes along, *China Beach* will be remembered as *the* TV series about Vietnam. The show's veterans, so to speak, also included Robert Picardo, of *The Wonder Years* and later of *Star Trek: Voyager,* as Dr. Dick Richard; Chloe Webb, in the show's first season, as USO singer Laurette Barber; Marg Helgenberger as a hooker with a heart of cold; and, from 1989–90, future talk-show host Ricki Lake as Holly the Donut Dolly.

Cisco Kid, The. *1950–56, syndicated.* In the original O. Henry story, "The Caballero's Way," the Cisco Kid was no Mexican do-gooder; in fact, he was an outlaw who killed Mexicans for sport ("It had been one of the Kid's pastimes," Henry wrote, "to shoot Mexicans 'to see them kick'"), and whose main activity in this one and only official, original Cisco Kid story was to trick a romantic rival into murdering their mutual love interest in cold blood. The basic Hollywood version, which eventually carried over to television, was lighter in tone, but the hero wasn't: the formula was inverted, making the Cisco Kid a devil-may-care, guitar-strumming, Mexican bandit, and eventually adding a gregarious and jolly sidekick. Production on the first Cisco Kid movie, *In Old Arizona,* began in 1928, with Raoul Walsh both directing and starring, but was halted when, driving back from a location shoot in Utah, Walsh's driver was startled by a jackrabbit. The animal jumped into and through the windshield, and both its carcass and the shattered glass smashed into Walsh's face— blinding him in one eye and being responsible for Walsh's subsequent trademark eye patch. The accident also was responsible for a new director and actor being hired for *In Old Arizona.* Irving Cummings took over as director, and Warner Baxter inherited Walsh's role of the Cisco Kid, winning a Best Actor Oscar in the process. Baxter reprised the Cisco Kid role three more times in the thirties, after which the film role was picked up by Cesar Romero, Gilbert Roland, and finally Duncan Renaldo, who stayed with the role when *The Cisco Kid* shifted from theatrical films to a syndicated TV series. Renaldo's dashing Cisco Kid and Leo Carrillo's comic but proud sidekick Pancho, like the Lone Ranger and Tonto, were Western adventurers of a similar sort; their respective TV showcases each told of a well-dressed hero and his faithful minority-group sidekick, roaming the West and doing good deeds. The syndication company behind *The Cisco Kid* also did good deals, because *The Cisco Kid* was the first Western series filmed in color, a bit of foresight that came in handy once that new TV technology caught on. The TV series was quite popular, and was one of the more sophisticated children's adventure shows of the fifties when it came to promoting and selling tie-in merchandise. In 1994, the TNT cable network revived the franchise and characters in a telemovie called *The Cisco Kid,* starring Jimmy Smits as the Cisco Kid and Cheech

Marin as Pancho. Smits was not a good Kidder, though, and was much more successful, later that same year, when he joined the cast of *NYPD Blue*.

Civilisation. *1970, PBS*. This thirteen-part BBC-TV program is the grand-daddy of the documentary miniseries, and every subsequent effort owes it a great debt. Kenneth Clark toured the roots and accomplishments of human society, and did so in a way that was neither condescending nor simplistic. The BBC administrator who commissioned Clark to make *Civilisation* in 1969, incidentally, was David Attenborough, who later returned to the field to make some great documentary miniseries of his own, including *The Trials of Life*, *The Living Planet*, and *Life on Earth*.

Civil War, The. *1990, PBS*. This eleven-hour, five-night PBS documentary series had such impact when it was broadcast that it helped change the direction, style, and face of PBS. However, that wasn't always a good thing. Since then, we viewers have been "treated" to abysmally dull—and long—documentary miniseries on such subjects as computers and Columbus, and every other documentary on every other network has employed the celebrated *Civil War* tricks of matching vintage photographs with music, sound effects, and actors reading from written letters from the period. But much less effectively. *The Civil War* was a work of art as well as of scholarship, and the efforts by writer-producer-director Ken Burns, writer-producer Ric Burns, and writer Geoffrey C. Ward were rewarded by a TV series as celebrated as it was popular. *The Civil War* gathered the largest audience for a single event in PBS history, and made an instant star—in PBS terms, at least—of author and historian Shelby Foote, whose easy manner and authoritative grasp of the subject made him to the Civil War what Joseph Campbell was to mythology. Years later, two sequences from *The Civil War* seem the most indelible. One, a highly personal selection, concerns the last words by a soldier who, severely injured on the battlefield and surrounded by his slain comrades, wrote one final note in the blood-stained diary found on his body. "June 4, 1864," it read. "I was killed." The other sequence, which closed the first episode of *The Civil War*, is one I'm sure will never be forgotten by anyone who saw it. Easily the most remarkable and remembered passage of the entire documentary, it has actor Paul Roebling reading, beautifully, the text of a letter sent by Civil War soldier Sullivan Ballou to his wife shortly before he was killed at the Battle of Bull Run. ("Sarah, do not mourn me dead; think I am gone and wait for me, for we shall meet again. . . . ") The letter is pure love, and the crafters of *The Civil War*, using vintage photographs, Jay Ungar's gorgeous "Ashokan Farewell" music, and Roebling's evocative voice, make it purer still. *The Civil War* not only enlivened history; in TV terms, it *made* history. And four years later, Ken Burns made *Baseball*, a grand, lengthy examination of America's pastime that was broadcast on PBS over nine nights, or "innings." The documentary was great, but the timing was lousy: *Baseball* came to bat while major-league baseball players were on strike, and during the first fall season in generations that would include no World Series.

Clutch Cargo. *1960–65, syndicated*. For some reason, the tag line from the opening credits of this horrendous cartoon series is something I've never been able to purge. Maybe it was the way the announcer *said* "Clutch Cargo—and his pals, Spinner and Paddlefoot!" More likely, it was a side effect of that cost-cutting "animation" process known as Synchro-Vox, which saved money by not animating the mouths of its characters. Instead, the lips of actors reciting the dialogue were photographed in closeup and superimposed onto the cartoon faces of Clutch, Spinner, and the rest. I don't remember any of the show's plots all these years later . . . but boy, those lips gave me the creeps. Yet one young boy's nightmare is another's inspiration. Robert Smigel, producer and head writer of NBC's *Late Night with Conan O'Brien*, drew upon his memories of old *Clutch Cargo* cartoons to create one of the funniest recurring segments on O'Brien's show: the sketches in which O'Brien "interviews" a celebrity photograph, whose lips (usually Smigel's lips, actually) are superimposed, and the dialogue inserted, in the old *Clutch Cargo* tradition.

Colgate Comedy Hour, The. *1950–55, NBC.* The title of this show may not have a secure place in TV posterity, but the various cohosts and their performances certainly do. This is where Dean Martin and Jerry Lewis did much of their very best work, over the course of five live and very lively years as occasional hosts. As surviving records of the series clearly demonstrate, live TV was the medium in which Jerry Lewis really *was* a genius. Another comedy team best known for its film work, Bud Abbott and Lou Costello, hosted many *Colgate* shows, too, as did such talented solo acts as Bob Hope, Donald O'Connor, Eddie Cantor, and Jimmy Durante. Martin and Lewis, though, squeezed the most fame out of this particular *Colgate* tube.

Columbo. *1971–77, NBC; 1989– , ABC.* A whole book could be written on *Columbo*—and, in fact, an excellent one has, by TV critic Mark Dawidziak. Richard Levinson and William Link, with no small help from actor Peter Falk, created a character so durable that, since that book about the 1971–77 mystery series was written, *Columbo* has risen again—as a series of two-hour telemovies, again starring Falk. In the fall of 1992, the new *Columbo* gained a new offstage coconspirator: Patrick McGoohan, who had played a hand, as well as a role, in some of the best *Columbo* episodes of both the seventies and nineties vintages. Columbo's "Oh . . . and just one more thing" is a recognizable catch phrase, but the most famous affectation of all is his ratty raincoat. As a character, as well as a series, *Columbo* stands distinctly away from, and above, most of the TV pack. Falk is so good as Columbo, he makes the part seem fresh after playing it for three decades. Falk was forty years old when he first played Lieutenant Columbo (whose first name is still hazy after all these years). That was in *Prescription: Murder,* a 1968 telemovie based on the Levinson-Link stage play. After one more telemovie, *Ransom for a Dead Man,* in 1971, *Columbo* became a recurring series later that same year. A quarter-century later, with the same rank, car, and coat, *Columbo* and Falk are still going strong. A list of best episodes from the original series would have to start with 1971's "Murder by the Book" (written by Steven Bochco and directed by Steven Spielberg, with Jack Cassidy as the untalented half of a mystery-writing team) and 1974's "By Dawn's Early Light" (with McGoohan as a maniacal military academy officer). Other memorable murderers from the original *Columbo* series were played by, among others, Robert Culp, Ruth Gordon, Robert Vaughn, and Roddy McDowall. From the new telemovie versions, the best so far has been 1990's "Agenda for Murder" (this time with McGoohan as a Machiavellian political operative), with other strong installments featuring Lindsay Crouse and Faye Dunaway. Oh, and one more thing. . . .

Combat. *1962–67, ABC.* This World War II series is known today as one of TV's most gung-ho pro-war series, and, along with *The Untouchables,* one of the titles most quickly tossed around in the sixties whenever TV violence came up. It's endured longer as a familiar TV title, and for its identification with actor Vic Morrow, than for its characters and stories—although some episodes and contributors were anything but ordinary. Director Robert Altman, for example, did many episodes of *Combat,* and the future director of the movie version of *M*A*S*H* liked to inject and reflect the reality of war by introducing a supporting character in one episode, having him reappear in the next few episodes, then kill him, suddenly and unexpectedly, as part of a minor subplot in a later episode. "That was unorthodox. . . . I used to get fired for it," Altman recalled. It would be decades before other dramatic series, most notably *Hill Street Blues* and *St. Elsewhere,* would adopt similar techniques.

Connections. *1979, PBS.* Until *Cosmos* came along a year later, this ten-part documentary series, a 1978 BBC-TV and Time-Life production imported to America a year later, was the most popular nonfiction series ever shown on PBS. That's not to imply it gathered a huge audience (all things are relative, especially on public television), but anyone who *did* see *Connections* is likely to have memories, or even nightmares, of the show's opening hour. Host James Burke had designed *Connections* as a series tracing the relationships of humans to the machines they invented, and of one invention to another, and he started off by examining the famous northeastern U. S. power blackout of 1965. Then he posed a particularly chilling hypothetical: what if it had been a disaster, nuclear or otherwise, rather than a freak technical problem, and the electricity had never been restored? Where would you go? How would you get there, if there was no electricity to drive the gas pumps, and no restocking of whatever gas you managed to get? And once you got there, how would you shelter, protect, and sustain yourself? Burke, who had anchored all of the BBC's coverage of the Apollo space flights, was an engaging host and original thinker, and what he was doing in most of his TV efforts, from *Connections* to *The Day the Universe Changed,* was serving as a one-man tour through various intersections of science, politics, and the arts. In a way, Burke was interactive before interactive was cool; it made perfect sense, in the midnineties, when Burke took his theories and insights to an even more suitable medium, and released *Connections* as a data-filled, time-tripping CD-ROM. He did not, however, forsake the medium with the most mass: in 1994–95, The Learning Channel coproduced and presented a series sequel, *Connections²*. Each thirty-minute episode was only half as long as ones from the original series, and production values were a lot less impressive. Burke's intellectual approach, however, was just as challenging and inspirational the second time around, even though it was the original *Connections* series, and especially that haunting first episode, that really packed, and continues to pack, quite a punch. Maybe I'm especially vulnerable, though, to this type of doomsday scenario: without electricity, TV critics would be pretty low on the postapocalyptic totem pole.

Cop Rock. *1990, ABC*. This series is to *Hill Street Blues* and *L.A. Law* co-creator Steven Bochco what *1941* is to Steven Spielberg: a widely acknowledged, high-profile failure from someone more associated with success. In the nineties, *Cop Rock* quickly attained the kind of "flop" status accorded to few other TV series—*My Mother the Car* and *Supertrain* being two other quick examples—and that's how it's most likely to be remembered in the future. Unlike those shows, though, *Cop Rock* wasn't that bad at all, and, by the conclusion of its brief four-month run, ended up being very good indeed. One problem is, no one was watching those later shows (for that matter, very few saw the *early* ones), but the insurmountable problem was that *Cop Rock*, despite some strong scenes and set pieces, never came close to the artistry of the two Dennis Potter masterpieces it was emulating, *Pennies from Heaven* and *The Singing Detective*. Randy Newman provided the show's theme song and wrote all the other songs for the pilot, but subsequent episodes were written by other, less biting lyricists. (The *Cop Rock* experience served, nonetheless, as a learning experience from which Newman could draw when writing his 1995 stage musical, *Randy Newman's Faust*.) As drama, *Cop Rock* did vault at least one performer to stardom: Peter Onorati, who played a loose-cannon cop on *Cop Rock* before starring in *Civil Wars*. Onorati's *Cop Rock* character, Vincent LaRusso, was a bigoted detective whose behavior in the field became a central issue when he had to testify in court—making him a kind of pre-O. J. Simpson trial version of a musical Mark Fuhrman.

COPS. *1989– , Fox*. Seen Paddy Chaycfsky's 1976 movie *Network* lately? The one about a struggling "fourth network" that rises in the ratings race because of its in-your-face "reality" programming? One of the programming innovations suggested by Faye Dunaway's TV-executive character in that film was to befriend a radical group that perversely filmed its crimes while committing them, then edit that footage into a weekly TV series. Flip that concept and have camera crews tagging along with the good guys, and presto: instead of *Robbers*, you've got *COPS*. The show's *video verité* style has been widely imitated, and widely parodied, but *COPS* remains the best and most gripping example of the genre. Some sequences exploit people (especially children) unnecessarily, but the show is one of the few "reality" shows that seems to bear any real resemblance *to* reality. *COPS*, like all other shows of this type, owes a huge and direct debt to Alan and Susan Raymond, the documentary filmmakers whose bold body of work includes *An American Family*, the 1973 PBS series in which William and Pat Loud and family were filmed going about their daily life—a life that, on camera, included Pat asking her husband for a divorce, and son Lance revealing his homosexuality. In 1977, the Raymonds created a similar stir with *The Police Tapes*, a ninety-minute documentary shot on videotape, without narration, following cops from the South Bronx's 44th Precinct as they went about their daily, and nightly, business. The setting of *The Police Tapes* was only nine precinct houses away from the 53rd Precinct housing the fictional cops of *Car 54, Where Are You?*, but the Raymonds were focusing on real life, and *The Police Tapes* became the prototype for all of the subsequent series based on the unscripted exploits of police officers, firefighters, emergency technicians, and just about every on-call road crew this side of D.A.P.S. (which sounds like a TV series but will never be one: the organization's initials stand for Dead Animal Pickup Squad). When Fox's New York station launched *COPS* as a local series in 1989, it did so by going a lot further south than the South Bronx, and filmed cops in and around Ft. Lauderdale—the tropical Florida setting being the reason for the show's reggae-flavored theme song. After Florida, when Fox took the series to its entire network, the focus switched to many different cities and countries, which literally was a good move. *COPS* proved successful enough to spawn many imitators of its own, and it also boasts Inner Circle's bouncy theme song that's hard to shake: "Bad boys, bad boys, whatcha gonna do? / Whatcha gonna do when they come for you?. . . . " In many respects, this is one TV cop show that's truly arresting.

Cosby Show, The. *1984–92, NBC.* This sitcom is an important part of TV history on several levels. As a success, it was unrivaled throughout the eighties. As a positive depiction of family life in general, and especially of an African-American family, *The Cosby Show* was of incalculable importance. It came at a time when the sitcom was thought to be dead on TV, and when a stable and nuclear family life—two parents, living in one home, raising their own children—was virtually nonexistent on prime-time television. Bill Cosby, the show's star, best performer, and guiding force, took unusual pains to ensure that the positive messages imbued in his shows would be neither too overt nor likely to be misperceived. The very first episode contained its most potent and crucial message, which was that *The Cosby Show* was going to be markedly different from the kids-know-best sitcoms that had proliferated during the previous decade. Cosby's Cliff Huxtable, a successful and financially secure doctor, was confronting his son, Theo (played by Malcolm-Jamal Warner), for bringing home a poor report card. Theo's defense was that he didn't need good grades to get a "regular job," and that not everyone could grow up to be as successful as his dad, who should love him no matter *what* grades he got in school. This type of TV speech was so common at the time, the studio audience sided with and applauded Theo's remarks. Then Cosby, knowing he was about to deliver the trump card, waited for a few seconds before staring at his TV son and saying, "That's the dumbest thing I've ever heard in my *life!* It's no *wonder* you get D's in everything!" The response from the crowd, and from viewers at home, was almost cathartic. An adult was taking charge on the tube again, going against the grain and setting a strong new example.

Cosby's TV wife, Phylicia Rashad's Clair Huxtable, was just as tough a parent, just as positive a role model, and just as successful in her own career (as an attorney). Together, they ran a household where there were a lot of laughs, but also a lot of rules and a lot of respect. This loving respect was directed even at the family grandparents—a rarity, sad to say, on prime-time television. One memorable episode of *The Cosby Show* had the entire Huxtable family performing for the grandparents by mounting a lip-synched, loosely choreographed version of a Ray Charles song, "Night Time Is the Right Time." Performing a song this way became a sort of *Cosby Show* tradition, along with the ever-evolving opening credits and theme song, which were produced anew each season to mark the growth in the program's cast and tone. Cosby and his show were attacked, in many quarters, for being unrealistic and unrepresentative, but that was a ridiculous charge. It was a realistic representation of his *own* lifestyle, which is all his show *had* to be, and it marked the passages of youth as capably, and humorously, as any other family sitcom, including such "unrealistic" and "unrepresentative" series as *The Adventures of Ozzie & Harriet* and *Leave It to Beaver*. In the ratings, *The Cosby Show* was so dominant that, after earning third place in its freshman year, it was TV's top-ranked series for the next five seasons—a feat only one other situation comedy has ever achieved, and that was *All in the Family*. It's no wonder that, even though Cosby proved much less successful at two subsequent series efforts outside the genre (mounting a syndicated revival of *You Bet Your Life* and an NBC comedy-drama hybrid called *The Cosby Mysteries*), CBS jumped at the chance to give Cosby a two-year commitment for a new sitcom series in 1996. He had almost singlehandedly rescued one network in the eighties; since at first he *did* succeed, why not let him try, try again for another network in the nineties?

Cosmos. *1980–81, PBS.* This PBS science series, like *The Civil War* a decade later, came on the scene and took everyone by surprise with the extent of its popularity. In the case of *Cosmos*, no small part of that was due to *Tonight Show* host Johnny Carson, an astronomy buff who invited Sagan on his show and endorsed *Cosmos* enthusiastically. Carson also made Sagan's speech pattern part of his standup monologue—and, quickly, part of the American consciousness—by poking good-natured fun at Sagan's "billions and billions of stars" line. Even though Sagan had been seen on the PBS series *Nova* prior to hosting *Cosmos*, it was *Cosmos* that made Sagan a scientific celebrity—a star among stars.

Crusader Rabbit. *1949–51, syndicated.* This was the first cartoon series created and animated specifically for television, and looked like it. The drawings were amateurish even by amateur standards, and the animators, especially in the early run of the series, saved effort (and money) by having characters talk offscreen, or with their backs turned, or with their mouths otherwise obscured. *Crusader Rabbit* was set up like a continuing serial, with five-minute episodes devoted to each step in a long-running "crusade." (The first crusade, "Crusader Rabbit vs. the State of Texas," had the heroic hare and his less intelligent buddy, Rags the Tiger, traveling to Texas to save his jackrabbit relatives from being deported.) With such loopy stories and crude animation, why does *Crusader Rabbit* rate a mention here? For the same reasons it's recalled by so many former kids today: it was different, and it was funny. And that was no accident, because one of the co-creators of *Crusader Rabbit* was Jay Ward, who years later would take the serial adventure form, and the pairing of a smart little hero and a tall dumb sidekick, and strike even richer gold with the characters of Rocky and Bullwinkle. The *Crusader Rabbit* characters were revived with new episodes in 1957–58, but without Ward, who had sold his share of the rights and moved on. For *Bullwinkle*-type looniness, stick with, and seek out, the ten Crusades from 1949–51.

Current Affair, A. *1986–96, syndicated.* If TV news and TV newsmagazines often went downhill in the late eighties and early nineties, and they did, *A Current Affair* is the rolling stone that gathered the first moss. Or first crept out from under a rolling stone, or something. It made its first host, Maury Povich, a star, and made even bigger stars of some of the subjects of its more lurid stories. Invariably, the most memorable of these were what might be called *America's Most Repugnant Home Videos*—"Preppie Murder" suspect Robert Chambers and his tasteless jokes with dolls, actor Rob Lowe and his blurry sex with a consenting nonadult, Amy Fisher and . . . well, take your pick. But not only did more respectable news operations pick up on and repeat these stories and videos, but many of them inspired major network docudramas. Well, maybe "inspired" isn't the right word. It certainly isn't for *this* show.

Dallas. *1978–91, CBS.* Outrating any Super Bowl ever played, outdrawing even the final episode of *Roots*, the episode of *Dallas* answering the question "Who Shot J.R.?" remains one of the most popular TV entertainment programs ever broadcast—topped, at this writing, only by the finale of *M*A*S*H*. The November 1980 installment was the third episode of the fourth season of *Dallas*, but the previous season's cliffhanger had created a seemingly insatiable demand for the resolution. Why was it *so* popular? Maybe it wasn't completely coincidental that Larry Hagman's J. R. Ewing was regaining power, and confronting his would-be assailant, the same month that Ronald Reagan was elected president: both Reagan and J. R. Ewing would spend the decade perpetuating the private-enterprise excesses of the eighties. Hagman relished the part, and was at his best when given devious things to do in the boardroom and the bedroom; similarly, Linda Gray's Sue Ellen shone most brightly in the latter years, when her character was the only one

LEFT: *Columbo*, with Peter Falk in trademark attire.
RIGHT: *The Cosby Show*, with Bill Cosby and Malcolm-Jamal Warner as father Cliff and son Theo.

LEFT: *Dallas*, with Larry Hagman's J. R. Ewing just after being shot in that cliffhanger.
RIGHT: *Davy Crockett*, with sidekick Buddy Ebsen and series star Fess Parker.

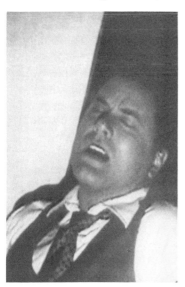

that wasn't stagnating. What hurt *Dallas* most through the years was that J.R.'s main adversary throughout the series, Ken Kercheval's Cliff Barnes, was about as cunning and credible as Wile E. Coyote on *The Road Runner*— and, over the long run, about as effective. And in terms of sheer ridiculousness, not even Barnes at his worst came close to the infamously absurd "dream season," in which the death of Patrick Duffy's Bobby Ewing, and the rest of the entire 1985–86 season of *Dallas*, was wiped away with a single stupid stroke—what I call the "Wake Up, Little Susie" ploy. Victoria Principal's Pam ended her traumatic "widowhood" by waking up to find a very live Bobby taking a shower. It was such an unimaginative way out of a dull dilemma, the only way the *Dallas* writers could have redeemed themselves was to have every subsequent season end the same way: by having a character wake up and start the story all over again. That way, every year of *Dallas* from that point on could be an exploration of alternate realities, without having to worry about long-range consequences. (As it was, the "dream season" gimmick became so famous that other, more imaginative TV writers alluded to it playfully in the final episodes of both *St. Elsewhere* and *Newhart*, where those entire *series* were dismissed as dreams.) If that idea sounds too fanciful, think of how the producers of *Dallas* actually ended the series itself: with Joel Gray as a demonic paranormal guide who took J.R. through a tour of alternate *Dallas* realities, after which J.R. raised his loaded gun, fired, and . . . may or may not have killed himself. Viewers saw only Bobby's reaction as he heard the gunshot and opened the door, and *Dallas* ended there, abruptly, as if awakened from some bad dream. Which, for at least one season, it *had* been. The durable *Dallas* spinoff, *Knots Landing*, lingered for a few seasons more, but its final seasons were just as disappointing and disjointed as those of *Dallas*. However, J.R. himself made enough of a major impact—internationally as well as in America—to become, and remain, a true TV icon, right up there with such instantly identifiable archetypes as Ted Baxter and Archie Bunker.

Daniel Boone. *1964–70, NBC.* Remember Fess Parker, exploring the Wild West as a famous American pioneer and setting off a national craze with his coonskin cap? Well, that was Parker in *Davy Crockett*—but Parker starred here, too, taking the super-successful Disney formula established on that show and transferring it to a character that *Parker* could control (and partly own). Although *Daniel Boone* ran for six years, Parker is still more closely associated with the much older, much briefer *Davy Crockett* series. A 1977 prequel, *Young Dan'l Boone*, lasted only a month before it was canc'led. Even so, *Daniel Boone* does have one strong tie to the teleliteracy canon: Boone's Indian sidekick, Mingo, was played by Ed Ames, who demonstrated his tomahawk-throwing ability in hilariously effective manner during a classic visit to *The Tonight Show Starring Johnny Carson*.

Danny Thomas Show, The. See *Make Room for Daddy*.

Dark Shadows. *1966–71, ABC; 1991, NBC.* This may be the only cult show on TV that was *about* a cult—as well as about vampires, werewolves, and other supernatural characters. The breakaway character was Jonathan Frid's Barnabas Collins, a vampire whose appearance in the show's second season made the gothic soap opera an instant hit—especially with teen viewers, who accounted for as much as 90 percent of the afternoon serial's audience. Even though Frid stumbled over his lines, and sometimes across the set, he stole the show and became its most identifiable character, sort of like the Fonz with fangs. The character of Angelique the witch, played by Lara Parker, was the show's sexiest and most interesting attribute, even though she, like Frid, displayed limited acting range. Kate Jackson and David Selby took part, and parts, in the series and one of its movie sequels (Jackson, later of *Charlie's Angels*, and Selby, later of *Falcon Crest*, costarred in 1971's *Night of Dark Shadows*), but their acting was no better. Even Joan Bennett (as Elizabeth Collins), who had the most prior screen experience of anyone in the cast, fluffed her *Dark Shadows* lines with the worst of them. In retrospect, the bad acting may have been an asset, because the tacky performances fit right in with the cheesiness of the show's sets, scripts, and not-so-special effects. If Ed Wood had made a TV series, it would have looked a lot like *Dark Shadows*. Yet the *Dark Shadows* cult never died—and was fueled, long after the show's cancellation, by reruns and eventually by home-video release. In 1972, a year after *Dark Shadows* was canceled, Dan Curtis redeemed himself in the occult genre by producing *The Night Stalker*, the excellent telemovie introducing Darren McGavin as Carl Kolchak. In the eighties, Curtis dove headfirst into the mainstream, and swam away with mammoth ratings for two equally mammoth miniseries projects, *Winds of War* and its *War and Remembrance* sequel. Then, in the early nineties, Curtis returned to his roots and, for NBC this time, remade *Dark Shadows*—casting it with actors superior, in every respect, to their counterparts in the original show, and presenting it in prime time. Ben Cross was the new Barnabas, and Lysette Anthony cast a great spell as the new Angelique, but the new series was doomed from the start because Curtis opted to revise old story lines rather than create new ones. It was a clear case of recycled television—and in that respect, the new series (which faded quickly) was a *Shadows* of its former self.

Dateline NBC. *1992–* , *NBC*. In its first season or two, this new NBC newsmagazine wouldn't have made the teleliteracy cut, even with Jane Pauley as cohost (with Stone Phillips), if not for a famous screwup: the televising of a rigged crash test of General Motors pickup trucks. It was a faked explosion that blew up in NBC's face, and, once GM blew the whistle in 1993, led to the resignation of then-NBC News President Michael Gartner and a reassessment of TV's responsibility in relying on "outside experts" to provide footage for news programs. The folks at *Dateline NBC* were in danger of being remembered as nothing more than crash-test dummies, but instead of becoming the latest in a long line of NBC newsmagazine failures, *Dateline NBC* instead reversed course and became its biggest newsmagazine success. *Dateline* did it by expanding—first to two nights in the summer of 1994, then to three nights that fall—and by tapping virtually its entire news staff, from a small army of reporters and correspondents to recurring "additional anchor" appearances by Tom Brokaw, Katie Couric, Bryant Gumbel, and Maria Shriver. As *Dateline NBC* got stronger and better, so did the network's entertainment series—a coincidental, but nonetheless beneficial, turn of events. Most important of all, though, was that in late 1995, both *ABC World News Tonight* and the stalwart CBS series *60 Minutes* became embroiled in controversy over what they reported, or decided not to report, in stories involving tobacco companies. When the smoke cleared, NBC had the only network news operation not tarred and feathered—or at least tarred—by tobacco-industry fallout over allegations of "spiked" levels of nicotine. *Dateline NBC*, after an explosively embarrassing start, had cleaned up its act just in the nicotime. Yet *Dateline NBC* had its own major low point in 1995: announcing, heavily promoting, then suddenly and sheepishly canceling, a live prime-time interview with a post-verdict O. J. Simpson.

Dating Game, The. *1966–70, ABC.* **The New Dating Game.** *1973, 1977–80, 1986, syndicated.* **The All-New Dating Game.** *1988, syndicated.* Look, there's no denying it. This Chuck Barris production is not without its contributions, minor though they may be, to the lexicon of teleliteracy. Certainly, the phrase "Bachelor number two" has stuck, as have the catchy Herb Alpert & the Tijuana Brass instrumentals used on the show: "Lollipops and Roses" and, appropriately, "Spanish Flea." There's also no denying that, though *The Dating Game* is not the first TV show to play matchmaker (that dubious honor probably belongs to a 1952 New York show called *First Date*), it's the one most directly responsible for the genre's obsession with double entendre questions-and-answers—a (lack of) development that reached its nadir in the eighties with the smarmy syndicated series *The Love Connection,* and in the nineties with the syndicated dating-show series *Studs* and MTV's mean-spirited *Singled Out.*

David Frost Show, The. *1969–72, syndicated.* This is the American talk-show platform that took Frost's popularity as host of *That Was the Week That Was* and pushed it to a whole new level, by giving him a one-on-one syndicated talk show similar in format to, and concurrent with, *The Dick Cavett Show.* Frost and his clipboard did well for three seasons, and scored many subsequent interview coups in a series of specials. The most famous of these was a four-part 1977 syndicated series called *The Nixon Interviews with David Frost* (see separate listing). Because of Nixon's general reticence, *The Nixon Interviews* were more infuriating than informative, but they also were unforgettable—and, at the time, very popular. And in the nineties, with the PBS series . . . *talking with David Frost,* the veteran talk-show host bounced back again, with a series of shows featuring such hot-as-they-could-be subjects as H. Norman Schwarzkopf, just back from the Persian Gulf War, and Salman Rushdie, not yet back from hiding in seclusion.

Davy Crockett. *1954–55, ABC.* "Born on a mountaintop in Tennessee / Greenest state in the land of the free / Raised in the woods, so's he knew every tree / Killed him a b'ar when he was only three: / Davy, Davy Crockett /

King of the wild frontier. . . . " When you think of *Davy Crockett*, that theme song, "The Ballad of Davy Crockett," is not only the first thing you think of. It's the first thing *they* thought of. When the first episodes of *Davy Crockett* were in the early planning stages for the anthology series *Disneyland*, Walt Disney commissioned staff composer George Bruns to work with the show's scriptwriter, Tom Blackburn, and create some music and lyrics that could serve to bridge the various scenes in the story. Bruns wrote the music and chorus, Blackburn wrote the rest of the lyrics, and a singer named Bill Hayes recorded and released the song as a record several months before the first episode of *Davy Crockett* was televised. The musical result was a surprise, runaway hit: seven million copies sold in the first six months, making it, at that time, the fastest-selling record in history. The mania continued when *Davy Crockett* premiered on *Disneyland*, catapulting Fess Parker to instant stardom—thus giving a whole new meaning to the term "Fess up." Buddy Ebsen, as sidekick George Russel, went along for the ride, and provided an early prototype for his Jed Clampett character on *The Beverly Hillbillies*. Disney-approved replicas of Davy's coonskin caps sold in the millions, but Disney was less astute when it came to capitalizing on the TV show itself. Originally, there were only three episodes of *Davy Crockett* planned, and in the last one, "Davy Crockett at the Alamo," he was killed. Shown a month apart, it wasn't until the final episode—the key word being *final*—that Disney realized what a hit he had on his hands. Unable to carry the story line forward, he followed it backward, and before long there were two additional *Davy Crockett* episodes dramatizing his *earlier* exploits. So in addition to "The Ballad of Davy Crockett" and the coonskin caps, Disney's *Davy Crockett* gave us two TV milestones. The first three episodes of *Davy Crockett*, with the very finite "Alamo" ending, formed network TV's first original miniseries. The later, "earlier" episodes (if that makes any sense) formed the first recorded instance of what's now known as the "prequel." And in one final example of Disney marketing savvy, all five episodes were recycled as theatrical films: the first three under the title of *Davy Crockett, King of the Wild Frontier*, and the final two under the title *Davy Crockett and the River Pirates*. With *Davy Crockett*, Walt Disney didn't waste anything—except a lot of raccoons.

Day After, The. *1983, ABC.* Question: When is a ratings bomb not a ratings bomb? Answer: When it's *The Day After*, ABC's 1983 day-after-doomsday telemovie. This drama, which dramatized life during, and after, a sudden nuclear strike on home soil, was neither the first or the last TV production of its type. The *American Playhouse* anthology series beat ABC to the punch by presenting *Testament*, starring Jane Alexander in a harrowing story about life after the bomb, in theaters and on PBS in the season before *The Day After* was televised. In Great Britain, the BBC followed suit a year after *The Day After* by presenting *Threads*, its own localized version of a domestic nuclear Doomsday. Like *Testament*, it was dark and disturbing, and well worth seeking out (eventually, *Threads* was imported by Ted Turner's TBS for its American premiere). Yet *The Day After*, with the backing and hype of a major network and a Cold War timing that couldn't have been better, wound up as the highest-rated telemovie of all time—a record it continues to hold. Dramatically, *The Day After* is thin on characterization, even though Jason Robards, John Lithgow, JoBeth Williams, and Amy Madigan do their best. It's strong, though, in its blatant antiwar position, and especially in its special-effects sequence of the bombs dropping across America, from Central Park in New York City to the missile silos of Kansas. The subliminal skeletal flashes, the shock waves and fire storms—all were approximated effectively under the direction of Nicholas Meyer. Today, the movie is a frozen-in-amber portrait of the country's greatest unspoken fear at that time, and many youngsters who saw *The Day After* then, or even those who saw only the previews, say those images have stayed with them ever since. One other legacy worth noting: when *The Day After* premiered, and drew such a gigantic TV audience, media critic Ben Stein complained that ABC ought to balance what he perceived as the drama's liberal slant by presenting another fictional drama, one that showed what might happen if America, hamstrung by its own pacifistic policies, came under Soviet control. ABC executive Brandon Stoddard liked the idea, and commissioned Donald Wrye to write and direct something along those lines. The result was 1987's *Amerika*, a fourteen-and-a-half-hour mini-series that generated more than its own share of controversy. *The Day After* and *Amerika* were flip sides of the same coin—a coin that, with the thawing of the Cold war, happily has been withdrawn from circulation. And not a mint too soon.

Days and Nights of Molly Dodd, The. *1987–88, NBC; 1989–91, Lifetime.* I'm being stubborn by putting *Molly Dodd* in here, because if enough people had cared about it at the time, it never would have had to relocate from NBC to the cable network Lifetime. Perhaps I could make a case that *Molly Dodd* is remembered as the no-laugh-track series for which the hybrid term "dramedy" was coined—as in half drama, half comedy. (Personally, I preferred the term "comma," but that never seemed to catch on, period.) But the truth is that this Jay Tarses series, starring the incomparable Blair Brown in the title role, was just too good for me to leave out. Neither Molly nor her job situation was very stable, and the series showed her reinventing herself, changing jobs, and checking out potential suitors with delightful unpredictability. The terrific supporting cast included James Greene as Molly's doorman, Allyn Ann McLerie as her mother, and, as Molly's three most memorable suitors, Richard Lawson (as Detective Nathaniel Hawthorne), David Strathairn (as bookstore owner Moss Goodman), and Tarses himself (as garbage man Nick Donatello). Near the end of the show's run, Molly became pregnant, and the father turned out to be Lawson's Detective Hawthorne— but on the same day he proposed marriage and gave Molly an engagement ring, the highly allergic detective had a fatal reaction to some bad seafood, leaving Molly pregnant and alone. (Given the circumstances, it was a pretty shellfish thing to do.) Molly decided to have the baby anyway, and did. This is worth mentioning because, in 1992, Dan Quayle attacked the fictional title character on *Murphy Brown* for making the same lifestyle decision that Molly had made on Lifetime, virtually unnoticed, the year before. Not only that, but Hawthorne, the father of Molly's baby, was an African-American. Clearly, Quayle wasn't a Lifetime *Molly Dodd* fan, or he might have gotten angry a lot earlier.

Days of Our Lives. *1965–   , NBC*. This series, NBC's most tenured daytime soap, has made its own stars as well as hired some stars of the future. In their *Days of Our Lives* roles, soap stardom has come to Macdonald Carey (as Tom Horton), Frances Reid (Alice Horton), Susan Seaforth Hayes (Julie Olson Williams), Bill Hayes (Doug Williams), Gloria Loring (Liz Chandler), and Diedre Hall (Marlena Evans). After leaving *Days,* prime-time stardom came, in a lighter vein, to Mike Farrell (Scott Banning, 1968–70) on *M*A*S*H,* and to Mary Frann (Amanda Howard, 1974–79) on *Newhart.* Recently, the show's most unforgettable story line was its silly satanic subplot, in which Hall's Marlena was possessed by a demon. For a few months, she ran around—or levitated—while controlling the dreams of others, shape-shifting into various people or beasts, manipulating machinery by telekinesis, seducing priests, burning churches, and generally having a hell of a time in Marlena's home town (which, as *Days of Our Lives* fans are well aware, is fittingly named Salem). After way too much of that nonsense, Marlena finally got her exorcise, putting an end to that devilishly dumb *Days* detour. Past that, and more positively, *Days of Our Lives* has one other gift to TV posterity—its opening line, which has remained unchanged for more than thirty years. "Like sands through the hourglass," it says, "so are the days of our lives." Or, to put it another way: Life's a beach.

Days of Wine and Roses, The. *1958, CBS*. This drama, about an alcoholic couple involved in a tragic love triangle (him, her, and the bottle), is one of the most famous surviving "Golden Age" dramas, though to many it's remembered more for the 1962 film adaptation, starring Jack Lemmon and Lee Remick, than for JP Miller's original, live *Playhouse 90* version, which starred Cliff Robertson and Piper Laurie. (John Frankenheimer directed *Days of Wine and Roses* for television, but when the Hollywood movie was made, the top job went instead to a pre-*Pink Panther* Blake Edwards.) But both versions survive, boast raw and riveting performances, and are worth treasuring. The TV version, preserved on kinescope and widely available on home video, includes one small bonus missing from the film: author Miller, who makes a cameo appearance in his own drama, saying "Shhh!" to a boisterous drunk at an Alcoholics Anonymous meeting. It proves there are no small parts—or perhaps, in Miller's case, it proves there's no business like Shhh!-ow business.

Dean Martin Show, The. *1965–73, NBC*. **Dean Martin Comedy Hour, The.** *1973–74, NBC*. In 1957, one year after breaking up with comedy partner Jerry Lewis, Dean Martin hosted an NBC variety special called *The Dean Martin Show,* which, to put it politely, was a lot less successful than his *Colgate Comedy Hour* triumphs with Lewis for the same network in the early fifties. (Then again, his ex-partner's *The Jerry Lewis Show,* a big-budget variety series bomb that lasted only three months in 1963, was a flop of much more major proportions.) But though at first Martin didn't succeed, he tried, tried again, with other *Dean Martin Show* specials in 1958–60. In 1965, one year after landing a Number One pop record with his recording of "Everybody Loves Somebody," Martin launched a new *Dean Martin Show*—a weekly series this time. He adopted "Everybody Loves Somebody" as his TV theme song, cementing it even further in popular memory. Other aspects of this series most likely to be recalled are Martin's sliding-down-the-fire-pole entrances, the drunk act by Foster Brooks, the occasional celebrity roasts, the Golddiggers lounging around Martin's couch, the surprise guests who knocked at Martin's door, and the intentionally loose feel of Martin's taping sessions. Only Jackie Gleason rivaled Martin in detesting rehearsals, but Gleason, at least, tried to make the performance itself look smooth. With Martin, messing up was part of the fun, and the audience was in on the joke—a joke that would be considered politically incorrect by the more sobering humor standards of the nineties. One other joke played by Martin back then was his annual summer replacement series, *Dean Martin Presents*—the 1968 edition of which, *Dean Martin Presents the Golddiggers*, was a memorably, laughably "mod" variety series cohosted by Frank Sinatra, Jr. and Joey Heatherton.

Death of a Salesman. *1966, CBS; 1985, CBS*. CBS mounted two different, yet equally superb, versions of Arthur Miller's seminal American play. The first, in 1966, had Lee J. Cobb and Mildred Dunnock reprising their roles of Willy and Linda Loman from the original 1949 Broadway production; for TV, new players included George Segal and James Farentino as Willy's sons, Biff and Happy. The second, in 1985, was a TV adaptation of a hit Broadway revival of *Death of a Salesman*, starring Dustin Hoffman as Willy Loman, with Kate Reid as Linda and John Malkovich and Stephen Lang as Biff and Happy. Two versions of the same play, a generation apart, each of them crackling with artistry and emotion. Comparisons, especially between the starring performances by Cobb and Hoffman, are fascinating but ultimately inconclusive. Both are astounding. Neither will be forgotten. And in the context of teleliteracy, Miller and *Death of a Salesman* deserve special credit for being decades ahead of the home-entertainment curve, especially when it comes to the phenomenon known as "time-shifting." In the play, written by Miller in 1948, Willy Loman visits the company firm to appeal to his boss—but instead of getting sympathy and understanding, gets treated to an impromptu and enthusiastic lecture about the virtues of modern technology's newest miracle, the wire recorder. Wire predated reel-to-reel tape, and Willy's boss was excited about its time-shifting possibilities . . . for radio. "You can't do without it," he tells Willy. "Supposing you wanna hear Jack Benny, see? But you can't be home at that hour. So you tell the maid to turn the radio on when Jack Benny comes on, and this automatically goes on with the radio! . . . You can come home twelve o'clock, one o'clock, any time you like, and you get yourself a Coke and sit yourself down, throw the switch, and there's Jack Benny's program in the middle of the night!" With the advent of television, VCRs, and timers, you didn't even need a maid to time-shift your favorite shows—

but otherwise, Miller's prophecy was a maid-to-order prediction worthy of the best of Nostradamus.

Death Valley Days. *1952–70, syndicated.* The stories in this long-running syndicated series were basically true ones, culled from oral histories collected by series creator Ruth Woodman; since this was an anthology series, some were rather dramatic and surprising. (So were some of the participants: Fess Parker played a U.S. Marshal in one episode that predated both Parker's *Davy Crockett* and the series about that most famous TV marshal of all, *Gunsmoke.*) But what's really surprising about TV's *Death Valley Days*, which was an offshoot of Woodman's radio series of the same name (the radio version ran from 1931–45), is that, despite all those years and all that history, the two things most likely to be remembered about *Death Valley Days* have nothing to do with the stories themselves. Instead, the most common associations are the name and image of the show's sponsor ("Twenty Mule Team Borax"), and the name and image of its most famous host: Ronald Reagan. Amazingly, given his widespread association with this show, Reagan had the job for only a year. He joined *Death Valley Days* in 1965, after the retirement of the show's original host, the pipe-smoking Stanley Andrews. In 1966, Reagan retired, too—to pursue a political career.

Defenders, The. *1961–65, CBS.* If you're looking for the true TV ancestor to *L.A. Law*, it isn't *Perry Mason*. It's *The Defenders*, which took a "Golden Age" drama approach to a weekly series about the law. The beauty and strength of *The Defenders* was that it wasn't just about murders and misdirection, like *Perry Mason*, but was about ideas: some of the most potent episodes concerned such touchy (and, for sixties TV, elusive) topics as abortion, civil rights, and blacklisting. And because *The Defenders* starred E. G. Marshall and Robert Reed as father-son lawyers (Lawrence and Kenneth Preston) working at the same firm, the most divisive issues of the time could be explored from both sides of the ever-widening generation gap. Marshall was as terrific here as Richard Dysart would later be on *L.A. Law*, and Reed, while no Harry Hamlin, was no ham, either (it's a shame, in a way, that he went from this stellar series to the black hole of *The Brady Bunch*). Today *The Defenders*, like *Lou Grant*, is remembered as an issues-conscious, issues-*conscience* kind of show. Yet its lineage is interesting in its own right: *The Defenders* was developed by writer Reginald Rose from his two-part 1957 *Studio One* drama called "The Defender," with Ralph Bellamy and William Shatner as the fraternal lawyers and Steve McQueen as their client. Three years earlier, Rose had bloomed by writing another *Studio One* courtroom drama, *Twelve Angry Men*.

Dennis the Menace. *1959–63, CBS.* Even if you tried to think of this series as a kind of *Eddie Haskell: The Early Years*, or a live-action *Bart Simpson* sitcom, it wasn't that impressive or entertaining. The main problem was that Jay North, who played Hank Ketcham's irrepressible cartoon character, was too old for the part when he started out, and, needless to say, didn't get any younger. But because the daily comic strip survived, so did this TV version of *Dennis,* which was repeated endlessly in syndication, then as part of the daily and nightly offerings on Nickelodeon. It was, in fact, one of the very first vintage reruns offered by Nick at Nite when that nightly Nickelodeon service was launched in 1985 (the others, for the record, were *The Donna Reed Show* and *Route 66).* That alone would guarantee it another generation's worth of teleliteracy status, but there's another reason, too: *Home Alone* writer-producer John Hughes mounted a *Dennis the Menace* movie remake in 1993, starring newcomer Mason Gamble—a boy much younger than North was—as Dennis. It turned out to be a poor Gamble, though: even without North, the new *Dennis the Menace* quickly went south.

Designing Women. *1986–93, CBS.* Speaking of going south: this situation comedy, set at an interior design firm in Atlanta, was one of the few TV sitcoms to treat southerners as having more innate intelligence than, say, Gomer Pyle or Luke Duke. (A later sitcom by the same *Designing Women* creative team, *Evening Shade,* was another.) But somewhere along the line, in the early nineties, two things happened that overshadowed the often skillful and funny work in this sitcom by its original five-member ensemble cast (Dixie Carter, Annie Potts, Jean Smart, Delta Burke, and Meshach Taylor). One was the eventual feud between Burke and the show's executive producers, Linda Bloodworth-Thomason and Harry Thomason, which resulted in Burke's leaving the show, and a season or two of further cast changes, bad blood, and fairly bad scripts. The other occurrence was Bloodworth-Thomason's high-profile 1992 efforts to help get her friend Bill Clinton elected President of the United States—efforts that, temporarily at least, took the focus away from *Designing Women* and all her other TV work, for her as well as for her audience. But as a "literate" sitcom driven almost entirely by a female cast, *Designing Women* earned, deserves, and will retain its place in TV history.

Dick Cavett Show, The. *1969–75, ABC; 1977–81, PBS.* Dick Cavett has hosted many more interview, documentary, and variety series than the ones listed above; in fact, well into the nineties, he was part of the nightly talk-show lineup for cable's CNBC. But it was in the late-night slot for ABC, and the prime-time slot for PBS, that Cavett did his most ambitious, interesting, and sometimes annoying work. On the positive side, he scored some remarkable coups with his interviews: conducting one-on-one conversations with the likes of Marlon Brando, Woody Allen, Katharine Hepburn, and Laurence Olivier, and refereeing one-against-one confrontations like the infamous literary-heavyweight bout between Norman Mailer and Gore Vidal. On the negative side, Cavett often led the conversations back to himself; in his Woody Allen interview, we learned almost as much about Cavett as we did about his reclusive friend (a trait carried on, in the nineties, by another well-respected PBS interview staple, Charlie Rose). Still, with Cavett, what counted most was his combination of intellect and enthusiasm. He was conversant, in every sense of the word, with everything from the Beatles to the Bard, from silent films to vocal politicians. (His on-air argument with Lester Maddox sparked Maddox to leave the show in anger, and also sparked Randy Newman to write the song "Rednecks" about it.) Like David Frost, who caught on in America at about the same time, Cavett has managed to remain in the public eye, and conduct in-depth TV interviews, every decade since.

Dick Van Dyke Show, The. *1961–66, CBS.* There's something warm and reassuring, as well as totally appropriate, in the Nickelodeon cable network's choice of Dick Van Dyke to serve as the on-air "Chairman" of Nick at Nite, the person and network accepting responsibility for "preserving our television heritage." *The Dick Van Dyke Show,* after all, is a crown jewel in that heritage, and has to rank on everybody's list as one of the ten best sitcoms of all time. (My own list would also include *The Honeymooners, Fawlty Towers, The Mary Tyler Moore Show, Taxi,* and *Cheers,* for starters.) Van Dyke as Rob Petrie, and Mary Tyler Moore as Laura, were the perfect couple for the Kennedy era, just as Rob's colleagues at *The Alan Brady Show* made for the funniest TV workplace until—well, until *The Mary Tyler Moore Show* came along. For many TV shows, catch phrases and theme songs are what linger the longest—and *The Dick Van Dyke Show* could claim its share, especially Laura's whiny "Ohhhhhhh, Rob," Rob's opening-credits tangle with the ottoman (will he trip over it or skip around it?), and the bouncy instrumental by Earle Hagen (coauthor of *The Andy Griffith Show* theme). Yet *The Dick Van Dyke Show* was so solid that entire *plots* are remembered fondly. In 1993, Van Dyke hosted a "Chairman's Choice" minimarathon, listing his five favorite episodes of the series: "That's My Boy??" (Rob thinks his baby was mistakenly switched with another at the hospital); "It May Look Like a Walnut" (an *Invasion of the Body Snatchers* takeoff, but with a closetful of nuts); "Never Bathe on Saturday" (Laura gets her toe caught in a hotel bathtub); "I'd Rather Be Bald Than to Have No Head at All" (Rob dreams of losing all his hair); and "Where Did I Come From?" (Rob recalls the day Laura gave birth). Also in 1993, Moore identified her own favorite *Dick Van Dyke Show* episode: "The Curious Thing About Women" (Laura can't resist opening up a package addressed to Rob). I'd agree with Van Dyke's first, second, and fifth choices, and add one of my own: "Coast-to-Coast Big Mouth," in which Laura reveals on a TV talk show that Rob's boss, the egomaniacal Alan Brady, wears a toupee. The scene with series creator Carl Reiner, as Brady, talking to his collection of hairpieces is an out-and-out classic. In the original pilot version of this series, Reiner had the Rob Petrie role—but though Reiner was prevented, outrageously, from starring in his own loosely based version of his own life (the former writer-performer on *Your Show of Shows* was told he was "too Jewish"), things worked out for the best. Reiner was a riot as Alan Brady, and Van Dyke turned Rob Petrie into the comedy role of a lifetime. Moore, of course, did more great work later, and Reiner had done much of his on *Your Show of Shows,* but for Van Dyke and the rest of the cast (Rose Marie's Sally Rogers, Morey Amsterdam's Buddy Sorrell, Richard Deacon's Mel Cooley, and the others), *The Dick Van Dyke Show* was as good as it got. And, frankly, TV sitcoms never got much better. CBS saluted this most classic of sitcoms with a 1994 reunion special, *The Dick Van Dyke Show Remembered,* but the title was a little unfair: who, after all, had forgotten? In 1995, Reiner appeared in an episode of NBC's *Mad about You,* portraying and reprising, for the first time since 1966, his old role of dictatorial TV talent Alan Brady. Reiner was fabulous all over again, and was nominated for an Emmy as best comedic guest actor—in a category also including, by a truly bizarre coincidence, his old *Your Show of Shows* boss Sid Caesar, who was nominated for his guest appearance on another sitcom, *Love & War.* Reiner went home with the Emmy that year, demonstrating that all things come to those who wait, and that all's fair, even in *Love & War.*

Diff'rent Strokes. *1978–85, NBC; 1985–86, NBC.* Forget *Amos 'n' Andy,* which at its core was a very funny show. *This* series exemplified all that was wrong with network television's portrayal of African-Americans. Not only was Gary Coleman's Arnold an impossibly rude little kid—a small, black Don Rickles—but he and his brother Willis (Todd Bridges) were happily adopted by a rich white man, played by Conrad Bain. *Diff'rent Strokes* introduced this sitcom premise a year after the premiere of *Roots,* which somehow made it all the more despicable. Coleman was such a singular performer, he'll be remembered—but you could say the same thing about Mr. T, and it wouldn't necessarily be any more of a compliment. This series gave birth to a spinoff, *The Facts of Life,* that was almost equally awful. These *Strokes* weren't just *Diff'rent.* They were disgust'ng.

Dinah Shore Chevy Show, The. *1956–63, NBC.* You must remember this: A kiss is still is a kiss. Dinah Shore sang a lot of songs, and acted in a lot of skits, in this long-running one-hour variety series, which was an outgrowth of her fifteen-minute *Dinah Shore Show* (1951–57) on the same network. It was on the *Chevy Show,* however, that Shore provided her two most durable trademarks: her sponsor-supporting "See the U.S.A. in your Chevrolet!" theme song, and her exaggerated "Mwahh!" kiss that ended each show. Why does a simple stage kiss earn a place in our collective memories thirty years later? Easy: The fundamental things apply, as time goes by.

Disneyland. *1954–58, ABC.* **Walt Disney Presents.** *1958–61, ABC.* **Walt Disney's Wonderful World of Color.** *1961–69, NBC.* **The Wonderful World of Disney.** *1969–79, NBC.* **Disney's Wonderful World.** *1979–81, NBC.* **Walt Disney.** *1981–83, CBS.* **The Disney Sunday Movie.** *1986–88, ABC.* **The Magical World of Disney.** *1988–90, NBC.* Take all of the *Disney* titles over the years, add them up, and what you have—after one massive uninterrupted streak from 1954–83 and a comparatively brief revival spurt from 1986–90— is the longest-running weekly series ever broadcast in prime time. CBS, NBC, and ABC all took at least one turn at televising a Disney showcase series, for a total run of thirty-four TV seasons. If fate and the Nielsen gods are kind, *60 Minutes* eventually will tie that record, as will *Monday Night Football*—but not until the years 2001 and 2003, respectively. Besides, one of those durable TV showcases comes from its network's news division, the other from sports; when it comes to attracting and holding an audience with a pure entertainment program, no other entity even comes close to the longevity of the various Disney TV series. When Walt Disney hosted the first episode of ABC's *Disneyland* in 1954, he started out by inaugurating a type of programming form that wouldn't become commonplace on TV until the nineties: the "infomercial." His entire one-hour opener, *The Disneyland Story,* was nothing but a one-hour commercial for his still-in-construction California theme park, which, not at all coincidentally, bore the same name as the TV series. That first season, in addition to establishing memorable rotating segments (with theme-park tie-ins, of course) called "Frontierland," "Fantasyland," "Tomorrowland," and "Adventureland," Disney went even deeper into Promotionland by pioneering the "making-of-the-movie . . . " genre. On one episode of *Disneyland,* he presented *Underseas Adventure,* a one-hour "documentary" about the new advances in underwater filmmaking. It was a flat-out, full-length promotional special for Disney's upcoming *20,000 Leagues under the Sea,* but it won an Emmy anyway. And with *Davy Crockett* as part of the first-year package, *Disneyland* became a hit show ABC's first TV series in the fifties to crack the Top 10, which explains why the fledgling network gave Disney such a long leash. By the time Disneyland the theme park opened in the summer of 1955, *Disneyland* the TV series already was a monster hit, and the success of one continued to fuel the other. (With the Disney Channel on cable, the company's penchant for promotion continues to thrive in the nineties, with Walt Disney World anniversary specials and *The Making of Beauty and the Beast* and *The Making of Toy Story* "documentaries" all over the place.) *Disneyland* gave many lasting contributions to teleliteracy: in addition to *Davy Crockett,* there were nature films and cartoon shorts, either recycled from Disney films or created especially for TV. Even more than *Crockett* and company, though, the show's most lasting and durable contribution was Walt Disney himself, making him as visible and durably famous as Alfred Hitchcock, who undertook similar hosting chores, starting a year later than Disney, on *Alfred Hitchcock Presents.* It was to emulate Hitchcock, no doubt, that Disney in 1958 renamed his own series *Walt Disney Presents.* That title change was superficial, though, compared to the revolutionary one signaled by *Walt Disney's Wonderful World of Color,* ushered in when Disney switched to NBC in 1961. NBC's parent corporation, General Electric, was proud as a (color) peacock to have Disney aboard. GE was a leading manufacturer of the newfangled color TV sets, but consumers needed a reason to buy them (fewer than one million color sets had been sold at the time), and few reasons were better than the cartoons, nature specials, and other offerings emanating from the Disney studio. "The world is a carousel of color," boasted the new show's theme song—and as Disney presented it, it was. Each week, Tinker Bell would wave her magic wand and splash vibrant colors all over the place . . . and the place was Disneyland. German-accented Professor Ludwig von Drake was one new Disney character introduced on *Wonderful World of Color;* he was billed, so to speak, as an occasional guest host, beginning with the series' inaugural episode. Walt Disney died in 1966, but the series kept going under the same format and title until 1969, when it was renamed *The Wonderful World of Disney*. *Disney's Wonderful World* followed in 1979; both shows, in their respective titles, reflected the studio as well as the man. Oddly enough, the next effort, when the Disney TV franchise relocated to CBS in 1981, reversed that trend and was called, simply, *Walt Disney*. For the final two network efforts of the eighties, ABC's *The Disney Sunday Movie* and NBC's *The Magical World of Disney*, the ghost of Walt Disney was brought back, in spirit, with the new head of Disney Studios serving, as had Walt himself, as on-air host. This time it was Michael Eisner— and in 1995, seven years after ABC canceled Eisner's *Disney Sunday Movie*, Eisner's Walt Disney Company turned around and acquired Capital Cities/ ABC. If a new prime-time *Disney* series, with or without Eisner at the helm, is not back on ABC's schedule prior to 1997, then something Goofy is going on. And if a new version does surface, stretching the Disney TV tradition across a total of five decades, then *60 Minutes* and/or *Monday Night Football*, in pursuit of tying and breaking those prime-time longevity records, will just have to wait. See also: *Davy Crockett*.

Dr. Kildare. *1961–66, NBC*. This successful medical series was spun off from an even more successful medical series: the *Dr. Kildare* movies from 1937–48, based on the short stories by Max Brand. Lew Ayres played young James Kildare in the film versions, and Lionel Barrymore was senior staff physician Leonard Gillespie. In the midnineties, though specific memories of the series have faded, millions of viewers have no trouble recalling Richard Chamberlain as the dashing young doctor, long before he become King of the Miniseries (thanks to *Shogun, Centennnial,* and *The Thorn Birds*). A bit older than Doogie Howser, Chamberlain's Kildare was similarly committed to his patients, and would have been right at home in the corridors of *ER*. In the TV version of *Dr. Kildare*, Raymond Massey played the paternal Dr. Gillespie, to whom young Dr. Kildare went for advice. Which reminds me: a syndicated spinoff sequel called *Young Dr. Kildare* was attempted in the seventies, but that operation was *not* a success. As for the "old" *Dr. Kildare*, it was a lot more watchable than its competition, *Ben Casey*, and even developed, in its final seasons, an overlapping story structure (many patients in one episode, with some plots and cases carried over to several different episodes) that would be echoed, decades later, by another medical series, *St. Elsewhere*.

Doctors, The. *1963–82, CBS*. And speaking of doctors. . . . With *Dr. Kildare* and *Ben Casey* both plying their trade successfully in prime time, daytime TV lost little time in establishing a medical practice of its own. In fact, both ABC's *General Hospital* and CBS's *The Doctors* premiered on the very same day—April Fool's Day, which is so obvious a joke even *I'll* resist it. For the first season, *The Doctors* was an anthology-type medical show, then switched to a more standard serial form with an all-new cast. Casting, as it turns out, was this series' strong suit: over the years, its regulars included Armand Assante (as Dr. Michael Powers, 1975–77), Julia Duffy (Penny Davis, 1973–77), Alec Baldwin (Billy Aldrich, 1980–82), Jonathan Frakes of *Star Trek: The Next Generation* (Tom Carroll, 1977–78), Valerie Mahaffey (Ashley Bennett,

1979–81), and Kathryn Harrold and Kathleen Turner, both in the role of Nola Aldrich (Harrold from 1976–78, Turner from 1978–79).

Doctor Who. *1970–89, syndicated.* And *still* speaking of doctors. . . . In England, the BBC launched this lighthearted fantasy series in 1963, one of the first TV entertainment programs offered when regular programming resumed in the aftermath of British coverage of the John F. Kennedy assassination. Within a few months, thanks to some silly-looking robotic creatures called the Daleks, *Doctor Who* became a major, majorly silly fad, just as *Batman* would in the States a few years later. Movie versions of the show, with different casts, appeared in the midsixties, but American viewers wouldn't get their first look at the BBC's *Doctor Who* until 1970, when it was first syndicated here—and it took until the late seventies for it to catch on. The show's electronic theme music is catchy enough to qualify as teleliteracy, as is the concept of a character so durable he can be played by many different actors over four different decades. Actually, by definition, he *must* be, because the deal with the time-traveling *Doctor Who* is that he occasionally must "regenerate" into a fresh body and personality. Counting an early incarnation of the Doctor who made his first and only appearance on the *Doctor Who* twentieth-anniversary special in 1983 (and was played by Richard Hurndall), eight different Doctors were presented during the show's duration—but in England, where the chronology really counts, only seven *Doctor Who* incarnations were given their own series. The BBC series began in 1963 with William Hartnell, commonly (and logically) referred to as "Doctor Who I," introduced as a Time Lord who hopped around time and space in a stolen, somewhat uncontrollable time machine called a TARDIS (an acronym for Time And Relative Dimension In Space). The "relative dimension" part explained, in a way, how the TARDIS could look like a phone booth—a British "call box"—on the outside, yet be a spacious spaceship on the inside. Hartnell was replaced in 1966 by "Doctor Who II," Patrick Troughton, who in turn was replaced in 1970 by "Doctor Who III," Jon Pertwee. The year 1975 saw the addition of "Doctor Who IV," played by Tom Baker, to the list, and Baker not only was the best *Doctor Who* star of all, and the one whose tenure on the show lasted the longest, but the most popular—in England and America alike. "Doctor Who V," Peter Davison, followed gamely in 1982, but the series lost steam with its final two protagonists, Colin Baker as "Doctor Who VI" in 1984 and Sylvester McCoy as "Doctor Who VII," whose tenure began in 1986 and ended, along with production of the series itself, in 1989. All seven of those TV Time Lords had assistants, usually young and pretty ones, but none really deserves mention here. What does deserve mention, though, is that Steven Spielberg's Amblin Entertainment revived the character, and perhaps the franchise, by producing a new Fox telemovie called *Dr. Who* in 1996 (the new title, like the doctor's visit, being relatively abbreviated). Instead of picking up where the British series had left off, this new *Dr. Who* went the prequel route, showing how Doctor Who became a Time Lord in the first place. This risked a major disruption of the accepted cast-list chronology (unless, that is, the star of the telemovie became known as "Doctor Who 0," or perhaps, in those pre-Time

Lord days, "Mister Who")—but in a series about time travel, how upset can you be when a plot takes you back to Doctor Who's past? As for the future of *Doctor Who*, it could go both ways: more adventures from the "early years," if there's sufficient demand, or else a resumption of the saga with "Doctor Who VIII." Because Time Lords are capable of living a total of thirteen different "lives," the good *Doctor*, or *Dr.*, could be around well into the new millennium—and, with older episodes widely available on home video, is in little danger of becoming *Doctor Who?*

Donahue. See *The Phil Donahue Show.*

Donna Reed Show, The. *1958–66, ABC.* This show is the female counterpart of *Father Knows Best:* the type of sitcom most remembered, and often ridiculed, as holding up an impossibly perfect view of middle-class suburbia. Donna Reed's character of Donna Stone had it all: she'd married a doctor (Alex, played by Carl Betz), given birth to good-looking, studious, talented kids, and lived in a beautiful and immaculately maintained home. It's worth noting that Reed herself later confessed "contempt for the two-dimensional, stereotyped woman" she had played for eight years, but that's not what people remember. What people remember most is a distressingly unattainable standard of harmonious family life—that, and the hit singles Reed's TV offspring managed to land on the music charts while appearing on *The Donna Reed Show.* Paul Petersen (Jeff) hit the Top 10 with "My Dad" in 1962, the same year in which future *Coach* costar Shelley Fabares, who on *The Donna Reed Show* played Mary, scored a Number One hit with "Johnny Angel." *The Donna Reed Show* not only was one of the inaugural vintage offerings on Nick at Nite (which rescued it from a decade of absence from TV syndication), and the one perhaps most identified with that particular cable lineup, but lasted longer than any other of the "original" reruns shown when Nick at Nite was launched in 1985. Nine years later, Nick at Nite scheduled a ten-hour, twenty-episode "Farewell Donna" night, and retired *The Donna Reed Show* with dignity and honor. Nick at Nite demonstrated that evening that it had, in the very best sense of the phrase, a heart of Stone.

Dragnet. *1952–59, 1967–70, NBC.* The Hemingway of law enforcement, Jack Webb's Joe Friday spoke softly and carried a heavy shtick: he never showed emotion, rarely raised more than an eyebrow, and worked hard to avoid commas. Each episode, after Walter Schumann's famous *"DUM-de-DUM-DUM"* opening theme, would begin with Webb's Friday saying, *"This* is the city. Los Angeles, California. I carry a badge. . . . " The end of the show was memorable, too, for each one ended with the announcer saying (recite after me): "The story you have just seen is true. Only the names have been changed, to protect the innocent." Even the hammer-and-chisel "A Mark VII Production" closing credit, one of the first "vanity-plate" TV-production tags, was terse and tough enough to imprint itself in our common cultural memories. Just the facts, ma'am—and the fact is, few TV series have been more influential, distinctive, imitated, or remembered than *Dragnet.* The show and the character had begun on radio in 1949, moved easily to TV two years later, and eventually inspired a trio of movie versions, all of which continued the *Dragnet* legacy. Two were Webb's "official" versions, each showcasing his TV costar at the time. The 1954 *Dragnet* film paired Webb with Ben Alexander as Frank Smith, while the 1969 *Dragnet* movie, released during the second incarnation of the series, showcased Webb and Harry Morgan, who played his new detective partner, Bill Gannon. Morgan, in fact, appeared in the final *Dragnet* movie as well, but that was a parody version in 1987, starring Dan Aykroyd as Joe Friday, and Tom Hanks as Friday's new partner. Neither that parody nor any other, however, matched the dead-on brilliance of that unforgettable *Dragnet* parody on *The Tonight Show*, in which Johnny Carson and Webb himself spoke monotonously—in matching monotones, that is—about the tongue-twisting case of the "copped copper clappers."

Dream On. *1990–96, HBO; 1995, Fox*. Next to *Mystery Science Theater 3000*, this is perhaps the most teleliterate series on television. Each episode, after all, is loaded with snippets from *other* TV shows—forgotten ones, usually, from the less glittery anthology shows of TV's "Golden Age." Brian Benben plays Martin Tupper, a child of television who, somewhat paradoxically, has grown up to be a book editor. Yet whenever he reacts to any odd, frightening, or even arousing situation, the first thing he thinks of—and therefore the first thing we viewers see—is an image or line of dialogue from some old TV show or movie. The technique is not unprecedented; in fact, it was used relatively recently, if notoriously ineffectively, in the X-rated 1970 movie version of Gore Vidal's *Myra Breckenridge*. In the case of *Dream On*, the impetus for the concept was practical: it was commissioned by MCA as a clever way to recycle some of the otherwise unused stuff in its vaults. Yet executive producer John Landis and series creators Marta Kauffman and David Crane (who moved on to collaborate, with Kevin S. Bright, on *Friends*) made sure it was clever in many more respects than that. The cast of *Dream On* is very good (especially Benben as Martin, Wendie Malick as his ex-wife Judith, and recurring cast member Michael McKean as Gibby, Martin's avaricious Australian publishing boss), the instrumental theme song is one of the best and bounciest in recent years, and the dialogue and stories are refreshingly adult, befitting its unedited cable home. In 1995, in a brief and puzzling experiment, Fox broadcast reruns of HBO's *Dream On*, but with some of its footage edited and with lots of the dialogue and action altered or reshot for commercial broadcast. Forget the diluted versions; HBO is the only acceptable place to turn on *Dream On*. Watch, in reruns, for an episode guest-starring Jennifer Tilly as a lesbian who competes with Martin in a very unusual romantic triangle, and another in which Martin ineptly initiates a heart-to-heart "birds-and-bees" talk with his teen son Jeremy, played by Chris Demetral. After the basic talk is begun and aborted, to the massive relief of them both, Martin soothingly tells Jeremy that if he ever has any specific questions, he should feel free to ask good old dad. So Jeremy, immediately warming to the offer, fires off a few questions in rapid succession, including the unexpected, unforgettable "What's smegma?" You think the commercial broadcast networks will be writing or approving stuff like that any time soon? *Dream On*.

Duel. *1971, ABC*. Steven Spielberg directed this visually stunning, relentlessly tense telemovie adaptation of a Richard Matheson short story—and even though *Duel* has reached the quarter-century mark in terms of its age, it still stands as one of TV's best and most exciting original movies. It's the story of a meek traveling salesman, played by Dennis Weaver, who is cut off on a lonely desert highway by a giant tanker truck, and gets angry enough to hit the gas and pass the guy (who, other than his outstretched arm, is never seen). That begins what turns into a deadly game of cat and mouse—or car and truck—on a largely unpopulated stretch of desert highway. Dennis Weaver is very expressive as the driver, especially given that he has so few lines of dialogue, and it's amazing how effectively Spielberg used camera angles, editing, sound effects, and music to turn the giant truck into a menacing monster. In many ways, *Duel* was a dry run—literally—for *Jaws*, which Spielberg would film four years later. (When, at the climax, a vehicle falls in slow motion over the edge of a cliff, both the sights and sounds are uncannily like those at the climax of *Jaws*, with the sinking shark carcass getting similar treatment.) *Duel*, one of the few telemovies from that early era to appear often on local and cable TV outlets in the nineties, survives not only as an early work by an accomplished movie director, but as a superb action drama in its own right. It's a natural for a modern remake, except that it's doubtful any young filmmaker today could improve upon the original.

Dukes of Hazzard, The. *1979–85, CBS*. This TV series, capitalizing at the time on the popularity of *Smokey and the Bandit*, led TV into a new action-comedy genre I once described, and dismissed, as "kinetic rednecks." If you extracted the slow-motion airborne autos from this series, you'd cut the running time in half, which would make it only half as wretched. *The Dukes of Hazzard* is gone now, but, unfortunately, not quite forgotten. John Schneider and Tom Wopat, who starred as Bo and Luke Duke, went on to more respectable careers—but short of instant retirement or untimely death, how could they not? Wopat, a decade after playing Luke Duke, was especially impressive: he was working for CBS again, but this time in the much less embarrassing role of Jeff Robbins, one of the ex-husbands on Cybill Shepherd's *Cybill* sitcom. Yet in teleliteracy terms, what's remembered most about *The Dukes of Hazzard* is General Lee, which is poetic justice. General Lee is a car, not a character.

Dynasty. *1981–89, ABC*. Like *Dallas* on CBS, this series wallowed in wealth, and rose and fell as greed went in, then out, of fashion in the eighties. Also like *Dallas*, *Dynasty* caught on big thanks to a central villain; in the case of *Dynasty*, it was Joan Collins as Alexis, who joined the series in its second season. Series creator Esther Shapiro told me once she saw the characters on *Dynasty* as the modern-day equivalents of the familial schemers of *I, Claudius*—but I, David, think that's aiming a little high. On its best days, *Dynasty*

The Dick Van Dyke Show, with Mary Tyler Moore and Dick Van Dyke as superb suburbanites.

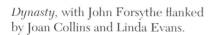

Dynasty, with John Forsythe flanked by Joan Collins and Linda Evans.

Dragnet, with Jack Webb and his very best police-force sidekick, Harry Morgan.

was never as good as *Dallas*, though it had, on balance, a more interesting cast. There was a four-hour *Dynasty* miniseries reunion in 1991, but that reunion generated almost as many yawns as a dream sequence on *Dallas*. Actually, both of those prime-time soaps could have benefited tremendously from a well-timed corporate merger. Imagine a *Dynasty vs. Dallas* show, with Alexis locking horns with J. R. Ewing, Heather Locklear's Sammy Jo Dean flirting with Bobby, and with John Forsythe's Blake Carrington running off with Miss Ellie. Instead, the *Dynasty* writers went off and machine-gunned half the cast in Moldavia, while the *Dallas* writers put their characters, and their audience, to sleep. Rock Hudson, in his last role before succumbing to AIDS, was featured as dashing Daniel Reece in 1984–85, and a *Dynasty* sister series, *The Colbys*, lasted from 1985–87. The true lasting legacy of *Dynasty*, though, came in the form of Locklear (and, to be sexist for one quick parenthetical, what a fine form it was). Just as Collins joined *Dynasty* in its second season and charged it with enough electricity to become a hit, Locklear eventually did the same thing, in the same second-season time frame, for *Melrose Place*.

E

Early Frost, An. *1985, NBC.* This telemovie often gets credit as the first prime-time dramatic treatment of the AIDS virus, although it wasn't. A 1983 episode of the series *St. Elsewhere*, predating *An Early Frost* by nearly two years, dealt with a married politician who had to deal with his mortality, and reveal his homosexuality, after testing positive for AIDS. A similar plot was used in *An Early Frost*, with Aidan Quinn as a young lawyer who returns to his middle-class family (Gena Rowlands and Ben Gazzara as his parents, Sylvia Sidney as his grandmother) to tell them he's gay—and dying. Because Hollywood films had yet to touch the topic, the well-written, compassionate *An Early Frost* garnered enough praise and attention to make a lasting impression. The first major Hollywood movie to touch the same subject, with Tom Hanks winning an Oscar for his trouble, was Jonathan Demme's *Philadelphia*—eight years after *An Early Frost*. For the record: in supporting *Early Frost* roles, John Glover and D. W. Moffett were especially good.

Edge of Night, The. *1956–1975, CBS; 1975–84, ABC.* The mayhem quotient of this long-running soap opera was a key to its success and durability. People not only kissed on this show; many of them killed, too, and audiences got swept up instantly by the murders, mysteries, and characters. (Fans of *Twin Peaks* might be particularly interested in one midsixties story line, in which Millette Alexander played an ill-fated young woman named Laura—then returned to the series shortly thereafter, playing the late Laura's lookalike.) The most famous alumnus of *The Edge of Night* is Larry Hagman, who played lawyer Ed Gibson for two years (1961–63), long before striking black gold and Texas tea on the nighttime soap opera *Dallas*. Among other familiar actors who once held *Night* jobs: Tony Roberts (as Lee Pollack, 1965–67), Ann Wedgeworth (Angela Talbot, 1966), John Cullum (David Gideon, 1966–67), Scott Glenn (Calvin Brenner, 1969), Dixie Carter (Brandy Henderson, 1974–76), and, as already familiar faces showing up in short-lived *Edge of Night* roles, Dick Cavett (as Moe Eberhardt, 1983) and Amanda Blake (Dr. Juliana Stanhower, 1984).

Ed Sullivan Show, The. *1955–71, CBS.* **Toast of the Town.** *1948–55, CBS.* In teleliteracy terms, this really *was* a "really big shew." This Sunday-night mainstay was broadcast TV in its broadest sense, a variety show offering so much variety that it was bound to, in the words of Abraham Lincoln, please all of the people some of the time. Ed Sullivan, who hosted *Toast of the Town* from the start in 1948 and worked his name into the revamped title seven years later, somehow managed to bridge four decades on nationwide TV while always seeming to be hosting for his very first time. Fumbling his way stiffly through every introduction, Sullivan became the celebrity impressionist's dream target: the variety-show equivalent of Rod Serling. Yet there's so much else to remember about *The Ed Sullivan Show*, from the sublime to the ridiculous—including, on the ridiculous side, Sullivan's cheesy conversations with the mouse puppet Topo Gigio, and those spinning-plate jugglers whose efforts, running around frantically while trying to keep several things in the air at once, provided a memorable metaphor for life as we know it. (Well, for life as *I* know it, anyway.) As for the sublime, there were the Broadway musical excerpts, the ballet and opera, the standup comics—and, most readily remembered after all these years, Elvis Presley and the Beatles. With both of those "rebellious" rock 'n' roll acts, Sullivan played the part of the tolerant old uncle, informing middle America that these mop-topped or pelvis-shaking youngsters were "really good kids." Presley's three appearances (the last one only from the waist up) sold records, and the Beatles, with their first *Ed Sullivan Show* appearance, *broke* records. That installment, on February 9, 1964, became the most-watched TV show of its era, and remains, more than three decades later, the second most popular TV variety program of all time—beaten only by the 1970 *Bob Hope Christmas Show*. Notably, the only other *Ed Sullivan Show* to land in the all-time Top 40 came a week after that landmark appearance by the Beatles—when John Lennon, Paul McCartney, George Harrison, and Ringo Starr returned for a second visit, broadcast from Miami. Talk to anyone over forty, and they'll tell you they were watching the Beatles on *Ed Sullivan* those two Sunday nights—and based on the ratings, they may not be lying. I remember watching the Beatles on that first *Ed Sullivan* appearance (at the impressionable age of ten), and loving the music, and laughing at the screaming audience members, and thinking how *long* the group's hair was. The movie *A Hard Day's Night* captured for posterity the essence of the Fab Four's *Ed Sullivan Show* appearances, as did a fabulous satirical documentary called *The Rutles*—and, of course, the actual Sullivan shows, which were served up in the nineties as syndicated specials and as a well-received set of prime-time retrospectives for CBS. Home-video releases and musical CDs collected and presented some of the best musical acts showcased on Sullivan's stage, and the stage itself figured prominently in two other TV events from the nineties. In 1992, McCartney revisited Broadway's Ed Sullivan Theater to record an *Up Close* music special for MTV, and in 1993, the "right here on our stage" site was remodeled to serve as broadcast headquarters for David Letterman's new *Late Show with David Letterman* series for CBS.

Elizabeth R. See *Six Wives of Henry VIII, The.*

Elvis. *1968, NBC; 1979, ABC; 1990, ABC*. Don't get all shook up. There *were* three different TV shows, in three different decades, all with the same and simple name of *Elvis*. The first, the only one to star the real Elvis Presley, is the best and best-known of the three: the 1968 music special that, with its stripped-down music and setting, marked the start of Presley's successful comeback. (Consider it the early prime-time prototype of a much more recent musical showcase: a sort of *Elvis Presley Unplugged*.) The second coming of *Elvis*, so to speak, was the 1979 telemovie, directed by John Carpenter and starring Kurt Russell as the Big E. Very stylish, and surprisingly convincing, this three-hour *Elvis* drama was a big hit when it first aired—which can't be said of the *third* coming of *Elvis*. That was a 1990 weekly ABC series focusing on young Elvis Presley, just as he was developing his musical style and notching his first successes. Michael St. Gerard played the midfifties-vintage Elvis, and did a good job, but the series never caught on. In January 1993, to coincide with the release of the "young Elvis" commemorative postage stamp, Ted Turner's TNT cable network presented all the *Elvis* episodes in a two-night marathon, including some that ABC had produced but not televised. Turner's TBS superstation countered by repeating the 1979 *Elvis* telemovie, which just goes to show you: when it comes to Elvis Presley, philately will get you everywhere.

Emmy Awards. *1955–64, NBC; 1965–86, rotated annually among NBC, CBS, and ABC; 1987–92, Fox; 1993–94, ABC; 1995, Fox, resuming annual rotation*. The first Emmy awards were handed out in 1949—but televised only in Los Angeles, and only because the fledgling Academy of Television Arts and Sciences was based there. New York established its own society and awards, but the tribute became bicoastal, and uniform, by the time the triumphant Emmy Awards were televised nationally for the first time in 1955. Since then, there's been no less—and no more—than one memorable Emmy telecast per decade. In 1960, a young comic named Bob Newhart got extra air time when a Mike Nichols-Elaine May skit was yanked at the last minute, and Newhart stole the show so effortlessly and completely that his own TV career as a headliner was launched as a result. In 1978, the memorable highlight was a preemption: President Jimmy Carter, flanked by Israeli Prime Minister Menachem Begin and Egyptian President Anwar Sadat, interrupted

The Ed Sullivan Show, with the host surrounded by a sampling of acts he presented.

the Emmys (and all other network programming) for almost a half-hour to announce and sign the Camp David peace-treaty agreement. In 1980, the year of an actors' strike, the Emmys were boycotted by all of the nominees—all except one, who stunned everyone in attendance, or watching on TV, by accepting his Emmy in person. It was Powers Boothe, who had won for best actor in a limited series by playing the title role in *Guyana Tragedy: The Story of Jim Jones.* "This is either the most courageous moment of my career, or the stupidest," Boothe said. Either way, it made for great television, and made him the only shining star on an otherwise dim night. In the nineties, the Emmy telecasts were memorable chiefly for their lack of restraint: Gilbert Gottfried went overboard with his off-color Pee-wee Herman jokes in 1991, and Vice President Dan Quayle's vocal protests regarding the single-mom "lifestyle choice" of Candice Bergen's character on *Murphy Brown* were countered on the 1992 Emmys by a barrage of Quayle-bashing jokes that amounted to excessive force. Not at all surprisingly, those last two awards shows, on Fox, led to the ceremony moving back to ABC, beginning a resumption of the annual rotation concept—but rotating, this time, among four networks, not three.

Entertainment Tonight. *1981– , syndicated.* This show's contributions to teleliteracy include, if nothing else, the show's theme song and its ubiquitous *ET* microphones. Technically, *Entertainment Tonight* pushed syndicated TV forward by distributing a breaking-news show via satellite. Journalistically, though *Entertainment Tonight* has gotten (and, on occasion, deserved) its share of scorn, it remains one of the best sources of stories *about* television *on* television, and has been widely imitated, especially in the nineties. Certainly, *ET* made millions of viewers more familiar with the inner workings, and lexicon, of Hollywood: ratings and shares, box-office opening weekends and home-video rental receipts, superstar salaries, and movies with legs. Speaking of which: as a walking example of the power of publicity, the legs of *Entertainment Tonight* cohost Mary Hart have become "famous" in their own right. (And left. . . .) John Tesh, the other *ET* cohost, has achieved his own measure of fame, of a sort, as a composer and performer of relentlessly mellow music.

ER. *1994– , NBC.* As if Steven Spielberg and Michael Crichton didn't enjoy enough cinematic success with their collaboration on *Jurassic Park,* viewers gave them the television equivalent by flocking in dinosaur-sized numbers to *ER,* the most phenomenally popular new TV drama series in nearly twenty years. The last weekly drama to attract so many viewers so quickly was *Charlie's Angels,* a comparison that speaks volumes about how TV shows and viewers have matured since the seventies. Yet *ER,* in concept, actually hails from that period: Crichton first wrote *ER* as a film script in 1974, but couldn't sell it. In 1990, he dusted it off and took it to Spielberg, whose enthusiasm about *ER* as a movie was overshadowed by his intense interest in Crichton's newest project, a novel about dinosaur DNA. When *Jurassic Park* finished filming and talk of *ER* resurfaced, it was as a TV series, not a movie—although the series remained proudly cinematic. The lengthy Steadi-Cam shots that give such energy to certain scenes in *ER* are the series' trademark. Instead of editing quickly among various emergency rooms to give a sense of urgency, *ER* lets the camera rush in and out as everything happens simultaneously. The speed of the show, the dozens of weekly subplots, and the appeal of such stars as Anthony Edwards (Dr. Mark Greene) and George Clooney (Dr. Doug Ross), all combined to make *ER* a stunning success. Creatively, the series pales when compared to *St. Elsewhere*, and on most weeks is neither written nor performed as well as *Chicago Hope*, the CBS medical series that premiered in the same time slot as *ER*—and was trounced, eventually surviving by retreating to a less competitive TV night. There are episodes of *ER*, though, that stand on their own as memorably excellent television. There's the two-hour pilot, for example, which breathlessly took us through one of Greene's typical sleep-deprived work shifts; and the superb "Love's Labor Lost," in which Greene makes some questionable decisions while trying to deal with a pregnant woman's dangerously high-risk delivery; and, from the second season, the poignant, thrilling episode in which Clooney's Ross struggled to rescue a child from a flooding culvert. Another *ER* coup was established when it played a game of chicken with two other quality dramas— David E. Kelley's aforementioned *Chicago Hope* on CBS, followed by Steven Bochco's *Murder One* on ABC—and forced them both to veer off the Thursday-night road and head for less competitive time slots. Finally, *ER* can claim a pop-culture crossover coup as well, by getting *Pulp Fiction* and *Reservoir Dogs* director Quentin Tarantino to direct a 1995 episode called "Motherhood." Not too surprisingly, the episode managed to make room for several Tarantino trademarks: designer sunglasses, blaring rock music, and even a severed ear.

Ernie Kovacs Show, The. *1952–53, CBS; 1954–55, DuMont local affiliate, WABD-New York; 1955–56, NBC; 1961–62, ABC.* Ernie Kovacs did many shows in addition to the ones listed above, which represent only the programs with that exact title. Kovacs is one of the few comedians to have series on four different networks, and almost certainly the only comedian to have four shows, on different networks and in different years, all named the same. ABC's *The Ernie Kovacs Show*, cut short by his untimely death in 1962, actually was a series of monthly specials, but the earlier efforts were more grueling. *The Ernie Kovacs Show* on CBS was a prime-time weekly show; *The Ernie Kovacs* on DuMont's New York station was a nightly, then biweekly, late-night comedy series; and *The Ernie Kovacs Show* on NBC was first a morning series running each weekday, then a prime-time series running once weekly. Other wonderful and memorable efforts by Kovacs and company included his tenure on the *Tonight!* show (1956–57) and his *Kovacs on Music* and *No Dialogue* Eugene specials, all for NBC. But by any other name, the TV series and specials of Ernie Kovacs were comic gems from one of the medium's first and most inventive geniuses. His comedy wasn't merely transplanted to television, nor did he just invent new jokes to *tell* on television. Kovacs played with the new medium as though he were one of *its* inventors, using special effects, comedy blackouts, and other fast-moving, fast-thinking techniques that had not been seen before, but certainly have been seen since. Not only do Kovacs's best shows and gags survive on videotape, and on such proper avenues of video posterity as Comedy Central, but he was the spiritual and comic forefather of everything from the quick-cut technique on *Rowan & Martin's Laugh-In* to the "Monkey-Cam" on *Late Night with David Letterman*. Teleliteracy in Ernie Kovacs includes too many images to present a complete list, but the top of any list would have to include the gravity-defying tabletops, the car-through-the-floor commercial spoof, the bathtubs that could hold or swallow anything, and, of course, the costumed musical "apes" of the Nairobi Trio, who would bash instruments, and occasionally each other, while playing "Solfeggio." (Edie Adams, Kovacs's wife and collaborator, played one of the apes on occasion, as did Jack Lemmon and Tony Curtis.) Ernie Kovacs deserves credit as one of TV's first teleliterates, too, for spoofing other TV shows and commercials as a constant part of his act. Yet while fluent in all of the medium's conventions and characters of the time, the shows of Ernie Kovacs also played against those conventions, literally from beginning to end: sometimes the programs started "cold," without opening titles, and even his closing credits were laced with jokes. It should be remembered, though, that for all of his pioneering playfulness with the technical side of television, Kovacs also created an impressive gallery of original and resonant comic characters, from giggly poet Percy Dovetonsils to his uncostumed, sarcastic, cigar-smoking self: Ernie Kovacs, the on-air host who conspired with viewers to defy expectations, break rules, and explore the strange new world of TV technology. He was doing all those things with his first on-air TV gig, hosting a daytime cooking show called *Deadline for Dinner* on Philadelphia's WPTZ, and merely increased and refined his act as he got more popular. A ninety-minute daily local daytime show for the same Philadelphia station, *3 to Get Ready*, was the first true Kovacs showcase; it ran from 1950 to 1952, boasted Edie Adams and other Kovacs loyalists, and interested the networks in hiring Kovacs as quickly as they could get him, which meant during his summer breaks from WPTZ. That's how *Ernie in Kovacsland*, his first prime-time network variety showcase, began on NBC in the summer of 1951, leading to a string of other TV and movie jobs that lasted, rather steadily, for more than a decade. We lost Ernie Kovacs way too early, but at least, thanks to kinescope and video, we didn't lose all of his comedy.

Eyes on the Prize. *1987, PBS.* Henry Hampton's six-part documentary, subtitled *America's Civil Rights Years, 1954 to 1965*, examined this century's most divisive internal conflict the same way *The Civil War* had done it with the nineteenth century—that is to say, with impeccable scholarship, sensitivity, and artistry. *The Civil War* became much more famous as a TV documentary miniseries, but *Eyes on the Prize* was just as impressive and powerful, and is sure to increase in value and importance as the years go by. Like its excellent 1990 sequel series, which carried the conflict into the mideighties, *Eyes on the Prize* used television itself as an invaluable resource. The vintage interviews and news clips, culled from local as well as national TV programs, provided a combination oral and visual history of the civil rights struggle, and also showed how TV itself helped identify and focus on the conflicts—particularly in the fifties, when both sides of the struggle were naive enough about television to display and reveal their most unguarded emotions and actions. Released on video and laser disc in 1992, the original *Eyes on the Prize* is a documentary resource every family should own, and prize.

F

Face the Nation. *1954–61, 1963– , CBS.* More than three decades old and counting, *Face the Nation* and its title are known even by those who have never seen the Sunday-morning public-affairs program itself—which, since 1983, has been moderated by Lesley Stahl. (Previous moderators included Howard K. Smith and Martin Agronsky.) Most historic installment in the show's long history: Nikita Khruschev's 1957 interview, direct from the Kremlin, which allowed the *Face the Nation* panel to face another nation's leader in the Soviet premier's first question-and-answer session on American television.

Faerie Tale Theatre. *1982–87, Showtime.* Using cable as her canvas, and fairy tales and famous painters and illustrators as her inspirations, Shelley Duvall spent most of the eighties becoming the modern female equivalent of Walt Disney. In fact, only after *Faerie Tale Theatre* ended its run did the Disney studio revive its own tradition of mounting full-length animated movies based on fairy tales and fables. The approaches were different in two major respects—Duvall used live actors rather than animation, and did not rework the stories as musicals—but otherwise quite similar. In both cases, characters are fleshed out fully and cleverly, and stories are presented with various levels of sophistication, so that parents and their children could be entertained simultaneously. But give Duvall credit: before Disney got to them, *The Little Mermaid, Beauty and the Beast*, and *Aladdin* all were covered by her *Faerie Tale Theatre*. Pam Dawber and Helen Mirren starred in *The Little Mermaid*, Susan Sarandon and Klaus Kinski played (respectively) *Beauty and the Beast*, and Robert Carradine, Valerie Bertinelli, James Earl Jones, and Leonard Nimoy all starred in *Aladdin and His Wonderful Lamp*, directed by Tim Burton. Other *Faerie Tale Theatre* installments, not yet covered by Disney in animated form, included Lee Remick as *The Snow Queen*, Robin Williams as *The Frog Prince*, and Herve Villechaize as *Rumpelstiltskin*. The twenty-six installments of *Faerie Tale Theatre* remain quite popular in video stores, and, in what perhaps is the best compliment of all, are offered regularly in reruns by The Disney Channel. Duvall went on to produce other imaginative quality TV for children, including the Showtime series *Shelley Duvall's Tall Tales & Legends* and *Shelley Duvall's Bedtime Stories*, but *Shelley Duvall's*

Faerie Tale Theatre (the show's original full title) would prove hard to beat—by her, or by anybody else. The best installments? The very best is *The Three Little Pigs*, starring Billy Crystal as the smart pig and Jeff Goldblum as the Big Bad Wolf. Also outstanding, though, are *Pinocchio*, with Paul Reubens in the title role and Carl Reiner as Geppetto; *Rapunzel*, with Duvall in the title role and Gena Rowlands as her guardian and captor; *The Princess and the Pea*, with Liza Minnelli and Tom Conti; and *Hansel and Gretel*, starring Joan Collins as the old witch. Like bedtime stories read aloud, they hold up beautifully to repeated exposure.

Family Feud. *1976–85, ABC; 1977–83, syndicated; 1988–95, CBS and syndicated.* "Survey *said.* . . . " "Good answer, good answer!" Richard Dawson, the *Hogan's Heroes* veteran, was the puckish and puckered-up host of the original network and syndicated versions of *Family Feud,* and it was Dawson who came up with most of the catch phrases associated with this series. Ray Combs, who took over in 1988, dutifully continued them, though he was a little more reticent than Dawson when it came to kissing the ladies and poking fun at astoundingly stupid answers. In 1994, Goodson-Todman released what it called *The New Family Feud,* but all it was, really, was a new version of the old *Family Feud,* with Dawson returning as host. He was older, but most of the contestants were no wiser. Yet that's what, in its heydey, made *Family Feud* watchable, and sometimes even enjoyable: it was a sort of anti-*Jeopardy!* On that dignified game show, part of the fun comes from marveling at how smart most of the contestants are; watching *Family Feud,* you marvel at how *stupid* most of them are.

Family Matters. *1989– , ABC.* Just as Henry Winkler's Fonz came from nowhere to become a core character on *Happy Days,* Jaleel White's Steve Urkel was added to *Family Matters,* a comedy about a modern African-American family, and completely dominated it. Adults may not care about, or even recognize, Urkel as TV's equal-opportunity nerd, but most kids *do* know him, and aren't likely to forget him—or his whiny signature line, "Did *I* do that?"

Family Ties. *1982–89, NBC.* Like *Family Matters,* this is another *Family* sitcom, in title and design, whose original family focus was usurped by a young member of the cast. When *Family Ties* was conceived by Gary David Goldberg (previously of *Lou Grant,* later of *Brooklyn Bridge*), it was intended as a look at former hippies who had evolved, or at least changed, into suburban parents. At least this time, when a child stole the spotlight, it was a member of the show's nuclear family: Michael J. Fox's Alex P. Keaton, who turned out to be an early representative of the fiscal greediness and political conservativeness of the Reagan era. It was Alex's me-first attitude, rather than any particular catch phrases, that stood out; he was like a younger-generation J. R. Ewing, and the two of those money-obsessed TV characters cruised through the eighties with equal aplomb, assurance, and arrogance. The show's best episode, without doubt, was "A, My Name Is Alex," an *Our Town*-type drama in which Alex searched his soul after the sudden death of a close friend. *Family Ties* ended, as the decade came to a close, with Alex taking a job on Wall Street, but he could just as easily have grown up to become Rush Limbaugh.

Fantasy Island. *1987–84, ABC.* "De plane" truth of this series is that, tacky and stupid though it was, it somehow wound its way into our national consciousness. Ricardo Montalban's too-too-suave Mr. Roarke and Herve Villechaize's Tattoo-cute Tattoo were the Mutt-and-Jeff hosts of this series, sporting matching white suits that looked like knockoffs from the John Travolta *Saturday Night Fever* collection. Though Mr. Roarke was in charge, tiny Tattoo got all the best lines—if, that is, you count "De plane, boss, de plane!" as durable prose. (And you almost have to, because Villechaize was starring in Dunkin' Donuts commercials a decade later, ordering "de plain" ones.) Several porn films, including the closely titled *Fantasex Island*, played with the wish-fulfillment premise of this series, and their existence (or, in this case, X-istence) underscored the show's most nagging flaw: the uninspired, G-rated nature of most of the "fantasies" bankrolled by visitors to this Anything-Can-Happen theme park. Here's a series that cries out for a modern remake—on the Playboy Channel.

Fatal Vision. *1984, NBC.* The most popular true-crime miniseries ever broadcast, this docudrama got the same rating as *Holocaust*, and set the standard for countless subsequent murder reenactments on television. (It's an excellent miniseries, even though it relies a bit too completely on the source book by Joe McGinniss.) Gary Cole, as the physician accused of murdering and mutilating his own wife and daughters, launched a successful career as a result, eventually displaying such impressive range that he appeared as both lovable Mike Brady in *The Brady Bunch Movie* and sinister Sheriff Buck in *American Gothic*. But *Fatal Vision* did more than propel an actor's career; the popularity of *Fatal Vision* increased both the quantity and production speed of fact-based TV crime dramas. For *Fatal Vision*, it was fourteen years from crime to dramatization; a decade later, the average time from real act to reenactment was closer to fourteen months, and sometimes only fourteen weeks. One other legacy of teleliteracy: Andy Griffith's portrayal of Victor Worheide, a crafty Southern lawyer, so delighted NBC executives that they commissioned a series in which Griffith would play a fictional variation on the same type of character. The result: *Matlock*.

Father Knows Best. *1954–55, 1958–62, CBS; 1955–58, NBC; 1962–63, ABC.* When *Father Knows Best* began on NBC radio in 1949, there was a question mark attached to the end of the title: in the comedy's original incarnation, the supremacy of Jim Anderson (played by Robert Young, the only cast member to stay with the show when it moved to television) was the exception, not the rule. Yet by the time the TV sitcom version was launched five years later, with Jane Wyatt as the perfect wife and Elinor Donahue, Billy Gray, and Lauren Chapin as the nearly perfect kids, Young's Jim Anderson was king of his suburban castle. Like *Ozzie and Harriet* and *The Donna Reed Show*, it idealized the nuclear family unit, and is remembered today more for the images it presented, and the stereotypes it perpetuated, than for specific episodic highlights. The show's very title—without the question mark, that is—now serves as shorthand for a bygone era in television land, when men were men, women were housewives, and little girls were Princesses and Kittens. Notably, this simplistic, moralistic series struck such a nerve with viewers that it prompted one of the first successful write-in campaigns in TV history. When CBS canceled *Father Knows Best* after its premiere season, fans of the show demanded it be renewed, and scheduled at an earlier hour so their children could watch it, too. CBS didn't listen, but NBC did, and picked up the series after CBS dropped it. The show grew so popular that, though Young stopped production of the series in 1960, reruns continued to be broadcast in prime time for another three years. Two *Father Knows Best* reunion telemovies were presented in 1977, the year after the cancellation of Young's subsequent hit series, *Marcus Welby, M.D.*, and the midnineties reflected a renewed interest in the *Father Knows Best* concept and characters—with Larry McMurtry, of *Lonesome Dove* fame, signing a deal to co-author a movie version of *Father Knows Best*. Some in Hollywood laughed at that announcement, but this may well be a case where McMurtry knows best.

Fawlty Towers. *1977, 1980, public television.* In 1972, the Monty Python comedy troupe stayed at "a seaside establishment in Devon" which, Python member John Cleese later recalled, featured a manager "so rude he was fascinating." Three years later, Cleese and his then-wife, Connie Booth, turned that memory into a brilliant six-episode comedy classic called *Fawlty Towers*, with Cleese as that fascinatingly rude innkeeper, Basil Fawlty; Booth played a maid, his one competent employee. The 1975 BBC sitcom proved such a hit that Cleese and Booth generated another half-dozen episodes four years later, then called it quits; the dozen shows quickly found their way stateside via a regional public television network. With only public-TV and home video exposure here, *Fawlty Towers* remains more of a cult item than a mainstream hit, yet its influence extends to one of TV's most mainstream comedies of all: *Cheers*, which its creators say was inspired by *Fawlty Towers*. (Rhea Perlman's sharp-tongued, reliably rude Carla, clearly, is a close kindred spirit of Basil Fawlty's.) Yet as a comedy concept, *Fawlty Towers*, like Basil Fawlty himself, all but stands alone: Basil is saddled with demanding or addled guests, a domineering and humorless wife (Prunella Scales), and a Spanish bellman (Manuel Sachs) with a very limited English vocabulary. Not until *Buffalo Bill*, a decade later, did a TV sitcom again revolve around such an irascible character as Basil, but Cleese made Basil Fawlty oddly endearing—partly because Basil never got the better end of things, and partly because Cleese was equally adept at verbal and physical comedy. The dozen episodes of *Fawlty Towers* rank among the finest sitcoms ever made. A best-episode list is tough, because all twelve are terrific, but "The Builders," "Gourmet Night," "The Hotel Inspectors," and "Waldorf Salad" may be the best among equals. Hint for new visitors to the inn: watch closely during the opening credits, for each episode features a new arrangement of some or all of the letters in the "Fawlty Towers" sign. My favorite: "Farty Towels."

Fernwood 2-Night. *1977, syndicated.* **America 2-Night.** *1978, syndicated.* Spun off from Norman Lear's soap opera satire, *Mary Hartman, Mary Hartman,* this outrageous talk-show satire lampooned *The Tonight Show* by reducing it to an intentionally mundane "local" level. (Ironically, *Fernwood 2-Night* was produced by Alan Thicke, who, before reviving his on-air career as the star of *Growing Pains,* all but killed it as the host of his own terrible talk show, *Thicke of the Night.)* In *Fernwood 2-Night,* Martin Mull played Barth Gimble, the smarmy host, with Fred Willard as Jerry Hubbard, Barth's overly eager and woefully unintelligent assistant. The ersatz talk show treated as celebrities the ultraordinary citizens of fictional Fernwood, Ohio. One such citizen was mechanic Virgil Sims, played by Jim Varney years before he became a simpleton star in earnest—that is, in his successful *Ernest* movies. A year after its original summer run, *Fernwood 2-Night* was relocated to California, retitled *America 2-Night,* and given a national scope with real celebrity guests (Charlton Heston, Robin Williams, Billy Crystal), who portrayed themselves and suffered through Barth's sarcasm and Jerry's idiocy. Both *Fernwood* and *America* poked fun at a genre ripe for satirical treatment, and *America 2-Night,* especially, provided the tone, if not the basic blueprint, for *The Larry Sanders Show,* Garry Shandling's sparkling talk-show satire of the nineties. At the end of 1995, Mull and Willard reunited, in very memorable form, on an episode of *Roseanne.* Mull, as recurring gay character Leon, and Willard, making a guest appearance as Leon's lover Scott, got married—to each other.

Fireball XL-5. *1963–65, NBC.* This 1962 British series, imported by NBC for its Saturday morning children's schedule, was the first sci-fi puppet series produced by Sylvia and Jerry Anderson in the process they called "Supermarionation." However, there was nothing "super" about it: on these marionettes, only their legs, arms, lips, and eyeballs moved, thereby providing the most wooden performances seen on TV until Jack Lord came along in *Hawaii Five-0.* Like the Anderson's later puppet-show efforts *(Stingray, Thunderbirds),* and their equally stiff live-action *Space: 1999,* their *Fireball XL-5* series was sci-fi for dummies only. Those who saw it, unfortunately, are doomed to recall it. It was that strange.

Firing Line. *1966–1971, 1976– , syndicated and/or public television; 1971–76, PBS.* Resolved: that William F. Buckley has presided over this structured-debate program longer than Mike Wallace has presided over *60 Minutes.* (No sense debating the point: it's a simple fact.) The longevity of the series, in syndication and on public TV, is due partly to its implied mandates to give conservatives equal time (at the very least). It's also due partly, however, to Buckley's eagerly imitated voice and mannerisms, impersonated through the years by everyone from David Frye to Robin Williams. Buckley himself, by the way, knows the value of artistic appropriation: his duly famous

Firing Line theme was lifted outright from Bach's Brandenburg Concerto No. 2.

Fisher, Amy, telemovies. See *Amy Fisher.*

Flintstones, The. *1960–66, ABC*. Some people think *The Flintstones* are deserving of their place in pop-culture history, and other people yabba-dabba-don't. (Personally, I never thought that much of the animation *or* the writing.) Yet even setting aside the indelible theme song (the show's best asset) and Fred Flintstone's "Yabba-dabba-doo!" catch phrase, *The Flintstones* has secured a comfortable place in the medium's overall history. It was the first cartoon series in prime time—and, along with *The Jetsons* and *The Simpsons,* one of the very few successful ones. *The Flintstones* was patterned as a stone-age variation on a previous sitcom classic, *The Honeymooners,* and itself later served as partial inspiration for another prehistoric comedy, *Dinosaurs.* It was its own animated cottage industry, spawning a Bedrock community of spinoff series and specials—including, in one nineties special, the wedding of the characters' respective children, Pebbles Flintstone and Bamm-Bamm Rubble, thus creating a cartoon dynasty that could last until, oh, the Cro-Magnon Era. Finally, the lasting appeal of *The Flintstones,* in teleliteracy terms, was demonstrated by the filming of a big-budget, live-action movie version, starring John Goodman as Fred and Rick Moranis as Barney Rubble, with Rosie O'Donnell as Betty, Elizabeth Perkins as Wilma, and another Elizabeth, Liz Taylor, as Wilma's mother, Pearl Slaghoople. The movie expended great effort to stage the live-action equivalent of the cartoon series' opening credits, but very little effort on concocting a worthwhile script. Despite its large budget and bloated promotional campaign, the 1994 movie version of *The Flintstones* sank like a flint stone.

Flipper. *1964–68, NBC*. This series was little more, and maybe even a little less, than a waterlogged *Lassie.* It featured the same formula: a boy and his amazingly intelligent pet, getting each other out of scrapes and generally enjoying the rural life. And Flipper was a dolphin, not a collie, which limited the routes by which the pet in this show could go get help, or even get in trouble. But because I grew up in southern Florida, as I kid I embraced both the series and its theme song: "They call him Flipper, Flipper, faster than lightning. . . . " The series remained afloat, so to speak, in syndicated reruns for decades, but the midnineties saw a sudden flurry of *Flipper* activity—a new syndicated *Flipper* series that premiered in 1995, and a big-screen *Flipper* movie set for release the following year. (The proximity of these two projects was coincidental, and was not done on porpoise.) The year 1995 also saw some sad *Flipper* news: a *USA Today* interview with dolphin trainer Scott Sharpe, in which he insisted the familiar "eek-eek-eek" noise emanating from the dolphin star of the old *Flipper* TV series was not a sound a real dolphin makes. "It was either a chipmunk or a gopher," trainer Scott Sharpe said of Flipper's familiar cry, apparently added in post-production, "but not a dolphin." (Where else but *USA Today* could you gopher information like that?)

This, I admit, was sad and shocking news to me: I knew Flipper was a mammal, so I wasn't on the lookout for anything fishy.

Flip Wilson Show, The. *1970–74, NBC*. I don't mean to be Flippant, but Flip Wilson wasn't the first African-American to headline a TV variety series; Nat "King" Cole, Leslie Uggams, and Sammy Davis, Jr., had preceded him. Flip, however, was the first whose show achieved major ratings success. For two seasons, *The Flip Wilson Show* was the second most popular series on television. Wilson was sharp and sassy without being confrontational, and the audience gleefully accepted his most outrageous character, the provocative and quick-tempered Geraldine. Squeezed into a Playboy Bunny outfit and flirting with the likes of a clearly astounded Bing Crosby, Wilson as Geraldine was TV's most beloved cross-dresser since Milton Berle. Two of Wilson's Geraldine catch phrases, "What you see is what you get" and "The Devil made me do it," have endured for more than a generation.

Flying Nun, The. *1967–70, ABC*. Sally Field's experience with *The Flying Nun* is one of show business' great success stories—not the series itself, but that she was able to live it down (and, after a few years and two Oscars, live it up). Its premise was so absurd, and its production values were so tacky (even George Reeves, in *The Adventures of Superman*, flew with more conviction and credibility than Field's Sister Bertrille), that perhaps the most amazing thing about *The Flying Nun* was that it survived for three seasons. Today, it survives mostly in name only: its title, like that of *My Mother the Car*, is virtually synonymous with terrible television. Otherwise, its lasting impact on TV history is best described as little to nun.

Ford 50th Anniversary Show, The. *1953, CBS and NBC*. When the Ford Motor Company decided to celebrate its golden anniversary on June 15, 1953, it did it in a huge way: by assembling some of the very best singing, dancing, and journalistic talent, and a wealth of movie and newsreel clips, to provide nothing less than a two-hour "panoramic capsule history of the past fifty years." Not only that, but it was shown on CBS and NBC at the same time. Legendary Broadway producer Leland Hayward put it all together, and emerged with one of the most ambitious, influential, and, to many, unforgettable specials in TV history—the kind of show that, even if you wanted to mount it today, you couldn't a-Ford it. Jerome Robbins provided choreography. Marian Anderson sang spirituals. Oscar Hammerstein II and Mary Martin performed a scene from *Our Town*. Edward R. Murrow gave an essay on the Ford assembly line, and he and Hammerstein, placed in front of a motion picture of an atomic bomb's mushroom cloud, discussed the future. "The people who invented war," Murrow said somberly, "had better invent peace." Other performers and journalists took part as well, but *The Ford 50th Anniversary Show* was stolen by Ethel Merman and Mary Martin, who sat on neighboring stools on a bare stage and, for twelve electrifying minutes, sang their way through a delightful medley of popular songs. Not only did Merman and Martin steal the show, but their manner of televised presentation influenced many other entertainers that followed in the years and decades to come. Most specifically, the influence was easy to see, and hear, in Judy Garland's 1955 TV debut on *Ford Star Jubilee;* the 1962 *Julie and Carol at Carnegie Hall,* the first of several musical specials teaming Julie Andrews and Carol Burnett; and Barbra Streisand's first TV special, 1965's *My Name Is Barbra.*

Forsyte Saga, The. *1969, NET (pre-PBS public TV).* This 1967 BBC-TV serialized drama, imported from England by National Educational Television two years later, often is cited as television's first miniseries. Wrong, wrong, wrong. In fact, not even close: the BBC's first miniseries, performed live in six successive installments, was 1953's *The Quatermass Experiment,* a sci-fi serial that spawned several sequels. And in the United States, the presentation of live serialized dramas had begun even sooner, with a four-part 1945 production (by NBC's New York station WNBT) of Cornell Woolrich's *The Black Angel* mystery. NBC also was first with the earliest full-fledged miniseries on a national network: a three-part 1952 dramatization of *Peer Gynt* on *Cameo Theatre.* Reacting, perhaps, to *Peer* pressure, other long-form dramas followed, including ABC's three-part *Davy Crockett* on *Disneyland,* several multipart dramatizations on the CBS and ABC versions of *Omnibus,* and, most famously, Patrick McGoohan's *The Prisoner* miniseries, produced in England the same year as *The Forsyte Saga.* On American TV, however, *The Prisoner* arrived in 1968, a full year before *The Forsyte Saga* finally was imported by public television. The delay, in the latter case, was because the public-TV executives were concerned that *The Forsyte Saga* was (1) too British, (2) too long, and (3) perhaps too "entertaining" for an educational TV network. Because this was long before the advent of VCRs, *Forsyte* fans in England reacted to the twenty-six-part serial by juggling social engagements, rescheduling vacation trips, and holding weekly *Forsyte* viewing parties. (One of those professed *Forsyte* fans, James Michener, was so taken with the miniseries form, he later wrote such novels as *Centennial* and *Space,* stories tailor-made for long-form adaptation.) In America, the audience for *The Forsyte Saga* was smaller, but the loyalty and fervor it generated were comparable. On both sides of the Atlantic, the impact was even more important. The British began cranking out other multipart serial dramas, and NET, which by then had evolved into PBS, began importing them in 1971—under the umbrella title *Masterpiece Theatre.* Meanwhile, ABC and NBC began developing more ambitious long-form dramas, such as ABC's *QB VII,* as a direct result of the imported drama's mainstream success. That's the true place of *The Forsyte Saga* in TV history: not as the first miniseries, but as one of the form's major early catalysts. As for its own merits, this adaptation of the John Galsworthy stories gave us Susan Hampshire, and not much else.

Frasier. *1993– , NBC.* In its few years on the air since providing Kelsey Grammer with a post-*Cheers* solo showcase, NBC's *Frasier* has more than earned its place in the annals of teleliteracy. To put it bluntly, and simply, *Frasier* is the best sitcom to be spun off from another sitcom in the entire

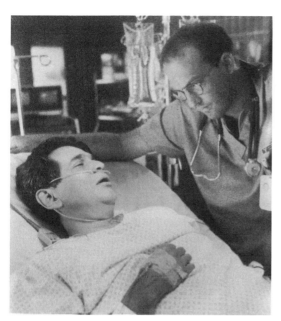

LEFT: *ER*, with Anthony Edwards looking in on patient Alan Rosenberg.
RIGHT: *The Ernie Kovacs Show*, with Kovacs in character as wide-eyed Percy Dovetonsils.

LEFT: *Fantasy Island*, with Ricardo Montalban and Herve Villechaize.
RIGHT: *The Flying Nun*, with Sally Field as the flighty Sister Bertrille.

history of television. In terms of quality humor, no one-two punch in TV history packs as great a punch as *Cheers* and *Frasier*. Line for line, performance for performance, laugh for laugh, nothing comes close. Please note, before launching into an argument, the careful wording of the phrase "best sitcom to be spun off from another sitcom." This eliminates such possible claimants to the throne as *The Honeymooners*, which was spun off from Jackie Gleason's variety series, as well as *The Simpsons*, which was spun off from Tracey Ullman's. It also eliminates *Lou Grant*. (Even though that series was a spinoff of a superb sitcom, *The Mary Tyler Moore Show*, and was itself superb, *Lou Grant* was a drama.) Technically, *The Andy Griffith Show* could qualify, because it was spun off from *The Danny Thomas Show*, but Griffith's Andy Taylor character appeared in only a single episode of Thomas's sitcom, and with the express intention of setting up the character for a spinoff. And then there's *Maude*, which certainly qualifies as a challenger—both as the best of all the spinoffs of *All in the Family* (*The Jeffersons* and *Good Times* among them), and as one sitcom series spun off from another. Yet with *Maude*, I can think of only a handful of episodes that have stood up really well over the years. Put the entire run of *Maude* up against what *Frasier* has been able to accomplish in its first few seasons, and *Frasier* already gleams by comparison. It also outshines all other challengers, including *Rhoda* (*The Mary Tyler Moore Show* had only one excellent spinoff, and we've already covered it), *Happy Days-Laverne & Shirley* (remember, we're looking for "best"), and even *December Bride-Pete & Gladys* (good shows, but not in the same league, and both already have lapsed from common memory). What made *Frasier* so brilliant from the start, besides the writing, was the inspired casting of David Hyde Pierce as Niles, Frasier's equally fussy and neurotic brother. (Both Grammer and Pierce won Emmy Awards in 1995, along with *Frasier* itself.) The rest of the cast, including John Mahoney as the Crane patriarch and Jane Leeves as the housekeeper, is equally gifted, but the sibling rivalry and comic similarity of the Crane brothers provide *Frasier* with many of its best plot lines. It's worth noting that *Frasier*, in its call-in segments for Frasier's radio show, have made room for the most celebrity cameo voices this side of *The Simpsons*, with such "callers" as Mel Brooks, Garry Trudeau, Lily Tomlin, Art Garfunkel, and Gary Sinise. It's worth noting, too, that various *Cheers* alumni have begun popping up on this spinoff series, including Bebe Neuwirth as ex-wife Lilith, Ted Danson as Sam Malone, and even Shelley Long in a quick cameo as Diane, Frasier's other ex-wife. Obviously, they recognize a quality spinoff when they see it—and years from now, when *Frasier* ends its run, NBC could do a lot worse than continue the string by showcasing Pierce in a spinoff spinoff called *Niles*. Three-peat! Three-peat! Three-peat!. . . .

French Chef, The. *1963–73, NET/PBS.* Here was a *real* Child of the sixties: Julia Child, whose recipes, advice, enthusiasm, and charming informality made her one of the first public-TV celebrity "superstars." In addition to propelling her cookbooks onto the bestseller lists, Child's *The French Chef*, according to the *New York Times* (which usually is loath to credit TV with anything other than the downfall of society), "made Francophiles of millions," "opened up opportunities for the best French chefs worldwide," and made French food so popular that "for years, *the* restaurants in this country were French." In 1993, on the thirtieth anniversary of *The French Chef*, chefs from all over the world gathered to cook a special meal for their guest of honor, Julia Child, who was celebrating her eightieth birthday (and still hosting occasional cooking specials and series). PBS televised parts of the affair, and had the good sense to season it with a pinch of the most teleliterate ingredient in Child's legacy: the *Saturday Night Live* cooking-show spoof in which Dan Aykroyd, dressing and sounding like a (Julia) Child, urged viewers to "save the liver," pretended to cut a finger with a giant carving knife, and, in a gruesomely funny and unexpected special effect, bled to death as the cameras rolled. Maybe you had to be there—but millions were, and never forgot it.

Friendly Fire. *1979, ABC*. Carol Burnett proved her dramatic acting prowess in this powerful docudrama, which told of a midwestern woman's tireless efforts to learn the circumstances surrounding her son's death in Vietnam. Eventually, she learned he was killed not by contact with the enemy, but by a tragic instance of "friendly fire"—accidental death by American artillery. Based on the book by C. D. B. Bryan, which told of Peg Mullen's one-woman fight against a military bureaucracy, this telemovie was popular and potent enough to make "friendly fire" a household word. Also potent: co-starring roles by Ned Beatty, Sam Waterston, and a pre-*Ordinary People* Timothy Hutton.

Friends. *1994–   , NBC*. Like *ER*, *Friends* was a surprise phenomenon that hit instantly, kept building, and emerged at the end of one season as a trend-setting audience favorite. *Friends* continued a dialogue-heavy sitcom trend that had begun on *Seinfeld*, with an even greater appeal to young viewers. It was during the summer, when college-age students flocked to the reruns, that *Friends* established its dominance as the year's biggest breakout comedy hit. Created by Kevin S. Bright and *Dream On* partners Marta Kauffman and David Crane, *Friends* presents a world in which attractive young people spend their endless hours of leisure time playing board games, watching TV, hanging out at a local coffee house, or converging at their absurdly large apartments. The well-written series makes fine use of its occasional guest stars (Jon Lovitz, appearing in one first-season episode as a rude and stoned restauranteur, was a riot), but the sextet of regulars really is all the show needs. *Friends* is surprisingly, impressively, almost amazingly democratic; male leads David Schwimmer (Ross), Matthew Perry (Chandler), and Matt LeBlanc (Joey) enjoy the same amount of screen time and punch lines as female leads Courteney Cox (Monica), Jennifer Aniston (Rachel), and Lisa Kudrow (Phoebe). One reason *Friends* makes the cut in this book, despite its youthfulness, is that all the networks tried desperately, though unsuccessfully, to cash in on the show's success by mounting their own thinly veiled variations on the *Friends* formula. The season after *Friends* premiered, all those networks, even NBC, decided to send in the clones, but *Friends* remained alone at the top. It also shared some common elements with previous watermarks in TV history. The hairstyle worn by Aniston became all the rage among fashion-conscious young women, much as, a generation before, Farrah Fawcett's *Charlie's Angels* shaggy mane was considered the 'do to do among well-tressed female fans. The show's theme song, "I'll Be There for You," became a hit song for the Rembrandts (reaching the top spot on the *Billboard* Hot 100 Airplay chart in 1995, even though it never was released as a single), rivaling the way in which the theme to *The Monkees* was embraced by a previous generation of young viewers. "I'll Be There for You," written by the Rembrandts as a quick opening-credits ditty, then expanded to a full-length song by popular demand, even *sounded* a little like The Monkees. The success of the theme song was good for *Friends*, but even better for all of television. ABC Entertainment President Ted Harbert had announced, a few months before *Friends* premiered on a rival network, that TV theme songs were literally a waste of time, and other executives seemed inclined to follow his lead—until the success of *Friends* and its Monkeelike theme song made monkeys of them all. Even so, it was a monkey of a different sort, the one that played Ross's pet during the first season of *Friends*, one that really connects this hit of the nineties to a previous TV era. After all, Monkey the monkey (whose sitcom name was Marcel) eventually was let go from the show because his human costars wearied of his wild antics and nasty attitude—the same complaints leveled against J. Fred Muggs, decades before, on the original *Today* show.

Frontline. *1983–   , PBS*. While other documentary showcases preferred the multitopic newsmagazine format, David Fanning's PBS series stuck with the old *See It Now* model: topical subjects, hard-hitting investigative journalism, full-length programs. Its installments on national and international politics rank among the best of the genre, and include *So You Want to Be President* (a behind-the-scenes look at Gary Hart's dark horse campaign in 1984), the 1988 and 1992 political biographies titled *The Choice* (profiling the presidential candidates), and the 1991 installment *The War We Left Behind* (which revisited the site of the Gulf War to gauge the aftereffects of the battle). But with other topics, ranging from abortion to oil spills, *Frontline* either got there first or did it best. Like *Nightline*, its similar-sounding champion of the serious examination of current events, *Frontline* has a familiar title and a sound reputation. *Nightline*, however, has millions more viewers.

F Troop. *1965–67, ABC*. This Western comedy starred Ken Berry as a man whose accidental battlefield "heroism" on horseback resulted in his being honored, promoted, and shipped out west—where he sought to interact and coexist with the native Indian population. Decades later, the same plot, with fewer laughs, would show up as the framework for *Dances with Wolves*. But on *F Troop*, with Forrest Tucker and Larry Storch as the naive captain's scheming underlings, the approach was strictly Fort Vaudeville, or Sergeant Bilko on the Prairie. Three memorable elements of this show stand out in memory, even *without* help from current cable reruns: the Indian tribe named the Hekawi (a lost tribe named after the phrase "Where the Hekawi?," a cleaner variation of a very old and dirty joke), the jaunty theme song, and the stunt man who jumps out of a lookout tower as it's toppled by cannon fire—making the longest opening-credits leap this side of the out-of-control skier on *Wide World of Sports*.

Fugitive, The. *1963–67, ABC*. This entire series, moody and well-acted, is worthy of discussion for its rather pessimistic take on the judicial system, its constantly changing setting (each week a different job, conflict, and supporting cast), and for David Janssen's brooding presence as the wrongly convicted Dr. Richard Kimble. But what really counts here is the finale, one of the most famous in the history of TV. Prior to *The Fugitive*, television series were like old soldiers: they just faded away. And when ABC notified executive producer Quinn Martin that the network was not renewing *The Fugitive* for the 1967 fall season, the general expectation was that the series would merely stop production and leave the story line dangling. Roy Huggins, the original creator of *The Fugitive* (as well as *Maverick* and other shows with morally ambiguous themes and protagonists), probably would have been happy if the series ended with Kimble still mistakenly accused, hunted, and at large, but Martin, a more law-and-order type whose other series included *The F.B.I.* and *The Untouchables*, was in charge of the show by then, and wanted to end with an episode showing justice prevailing and Kimble clearing his name. Hence the summertime two-parter, in which Kimble, Barry Morse's Lieutenant Gerard, and Bill Raisch's one-armed man all converged at a water tower to give the four-year series a concrete resolution. (In the case of the murderous one-armed man, who fell to his death on the pavement below, it was *literally* a concrete resolution.) Audiences were so enthralled by the idea of seeing Kimble's quest actually end, that the finale became the most-watched TV program in history up to that time. Even today, the only episodes of a weekly series to rank higher in the all-time ratings are, like *The Fugitive* finale, resolution shows: the answer to the "Who Shot J.R.?" mystery on *Dallas*, and, at the top, the last episode of *M*A*S*H*. The series remains in syndication today, and the depth of its influence can be measured in homages both small and large. On the small side, there's the one-armed man character in *Twin Peaks;* on the large side, there's the 1993 movie remake of *The Fugitive*, with Harrison Ford as Richard Kimble—a watermark of major teleliteracy status if ever there was one. It was a fine film, with only one flaw. Tommy Lee Jones, as the indefatigable Lieutenant Gerard, was more interesting and lively a character than Ford's brooding doctor—which is a little like having a movie version of *Perry Mason* stolen by the actor playing Hamilton Burger.

Full House. *1987–95, ABC*. There's no avoiding it, I guess. In future generations, this family sitcom will be recognized—though not, if there's any justice, revered—as its era's equivalent of *The Brady Bunch*. It's that universal a viewing experience for young kids, who someday will be reminiscing about the likes of Jodie Sweetin's little Stephanie muttering, "How rude!" Bob Saget, John Stamos, David Coulier, and Lori Loughlin were the alleged role models on this show, but the standout scene-stealer was the character of young Michelle, alternately played by young twins Mary-Kate and Ashley Olsen. The Olsen twins went on, as preteens, to start their own production company and star in several network specials and telemovies, but despite their undeniable popularity among young viewers, something about those little twin girls, frankly, gave me the creeps. Perhaps they reminded me of those twin girls in the hallway in Stanley Kubrick's film version of *The Shining*. Then again, maybe it was that dream I had—the one about lifting the bangs from one of their foreheads and finding the number "3–3–3."

Garry Moore Show, The. *1950–64, CBS.* Along with Perry Como and Dean Martin, Garry Moore was one of the most laid-back of all variety show hosts; Moore was as quiet as his jackets were loud. *The Garry Moore Show* lasted eight years on daytime TV, and six more in prime time. Carol Burnett, one of Moore's many big talent finds, appeared on both the daytime and evening shows, but it was on his nighttime series that she made her big splash. Others who entered television through Moore's show included Don Adams, George Gobel, Jonathan Winters, and Don Knotts, who made his first appearance on the show impersonating CBS programming executive Harry Ommerle. (At the time, Knotts was as relatively anonymous as the man he was impersonating, so the trick worked beautifully. More than a decade later, Pat Paulsen would pull the same trick, just as successfully, by initially introducing himself to viewers of *The Smothers Brothers Comedy Hour* as a CBS executive.) Most of those contributors to Moore's show made more permanent marks in later TV vehicles, and most of *The Garry Moore Show* has faded from cultural mass memory. However, some lingering traces remain, including the show's *Candid Camera* feature pieces and Moore's cohost Durward Kirby, whose name, at least, was saluted for posterity when a "Rocky and Bullwinkle" sequence featured an intelligence-increasing hat called the "Kirwood Derby." Kirby objected strenuously at the time—but that's only because he wasn't wearing his derby.

General Electric Theater. *1953–62, CBS.* Fittingly, given its corporate sponsor, this series was a sort of "dim bulb" of anthology series: lots of stars, but not all that much substance. The most resonant episode, many decades later, probably is 1958's *Auf Wiedersehen*, which featured the dramatic debut of Sammy Davis, Jr., and became prominent in most of the entertainer's televised tributes and obituaries. (Ironically, *Auf Wiedersehen* was written by Kurt Vonnegut, who had quit his job as a publicist for General Electric seven years earlier.) This anthology series earns its spot in TV posterity, however,

Friends, with Matthew Perry, Jennifer Aniston, David Schwimmer, Courteney Cox, Matt LeBlanc, and Lisa Kudrow.

LEFT: *The Fugitive,* with a rare group shot of Barry Morse's Lieutenant Gerard, David Janssen's Richard Kimble, and Bill Raisch's one-armed man.
RIGHT: *Get Smart,* with Don Adams and shoe phone.

chiefly because of its host. How many other TV series can lay claim to being hosted by a future president of the United States? Actually, *two* others: both *Death Valley Days* and the little-known 1953 ABC variety series *The Orchid Award*, like *General Electric Theater*, were hosted (at least in part) by Ronald Reagan.

General Hospital. *1963–   , ABC*. Three words, and one story line, made this the most famous soap on TV: Luke and Laura. As positive role models go, though, Anthony Geary's Luke Spencer fell a little short. To "seduce" Genie Francis's Laura Baldwin, a young newlywed, Luke threw her down on the dance floor and raped her—the beginning, improbably, of a beautiful friendship. He got tender, she got divorced, and, in 1981, they got married. Elizabeth Taylor attended the ceremony in person (portraying an evil schemer named Helena Cassidine), and enough viewers watched it on TV to generate the highest ratings in the history of daytime soaps. In addition to Taylor, some of the other big-name stars who checked into *General Hospital* for quickie guest roles included Milton Berle and Sammy Davis, Jr., and the series attracted future stars as well. In 1982, the year after the Luke and Laura nuptials, Janine Turner (later of *Northern Exposure*) and Demi Moore joined the cast, portraying sisters Laura and Jackie Templeton. Two future *Hill Street Blues* stars appeared on the soap: Daniel J. Travanti (as Spence Andrews, 1979) and James B. Sikking (Dr. James Hobart, 1973–76). Other future celebrities included Mark Hamill (Kent Murray, 1972–73), Richard Dean Anderson (Dr. Jeff Webber, 1976–81), John Stamos (Blackie Parrish, 1982–84), and, stretching the definition a bit, Rick Springfield (Dr. Noah Drake, 1981–83). The then-unknown Richard Simmons, playing himself in 1979, got such instant acceptance after playing a fitness guru on *General Hospital* that it made him what he is today—whatever that is. But it was the furor over Luke and Laura, coming only a year after the "Who Shot J.R.?" obsession on *Dallas*, that imported a similar measure of media mania to the once-neglected world of the daytime serial. Both Francis and Geary left *General Hospital* in 1984, but never duplicated their success as a daytime pair, and eventually reunited. Geary returned to *General Hospital,* and the role of Luke, in 1991, and Francis, after a string of telemovies, guest appearances, and different roles on rival soaps, checked back in to *General Hospital* in 1993, and Luke and Laura were an item again.

George Burns and Gracie Allen Show, The. *1950–58, CBS*. Four decades after they were made, episodes of this sitcom continue to show up on cable and in syndication—and continue to look like one of the freshest sitcoms around. Almost before there *was* an established set of sitcom conventions (the premiere of *I Love Lucy* wouldn't occur for another season), Burns was lampooning and ignoring those rules by breaking the "fourth wall" and addressing the audience directly. It was a gimmick he admitted to stealing from Thornton Wilder's *Our Town,* and he did it so successfully that other shows later stole it from him, including *The Many Loves of Dobie Gillis* and *It's Garry Shandling's Show.* Burns and his wife, Gracie Allen, had honed their act already in vaudeville and, from 1933 until television beckoned, their own popular radio show. The comedienne's scatterbrained comic persona would be echoed, a generation later, by Goldie Hawn on *Rowan & Martin's Laugh-In* (Burns himself, once, fittingly appeared as her straight man on one installment of that series), and, in spirit, by both Nicholas Colasanto's Coach and Woody Harrelson's Woody on *Cheers*. Although *The George Burns and Gracie Allen Show* stopped abruptly once Allen announced her retirement, Burns as a solo act would keep his career going, and her memory alive, well into the nineties. It's worth noting that, though Burns informed viewers of all other backstage events during the run of his sitcom (going so far as to replace one defecting cast member with his replacement as the cameras rolled), there was no official "final" episode of the Burns and Allen sitcom, or on-air acknowledgment of his wife's sudden, final retirement from television. Then again, Burns had allowed her to say farewell in every show they made, in what became the series' most quoted and paraphrased contribution to teleliteracy: "Say good night, Gracie."

George Gobel Show, The. *1954–59, NBC; 1959–60, CBS.* Long before Rodney Dangerfield didn't get no respect, neither did "Lonesome George" Gobel, whose own memorable mantras included "Well, I'll be a dirty bird!," and countless monologues about his wife Alice and friend "Packie." After this popular variety show faded, Gobel eventually resurfaced as a fixture on *Hollywood Squares,* but the genre he headlined on TV fell onto hard times in the eighties. When it comes to variety series today, as Gobel used to say, "You don't hardly get those no more."

Geraldo. *1987– , syndicated.* Who knows what evil lurks in the hearts of daytime talk shows? Geraldo Rivera nose—and it's a nose that was broken when one of his typically angry guests threw a chair (which Rivera caught with his face) at another angry guest. Rivera trafficked in the same general topics and types of guests as such syndicated competitors as Phil Donahue and Oprah Winfrey—in other words, his program, like theirs, was part therapy session and part geek show—but Rivera took much of the heat, thanks to his sensationalistic approach and, in his prime time specials at least, sensational ratings successes. *Geraldo,* shown on a daily basis, cemented for posterity Rivera's reputation as The P. T. Barnum of talk show hosts. In the early nineties, he became as shrill and overzealous as a carnival barker—all barker and no bite. Yet two things happened to energize Rivera in the midnineties, and bring him back, at least on occasion, to the more solid and serious reporting of his early career with ABC. One, a new generation of talk-show competitors, led by *Ricki Lake,* actually made their reputations by sinking a lot lower than *Geraldo* ever had, thereby allowing Rivera to rise above the bottom of the barrel. Two, the O. J. Simpson trial, of all things, became to Rivera what the Persian Gulf War was to CNN—a daily, reputation-enhancing specialty and obsession. While Rivera continued to interview a parade of daytime dysfunctionals on *Geraldo,* his nightly talk show on CNBC, *Rivera*

Live, was one of the best and most thoughtful sources, outside of Court TV, for discussion of the legal and social ramifications of the Simpson case.

Get Smart. *1965–69, NBC; 1969–70, CBS*. Prior to *Rowan & Martin's Laugh-In* and *Saturday Night Live*, this sitcom was one of TV's most prolific factories for popular catch phrases. No wonder, since its writing and production staff, in addition to co-creators Mel Brooks and Buck Henry, included writers whose individual credits included *The Honeymooners, The Ernie Kovacs Show, The Bullwinkle Show,* and *That Was the Week That Was*—virtually an all-star gallery of clever and creative TV offerings. *Get Smart* hit the air while the James Bond movie series was at its *Goldfinger*-era peak, and the first few seasons of this spy spoof, especially, were delightful. Don Adams, as Secret Agent 86, generated more quotable lines than you could shake a *shtick* at: "Sorry about that, chief," "Would you believe . . . ?," " . . . And *loving* it," and "Missed it by *that* much!" The opening sequence, with its series of giant doors opening and closing, and with Smart eventually falling through a trap door "entrance" in a phone booth, is as memorable as the theme music that accompanied it. The show's gadgets, too, seem to have a cultural half-life of sorts, especially the Cone of Silence and Max's shoe phone (which must seem especially baffling, in these days of cellular telephones, to young viewers watching *Get Smart* on Nick at Nite). Barbara Feldon's character, named— or, to be more precise, numbered—99, raised some viewers' temperatures at least that high, and due credit should also be given to Dick Gautier's Hymie the Robot, the original Robocop. A *Get Smart* movie sequel, 1980's *The Nude Bomb*, was a bomb no matter how it was attired—and was ruined by some really attired writing. Yet eventually, *Get Smart* appeared again in *Get Smart, Again!*, a 1989 telemovie that was another major disappointment. The franchise appeared to be torpedoed for good, though, by a new series remake of *Get Smart*, which the Fox network premiered in 1995. Adams was back as Maxwell Smart, and Feldon made token appearances as Agent 99, but the focus of the new series was their son Zachary (played by Andy Dick), a fledgling spy with a sexy new partner named Agent 66 (Elaine Hendrix). Fox got smart, and canceled its losses after six awful episodes.

Gidget. *1965–66, ABC*. When the first *Gidget* film premiered in 1959, starring Sandra Dee as a surfboard-toting beach bunny, it actually was ahead of the wave when it came to the surfer craze. After all, the Beach Boys wouldn't score their first Top 20 hit, "Surfin' Safari," until 1962. But by the time this sitcom version was launched in 1965, two full years after Frankie Avalon and Annette Funicello starred in *Beach Party*, the surfer craze had crested. *Gidget* is remembered, though, as one of the two worst TV series Sally Field had to endure, and outlive, before attaining TV respectability and movie stardom. See also: *Sybil, The Flying Nun*.

Gilligan's Island. *1964–67, CBS*. So little time, so much to ridicule. Start with the theme song, which is hopelessly inane yet maddeningly unforgettable—a perfect reason for some enterprising scientist to invent a mental "purge button" for unwanted memories. Perhaps, though, it is the stupendous stupidity of this show, and its insipid simplicity, that has made it stand out all these years. But that's slightly unfair, because, bad as the *Gilligan's Island* series was, there was more bottom to that barrel: the *Harlem Globetrotters on Gilligan's Island* reunion telemovie, for example, and the short-lived, amazingly unfunny 1992 series *Woops!*, which transplanted the sole-survivors concept to a *Day After* postnuclear scenario. On the one hand, *Gilligan's Island* was an intentional microcosm, with Jim Backus's millionaire Thurston Howell III a harbinger of the Wall Street greed and woes of the eighties, long before even *Family Ties* suggested it. On the other hand, it was unintentionally macrostupid, with no internal logic and only one arguably clever episode: "The Producer," in which Phil Silvers guest starred as a visiting Hollywood producer who was, quite literally, all washed up. To impress him, the castaways, using old instrumental recordings of famous operas (no three-hour cruise would be complete without them) and adding their own lyrics, staged a musical version of *Hamlet*. Bob Denver as Gilligan as Hamlet has to be seen to be disbelieved, and Tina Louise as Ginger as Ophelia—well, Ophelia getting as weary of this entry as I am. Granted, Ginger was my major reason for watching as a youngster (the "Ginger or Mary Ann" debate in that recent teleliterate beer commercial was, in my pubescent mind, about as tough a call as "Ginger or Roseanne"), but adults might still enjoy the strangeness of the 1964 "Gilligan Meets Jungle Boy" episode, with a very young Kurt Russell sharing top billing. Since its three-season original run, *Gilligan's Island* has proven inescapable in syndication, and many of the surviving principals have taken part in recent dream-sequence homages on other shows, including *ALF* and *Baywatch*. The teleliteracy quotient of *Gilligan's Island*, though, is highest when it comes to the names of the "seven stranded castaways"—and the other lyrics in that unsinkable theme song. Expect to hear it someday soon at a movie theater near you: with *The Brady Bunch Movie*, a big-screen remake of another Sherwood Schwartz series, proving such a hit, a *Gilligan's Island* movie can't be far behind. Start with Geena Davis as Ginger, and even I'd buy a ticket.

Goldbergs, The. *1949–51, CBS; 1952–53, NBC; 1954, DuMont; 1955–56, syndicated.* In more than one respect, Gertrude Berg's Molly Goldberg was the mother of all TV sitcoms. Technically, *The Goldbergs* wasn't the first live sitcom on TV—it was predated by a handful of others, including DuMont's *Mary Kay and Johnny*, which premiered in 1947. Also, it technically was not a TV "original": like many TV series after it, *The Goldbergs* was a carryover from radio, where the comic exploits of these fictitious, identifiably Jewish residents of the Bronx already had delighted audiences for more than fifteen years. But it predated, by at least half a year, the other two familiar sitcom titles from 1949, *Mama* and *The Life of Riley*—and, nearly half a century later, surviving kinescopes and films of *The Goldbergs* make a strong case for how visionary it really was. Berg, who wrote every script, stressed commonplace everyday events in her stories, refused to include a laugh track, and provided a program in which *mother* knew best. *The Goldbergs* is the trunk of a sitcom family tree whose branches have extended, in recent years, to the ethnic sensibilities of *Brooklyn Bridge*, the "dramedy" sensibilities of *The Days and Nights of Molly Dodd*, and the minimalistic sensibilities of *Seinfeld*. Elder viewers may well remember Molly's famous call of greeting to her neighbor ("Yoo-hoo, Mrs. Bloom!"), but the most commonly recalled aspect of *The Goldbergs*, sadly, is the blacklisting of Philip Loeb, who played Molly's husband, Jake, until his name was published in the infamous *Red Channels*, which claimed to list show-biz personnel with Communist leanings. Loeb insisted the charges were false, and Berg stood by her costar. However, the sponsor didn't, so *The Goldbergs* disappeared for a year, and resurfaced on another network, with another actor playing Molly's husband, in 1952. Three years later, in an act that would be linked in broadcast history to his dismissal from *The Goldbergs*, Loeb committed suicide. One happier final note: in 1950, between seasons during the show's successful run on CBS, Berg mounted a separate film version of *The Goldbergs*—making it television's very first program to be adapted for film.

Golden Girls, The. *1985–92, NBC*. This sitcom, which in time spawned the spinoff *Empty Nest*, earned a niche in the teleliteracy canon by proving that a show populated entirely by elderly women *could* be a big hit on TV—at least when those women included the impeccable comic talents of Beatrice Arthur and Betty White. Those two, in particular, were a lot funnier than the scripts, and helped make the title *The Golden Girls*, which also costarred Rue McClanahan and Estelle Getty, synonymous with almost any subsequent TV project starring mature performers. Similar shorthand had been used, prior to the success of this sitcom, regarding the film version of Neil Simon's similarly titled comedy, *The Sunshine Boys*—which gave George Burns his big "comeback" film role in 1975. Ever wonder where *The Golden Girls* got the inspiration for its title?

Gomer Pyle, U.S.M.C. *1964–69, CBS*. What goes around, comes around. It was television's *The U.S. Steel Hour*, by showcasing Andy Griffith in a 1955 version of *No Time for Sergeants*, that beat both Broadway and the movies to the punch. Those subsequent adaptations, like the TV version of Mac Hyman's comic novel, made fine use of Griffith, who played an affable country bumpkin shipped off for military service. Once Griffith hit it even bigger on *The Andy Griffith Show*, he and his producers had a choice of several stars and characters to spin off into their own series, and their choice was Jim Nabors as Gomer Pyle—who, in the spinoff pilot, was sent to Marine boot camp, thereby becoming an affable country bumpkin shipped off for military service. Before you could say "Shazam!," or certainly before you could say Gomer's three-syllable "Gaw-awl-lee!," *Gomer Pyle, U.S.M.C.* was a hit. Those two catch phrases, and the occasional occurrence (as enacted in the movie *Splash*) of insulting someone by calling him a "Gomer," are about all that linger from this sitcom, which is just as well.

Gong Show, The. *1976–78, NBC; 1976–80, syndicated*. This is the worst, and therefore arguably the best, of the tasteless game shows produced by Chuck

Barris. It came not to praise contestants, but to bury them, and Barris himself, as the talentless host of a largely talentless talent show, led the charge. In retrospect, *The Gong Show* gave us an early peek at the type of publicity-hungry, charisma-starved "performers" who would flock to cable's public-access channels (not to mention talk shows) in the eighties and nineties. Watching the show, though, was like being behind the wheel of a car and seeing an accident, or an animal carcass, on the side of the road—it was hard not to slow down and look at it, yet you felt both ashamed and sickened once you did. The celebrity panelists were as devoid of enviable skills as the contestants, and the show encouraged a level of cruelty not encountered again on a regular TV series until *The Morton Downey, Jr. Show*. Historically, Barris gets a smidgeon of credit for excavating and perpetuating the concept of "gonging" contestants—established on radio's *Major Bowes and His Original Amateur Hour* as an aural equivalent of vaudeville's hook—and for providing a national TV audience with its first glimpse of Paul Reubens as Pee-wee Herman. But any credit Barris deserves is dwarfed by the blame of creating such a mean-spirited satirical series. The show's title, and the "gong" idea itself, remain familiar, but other elements of this series, thank goodness, are *Gong* with the wind.

Good Times. *1974–79, CBS.* The good things about *Good Times* have long since been forgotten. The sitcom, a spinoff of *Maude* (itself a spinoff of *All in the Family*), invited Americans to spend time with a working-class, nuclear African-American family. The parents, James and Florida Evans (played by John Amos and Esther Rolle), were loving but demanding, and the youngest child was so aware of his heritage and ethnic identity—years before *Roots* was presented on TV—that he wrote school papers on Malcolm X. In the earliest shows, the punch lines on *Good Times* were accompanied by jabs at the political status quo and the difficulty of making ends meet on a tight budget; in that respect, *Good Times* was a soul sister of *Roseanne*. But *Roseanne* never allowed one of the child actors to run away with the show, and once Jimmie Walker, as J. J., became a breakout character with his Stepin Fetchit buffoonery and "Dyn-O-Mite!" catch phrase, *Good Times* lost all claims to relevance and artistry. From the time the still-remembered "Dyn-O-Mite" fuse was lit, *Good Times* became a real bomb. The only performer to thrive after its cancellation was Janet Jackson, who played an abused child adopted by Florida during the show's final two seasons.

Good Morning America. *1975– , ABC.* ABC's morning show doesn't have the tenure or pedigree of NBC's *Today*, but it's been around long enough to establish its own niche in daytime TV history. David Hartman, the host from 1975–87, became a bigger star as a *GMA* host than he ever was as an alleged TV star on such shows as *Lucas Tanner* and *The Virginian*. Joan Lunden, the program's cohost since 1980, has been partnered since 1987 with the very affable Charles Gibson, and the two share a congenial and notably equal partnership. Once a mere also-ran in the morning-show race, *GMA* finally lapped *Today* in the ratings after Jane Pauley left that NBC series, and the two shows have fought it out ever since, with *GMA* drawing more viewers for the first half of the nineties, but with *Today* making it an increasingly tighter race. So tight, in fact, that for one week during the November 1995 ratings sweeps, *Good Morning America* and *Today* were tied, with each show earning a 4.6 rating.

Goodyear TV Playhouse. See *Philco Television Playhouse, Marty.*

Great American Dream Machine, The. *1971–72, PBS.* This eclectic, short-lived PBS anthology variety series makes the list out of sheer stubbornness on my part. The likelihood of this series ever being repeated, and revered for the breakthrough TV series it was, is frustratingly slim. Yet to those of us who became addicted to its spirit of all-inclusive anarchy, *The Great American Dream Machine* was an unforgettably rich and delightful pop-culture pot-pourri—a sort of "Anything Can Happen Day" for adults. Comedy skits shared time with film shorts and minidocumentaries; contributors included Chevy Chase, Andy Rooney, Studs Terkel, and Marshall Efron, whose eccentric lectures were a special highlight. Long before Rooney took roost on *60 Minutes*, Efron was puzzling over such memorable minutiae as which black olives were larger: jumbo or colossal? For one lecture, titled "Is There Sex after Death?," Efron walked to the podium, recited the title, opened his textbook, peered into the camera, and said, "No." End of lecture.

Great Performances. *1974– , PBS.* After bringing stage plays to TV in the ambitious and successful *Theatre in America* (well, successful in public television terms, anyway), Jac Venza launched this even more ambitious series, which made room for dance, music, drama, comedy, and even the occasional telemovie and miniseries. Some of the stage and concert works were commissioned, but most were broadcasts of existing theatrical presentations. The 1978 *Great Performances* original telemovie called *Verna: USO Girl*, starring Sissy Spacek, was an early triumph for both the series and the actress; in the miniseries arena, *Great Performances* made a lasting impact, and earned name recognition, by importing such wonderful presentations as *Brideshead Revisited* (see separate listing), Tom Conti in 1978's *The Norman Conquests*, and Alec Guinness in 1980's *Tinker, Tailor, Soldier, Spy.* Ranking the most memorable stage, musical, and dance specials is entirely a matter of taste; my own tastes, among the more recent productions at least, favor 1990's *Hamlet* (with Kevin Kline) and 1993's *Sondheim: A Celebration at Carnegie Hall.*

Green Acres. *1965–71, CBS.* It doesn't say much for this series, but says just about enough, that its two most memorable components have proven to be its theme song and its pig. Vic Mizzy, who wrote the equally catchy *Addams Family* theme, also composed the music and lyrics for *Green Acres* ("Green Acres is the place to be / Faa-arm livin' is the life for me!"). As for Arnold Ziffel, the infamous (and, some say, postmodern) pig that brought new meaning to the term "ham actor," there were actually about a dozen pigs, male and female, who played Arnold over the course of the series. Obviously, there were no such reinforcements for Eddie Albert and Eva Gabor, who starred throughout the series as the city folk (and, in retrospect, proto-Trumps, with Albert's Oliver as Donald and Gabor's Lisa as Ivana) who moved to the country. Though the plot sounds like *The Beverly Hillbillies* in reverse, *Green Acres* actually was created by Jay Sommers as a TV version of his 1950 radio series, *Granby's Green Acres*, which starred Gale Gordon (later of *The Lucy Show*) and Bea Benaderet (who wound up starring in *Petticoat Junction*). Paul Henning was the executive producer of all three rurally rooted sitcoms—*Petticoat Junction, The Beverly Hillbillies,* and *Green Acres*—with *Green Acres* the strangest and silliest of the bunch. And speaking of "bunch": more than twenty years before a theater company mounted live versions of *The Brady Bunch* in Chicago and New York, a 1967 episode of *Green Acres* had the citizens of Hooterville mounting a local stage production of *The Beverly Hillbillies* (which was still on CBS at the time). For the record, Gabor's Lisa played Granny, while Albert's Oliver played Jethro. *Green Acres* has such a fanciful and farcical flavor, and is populated with such outrageous characters, that the series has been compared to *The Simpsons*—which might seem unfounded, except that the comparison was made by none other than Matt Groening, the creator of *The Simpsons*, who lovingly describes *Green Acres* as "the story of Oliver Douglas in Hell." When Nick at Nite promoted its *Green Acres* reruns, it did so with the slogan, "Remember: it's not dopey, it's surreal." Which, given its rural setting, made *Green Acres* surreal McCoy.

Green Hornet, The. *1966–67, ABC.* This entry just barely makes the cut, and does so thanks to Al Hirt's breathless theme song (an arrangement of Rimsky-Korsakov's *Flight of the Bumblebee* on trumpet) and to the presence of Bruce Lee, who had a supporting role as Kato, the martial-arts assistant to Van Williams's Green Hornet. It's no accident that *The Green Hornet* has so much in common with *The Lone Ranger:* a musical theme pulled from the classical canon, a hero with a faithful sidekick, and the fact that, when not in disguise, both protagonists have the last name of Reid (the Green Hornet was Britt Reid, and the Lone Ranger's real name was John Reid). Both of these costumed heroes were created by George W. Trendle and writer Fran Striker, and at least one link between the two protagonists was intentional: the Green Hornet was identified as the Lone Ranger's grand-nephew. The *Green Hornet* radio series began in 1936, with several vocal actors (beginning with Al Hodge as Britt Reid) sharing the two leading roles, and lasted on radio all the way until 1952. On television, when *Batman* became a hit for ABC in 1966, the network quickly revived the Green Hornet and Kato radio characters and injected them into an episode of *Batman*, with Williams and Lee in the roles; after that, ABC launched *The Green Hornet* as its own, less enjoyable spinoff. Lee's fighting moves were fluid, but his acting was as stiff as everything else about this series. It's worth noting that, back during the radio tenure of *The Green Hornet*, Kato the Japanese valet suddenly became "Reid's faithful *Filipino* valet" right after the 1941 Japanese attack on Pearl Harbor. It's also worth noting that, when *The Green Hornet* was made for television, Hong

Kong imported it—but retitled it *The Kato Show*. A scary thought, now that we're on the other side of the O. J. Simpson trial.

Guiding Light. *1952– , CBS.* It would be impressive enough merely to identify this as TV's longest-running current soap opera. The only other surviving soap from the fifties, in fact, is *As the World Turns*, which premiered four years after the *Guiding Light*. But the history of the *Guiding Light* goes back all the way to 1937, when it first appeared as a fifteen-minute serial on NBC radio. Though it was common for sitcoms and variety shows to make the leap from radio to television, no other soap opera made the transition successfully. Put the two media together, and the *Guiding Light* stakes a claim—an irrevocable one—as being the most durable drama in broadcast history. Given that, you'd expect the show to also claim a long roster of star alumni, but you'd be wrong. However, Mercedes McCambridge did play the key character of Mary Rutledge on the radio version, and the TV troupers through the years have included Christopher Walken (as young Mike Bauer, 1954–56), Sandy Dennis (Alice Holden, 1956), Joseph Campanella (Joe Turino, 1959–60), Chris Sarandon (Tom Halverson, 1969–70), and JoBeth Williams (Brandy Shelooe, 1977–81), Kevin Bacon (T. J. Werner, 1980–81), and *ER* regular Sherry Stringfield (Blake Marler, 1989–92). The best and most surprising casting of all, though, occurred in the midsixties, when an African-American doctor and his wife were written into the storyline. When the characters of Dr. Jim and Martha Frazier were introduced in 1966, they were played by Billy Dee Williams and Cicely Tyson. And when those performers left the *Guiding Light* within a year, their roles were inherited by a slightly older, but no less impressive, pair of performers: James Earl Jones and Ruby Dee.

Gulf War, The. See *Persian Gulf War, The*.

Gumby. *1957, NBC; 1966, syndicated.* This popular idol with feet of clay was spun off into his own show after attaining stop-action stardom on *The Howdy Doody Show*—thereby proving, contrary to the familiar complaint by Kermit the Frog, that it *was* easy being green. And when Eddie Murphy showed up on *Saturday Night Live*, wearing a big green Gumby suit and talking about launching a comeback, Art Clokey's character of Gumby, and all the accompanying toy paraphernalia, was embraced all over again by a new generation. Personally, though, I thought most of the tabletop adventures on *Gumby* were a little Pokey. In 1995, Gumby and Pokey made a big comeback, at least in terms of screen size, by starring in their first full-length feature film, *Gumby—The Movie*. Other than its projected dimensions, it was no big deal.

Gunsmoke. *1955–75, CBS.* This Western holds one record that, most likely, will stand forever. With twenty seasons of shows under its gun belt, *Gunsmoke* is (and, I suspect, forever shall be) the longest-running network drama series in prime time. Its roots actually go back a few years further, to 1952—when CBS launched *Gunsmoke* on radio, starring William Conrad as Sheriff Matt

LEFT: *Gilligan's Island*, with Bob Denver and Alan Hale, Jr.
RIGHT: *Gunsmoke*, with James Arness and Amanda Blake.

Happy Days, with Henry Winkler as the Fonz and Ron Howard as Richie.

Dillon. Unlike other radio Westerns, which were aimed largely at kids, *Gunsmoke* was mature in both tone and subject matter. When *Gunsmoke* moved to TV with James Arness in the Dillon role, it was the medium's most popular Western for years (until *Bonanza* came along), and remained a viewer favorite because its plots were as distinctive as its characters. *Gunsmoke* used its period setting as *Star Trek* used its futuristic one: to explore themes of bigotry, violence, loyalty, responsibility, and so on, presenting the touchy and often relevant subjects in a manner that was more comfortable to watch simply because the conflicts took place in a distant time and place. (Actually, the stoic, heroic characters of Sheriff Dillon and Captain Kirk are quite similarly motivated and presented, as are their physician sidekicks: Milburn Stone's "Doc" on *Gunsmoke* and DeForest Kelley's "Bones" on *Star Trek*.) In 1987, a dozen years after *Gunsmoke* rode off into the sunset, Arness climbed back into the saddle again for a CBS telemovie called *Gunsmoke: Return to Dodge*—starring opposite Amanda Blake, reprising her role as the independent yet loyal Miss Kitty. Several more *Gunsmoke* telemovies followed, but by 1994's *Gunsmoke: One Man's Justice*, they couldn't be considered reunions at all, because Arness was carrying the franchise virtually alone. (And playing the same TV character, amazingly, over a forty-year span.) From the old *Gunsmoke*, though, the entire company contributed greatly to the show's success, and the characters and relationships, not any catch phrases or recurring bits of business, are what survive most vividly. One highlight was the always electric, never overt relationship between Dillon and Blake's Miss Kitty; others were provided by the show's long succession of deputies and town characters, including the backwoods deputy Festus (Ken Curtis, 1964–75), the half-breed blacksmith Quentin (played, from 1962–65, by a prefame Burt Reynolds), and, most memorably of all, Dillon's original deputy, the limping Chester (portrayed from 1955–64 by Dennis Weaver, who went on to star in *McCloud*). One little-noted possible side effect of Chester's popularity was Chuck Berry's "Johnny B. Goode," which became a Top 10 hit in 1958, three years after *Gunsmoke* premiered on TV. The connection? Berry didn't shoot the deputy, but he may have borrowed from him: Chester's full name was Chester B. Goode.

Hallmark Hall of Fame. *1952–1978, NBC; 1979–   , divided among CBS, NBC, ABC, and PBS.* The longevity and continued success of this series of specials should (but never will) persuade network programmers of the substantial appetite for quality fare on TV. *Hallmark Hall of Fame* is by no means a nostalgia item: its 1991 drama *Sarah, Plain and Tall*, with Glenn Close and Christopher Walken, was the highest-rated presentation in the four-decade history of the series. Long after the quiz show scandals discouraged the practice of full sponsorship of network programs, Hallmark continued the tradition, timing the release of each special to precede a key holiday card-buying season. Yet that pragmatic marketing ploy was (and is) accompanied by an unusually altruistic and optimistic faith in the drawing power of "good" television, and, over the years, *Hallmark Hall of Fame* has presented some truly outstanding work, including the 1986 drama *Promise*, one of the finest telemovies ever made (it starred James Woods and James Garner as a schizophrenic and his brother). Other "hall of fame" *Hall of Fame* offerings through the years include 1953's *Hamlet* with Maurice Evans, 1955's *Alice in Wonderland* with Eva LeGallienne and Elsa Lanchester, 1956's *Born Yesterday* with Mary Martin, 1959's *A Doll's House* (starring Julie Harris, Hume Cronyn, and Christopher Plummer), 1964's *The Fantasticks* (with John Davidson, Bert Lahr, and Ricardo Montalban), and 1972's *The Man Who Came to Dinner*, which NBC ought to dig out from the archives. Its astoundingly eclectic cast included Orson Welles, Lee Remick, Joan Collins, Don Knotts, and Marty Feldman. See also: *Amahl and the Night Visitors*.

Happy Days. *1974–84, ABC*. In a direct sense, *Happy Days* came out of "Love and the Happy Day," an unsold sitcom pilot by producer Garry Marshall that was broadcast in 1972 as an episode of *Love, American Style*. George Lucas, seeing Ron Howard as the squeaky-clean fifties teen in that pilot, cast him in virtually the same role in *American Graffiti*, the 1973 film that ignited the nostalgia craze—and, as a result, prompted ABC to reverse its decision on Marshall's project and give the go-ahead to a series called *Happy Days*. That's the direct lineage of the show. Indirectly, though, *Happy Days* came about as a counterprogramming reaction by ABC to the more mature and relevant sitcoms on CBS, the home of such dominant series as *All in the Family* and *M*A*S*H*. ABC countered with youthful escapism, and *Happy Days* led the charge. Before long, the show had generated one genuine TV icon—Henry Winkler as the Fonz, a mixture of James Dean and a cuddly panda—and several successful spinoffs, including *Laverne & Shirley* and *Mork & Mindy*. For a while, the leather-jacketed Fonz had more impact with his "thumbs up" gesture than anyone this side of Gene Siskel and Roger Ebert, but his once-rebellious character got too popular for his own good—or, more specifically, too *good* for his own good. As Winkler became more of a star on the show, Fonzie became more of a role model, and ended up as a rebel with a cause. By the end of the show, he was virtually interchangeable with Howard's Richie Cunningham. Yet the earliest episodes of *Happy Days*, done on film, largely on location, and without a laugh track, had a much more satisfying, *American Graffiti*-style flavor than the more standard sitcom episodes that followed. Marion Ross, who reprised her role from the *Love, American Style* episode, played Richie's mom as a virtual carbon copy of the type of suburban housewife on *The Donna Reed Show* and *Father Knows Best*—which made her subsequent sitcom role, as the quintessential Jewish grandmother on *Brooklyn Bridge*, that much more of a contrast, shock, and pleasant surprise. Coincidentally, both Marshall's *Happy Days* and Gary David Goldberg's

Brooklyn Bridge were set during the same general period in the fifties, yet they couldn't have been more different. *Brooklyn Bridge* was constantly aware of the era in which it was set, was true to both the events and concerns of the times, and was superb. Aside from the sets, costumes, and slang, about the only times *Happy Days* referred directly to its own era were when it wanted to demonstrate teleliteracy, and make room for such fifties-vintage guest stars as Jack Smith of *You Asked for It* or "Buffalo" Bob Smith of *Howdy Doody*. Robin Williams, making a return guest appearance as Mork on a 1979 episode of *Happy Days*, summed it all up nicely at the end of that show: "I went back to visit the Cunninghams and their friends," he reported to Orson, as though concluding an episode of his own *Mork & Mindy*. "They're really nice people, but a little mondo-mundane. . . . I'm talkin' white bread and mayonnaise." A *Happy Days Reunion Special* was televised in 1992, the same year Howard also reunited on TV with the cast of *The Andy Griffith Show*.

Hart to Hart. *1979–84, ABC*. This allegedly romantic, inexplicably popular series, starring Robert Wagner and Stefanie Powers as rich amateur sleuths, was designed as a modern TV variation on *The Thin Man*, those classic comedy mysteries starring William Powell and Myrna Loy as Nick and Nora Charles. In one way, at least, the writers of *Hart to Hart* succeeded, because their plots were thin, man. Yet this series stuck around, and stuck, long enough for its title to enter the pop-culture memory bank, and to earn one of the clearest measures of teleliteracy status: a reunion telemovie, *Hart to Hart Returns*, broadcast by NBC in 1993. Two years later, cable's Family Channel paired the Harts, and guest star Joan Collins, in another new *Hart to Hart* telemovie. By then, though, the concept clearly was in dire need of a couple of *Hart* transplants.

Harvest of Shame. *1960, CBS*. This *CBS Reports* special is one of the most famous TV documentaries of all time, and is the only one, to my knowledge, to have inspired follow-up documentaries every ten years since its premiere. The original *Harvest of Shame* detailed the sad plight and miserable working conditions of migrant workers—and got a lot of attention, in part, because it was televised the day after Thanksgiving, when stomachs were full and consciences were ripe for the pricking. Edward R. Murrow narrated the hour, and he and executive producer Fred W. Friendly have gotten most of the credit for it, but the aggressive reporting and agonizing photography were what gave *Harvest of Shame* such impact, and those were provided, respectively, by producer David Lowe and camera operators Martin Barnett and Charles Mack. All these years later, it remains a potent, disturbing, and clearly subjective program, all but begging for legislation to change the existing conditions. It's a sad postscript, but an unavoidable one, that other teams of reporters, producers, narrators, and photographers have been able to revisit the same story, at ten-year intervals, and find similarly *Shame*-ful conditions. In 1970, on the tenth anniversary of *Harvest of Shame*, rival network NBC noted the occasion by presenting *Migrant*, narrated by Chet Huntley—by most accounts, the first time any network had blatantly and unapologetically broadcast a sequel to a competitor's news special. A decade later, NBC struck again, this time with a Chris Wallace report called *The Migrants, 1980*. In 1990, the PBS series *Frontline* picked up the baton, presenting an installment titled *New Harvest, Old Shame*. And finally, in 1995, CBS finally acknowledged the value of its own history by presenting *Legacy of Shame*, a special *CBS Reports* hosted by Dan Rather (who, in one scene taped in a furrowed Florida field, almost literally followed in Murrow's footsteps), reported by Randall Pinkston, and produced by Christina Borjesson and Maurice Murad. By so doing, CBS finally reclaimed one of its own legacies—one of its very best. After thirty-five years since the original *Harvest of Shame* telecast, CBS completed the circle: *Shame* time, *Shame* station.

Have Gun, Will Travel. *1957–63, CBS.* The title of this show, and its "Ballad of Paladin" theme song, are the two elements most remembered about this brooding Western. And that's baffling and almost infuriating, because *Have Gun, Will Travel* is one of the most singularly stylish series of its day, and ought to be thriving today in reruns on syndication or cable. Richard Boone, as hired gun Paladin, advertised his services with a business card that carried his symbol (a chess knight, also called a paladin) and read, "Have Gun—Will Travel. Wire Paladin, San Francisco." Intelligent and tough, Paladin was, in effect, a Wild West version of *The Equalizer* (and, in fact, the original outline for *Have Gun, Will Travel* placed Paladin in modern-day New York, the precise premise of *The Equalizer*), and had just as strong a moral code. He even disliked, and was troubled by, the violence he encountered and often initiated, making him an early prototype for the character played by Clint Eastwood in the 1992 film *Unforgiven*. Like Pernell Roberts's Adam Cartwright on *Bonanza*, Boone's Paladin was a good guy who wore black, spoke softly, and carried a heavy attitude. *Have Gun, Will Travel* was especially fair when it came to depicting people of other cultures—and, like *Bonanza, Gunsmoke*, and *Star Trek*, used their different-era settings to address problems and attitudes relevant to modern viewers: one episode had Paladin defending, rather forcefully, a schoolteacher's right to teach unpopular or controversial subjects. In this case, the *Star Trek* comparison is especially apt, because Gene Roddenberry, the creator of *Star Trek*, served as head writer on *Have Gun, Will Travel*, one hour of which featured DeForest Kelley (who surfaced later as Scott "Bones" McCoy on *Star Trek*). Like many Westerns of the era, *Have Gun, Will Travel* had a radio counterpart; unlike almost all the others, the TV version, in this case, came first, with CBS Radio adapting the television scripts, with John Dehner as Paladin, from 1958–60. On television, the show's guest stars included Charles Bronson, Peter Falk, Robert Blake, Vincent Price, James Coburn, William Conrad, Harry Morgan, Ben Johnson, and even, in uncharacteristically dramatic TV turns, June Lockhart and Elinor Donahue. To TV programmers out there in rerun land, I offer this promise regarding your acquisition of this program and its effect upon your competitors: Have *Gun*, Will Trample.

Hawaii Five-O. *1968–80, CBS.* This series set out to be a sun-baked *Dragnet*, and halfway succeeded. That is, it got the *drag* part right. Despite a dozen years on the air, *Hawaii Five-0* earns its appearance in this collection for only two reasons: its hard-driving, drum-heavy theme song, and the laughably memorable phrase with which Jack Lord's McGarrett, instructing his sidekick (James MacArthur's Danny Williams), would end seemingly every show. Perhaps McGarrett was thinking literally, about future inclusion in this *Dictionary of Teleliteracy*, when he said, "Book 'em, Dan-o!"

Hee Haw. *1969–71, CBS; 1971–93, syndicated.* Here's one measure of the durability of this country-music variety show: it premiered on CBS just as the network dumped *The Smothers Brothers Comedy Hour*, and survived for almost a quarter-century. CBS dumped *Hee Haw*, too, as part of its "rural purge" of 1971 (other victims included *The Beverly Hillbillies* and *Green Acres*), but *Hee Haw* moved immediately and successfully to first-run syndication. *Hee Haw* was designed like *Laugh-In* with musical interludes, but the fast-paced jokes in *Hee Haw* were decidedly and deliberately not topical. In fact, the cornball humor was so irrelevant and undated that it eventually became the cause of the show's undoing: a year's worth of vintage *Hee Haw* shows performed so well in syndication that the program's distributors decided in 1993 to shut down production and stop making new ones. Buck Owens and Roy Clark cohosted the series until 1986, when Clark took over solo; the music was as good as the jokes were bad, but eventually the mainstreaming of country music gave artists other outlets—including the entirety of cable TV's The Nashville Network—that were unavailable when *Hee Haw* began. One little-known *Hee Haw* fact I can't resist sharing: in 1978, *Hee Haw* launched a syndicated sitcom-variety show spinoff, *Hee Haw Honeys*, that lasted two seasons. The star of this horrible show was actress and singer Kathie Lee Johnson, who played Kathie Honey—and who is better known today under her married name, Kathie Lee Gifford, cohost of *Live! with Regis & Kathie Lee*.

Highway Patrol. *1955–59, syndicated.* Broderick Crawford cut such a striking no-nonsense figure as the star of this low-budget cop show that, in the decades since, only Jack Webb's Joe Friday has been lampooned more by comics and filmmakers poking fun at the genre. The theme music, remembered by many, is less distinctively original: in fact, it was the same exact theme used for radio's *Mr. District Attorney* series sixteen years previously. On *Highway Patrol*, Crawford's Dan Matthews was just about the whole show, barking into his squad-car radio with the kinds of coded commands kids loved to imitate, including "Twenty-one fifty bye!" and the one he helped make famous, "Ten-four!" In 1992, a syndicated series appeared called *Real Stories of the Highway Patrol*, but it was merely another "reality TV" variation of *COPS*. Before too long, perhaps even by the time this is published, that new *Highway Patrol* is bound to be "ten-four"—over and out.

Hill Street Blues. *1981–87, NBC.* It's hard to remember, but there was a time when hand-held camerawork on a drama series was more innovative than imitative. Although *St. Elsewhere* edged it out as the best drama series of the eighties, *Hill Street Blues* stands alone as *the* most influential series of its decade. Creators Steven Bochco and Michael Kozoll based the look and feel of the show on *The Police Tapes*, a striking documentary by Alan and Susan Raymond which profiled and tagged along with cops from the South Bronx. (Eventually, the series *COPS* would cop a similar attitude.) The documentary feel of the precredits sequence of *Hill Street*, with the jerky camerawork and Altmanesque overlapping dialogue, made the show stand out immediately, and favorably, from other offerings at the time it premiered. That opening sequence also gave *Hill Street* its most lasting and quotable moment: the late Michael Conrad, as Sergeant Phil Esterhaus, warning his troops, "Let's be *careful* out there!" Only the theme song by Mike Post, with its quiet piano opening, is as resonant today. The importance of *Hill Street* hardly can be overstated, yet this much-admired, often-imitated cop show didn't emerge from a vacuum. Its tricky mixture of comedy and drama had been established in *Lou Grant*, the messy and unpredictable resolutions to dramatic situations was an outgrowth of Bruce Paltrow's *The White Shadow* (for which Bochco wrote) and Bochco's own *Paris*, and the seeds of what became *Hill Street* were sown rather directly in an unsold 1978 pilot project, *Operating Room*, written by Paltrow and Bochco and featuring future *Hill Street* players Barbara Bosson and Barbara Babcock. The latter's portrayal of the unabashedly sensual Grace Gardner was a highlight of *Hill Street*, as were scenes of Daniel J. Travanti's Captain Frank Furillo showing up unexpectedly at an Alcoholics Anonymous meeting and inside a Catholic confessional, and Dennis Franz's portrayals of two different black-sheep cops, and strong weekly work by so many regulars that they may as well be praised as a whole, rather than by name. (To go without praising Veronica Hamel as Joyce Davenport, Furillo's eventual wife, would be an unforgivable oversight.) The formula of lacing and overlapping plot lines throughout several episodes, so that major stories and smaller subplots kept propelling the series forward, made *Hill Street Blues* a novel TV show in more ways than one. The precinct house was burned down in the finale, but the flames from *Hill Street* will continue to flicker for a long, long time. It set a standard to which all new ensemble drama series continue to aspire, and which only a few have managed to equal or surpass.

Hogan's Heroes. *1965–71, CBS.* This certainly ranks as one of the most politically incorrect sitcom premises of all time: laughs and hijinks at a German P.O.W. camp. *Hogan's Heroes* borrowed its basic premise from the 1953 film *Stalag 17*, but exaggerated the comedy to make the show's base of operations, Stalag 13, look more like a day camp for the multiethnic prisoners "guarded" by the inept Nazis. John Banner's cuddly Sergeant Hans Schultz, with his persistent "I see nothing, *noth*-ing!" disavowals, was about as menacing as Barney the Dinosaur, and the whole series trivialized the Nazi regime in a way that seems almost unthinkable, and certainly unacceptable, a few decades later. For World War II to get stuck with *Hogan's Heroes* as one of its most successful representative sitcoms, while the Korean War got *M*A*S*H*, hardly seems fair. *Hogan's Heroes* was quite popular, though, even among the veterans' groups that would have been most justified in raising objections.

Werner Klemperer's Commandant Wilhelm Klink and Bob Crane's Robert Hogan were accepted, and enjoyed, as the cartoonish caricatures they were. Klink, in a way, was Sylvester the Cat to Hogan's Tweety Bird: the former kept the latter caged, but the latter clearly ran the roost.

Hollywood Squares. *1966–80, NBC; 1972–80, 1986–89, syndicated.* For much of its run, this series presented a gallery of such past-their-prime celebrities that the title could be taken to mean more than just tic-tac-toe. But long before *The Love Boat* or *Fantasy Island* established themselves as welcome ports of call for stars whose trajectories were past their zenith, *Hollywood Squares* reserved room (albeit a relatively small amount of square footage) for the likes of George Gobel, Cliff Arquette (a.k.a. Charley Weaver), Wally Cox, and Rose Marie, and literally put them on pedestals. The show also enhanced, as well as prolonged, some careers, as in the cases of Paul Lynde and, inexplicably, John Davidson and Shadoe Stevens. With its yes-or-no format, neither the celebrities nor the competing contestants were required to demonstrate any actual knowledge, other than to decide whether "X" or "O" marked the spot. It was no great loss, therefore, when *Hollywood Squares*—after nearly a quarter-century on television—became an ex-show. Or, more appropriately, an "X" show.

Holocaust. *1978, NBC.* Written specifically for television by Gerald Green, *Holocaust* was, like *Roots*, one of the few ambitious and important miniseries to make a major impact. To this day, *Holocaust* ranks tied for seventh (with *Fatal Vision*) on the list of highest-rated miniseries of all time. More an historical tapestry than a docudrama, it created fictional characters—stressing two Jewish families and one German clan—and placed them in proximity to actual events and figures from the German campaign in World War II. Two relative unknowns, Michael Moriarty (as a budding Nazi) and Meryl Streep (as one of many victims of the Nazi reign of terror), were among those winning Emmys for their roles; James Woods, as Streep's devoted husband, should have won one too. Sam Wanamaker, Fritz Weaver, Rosemary Harris, David Warner, and Blanche Baker (another Emmy-winner) were impressive also, and of all the subsequent TV dramas exploring the Nazi concentration camps, only two equal *Holocaust* in their intensity. One is 1980's *Playing for Time*, a telemovie starring Vanessa Redgrave and Jane Alexander; the other is *War and Remembrance*, where the scenes of internment are as harrowing as the other scenes are unintentionally laughable.

Homicide: Life on the Street. *1993–   , NBC.* This outstanding cop series premiered immediately after *Super Bowl XXVII*, but, despite appearing on several nights and in many different time slots, never has drawn or held a sizable audience; it was only in late 1995 that it began to regularly outdraw any of its network competitors. Yet the show's quality is so high, and its acting, direction, and writing so distinct, it deserves inclusion here. Despite all the headlines and attention given to *NYPD Blue*, its contemporary counterpart at ABC, *Homicide* is the superior program. Series creator Paul Attanasio, who also wrote the film *Quiz Show,* based the series on David Simon's book *Homicide: A Year on the Killing Streets,* and teamed with executive producers Barry Levinson and Tom Fontana to mount one of television's all-time best police series. Set in Baltimore, the boyhood home Levinson embraced as far back as his film *Diner, Homicide* crackles with strong characters, lively writing, and an unusually high level of intensity and wit—virtues associated strongly with Fontana, one of the key writer-producers on *St. Elsewhere.* Visually, the hallmark of *Homicide* is its "stutter-step" style of editing. During production, scenes are filmed completely from start to finish using a single camera, then repeated again and again with the camera placed at different angles. When the pieces are assembled in the editing room, key lines of dialogue or bits of action and reaction are repeated, like a truly instant replay, from one of those different angles. The jarring effect is intentional and incredibly effective, especially during the interrogation-room sequences in which *Homicide* has no peer. One first-season, Emmy-winning episode written by Fontana, "Three Men and Adena," was devoted wholly to a volatile session "in the box," with detectives Frank Pembleton (Andre Braugher) and Tim Bayliss (Kyle Secor) given twelve hours to extract a confession from a suspected murderer (guest star Moses Gunn) or let him walk. Because of the show's production style and the superb acting of the three men, that *Homicide* episode was unforgettably riveting, credible, and surprising—especially since, in the end, the detectives failed. The "win some, lose some" universe of *Homicide* is reflected, constantly and unblinkingly, by the precinct's assignment board, on which are listed the names and file numbers of each detective's murder cases. When a new case is entered on the board, the name is written in red; if and when the murder is solved, the name is erased and rewritten in black (the more red on the board, the more unavenged blood on the streets). And unlike most cop shows, *Homicide,* borrowing a page from *St. Elsewhere,* occasionally puts its characters in genuine jeopardy. One three-part episode, in which three of the detectives were gunned down during a routine arrest, spent several episodes dealing with the physical and emotional consequences of that violent attack. None of the characters died that time, but *Homicide* has lost several detectives, and actors, over the years: Jon Polito's Steve Crosetti committed suicide, and both Ned Beatty's Stanley Bolander and Daniel Baldwin's Beau Felton were suspended after inappropriate behavior at a police convention. Losing actors of that caliber would cripple a lesser show, but *Homicide* still boasted such fine performers as Yaphet Kotto (as Al Giardello), Melissa Leo (Kay Howard), and Richard Belzer (John Munch). Beatty, especially, is missed, but Secor and Braugher, as partners Bayliss and Pembleton, are the real stars of *Homicide.* Secor is excellent in every scene, and Braugher, quite simply, is the best dramatic actor working on TV in the nineties. *Homicide* also has the benefit of some superb guest stars, including some who have worked previously with Levinson or Fontana. Robin Williams *(Good Morning, Vietnam)* was featured in one potent episode as a Baltimore tourist whose wife was killed before his eyes, and Bruno Kirby, also of *Good Morning, Vietnam,* played an ex-convict determined to kill Pembleton for sending him to prison. Another series triumph, "Colors," was an engrossing episode about bigotry, and its guest star was David Morse of *St. Elsewhere*. (One other *St. Elsewhere* connection was the "inside joke" quotient, employed sparingly but still cleverly by Fontana: in one *Homicide* episode, a visit to a local hospital included an announcement on the loudspeaker paging "Dr. Ehrlich," a sly reference to one of the former *St. Elsewhere* physicians.) Other classic *Homicide* episodes include the three-parter about a female serial killer (with, again, some absolutely stunning interrogation work by Braugher as Pembleton), and the episode in which guest star Adrienne Shelly played an S&M shopkeeper who lured the straitlaced Bayliss to take a walk on the wild side. *Homicide*, too, is on the wild side—raw, powerful, and unpredictable.

Honeymooners, The. *1955–56, CBS.* Baby, it's the greatest. When it comes to TV entertainment, there isn't a better example of televiteracy than this classic sitcom, which has become so ubiquitous, familiar, and beloved in syndication that it ranks as a genuine TV treasure. Jackie Gleason's Ralph Kramden, as much as Willy Loman in *Death of a Salesman,* epitomizes the American working-class man as perpetual dreamer and underdog. Art Carney's Ed Norton, the perfect TV sidekick, forged with Gleason a comic partnership every bit the equal of such great comedy teams as Laurel and Hardy—and they were but two sides of a potent triangle, since Audrey Meadows as Alice, Ralph's understanding yet strong-willed wife, was just as seminal an ingredient. (Joyce Randolph as Trixie, Norton's wife, pulled the least weight among the starring quartet.) From Ralph's roaring threats ("Bang! Zoom!," "One of these days, Alice, pow!—Right in the kisser!") to his bear-hug compliments ("Baby, you're the greatest") and his endearing nervous stutter ("Hummana-hummana"), and from Norton's fussy hand gestures to his friendly greeting ("Hey there, Ralphie boy!"), much of the thirty-nine episodes of *The Honeymooners* have passed into what might be called *public domain*. The theme song, the dingy Brooklyn apartment, Norton's inimitable way of addressing the ball in golf ("Hello, ball!"), the Raccoon lodge, the schemes and dreams—all of it, by now, is an indelible part of popular culture. So much has been written about Gleason and *The Honeymooners,* including John O'Hara's description of Ralph Kramden as "a character that we might be getting from Mr. Dickens if he were writing for TV," there seems little point in adding more. Except that, to pursue the literary parallel, the legacy of *The Honeymooners* has been enhanced in more recent years by the discovery of long-dormant equivalents of sequels and rough drafts. The "lost" episodes, culled from kinescopes of the CBS variety series *The Jackie Gleason Show,* were "Honeymooners" sketches of varying lengths, starring the identical cast as the one-season sitcom; some predated the "official" version of the series, while others came after *The Honeymooners* was canceled. The Museum of Television & Radio (then known as the Museum of Broadcasting) located four such sketches in the CBS program vaults, mounted an exhibition in 1985 generating substantial excitement and acclaim, and then learned that Gleason himself had preserved copies privately of all his CBS variety shows, including the ones with "Honeymooners" sketches. These were released to TV as the so-called lost episodes, though other such skits—from Gleason's pre-*Honeymooners*, pre-CBS showcase, DuMont's *Cavalcade of Stars*—were thought to be *truly* lost. In fact, it was because of DuMont's unwillingness to archive its programs that Gleason began stockpiling his own at CBS. Yet in 1993, the Museum of Television & Radio struck another mother lode, locating and exhibiting the private kinescope collection of Snag Werris, a veteran Gleason writer who had preserved many of the *Cavalcade* shows from the early fifties. These included such "rough draft" treats as the very first "Honeymooners" sketch from October 5, 1951, starring Pert Kelton as Alice and featuring Carney not as Ed Norton, but as a confused policeman. (Another trivia bonus: when Carney did appear for the first time as Ed Norton, on the second "Honeymooners" sketch televised on November 2, 1951, Norton's wife Trixie was played, for that initial appearance, by Elaine Stritch.) The unearthing and viewing of these early treats is a feast for scholars of the medium, and certainly for the fan-club members of R.A.L.P.H. (Royal Association for the Longevity and Preservation of the Honeymooners); The Disney Channel made the feast available to all of its subscribers by televising a collection of the sketches, seen on TV for the first time in more than forty years, in a special called *The Honeymooners Really Lost Debut Episodes*. But it will forever be the "classic thirty-nine," the episodes that have been in syndication for decades, that define *The Honeymooners* and protect its claim to TV immortality. When Gleason himself was asked why *The Honeymooners* sitcom episodes had been embraced by so many for so long, his explanation was a lot shorter than this entry. It was, in fact, four words long: "Because they were funny."

Hopalong Cassidy. *1948–49, 1952, syndicated; 1949–51, NBC*. As both on-screen hero and off-screen entrepeneur, William Boyd was bold and victorious. Boyd appeared for the first time as Hopalong Cassidy ("Hoppy" to friends and fans), the original Western hero to wear black, in 1935, and made sixty-five subsequent "B" Western features as the same popular character. As early as 1945, when only a few hundred TV sets had been produced for general consumption, some of these *Hopalong Cassidy* films were being shown on New York television. By 1948, edited versions of Hoppy's old adventures, complete with new narration and sometimes a bit of fresh footage, were offered to local stations as a package of sixty-minute film features—making *Hopalong Cassidy* the first one-hour drama series in syndicated TV history. Boyd mortgaged everything he owned to buy the *Hopalong Cassidy* television rights that year, and soon became a millionaire. Boyd's heroic cowboy character, he was Hoppy to learn, caught on so quickly and fervently that he became TV's first big Western hit. Meeting the seemingly insatiable demand for new adventures of Hopalong and his horse, Topper, Boyd took the unprecedented step of filming a *new* series of *Hopalong Cassidy* adventures specifically for TV in 1952—at age sixty. You'd think, by that time, the hero should have been renamed Limpalong, yet Boyd looked as fit as when he first played the character seventeen years earlier. Boyd also maintained interest in the series, and increased his own principal, by merchandising everything from bread and bicycles to watches and wallpaper with the Hopalong Cassidy name and image. Before either *The Lone Ranger* or *Davy Crockett*, Boyd proved exactly how much gold was in them thar TV hills.

Howdy Doody Show, The. *1947–60, NBC*. In all of TV history, there are two programs whose massive initial samplings were at least partly attributable to major winter snowstorms. *Roots*, in 1977, was one; *Puppet Playhouse Presents*, thirty years earlier, was the other. The night it premiered, two days after Christmas, so much snow fell in Manhattan that Broadway went dark that night, and vaudeville and movie palaces closed their doors. Up and down NBC's northeastern corridor of stations, the weather wasn't much better—so when *Puppet Playhouse* was unveiled that afternoon at five, giving housebound kids something to watch before dinner, the response was immediate and amazing. So, in retrospect, was the approving tone of the *Variety* review it generated, reflecting more relief than apprehension at the new medium's potentially mesmerizing effect on young viewers. "In the middle-class home, there is perhaps nothing as welcome to the mother as something that will keep the small fry intently absorbed and out of possible mischief," *Variety* wrote. "This program can almost be guaranteed to pin down the squirmiest of the brood." In 1949, that still-snowballing show would be retitled *The Howdy Doody Show*, reflecting the popularity of its main marionette. (The year before, as a phenomenally successful publicity stunt, Howdy had run for president, campaigning as "the only candidate *completely* made of wood.") "Buffalo" Bob Smith was the creator and host of the show, and therefore the man most responsible for the unforgettable elements in this pioneering children's program. One of his best ideas was to get a bunch of little kids into the studio to serve as a live audience—then and forever known as the Peanut Gallery. Other *Howdy Doody* highlights included Clarabell the silent clown (played over the run of the series by three different actors, including future *Captain Kangaroo* Bob Keeshan), squirting seltzer and honking horns as the Peanut Gallery squealed with delight. And Buffalo Bob's opening line—"Say, kids! What time is it?"—to which the Gallery, and all the young viewers at home, would respond by screaming, "It's *Howdy Doody* time!" And the theme song, and the beautiful Princess Summerfall Winterspring (played by Judy Tyler, who went on to star opposite Elvis Presley in *Jailhouse Rock*), and the enthusiastic cry of "Kowabunga!" by Bill LeCornec's Chief Thunderthud, and the no-strings-attached character of Gumby, who was spun off into his own series (see separate listing), and a lot, lot more. In 1960, after thirteen years on the air, NBC cut Howdy's strings, but Smith and company went out with a poignant parting gesture that ranks among TV's finest finales. All during that last show, Smith had promised that Clarabell, then played by Lew Anderson, would have a special surprise—and the program concluded with a closeup of the formerly silent clown, who had uttered not a word in the history of *Howdy Doody*. Fighting back tears, in a choked whisper, Anderson's Clarabell looked right into the camera and said, "Good-bye, kids." The show, like the series, was over—and there wasn't a dry eye in Doodyville.

Huckleberry Hound. *1958–61, syndicated*. This was the first full-length cartoon series created by William Hanna and Joseph Barbera, and was the show that first featured their most popular creation, Yogi Bear—whose "smarter than the average bear" catch phrase and "Hey, Boo Boo!" call to his little buddy became as familiar as their animated habitat of Jellystone Park. Personally, I preferred the next Hanna-Barbera effort, the 1959–61 *Quick Draw McGraw*, which starred a Western six-gun hero who happened to be a horse. (Somehow, this worked a lot better than the recent CBS cartoon series *The C.O.W.-Boys of Moo Mesa*, which had *cows* as the heroes, and even featured a comely cowgirl with cleavage, a sight that was udderly ridiculous.) Sometimes, in a *Zorro*-type disguise, he did double duty as a caped crusader named El Kabong. *Quick Draw* featured a line I still quote regularly—"*I'll* do the thinnin' around here, Baba Looey!"—as well as the singularly silly Snagglepuss, the lisping Shakespearean lion who left every scene with a jaunty, and much-imitated, cry of "Exit, stage left!" Actually, Snagglepuss, like Yogi, exited to the *Yogi Bear* spinoff show in the sixties, but the original shows that spawned them deserve the lion's share of the credit. After all, there ain't nothin' like a *Hound* dog.

Hullabaloo. *1965–67, NBC*. These days, despite a set of home-video compilations in the midnineties, there isn't that much hullabaloo about *Hullabaloo*, the prime-time midsixties music series that was on the air concurrently with *Shindig!* ABC's *Shindig!* had a better roster of guests, was a better show, and enjoys a more resonant reputation. (Some of the things that made *Hullabaloo* stand out are things best left forgotten, like Jerry Lewis and his son Gary teaming for an inimitable version of "Help.") *Hullabaloo*, though, had one memorable attribute that *Shindig!* lacked: those dancing ladies in suspended cages, a memory that persists even though this series vanished long a-go-go.

Huntley-Brinkley Report, The. *1956–70, NBC*. Still the most famous news team in broadcast history, Chet Huntley and David Brinkley were paired as a tandem act at a time when the move was more motivated more by desperation than innovation. CBS already had pegged Walter Cronkite, rather than star newsman Douglas Edwards, as the "anchor man" of its 1956 Republican political convention coverage, and NBC felt it necessary to pull talent from within its ranks as well. But instead of going with one talking head, NBC went with two, and the contrast between Huntley's mature solemnity and Brinkley's acerbic wit made NBC's news team an immediate hit. How immediate? So immediate that when it came time for the Democratic convention, CBS recruited Edward R. Murrow to coanchor with Cronkite, an arrangement no more popular with either of them than with most of the viewers. At NBC, a mere two months after the conventions were concluded, so was the seven-year run of John Cameron Swayze on *Camel News Caravan*. In its place was *The Huntley-Brinkley Report*, which ran for fourteen years, each night with the same familiar opening and closing. The program started with majestic theme music—lifted outright, of course, from the start of the second movement of Beethoven's Ninth Symphony. It closed with that popular pop-culture signoff, the "Good night, David," "Good night, Chet" exchange between Huntley and Brinkley that was endlessly parroted and parodied. The closing proved so durable that it was recycled as an homage, word for word, at the end of the inaugural broadcast of *The CBS Evening News with Dan Rather and Connie Chung* in 1993 (Chung took the "Good night, Chet" line, Rather the "Good night, David" reply). The good-luck charm didn't work, though, because the Rather-Chung anchor duo lasted only two years, twelve fewer than the Huntley-Brinkley pairing. Huntley broke up the team, and *The Huntley-Brinkley Report*, by retiring in 1970. Brinkley, whose outspokenness and playful grumpiness became even more charming with age, found a new career at ABC, revitalizing the Sunday morning public affairs show with his lively and informative *This Week with David Brinkley*. At the end of 1995, a generation after the cancellation of *The Huntley-Brinkley Report*, Brinkley wasn't finished Chet.

I

· ·

I, Claudius. *1977–78, PBS.* In 1937, Charles Laughton undertook the role of the stuttering, seemingly simple farmer who ultimately became emperor of Rome. His performance was mesmerizing, but, unfortunately, incomplete. That version of *I, Claudius*, beset by all sorts of production and personal problems, folded midway through filming; the often brilliant outtakes survive thanks to a 1965 BBC-TV documentary, *The Epic That Never Was*. In 1976, the BBC used that documentary, and the original novels by Robert Graves, as inspiration, and mounted its own version of *I, Claudius*. This one was complete, and was a complete success as well. Imported by *Masterpiece Theatre* the following year, it made Derek Jacobi, who starred as Claudius, an internationally respected star. Even though some of the makeup and technical direction verged on sloppiness, the devious doings of *I, Claudius* were so refreshingly atypical of public television that the thirteen-part miniseries was a major hit with viewers and critics alike. What else on PBS was nasty, funny, *and* kinky, other than William F. Buckley on *Firing Line?* John Hurt as the demented Caligula, and Sian Phillips as the livid Livia, contributed performances as potent as Jacobi's, and watching reruns these days offers the added treat of watching a younger and hairier Patrick Stewart, long before he took command of the *Enterprise* on *Star Trek: The Next Generation,* in the key supporting role of Sejanus.

I Dream of Jeannie. *1965–70, NBC.* The season after ABC's *Bewitched* caught viewers in its fantasy-female spell, NBC uncorked its own version, starring Barbara Eden as a genie named Jeannie. *Bewitched* had the better actress in Elizabeth Montgomery, but *I Dream of Jeannie* had the better costar in Larry Hagman, who was as charmingly silly here as he was charmingly sinister on *Dallas*. Both *Bewitched* and *I Dream of Jeannie* presented

LEFT: *Hill Street Blues,* with Daniel J. Travanti and Veronica Hamel.
RIGHT: *Holocaust,* with Meryl Streep and Blanche Baker.

LEFT: *I, Claudius,* with Derek Jacobi as the stuttering emperor.
RIGHT: *I Love Lucy,* with Lucille Ball and Desi Arnaz in a backstage moment from 1952.

beautiful, all-powerful women who were more than happy to be subservient to their mortal and rather unimaginative men—but interestingly, both of these sitcoms found ways to placate their female stars, and perhaps the viewers, by having their leading ladies show up occasionally in lookalike dual roles. Eden's Jeannie II, like Montgomery's Serena, was flagrantly sexy, disdainful of mere mortal men, and more than willing to use her powers for personal gain and pleasure (which, naturally, makes a lot more sense). In the case of *I Dream of Jeannie*, this female duality harks back to *The Patty Duke Show*—which, like *Jeannie*, was devised by Sidney Sheldon, later to gain best-seller fame with such glamorous gunk as the book and miniseries versions of *Rage of Angels*. Time was less kind to Sheldon's bottled-up creation, though. Even with Eden's formerly obscured navel in full view, her subsequent telemovie sequels, 1985's *I Dream of Jeannie: 15 Years Later* and 1991's *I Still Dream of Jeannie*, were more like nightmares.

I'll Fly Away. *1991–93, NBC; 1993, PBS.* It may be wishful thinking to put this high-quality, low-rated drama series on the list—but even if it *isn't* rediscovered and cherished in the coming years, it deserves to be. *I'll Fly Away* explored the civil rights movement in the late fifties through two very different points of view: a white attorney in the Deep South, and his "colored" domestic. Sam Waterston and Regina Taylor starred, and their portrayals were as subtle, challenging, and engrossing as the scripts. One scene, in which Taylor's Lilly Harper pushed Waterston's Forrest Bedford for a meager raise, generated as much tension and drama as anything else on TV that season. In other episodes, when Forrest got involved with investigating the local Ku Klux Klan, *I'll Fly Away* probed at the roots of racism in the fifties just as the nation in the nineties was being tested by the verdict in the Rodney King case. After NBC canceled *I'll Fly Away* in 1993, PBS made room for a repeat run, and even committed enough money to mount a two-hour telemovie finale later that year. Written by series creators Joshua Brand and John Falsey, the *I'll Fly Away: Then and Now* telemovie wrapped up the series by vaulting forward, in certain scenes, to the present day—and revealing, at the climax, that Lilly had left the Bedford household to become a published, well-respected writer. Miss Jane Pittman would have been proud.

I Love Lucy. *1951–57, CBS.* Simply put, Lucille Ball did as many singularly memorable things in front of the cameras as behind them. Her performances helped create a handful of true TV classics, where just a few words of description evoke an utterly hilarious set piece of small-screen comedy. What's no less impressive, those "best of the best" episodes are spread rather evenly throughout the six-season run of the series, attesting to its overall comic consistency. There was 1952's "Lucy Does a TV Commercial" (and gets drunk on Vitameatavegamin), the same year's "Job Switching" (in which Lucy and Vivian Vance's Ethel try to keep up with the conveyer belt at a candy factory), 1953's "Lucy Goes to the Hospital" (and gives birth to Little Ricky), 1955's "Harpo Marx" (in which Harpo and Lucy, dressed identically as Harpo, reenact the mirror scene from *Duck Soup*), and 1956's "Lucy's Italian Movie" (in which Lucy stomps grapes and gets a bunch of laughs). Harpo's guest appearance was especially fitting, because Lucille Ball did enough comedy, verbal and physical, to qualify as a Marx Sister—or as TV's closest female equivalent of a Charlie Chaplin, Harold Lloyd, or Buster Keaton. As for her husband and costar, Desi Arnaz, he contributed a mean version of "Babalu," dozens of different line readings of the word "Lucy," and managed to immortalize one of the most seemingly forgettable lines in all of TV history: "Hi, honey, I'm home!" However, his character of Ricky Ricardo had less impact, in the long run, than Arnaz's insistence that *I Love Lucy* be produced on the West Coast rather than in New York, with each episode's performance captured by multiple cameras and distributed on film rather than kinescope. Those technical innovations changed the TV industry, hastened its transplantation to Hollywood, and guaranteed that *I Love Lucy* would be repeated endlessly, and very profitably, in syndication. When it premiered, *I Love Lucy* benefited greatly from following the era's most popular prime-time series, *Arthur Godfrey's Talent Scouts*, and was an instant hit. By the time Lucy Ricardo was shown in the family way in 1953 (an unprecedented plot line at a time when even the word "pregnant" was forbidden on TV), *I Love Lucy* was so popular that it regularly was drawing ninety percent or more of the viewers watching TV at that hour. More than forty years later, *I Love Lucy* remains, with *The Honeymooners*, one of the medium's most famous and familiar sitcoms, with its style saluted and parodied on everything from *Kate & Allie* to "Weird Al" Yankovic's "Ricky" video parody. After *I Love Lucy*, Lucille Ball moved on, without Arnaz, to *The Lucy Show* (1962–68) and *Here's Lucy* (1968–74), but the *Lucy* I loved most was the original series, with that fabulous theme song, those outrageous physical gags, and Lucy's trademark "Waaaaah!" One fast footnote: many of the early scripts for *I Love Lucy* were strongly "inspired" by stories from the CBS 1948–50 CBS radio comedy *My Favorite Husband*, which starred Lucille Ball as the rather ditzy housewife and was concocted by writers who moved on to *I Love Lucy*. Meanwhile, a more "official" TV version of *My Favorite Husband*, with that identical title, was televised in 1953, starring Joan Caulfield, but was nobody's favorite at all. We loved *Lucy*.

Incredible Machine, The. See *Nova*.

In Living Color. *1990–94, Fox.* When at its outrageous best, this series earns "two snaps up"—one of many quotable remarks from its flagrantly gay "Men on . . . " critics Blaine and Antoine, played by Damon Wayans and David Alan Grier (as, basically, the modern counterparts of Ernie Kovacs's Percy Dovetonsils). No sketch-variety series since *Saturday Night Live* and *Second City TV*, and no minority-dominated series ever, generated as many breakout characters and sketches as this refreshingly irreverent Keenen Ivory Wayans series. No other show on TV would have the audacity, much less the talent, to imitate Mike Tyson, Sugar Ray Leonard, and Muhammad Ali (played by Keenen Ivory Wayans, Tommy Davidson, and Grier, respectively) in a skit called "Three Champs and a Baby," or to lampoon *Star Trek* characters and a controversial Islamic leader in a sketch titled "The Wrath of Farrakhan." *In*

Living Color, in its original incarnation, also gave us, among other things, Damon Wayans as sour old Homey the clown ("Homey don't play that"), Kim Wayans as a frighteningly close approximation of Grace Jones, and the hip-hop Fly Girls, choreographed very memorably indeed by Rosie Perez. Its most famous alumnus, though, was Jim Carrey, who had begun the series as the token white guy and ended it, following the departure of the Wayans clan in 1992 and 1993, as the show's star. Within two years, Carrey would be one of Hollywood's biggest stars as well, thanks to a string of hit comedy films.

Iran-Contra Hearings. *1987, various networks.* After months in which his only comments to reporters were variations on "Have a nice day," Oliver North took the oath instead of the Fifth and testified for seven days in July as the key witness in the government hearings investigating a possible "arms for hostages" deal. The hearings made temporary celebrities of North's secretary (Fawn Hall) and lawyer (Brendan Sullivan, who responded to a committee member's objection to *his* many objections by saying he was not "a potted plant"), and a permanent celebrity of North, who played to the cameras emotionally and flawlessly, if not necessarily convincingly. Instead of the made-up legal wranglings of *L.A. Law,* it made for a riveting summer series that could have been called *D.C. Law,* and, once North took the stand, all the networks covered it. Two years later, David Keith starred as the former lieutenant colonel in a (not very good) CBS miniseries called *Guts & Glory: The Rise and Fall of Oliver North;* in 1992, North himself showed up in prime time, playing himself as a guest star on NBC's *Wings*—his first move in years that was announced in advance and conducted in plain sight. He sought, and won, the Virginia Republican Party nomination for the United States Senate in 1994, but lost the election. He did, however, win a seat elsewhere, hosting his own nationally syndicated radio talk show—as did fellow conservative (and covert) Washington insider G. Gordon Liddy.

I Spy. *1965–68, NBC.* As a secret agent show at the apex of the James Bond craze, *I Spy* was fun on several counts. It was shot each week at a different foreign location (real ones, too, unlike those ersatz backlot "countries" seen on *Mission: Impossible* and *The Man from U.N.C.L.E.*), its spies had hedonistic cover identities—as a tennis pro (played by Robert Culp) and his physical trainer (Bill Cosby)—and there was a freewheeling, improvisational feel to the conversations between the two characters that made *I Spy* seem almost as much an attitude as an adventure series. The theme song, with its gunshot accents, is still remembered, but nothing about *I Spy* is more memorable or important than its status as the first prime-time drama series to give equal, costarring status to an African-American. Previously, executive producer Sheldon Leonard had helped break down barriers with the "That's My Boy??" episode of *The Dick Van Dyke Show,* in which Rob's fears that he had been given the wrong baby at the hospital were calmed when he set up a confrontational meeting with the "other" family, only to learn they were black. (The resultant laugh was the series' longest.) For *I Spy,* Leonard relied upon the stand-up comedy skills of young Cosby, as well as his good looks and obvious intelligence, to make his character of Alexander Scott acceptable to a mass audience, and Cosby learned on the job and delivered magnificently. Robert Culp's playful and generous portrayal of Kelly Robinson was just as important an ingredient, and the show worked chiefly because of them, not because of the show's locations or plots. A quarter-century after *I Spy* folded up shop, Culp and Cosby teamed up again for a CBS reunion telemovie, 1994's *I Spy Returns*, which turned the reins over to a new generation of characters: Scott's daughter Nicole (played by Salli Richardson) and Robinson's son Bennett (George Newbern). The telemovie was a tepid one, though, and the reins stopped there.

I've Got a Secret. *1952–67, 1976, CBS; 1972, syndicated.* One secret about this long-running game show is that it was co-created by Allan Sherman of "Hello, Muddah" fame. Another is that this lightest of formats was staffed by one of the sharpest and funniest of celebrity panels, including lengthy stints by Bill Cullen and Steve Allen (both of whom ended up hosting), Faye Emerson, Jayne Meadows, Henry Morgan, Bess Myerson, and Betsy Palmer. Garry Moore hosted for the first dozen years, then quit this series and *The Garry Moore Show* at the same time—Moore or less.

J

Jack Benny Program, The. *1950–64, CBS; 1964–65, NBC.* In 1951, after completing his first two TV shows, Jack Benny wrote an article in *Collier's* magazine, asking—but seriously, folks—"Can a comedian who is accepted week after week for ten or fifteen years on radio repeat the same record on television?" With all due humility, Benny thought it was possible, and he went out and proved it. Not only did Benny's show outlast *Collier's*, it lasted for fifteen seasons, making it the most durable sitcom in TV history. (Notably, the runner-up in this "tenured TV" category is *The Adventures of Ozzie & Harriet*, which ran for fourteen seasons, and, like Benny's TV show, previously had enjoyed a lengthy reign on radio.) *The Jack Benny Program* came to television two weeks after Benny's close friend, George Burns, began *his* show with Gracie Allen on CBS, and both shows played impishly with TV's conventions from the start. Benny, like Burns, used his own name for his TV "character," and during each week's show slipped effortlessly from the "real world" of hosting to the "sitcom world" of his fictional private life. Year after year, Benny established and exploited his comic trademarks—his character's cheapness, vanity (thirty-nine years old and holding), intentionally bad violin playing (even of his theme song, "Love in Bloom"), and hand-on-face stare—to classic heights. His sense of timing, particularly in how to hold and ride silences to milk the most laughs, was the best in the business; a generation later, only Bob Newhart comes close to embracing and embodying Benny's silence-is-golden work ethic. Eddie Anderson's gravel-voiced Rochester was Benny's best foil, but Mel Blanc, Don Wilson, Dennis Day, and Benny's real-life wife, Mary Livingstone, added considerable charm, and Benny's guest list .was one of the best in the business: Humphrey Bogart, Marilyn Monroe, Bing Crosby, Bob Hope, Milton Berle, Ginger Rogers, Nat "King" Cole, Jimmy Stewart, Carol Burnett, even Mike Wallace. Most of that, of course, is common knowledge, since *The Jack Benny Program* remains popular on cable even today. However, there is one area in which *The Jack Benny Program* has yet to receive its due credit: its remarkably early and energetic displays of teleliteracy. On his own show, Benny spoofed and re-created many other TV programs, with an uncanny eye for appreciating the best. He took Jackie Gleason's part of Ralph Kramden in a spoof of *The Honeymooners*, Gracie Allen's part (opposite her real-life husband) in a parody of *The George Burns and Gracie Allen Show*, appeared as a contestant on an ersatz version of Groucho Marx's *You Bet Your Life*, and had his staff construct fake *Tonight* show sets so he could pretend to be a guest visiting Jack Paar—and, later, Johnny Carson. Benny was so TV-savvy, in fact, the guests on his final show in 1965 were Tom and Dick Smothers, whose own variety series would have a major impact on TV two years later. Well into the nineties, the spirit of *The Jack Benny Program* was alive, and very well indeed, on *Seinfeld*. In 1995, NBC presented a fine prime-time retrospective special with a self-explanatory title: *Kelsey Grammer Salutes Jack Benny*. As Benny himself might have said: "Well, *I'll* be!"

Jackie Gleason Show, The. *1952–55, 1956–57, 1962–70, CBS.* Just headlining *The Honeymooners* would have been enough to ensure its star one of the top places in TV history, but Jackie Gleason had plenty of other characters up his ample sleeve—Joe the Bartender, Reginald Van Gleason III, and the Poor Soul, just to name a few. Even out of character, as the host of his own variety series, he churned out memorable bits of business, like "How sweet it is!" and, to kick off each show, the exit line, "And awaaaay we go!" The early CBS shows, following on the heels of Gleason's successful stint on *Cavalcade of Stars*, featured fellow *Honeymooners* Art Carney, Joyce Randolph, and Audrey Meadows; Carney returned for the last few seasons, which also featured Sheila MacRae and Jane Kean. The middle years of *The Jackie Gleason Show* included Frank Fontaine as Crazy Guggenheim, a daffy-talking, syrupy-singing performer, but, like the entire stretch after the fall of 1964, are most remembered for being broadcast from Miami, where Gleason had the entire production relocated in a rather astounding example of celebrity clout. (Subsequently, that type of TV-host clout transferred to late-night television, where Johnny Carson, then David Letterman, amassed the popularity and power to call their own shots.) Over the years, Gleason's variety show proudly reflected the tastes and pace of vaudeville and musical theater, down to the Busby Berkeley-style June Taylor Dancers and the curtain-call finale. That dated sensibility eventually spelled curtains for *The Jackie Gleason Show,* although his characters of Reggie and the Poor Soul, especially, have attained a sort of immortality of their own.

Jack LaLanne Show, The. *1958–78, syndicated.* Long before Arnold Schwarzenegger began pumping iron, or Jane Fonda led her first video workout, TV's original fitness freak, Jack LaLanne, was pushing an exercise regimen in his nationally syndicated series. Running for decades, *The Jack LaLanne Show* proved almost as indefatigable as its host. A syndicated TV fixture for years even before Johnny Carson began imitating and lampooning him, LaLanne kept going and going and going . . . and was still going into the nineties (the century's, not his), cohosting an *Amazing Discoveries* infomercial that pushed a power blender known as the Juice Tiger. One thing you've got to say about LaLanne: He's not LaLazy.

Jeffersons, The. *1975–85, CBS.* The theme song of this series was "Movin' on Up," and it was the theme of the plots as well. Sherman Hemsley's George Jefferson, having made a tidy profit in the dry-cleaning business, transplants his family from street-level Queens to high-rise Manhattan. What made this series possible, though, is the neighborhood he left behind. Originally, the Jeffersons were neighbors of the Bunkers, and this series, like *Maude* and *Good Times,* was a successful spinoff of *All in the Family.* On that series, George was a funny acerbic foil to Carroll O'Connor's Archie—a bigot of a different color, just as wrongheaded and spirited in his opinions as his blue-collar, white-skinned adversary. By moving to center stage, and to Manhattan, Hemsley's George Jefferson (and Isabel Sanford's Louise, George's wife, affectionately known as Weezie) notched another small victory when it came to showcasing minorities on prime-time TV, but George, like the show itself, was all bark and no bite. Poorly written and overly strident, *The Jeffersons* was a sitcom for which I never cared very much, although millions of viewers were much more enthusiastic. After many years apart, Hemsley and Sanford began teaming up again in the nineties. In 1993, they reprised their seventies sitcom roles in a touring stage show of *The Jeffersons,* and in the following two years appeared on TV together in guest roles on *Lois & Clark: The New Adventures of Superman, The Fresh Prince of Bel-Air,* and *In the House.* Their career path at that point, you might say, was movin' on down.

Jeopardy! *1964–75, 1978, NBC; 1984– , syndicated.* The category is "game shows for $100." The answer is "the smartest, best, most entertaining game show of all time." The question, of course, is: "What is *Jeopardy!*?" No contest. Just think of what this cerebral contest has given us over the years. There's Don Pardo, whose chores as announcer on *Jeopardy!* led directly to his similar duties on *Saturday Night Live.* There's the unforgettable "think music" played during the Final Jeopardy round—music written by Merv Griffin, who also created the series. There are those harsh buzzer sounds for wrong answers (a sound used by many other game shows as well, but driven by *Jeopardy!* into the common vernacular). And, of course, there are those twin towers of *Jeopardy!* hosts, Art Fleming (for the NBC years) and Alex Trebek (for the still-popular syndicated version). I love the esoteric nature of the show, which is the only game show on television where contestants are expected to display expertise in such categories as "Those Darned Etruscans." Speaking of esoteric: it may or may not come as a surprise that Griffin concocted *Jeopardy!* in direct response to concerns over the quiz-show scandals (by giving the contestants the answers right up front, and making them guess the questions instead). Similarly, it may be relatively common knowledge that NBC nearly passed on the *Jeopardy!* concept as too tough for TV, until an assistant programmer urged his boss to buy the show. But here's the surprising part: that assistant, in the standard *Jeopardy!* form of a question, can be identified by the phrase, "Who is Grant Tinker?" It may have been Tinker's first major lesson that quality, intelligent TV could reap big dividends—a lesson he would later apply to everything from *The Mary Tyler Moore Show* (the first sitcom from his MTM Productions) to *St. Elsewhere* and *Cheers* (shows he nurtured patiently once becoming president of NBC). In the nineties, Trebek began hosting and televising special celebrity *Jeopardy!* tournaments for charity every November. In 1994, that tournament drew one memorable panel composed of Tony Randall, Stefanie Powers, and former General H. Norman Schwarzkopf. As the panelists entered the high-stakes Final Jeopardy round, Powers was basically powerless with $600, but Randall and Schwarzkopf were only $100 apart, with Schwarzkopf boasting $7,000 to Randall's $6,900. All three contestants correctly supplied the question to the Final Jeopardy answer, so the winner that day would be the player who risked the most. Randall wagered $3,000, giving him a temporary taste of victory—but only for a moment, because the former military strategist had bet his entire $7,000, and handily won the game. All's fair in love and war—and *Jeopardy!*

Jetsons, The. *1962–63, ABC; 1985, syndicated.* The most teleliterate thing about this prime-time sci-fi cartoon sitcom is its inexplicably unforgettable theme song, complete with all eleven words of the lyrics: "Meet George Jetson; his boy Elroy; daughter Judy; Jane, his wife." Given that the wife got bottom billing, *The Jetsons* clearly presented an unenlightened perspective, though it was encouraging to note that, in the twenty-first century, George's job at Spacely Sprockets required only a three-day work week, three hours per day. The futuristic flip side of *The Flintstones, The Jetsons* lasted only one season in prime time on ABC, yet those original twenty-four episodes were rerun endlessly on Saturday mornings and in syndication, and eventually found their way to cable's Cartoon Network. In 1985, an inferior second batch of *Jetsons* episodes finally was added to the mix, but that same year the original episodes were improved—relatively speaking—by having their laugh tracks removed. Either way, the only way to truly enjoy this series was to be an indiscriminate Astro-nut. A big-screen version, *Jetsons: The Movie,* appeared in 1990, but its unenthusiastic reception suggested that, when it came to *The Jetsons*, not many people were willing to pay admission to go back to the future.

Jewel in the Crown, The. *1984–85, PBS.* Produced by England's Granada Television in 1983, this fourteen-part miniseries was imported by *Masterpiece*

Theatre the following year, and gave that anthology series a jewel in its crown to rival that of *Brideshead Revisited*, which had been presented in America by *Great Performances* in 1981. The first *Jewel in the Crown* episode, set in India in 1942, unfolded with an interracial romance and a violent rape, setting the stage for a mammoth restaging of the events presented in Paul Scott's *Raj Quartet* books. *The Jewel in the Crown* was embraced at the time as another sterling example of how only the TV miniseries could do true justice to a sprawling and involved narrative, but its reputation now looms larger than any other residual aspect, and its major players, including Charles Dance and Art Malik, have all but abdicated their stellar trajectories.

Jimmy Durante Show, The. *1954–56, NBC.* Most of what "The Great Schnozzola" brought to this TV variety series was carried over from his vaudeville and Broadway days—the catch phrases ("Stop da music!," "I'm mortified!"), the nonsensical asides ("Hot-cha-cha!," "Inka-dinka-doo!"), the rambling song lyrics ("Didja ever have da feelin' dat ya wanted ta go, and still had da feelin' dat ya wanted ta stay?"). But the ending of *The Jimmy Durante Show* provided two treats, one each for the eyes and ears, that were both original to television and destined to live on in the annals of teleliteracy. At the conclusion of each program, Durante would look into the camera and say, somewhat mysteriously but with great flourish, "And good night, Mrs. Calabash, wherever you are." ("Mrs. Calabash" was one of several fictional characters often referred to by Durante, but never heard from directly, on his 1943–50 radio program, also called *The Jimmy Durante Show;* most radio episodes ended with that same cryptic farewell.) On television, Durante would say good night, turn, and walk away from the camera, passing through a series of overhead spotlight beams as he got farther and farther away. It was, and remains, one of the most striking and classy closings to a weekly TV series. Good night, Mr. Durante, wherever you are.

Joe Franklin Show, The. *1950–93, New York local TV. (Titled Joe Franklin's Memory Lane, after first few shows until 1954.) WJZ (now WABC), then WOR (now WWOR).* Nothing made Joe Franklin more famous, or captured his essence more perfectly and lovingly, than Billy Crystal's dead-on impersonation of him on *Saturday Night Live*. "Yes, my friends, this is one for the time capsule. . . . " On *The Joe Franklin Show*, every guest was treated like royalty, even though many of them were like the ex–vaudevillian losers represented by Woody Allen's talent-agent character in *Broadway Danny Rose*. The program was like a daily dose of Jerry Lewis's Labor Day telethon, with show-biz talents and no-talents run together, and often run amok. Yet through sheer longevity, as well as an eagerness to surrender air time to undiscovered artists, Franklin's guest list ended up being impressive as well as eclectic. Everyone from Bing Crosby to Bill Cosby showed up over the years to entertain Franklin's often unrelated questions, as did Ronald Reagan and Madonna. Those two weren't on the same show, but Jack LaLanne and Barbra Streisand were—waiting patiently as Franklin delivered a live testimonial for Royal gelatin. However, on the night in 1958 that Franklin conducted a ninety-minute solo interview with his idol, Eddie Cantor, there were no commercials: Cantor, Franklin thought, deserved to be presented uninterrupted. Franklin's appreciation of show-biz history, from silent films to stage and musical stars, was so strong from the start that he predated teleliteracy. He was, in essence, a walking, talking celebration of vaudevilliteracy. Watching him wend his unpredictable way through each program was a guilty pleasure, but a pleasure nonetheless. On August 6, 1993, *The Joe Franklin Show* finally closed up shop, but Franklin seemed uncharacteristically reluctant to walk down his own memory lane. Instead of clips from past shows, the finale was a representative everyday edition of *The Joe Franklin Show*, with a guest list including journalist Alan Miller and "triviologist" Richard Ornstein. And yes, my friends, it was one for the time capsule.

Jonny Quest. See *Adventures of Jonny Quest, The.*

Joseph Campbell and the Power of Myth. See *Moyers: Joseph Campbell and the Power of Myth.*

Julia. *1968–71, NBC.* The one thing for which this show is most famous— being the first prime-time sitcom to star an African-American woman—actually is a fallacy. That recognition belongs instead to *Beulah*, the 1950–53 TV spinoff showcasing the character of the maid from radio's *Fibber McGee and Molly*. Ethel Waters, Hattie McDaniel, and Louise Beavers all took turns playing *Beulah*, but *Julia* belonged to one woman alone: Diahann Carroll, who played a widow with a young son and a full-time job as a nurse. In one sense, this series was more nineties than sixties: her child's day-care concerns anticipated the problems of single working mothers, and the overall tone of the series drowns in what would now be called political correctness. Offered a nursing job sight unseen over the phone, Julia feels compelled to tell her prospective employer (played by Lloyd Nolan), "I'm colored." "What color are you?" he asks. When she replies "A Negro," he shoots back, "Have you always been a Negro, or are you just trying to be fashionable?" To the enlightened doctor, race was not an issue. Unfortunately, it wasn't an issue anywhere in *Julia*, either, to the point where many episodes could just as effectively have starred Mary Tyler Moore in the title role. Yet *Julia* has been credited and remembered, rightly or not, as a groundbreaking TV series, so here it is. Half of what I say is meaningless—but I say it just to reach you, *Julia*.

Kefauver Crime Commission Hearings. *1951, ABC, DuMont, and local TV.* Tennessee Senator Estes Kefauver, mob "moll" Virginia Hill, and the hands of reputed gambler Frank Costello all gained notoriety as a result of TV

LEFT: *I Spy*, with Robert Culp and Bill *Cosby*.
RIGHT: *Kukla, Fran & Ollie*, with puppeteer Burr Tillstrom, host Fran Allison and friends.

In Living Color, with two views: At left, Damon Wayans and David Alan Grier as critics Blaine and Antoine; at right, Jim Carrey as a post-scandal Pee-wee Herman.

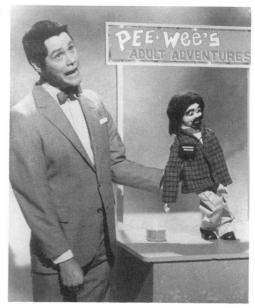

coverage of these hearings, which *Life* magazine called "the first big television broadcast of an affair of . . . government." A *Broadcasting* editorial, even more enthusiastically, insisted the hearings had "promoted television in one fell sweep from everybody's whipping boy—in the sports, amusement, and even retail world—to benefactor, without reservations. Its camera eye had opened the public's." The Special Senate Committee to Investigate Organized Crime in Interstate Commerce held hearings in fourteen different cities, half of which provided television coverage. In New York, where the hearings were most potent and most popular, five of the city's seven TV stations presented all or part of the hearings; ABC and DuMont, with the weakest program lineups and thus the least to lose, televised the New York hearings live to as many affiliates in the Northeast as they could reach. Amazingly, estimates by the Hooper ratings service indicated that, at times, the hearings attracted not just a majority of the audience watching TV, but a totality. And no wonder, because a lot of fascinating stuff was crammed into the Kefauver hearings. There were the often uncooperative witnesses, refusing to incriminate themselves on so many occasions that "taking the Fifth," as in invoking the Fifth Amendment of the U.S. Constitution, soared from arcane legal language to a well-known national catch phrase. There was the sexy, sometimes playful Virginia Hill. There was Kefauver, who became so popular as a result of chairing the hearings that he received an Emmy (no kidding), ran for president the following year (again, no kidding, but he lost the Democratic nomination anyway), and, also in 1952, turned right around and conducted a Senate inquiry into the relationship between radio and TV violence and juvenile delinquency. Finally, there was Frank Costello, a reluctant witness who wanted to be heard but not seen—prompting the visually compelling television compromise of focusing solely, and closely, on his hands, as he poured water, fingered his eyeglasses, and gestured for emphasis. In 1991, those dramatic Costello images were echoed, in a way, during TV coverage of the trial in which William Kennedy Smith was accused of rape. His then-unidentified accuser, to maintain her anonymity, testified on TV with an electronically generated "blue dot" obscuring her face. With her, as with Costello, the minimalism of the visuals made audiences pay maximum attention to the verbal testimony. However, the woman, Patricia Bowman, eventually revealed her own identity, ironically using television (specifically, ABC's *PrimeTime Live* newsmagazine) to do so.

Kennedy, John F., Assassination and Funeral Coverage. *1963, all networks.* If there were only one teleliteracy item, rather than hundreds, in this book, this, even more so than Neil Armstrong's walk on the moon, would be the one—the most important, durable, and memorable contribution television has ever made to American society. For the days following the November 22, 1963, assassination of JFK, television held the nation together just as it was threatening to rend apart. The TV channels became a place for viewers to channel their grief, and witness firsthand the outpouring of affection for the slain president and the succession of power by the new president, Lyndon Baines Johnson. In addition, astoundingly, there was the murder of alleged assassin Lee Harvey Oswald, shot by Jack Ruby on live television—live, that is, on NBC, the only network to have a camera aimed and running as police attempted to transfer Oswald from the Dallas jail. The networks had pooled resources for that fateful weekend, and CBS and ABC quickly responded by replaying the tape—ad infinitum, as did NBC. The image of Ruby stepping forth and shooting Oswald, with Oswald's pained grimace as the bullet finds its mark, became one of many indelible images from those days in November. Others, as if they needed to be renumerated, included Jackie Kennedy's blood-stained dress, the long lines of mourners, the caisson, the riderless horse, the flag being folded, the surviving Kennedys huddled together, and most heartbreaking of all, the proud and silent salute by young John-John as his father's body was drawn past. Sights, not sounds, are what remain most resonant from those days of TV coverage, unless you count the music: the strained bugle notes of "Taps," the haunting bagpipes, and the rumbling drums played during the funeral procession. The pictures said it all, and, to this day, the pictures, not the words, are what people remember. Ninety-three percent of American homes with television watched that solemn tribute, making it, at that time, the most-viewed TV event ever measured by the Nielsen rating service. Twenty-three other countries watched via satellite, and watched American television come of age. TV critic Jack Gould of the *New York Times* wrote at the time, "When the day's history is written, the record of television as a medium will constitute a chapter of honor." Mythologist Joseph Campbell called the coverage a "deeply significant rite of passage," with the mass medium of television facilitating "an enormous nation, made those four days into a unanimous community, all of us participating in the same way, simultaneously, in a single symbolic event." Perhaps the most significant assessment of all was printed in *TV Guide* a few weeks after JFK's assassination: "On that unforgettable weekend in November 1963, television provided a personal experience which all could share, a vast religious service which all could attend, a unifying bond which all could feel. I take this opportunity to add my voice to those who already have recognized television's historic contribution." The review was signed: Lyndon B. Johnson, president of the United States. Walter Cronkite, who had become anchorman of *The CBS Evening News* only the year before, became "the most trusted man in America" largely because of his solid work during those four days. Even though NBC had the Oswald murder first, CBS and Cronkite ended up owning the story to such an extent that, decades later, *60 Minutes* executive producer Don Hewitt referred to the coverage as "Walter's ministry." I firmly believe, having seen that coverage firsthand, that the trust and respect invested in Cronkite stems directly from his reading of the bulletin pronouncing the president dead. "From Dallas, Texas," he said, "a flash, apparently official: President Kennedy died at 1 P.M., Central Standard Time, 2 o'clock, Eastern Standard Time . . . Some 38 minutes ago." The words aren't that important, and most people can't recall them—but no one who saw Cronkite at that moment failed to see, or later forgot, that his voice broke, and he fought back tears, as he made the announcement. Thirty years later, Cronkite appeared in a retrospective special hosted by Dan Rather (Cronkite's successor, and another newsman who did memorable work during the assassination coverage; Rather, in fact, was the first to report Kennedy's death, on CBS Radio). When asked by Rather to conjure the images of the JFK funeral, Cronkite said nothing; instead, he sat there as his eyes welled with tears. Finally, he sniffed and smiled, and said, "Anchormen shouldn't cry." But sometimes they should, if they are men first and anchors second, and Cronkite won the nation's heart in 1963 by revealing his own. One significant note: the most dramatic and important pictures taken of the JFK assassination, photographed on eight-millimeter film by amateur photographer Abraham Zapruder, were not shown at the time by TV at all, even though they contained the only filmed record of Kennedy actually being shot. *Life* magazine quickly bought the rights, and printed some frames in a subsequent issue, but otherwise controlled and denied access for years. Bootleg copies began to circulate, and were shown on some college campuses in the early seventies; CBS finally broke the unofficial prime-time ban by showing and analyzing frames of the Zapruder film in its four-part 1975 documentary, *The American Assassins*, with Rather as the correspondent. The first time the Zapruder film had been shown in its entirety on network television, though, was a year earlier, on a short-lived 1974 late-night ABC series called *Good Night America*. The host of that controversial program? Geraldo Rivera. Finally, this sad postscript: on May 23, 1994, cancer victim Jacqueline Kennedy Onassis was buried at Arlington National Cemetery, next to her martyred first husband. Only thirty-four years old at the time of his death, the widow known endearingly as Jackie was laid to rest in a televised Monday afternoon ceremony revisiting many of the moments and mourners from her husband's funeral thirty-one years earlier. The eternal flame was there, and the restrained yet heartrending graveside anguish, and even young John-John and Caroline, all grown up now and known, respectively, as John F. Kennedy, Jr., and Caroline Kennedy Schlossberg. "During those four endless days in 1963," Senator Edward M. Kennedy said in his eulogy to Jackie, "she held us together as a family and a country. In large part because of her, we could grieve and then go on." In large part because of her, yes—and in small part because of television, who brought her example to us, and brought us together as a result.

Kennedy, Robert F., Assassination and Funeral Coverage. *1968, all networks.* One of the ghoulish lessons learned by the networks after the assassination of JFK was that political leaders, especially presidents and aspirants to that post, had to be covered by film or videotape at all public appearances—just in case tragedy, in the form of a killer, struck again. On June 5, 1968, it did. Senator Bobby Kennedy, having just won the California primary in his pursuit of the Democratic presidential nomination, was celebrating with his political supporters at the Ambassador Hotel in Los Angeles. He delivered his victory speech, smiled and waved good-bye, and was led offstage—where, in the pantry just out of sight of network cameras, he was shot (a gunman named Sirhan Sirhan was apprehended on the spot and charged with the crime). Within moments, CBS's Jim Wilson and other cameramen on the scene were capturing the tragic action, photographing Kennedy's friends and associates who hovered around him, cradling his head, as he lay in an expanding pool of his own blood. Kennedy lost consciousness and never regained it; for the next few days, America's collective consciousness was assailed yet again, as the networks televised another funeral procession and series of tributes, with its own array of solemn images. Perhaps the most emotional images of all were the literally moving pictures taken from the train transporting Kennedy's body from New York City (where his bier had been on display at St. Patrick's Cathedral) to Washington, where he was to be interred. Thousands of mourners, unable to attend the services in New York, lined the tracks along the entire route to pay their silent respects as the train chugged by—and their faces, photographed by film and TV cameras aboard the train itself, said it all.

King, Martin Luther, Jr., Funeral Coverage and Aftermath. *1968, all networks*. It's depressing, as well as coincidental, that these three murders from the sixties—those of John F. Kennedy, Robert F. Kennedy, and Martin Luther King, Jr.—follow one another alphabetically in this compendium of memorable TV shows and events. Yet in retrospect, that was the way it seemed to unroll back then: one senseless death after another. On April 4, 1968, with no TV cameras present, the nonviolent civil rights leader was shot and killed by a sniper while standing on his motel balcony in Memphis, Tennessee. Once again, the loss of a leader was mourned via television, with a seven-hour service broadcast nationally, and sent by satellite to countries overseas. Among the mourners at King's old Ebenezer Baptist Church in Atlanta that day was Bobby Kennedy, who, in the moments after learning of King's death, had spoken publicly, delivering an exceptionally personal and passionate plea for peace; two months later, Kennedy, too, would be shot and killed. The television coverage of King's funeral included many evocative moments— again, as with JFK, more visual than verbal. King's coffin, drawn to the cemetery on an ordinary farm wagon pulled by a pair of mules, spoke volumes about his roots, just as the hundreds of thousands of mourners walking behind that wagon spoke eloquently of his impact and high regard. After King's death, TV also relayed scenes of a less passive sort, as the anguish over the loss of a beloved minority leader sparked riots in more than sixty cities. Along with the buildup in Vietnam, the death of Bobby Kennedy and the demonstrations in Chicago during the Democratic National Convention, the riots following King's death were part of what might be called the summer of our discontent. The man eventually convicted of King's murder, James Earl Ray, finally was located and arrested in London on June 8, three days after Bobby Kennedy was murdered.

King, Rodney, Video, Verdict, and Aftermath. *1991, 1992, 1993, network, local, and syndicated TV*. The amateur filmmaker who photographed JFK's assassination found his name forever linked with the footage he shot, which thereafter was referred to as "the Zapruder film." That was not the case with George Holliday, who, from inside his home, videotaped motorist Rodney King being surrounded, overpowered, and beaten by Los Angeles police on March 3, 1991, after King had attempted to evade arrest in a high-speed car chase. The video's grainy, blurry, but indisputable images showed three patrolmen beating an apparently subdued man as a dozen other officers stood by and watched. Holliday sold the video to a Los Angeles TV station for five hundred dollars; once televised locally in California, it quickly was copied, replayed and relayed nationally (and endlessly) by network and local news programs, talk shows, Cable News Network, and almost every broadcast outlet in between. The soon painfully familiar visual record of the beating became known as "the Rodney King video," and was the central piece of evidence in King's 1992 lawsuit against four of the arresting officers. When all four white policemen were acquitted of nearly all the state charges against the African-American King, news of the "not guilty" verdicts on April 30, 1992, led to widespread rioting and arson in portions of South Central Los Angeles and elsewhere—the worst outburst of national urban violence, according to news reports, since the days after the murder of Martin Luther King, Jr., in 1968. In 1992, many Los Angeles TV stations covered the street-level reactions live, using helicopters to follow and photograph them from a safe distance; their breaking news coverage was picked up and relayed by local independent stations as far away as New York, as well as by CNN. The most horrific image, broadcast live, was of a white truck driver, later identified as Reginald Denny, being dragged from his vehicle and brutally beaten by angry blacks. It was like watching the Rodney King video all over again, only from an aerial view and with the races reversed. As reported later on *Nightline*, Denny was rescued by nearby residents who had seen the local TV coverage, recognized the intersection where he had been stopped and attacked, and rushed to his aid. The Los Angeles police force, it turned out, had no TV sets at nearby precincts, making them just about the only people in the area who lacked that particular perspective and information. After days of unrest and a state-imposed curfew, tensions eased somewhat, especially with a decision by federal authorities to pursue other means of justice. In April 1993, the same four officers cleared of the King beating at the state level faced federal civil rights charges; when those verdicts were handed down, local and network TV news organizations were steeled for the worst, but two of the four officers were convicted, defusing the potential for another round of riots. For once, no news was good news—and both King and Denny emerged from the two-year ordeal as proponents of nonviolence and understanding. In November 1993, Denny appeared on *Donahue* alongside one of the men who brutalized him, and hugged the young man's mother as a gesture of forgiveness. A month later, Damian M. Williams, whom TV helicopter crews had photographed attacking Denny, was sentenced to ten years in prison. And King, while maintaining a low profile, remained famous not only for the "Rodney King video," but for emerging, visibly shaken, the day after the 1992 riots, to ask the most poignant and oft-repeated—and oft-misquoted—question of the entire saga. King's plea for tolerance has come to be lodged in public memory as, "Can't we all just get along?" To be precise, though, what he really said that day was this: "People, I just want to say, can we all get along? Can we get along?"

Knots Landing. *1979–93, CBS.* After two Kennedys and two Kings, it's nice to get away from grim reality for a minute and shift over to harmless, meaningless fantasy. *Knots Landing* was such a durable prime-time serial, and such a successful spinoff of *Dallas*, that it outlasted its parent program and became the longest continuing prime-time soap opera in American TV history. Why, I have no clue, except that its allegedly "everyday folks" (with Gary Shackelford as Gary, the world's poorest Ewing) may have worn better on the nerves, in the long run, than their richer and showier counterparts on *Dallas* and *Dynasty*. But I question that theory, even if it's mine, because the most memorable characters on *Knots Landing* were the rich and powerful and unscrupulous ones: William Devane's craggy Greg Sumner and Donna Mills's bitchy Abby. Abby returned to the show, and the neighborhood cul-de-sac, for the series finale, and Mack (Kevin Dobson) and Karen (Michele Lee), the longtime rock-solid married couple, reunited, tentatively but tenderly, just in time for the series to end. But for me, the best moments for this series had come and gone years before—with the death of Laura Avery (Constance McCashin) and the stalking of Val (Joan Van Ark) by crazy Jill Bennett (Teri Austin). In the end, what may be most memorable about *Knots Landing* is the year the writers forgot to forget. When *Dallas* erased one laughably bad season by having Bobby Ewing's death on that show be dismissed as a "bad dream," the writers of *Knots Landing* made no such adjustment, even though events after Bobby's "death" had influenced events on their spinoff show as well. I guess they figured it wouldn't really matter to viewers who were all tied up in *Knots*. As with daytime soaps, some of the alumni from *Knots Landing* have since attained greater glory, including Alec Baldwin (who played Joshua Rush, 1984–85), Lisa Hartman (who played two roles, Cathy Geary Rush and Ciji Dunne, in four years), Marcia Cross (Victoria Broyard, 1991–92), and Halle Berry (Debbie Porter, 1991).

Kojak. *1973–78, CBS*. Who loves ya, baby? Telly Savalas became an international telly sensation as Theo Kojak, the lollipop-sucking, bald-headed, order-growling New York police lieutenant who, when things got tough, shouted "Crocker!" to summon his second-banana lieutenant. Bobby Crocker was played by Kevin Dobson, who spent five years on this show before spending another fourteen on *Knots Landing*—which means the guy spent nearly two decades in prime-time series TV without ever leaving the K's. *Kojak*, the character and the show, began (without Dobson or Crocker) as *The Marcus-Nelson Murders*, a 1973 telemovie introducing Savalas as Theo Kojak. CBS showed the telemovie in March, and was so encouraged by the response that it had a full-blown *Kojak* series up and running seven months later. Before *Hill Street Blues* hit the air and redefined the genre, *Kojak* was credited by critics, and even by police, for its credible depiction of police work. The series was an instant hit, and soon used its clout to film more extensively on location around New York City, which made *Kojak* even more distinctive. In 1989, ABC revived the character, and the show, as a series of telemovies, but by then the Kojak character had lapsed almost into self-parody. However, Andre Braugher, the actor playing his new second-in-command, did such a fine job that good things were predicted for him in the future (at least by me). He got one good thing, soon afterward, by landing a plum role among the ensemble cast of Barry Levinson's 1993 Baltimore cop series, *Homicide: Life on the Street*.

Kolchak: The Night Stalker. See *Night Stalker, The*.

Kraft Television Theatre. *1947–58, NBC; 1953–55, ABC*. When you talk about the so-called Golden Age of live TV drama, you can't go back much further than *Kraft Television Theatre*. In fact, you can't go back *any* further, at least on a regularly scheduled level. Because NBC was owned by RCA, there was an obvious ulterior motive to advance the cause and popularity of television: the better the programming NBC presented, the more TV sets RCA was likely to sell. NBC had launched its experimental flagship TV station, New York's W2XBS, way back in 1930, when radio was king, and was tinkering with live dramatic presentations on that station even before TV was "unveiled" at the 1939 New York World's Fair. A version of Arthur Conan Doyle's *The Three Garridebs* was telecast in 1937, and Thomas Hutchinson's *The Mysterious Mummy Case* in 1938. World War II sidelined almost all TV experimentation until 1945, after which NBC's New York station, by then renamed WNBT, began to pursue live dramatic TV with a vengeance. By 1946, WNBT was presenting a monthly showcase of full-length plays under the umbrella title *Television Theatre*. Many of them were directed by a young man named Fred Coe, and if you're looking for the true birthplace of "Golden Age" TV drama, that local Sunday showcase was it. Inspired by its success, NBC borrowed the title, found a regular sponsor, and launched *Kraft Television Theatre*—which, when it premiered on May 7, 1947, became television's first weekly hour-long dramatic series, and set the standard for all that followed. Similarly inspired by WNBT's *Television Theatre*, but heading in another direction, Coe went off on his own, and went on to produce some of television's other most significant "Golden Age" series: *Goodyear TV Playhouse, Philco Television Playhouse*, and several seasons of *Playhouse 90*. But *Kraft Television Theatre* enjoyed a longer run than them all, missing only three live telecasts in eleven years (because of preemptions by coverage of political conventions). In fact, the series became such a success on Wednesdays that Kraft added another weekly installment on Thursdays—on rival network ABC, which ran its own *Kraft Television Theatre* from 1953–55. That made for a grand total of six hundred and fifty shows, most of which emanated from NBC's Studio 8H—the previous home of NBC Radio's famed orchestral concerts led by Arturo Toscanini, and the future home of *Saturday Night Live*. E. G. Marshall appeared in enough productions (including the title role in a 1950 condensation of *Macbeth)* to be considered almost a repertory player, and other noteworthy stars over the years included Jack Lemmon, Jack Klugman (who even wrote one teleplay, 1958's *Code of the Corner)*, Cliff Robertson, Lee Grant, John Forsythe (who starred in a 1948 adaptation of *Wuthering Heights)*, Grace Kelly, Leslie Nielsen, Cloris Leachman, Roddy McDowall, Rod Steiger, Rip Torn, Richard Kiley, Robert Culp, Eva Gabor, Warren Beatty, Lorne Greene, and Wally Cox; writers included Truman Capote, JP Miller, and Rod Serling. James Dean starred in a 1953 drama called

A Long Time Till Dawn, and other special offerings included Art Carney and Edgar Bergen (complete with his wooden sidekick, Charlie McCarthy) in 1954's *Alice in Wonderland,* Ossie Davis in a 1954 adaptation of Eugene O'Neill's *The Emperor Jones,* and Lee Remick and Elizabeth Montgomery in a 1955 version of F. Scott Fitzgerald's lighthearted *The Diamond as Big as the Ritz.* Productions getting even more notice were an ambitious retelling of the *Titanic* disaster (in 1956's *A Night to Remember,* directed by George Roy Hill), a 1965 drama called *A Profile in Courage* (introduced by a thirty-eight-year-old John F. Kennedy), and a two-part 1958 retelling of *All the King's Men,* starring Neville Brand. However, the most famous *Kraft Television Theatre* presentation by far was Serling's *Patterns,* starring Ed Begley, Sr., and Richard Kiley. Performed live in 1955 (and made the next year into a feature film), it was a scathing drama about corporate Darwinism, and instantly (though it was hardly his first effort) made Serling's reputation as one of the medium's best writers. Despite the anthology show's loyal sponsor, *Kraft Television Theatre* was anything but cheesy.

Kukla, Fran & Ollie. *1948–54, NBC; 1954–57, ABC.* Burr Tillstrom, the puppeteer-producer behind *Kukla, Fran & Ollie,* was another early TV pioneer—a *very* early one. Along with puppet creations Kukla (named by Russian prima ballerina Tamara Toumanova, who saw its cute clown face and shouted "Kukla!," an affectionate Russian term for doll) and Ollie (a friendly dragon with a long protruding tooth), Tillstrom performed two thousand shows demonstrating television to visitors at the RCA-TV exhibit of the 1939 New York World's Fair. In 1941, he and his puppets were among the guests during the opening-day TV broadcasts of Chicago's WBKB; in October 1947, the same station gave Tillstrom and his make-believe menagerie their own one-hour children's show, *Junior Jamboree*—a series that predated *Howdy Doody* by two months. To help him ad lib his way through each show, puppeteer Tillstrom hired Fran Allison as on-air host, and the show soon adopted the name of its three leading players: *Kukla, Fran & Ollie.* In 1948, the series went regional over NBC's Midwest network (RCA, the owners of NBC, had been sold on Tillstrom's puppets since the World's Fair), and went national on NBC when the coaxial cable came to Chicago in 1949. The first generation of young TV viewers may still remember the theme, with such lyrics as "Yes, by gum, and yes, by golly, Kukla, Fran, and dear old Ollie. . . . " They may also remember the often outrageous (and crowded) operas, plays, and variety shows put on by the "Kuklapolitan Players," which also included Beulah the Witch, Madame Ophelia Oglepuss, and Cecil Bill. But how many remember that the announcer for *Kukla, Fran & Ollie* was . . . Hugh Downs?

Kung Fu. *1972–75, ABC.* Inspired by the slow-motion violence ballets of *Bonnie and Clyde* and the films of Sam Peckinpah, and by the martial-arts techniques and popularity of Bruce Lee, ABC set out to make a Western that combined both. Actually, Lee was supposed to star in the series, which had been developed with him in mind, but the part was recast, with David Carradine in the lead, midway through development. The whole concept was like a barefoot *Billy Jack*, with Carradine's Kwai Chang Caine preaching tolerance and pacifism until backed into a corner, at which time he would quietly but efficiently (and in slow motion) reduce all adversaries to groaning or unconscious pulps. Many viewers seriously embraced the show's "Eastern philosophy," as espoused in its frequent flashbacks to Caine's days of childhood instruction—back when he was called "Grasshopper," which remains the single most joked-about element from the show. Yet except for overtly encouraging brotherhood among various racial groups, *Kung Fu* was about as filling and deep as a fortune cookie. Ironically, two efforts at sequels, a 1986 telemovie and a 1987 series pilot, teamed Carradine with Brandon Lee, the son of the man whom Carradine had inexplicably beaten out for the lead. In 1993, a new syndicated series starring Carradine, *Kung Fu: The Legend Continues*, was more successful as sequels go, but even less impressive. If Carradine's *Kung Fu* legend is to continue anywhere, it'll probably be thanks to late-night TV ads for his 1993 home video production, *David Carradine's Tai Chi Workout*—unavailable in stores.

L

Lace. *1984, ABC.* At this writing, *Lace* and another miniseries from 1984, *Fatal Vision*, have drawn higher ratings than any long-form dramas since; *Fatal Vision* is tied for seventh place on the list of all-time Top 10 miniseries, and *Lace* just misses the cut, ranking eleventh. Not even *Lonesome Dove* got as high a Nielsen rating, which is an absolute travesty—especially when compared to *Lace*, which would have to improve by 50 percent to qualify as awful. Its only claim to fame is what got it such a big audience in the first place: the scene in which Phoebe Cates, as a wayward starlet confused about her parentage, confronts three women and asks, "All right, which one of you bitches is my mother?" And yes, ABC presented a sequel the following year, imaginatively called *Lace II*, and just as imaginatively having Cates ask the inevitable follow-up question, "Which one of you bastards is my father?" The only comforting thought is that the concept ran out of steam before descending into *Lace: The Next Generation*.

L.A. Law. *1986–94, NBC.* A year before Oliver Stone's *Wall Street* captured the runaway greed of the eighties, Steven Bochco and Terry Louise Fisher presented this aggressively upscale lawyer show. In its execution as well as its creation, *L.A. Law* had direct ties to *Hill Street Blues*, with its overlapping stories, large ensemble cast, and occasional forays into the humorous and the unexpected. One of the most talked-about aspects of the entire series was the episode in which Michael Tucker's meek Stuart Markowitz was taught a mysterious (and, unfortunately, fictitious) sure-fire sexual technique called the

"Venus Butterfly." Another was the time Rosalind Shays, a contentious and disliked law partner played by Diana Muldaur, literally was given the shaft by stepping into an empty elevator shaft and falling to her death. A third was the time Amanda Donohoe's C. J. Lamb surprised Michele Greene's Abby Perkins by kissing her—a plot line that, like many others on this series, never reached full fruition. The courtroom scenes in *L.A. Law* remained a consistent strength, but romantic and dramatic subplots got more convoluted and less satisfying after a while; the stars, it seemed, got even more restless than viewers, and many of them, including Jimmy Smits, Harry Hamlin, and ex-*Partridge Family* member Susan Dey, left (some more than once) partway through the show's run. The seventh season, which had Markowitz suffer a head injury during the South Central Los Angeles riots after the Rodney King verdict, was the all-time *L.A. Law* low point, but the series made a strong comeback in the fall of 1993 by adding two characters from *Civil Wars*, Debi Mazar's Denise Iannello and Alan Rosenberg's Eli Levinson, to its roster. *Civil Wars* had been created by William L. Finkelstein, a supervising producer on *L.A. Law* who had left after four seasons to start his own courtroom show on ABC. When he returned to *L.A. Law*, it was as executive producer, and the first thing he did after the cancellation of *Civil Wars* was to import two of that show's popular characters—an unprecedented display of cooperation between nonspinoff series from different networks. Speaking of cooperation: during Finkelstein's initial stint on *L.A. Law*, his writing partner most of the time had been David E. Kelley, who had taken over as executive producer when Bochco left the show in 1989. Three years later, Kelley, like Finkelstein before him, left the womb of *L.A. Law* to create his own series—in Kelley's case, the superb *Picket Fences* and the often outstanding *Chicago Hope*. The finale episode of *L.A. Law* was less bang than whimper; it set the stage for possible reunion telemovies, but didn't put any effort into even temporarily lowering the curtain.

Larry King Live. *1985–   , CNN.* On February 22, 1992, *Larry King Live* changed from one of the Cable News Network's softer hours to one of its hardest, at least in terms of the potential to deliver hard news. That was the night Texas billionaire H. Ross Perot, responding to King's persistent and direct questioning ("Is there any scenario in which you would run for President?"), announced spontaneously he would agree to run as an independent if supporters registered him in all fifty states. The dynamics of the 1992 presidential campaign, and the way the battle for voters was fought on national television, received a major overhaul that night. Candidates, either reluctantly or eagerly, ended up appearing on everything from *Donahue* to MTV, and fielding calls from viewers on every TV platform from *Nightline* to the CBS *Morning* show. Perot loved the "national town meeting" format so much, he almost single-handedly pushed that phrase into everyday use—and King, with his phone-in show and freewheeling conversational style, was at the epicenter of this new type of political platform. (Well, not all that new: *America's Town Meeting*, a public-affairs program featuring guest speakers and encouraging input from the studio audience, was a regular radio show as

far back as 1935, and ABC presented prime-time versions, hosted alternately
by George V. Denny and John Daly, between 1948 and 1952.) Shortly before
the 1992 election, George Will wrote in his syndicated column, somewhat
grudgingly, that King was "the master of ceremonies of the 1992 campaign."
Before King had such an impact on political media strategies, it was easier to
denounce or dismiss him as a softball questioner who prided himself on *not*
doing research. But lazy or not, he listens, and so does his TV and radio
audience, which often asks questions as tough and direct as the Washington
press corps. As a result, *Larry King Live* has emerged as one of the mandatory
whistle stops for any politician with a voter to woo or an issue to sell. In
November 1993 King got the highest ratings in his program's history by
hosting a freewheeling debate on the North American Free Trade Agreement
(NAFTA), during which Perot and Vice President Al Gore engaged in ninety
minutes of *insultus interruptus*. "Can I finish? . . . Can I finish? . . . " I'll
finish, though, with King's "most memorable" interview as judged by King
himself: his ninety-minute chat with Frank Sinatra.

Larry Sanders Show, The. *1992–   , HBO.* From 1986–90, Garry Shandling
starred in a very funny and unusual sitcom, produced for the Showtime cable
network and subsequently rebroadcast on Fox, called *It's Garry Shandling's
Show*. He played himself, a character blissfully self-aware of his "role" as star
of his own sitcom—a modern variation on the gimmick established by George
Burns on his series in the fifties, except that on Shandling's show, *everyone*
was aware of the cameras, and the audience, and of being characters in a TV
sitcom. A few years later, Shandling returned to cable TV—Home Box Office,
this time—with a show that was even *more* obsessed with television. *The
Larry Sanders Show*, like the Martin Mull showcase *Fernwood 2-Night*, is a
sitcom about the fictional host of a make-believe TV talk show. This time, too,
Shandling added something to the formula: namely, presenting the talk show
host's home life, and backstage activities and concerns, as well as his on-air
"program." This makes it a kind of distant relative to *The Dick Van Dyke
Show*, only with its focus on the star of the show-within-a-show, rather than
its head writer. What makes *The Larry Sanders Show* such a treat from the
start, though, is not only the concept, but also the casting, the writing, and
the timing. As the self-absorbed Sanders, Shandling is wonderful: assured
and funny on air, distant and insecure in private. Rip Torn, as his producer
Artie, and Jeffrey Tambor, as sidekick Hank "Hey now!" Kingsley, are equally
brilliant, and the scripts give all these players, and more, a chance to shine
and stretch. Special standouts among the other regulars include Janeane Garofalo, as Paula the talent booker; Wallace Langham, as Phil the head writer;
and Scott Thompson as Brian, Hank Kingsley's feisty assistant. They're terrific, and so are the guest stars, who have included everyone from Sharon
Stone and Farrah Fawcett to Carol Burnett and Doc Severinsen. Because *The
Larry Sanders Show* resides on HBO, it often uses language and situations
deemed too "adult" for network TV, and uses them to hilarious and very
believable effect. Best of all, though, are the endless "inside jokes" about TV's
talk-show wars of the nineties. Shandling and the producers and writers of

The Larry Sanders Show assume viewers have a firm grasp of such trade-paper fodder as ratings, shares, time slots, lead-ins, superagents, affiliate clearances, contract ploys, show bookers, and midlevel network executives—and these days, thanks to a proliferation of magazines and TV shows covering the entertainment industry, most viewers do. The stories are so intelligent, believable, and close to the bone that the show has become one of the hottest guest-shot tickets of the nineties, and most of the fictional Sanders's real competitors have guest starred as themselves, including David Letterman, Jay Leno, and even Martin Mull, who appeared in one episode to guest host the fictional Sanders show—but was ridiculed by second banana Hank for not being good enough to host a "real" TV talk show. Mull over that for a minute, and you'll understand why *Sanders* is worth savoring. Even better was the 1993 episode in which Sanders prodded Letterman into revealing his secret choice to host a late-night companion show. After repeated refusals to answer the question, Letterman finally whispers to Sanders: "Tom Snyder. But don't tell anybody." That episode ended with Sanders hiring Snyder himself, and with the real Snyder capping the show by showing up and announcing that it was a "pleasure to be back at the network . . . and back at the old 12:30 A.M. saddle." Two years later, Snyder indeed was back on network TV, in the time slot following Letterman, as the host of *The Late Late Show with Tom Snyder*. The foresight and timing of *The Larry Sanders Show* have been that good from the start: Shandling's series premiered just as the late-night landscape was changing irrevocably, and with Johnny Carson stepping down, Letterman stepping forward, Leno stumbling but not falling, and Chevy Chase landing flat on his face, it couldn't have been better. Neither, for that matter, could the series itself.

Lassie. *1954–71, CBS.* Forget *The Adventures of Rin Tin Tin*, which ran a mere five years on ABC in the fifties. *Lassie*, without question, was TV's top dog. Except for *Gunsmoke*, which lasted twenty seasons, *Lassie* is the longest-running dramatic series in network TV history; it lasted seventeen seasons, which is nothing to bark at. I watch reruns of *Lassie* on Nickelodeon these days and almost cringe at how taken I was, as a kid, by such tacky production values and stories. Lassie's patented whine obviously was added in post-production much of the time, and the shows never strayed (so to speak) from the same "Dog Knows Best" formula. Yet my own children watch these same dusty old black-and-white *Lassie* shows, especially the ones with Jon Provost as Timmy, and enjoy them without any sense of irony or superiority. There's something timeless, I guess, about a boy and his dog, especially when the dog is so totally loyal, brave, smart, and cheerful (after all, what good is a melancholy collie?). The first live-action *Lassie* adventure, based on the book by Eric Knight, was the 1943 film *Lassie Come Home*, with Roddy McDowall and Elizabeth Taylor. It made Rudd Weatherwax's trained dog an overnight star, and Lassie barely pawsed before starring in several movie sequels, and, from 1946–49, in his own ABC radio series called *Lassie*. (If it sounds ridiculous for a dog to have its own radio show, remember that this was the era when two of the medium's biggest stars were a ventriloquist and his dummy.)

The TV *Lassie* began on CBS in 1954, and, with Campbell's Soup as the sole sponsor, spent the next seventeen years cranking out episodes that were, for the most part, Mmmm-mmmm good. (Tommy Rettig as Jeff, the original TV owner of Lassie, was first, Provost's Timmy—with June Lockhart as his mom— was best, and the "Ranger" years, which intentionally served up proenviron-mental sermonettes, were a little heavy-handed.) Separate, though equally inferior, syndicated revivals were mounted in the seventies and eighties, but reruns of the old *Lassie* shows on cable kept the old legacy alive, enough to warrant a new big-screen *Lassie* movie, costarring Helen Slater and Richard Farnsworth, in 1994. That's a stretch of stardom covering fifty-one years—or three hundred and fifty-seven, if you're counting in dog years—so several generations of collies, all descended from the original screen star, have played the role. Pal, also known as "Lassie I," starred in all the old MGM movies, the radio show, and the first two TV episodes. Lassie, Jr., took over at that point, dogging it through all the Jeff years and the first two with Timmy; Baby, or "Lassie III," finished the Timmy years, and Mire, or "Lassie IV," closed out the run on CBS. The next three generations of dogs starred in subsequent syndicated and movie versions, and Howard, the great-great-great-great-great-grandson of Pal, headlined the 1994 revival movie. It's no secret that, although the character of Lassie was female, all the dogs who played her were male. But here are two lesser-known *Lassie* tricks. When an onscreen Lassie had to fight, Weatherwax used painted rubber bands to hold up its upper lip, baring the dog's teeth for a more fierce look. And to make it easier to film long shots of Lassie at rest, or to set the lighting using an endlessly patient test subject, the TV production crew had a stuffed collie, captured for eternity in a comfortable supine position, ready to toss out in the fields and photograph. I know that only because I once visited producer-director Mark Tinker on the set of *St. Elsewhere*, where the stuffed collie, in a constantly comfortable state of Lassie repose, had become part of his office decor. However, Tinker had given his passive pet a new name: "Stay the Wonder Dog."

Late Night with David Letterman. *1982–93, NBC.* In 1980, two years before this late-night show was launched, NBC presented a daytime talk series called *The David Letterman Show.* Letterman pointed cameras out on the streets of New York City, did stupid stunts, played host to occasional pets who per-formed tricks, visited various stores and conventions in and around town, and joked with whichever celebrities and "civilians" could be persuaded to visit the set that day. In terms of ratings, the show was an immediate flop, and NBC canceled it after four months. Yet in those four months, Letterman already had forged a style, and found an audience, that would reap major dividends down the road. On the penultimate daytime *David Letterman Show,* Letterman began by announcing, "There are two people in my life that I've always respected and admired, and these are people who make me laugh really hard. One of them is Johnny Carson, and the other one is here this morning: Steve Allen." In hindsight, it's a fascinating show to watch, because the mutual admiration society revealed Letterman's past influences as well as his future direction. During the interview, he asked Allen about such *Tonight!* and *Steve Allen Show* stunts as the time he dressed as a "Human Tea Bag," and pointed a TV camera outside to watch pedestrians pass by, and so on. "I've been a big fan of yours forever," Letterman told Allen, who in turn told Letterman he was impressed with the particular demographics of his midmorning studio audience. "They are all hip young people," Allen noted, "out of work." Letterman, with less than two shows to go before cancellation, grinned at Allen and replied, "I can sort of relate to that." But NBC kept paying Letterman, and eventually dumped Tom Snyder and *Tomorrow* in favor of *Late Night with David Letterman*, where Carson's *Tonight Show* served as Letterman's lead-in, and Letterman's loyal audience of "hip young people" made him a campus and cult hit. Over the next eleven years, the cult got much bigger and Letterman's interviewing skills got much better, but Letterman's strengths always were the more playful things he appropriated and adapted from previous TV hosts. For example: Carson's winning way of poking fun at his own jokes when they bomb; Allen's delight with freewheeling conversation, silly skits, and outrageous stunts; a fascination with using TV technology to comic effect, a curiosity traceable to the pioneering work of Ernie Kovacs; and even a genuine love of interacting with animals and small kids, a trait shared by both Carson and Art Linkletter. While drawing upon all those influences, Letterman brings two pricelessly comic traits of his own: a willingness to cut through the polite veneer of usual show-biz chat, and the liberating perspective that, no matter what he does, "It's only television." What other TV host would be able to claim as a highlight, much less with pride, the night Cher called him an "asshole"? (She returned, though, to reunite with Sonny Bono for an impromptu "I Got You Babe" on another memorable *Late Night* show.) In late-night annals, only Carson's *Tonight Show* can claim as many notable or quotable elements as Letterman's silly circus: Paul Shaffer and the World's Most Dangerous Band, the nightly "Top Ten" lists, dropping fruit from a rooftop, the Monkey-Cam and Thrill-Cam, Calvert DeForest as Larry "Bud" Melman (who always managed to look like he'd just walked off the set of *Plan 9 from Outer Space*), Chris Elliott as any number of wild and crazy guys (including, of course, The Guy Under the Seats), Stupid Pet Tricks, shopping and walking around New York City, and delivering a fruit basket to NBC's new corporate owners, a classic General Electric *faux pax* sowing the initial seeds of Letterman's discontent. Once NBC gave Carson's vacating *Tonight* throne to Jay Leno instead of him, Letterman was amenable to a corporate takeover of his own, and left *Late Night* in 1993 to launch a similar new show for CBS in an earlier time slot. By then, the "late night wars" were beginning to brew, and Letterman, despite his lame-duck *Late Night* status, worked hard to make those final shows especially entertaining and freewheeling. One night he left Cindy Crawford stranded in the Green Room so he could spend more on-air time chatting with (and delightedly repeating the name of) audience member Herb Clumpy III. Only in Letterman's elliptical universe would supermodel Crawford rank below supernormal Herb Clumpy III, but Letterman's different-drummer attitude is what made him such a pleasure, and a treasure, in the first place. His last original

Late Night installment took place on June 25, 1993, with Tom Hanks imitating Slappy White ("Stop bendin' the shaft!") and Bruce Springsteen teaming with Shaffer and the band for a rousing rendition of a most appropriate song: "Glory Days." On September 13, 1993, a young writer-producer for *The Simpsons* inherited Letterman's old show, which, fittingly, was retitled *Late Night with Conan O'Brien*. The show proudly germinated its own skits and comedic style, even while O'Brien and sidekick Andy Richter, by doing things like having Richter broadcast live from a blimp, maintained just enough of the zaniness of late-night TV to make *Late Night with Conan O'Brien* a worthy and doubtlessly durable successor to Letterman's version. At this writing, though, *Late Night with Conan O'Brien* has yet to earn its own separate entry.

Late Show with David Letterman. *1993–   , CBS*. This show, however, already has. By moving to CBS, and into the grandly refurbished Ed Sullivan Theater, Letterman instantly grabbed the up-for-grabs crown as the new king of late-night TV. No longer merely a fan of Johnny Carson's and Steve Allen's, David Letterman was, at CBS, their next-generation equal: to the nineties, he *was* Carson and Allen, and broadcasting direct from Broadway, from the very theater where *The Ed Sullivan Show* originated, was a master stroke of teleliterate continuity and appreciation. From opening night on August 30, 1993, when Paul Newman stood up in the audience and asked "Where the hell are the singing cats?," *Late Show* solidified its own very secure place in TV history—and on the CBS schedule. It wasn't that different a show—the "Top Ten" lists made the transition intact, as did Paul Shaffer and bandmates (now playfully renamed The CBS Orchestra)—but Letterman's relaxed and confident air, and the effort and wit displayed not only by him, but by his writing and production staff, made *Late Show* the best post-Carson talk show on television. Already, *Late Show* has made stars of neighboring salesmen Mujibur Rahman and Sirajul Islam, and of Letterman's own mother Dorothy. Meanwhile, celebrities have come on to have fun, make conversation, and sometimes make waves. Debra Winger stripped to reveal a Wonder Girl costume from her old *Wonder Woman* days, Demi Moore stripped to a bikini for a quick, PG-rated dance; Drew Barrymore, in honor of Letterman's birthday, faced her pleasantly surprised host and bared not her soul, but her chest; and Madonna showed up only to swear up a storm. By the end of 1995, Letterman had been usurped, at least for the moment, by *The Tonight Show with Jay Leno* in the ratings race, but *Late Show* remained the better of the two programs.

Laverne & Shirley. *1976–83, ABC*. You could make a case that Penny Marshall and Cindy Williams, as blue-collar buddies Laverne and Shirley, carried on the physical-comedy tradition of *I Love Lucy* while simultaneously providing a female equivalent of the Ralph Kramden-Ed Norton friendship on *The Honeymooners*. You could make that case, but I won't, because I was too put off by the insipid scripts and school-revue acting. But with the nostalgic sitcom *Laverne & Shirley* being a spinoff of *Happy Days*, and paired with it

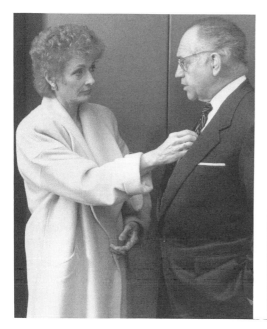

LEFT: *L.A. Law*, with Diana Muldaur and Richard Dysart, just before Muldaur's Rosalind got the shaft.
RIGHT: *Late Show With David Letterman*, with David Letterman.

The Larry Sanders Show, with Jeffrey Tambor, guest Sharon Stone, and Garry Shandling.

on the ABC schedule, *Laverne & Shirley* immediately shot to the number-two slot in the prime-time ratings, right behind *Happy Days;* for two seasons after that, *Laverne & Shirley* outdid its parent program and was the most popular series on television. (Remember, this was right in the middle of what I like to call TV's "Tarnished Age.") Michael McKean, as the taller half of the Lenny and Squiggy supporting team, did well for himself later in *This Is Spinal Tap!* and fine work in such superior sitcoms as HBO's *Dream On* and *Sessions*. (David L. Lander, as Squiggy, wound up years later as a featured character on two David Lynch-Mark Frost TV series, *Twin Peaks* and *On the Air.*) The most successful survivor of *Laverne & Shirley*, though, was Marshall, who, like her brother Garry (who was executive producer and creator of *Happy Days, Laverne & Shirley,* and *Mork & Mindy*), became a successful film director. Penny Marshall's films included *Big* and *A League of Their Own;* Garry Marshall's included *Pretty Woman* and *Frankie and Johnny.* Ironically, Garry Marshall ended up going in the opposite direction of his sister Penny, by eventually landing a very funny recurring role as a network executive on *Murphy Brown.* And the most resonant portions of *Laverne & Shirley* after all these years? There are none, even though ABC tried to jog our memories with a 1995 *Laverne & Shirley Reunion* special. The original show's theme song and the title, unfortunately, are impossible to forget. "One, two, three, four / Five, six, seven, eight / Schlemiel, Schlimazel, Hasenpfeffer Incorporated. . . . "

Lawrence Welk Show, The. *1955–71, ABC; 1971–82, syndicated.* At least three aspects of Welk's long-running music series remain lodged in memory to this day—one musical, one visual, one verbal. The musical memory is Welk's "Bubbles in the Wine" theme (a.k.a. "I'm Forever Blowing Bubbles"). The visual one is the image of those forever-blowing bubbles, released as part of each festive episode of *The Lawrence Welk Show.* The verbal one, of course, is the heavily accented bandleader's count-in—"a-one, a-two . . . "—which he employed on TV for a-three decades on ABC and another decade in syndication. His broadcasting career began on ABC radio in the late forties, as bandleader and headliner of *The Lawrence Welk High Life Revue* (the *High Life* in the title referring not to Welk's image, but to his Miller Brewery sponsor). On local TV, and then on ABC, Welk added dancers to the singers and musicians and presided over his "TV family" until 1971, when the same rural purge that bounced *Hee Haw* into syndication did the same thing to Welk's ultrawholesome variety show. Like Arthur Godfrey, Welk was sufficiently popular to have two weekly network series running simultaneously in the fifties. Back in 1956, when Welk's primary Saturday showcase was still known as *The Dodge Dancing Party* (the name change to *The Lawrence Welk Show* didn't take effect until 1959), ABC imitated Godfrey's success and added a *Talent Scouts*-type show on Mondays: *Lawrence Welk's Top Tunes and New Talent,* which lasted two seasons. On the main *Lawrence Welk Show,* the new talent Welk showcased included the Lennon Sisters and clarinet player Pete Fountain (who reunited with other bubbly alumni in a 1993 PBS tribute to honor Welk, who had died the previous year). The one major note of discord surrounding *The Lawrence Welk Show* occurred in 1959, when the show's original "Champagne Lady," Alice Lon, was fired by Welk for showing "too much knee" in her role as a member of his TV family. Responding to viewer complaints, Welk tried to rehire her, but she refused to return; Norma Zimmer became the new "Champagne Lady" a year later, and fulfilled that kneedy function for the rest of the show's run. If the loss of the original "Champagne Lady" upset Welk privately, he never showed any hint of it on the air. He was, as always, polka-faced.

Leave It to Beaver. *1957–58, CBS; 1958–63, ABC.* Golly, Beav, what is there to say about *this* sitcom that most people don't already know? Gee, I dunno, Wally. Given this show's central spot in the pantheon of pop culture, perhaps the most surprising thing is that it never once cracked the Top 25 in Nielsen's end-of-season rankings. So many things remain fresh in memory, and have been embraced all over again after decades of syndicated reruns, that *Leave It to Beaver* has become one of the primary sources for straight-from-TV quotations—most of them the smallest of small talk, used in modern everyday conversation with an ironic and self-aware twist. Some boyfriends and husbands jokingly call themselves Ward, and their girlfriends and wives June, or vice versa, and it's equally common for working men and women to return after a day's work and announce, as Hugh Beaumont's Ward invariably did to Barbara Billingsley's June, "Hi, honey, I'm home!" (The staked claim on that particular line goes at least as far back as Desi Arnaz's Ricky Ricardo on *I Love Lucy*, but Ward Cleaver said it almost as a daily mantra.) Even the final line in the opening credits, announcing " . . . And Jerry Mathers as the Beaver," somehow has stuck in our collective minds. (On *Second City TV*, the repertory member to be named last in its opening credits was described, " . . . And Dave Thomas as the Beaver.") Mathers and Tony Dow, who played his older brother Wally, were the most natural child actors on sitcom TV, and embodied a credible and likable look at middle-class boyhood that wouldn't be approached again for three decades, until ABC's *The Wonder Years*. Surprisingly, *Leave It to Beaver*, this quiet little dissection of white-bread America, was created and produced by Bob Mosher and Joe Connelly, who had written more than one thousand scripts for the radio and TV versions of *Amos 'n' Andy*. Although it's remembered mostly as an idyllic suburban world, *Leave It to Beaver* actually broke a bit of ground by showing the parents disagreeing in private, and even arguing, about how to treat or punish the boys from week to week. True, June wasn't exactly a potential poster girl—or poster woman—for the future feminist movement, but there was a constant undercurrent in the show that the parents, like the kids, were figuring out a lot of life as they went along. The jokes were reserved, the conflicts small, which may be what, in the long run, makes *Leave It to Beaver* loom so large. Telemovie and series sequels, including the horrid *Still the Beaver* and *The New Leave It to Beaver*, are best left unmentioned and unwatched; instead, remember and seek out the old classic shows, like "Captain Jack" (Beaver and Wally secretly rear a baby alligator); "The Haircut" (Wally and Beaver try to cut Beaver's hair); "Beaver's Crush" and "Miss Landers's Fiancé" (two great episodes about Beaver's crushes on his attractive teachers); and "In the Soup" (Beaver climbs into a billboard prop to see if a steaming cup contains real soup). And don't forget (but who could?) about Ken Osmond's Eddie Haskell, a subversive and sarcastic delinquent when alone with Wally and the Beav, but transparently unctuous in front of their parents: "Mrs. Cleaver, you've done something new to your hair!"). Eddie always stirred up trouble, but it never boiled over, not with Wally and Beaver looking out for one another. "You know something, Wally?" Beaver asked his big brother, in another quietly quotable moment. "I'd rather do nothin' with you than somethin' with anybody else." My favorite quote of all, though, is some parental advice from Ward: "Well, Beaver, this may be hard to believe, but life isn't exactly like television."

Let's Make a Deal. *1963–67, NBC; 1968–76, ABC; 1971–76, 1980, 1984–85, syndicated.* The name of this long-running, ultratacky game show, like that of its host Monty Hall, remains a synonym for silly greediness—or greedy silliness. Audience members dressed up in silly costumes (more frequently as animal or vegetable than mineral), hoping to catch Hall's eye and be selected as a contestant. The way everyone was outfitted, though, the most effective tactic for catching Hall's eye might have been to dress normally. When the lucky people were chosen, they then learned just how lucky—and how greedy—they really were. In a sort of concentrated Las Vegas laboratory setting, each contestant was allowed to build (or lose) his or her winnings by betting them, time and again, against the promise of still greater treasures—many of those treasures, hidden behind curtains, as disparate as a trip to Bimini or a trip on a burro. Hall's request that contestants choose from "Door number one, door number two, or door number three" is where that venerable catch phrase originated—just as their flustered indecision is the origin of the phrase "Oh, Monty, Monty," commonly used today by teleliterates confronted with a tough choice.

Life and Adventures of Nicholas Nickleby, The. *1983, syndicated.* The Royal Shakespeare Company adapted this Charles Dickens novel into a mammoth theatrical event—dozens of actors playing more than one hundred roles, acting out a story that took nine hours to tell. Onstage, at the RSC and on Broadway, the scope and ambition of the play thrilled and drained performers and theatergoers alike. (During the standing ovation at the performance I attended, one audience member drew hearty laughs from the actors by jokingly shouting, "Encore!") On TV, where it was filmed and packaged as a four-night drama, *The Life and Adventures of Nicholas Nickleby* revealed itself, quite naturally, as a literary miniseries; in a way, television was its natural home. What you missed on TV, of course, was the incomparably involving feeling of being there, having RSC members running all around you, and basically running the theatrical equivalent of a marathon. Yet the TV version, with its clever camerawork and effective closeups, took advantage of the intimacy of television, and emerged with one of the best miniseries ever broadcast. Roger Rees, who starred in the title role, later appeared as rich

Robin Colcord on *Cheers*. The miniseries was syndicated and presented via the Mobil Showcase Network after being rejected by CBS, NBC, and ABC, and attracted much attention at the time for being "too good for network TV." Herb Schmertz, Mobil's longtime publicist, later admitted the submission to the networks was a ploy. "I knew they'd turn it down," he told me. "I just wanted the record to be clear that they'd had a shot at it. It made good copy in manipulating the press. The print press hates television." Why the Dickens would he think that?

Life of Riley, The. *1949–50, 1953–58, NBC*. On TV, *Riley* actually had two lives. The first began in 1949, as one of television's earliest situation comedies. A thin Jackie Gleason, whose success on DuMont's *Cavalcade of Stars* was still a season away, starred as blue-collar worker Chester A. Riley, but the TV spinoff of the popular NBC radio series didn't catch on, and was canceled after one season. Perhaps it was because William Bendix, who had attained stardom in the role on radio in the forties, had become too closely associated with the role. When NBC relaunched *The Life of Riley* on TV again three years later, with Bendix himself heading an all-new cast, the sitcom shot immediately into the Top 20, and lasted five years—making the title phrase, and Riley's signature remark ("What a revoltin' development *this* is!") even more familiar. It's noteworthy, perhaps, that the *radio* version of *The Life of Riley* had two Rileys as well: before Bendix, the part was played by Lionel Stander, who went on to play Max the valet in *Hart to Hart*, but only after a very long stretch in which his career was torpedoed by the Hollywood blacklist. What a revoltin' development *that* was. . . .

Lifestyles of the Rich and Famous. *1984–88, syndicated; 1986, ABC*. One of the most imitated narrative voices of the eighties, Robin Leach burst onto the TV scene with a series of posh programs celebrating the wretched excesses of the world's wealthy celebrities and minor foreign royalties. Leach's style was pure hyperventilated overenthusiasm: every person profiled was a star, every abode and yacht a palace, every sentence at least partly *shouted!* "Look at *this!*" Leach would scream, as cameras peeked into a bathroom the size of West Virginia. The series was so over-the-top, and so uncritically accepting of every extravagance, it may as well have been titled *Thou Shalt Covet Thy Neighbor's Goods*. Leach, TV's most famous and fawning toady, bellowed and salivated all the way to the bank (the one in Monaco, no doubt), and, when shameful overindulgence fell into disfavor near the end of the eighties, churned out more "reserved" sister shows like *Runaway with the Rich and Famous*, and eventually retitled the parent show *Lifestyles with Robin Leach and Shari Belafonte*, as a nod to both the less ostentatious focus and Leach's new cohost. But no matter where Leach travels, or with whom, he sticks out like a "Have Volume, Will Travel" sycophant, a passport-brandishing, name-dropping Crazy Eddie. His programs are *in-saaane!*

Little House on the Prairie. *1974–83, NBC*. After fourteen years as the youngest son on *Bonanza*, Michael Landon took a year off and returned with another period Western series, one that would occupy him for the next nine years—as creator, executive producer, writer, director, and, for all but the final season, star. This time he was the patriarch, playing Pa Ingalls, famed father figure from the autobiographical books by Laura Ingalls Wilder. Melissa Gilbert, as Laura, narrated the shows, and wound up as the central star; the final season, retitled *Little House: A New Beginning*, left her in charge, with Landon's Pa and costar Melissa Sue Anderson's Mary Ingalls having left the spotlight for Laura alone. For many, including myself, *Little House* was too anachronistic, preachy, predictable, and saccharine (or, these days, too Nutra-sweet.) That formula, however, was no less successful for *Little House* than it had been for *The Waltons,* or for Landon's next series, *Highway to Heaven,* which ran from 1985–89. (In the midnineties, other unabashedly wholesome TV series would taste significant success by presenting thin variations on familiar Landon themes: *Dr. Quinn, Medicine Woman* was a little like a distaff *Little House on the Prairie,* while *Touched by an Angel* was a lot like a distaff *Highway to Heaven.)* Before the term was bludgeoned into meaninglessness in the nineties, *Little House* espoused "family values," and stood for years as a prime example of intentionally wholesome programming—stood, that is, until the 1984 telemovie *Little House: The Last Farewell,* in which writer-director Landon, returning for one last appearance as Pa Ingalls, watched as the whole town of Walnut Grove was burned to the ground. It was torched by its residents in an act of defiance against a land baron, the *Little House* equivalent of destroying the village in order to save it. In that final season and those final telemovies, the part of Laura's orphaned niece was played by Shannen Doherty, whose TV address subsequently changed from Walnut Grove to *Beverly Hills, 90210*.

Live Aid. *1985, MTV, ABC, syndicated.* In the summer of 1971, George Harrison and Ravi Shankar hosted a pair of benefit concerts at New York's Madison Square Garden, aimed to raise money for famine victims in Bangla Desh. It was an all-star concert and major musical success, featuring Harrison, Shankar, Eric Clapton, Bob Dylan, Ringo Starr, Leon Russell, and others, and was captured for posterity in the 1971 album *The Concert for Bangla Desh* and in a 1972 film version. More than a dozen summers later, rocker Bob Geldof decided to mount another superstar concert to benefit famine victims—in Africa this time—and enlisted the live aid of Paul McCartney, Mick Jagger, The Who, Phil Collins, David Bowie, Sting, Madonna, and dozens of others. (With the video and single of "We Are the World," another all-star musical effort to provide African famine relief, having topped the charts a few months earlier, it was a relatively easy sell.) Staged simultaneously in London and Philadelphia, *Live Aid* relied on satellite TV to feed performances from one arena to another, and to an international audience as well: one way or another, most, but not all, of the sixteen-hour event was televised. (Collins, by flying via Concorde, managed to perform at both Live Aid sites during the concert's duration.) One memorable, and ironic, technical glitch occurred during The Who's performance of "My Generation," with sound and picture both being lost just as Roger Daltrey was singing, "Why don't you all f-f-f-fade away. . . . " *Live Aid* raised lots of money, and also raised consciousness about using rock music as a social force once again: Willie Nelson staged the first of several *Farm Aid* concerts (fund-raisers for needy American farmers) later that same year.

Live! with Regis and Kathie Lee. *1988–   , syndicated.* When this informal TV talk show was syndicated nationally on Labor Day 1988, a few years after becoming the dominant local morning program in New York, Regis Philbin officially went from second banana (on *The Joey Bishop Show* in the sixties) to top dog. In between, he had attained major TV success in another local market, on the opposite coast, as cohost (with Cyndy Garvey) of *A.M. Los Angeles*. New York imported him, teamed him with actress-singer Kathie Lee Johnson (now Gifford), and their somewhat peculiar chemistry took hold almost immediately. It's no surprise that another New York talk-show host, David Letterman, mentions and utilizes Philbin so often; their grumpy senses of humor, and their wary senses of show business as a somewhat silly line of work, are pretty much the same. And Gifford, though she isn't married to Philbin, might as well be: she's that familiar with his rhythms and obsessions, and with just what it takes to support, insult, inspire, or derail him. (And vice versa.) Every day, *Live!* opens with its best segment: Philbin and Gifford talking, unscripted, about whatever happened the night before. It's the same sort of unguarded and endearing banter in which Bryant Gumbel, Katie Couric, and company engage a few times daily on *Today*, except that most local stations preempt those conversations to present their own local newsbreaks and traffic updates. On *Live!*, they know better than to treat informality as filler: that loose chatter *is* the show. It's more radio than television, except both of the hosts play to the cameras with winks, scowls, smiles, and, when appropriate, yawns. The subsequent celebrity interviews are informal, and somewhat entertaining, but the opening section of *Live! with Regis and Kathie Lee* is what makes it such a guilty pleasure. And when I wrote *that* in my TV column for the *New York Daily News*, Philbin complained on his show the next morning, grumbling about how I could possibly feel *guilty* about liking the show. "Aw, David, c'mon! You've owned up to it," he said, shouting as he stared into the TV camera. "Stand up! Be tall! Be *proud* of watching this show, David!" Then he laughed, not even able to take *himself* seriously. Which is why, I guess, I have decided to use this space to tell *Regis and Kathie Lee:* "I like you, I really like you!"

Lonesome Dove. *1989, CBS.* What a wonderful miniseries this was. It came to TV just as the form had fallen out of favor (the miniseries form, that is; the Western, according to conventional wisdom, had been dead for decades), and became the highest-rated miniseries in years. Part of the reason had to do with Larry McMurtry's story and script, which made full use of the miniseries genre's major strengths: the ability to put even its leading characters in credible dramatic jeopardy, and to develop those characters with the depth and subtlety that only a long-form narrative can allow. In the late seventies, McMurtry published an essay on just this topic, arguing that the TV miniseries form "allows writers to keep rhythms and textural details that are usually lost in the cuttings and budgetings of movie scripts." Certainly, he proved it with *Lonesome Dove*, and so did the stars of the show. Robert Duvall, as former Texas Ranger Augustus McCrae, gave one of television's all-time best performances—and Tommy Lee Jones, as his quiet but ultimately explosive partner, Woodrow Call, gave another one, quite a few years before most of Hollywood awakened to his full dramatic range and power. Anjelica Huston, as rancher Clara Allen, gave a similarly subtle and touching portrayal, as did Rick Schroder as Call's unacknowledged son, Newt. The acting, the scenery, and the unpredictable turns of events made *Lonesome Dove* a memorable TV milestone—and brought the Western back in vogue, a year before the large-screen *Dances with Wolves*. In 1993, CBS presented a miniseries sequel, *Return to Lonesome Dove*, that was not written by McMurtry and did not star any of the three principals. Duvall's Gus, like Francisco Franco, was still dead, and Jones and Huston declined to reprise their respective roles as Call and Clara; they went instead to Jon Voight and Barbara Hershey. Predictably, *Return to Lonesome Dove* paled beside the original—but on its own, judged purely on its own story, performances, and merit, it was surprisingly good, and Oliver Reed, as a greedy land baron, all but stole the show. Two years later, CBS took the unusual step of reversing course and presenting McMurtry's "official" *Lonesome Dove* sequel, *Larry McMurtry's Streets of Laredo*. That five-hour 1995 miniseries gave the role of Call to James Garner, who was every bit as good, and stoic, as Jones had been; Sissy Spacek played Clara, and the best supporting performances were turned in by Sonia Braga and—in an effective dramatic performance almost as unexpected as when Ed Wynn appeared in *Requiem for a Heavyweight*—comedian George Carlin. *Laredo* was even better than *Return*, but neither came close to the artistic perfection of the original *Lonesome Dove*. Without McMurtry's involvement, a weekly syndicated series (called, in its first season, *Lonesome Dove: The Series*) popped up in 1994, following the exploits of Newt—now played by Scott Bairstow. By the show's second season, though, the show took on a darker edge, propelling Newt into a career as a somewhat ruthless bounty hunter, and renaming the series *Lonesome Dove: The Outlaw Years*. McMurtry had no interest in propelling the saga forward, but apparently was quite interested in examining its past. He wrote *Dead Man's Walk*, a *Lonesome Dove* prequel showing young rookie Texas Rangers Gus McCrae and Woodrow Call on their first mission together, and cowrote (with Diana Ossana) the four-hour ABC miniseries adaptation scheduled for telecast in 1996. David Arquette plays Gus this time around, and Jonny Lee Miller gets the call as Call.

Lone Ranger, The. *1949–57, ABC; 1953–57, CBS.* The strains of Rossini's *William Tell Overture*. The masked man, majestically astride a white horse, shouting, "Hi-yo, Silver!" The opening narration, which many can recite from memory decades later: "A fiery horse with the speed of light, a cloud of dust, and a hearty 'Hi-yo, Silver!' The Lone Ranger! With his faithful Indian companion, Tonto, the masked rider of the plains led the fight for law and order in the early West. Return with us now to those thrilling days of yesteryear. The Lone Ranger rides again!" The quintessential TV Western, *The Lone Ranger* was created for radio in the thirties by George W. Trendle, who concocted the show as a way to draw listeners to his Detroit radio station—and intentionally devised both the radio and TV versions as "a good, clean show to keep the Parent-Teacher Association off our neck." Writers for episodes of *The Lone Ranger* were given a handbook of guidelines to follow, which explained that the hero in this particular Western series did not smoke, use profanity, drink intoxicating beverages, make love, or shoot to kill—and that, at all times, "his grammar must be pure." (Probably his grandpa, too.) The origin of the Lone Ranger was an episode repeated every season, explaining just why John Reid ran around with a mask and silver bullets, and how he came to link up with his faithful Indian companion. Like Gus McCrae and Woodrow Call in *Lonesome Dove*, John Reid was a Texas Ranger. When he and five other Rangers were trapped in an ambush, Reid was the only one to survive. Left for dead, he was nursed back to health by Tonto, and thereafter sought frontier justice by donning a mask and riding in memory of his slain colleagues, as the "lone" Ranger. He used silver bullets not because he feared werewolves, but because his sole source of income was a silver mine—and because, theoretically, silver bullets were less destructive than lead ones. At least, that's what viewers of *The Lone Ranger* were "lead" to believe—and there were an awful lot of those viewers. Until *Disneyland* came along in 1954, it was the only ABC series to rank in TV's Top 10. Jay Silverheels was the only Tonto throughout the TV run, and Clayton Moore the Lone Ranger we all remember (even though John Hart replaced him for two seasons during a contract dispute). CBS reran episodes of the ABC show as part of its Saturday morning schedule, an unusual arrangement that doubled the pleasure, and doubled the fun, of many *Lone Ranger* fans during the fifties. Besides the theme song and opening credits, one other thing from *The Lone Ranger* is universally familiar: Tonto's friendly nickname for the Lone Ranger, "Kemo Sabe." No matter what Lenny Bruce claimed in his famous comedy routine, that Indian phrase, according to the "origin" *Lone Ranger* show, actually translates to "trusty scout."

Loretta Young Show, The. *1953–61, NBC.* Just as Jimmy Durante is best remembered in TV terms by the way he ended his shows, Loretta Young, the actress whose familiar film roles include *The Stranger* and *The Farmer's Daughter*, is most famous for the way she began hers: with the grandest of grand entrances, entering a doorway with a swirling skirt and a dazzling smile. In syndication, ironically, those memorable introductions were deleted, solely because Young feared that her fashions and hairdos had become unflatteringly dated. So much for being forever Young. . . .

Lost in Space. *1965–68, CBS.* "Warning! Warning! Danger! Danger!" That's the way the bubble-headed Robot used to warn Billy Mumy's Will Robinson about impending trouble—and it's easily the most commonly quoted line of dialogue from this camp sci-fi series. Actually, when Irwin Allen created this series, "camp" was not what he had in mind. He intended *Lost in Space* to be serious, and was angered when CBS executives roared with laughter while screening the pilot (which, by the way, included neither the Robot nor Jonathan Harris's cowardly Dr. Smith). He was angered, that is, until they bought it anyway. *Lost in Space* deserves credit for popularizing "camp TV," and tongue-in-cheek prime-time cliff-hangers, three months before TV's *Batman*, but that's about as much credit as it deserves. The *Lost in Space* cast included a former *Zorro* (Guy Williams) and one of the former moms on *Lassie* (June Lockhart), but gave them absolutely nothing to do. The series, instead, was about a boy and his robot—named, in this case, Robot—and their adventures with Dr. Zachary Smith, the world's (universe's?) worst role model. "Best" episode, in terms of outrageousness? "The Great Vegetable Rebellion," in which the Robinsons are attacked by giant alien veggies who turn them into walking, then rooted, vegetables. (The giant celery, naturally, was the big stalker.) The series, now shown on The Sci-Fi Channel, is less interesting in retrospect than some trivial facts about it. For example, the first episode's story line had the Robinsons shot into space (aboard the junky-looking Jupiter 2) to colonize Alpha Centauri, because the Earth was at that time immensely overpopulated. That time—that year—was 1997. Then there's the musical trivia: a more mature Mumy, as half of the rock duo Barnes & Barnes, wrote and performed the novelty cult single "Fish Heads" in the late seventies (well, maybe not *that* much more mature: the primary lyrics were "Fish heads, fish heads, roly-poly fish heads / Fish heads, fish heads, eat them up, Yum!"). In the nineties, Mumy went back to outer space, playing an alien named Lennier as a regular on the syndicated series *Babylon 5*. And before I Babylon much longer, I'll close on another musical note: The *Lost in Space* theme was written by John Williams, who later returned to outer space as the composer of the scores to *Close Encounters of the Third Kind* and *E.T.: The Extra-Terrestrial*.

Lou Grant. *1977–82, CBS.* So many of the best one-hour shows of the nineties are so adept at mixing comedy and drama—shows such as *Northern Exposure, Picket Fences,* and *NYPD Blue*—that it's hard to imagine a time when they didn't exist. Yet it was only in the late seventies, a year or two before *The White Shadow* and *Hill Street Blues*, that yet another series from MTM Productions, *Lou Grant*, all but invented this particular hybrid. Transplanting Ed Asner's gruff but lovable Lou Grant from the classic sitcom *The Mary Tyler Moore Show* to his own dramatic series was risking a lot: *Lou Grant*, set in a newspaper newsroom instead of a TV newsroom, had no laugh track, no other on-camera personnel from *The Mary Tyler Moore Show*, and no successful precedents at having a familiar TV character make such an abrupt comedy-to-drama transition. Imagine if *Frasier* had been a one-hour dramatic spinoff of *Cheers*, rather than a half-hour sitcom, and you've got a pretty good sense of what a risky endeavor it was. Co-creator James L. Brooks described the formula for which they were aiming in *Lou Grant* as "about 70 percent drama, 30 percent comedy," and the mixture worked perfectly—largely due to Asner, who was equally skilled at both ends of the spectrum. *Lou Grant* was a special favorite of mine because it took place in a newsroom, and captured

LEFT: *Leave It to Beaver,* with Barbara Billingsley, Hugh Beaumont, Jerry Mathers, and Tony Dow.
RIGHT: *Lonesome Dove,* with Robert Duvall and Tommy Lee Jones.

The Lone Ranger, with Clayton Moore atop Silver and Jay Silverheels on Scout.

the relationships and office politics beautifully—even if it was too large a paper to rely so heavily on one photographer and a pair of reporters. The show also was a favorite because the drama of putting out a daily paper gave the show's characters, and hence its writers and producers, a perfect excuse to address and analyze topical and significant issues. In the ensuing years since the cancellation of *Lou Grant*, only a handful of prime-time shows, among them *L.A. Law* and *Picket Fences,* have eagerly addressed volatile and complex ideas and conflicts—and *Lou Grant* itself, ironically, was taken from the air partly because of Asner's off-screen but very vocal opposition to America's political policies in Central America. The show was canceled so summarily and unjustly, in fact, that *Lou Grant* never got to close up shop with what would have been the perfect final episode: the folding of the *Los Angeles Tribune,* with all the characters watching the presses roll for the last time.

Love Boat, The. *1977–86, ABC.* Any Hollywood actor or actress who ever cashed a paycheck, in any decade, seemed automatically eligible for a guest spot on either this show or its sister series, *Fantasy Island.* Gavin MacLeod, like Ed Asner, had just come from the WJM newsroom of *The Mary Tyler Moore Show* into a one-hour show, but MacLeod's Captain Stubing was no Lou Grant, and *The Love Boat* was no comedy-drama hybrid. In fact, it had no drama, no comedy, and no reason for staying afloat as long as it did (not even with Teri Hatcher, later of *Lois & Clark: The New Adventures of Superman,* as one of the "Love Boat Mermaids" in its final season). The most memorable thing about *The Love Boat* was the on-air promotional campaign by ABC, for which the announcer pronounced the word "love" in the title as though it were three syllables long ("Stay tuned for *The Loooooooooooove Boat!*"). In retrospect, there certainly was something memorable, also, about Fred Grandy, who played Gopher. During the show's final season, Grandy announced he was returning to his first love—politics—and was finished with show business. (Anyone who had seen him act could well have wondered, "When had he *started?*") In November 1986, exactly two months after *The Love Boat* sailed its final voyage as a weekly series, Grandy, an Iowa Republican, was elected to the U.S. House of Representatives. Grandy declined to participate in the 1990 reunion telemovie, *The Love Boat: A Valentine Voyage,* but MacLeod defended his former costar's absence, and his intellectual qualifications, during a TV press conference keyed to the reunion special. Grandy, MacLeod said, was overqualified to play the role of Gopher—at which point Ed Bark, TV critic for *The Dallas Morning News,* asked MacLeod, "Could you name an actor who is *not* overqualified to play the role of Gopher?" I *loooooooooooove* that question.

Love of Life. *1951–80, CBS.* Lasting nearly thirty years, *Love of Life* perhaps is most remembered today merely for its title, even though its claim to hiring future stars is better than a lot of other daytime serials. Warren Beatty worked on this soap for a few weeks in the late fifties, and actors staying around for a longer lease on *Life* included Bonnie Bedelia (as Sandy Porter, 1961–67),

Roy Scheider (Jonas Falk, 1965–66), Ray Wise (Jamie Rollins, 1970–76), Paul Michael Glaser (Dr. Joe Corelli, 1971–72), Marsha Mason (Judith Cole, 1972), Christopher Reeve (Ben Harper, 1974–76), and, last but by no means least, Dana Delany (Amy Russell, 1979–80).

M

MacNeil/Lehrer NewsHour, The. *1983–95, PBS.* **The MacNeil/Lehrer Report.** *1975–83, PBS.* In the sixties, Robert MacNeil was a correspondent for NBC's *The Huntley-Brinkley Report*. By the nineties, MacNeil and Jim Lehrer would generally be acknowledged as the classiest descendents of the Huntley-Brinkley tradition—the best news anchor duo in the business. They initially had been paired to coanchor PBS coverage of the Senate Watergate Hearings in 1973. Two years later, they reteamed for a locally produced New York public television newscast, *The Robert MacNeil Report*, with Lehrer as the Washington correspondent. In a few months, with the two men remaining in their respective cities, PBS gave them equal billing and launched the show nationally. Using satellite TV technology to great advantage, MacNeil and Lehrer communicated with one another, and with guests around the country, to produce one of the most intelligent news programs on the air. When it doubled its length in 1983, the program became even more thorough and valuable. Ted Koppel freely admitted that ABC had copied the *MacNeil/Lehrer Report* formula when creating *Nightline*, but that's only fair. Back in 1952, ABC had experimented with a short-lived prime-time, one-hour newscast called *All Star News,* which, like *MacNeil/Lehrer* decades later, combined breaking news and interviews with commentary and feature pieces. On October 20, 1995, the PBS mainstay, which had begun life as *The Robert MacNeil Report* exactly twenty years earlier, said farewell to the retiring MacNeil—after which *The MacNeil/Lehrer NewsHour* was retitled, quite sensibly, *The NewsHour with Jim Lehrer*. Predictably, the no-nonsense approach of Mac-Neil and Lehrer extended to their final joint appearance, which had only a touch more emotion than their everyday balanced-budget discussions. For twenty years on *MacNeil/Lehrer,* the calm coanchors served PBS and its viewers admirably and stoically—and on the night they ended their on-air partnership and said good-bye to one another, there wasn't a wet eye in the house.

McClure, Jessica, Rescue Coverage. *1987, CNN and other networks and local stations.* A little girl falls in a well, and the attempts to rescue her become, for days, the stuff of live television drama. Sound familiar? Maybe it's deja vu: that description matches not only the case of eighteen-month-old Jessica McClure, trapped twenty-two feet below ground in rural Texas in 1987, but also describes what happened to young Kathy Fiscus in San Marino,

California, in 1949, when television was in its infancy. One Los Angeles station, KTLA-TV, broadcast rescue efforts nonstop for more than twenty-seven hours then, and competing station KTTV was not far behind. The coverage was so riveting that people without TV sets crowded around appliance stores and stared for hours at the televisions in the display windows. "The telecasts of the tragedy gave a glimpse into the future coverage of big news events by video once the coaxial cable is laid across the country," an unsigned *Variety* report suggested at the time, noting that "nearly every tele receiver within signal range of the two TV stations was turned on" as people monitored the ongoing ordeal. "Interest was so great in the heroic rescue work . . . that it would have attracted millions on interconnected networks." Cut to thirty-eight years later, and *Variety* was proven right. In Texas, local stations provided major coverage again, but this time the Cable News Network was in place to cover the story nonstop and relay it nationwide. CNN was rewarded for its efforts with a Nielsen rating of 6.6—the highest in its history, up to that time—and the beginning of a reputation that it was indeed a valid place to turn for lengthy coverage of breaking news. The major broadcast networks, seeing how big the story had become, generated more and more updates, and CBS, NBC, and ABC all interrupted prime-time programming that Friday night to relay live coverage of what turned out to be a happy ending: unlike Kathy Fiscus, Jessica McClure emerged alive. The coverage was indeed riveting—and so, surprisingly, was *Everybody's Baby: The Rescue of Jessica McClure,* a 1989 docudrama presented by ABC. The rating for that telemovie, in which art imitated life? Nielsen estimated it at 22.9, more than three times as large an audience as CNN had gotten for the actual rescue. Oh, well. . . .

McHale's Navy. *1962–66, ABC.* This World War II sitcom was a clear and pale imitation of *The Phil Silvers Show* and his Sergeant Bilko character, but this time the bilker was a Navy lieutenant: Quinton McHale, likably played by Ernest Borgnine (who had won an Oscar for his film portrayal of *Marty,* a character and drama originally written by Paddy Chayefsky for television). Joe Flynn was Captain Binghamton, the butt of most of McHale's jokes and schemes, and the actors playing McHale's cohorts included such strong comic character actors as Tim Conway, Carl Ballantine, and Gavin MacLeod. The most impressive and amazing thing about *McHale's Navy,* though, is that one of the episodes was written by, though not officially credited to, Joseph Heller, who penned the TV script *after* the publication of his classic wartime novel, *Catch-22.*

McLean Stevenson Show, The. *1976–77, NBC.* Just kidding.

McMillan and Wife. *1971–76, NBC.* This was a mindless, ridiculous program—if the loving couple on *Hart to Hart* had less money, they'd act like Rock Hudson and Susan Saint James did on this silly show about a police commissioner and his wife. Except that when Saint James decided to leave the series in 1977, Hudson killed off his costarring character and proceeded for another season, in a series renamed *McMillan.* Can you imagine Robert

Wagner squeezing out one more year in a show called *Hart?* No—he's not that *Hart*-less. The main contribution of *McMillan and Wife* to teleliteracy is a tragic one: it was this successful series, as much as Hudson's movies, that enabled that actor to reach and touch so many millions, and thus get and hold their attention when becoming the first Hollywood celebrity to publicly acknowledge he had contracted the AIDS virus. Hudson died in 1985—and, typically, TV had a docudrama, *The Rock Hudson Story*, up and running five years later. It was so awful, even *McMillan and Wife* was more dramatically credible.

Magnum, p.i. *1980–88, CBS.* Tom Selleck's winning personality and seemingly effortless acting style had almost everything to do with why *Magnum, p.i.* became and remained a top-rated detective series. Like James Garner's Jim Rockford in *The Rockford Files*, Selleck's Thomas Magnum was self-deprecating, sarcastic, and, though brave and noble when driven to it, very bullish on self-interest and self-preservation. (The Selleck-Garner connection was most obvious in a wonderfully witty episode of *The Rockford Files*, in which Selleck guest starred as Lance White, a naive yet invariably successful rival private eye.) Some of the most memorable episodes of *Magnum, p.i.* were its misguided attempts to end the series—first with a die-and-go-to-heaven finale that was dismissed as a dream sequence, *Dallas* style, after CBS unexpectedly renewed *Magnum* for one more season, and then with a *final* finale that suggested, among other things, that John Hillerman's haughty Higgins was indeed the same man as Magnum's mysteriously unseen employer, author Robin Masters. This flew in the face of several clues planted along the way during the run of the series—not the least of which was the fact that during the show's first five seasons, the voice of Masters (heard via telephone) was provided by none other than Orson Welles.

Make Room for Daddy. *1953–56, ABC.* **The Danny Thomas Show.** *1956–57, ABC; 1957–65, CBS.* Oh, Danny boy, the pipes, the pipes are calling. . . . Over its long run, this series had two titles and two wives, but only one father figure: Danny Williams, the nightclub entertainer played by, and patterned after, Danny Thomas. For a fifties sitcom, the show had a decidedly modern sensibility. Its original title reflected the father's guilt about being on the road and away from his kids so much that his presence in the household was a relative novelty. The title was changed after three seasons when *Singin' in the Rain* comedienne Jean Hagen, who on the sitcom played Danny's wife Margaret, left the show. Rather than replace her character, Thomas merely killed her off, a very unusual thing to do in the soothing sitcom universe of that era. After one season as a widower, Danny Williams remarried, with the more suitably cast Marjorie Lord playing his second wife (and with Angela Cartwright coming along as her daughter). These days, the durable Thomas sitcom is remembered most for its buffoonish supporting players—Hans Conreid as Danny's boisterous Lebanese patriarch Uncle Tonoose, and Bill Dana as the Hispanic elevator operator who introduced himself by saying, "My name José Jimenez" (a name, and bit, carried over from Dana's appearances on *The Steve Allen Show)*—and for the traditional "Danny Boy" ballad that ended each show. It was a cleverly written series (Larry Gelbart, for example, did his first comedy writing on Thomas's sitcom), but Thomas deserves special credit for his business acumen behind the scenes. With partner Sheldon Leonard, he launched *The Andy Griffith Show* as a spinoff of *The Danny Thomas Show,* and also presented *The Real McCoys* and *The Dick Van Dyke Show;* later, with Aaron Spelling, Thomas was part owner of *The Mod Squad.* And in February 1965, a mere five months after CBS folded *The Danny Thomas Show,* Thomas was back on NBC with a one-hour special called *The Danny Thomas TV Family Reunion*—television's very first official reunion show. Off-screen, Thomas's real family reunions included daughter Marlo, who grew up to star in her own sitcom, *That Girl.* And to complete the Thomas TV family portrait, Danny Thomas's real-life son Tony, the Thomas in Witt-Thomas-Harris Productions, was part owner of such popular sitcoms as *Soap* and *The Golden Girls.* For a while, the family patriarch busied himself by starring in occasional (and less successful) sitcom efforts, such as 1970's *Danny Thomas in Make Room for Granddaddy.* Eventually, and proudly, the elder Thomas stopped his active involvement in TV production—and made room for sonny.

Mama. *1949–57, CBS.* This popular sitcom was to Norwegians what *The Goldbergs* was to Jews: an affectionate look at their cultural heritage, rich family life, and proud status as hardworking American immigrants. But where *The Goldbergs* was a contemporary comedy, *Mama* was a period piece, set in turn-of-the-century San Francisco. Except for its final season, *Mama* was performed live, so the majority of the series' episodes exist only in memory— a neat irony, since the sitcom is based on the 1948 movie *I Remember Mama* (which, in turn, was based on a Broadway play, which was based on a novel). On television, Rosemary Rice's Katrin opens each show by flipping through a family photo album and saying fondly, "I remember my brother Nels, and my little sister Dagmar, and, of course, Papa. But most of all, I remember Mama." The TV *Mama* is loaded with firsts: it's the first TV spinoff series based on a movie (beating CBS's *The Front Page* and NBC's *The Life of Riley* to the punch by several months), the first instance of popular support from viewers reinstating a canceled TV show (when CBS dropped the series in 1956, so many fans complained that the network reversed its decision), and the first instance of a TV series getting its act together and taking it on the road. Peggy Wood, the titular star of *Mama,* toured regional summer theaters with a stage version of her TV show and, according to one account at the time, "broke box-office records"—a startlingly early precursor of the TV-to-stage phenomenon later presented by the likes of *The Real Live Brady Bunch.* Other *Mama* legacies include the character of Dagmar (one of the actresses who played the role is now better known as feminist writer Robin Morgan), whose *Dagmar* name was appropriated for the buxom sidekick played by Jennie Lewis on *Broadway Open House,* and a youngster named Dick Van Patten, who played the rather geeky-looking son, Nels. Van Patten would grow up, of course, to head his own TV family, as the patriarch of *Eight Is*

Enough. And regarding *Mama*, that's about enough, too—except to note one *Mama* legacy that, unfortunately, was not embraced by subsequent sitcoms. On *Mama*, commercials appeared only at the start and end of each program, and never were permitted to interrupt the action. *Mama* mia!

Man from U.N.C.L.E., The. *1964–68, NBC.* "Open Channel D! Open Channel D!" Like Dick Tracy speaking into his two-way wrist radio, Robert Vaughn's Napoleon Solo and David McCallum's Illya Kuryakin communicated with each other, and with U.N.C.L.E. headquarters, by talking into their spiffy, streamlined, pen-shaped communicators. Illya, a blond Russian, had a Beatle haircut, and both he and Napoleon spoke sarcastically and carried big guns. Inspired by the spy craze in general and Ian Fleming's novels in particular (Fleming, in fact, was involved in helping to concoct the original series premise, and even contributed the name of Solo, which also appeared as a minor character in *Goldfinger)*, *The Man from U.N.C.L.E.* started out as a gun-crazy, paranoid, but stylish adventure series that, like *Mission: Impossible*, got more fanciful and less realistic after its first season. One year before *Get Smart* and two years before *Batman*, *The Man from U.N.C.L.E.* was a camp cult hit, and attracted as much interest, and as many high-profile guest stars, as either of those other crime spoofs. An allegedly feminist counterpart, *The Girl from U.N.C.L.E.*, was launched in 1966, starring Stefanie Powers and Noel Harrison, but it lasted only a season. Leo G. Carroll, the gruff costar of *Topper*, appeared in both series as U.N.C.L.E. boss Mr. Waverly, and guest stars included an incredible roster of players from TV's past, present, and future: William Shatner and Leonard Nimoy (in the same episode), Sonny and Cher, Angela Lansbury, Barbara Feldon, Don Adams, Eve Arden, Joan Collins, Carroll O'Connor, June Lockhart, Jack Palance, Jack Lord, Yvonne Craig, Telly Savalas, Rip Torn, and—dressed in drag in a memorably camp turn for "The Mother Muffin Affair"—Boris Karloff. The false-front tailor shop of U.N.C.L.E. headquarters was lampooned in the labyrinthine opening credits of *Get Smart*, just as their communications devices were exaggerated as Maxwell Smart's infamous shoe phone. Neither U.N.C.L.E. nor its no-periods rival, THRUSH, began with workable matchable acronyms, but the former quickly was explained as shorthand for United Network Command for Law Enforcement. (In the *Man from U.N.C.L.E.* novelizations, THRUSH got its own matching definition, a rather pathetic one: the Technological Heirarchy for the Removal of Undesirables and the Subjugation of Humanity.) Fifteen years after *The Man from U.N.C.L.E.* was canceled, Vaughn's Solo and McCallum's Kuryakin reunited, with *Avengers* star Patrick Macnee as their new boss, in a 1983 telemovie called, straightforwardly, *The Man from U.N.C.L.E.: The Fifteen Years Later Affair*. There was no return for *The Girl from U.N.C.L.E.*, which, all things considered, was just as well.

Mannix. *1967–75, CBS.* This detective series, starring Mike Connors as private eye Joe Mannix, was one of the most violent TV shows of the sixties and early seventies—and remains memorable, if at times laughable, because most of that violence was perpetrated upon poor Mannix himself. Until Jim Rockford and *The Rockford Files* came along, Mannix was the biggest punching-bag detective on series TV. At being beaten, he couldn't be beat.

Man on the Moon. See *Moon Landing*.

Many Loves of Dobie Gillis, The. *1958–63, CBS.* Long before the young hero of *Doogie Howser, M.D.* bared his soul in his computerized diaries, or the cocky protagonist of *Parker Lewis Can't Lose* finessed his way through high school, Dwayne Hickman's Dobie Gillis laid out his alienated teenaged angst for all to see—often speaking directly to the viewer, pondering the mysteries of life and love while seated beneath a copy of Rodin's famous *The Thinker* (made all the more famous, art historians may cringe to hear, by its weekly appearance on *Dobie Gillis*). This sitcom, like George Burns's, broke the "fourth wall," and added its own stylized trick of panning and zooming quickly between scenes, giving the show a pace that nowadays seems surprisingly close to that of *Seinfeld.* Its most subversive contribution, though, was serving up a beatnik as a second banana, even though Bob Denver's Maynard G. Krebs was less of a counterculture poet than a cuddly puppy—less likely to recite *Howl* than to howl, period. Denver, who would resurface as the even more neutral and neutered goofball on *Gilligan's Island,* made a lasting impression as Krebs, thanks mostly to slang that didn't last ("like, cool, daddy-o") and fashions that did (sneakers and torn sweatshirts, a radical departure from TV's button-down young role models, Dobie included). Also remembered from the show, even though they appeared only during the first season, were Tuesday Weld as Thalia Menninger and Warren Beatty as Milton Armitage—the ingenue with whom Dobie was obsessed, and the rich rival for her affections. Though both were depicted as vain and shallow, Dobie envied him and adored her, which sent mixed messages to the show's impressionable young audience. Yes, *Dobie Gillis* presented Sheila James's brainy but mousy Zelda Gilroy as the obvious ideal mate for Dobie, and also paired him with a best buddy well outside the in-crowd mainstream, but Dobie kept coveting the establishment status quo: all he wanted was to fit in, get rich, and attract a beautiful woman. Two telemovie reunions, 1977's *Whatever Happened to Dobie Gillis?* and 1988's *Bring Me the Head of Dobie Gillis,* answered the question in the former telemovie's title: Dobie ended up marrying Zelda and taking over his father's grocery store, the very place he used to hate working as a teenager. Happy ending? You be the judge, daddy-o.

March on Washington. *1963, CBS, NBC, and ABC.* In the summer of 1963, five years before he was murdered, Martin Luther King, Jr., delivered the famous climax to the well-organized March on Washington, in which an estimated two-hundred-thousand civil-rights activists and concerned citizens (only one out of five of which were white) migrated to Washington, D.C., and the Lincoln Memorial, for a day of solidarity and speeches. Radio and television came in and out of coverage all day, and the activities were considered important enough to preempt many national TV programs and to be broadcast on radio internationally. Forty-nine network TV cameras, including twenty-three different pool cameras, were set up to record and relay the civil rights march and the day's events, with such reporters at the scene as Howard K. Smith for ABC and Roger Mudd and Marvin Kalb for CBS. The highlight of the TV coverage, and of the demonstration, was King's "I have a dream . . ." speech on August 28, now regarded as one of the most famous public addresses of the twentieth century. At the start of his oratory, King correctly predicted the March on Washington would "go down in history as the greatest demonstration for freedom in the history of our nation," but other of King's remarks became indelibly etched in national memory. "I have a dream," King said, in one of many sentences repeating that now-famous phrase, "that my four little children will one day live in a nation where they will not be judged by the color of their skin, but by the content of their character." The conclusion to King's speech, calling for solidarity and equality, was another strong moment, powerful at the time and repeated in countless documentaries since. "Let freedom ring!" King said. "And when this happens, when we let it ring from every village and every hamlet, from every state and every city, we will be able to speed up that day when all of God's children—black men and white men, Jews and gentiles, Protestants and Catholic—will be able to join hands and sing, in the words of the old Negro spiritual, 'Free at last, free at last, Thank God Almighty, we are free at last!' " Twenty-two years later, on October 16, 1995, there was another march on Washington, as a mass of well-behaved protesters, most of them African-American males, converged upon the same National Mall with their "Million Man March." Crowd estimates ranged from four hundred thousand to one million and more, but this time the commercial networks paid little attention on live TV. On cable, C-SPAN pointed one camera at the podium and served as the network of record for all the day's speeches, while CNN and Black Entertainment Television came in and out of coverage all day. The event's centerpiece, a late-afternoon speech by controversial Nation of Islam Minister Louis Farrakhan, proved so lengthy (two-and-a-half hours) that both CNN and BET cut away before it was concluded. King's famous "I have a dream" speech, by comparison, clocked in at about sixteen minutes long.

Marcus Welby, M.D. *1969–76, ABC*. In this inexplicably popular series, Robert Young went from *Father Knows Best* to Doctor Knows Best, and portrayed his compassionate Dr. Welby as the kind of general practitioner who involved himself in the lives of his patients, never made an inaccurate diagnosis, and still made house calls. The name *Marcus Welby* came to personify, and be verbal shorthand for, the perfect doctor, just as *Perry Mason* had come to stand for the perfect lawyer. The widespread acceptance of that medical image, and that type of role model, was eradicated (at long last) when the more mortal physicians of *St. Elsewhere* started making their rounds in prime time. And by the time *ER* rolled around, *Marcus Welby* was a visual punch line— shown as something Anthony Edwards's Dr. Mark Greene watched on late-night TV with wry amusement.

Mark Twain Tonight! *1967, CBS*. By the time Hal Holbrook brought his one-man Mark Twain show to TV, he already had been impersonating Sam Clemens on stage for twenty years (including successful off-Broadway and Broadway runs in the late fifties and early sixties), and appeared briefly as the famous author on *The Ed Sullivan Show* and Steve Allen's *Tonight!* show. But it was his triumphant full-length special on TV—a medium Holbrook previously had decried as having "done more to soften the backbone of America than any single thing, even Joe McCarthy"—that made Holbrook a national celebrity. Though Holbrook was only forty-two when he appeared as a seventy-year-old Twain for the CBS version of *Mark Twain Tonight!*, he carried off his impersonation of the white-haired, rusty-voiced author to perfection. More than a quarter-century later, Holbrook continued to tour with constantly revised versions of the stage show, personally adapted from Twain's voluminous and brilliant output. In 1995, Holbrook toured *Mark Twain Tonight!* and reached a very significant milestone: he was seventy years old, the same age at which he had been portraying Twain all these years. Even though the silver anniversary of the televised 1967 *Mark Twain Tonight!* production has come and gone, I hold out hope that Holbrook, who went on to star in TV's *The Senator* and costar on *Evening Shade* (apparently having softened his attitude about television), will reprise his most famous role in a new television special—perhaps complementing his new, more mature portrayal of Mark Twain with footage from his previous show. I'd love to see that happen, but it's more likely, given the ferocity with which Holbrook guards his past and present portrayals of Sam Clemens, that never the Twains shall meet.

Married . . . with Children. *1987–   , Fox.* Popularity, like familiarity, breeds contempt—and when *The Cosby Show* became TV's runaway hit in the mid-eighties, the inevitable (and predictably unsuccessful) copycat sitcoms were followed by the equally inevitable (but more successful) "backlash" sitcoms, which displayed family life in a much less flattering light. *Roseanne* was the best and most popular of the bunch, but Fox's *Married . . . with Children* was first, and was the network's first show to define and embody its "outlaw" image as a more risque network than its established competitors. Usually more crude than creative, and more lewd than amusing, *Married . . . with Children* became Fox's first big hit, as well as the longest-running show in its brief history. Ed O'Neill's hapless Al Bundy, and Katey Sagal's brassy Peg, fought their way through every show, and daughter Kelly paraded around in such skimpy outfits, and acted so wantonly, that the actress portraying her, Christina Applegate, quickly, if briefly, joined the ranks of new-generation sex symbols. Any other symbolism on *Married . . . with Children* was impossible to find, so moronic were most of the jokes and plots—athough one Christmas episode, a takeoff on *It's a Wonderful Life* featuring Sam Kinison as the acerbic angel who takes Al on a tour of what his family's life would be like without him, was deliciously warped (Al's family, he discovered, would be much better off). The funniest thing of all about *Married . . . with Children*, though, was the 1989 boycott organized by housewife Terry Rakolta, who complained that the show was rude and crude and totally inappropriate for family viewing. After her widely repeated and reported rantings, *Married . . . with Children* became more popular than ever.

Marty. *1953, NBC.* This Paddy Chayefsky story is one of the most famous TV dramas of all time—probably *the* most famous—and yet there's widespread, and somewhat maddening, confusion regarding exactly which anthology drama series gets to claim it. Was this live television classic presented on NBC's *Philco Television Playhouse?* Or was it staged instead on *Goodyear TV Playhouse,* the sister series that rotated in the same time slot? Even the best reference books are split evenly down the middle, and thus are little help; *The Collected Works of Paddy Chayefsky: The Television Plays* doesn't mention either *Philco* or *Goodyear;* Shaun Considine's 1994 biography, *Mad as Hell: The Life and Work of Paddy Chayefsky,* skirts the issue by adopting the catch-all title *Philco-Goodyear;* and contemporaneous TV listings from the *New York Times* and *TV Guide* are just as useless, for they referred to the anthology series only as *TV Playhouse* (having dropped all sponsors' names from the titles as a matter of policy). However, these corroborating pieces of evidence should settle the *Marty* lineage issue once and for all: the closing credits on existing kinescopes of the original *Marty* telecast are displayed in front of a Goodyear logo, and the original NBC press release, sent out in advance to promote *Marty,* credits it as a *Goodyear TV Playhouse* production. So it was *Goodyear,* not *Philco,* which on May 24, 1953, presented the play that would change Chayefsky, and television, literally overnight. Its working title had been "Love Story," but NBC requested a title change, so it went on the air as *Marty,* starring Rod Steiger as a lonely Bronx butcher and Nancy Marchand as Clara, the homely woman with whom Marty feels unexpectedly at ease. Steiger and Marchand were brilliant, as was the direction by Delbert Mann, and kinescopes of TV's *Marty* attest to the power of this particular live drama. It won no awards, yet it didn't exactly go unnoticed. *Marty* became the first original TV drama to be adapted as a film. Hollywood hired Chayefsky and Mann to write and direct the expanded movie version, but replaced Steiger with Ernest Borgnine. Released in 1955, the movie *Marty*—this former live TV show—won four Oscars, including best screenplay, best actor, and best picture. The path to Hollywood defection having been blazed by *Marty,* TV directors of other anthology dramas soon followed suit, leading to a premature end to TV's so-called Golden Age. But *Marty* remains part of our common TV vocabulary to this day; it was the first drama to propel a television writer to national prominence, and many of those who remember nothing else about *Marty* recall the classic exchange of dialogue in which Marty and his pal, Angie (played by Joseph Mantell), repeat the same boring, bored mantra: "Well, what do you feel like doing tonight?" "I don't know . . . What do *you* feel like doing?"

Mary Hartman, Mary Hartman. *1976–77, syndicated.* This series not only satirized a specific TV genre, but spawned equally inventive spinoffs satirizing a different TV genre. The genre spoofed by *Mary Hartman, Mary Hartman* was, of course, the soap opera. (Its spinoff series, *Fernwood 2-Night* and

America 2-Night, ridiculed, respectively but not respectably, the local and national TV talk-show format.) The serialized daily format and the intimate, outrageous, often minimalist plot lines of *Mary Hartman, Mary Hartman* poked fun at the soap-opera form, but other elements of the series targeted the stereotypical soap-opera viewer. Mary, the depressed and insecure house-wife played by Louise Lasser, obsessed about "waxy yellow buildup" and wondered why her kitchen, meals, and love life were less attractive than the ones she watched on TV. Like human versions of *The Simpsons,* Mary and her doltish husband Tom (Greg Mullavey) interacted clumsily with friends and relatives, had little control over their offspring, and watched a lot of television. To give the show its warped yet familiar flavor, executive producer Norman Lear teamed writers from different perspectives, including Ann Marcus (a head writer for the real soap opera *Search for Tomorrow)* and Gail Parent (who wrote the continuing soap spoof "As the Stomach Turns" for *The Carol Burnett Show).* His biggest contribution, though, was in assembling an ad hoc network of independent stations to televise *Mary Hartman* nationwide. On camera, the serialized spoof launched the careers of Dabney Coleman (as Fernwood's nasty mayor, Merle Jeeter, an early template for Coleman's *Buffalo Bill),* Mary Kay Place (as country singer Loretta Haggers and, stricken by amnesia, Loretta's sexy alter ego, Lulu), and Martin Mull (as both Garth Gimble, a wife beater who died when he was impaled on a Christmas tree, and Barth Gimble, Garth's unctuous twin brother, who went on to host *Fernwood 2-Night). Mary Hartman, Mary Hartman* was very funny, very funny, and paved the way for Susan Harris's *Soap,* which came to TV just as *Mary Hartman* was leaving it. *Mary Hartman* also displayed a macabre sort of prescience in one of its most controversial story lines, in which Loretta's husband Charlie (Graham Jarvis) lost part of his private parts after an unexpected below-the-belt attack. Charlie was shot, not shorn, and his wife was not the culprit, but it still was as uncomfortably unforgettable, in its day, as the more recent and real fate of John Wayne Bobbitt.

Mary Tyler Moore Show, The. *1970–77, CBS.* TV series don't get much more successful, influential, or flat-out funny than this. For Mary Tyler Moore to go from *The Dick Van Dyke Show* to *The Mary Tyler Moore Show,* and follow one witty, well-written, classic comedy with another, is an amazing feat; having the two sitcoms sharing space on Nick at Nite, as celebrations of their respective achievements, is a just reward, ensuring that the female star of those programs will be remembered and revered for Moore generations to come. (One fraternal bit of trivia: Dick Van Dyke's brother, Jerry, guest-starred on a pair of *Mary Tyler Moore* shows, playing a despondent TV writer.) Backstage, the creators, producers, and writers of *The Mary Tyler Moore Show* eventually divided and conquered, creating such subsequent stellar series as *Taxi, Cheers,* and *The Simpsons,* as well as such official spinoffs as *Rhoda, Phyllis,* and *Lou Grant. The Mary Tyler Moore Show* gave us one towering TV icon (the insipid anchorman Ted Baxter, played so wonderfully by Ted Knight), and one character so real and strong, Ed Asner's Lou Grant, that he was able to be transplanted intact from a sitcom TV newsroom to a dramatic newspaper newsroom. The initial job-interview exchange between Lou Grant and Moore's Mary Richards passed instantly into the annals of TV immortality. "You know what? You've got spunk," Lou tells Mary. As she smiles and blushes, accepting the compliment, he snarls, "I *hate* spunk." Though Mary Richards was both embraced and attacked by feminists in the seventies (embraced because she was a single career woman, a small step forward for TV womankind; attacked because, for one thing, she always addressed her boss using the deferential "Mr. Grant"), her greatest value was her consistency. Whatever she did over the course of the series, it was totally true to character—even her brief, disastrous flirtation with Lou. The quality of the writing, and the ensemble acting, made the WJM newsroom a credible, wonderful work environment, and yielded such rich characters as Betty White's Sue Ann Nivens ("The Happy Homemaker") and Gavin MacLeod's Murray. At home, Mary Richards was surrounded by a whole other set of memorable characters, from Valerie Harper's boisterous Rhoda to Cloris Leachman's flighty Phyllis. In addition to the pilot, the most classic episodes of *The Mary Tyler Moore Show* were "Chuckles Bites the Dust" (with that clown's durable eulogy line, "A little song, a little dance, a little seltzer down your pants"), and the finale, one of the best closing episodes in the history of series television. The key elements of that finale—the group hug, the turning out of the lights—have been intentionally and lovingly echoed in the finale episodes of other series, including two other MTM Productions, *St. Elsewhere* and *Newhart*. What I remember most from that finale, though, is Asner's emotional delivery of the line when he says to his fellow cast members, "I treasure you people." For seven seasons, so did we all.

M*A*S*H. *1972–83, CBS.* If this book were organized by popularity, not by alphabet, the finale of *M*A*S*H* would put this entry at the front of the list: its expanded concluding episode, "Goodbye, Farewell, and Amen," attracted 77 percent of all TV viewers that night, and earned a Nielsen rating of more than 60—something no Super Bowl has ever done. Even more so than the "Who Shot J.R.?" furor over *Dallas*, the ending of *M*A*S*H* upped the ante for the perceived value of entertainment as news; an advance copy of the final script was obtained and leaked by *The National Enquirer*, which treated it like the tabloid equivalent of the Pentagon Papers. This left the more legitimate media grappling with a rather sticky question: whether 'tis nobler to ignore the plot details divulged by a usually unreliable source, or to acknowledge them—and by so acknowledging, repeat them. Most newspapers came down on the "this is news, regardless of the source" side, and reprinted the major details, including the central plot surprise that Alan Alda's Hawkeye Pierce would suffer a nervous breakdown. It was the uncredited precedent for the now-common practice of major media outlets trolling national (and, later, TV) tabloids for high-profile news, innuendo, and rumors. Other, more direct achievements by *M*A*S*H* included its tasteful and somewhat daring use of a laugh track (when the action took place inside the operating room, there were no laughs to be heard), its status as one of the most successful and artistic TV series ever to be spun off from a movie (its own sequel, TV's

AfterMASH, was deservedly a flop), and, of course, the *M*A*S*H* finale's claim as the most-viewed TV episode of all time. Over its eleven-year run, it established dozens of strong characters and showcased some truly talented actors—none more so than Gary Burghoff's affable Radar, Harry Morgan's sensible Sherman Potter, David Ogden Stiers's haughty Charles Winchester, and Alda himself. The list of memorable episodes is a long one, from the departure and unexpected death of McLean Stevenson's Henry Blake to the one in which Radar stopped idolizing Hawkeye. The all-time best, though, was "The Interview," a black-and-white episode in which Clete Roberts, as a visiting documentary newsman, echoed Edward R. Murrow's 1952 visit to the real Korean War for the *See It Now* special *Christmas in Korea*. Roberts "interviewed" the *M*A*S*H* characters about their wartime experiences, and the most unforgettable response, by William Christopher's Father Mulcahy, was based on an actual army doctor's recollections, recorded and utilized by the show's writers. "When the doctors cut into a patient—and it's very cold here, you know—steam rises from the body," Mulcahy quietly and movingly says to his interviewer. "And the doctor will warm himself over the open wound. Could anyone look on that and not feel changed?" No more so than they could see and hear that story told on TV and not feel changed. At times like that, and they were the best of times, *M*A*S*H* mattered. And its record as the most popular TV show in history? Expect it to last forever.

Masterpiece Theatre. *1971–   , PBS*. This durable PBS anthology series rode to success on the wave of one TV revolution and was all but drowned by another. The first was the development and popularity of the miniseries TV form, which provided both the grist and the impetus for Mobil to snatch up American rebroadcast rights of British long-form costume dramas. The second was the cable revolution, which ended the virtual monopoly of the series, thus greatly reducing its potential percentage of masterpieces. The first *Masterpiece Theatre* triumph, *The Six Wives of Henry VIII*, actually was a hand-me-down: it was broadcast on PBS in 1972, five months after premiering on CBS. But next came Glenda Jackson in the wonderful *Elizabeth R*, and the first true *Masterpiece Theatre* hit, 1974's *Upstairs, Downstairs*, and the series was off and running. Over the years, the best productions have included Derek Jacobi in *I, Claudius* (1977), Alan Bates in *The Mayor of Casterbridge* (1978, for which the Thomas Hardy novel was adapted by Dennis Potter), Anthony Andrews in *Danger UXB* (1981), Bob Hoskins in *Flickers* (1982), Michael Elphick and Ian Richardson in *Private Schulz* (1983), and its crown jewel, 1984's *The Jewel in the Crown*. Since then, its *Masterpiece* ratio has dwindled even lower, with only 1989's *A Very British Coup*, 1991's *A House of Cards* (with Richardson again), and its initial sequel, 1994's *To Play the King*, as unqualified successes. All three of them dealt with modern British politics, and were strikingly unlike the types of dramas that made *Masterpiece Theatre* famous. In 1995, *Masterpiece Theatre* even resorted to sister-series theft, stealing the latest batch of *Prime Suspect* dramas from *Mystery!* The most famous *Masterpiece Theatre* element of all, through the years, was the host, Alistair Cooke, whose drawing-room pontifications eventually were lam-

Mary Hartman, Mary Hartman, with Louise Lasser and Greg Mullavey as the Hartmans.

LEFT: *The Mary Tyler Moore Show,* with Mary Tyler Moore's Mary Richards and Ed Asner's Lou Grant.
RIGHT: *M°A°S°H,* with Alan Alda and guest star Clete Roberts in an Edward R. Murrow-inspired show.

pooned by everyone from the Muppets ("Monsterpiece Theatre") to The Disney Channel (with George Plimpton hosting a collection of old Disney cartoons under the umbrella title *Mouseterpiece Theatre*). Always brandishing a leather-bound volume (or, if you prefer, a Cooke book) as he commented on the miniseries to come, Cooke was as much a part of *Masterpiece Theatre* as Mouret's Rondeau, the fanfare theme that opened each program. Yet Cooke, like Walter Cronkite, Johnny Carson, and other TV icons, eventually called it quits, and was replaced by Russell Baker in 1993. Baker's first task in succeeding Cooke was, somewhat ironically, to host a drama called *Selected Exits*. See also: *I, Claudius; Jewel in the Crown, The; Prime Suspect; Six Wives of Henry VIII, The; Upstairs, Downstairs*.

Maude. *1972–78, CBS*. Archie Bunker is one of TV's most famous and durable characters. . . . And then there's Maude. Bea Arthur's character of the loudmouthed liberal Maude, spun off from *All in the Family* into her own popular series, doesn't wear well with the passage of time. Like the characters in most Norman Lear sitcoms of that era, she's shrill crazy after all these years. Rue McClanahan, who later played opposite Arthur on *The Golden Girls*, was a charter member of the *Maude* squad, playing Maude's conservative neighbor, but other lingering aspects of this particular sitcom are few. One episode worth remembering demonstrated Arthur's estimable talents by confining itself to one of Maude's therapy sessions; another, a two-part episode, sparked a controversy that was foreshadowed by its title, "Maude Gets an Abortion." That particular show, by the way, was written by Susan Harris, who went on to create *Soap*.

Maverick. *1957–62, ABC*. The season that *Maverick* premiered, there were five Westerns in the Top 10. The following year, seven out of the Top 10 were Westerns, and one of those was *Maverick*, despite (or, more likely, because of) the fact that it ostensibly, and sometimes directly, spoofed all the others. Series creator Roy Huggins and star James Garner, who would rely on a similar magic formula when teaming later for *The Rockford Files*, cast Garner as a TV hero in a different mold: poker-playing Bret Maverick was wry and sarcastic, selfish and cowardly, yet somehow, for the most part, likable and even noble. (Bruce Willis, in *Moonlighting*, could have used Garner's Bret as his template.) Jack Kelly as Bret's brother Bart, and Roger Moore as brother Beauregard, had their own followings, but Garner was the one who made this series a weekly best Bret; when he rode off into the sunset after three seasons, he took a good part of this show's heart and soul with him. All-time keepers included "Shady Deal at Sunny Acres," in which Bret literally whittled away most of the hour while surreptitiously plotting to retrieve his money from an unscrupulous banker, and any of the show's wicked parodies, including "Gunshy" (a full-length satire of the top-rated *Gunsmoke*), and loopy variations on *Bonanza* and, believe it or not, *Dragnet*. Several attempts to revive *Maverick* in TV form, with and without Garner, appeared over the years, but the biggest and most recent measure of this show's continued appeal was the 1994 film remake starring Mel Gibson and Jodie Foster, with Garner himself costarring as lawman Zane Cooper. The twist ending to that movie had several possible interpretations, including the one I believe to be true: that Garner's character was revealed at the end to be the original Bret Maverick, an older version of the very same character Garner had played on TV, while Gibson's Bret Maverick was his similarly named son, quoting his "Pappy" the same way Garner's Maverick had quoted *his*. Speaking of quotes: I recently mentioned to Garner that my friends and I had argued about his true role in the *Maverick* movie, and I laid out the contrasting interpretations. Garner smiled and said, *"You were right."* The defense rests.

Max Headroom. *1987, ABC.* **The Max Headroom Show.** *1985–86, Cinemax.* The title character of these series personifies both the intensity and fickleness of late twentieth-century pop culture. At a time when MTV's influence was wide and its taste and hosts were equally bland, Crysalis Records presented Max Headroom as a way to get more exposure for its artists' videos. On England's Channel 4, and then on America's Cinemax, *The Max Headroom Show* was a half-hour, self-contained mini-MTV, hosted by a startlingly futuristic and refreshingly sarcastic character (portrayed by Matt Frewer). Max Headroom was to rock music what Martin Mull's Barth Gimble, on *Fernwood 2-Night*, was to small-town America. Max looked like a white Ray Charles, but with unnaturally gleaming teeth, a sculpted and furrowed skull, and a visual and verbal stutter that was computer-generated. Purportedly, so was Max himself. A British telemovie, called *The Max Headroom Story* and quite fittingly produced in the year 1984, explained the origin of the high-tech video wise guy. A TV reporter named Edison Carter (also played by Frewer) was chasing down a hot story in the near future, only to be involved in a serious auto accident involving a menacingly low parking-garage overhang (the last thing Edison saw before losing consciousness is a sign warning, "Max. Headroom 2.3 meters"). The real Carter survived, but not before his personality was injected into, and "enhanced" by, an untested computer program. That personality, a head-and-shoulders video image known as "Max Headroom," also survived to live another day—as a music-video host and interviewer. It was that incarnation of Max Headroom that became a cult figure in England and America. He made fun of the videos he presented, rarely showed them in complete form, and stood apart from his less animated, less irreverent counterparts on MTV. He was, in short, *Beavis and Butt-Head: The Previous Generation*. Success soon went to Max's head (though, come to think of it, where else *could* it go?). He became the stuttering spokesman for Coca-Cola, added a studio audience to his watered-down TV show, and landed on the covers of national newsmagazines—all *before* a weekly science-fiction series, picking up where the British telemovie had left off, was launched by ABC. The series, which had its strong and weak points, didn't last long, but the memory of *Max Headroom* will—especially since a 1993 MTV Christmas special showed an understandably befuddled Beavis and Butt-Head trying to make sense of an old video of Max Headroom crooning a carol. Needless to say, they failed.

Meeting of Minds. *1977, 1978, PBS.* In 1959, Steve Allen and Nat Hentoff collaborated on an ambitious nineteen-minute segment for *The Steve Allen*

Show, Allen's popular prime-time variety series. The idea was to cast guest stars as Sigmund Freud, Aristotle, Feodor Dostoevsky, and others, and have them debate their respective philosophies in a roundtable discussion called "Meeting of Minds." NBC executives, concerned in part about Allen's outspoken remarks on several controversial issues, refused to televise the sketch, but Allen didn't give up. "Eventually," he wrote in his 1960 autobiography, "*Meeting of Minds* will go on the air somewhere." And it did, with a syndicated one-shot effort in 1964, a more sophisticated version shown only in Los Angeles in 1971, and finally with the two-season, twelve-episode series presented on PBS. In these shows, great minds did *not* think alike, which was what made the conversations so entertaining. Allen served as moderator, and gave his wife Jayne Meadows Allen the plum roles of Cleopatra, Marie Antoinette, Susan B. Anthony, and Florence Nightingale; on the male side, Alexander Scourby played both Galileo Galilei and Socrates. Other actors played one role apiece, including Katherine Helmond as Emily Dickinson, Roscoe Lee Browne as Frederick Douglass, and Stefan Gierasch as the Marquis Donatien Alphonse François de Sade. Watching these characters debate one another was a treat, and a lingering TV memory, even if it often was difficult to de Sade who was right.

Meet the Press. *1947– , NBC.* This is one of the oldest TV series mentioned in this book, which is one testament to its lasting impact. The real testament, though, is that it's still *on* TV, and at this writing remains the longest-running series on network television, as well as the basic model for most other public-affairs discussion shows. Laurence Spivak, who co-created the show with original moderator Martha Rountree, eventually promoted himself from panelist to moderator, and served for an additional ten years. In his era, Spivak was one of the better-informed inquisitors of politicians on TV, a function performed no less ably, since 1991, by current *Meet the Press* moderator Tim Russert. The full roster of moderators serving during this program's impressive (and still expanding) life span: Rountree (1947–53), Ned Brooks (1953–65), Spivak (1965–75), Bill Monroe (1975–84), Marvin Kalb (1984–87), Chris Wallace (1987–88), Garrick Utley (1988–91), and the aforementioned Russert.

Melrose Place. *1992– , Fox.* What *Peyton Place* was to the sixties, *Melrose Place* is to the nineties: a prime-time soap filled with enough romances and rivalries to make it a happy addiction, or guilty pleasure, for tens of millions of loyal viewers. Created by Darren Star, *Melrose Place* was spun off from *Beverly Hills, 90210,* but given a slightly older tone—twentysomething as opposed to teensomething. The first season, though, was a total tossaway, entertaining only for the laughably inconsistent Southern accent of Amy Locane as Sandy (there one week, gone the next). Sandy was benched for the second season, and other players were added—including Heather Locklear as Amanda, who came in and energized *Melrose Place* just as completely as Joan Collins had on *Dynasty,* another prime-time soap on which Locklear had been featured. (Both of those shows also have as their coexecutive producer Aaron Spelling, whose TV dynasty was carried into the nineties by

Masterpiece Theatre, with original host Alistair Cooke.

LEFT: *Maverick*, with James Garner as the sharp cardsharp.
RIGHT: *Miami Vice*, with Don Johnson and Philip Michael Thomas.

90210 and this *Melrose* spinoff.) Locklear's super-schemer is at the core of the success of this series, even though the most memorable, over-the-top episodes have other video vixens at center stage: Laura Leighton's Sydney stripping as "Jungle Jane," guest star Traci Lords as a combination temptress and terrorist, and, as the most famous and entertaining *Melrose* moment to date, Marcia Cross's crazy Kimberly flipping her wig to reveal a sinister-looking scar on her skull. Grant Show's Jake and Thomas Calabro's Michael are there as partial fulfillment of the hunk quotient, but at work and at home on *Melrose Place*, the women (especially Amanda) have all the power, and are the reason this series is such a hit. A deservedly unsuccessful spinoff attempt, *Models Inc.*, came and went quickly in 1994–95, though not quickly enough.

Merv Griffin Show, The. *1965–69, 1972–86, syndicated.* When *Second City TV* presented skits about a laughably affable talk-show host named Sammy Maudlin, Merv Griffin undoubtedly was one of the role models (an even more direct inspiration, though, was the syndicated midseventies series *Sammy and Company*, hosted by the famously fawning Sammy Davis, Jr.). Griffin was an early, obvious, and successful daytime imitator of Johnny Carson and *The Tonight Show* (in an unusual case of sibling rivalry, Dick Carson, Johnny's brother, served as Griffin's director). Instead of jovial Ed McMahon, though, Griffin's sidekick was snarly old Arthur Treacher, a grumpy Eeyore to Griffin's bouncy Tigger. The contrast worked nicely on TV, and the long-running success of *The Merv Griffin Show* supported the pair's independent off-camera ventures: Griffin created *Jeopardy!* and *Wheel of Fortune* and eventually bought casinos in Atlantic City, while British character actor Treacher went the fast-food route with a chain of fish 'n' chips restaurants bearing his name. After a while, both Griffin, with his casinos, and Treacher, with his restaurants, were raking in the chips.

Miami Vice. *1984–89, NBC.* This rock-driven, fashion-conscious, Uzi-filled cop show did a lot in the mideighties to popularize, in no particular order, pastels, TV violence, and Don Johnson. The synthesized drums of Jan Hammer's pulsating theme song set the mood, and the fast cars, flashy women, and furious gunfire did the rest. To *Miami Vice* and executive producer Michael Mann, style and look was more important than substance and plot, and the sound was an integral part of that style. *Miami Vice* did for modern rock what *American Graffiti* had done for vintage rock: it showed how the music could be used, very prominently, as part of the dramatic equation. In the telemovie premiere, Johnson's Sonny Crockett was shown tooling his Ferrari down the Miami causeway at night, heading for a dangerous nighttime rendezvous as Phil Collins's "In the Air Tonight" set the mood for the scene, and for the entire series. *Miami Vice* inspired several uninspired copies—remember *Hollywood Beat?* (I didn't think so)—and ran out of gas long before it ended, but nevertheless made a lasting mark in the annals of TV detective shows. Philip Michael Thomas, as Crockett's partner Ricardo Tubbs, didn't do much of note after *Miami Vice*, but others did. Edward James Olmos, after playing Lieutenant Martin Castillo, went on to *Stand and Deliver*, and many of the guest stars on *Miami Vice*, from Jimmy Smits to Wesley Snipes, went on to become stars in their own right—or were noteworthy already, as in the cases of G. Gordon Liddy and Frank Zappa.

Michael Jackson Talks to Oprah. *1993, ABC.* Not since David Frost presented a series of taped conversations with Richard Nixon in 1977 has a prime-time interview special caused so much fuss. Oprah Winfrey's ninety-minute chat on Jackson's home court, all the more compelling because it was live, drew a 39.3 Nielsen rating and a 56 percent audience share when it was televised on February 10, 1993. Jackson's first one-on-one TV interview in a decade attracted a bigger audience than watched that year's Oscars; for that matter, it was the highest-rated entertainment special in more than ten years. At the time, viewers buzzed the next day about Jackson's explanation of his congenital skin disorder (later identified as vitiligo) and his denials of extensive plastic surgery. Six months later, though, the buzz about Jackson increased in volume, and deepened in tone, after a thirteen-year-old boy accused him of child molestation—a charge Jackson eventually settled out of court. "People always wonder why I have children around," Jackson told Winfrey during that live ABC telecast, explaining it was to experience the childhood he felt he had missed. "I find a thing I never had," he said, "through them." On June 14, 1995, Jackson again appeared on ABC for a live TV interview, this time on *PrimeTime Live*, with Diane Sawyer as his questioner and with his new bride, Lisa Marie Presley, at his side. The year's most shameful TV interview (and 1995, remember, was a year filled with O. J. Simpson stories), Sawyer's handling of the hour was so bad that not only did critics roast it at the time, but *Vanity Fair* writer Maureen Orth dissected it point by point in a September 1995 article, challenging Sawyer's and Jackson's statements of the "facts" in the child-molestation case. Having said on live TV that Jackson had been "cleared of all changes," Sawyer later admitted to the print press that she "misspoke." For ABC News, even though that edition of *PrimeTime Live* was the week's top-rated show, the Saywer interview with Jackson clearly was a major mistake.

Mickey Mouse Club, The. *1955–59, ABC.* "M-I-C . . . " "See ya real soon." "K-E-Y . . . " "Why? Because we *like* you!" "M-O-U-S-Eeeeeeee. . . . " The Mouseketeers reverently spelled out the words, and Jimmy Dodd, who had written that "Mickey Mouse Club Alma Mater," enthusiastically sang the solo rejoinders. That was the unforgettable way each *Mickey Mouse Club* show ended, just as each had begun, reliably and memorably, with another Dodd tune: "The Mickey Mouse Club March" ("Who's the leader of the club that's made for you and me? M-I-C-K-E-Y M-O-U-S-E . . . "). In between those two songs each day was a variety of delightful offerings, especially on "Anything Can Happen Day," when, well, anything could happen. Disney cartoons, nature shorts, musical numbers, guest stars, rotating serials (including *The Hardy Boys* and *The Adventures of Spin and Marty*) made it one of the most dizzyingly diverse children's shows in the history of television. And in addition to adult hosts Dodd and Roy Williams, kids were empowered as on-air

Mouseketeers, many of whom became stars, or broke hearts, in their own right. Annette Funicello became the standout star, and transferred her pubescent popularity to a subsequent series of *Beach Blanket Bingo* movies. (Eventually stricken with multiple sclerosis, Funicello portrayed herself, and narrated a story in which younger actresses portrayed her as a child and younger woman, in the CBS 1995 biographical telemovie, *A Dream Is a Wish Your Heart Makes: The Annette Funicello Story.*) Among the almost three dozen Mouseketeers who came and went over the show's four-year run, eight other kids joined Annette in going the whole way. The roll call for those tenured Mouseketeers would go like this: Annette! Sharon! Bobby! Lonnie! Tommy! Darlene! Cubby! Karen! Doreen! (Their last names at the time, for completists, were Funicello, Baird, Burgess, Burr, Cole, Gillespie, O'Brien, Pendelton, and Tracey, respectively.) One of the original Mouseketeers, Johnny Crawford, would not go the distance; instead, he'd go to another and more violent ABC series, playing the son of Chuck Connors in *The Rifleman*. One of the later Mouseketeers, Don Agrati, would move on to something much more wholesome: as Don Grady, he played Robbie on *My Three Sons*. The series stopped after three seasons not because it was falling in popularity, but because ABC wanted to increase the amount of commercial time in each episode; Walt Disney refused, and that was the end of *The Mickey Mouse Club*. Several attempts have been made, over the ears, to update *The Mickey Mouse Club*, including a syndicated version in the seventies and a Disney Channel version that has run, with various casts and permutations, since 1988. All of them have been more racially diverse, yet less entertainingly diverse, than the original, which prods more fond memories among aging Baby Boomers than most other shows of its era. Why? Because we *liked* it. . . .

Mighty Morphin Power Rangers, The. *1993–   , Fox.* Putting it into historical and cultural perspective doesn't make *Mighty Morphin Power Rangers* any less inane, but here goes. In the midsixties, Japanese TV produced—and syndicated internationally—a terrible superhero action series called *Ultraman*. The title character was a guy who could metamorphose from mild-mannered human size to a towering (as in sixty meters), helmeted martial arts hero, battling tacky "creatures" on a set of an even tackier Tokyo miniature. Awful as that sounds, it was mighty good next to *Mighty Morphin*, which took footage from a modern Japanese variation on the *Ultraman* genre, combined it with new footage featuring English-speaking teens, dubbed the rest, and—presto—emerged with the most inexplicably popular kiddie TV series since *Teenage Mutant Ninja Turtles*. The Japanese stuntpeople wear helmets and body suits that obscure their features, so the mix-and-match editing works—at least as well as anything else on this show, what with its cardboard skylines, rubber suits, Transformer-like "Zord" vehicles, unmatched dubbing, and villains with names like Rita Repulsa. American kids took to *Mighty Morphin Power Rangers* with enough enthusiasm, and spent enough millions on its action-figures toy line, to warrant its inclusion here, but that doesn't mean I don't find the whole program rather Repulsa. I take solace, though, in the fact that the show's spell was destined to fade quickly—and, in fact, interest in the series crested well before *Mighty Morphin Power Rangers—The Movie* arrived (and flopped) in 1995. It was, for children as well as their parents, a valuable lesson in pop-culture transience: live by the Zord, die by the Zord.

Mighty Mouse Playhouse, The. *1955–67, CBS.* A lot of cartoon characters and shows don't quite make the teleliteracy cut, but this long-running series about a super-powered singing rodent makes it for two reasons. One is the operatic mouse's most famous line, the loud and lyrical "Here I come to save the daaaay!"—a tenor of our times in more ways than one. The other is Andy Kaufman's classic use of the *Mighty Mouse* theme song, in which he lip-synched the aforementioned line, and *only* that line, on *Saturday Night Live*. The skit worked only if the audience knew the song, and *everyone* seemed to know it.

Mike Douglas Show, The. *1963–82, syndicated.* Like Merv Griffin, Mike Douglas was a former singer who became a successful talk-show host. Like Griffin, he seemed enthusiastic about everything and everyone. Like Griffin, he—well, he was a lot like Griffin, period. And after that period, here's the exclamation point: one executive producer of that series was Roger Ailes, who, decades later, returned to his talk-show roots to oversee the operation of CNBC and its (temporary) sister talk-show cable network America's Talking. The main TV contribution by *The Mike Douglas Show*, though, was the concept of celebrity cohosts, which made room, at a time when outlets for casual conversation among show-biz folk were comparatively few, for week-long visits by Muhammad Ali, Jackie Gleason, Ray Charles, Barbra Streisand, John Lennon, and, in a memorable tandem stint, Gene Kelly and Fred Astaire.

Millionaire, The. *1955–60, CBS.* Each week on this series, John Beresford Tipton, a rich, eccentric and unseen benefactor, handed his distinguished manservant Michael Anthony (played by Marvin Miller) a cashier's check for one million dollars—with instructions to turn it over to a total stranger selected somehow by Tipton. The recipient could spend the money any way he or she wished, and the only catch was that the source of the gift could not be revealed. It was an expensive way to conduct a sociological study on the effects of sudden wealth: at the rate Tipton was giving money away, he had spent $188 million by the time the series was over. (The voice of the camera-shy Tipton, by the way, was provided by Paul Frees, who played Boris Badenov on *The Bullwinkle Show.*) What I was, and remain, unclear about, though, is this: how much money did Michael Anthony earn from Tipton for handing out those checks each week? If his salary was a lot less than a million, why didn't he resent it? And if it wasn't, why didn't he stop?

Miracle of Life, The. See *Nova*.

Miracle Worker, The. See *Playhouse 90*.

Miss America Pageant, The. *1954–56, ABC; 1957–65, CBS; 1966– , NBC.* If you didn't see the first televised *Miss America Pageant*, you didn't Miss much—except for the crowning of Lee Meriwether, who went on to star opposite Buddy Ebsen in *Barnaby Jones*. (Bess Myerson, the most TV-familiar Miss America of all, had been crowned back in 1945, and owed her continued celebrity largely to her seat on *I've Got a Secret*.) It wasn't until 1955, the second year the contest was broadcast live from Atlantic City, that new master of ceremonies Bert Parks first sang, "There she is, Miss America . . . ," launching what was to become a well-known annual TV tradition. It was annual, that is, until 1979, when pageant officials unceremoniously replaced Parks with Ron Ely—who was himself replaced by Gary Collins, who eventually was replaced by the daytime TV team of Regis Philbin and Kathie Lee Gifford. Since Parks was demoted, the only noteworthy aspects to the pageant have been its public-relations disasters. Its first African-American winner, Vanessa Williams, was stripped of her title, like Chuck Connors in *Branded*, as an overreaction to old nude photos subsequently printed in *Penthouse*. (Williams responded by building a successful career as a recording artist, then triumphing on Broadway in *Kiss of the Spider Woman*.) And in one lame attempt after another to justify and "update" the sexist and superficial premise of the pageant itself, pageant officials talked of making the proceedings "less giddy" for the nineties, and of rewarding contestants for "substance" as well as appearance. In 1993, producers went so far as to present a 900–number during its annual telecast, asking viewers to vote on whether *The Miss America Pageant* should consider eliminating the swimsuit portion of the competition. The vote was 60 percent no (no elimination, that is), 40 percent yes. During the 1995 telecast, another 900–number poll was established, this one a firm viewer vote on whether the swimsuit portion of the pageant *would* continue. Big surprise: viewers already tuned in to watch that year's *Miss America Pageant* voted to keep the swimsuits. If you think about it, it's a little like polling customers inside a McDonald's to see whether they want to Just Say Yes to fries.

Missiles of October, The. *1974, ABC*. Producers Buzz Berger and Herbert Brodkin, whose credits include both *The Defenders* and *Holocaust*, presented this outstanding early docudrama, written by Stanley R. Greenberg and directed by Anthony Page. A behind-closed-doors reenactment of the leadership decisions during the 1962 Cuban Missile Crisis, this drama was taut, clever, credible, and, unlike most docudramas to follow, impeccably researched. It benefited, too, by the incendiary talents of the three actors portraying the central figures: William Devane as John F. Kennedy, Martin Sheen as Robert F. Kennedy, and Howard da Silva as Nikita Khruschev. Sheen had starred in another superb docudrama, *The Execution of Private Slovik*, earlier that year. In 1983, nine years after playing Bobby Kennedy, Sheen would star as JFK in the surprisingly good *Kennedy* miniseries for NBC. Then in 1994, twenty years after the premiere of *The Missiles of October*, director Joseph Sargent and writer David Rintels would adapt the formula for a gripping docudrama about three other powerful men at a key time in world history: the NBC miniseries *World War II: When Lions Roared*, starring John Lithgow as Franklin Delano Roosevelt, Bob Hoskins as Winston Churchill, and Michael Caine as Joseph Stalin.

Mission: Impossible. *1966–73, CBS; 1988–90, ABC*. It's possible to remember a lot about the original *Mission: Impossible*, which each week dispatched a cadre of top-secret "Impossible Missions Force" (IMF) agents to depose foreign leaders, sabotage enemy guerrilla groups, and engage in other, similarly covert activities. Each week's opening was like a familiar mantra. The head of the IMF would receive his recorded instructions, listen to the disclaimer at the end of every assignment ("As always, should you or any of your IM Force be caught or killed, the secretary will disavow any knowledge of your actions"), and either destroy the evidence or watch as it destroyed itself. Lalo Shifrin's powerful theme music would kick in, a lit match would ignite a fuse, and *Mission: Impossible* would run through almost subliminal snippets from the episode to come—a stylistic forerunner to the hyperkinetic movie trailers of the eighties and nineties. Except for the team's stoic leaders (played first by Steven Hill as Dan Briggs, then by Peter Graves as Jim Phelps), the team members made memorable impressions within rather narrowly set parameters. Martin Landau's Rollin Hand, like Ross Martin's Artemus Gordon on *The Wild Wild West*, had fun with his master-of-disguise duties; so did Leonard Nimoy as Paris, when he joined the show after Landau's departure. Peter Lupus's strongman Willy wore good sweaters, while Greg Morris's Barney *was* a good sweater; and Barbara Bain's Cinnamon was the show's first and best sex symbol (others to follow included Lesley Ann Warren as Dana, but Cinnamon was the spiciest). Like *The Mod Squad, Charlie's Angels*, and *The A-Team, Mission: Impossible* was a weekly caper story in which loyal operatives got their assignments and ran, but *Mission: Impossible* was, in terms of plot twists and gimmicks, much more complex—closer to *Columbo*, except without that show's all-important depth of characterization. In retrospect, the anything-goes, nothing-admitted approach of the IMF prefigures Oliver North's behavior during the Iran-Contra affair and its televised hearings—and though hindsight makes that obvious, at least one TV critic objected to *Mission: Impossible* at the time on precisely those grounds. When the series premiered in 1966, Robert Lewis Shayon of *Saturday Review* called it "the season's most harmful program," pointing out that the IMF agents, "for pay and at government instigation, interfere directly in the affairs of foreign nations with whom we are at peace and from whom no direct threat to our safety emanates. They break the laws of these nations, yet are never brought before any bar of justice." Ironically, though it was never produced, NBC had commissioned and rejected a rather prescient *Mission: Impossible* sequel script long after the original series had shut down. According to Patrick J. White, author of *The Complete Mission: Impossible Dossier*, that story opened with IMF agent Phelps being released after a six-year prison term, having been convicted of conspiracy, wiretapping, burglary, and refusing to testify before a Congressional committee. The telemovie was written in 1980—the same year Ronald Reagan was elected President. In 1988, after the Iran/Contra hearings were over, a lengthy strike by the Writers Guild "inspired" ABC to dust off old scripts of *Mission: Impossible,* recast them, and present them for a new generation of TV viewers. The idea was a brilliant one, but the network soon lost the courage of its convictions; that, and the conclusion of the strike, led to only a handful of old scripts being used in the sequel series, and even those were reworked substantially. Graves returned as the IMF leader, Greg Morris's son Phil portrayed Barney's son Grant, and other touches were aimed at bringing *Mission: Impossible* up to date. The reel-to-reel tapes that self-destructed in the old series were replaced by equally flammable laserdiscs, while the fast-paced teaser sequence was dropped—an egregious lack of respect for a true TV tradition. The new series sank, deservedly, after a season or two; perhaps Brian De Palma, the director who did justice to a large-screen adaptation of *The Untouchables,* will fare better with his own version of *Mission: Impossible,* a big-budget movie, starring Tom Cruise, scheduled for 1996. At any rate, true devotees of the *Mission: Impossible* TV series can, and do, remember the original. Recalling Nimoy's character in particular, we'll always have Paris.

Mister Ed. *1961, syndicated; 1961–66, CBS.* For five years in the sixties, and more years than that on Nick at Nite in the eighties and nineties, the face, and the voice, were familiar: "Welll, Willl-bur. . . . " That drawling baritone, straight from the horse's mouth, is one of the two indelible remnants of this silly sitcom—one of the few TV shows to be produced for syndication, then promoted to prime-time network status. The other unforgettable feature of *Mister Ed* is, of course, of course, its theme song, which began: "A horse is a horse, of course, of course / And no one can talk to a horse, of course / That is, of course / Unless the horse / Is the famous Mister Ed." Jay Livingston, who wrote the theme with Ray Evans, was the vocalist as well, and didn't even get hoarse. He did, however, write other, equally durable songs, including "Mona Lisa," "Que Será, Será (Whatever Will Be, Will Be)," and the *Bonanza* theme. In retrospect, the most unusual aspect of *Mister Ed*—leaving aside the issue of a talking horse—is how much time the title character spent watching TV, an activity rarely reflected by most television shows of the time. (Mister Ed especially, and understandably, enjoyed TV Westerns.) It was the popularity of the *Francis the Talking Mule* movie series that had led to *Mister Ed* being sold and produced, even though the Walter Brooks short stories about a talking horse named Mister Ed had predated David Stern's 1946 novel *Francis* by several years. The links between the movie mule and the TV palomino included Arthur Lubin, who directed most of the *Francis* movies and *Mister Ed* shows, and actor George Burns, who thought the success of the *Francis* franchise was so obviously adaptable for TV that he bet $75,000 on a long-shot horse—and financed the TV pilot of *Mister Ed.* Alan Young played Wilbur, the only person who could hear Mister Ed talk; former Republic Pictures cowboy serial star Allan "Rocky" Lane provided the horse's voice, and Bamboo Harvester played the title role on-camera. During the run of the series, guest stars included Mae West (in, bizarrely, her only TV role) and Clint Eastwood, whose 1962 appearance on "Clint Eastwood Meets Mister Ed" somehow has been overlooked on his résumé. As to the question,

"How did Mister Ed 'talk'?" there are conflicting reports. According to most accounts, it was by a combination of hidden nylon wires and the spreading of peanut butter on the horse's gums—the same technique allegedly used on Gerald Ford during the 1976 presidential debates. The biggest *Mister Ed* secret of all, though, was the death of the four-legged star, Bamboo Harvester, two years after the series had been canceled. Because the show was doing so well in syndication, especially among impressionable young audiences, news of the death of Mister Ed was, like the horse himself, buried. The death of "Mister Ed" finally made headlines in 1979, but the horse honored in that misguided string of news reports actually was a lookalike. (A corpse is a corpse, of course, of course.) Oddly enough, the original Mister Ed had died, and a double inserted in his place, at about the same time a similar fate was rumored to have befallen Paul McCartney. There is no truth, however, to the assertion that playing the *Mister Ed* theme song backwards will yield the ominous phrase, "Turn me on, dead mane."

Mr. Peepers. *1952–55, NBC.* This delicate little sitcom, starring the equally delicate and little Wally Cox, launched or furthered the careers of several gifted comedic character actors. Cox, as meek science teacher Robinson Peepers, was aided and abetted in this classy live TV production by the likes of Jack Warden, Marion Lorne, and, most notably of all, Tony Randall. Some elements of *Mr. Peepers,* such as the protagonist's continual bouts with seemingly animated inanimate objects, were close to the playfulness of Ernie Kovacs; others, such as Mr. Peepers's patient removal of an endless array of straight pins while unwrapping a new shirt, are much closer to the found humor in everyday minutiae of *Seinfeld,* a few TV generations later. Most plot lines were, by design, minor, but one was major: the wedding of Mr. Peepers to Patricia Benoit's Nancy Remington, the school nurse who in 1954 became Mrs. Peepers. That TV event caused almost as big a stir as had the birth of Little Ricky on *I Love Lucy* the year before, and established TV weddings as no less reliable a publicity stunt than TV births. The Peepers wedding, however, had almost never come to pass. Despite thousands of letters and phone calls protesting its announced demise, *Mr. Peepers* was canceled after its initial eight-week summer season, and reinstated only after another NBC series proved an immediate disaster when the fall season began. NBC should have known what a talented cast, quality series, and loyal fan base it had in *Mr. Peepers*—but, in the network's defense, this audience-measurement miscalculation took place long before the invention of Peeper meters.

Mister Rogers' Neighborhood. *1968– , NET/PBS.* Parodied by everyone from Johnny Carson to Eddie Murphy, Fred McFeely Rogers is a true TV original—one of the medium's most adept communicators at reaching and holding a very young audience. Most politicians would trade their matching election funds to learn the secret of projecting intimacy and friendliness so effectively, yet Rogers doesn't operate in a calculated or conniving manner. On television, he moves so slowly, talks so quietly and acts so naturally, the obvious assumption is that he's scaling back his entire persona to suit the needs of his young audience. Yet from the very beginning of his TV performing career, back when he was seen but not heard, he spoke and conducted himself the same way. Rogers began his children's TV career in 1953 as the producer, puppeteer, and off-camera pianist for *The Children's Corner*, a delightful local series (hosted by Josie Carey) for Pittsburgh's WQED-TV. Daniel Striped Tiger and "X" the Owl were only two of the familiar puppet characters introduced on that series, and they, among others, went with Rogers to Canada when he became the on-camera host of a series called *Misterogers*. In 1966, Rogers returned to Pittsburgh to develop the format of his current series, which was shown on the Eastern Educational Network for two years before going national on public television, when its famous theme ("It's a beautiful day in this neighborhood / A beautiful day for a neighbor / Would you be mine? / Could you be mine? . . . ") was introduced, along with Rogers the not-so-quick-change artist switching from dress shoes and suit jacket to loafers and a cardigan. Other durable elements from Rogers's Land of Make Believe include puppets King Friday XIII and Henrietta Pussycat, and human supporting players Betty Aberlin (as Lady Aberlin) and David Newell (as Speedy Delivery man Mr. McFeely). At this writing, *Mister Rogers' Neighborhood*, with more than a quarter-century under its belt, is the longest-running program on PBS, although the record demands an asterisk. Only a week or two of new shows is produced each year to complement the reruns, and for several years Rogers produced no new shows at all. Rogers's delivery has gotten more polished in recent years, his guests have included more high-profile visitors (cellist Yo-Yo Ma, for example), and his topics and productions have gotten more ambitious, yet his on-air personality has not shifted one iota. The honesty and sincerity of Fred Rogers are an apparent constant, and as each TV generation outgrows him, another is there to fall under his spell, and learn, all over again.

Mr. Wizard. See **Watch Mr. Wizard.**

Mod Squad, The. *1968–73, ABC*. Flying in the face of the Summer of Love counterculture, ABC presented this contrived police series about three young undercover cops—as the network's ads described them, "One white, one black, one blonde." Michael Cole was the overly earnest, long-haired white guy, Clarence Williams III was the Afro-sporting black guy (whose favorite expression was the affirmative catch word "Solid!"), and Peggy Lipton, the only real reason for watching, was the blonde, long-haired flower child. This was a big, early hit for executive producer Aaron Spelling, who had presented this series in partnership with Danny Thomas. It was created by Bud Ruskin, a real-life member of a similarly youthful undercover squad (assigned, in that case, to the narcotics division) in the fifties. He first proposed a series about young operatives in 1960, but it wasn't until 1968, when the word "narc" was anathema to millions of young hippies, that ABC courted young audiences by giving the green light to *The Mod Squad*. Paradoxically, it was those same young viewers who made the series a "solid" hit from the start. The same trio of *Mod Squad* stars, along with Tige Andrews as their establishment boss,

LEFT: *Mr. Peepers*, with Patricia Benoit's Nancy (the eventual Mrs. Peepers) and Wally Cox.

RIGHT: *Mister Rogers' Neighborhood*, with Fred Rogers and a very special, typically welcome neighborhood friend.

LEFT: *Mission: Impossible*, with Peter Graves and his self-destructive tape recorder.

RIGHT: *The Mod Squad*, with Michael Cole, Peggy Lipton, and Clarence Williams III.

reunited for a 1979 telemovie, *Return of the Mod Squad,* but the times, they had a-changed. In 1987, though, Fox Broadcasting inaugurated its "fourth network" with *21 Jump Street,* a high-school variation on the *Mod Squad* formula, which starred, and launched the career of, Johnny Depp.

Monday Night Football. *1970–   , ABC.* The National Football League had experimented with televising Monday night games in the sixties, all but forcing regular NFL broadcasters CBS and NBC into presenting a "special" game or two. But the CBS Monday comedy lineup was too strong to justify regular preemptions during football season, and NBC's Johnny Carson, who refused to participate in any *Tonight Show* delayed by prime-time football, was even stronger. That's largely how *Monday Night Football* ended up in the lap of ABC and executive producer Roone Arledge, who with director Chet Forte set out to produce a sports telecast whose popularity hinged not only on the game on the field, but on other elements: sophisticated slow-motion and special effects, intrepid camerawork, dazzling highlights packages, in-depth personality profiles, and, most of all, commentary and chemistry from the broadcasters covering the game. The recipe succeeded so well that when you think of *Monday Night Football,* you tend to think of everything *but* football. You think instead, during its salad days, of Howard Cosell, providing the sort of opinionated commentary that was rare, if often irritating, in TV sports coverage. And of "Dandy" Don Meredith, Cosell's foil during the formative years of *Monday Night Football,* whose lasting contribution was to sing "the party's over" at the moment one team all but locked up a victory over its opponent. And of the snazzy NFL Films half-time highlights, which, with Cosell providing breathless narration, were for years the place to go for next-day highlights of each Sunday's pro games. Cable TV and satellite technology, however, eventually made that particular feature obsolete, as ESPN, CNN, and the broadcast networks presented highlights and results almost as they occurred. Frank Gifford, however, has remained a constant almost from the beginning. He joined *Monday Night Football* in its second season, and has stayed ever since, sharing booth duties with everyone from Joe Namath and O. J. Simpson to current cohorts Al Michaels and Dan Dierdorf, who completed the Monday-night trio in 1987. All networks now routinely package their football telecasts using ABC's once-innovative approaches, but *Monday Night Football* remains something special, even if Meredith's "the party's over" has given way to Waylon Jennings's "Are you ready for some football?" One thing about *Monday Night Football* is as true today as it was in 1970— it's one prime-time show that *never* pops up in reruns.

Monkees, The. *1966–68, NBC.* In August 1966, the Beatles appeared at San Francisco's Candlestick Park, playing their last live set for a paying audience. The popularity of their musical-comedy films, 1964's *A Hard Day's Night* and 1965's *Help!,* and their unusual but successful attempts to promote such recent releases as 1966's "Paperback Writer" and "Rain" by providing lip-synched film shorts instead of guesting on music shows, had persuaded the group members to focus their efforts solely on the recording studio instead.

That same August, a record was released by The Monkees, an American group—assembled specifically for television—whose TV show would premiere the following month. By November, the group's debut single, "Last Train to Clarksville," was number one on the *Billboard* charts, and, just as *The Monkees* echoed the playful anarchy of Richard Lester's Beatles films, Monkeemania soon took hold as a calculating but clear cousin of Beatlemania. Although it's true that only two of the four Monkees, Michael Nesmith and Peter Tork, were true musicians (Davy Jones was a singer-actor, while Mickey Dolenz was the former child star of *Circus Boy*), and that session musicians provided the rhythm tracks for their first two albums, the group and the show deserves more credit than it generally receives. The TV series constantly broke the "fourth wall," and its overall sensibility, with its frenetic pace and cartoonish feel, owed as much to Marx as to Lennon—or, in other words, was as much Groucho as Ringo. The show's self-contained music videos, clear forerunners of MTV, propelled the group's first seven singles to enviable positions on the pop charts: three number ones, two number twos, two number threes. (Surprisingly, the show's theme song, with its well-known "Hey, hey, we're the Monkees" lyric, never was released as a single.) And musically, from start to finish, The Monkees associated themselves with some inarguably talented collaborators. Songs were provided by Carole King and Gerry Goffin ("Pleasant Valley Sunday"), Neil Diamond ("I'm a Believer"), and Harry Nilsson ("Cuddly Toy"), as well as by studio songsmiths Tommy Boyce and Bobby Hart, who wrote the group's early hits "Last Train to Clarksville" and "(I'm Not Your) Steppin' Stone." Musicians on the first Monkees album included Billy Preston (three years before The Beatles would invite him to play during *their* sessions), Glen Campbell, and Leon Russell; later in their careers, when they laid down their own instrumental tracks, the Monkees made room in the studio for such guest artists as drummer Buddy Miles and guitarists Danny Kortchmar, Ry Cooder, and Neil Young. Sometimes the alliances were in direct conflict with the group's bubblegum TV image. Frank Zappa, a guest on one of the last episodes of *The Monkees*, also appeared in the group's 1968 movie *Head*, which was cowritten and coproduced by Bob Rafelson and Jack Nicholson, choreographed by Toni Basil, and featured, among others, Annette Funicello and Teri Garr. Most jarring of all, perhaps, was the rock group selected as the opening act for the Monkees' summer 1967 concert tour: the Jimi Hendrix Experience. (I believe this only because I was in attendance at one Miami concert and saw Hendrix, fresh from the Monterey International Pop Festival, for myself.) In 1986, twenty years after *The Monkees* first appeared on TV, the series was repeated in marathon form by MTV, launching a Monkees nostalgia wave. The TV shows held up nicely, and, except for Nesmith, the group reunited, released a new album, and toured, while old Monkees recordings were rereleased on CD (then, a few years later, rereleased, this time with bonus tracks). In 1987, a syndicated series, *The New Monkees*, cast four unknowns and tried to duplicate the magic and success of the original series. It proved, instead, that it wasn't all that easy to make a Monkee out of somebody.

Monty Python's Flying Circus. *1974–80, public television and syndication.* No sense minimizing the historical significance of this series, which was produced for England's BBC-1 between 1969 and 1974, and presented on American public TV just as the series was coming to a close in its country of origin. In England, *Monty Python's Flying Circus* was a riotous, ambitious spiritual descendent of radio's *The Goon Show*, the *Beyond the Fringe* and *Cambridge Footlights Revue* stage shows, and, more directly, several TV comedy series featuring the bizarre contributions of future members of the Monty Python troupe. These programs included *That Was the Week That Was* (the 1962–63 British version, for which John Cleese was a writer), the 1966–67 *Frost Report* (hosted by David Frost, with Cleese as writer-performer and Graham Chapman, Michael Palin, Terry Jones, and Eric Idle among the writers), and the 1968–69 *Do Not Adjust Your Set* (with Idle, Jones, and Palin as writer-performers and Terry Gilliam providing the first TV glimpses of his now inimitable animation style). In England, therefore, there was some frame of reference for the oddball comedy presented by Monty Python. But on American TV, arriving at a time when comedy-variety was defined by *The Carol Burnett Show, Monty Python's Flying Circus* was, among the cult audience that almost instantly embraced it, a second British Invasion. What the Beatles had done to shake up rock 'n' roll, Monty Python did to TV comedy. On these shores, *Monty Python's Flying Circus*—with its amazing collection of talent and its energetic disregard of established comedy "rules"—can be linked spiritually to very few (but very wonderful) TV precedessors, including *Your Show of Shows*, early work by Ernie Kovacs and Steve Allen, *The Smothers Brothers Comedy Hour,* and *Rowan & Martin's Laugh-In*. Yet every quality comedy-variety show that came after *Monty Python's Flying Circus,* from *Saturday Night Live* and *Second City TV* to *The Tracey Ullman Show* and *The Kids in the Hall,* owes a great debt to what that comedy sextet was able to do in the confines of television. Sketches could lead anywhere, or be interrupted midway through by representatives of the Spanish Inquisition. Terry Gilliam's animated film shorts—showing, for example, a giant foot stomping free-floating talking heads—might (or might not) link one skit to another. And the cast members were equally inclined, for the sake of a laugh, to quote Proust, cross-dress, or hit one another with dead fish. Most Americans got their first glimpse of the troupe's antics in *And Now for Something Completely Different,* a 1971 compendium of skits, with new animation, from the British series' first two seasons. In a way, it was like *Ten from Your Show of Shows* in reverse, with the movie *preceding* the broadcast of the series (in America, anyway), except that the skits in the Monty Python movie, though based on scripts from the British TV series, actually were filmed anew for the movie collection. One fan of that film, a local public TV executive in Dallas, went out and secured American rights to broadcast the original shows, and a similar deal soon was struck by other public and commercial stations. Then, when *Monty Python and the Holy Grail* established the troupe as a film-comedy franchise in its own right, the *Flying Circus* series—already finished and off the air in England, but just starting in America—really took off. Memorable bits? Well, *Bartlett's Quotations* lists among the show's lasting cultural contributions its Dead Parrot sketch ("This is an *ex*-parrot!") and a typically naughty verse from "The Lumberjack Song," in which a rugged lumberjack shocked his cohorts by singing of unexpected pursuits ("I cut down trees, I skip and jump / I like to press wildflowers / I put on women's clothing / And hang around in bars"). However, *Bartlett's* overlooks Idle's "nudge-nudge, wink-wink, say-no-more" character, Cleese's Minister of Silly Walks, dozens of still-quoted phrases—including "Nobody expects the Spanish Inquisition!" and the all-purpose transition line "And now for something completely different!"—and other bits of business that are every bit as durable as, say, John Philip Sousa's *Liberty Bell March,* which the Monty Python troupe effectively appropriated as its TV theme song. The forty-five *Flying Circus* shows, a current staple on Comedy Central, are lasting testament to the group's originality and unpredictability, even though the shows almost didn't last at all—*Monty Python's Flying Circus* was one of the first BBC entertainment programs to be preserved on videotape. As individuals or in smaller groups, the various Python members have, in addition to their various movie credits *(A Fish Called Wanda, Time Bandits, Brazil)* made other wonderful contributions to television, including Cleese's *Fawlty Towers,* which makes this book's final cut, and two fine shows that, by the merest of margins, do not: the *Ripping Yarns* literature-spoof series by Palin and Jones, and *The Rutles—All You Need Is Cash,* a brilliant Beatles documentary parody by Idle. Another, much more recent media triumph was 1994's *Monty Python's Complete Waste of Time,* an utterly brilliant CD-ROM that takes the group's outrageous humor to new, interactive levels. I could go on and on about *Monty Python's Flying Circus* and its many offshoots, but I know what you're thinking: nudge-nudge, wink-wink, and, especially, say-no-more.

Moon Landing. *1969, CBS, NBC, and ABC.* Watching a man land on the moon on live TV—there was nothing in the world like it. (The front-page *Variety* headline said it best: "Greatest Show off Earth!") And even though Neil Armstrong planted that first lunar footprint at 10:56 P.M. (Eastern Earth Time) on July 20, 1969, that relatively late hour didn't deter many viewers from tuning in: Armstrong's descent from the Apollo 11 lunar module ladder, and his first words as a man on the moon, were witnessed live by an estimated forty million American viewers, with a combined audience (counting replays) of 94 percent of all American TV homes, or 125 million viewers, and as many as a billion total viewers worldwide. In America, CBS and NBC followed the story for thirty-one consecutive hours, and ABC thirty. Frank Reynolds and Jules Bergman anchored ABC's coverage and Chet Huntley, David Brinkley, and Frank McGee were responsible for NBC's, but most of the country was tuned to, and most clearly recalls, Walter Cronkite's marathon anchoring chores for CBS (more than seventeen straight hours, with former astronaut Wally Schirra at his side throughout). Here was Cronkite, the newsman most remembered, and revered, for his emotional reaction to the assassination of John F. Kennedy in 1963, displaying emotion once again, this time during the tense but happy occasion fulfilling Kennedy's pledge to get a man to the moon and back before the end of the decade. The words "The Eagle has landed," relayed back to Earth, were as thrilling to Cronkite as they were to his enthralled viewers. "Oh, boy!," Cronkite exclaimed when the Eagle,

Apollo 11's lunar module, touched down on the moon's surface at 4:17 P.M., relaying TV pictures all the way. "Hot diggity dog!" he exclaimed at the end of the lunar visit, when the Eagle, with Armstrong and fellow moon-rock collector Buzz Aldrin safely back inside, fired its rocket engines and headed back towards Michael Collins and their ride back to Earth. In between, viewers saw and heard perhaps the most resonant and lasting moment from the entire history of television: Armstrong's first words after stepping on the moon. "That's one small step for a man, one giant leap for mankind." Unfortunately, because of the static and Armstrong's phrasing, that rather important article *a* in his carefully prepared remark went largely unheard and unreported, making Armstrong's phrase, even after the astronaut himself set the record straight, one of the most widely quoted *and* misquoted phrases ever uttered. (That little *a*, you might say, had been lost in space.) Also overlooked, for the most part, was the more diminutive Aldrin's message to mission control as he became the *second* man on the moon. "That may have been a small step for Neil," Aldrin said dryly after descending the ladder, "but it was a long one for me." Yet the images of the lunar landing, of Armstrong and Aldrin hopping around and planting flags, and of the takeoff from the lunar surface, arrived intact, and are indelibly etched in the memories of anyone old enough to have seen them broadcast in that summer of '69. Slightly younger viewers might recall them, too, but in a different context—as key components of the "living logo" used during the early years of MTV. See also: *Space Exploration Coverage*.

Moonlighting. *1985–89, ABC*. This is the series that revived Cybill Shepherd's career, established Bruce Willis's, and, for a while, was one of the most playful romantic comedy-dramas on television. Because series creator Glenn Gordon Caron's tastes ran from Harold Lloyd to the Three Stooges, from Howard Hawks to Humphrey Bogart, and from old musicals to film noir, he had *Moonlighting* reflect them all. Shepherd's Maddie Hayes, the fast-talking Snow Queen, and Willis's David Addison, developed such a volatile and intriguing will-they-or-won't-they? sexual chemistry that, for years afterward, any TV show built around a bickering but mutually attracted couple was referred to as a variation on the *Moonlighting* formula. Willis provided most of the energy, and Caron and the show's other writers provided the ideas that made *Moonlighting* so much fun: the intermittent direct remarks to the audience, the convoluted plots, the stylish photography, and the occasional special-event episodes. There was the *Taming of the Shrew* show, done completely in verse; the black-and-white film noir salute show, narrated by Orson Welles; a minimusical, sizzlingly choreographed to Billy Joel's "Big Man on Mulberry Street"; and so on. The series' endless production delays and behind-the-scenes squabbles led to the show's premature burial, as did the clumsy culmination of the leading couple's long-awaited coupling (the most anticlimactic climax this side of Joel and Maggie on *Northern Exposure*). Worst of all, though, was the resolution of a romantic-triangle story line in which Maddie had to choose between David Addison and Sam Crawford, an apparently flawless suitor played, over several episodes, by guest star Mark Harmon. In rejecting Sam, Maddie clearly chose the wrong man; had the writers gone the other way, *Moonlighting* might have painted itself into a much more satisfying corner. Shepherd returned to TV six years later as the star of a successful sitcom called *Cybill,* but it was Willis, who went on to star in the *Die Hard* franchise and costar in *Pulp Fiction,* whose star shone more brightly after *Moonlighting.* For watching Willis and catching a rising star in action, *Moonlighting* reruns are as instructive and entertaining as, say, watching Tom Hanks in *Bosom Buddies* or Robin Williams in *Mork & Mindy.* Speaking of which. . . .

Mork & Mindy. *1978–82, ABC.* This series grew out of a fantasy episode on *Happy Days,* in which Robin Williams played outer-space visitor Mork from Ork—and injected *Happy Days* with so much frenetic energy that series creator Garry Marshall decided to build a series around him. That's how *Mork & Mindy* began. Here's why it took off so quickly. In the summer of 1978, at the semiannual press tour for the nation's TV critics, ABC presented a one-man comedy concert by one of its unknown sitcom stars, Robin Williams. In that most pressure-filled of settings, facing that most jaded of audiences, Williams blew everyone away, and from that one standing-ovation performance generated a nationwide buzz of critical good will: we don't know about the show, ran the general consensus, but this Williams guy is terrific. Viewers thought so, too, and made *Mork & Mindy* an instant Top 10 hit. Pam Dawber, as Mindy, didn't have much to do, and didn't do what she did that well. For that matter, the only supporting player who earned his keep against Williams was Jonathan Winters, who joined the show in its final season, playing Mearth, the big-bodied, small-brained baby of the title couple. Winters, like Williams, ran around and ad-libbed like a Tazmanian Devil of sitcoms. Williams also popularized, among his youngest fans, such nonsense Orkan catch phrases as "nanoo, nanoo" and "shazbot." But after one stellar season, ABC gambled big by taking its new hit and moving it from Thursdays to Sundays, where it was placed opposite CBS's *Archie Bunker's Place,* and was creamed. In a shameless quest to regain viewers, it presented one truly awful, regrettably memorable episode, in which Raquel Welch and two equally endowed Playboy playmates guest-starred as evil aliens who kidnapped Mork and "tortured" him by fondling him in a hot tub. Nice Ork if you can get it.

Morton Downey, Jr., Show, The. *1988–89, syndicated.* In 1949, a singer named Morton Downey hosted a musical variety show called *Mohawk Showroom* for NBC. Four decades later, his son hosted a syndicated talk show that was a lot less civilized. *The Morton Downey, Jr., Show* was, in one respect, merely the latest edition in a string of bellicose TV talk-show personalities, a tacky syndicated-TV staple stretching back to *The Joe Pyne Show* in 1966–69 (with an angry Los Angeles host who called his own audience "meatheads," long before Archie Bunker popularized the phrase), and *The Alan Burke Show,* a 1967 New York variation on the same theme. Mike Wallace's *Night Beat,* the granddaddy of them all, was just as confrontational, but infinitely more intelligent. The local New York show, which premiered in 1956 on

DuMont's WABD-TV, used its stark set, smoky atmosphere, extreme close-ups, and Wallace's prodding interviewing style to present what amounted to live cross-examinations of such guests as Salvador Dali, William F. Buckley, Jr., and Norman Mailer. *The Morton Downey, Jr., Show,* by contrast, had no-name guests and, on most nights, no-brain arguments. Downey came to prominence after Paddy Chayefsky's visionary 1976 movie *Network,* so the parallels between the real Downey, Jr., and the fictional Howard Beale—the *Network* character (played by Peter Finch) who screamed at his viewers to get out of their chairs, open their windows, and yell, "I'm mad as hell, and I'm not gonna take this anymore!"—are, to say the least, interesting. Downey, like Beale, came from nowhere (actually, Downey came from New York's WWOR, which had launched the show locally the year before), played to people's anger and frustration, and encouraged them to get out of their seats and yell. The microphoned podiums in Downey's studio, where audience members "addressed" the guests, were called "The Loudmouths." Sneering and smoking, prodding and poking, Downey was a TV showman who knew just what he was doing, but his studio audience was much less controlled. It was more like a horror-movie mob, minus the torches. Television improved a little when Downey's show was canceled. It's worth noting, in closing, that the following year, WWOR launched another local series: *The Howard Stern Show.*

Motown 25: Yesterday, Today, Forever. *1983, NBC.* This live special is famous for one thing and one thing only: Michael Jackson's performance of "Billie Jean," during which he stunned the concert audience, and a nation of TV viewers, by introducing the dance step in which he seemed to move backwards and forwards at the same time. The day after *Motown 25* was televised, Fred Astaire phoned Jackson and told him, "You're a hell of a mover." Next to Neil Armstrong's performance fourteen years earlier, it was TV's most memorable moonwalk.

Moyers: Joseph Campbell and the Power of Myth. *1988, PBS.* Mythologist Joseph Campbell is better known in death than he was in life, thanks to this superb six-part interview series with Bill Moyers. It was not at all unusual for Moyers to tap an author, poet, or philosopher whose works subsequently find their way into the cultural mainstream. In 1991, for example, two entries on the *New York Times Book Review* best-seller lists—*Iron John* by Robert Bly (#1) and *Fire in the Belly* by Sam Keen (#6)—owed much of their popularity to Moyers, who had interviewed them previously in well-received, reputation-enhancing specials. Yet *The Power of Myth,* which propelled some of Campbell's books onto the best-seller lists, was, and probably always will be, Moyers's finest career triumph, a once-in-a-lifetime special event. The "lifetime" description can be taken literally: Moyers interviewed Campbell in a series of taped interviews during 1985 and 1986, the year before the mythologist died of cancer. Campbell's theories and observations, linking the world's religions, myths, and folktales into some coherent whole, was more than just captivating conversation; it was the distillation of a life's work, presented in a form that made it both understandable and inspirational. Campbell's final words of advice, "Follow your bliss," became part of the language, and there was the definite sense that both Moyers and Campbell, while engaging in those televised conversations about life and death and love and art and everything else, were indeed following their bliss. *The Power of Myth* was a dual labor of love, and a truly lovely series.

The Munsters. *1964–66, CBS.* This series premiered less than a week after ABC's *The Addams Family,* making it a week imitation in more ways than one. *The Addams Family* was witty; *The Munsters* was largely witless, yet its name, and the image of Fred Gwynne and Yvonne DeCarlo as Herman and Lily, who resembled Frankenstein's monster and Vampira, somehow survives. Gwynne's Herman was such a precise and goofy characterization that Edward Herrmann, in a 1995 Fox telemovie remake called *Here Come the Munsters,* was able to appropriate, and imitate perfectly, the walk, the smile, and even the laugh of Gwynne's childlike monster. Despite a shockingly talented cast— Herrmann as Herman, Veronica Hamel as Lily, and Robert Morse as Grandpa—that telemovie prequel, explaining how the Munster clan got from Transylvania to California, was a total dud, as inferior to the clever *Addams Family* movies as the original *Munsters* TV show was to the original *Addams Family* TV series. Al Lewis, as the original Grandpa, came to *The Munsters* as had Gwynne, from the much more amusing *Car 54, Where Are You?* For that matter, even the creators and writers of *The Munsters* boasted impressive résumés: creators Joe Connelly and Bob Mosher had teamed earlier on *Leave It to Beaver* (which explains why characters on *The Munsters* referred to it often in conversation), and writer Gene Reynolds later wrote for *M*A*S*H*. *The Munsters,* though, was far inferior to their best work. The series spawned a 1966 theatrical film, *Munster Go Home,* as well as a 1981 reunion telemovie called, fittingly, *The Munsters' Revenge.* A syndicated remake featuring a different cast, *The Munsters Today,* ran in syndication from 1988–90, casting John Schuck and Lee Meriwether as the monstrous couple. However, *The Munsters Today* was even less funny than *The Munsters* yesterday.

Muppet Show, The. *1976–81, syndicated.* In 1955, a college freshman named Jim Henson persuaded a local TV station in Washington, D.C., to let him mount a children's show. It was called *Sam and Friends,* and the puppet TV show ran successfully until 1961. In its second year, one of Sam's new friends was introduced, and Kermit the Frog was born. In 1969, along with several other characters, Kermit established himself as a star of public television's *Sesame Street,* but Henson and company always felt the Muppets, as their loony and lively creations were called, could appeal to a full-family audience, not just children. In 1974 and 1975, ABC presented a pair of prime-time specials, one featuring guest star Mia Farrow, the other a theme special given the typically playful title *The Muppet Show: Sex and Violence.* But ABC turned down both those potential pilots, and CBS was no more interested. So Henson and the Muppets attacked on other fronts, creating scruffy garbage-heap characters for the first season of *Saturday Night Live,* and turning the *Sex and Violence* concept into a syndicated series called *The Muppet Show*. Kermit, doing double duty from *Sesame Street*, played the emcee of an eccentric troupe intent upon mounting a weekly show—thus following in the footsteps, if not the frog's legs, of the TV shows of Milton Berle and George Burns. Both Berle and Burns, incidentally, guest-starred on *The Muppet Show* during its phenomenally successful five-year run, as did an impressively eclectic stream of singers, dancers, and other performers. From the comedy field alone, other guest stars included Bob Hope, Carol Burnett, Steve Martin, John Cleese, and Peter Sellers, during whose appearance Kermit stepped forward and sang his trademark song, "It's Not Easy Being Green." As for the Muppets themselves, the biggest star, next to Kermit, was puppeteer Frank Oz's Miss Piggy (and she wouldn't be at all pleased to be ranked "next to Kermit," unless it was at an altar). Her affectatious *"Moi?"* is a durable catch phrase, and there are so many characters and skits and punch lines that each *Muppet Show* viewer should remember a few, though not necessarily the same ones. Gonzo the Great, Scooter, "Pigs in Space," Fozzie Bear, Sam the Eagle—they all have their major fans. Personally, I've always been most partial to the blatherings of the Swedish Chef ("hiffany blarney blarney . . ."), the high-pitched way Kermit screamed "Yaaaaayyy!," and those acerbic old hecklers from the balcony, Statler and Waldorf, who watched the *Muppet Show* production numbers and said things like, "I've seen *detergents* that left a better film than this." On TV, Henson and the Muppets continued with such ambitious shows as HBO's *Fraggle Rock* and NBC's *The Storyteller* and *The Jim Henson Hour*. In other media, they sold zillions of stuffed animals, became stars of a hit attraction at Walt Disney World, and, of course, starred in *The Muppet Movie* and all its successful sequels. Henson's sudden death from pneumonia in 1990 was no less sad and shocking a blow to family entertainment than was Walt Disney's death a generation before. Yet Henson's family and colleagues, like Disney's, kept the dream and franchise alive—and sold an all-new *Muppet Show* sequel series, with Kermit and company running a TV station instead of a theater, to ABC for a 1996 premiere.

Murder, She Wrote. *1984– , CBS*. Before teaming with Peter S. Fischer to create this relatively sedate mystery series, writer-producers Richard Levinson and William Link already had amassed one of the most impressive success records in television. Their partnership had generated some of the medium's most dramatic and groundbreaking telemovies, including 1970's *My Sweet Charlie* (a story about interracial love, starring Patty Duke and Al Freeman, Jr.); 1972's *That Certain Summer* (TV's first homosexual love story, starring Hal Holbrook and Martin Sheen); and 1974's superb *The Execution of Private Slovik*, again starring Sheen. Before those telemovie successes, though, Levinson and Link had toiled long and hard in the vineyards of episodic television, writing scripts for everything from *Burke's Law* and *The Fugitive* to *Dr. Kildare* and *The Man from U.N.C.L.E.*. That prime-time apprenticeship served them well, for once they began creating and overseeing their own weekly and "rotating" series franchises, Levinson and Link had learned enough about structure, style, and casting to generate one popular TV sleuth after another.

Mike Connors lasted eight years as *Mannix*, Dennis Weaver lasted seven years as *McCloud*, and Peter Falk, as *Columbo*, has been around, off and on, since the sixties. In terms of a continuous weekly run, though, no other Levinson-Link sleuth comes close to Angela Lansbury's Jessica Fletcher in *Murder, She Wrote*. Neither does any other TV sleuth, period, unless you count Jack Webb's Joe Friday, who logged twelve seasons on *Dragnet*. At this writing, that's exactly how long Lansbury has been playing Jessica Fletcher—and if CBS renews *Murder, She Wrote* for the 1996–97 season, Lansbury will stand alone as series television's most durable detective. Already, *Murder, She Wrote* holds the record as the longest-running dramatic show with a female lead; the closest competitor in that particular category is *Cagney & Lacey*, which ran for seven seasons. Add, to all this, the fact that *Murder, She Wrote* has been in the Top 20 every year, and in the Top 10 more years than not, and it's no wonder Lansbury felt hurt and a little betrayed by the network's decision to chase after younger viewers in 1995 and move *Murder, She Wrote* from its long-established Sunday time slot. The secret to the show's success? Lansbury is the biggest part of it—she's a wonderful actress, even if the part of Jessica is not exactly taxing—but the neatly resolved mystery plots, and the ample guest-star rosters, are other key ingredients (one noteworthy guest star in 1994 was Mickey Rooney, who played a horse trainer—the same occupation he had portrayed fifty years earlier in *National Velvet*, a film also featuring Lansbury). When Lansbury read the first *Murder, She Wrote* script about mystery writer and amateur sleuth Jessica Fletcher, she described the Cabot Cove resident, quite accurately, as "an American Miss Marple," referring to the popular Agatha Christie character. One little-known fact is that before Lansbury read that script and agreed to star in the series, Jean Stapleton read the same script and passed. Why? It's a mystery.

Murphy Brown. *1988–   , CBS.* This series is most famous for two things: incorporating "real" TV newspeople into its fictitious sitcom world, and for angering then-Vice-President Dan Quayle because its title heroine, played by Candice Bergen, had the audacity to have a baby out of wedlock. Neither of these events was as unprecedented as widely thought, or deserved the amount of attention received. As to the first "breakthrough," Walter Cronkite had appeared as himself, and visited the WJM newsroom, way back in the seventies on *The Mary Tyler Moore Show*—and Linda Ellerbee, the first actual TV newsperson to appear on *Murphy Brown*, previously had portrayed herself on HBO's *Tanner '88*. As to the second point, Quayle must not have had cable, or he would have seen, and reacted, to Blair Brown's single-woman character having a baby on *The Days and Nights of Molly Dodd*. Instead, Quayle selected *Murphy Brown* as a target, and went after the show and its title character during a May 1992 campaign speech in San Francisco. "It doesn't help matters," Quayle said, "when prime-time TV has Murphy Brown—a character who supposedly epitomizes today's intelligent, highly paid professional woman—mocking the importance of fathers by bearing a child alone and calling it just another 'life-style choice.' " Both the Vice President and the CBS sitcom became, for a while, much more visible and vociferous as a result. When *Murphy Brown* returned with its season premiere that September, series creator Diane English fired back a return salvo by having Bergen's Murphy watch Quayle's speech, then reply in kind on her own forum, the fictional *F.Y.I.* newsmagazine. "These are difficult times for our country," she said, "and in searching for the causes of our social ills, we could choose to blame the media, or the Congress, or an administration that's been in power for twelve years, or we could blame me." Ironically, that particular show was the first *Murphy Brown* Quayle had ever seen; his previous criticisms were made about a show he had never watched. Nice TV-critic work, if you can get it. In 1995, the fictional world of *Murphy Brown* intersected with the real world once again, as John F. Kennedy, Jr., made a cameo appearance as himself, visiting the *F.Y.I.* offices to present Murphy with an advance copy of his new political magazine, *George.* The show was energized more significantly, though, thanks to recurring appearances by Garry Marshall and Paul Reubens as, respectively, a bullying network executive and his sycophantic relative—the best characters, and performances, in the entire *Murphy Brown* canon.

Muscular Dystrophy Association Jerry Lewis Labor Day Telethon. *1966–   , syndicated.* The history of this telethon is a long, controversial, and inconsistent one. How and when Jerry Lewis got involved, and turned the fund-raiser into a plea to help "Jerry's kids," long predates the official start of the national *Labor Day Telethon,* and has a lot to do with the evolution of the joint and solo careers of Lewis and Dean Martin. In the early fifties, when they were a white-hot comedy team wowing audiences on *The Colgate Comedy Hour,* Martin and Lewis also donated their time and talents to several charities, many of whom used television as a fund-raising mechanism. In 1952, Martin and Lewis hosted an eighteen-hour marathon for the New York Cardiac Hospital, a local event broadcast live by what is now WNBC-TV. The following year, they headlined a two-hour Muscular Dystrophy Association (MDA) fund-raiser on the fledgling ABC network, broadcast on Thanksgiving Day and titled *The Martin and Lewis Thanksgiving Party.* A condensed blueprint for telethons to come, its parade of show-biz talent included Eddie Cantor, Spike Jones, and a very young Danny Thomas. (A kinescope of this 1953 special is available on home video, but is retitled *Dean Martin and Jerry Lewis Muscular Dystrophy Party* and incorrectly identified as a 1951 production.) In 1955, the year of much friction between Martin and Lewis, New York DuMont station WABD-TV presented a local, nineteen-hour MDA telethon—but with George Jessel, not Martin and/or Lewis, as emcee. The comedy duo, meanwhile, was splitting at the seams; their last appearance on *The Colgate Comedy Hour* was in November 1955, and they engaged in a fairly public feud for most of that and the following year. Therefore, when DuMont mounted another MDA telethon in June 1956, and got Martin and Lewis to host the twenty-one-hour affair, it was sufficiently newsworthy for *Variety* to review the event as a big-deal reunion: "The feuding duo was seemingly united under the common bond of charity," it reported, adding, "during several occasions, the teamwork was again evident." But not for long: their split became official on July 25, 1956, a decade to the day since they had joined forces, and they went their separate ways. Lewis became national chairman of the MDA and hosted, among other things, a one-hour 1961 MDA fundraising special on local TV in Chicago. In 1963, Lewis came to TV, amid much publicity, for an extravagant two-hour ABC variety series called *The Jerry Lewis Show*, but it was excoriated by critics, ignored by viewers, and canceled after three months. Shortly thereafter, in 1965, Martin launched his own variety series, *The Dean Martin Show*, which hit as quickly as Lewis's series had flopped, and ran on NBC for nine years. Hardly by coincidence, Lewis regrouped in 1966 and launched the first annual *Muscular Dystrophy Jerry Lewis Telethon*, presented by the same New York station that had run the Martin and Lewis cardiac benefit fourteen years before. That local production raised only eleven thousand dollars, but it also raised interest in syndicating the production nationally, which made the telethon a successful and durable Labor Day Weekend TV event: by the midnineties, the fundraiser was broadcast annually by more than two hundred stations, and money raised up to 1995, according to Lewis, amounted to $1.4 billion overall. In show-biz terms, the most memorable telethon highlight occurred in 1976, when Frank Sinatra surprised Lewis by bringing Martin onstage and staging a teary reunion—precisely twenty years, as it turned out, after Martin and Lewis *first* reunited on a MDA telecast. (In 1983, Lewis used the MDA forum to reunite Tony Orlando with Dawn, but somehow it didn't have quite the same impact.) Although Lewis raised both money and consciousness for the MDA, his efforts—including the almost annual singing of "You'll Never Walk Alone" from *Carousel*, the parading of the handicapped, photogenic "Jerry's kids" (who sang "Look at me, I'm walking . . . "), the periodic updating of the tote board, and the endless patter and fatiguing structure of the telethon itself—also generated their fair share of ridicule and ire. On his own TV show, Steve Allen lampooned Lewis's efforts by staging a "Telethon for Prickly Heat." In 1981, the American Coalition of Citizens with Disabilities attacked the MDA host's depiction of the handicapped as "helpless, childlike, and dependent," and in 1992, leveling the same charge, a group of disaffected, disabled adults, including some former MDA poster children, presented themselves to the media as "Jerry's orphans" and picketed dozens of local stations carrying the telecast. The results that year? Stung by charges of exploiting both the MDA and the children, Lewis nonetheless proceeded with the twenty-seventh annual telethon, and viewers showed their support by pledging a record forty-five million dollars. Whatever his initial motives, and however cloying the performances of the emcee and his guests, Lewis has given so much of himself to the MDA, and raised so much money for them, that it seems perhaps unfair to attack his efforts and methods under some new banner of political correctness—except that, if you see any given hour of any given MDA telethon, you can easily see another point of view.

Mutual of Omaha's Wild Kingdom. *1963–1971, NBC; 1971–   , syndicated.* Marlin Perkins literally turned his career inside out once he got involved with television. As curator of the Lincoln Park Zoo in Chicago in 1947, he suggested a weekly TV show about the animals there. City officials vetoed the idea, but Beulah Zachary, producer of the local show that would become nationally famous as *Kukla, Fran & Ollie*, loved it, so Perkins smuggled zoo animals into the studios for occasional live, unapproved, and unscheduled specials. Those guerrilla (and sometimes gorilla) specials caught on, and led to Perkins and Jim Hurlbut cohosting an NBC nature series called *Zoo Parade*, which ran from 1950 to 1957. By the end of that show, Perkins had decided that watching animals in their natural habitats, rather than having them penned in cages and confined to TV studios, was where the action was, so he went from inside to outside and launched *Mutual of Omaha's Wild Kingdom* in 1963. Like the *National Geographic Specials*, Walt Disney's nature shorts, and *The Undersea World of Jacques Cousteau*, Perkins and *Wild Kingdom* relayed images reflecting, overtly or implicitly, a love of nature that surely enhanced our awareness and appreciation of animals and the environment. The title of the show remains familiar, as does the show's cohost and eventual solo host, Jim Fowler, a zoo curator who used to "smuggle" animals into the TV studios for *The Tonight Show Starring Johnny Carson*. It seems that nature TV, like nature itself, runs in complete cycles.

My Favorite Martian. *1963–66, CBS.* Back when televisions had antennae, Ray Walston's intermittently extending Martian appendages were the most famous antennae on television. Walston's bouncy headgear as Uncle Martin the Martian was the spiritual forefather of the similarly designed antennae adorning John Belushi and company during the "killer bee" skits on *Saturday Night Live*. They're the only thing truly memorable about this silly sitcom, which costarred Bill Bixby, but they're memorable enough. During a first-season episode of *Picket Fences*, Walston, featured as the very somber Judge Henry Bone, alluded to his previous TV role, and got a big laugh from televiterate viewers, by attending a Halloween party wearing those very same antennae.

My Mother the Car. *1965–66, NBC.* The history of television is littered with classic failures—shows so bad that their wretchedness is a matter of almost universal agreement. But even when they're yanked after a single episode, as in the cases of 1969's *Turn-On* (a horrid imitation of *Rowan & Martin's Laugh-In*) and 1961's *You're in the Picture* (in which host Jackie Gleason had celebrities stick their heads through holes in illustrated cardboard cutouts and guess their new "identities"), bad shows tend to fade from memory, and lose their bottom-of-the-barrel reputation, after a generation. Even 1972's *Me and the Chimp* has, by now, seen its sins mostly forgotten, if not forgiven, along with McLean Stevenson's limp *Hello, Larry* from 1979. But *My Mother the Car* was to the sixties what *Supertrain* was to the seventies: a show too awful to ignore, even in retrospect. Jerry Van Dyke, since redeemed by *Coach*, played the owner of a 1928 Porter, an old car that, it turned out, was possessed by the spirit of his late mother (whose voice was provided by Ann Sothern). That concept is auto-matically bad, but the writing and performing made it even worse: even *Knight Rider* got more mileage out of the talking-car concept.

My Mother the Car is still recalled and ridiculed because it lacked, in a word, engine-uity.

Mystery! *1980–   , PBS.* Like *Masterpiece Theatre,* this PBS anthology series is cobbled together, quite successfully, by importing a variety of mostly British dramas. Some are brief series which, because of their popularity abroad, generate sporadic bursts of additional episodes; others are stand-alone telemovies, which the British refer to as "one-offs." Boston's WGBH-TV commissioned fanciful animation by Edward Gorey to open and close *Mystery!*, and hired Gene Shalit as host, and presto: this less tony cousin of *Masterpiece Theatre* was born. Vincent Price took over as host in 1981, and Diana Rigg in 1989; unlike *Masterpiece Theatre,* though, where the host is (or at least used to be) the most identifiable thing about the series, on this show it's the mysteries, and the sleuths, who count most. Leo McKern in John Mortimer's *Rumpole of the Bailey,* first imported in 1980, was the earliest hit, and, with its many sequels, remains one of the most popular; Rumpole's description of his wife as "She Who Must Be Obeyed" (taken from H. Rider Haggard's female tyrant in *She)* struck a popular chord here as well as in England. Other *Mystery!* triumphs include Sam Neill in *Reilly: Ace of Spies* (1984), Jeremy Brett in *The Adventures of Sherlock Holmes* (a continuing series beginning in 1985), and David Suchet in *Poirot* (beginning in 1990). What's most impressive about this particular anthology series, though, is its penchant for showcasing women in strong, complex roles not usually presented on American television. Cherie Lunghi in *Praying Mantis* (1985) was wonderful, hostess Rigg in *Mother Love* (1990) was astounding, and Helen Mirren, as both suspect and detective, provided some of the best and most memorable moments from this entire anthology. In 1988, she played prime suspect Alma Rattenbury in *Cause Célèbre,* and, beginning in 1992, starred as detective Jane Tennison in three annually presented, totally absorbing *Prime Suspect* miniseries. After that, the *Prime Suspect* franchise moved abruptly to *Masterpiece Theatre.* Whodunnit? Mobil, the corporate underwriter of both series, was the culprit; its motive was the same as that of sponsors anywhere. It wanted to reach a larger audience, and that's no *Mystery!* See also: *Prime Suspect.*

Mystery of Al Capone's Vaults, The. *1986, syndicated.* Geraldo Rivera calls this live two-hour special "the most embarrassing thing that ever happened to me on television"—which, considering Rivera's career achievements, is really saying something. The purpose of the show was to rip down or blow up a wall or two in the basement of Chicago's abandoned Lexington Hotel, the location of gangster Al Capone's not-so-secret vault. The lure was to broadcast it live, which is where Rivera—reportedly a replacement for Robert Stack (whose appointment as host, given his *Untouchables* connection, would have made perfect sense)—struck real gold. The show, televised on April 21, 1986, attracted an estimated thirty million viewers, making it the most-viewed syndicated TV special in history (a record that, as of this writing, still stands). The reason most people remember it, though, is because Rivera came up with a bad case of withdrawal. In other words, the so-called vault was empty, except for an empty bottle and a bunch of dirt. "What can I say? I'm sorry," Rivera said to his audience, and spent the last moments of the special singing "Chicago." Ironically, it was this laughable failure, seen by so many and talked about for so long, that revived Rivera's career and led to his subsequent series in syndicated and cable TV. It also proved, along with the syndicated *A Current Affair* series premiering that same year, that an audience could be built for just about anything if the hype was shrill and shameless enough. Yet most viewers didn't blame Rivera for that, or for his unsuccessful excavation in Chicago, because they knew, in the end, it wasn't his vault.

Mystery Science Theater 3000. *1989–91, The Comedy Channel; 1991–96, Comedy Central.* The best TV series ever to emanate from Eden Prairie, Minnesota, *Mystery Science Theater 3000* began as a local production on Minneapolis UHF station KTMA-TV in 1988, and was distributed nationally via cable comedy networks the following year. Joel Hodgson, who created the series, was its on-camera star until 1993, when head writer Mike Nelson took over. (Film critic Richard Corliss, one of many fervent *MST3K* fans, likened that changing of the guard, in typical *MST3K* show-biz shorthand, to "Carson replacing Paar.") The premise, regardless of who's starring, is that some hapless guy is shot into space by evil scientists and forced to watch bad movies so they can monitor his reactions. He and his robot pals, seen in silhouette at the bottom right of the TV screen, crack jokes while watching films like *Godzilla vs. Megalon* and *Viking Women and the Sea Serpent*, making *MST3K* a sort of interactive viewing experience, like *The Rocky Horror Picture Show* without props. The premise sounds dumb—and, in truth, is—but the hundreds of jokes and allusions spouted each week by the wise guys (Hodgson, Nelson) and wiser robots (Tom Servo, Gypsy, and Crow) make *MST3K* the place to find more pop-culture references per minute than anywhere else on TV, HBO's *Dennis Miller Live* notwithstanding. Exteriors of castles or mansions are routinely described by the silhouetted hecklers as "stately Wayne Manor," an allusion to TV's *Batman.* A typical episode might also refer, however obliquely, to Firesign Theatre, Harold Pinter, Pia Zadora, *Deliverance, The Mary Tyler Moore Show,* and *Sea Hunt.* A typically obscure reference goes something like this: during *Cave Dwellers,* there's a closeup of a hammer coming down on an anvil, and the off-screen wisecrack is, "A Mark VII Production," referring to the visual tag at the end of *Dragnet* with which Jack Webb identified his production company. Other jokes, though, are the kind that everyone can get and enjoy. When an Amazon in *Robot Holocaust* says, "We have no history; we have always been here," Crow shouts at the screen, "Then you have a history." The show's more loyal and intense fans call themselves "MiSTies," overload the Internet with their on-line conversations about the series, and trade bootleg tapes and arcane information with the same fervor as fans of the Grateful Dead. By turning bad movies into good television, *Mystery Science Theater 3000* simultaneously recycled, ridiculed, and revered popular culture, and did a great job. Even though the series was nearly as obscure as some of its punch lines, and eventually was dropped by Comedy Central after a lengthy run, its fan base remains loyal and widespread

LEFT: *Monty Python's Flying Circus*, with John Cleese as a member of the Ministry of Silly Walks.

RIGHT: *Mystery Science Theater 3000*, with original host Joel Hodgson, his robot pals, and Mad Scientists Frank Conniff and Trace Beaulieu.

Murphy Brown, with Candice Bergen surrounded by, clockwise from left, Charles Kimbrough, Robert Pastorelli, Pat Corley, Joe Regalbuto, Faith Ford, and Grant Shaud.

enough to earn *MST3K* a place in teleliteracy history, and to justify the production of a planned *Mystery Science Theater 3000* movie. Meanwhile, the fans of the series know the show's theme song by heart, so play MisTie for them. . . .

My Three Sons. *1960–65, ABC; 1965–72, CBS.* No reflection on Fred Mac-Murray, or anyone else in this long-running sitcom, but the first things that come to mind when you say *My Three Sons* are the bouncy, instrumental theme song by Frank DeVol, and the visually striking opening credits accompanying that theme. In the beginning, the opening image was a simple drawing of three sets of legs, with one foot tapping along in time. Later on, the most resonant image was of the titular three sons peeking their heads around a corner, looking like a suburban totem pole, with their shaggy dog completing the picture. As to its place in TV history, *My Three Sons* was one of the first single-parent sitcoms—of which all the early ones, curiously enough, featured men, not women, as the protagonists. The very first, John Forsythe in *Bachelor Father*, had premiered in 1957; the next two, *My Three Sons* and *The Andy Griffith Show*, were unveiled within a month of one another in 1960. To help MacMurray's Steve Douglas run his all-male household, he had live-in help: first "Bub" O'Casey (played by William Frawley of *I Love Lucy*), then Bub's brother, Uncle Charley (William Demarest, who joined the show after Frawley died in 1965). Naming the Douglas brothers is like naming the seven dwarfs; you might forget one or two, but not all of them. For the record: Don Grady was Robbie, Tim Considine played Mike, Stanley Livingston was Chip, and Barry Livingston, Stanley's real-life little brother, joined the cast as adopted brother Ernie in 1963. Like *Leave It to Beaver*, the show was very moral, fairly funny, and uncloyingly wholesome. One behind-the-scenes footnote worth repeating: because MacMurray was reluctant to devote too much time or energy to television, the producers agreed to shoot all of his scenes in only sixty-five days of filming each year. This contractual requirement led to the development of what came to be called "the MacMurray system," in which all of a season's episodes were written in advance and photographed out of sequence, so that, for example, all the kitchen scenes could be shot in a row. Also, when necessary, the action would be blocked and photographed so that MacMurray didn't need to be there: MacMurray could eat his breakfast and recite lines at one end of the table in March, his TV sons could sit at the other end and record their replies months later, and the scenes would be edited together in postproduction. With MacMurray, "the MacMurray system" worked for a dozen years; without him, needless to say, it hasn't widely been used since.

My World and Welcome to It. *1969–70, NBC.* Until *The Simpsons* came along, this was the last intelligent use of animation on weekly prime-time TV. The animation, based on the fluid and very funny drawings by James Thurber, was only a small part of this sitcom, but a crucial part: William Windom played writer-cartoonist John Monroe (an obvious approximation of Thurber), who, like Thurber's Walter Mitty, often retreated into fantasy, in this case using his own illustrations as his escape hatch. This series was so unusual, and so well-written, that it remains strong in the minds of those who saw and enjoyed it—even though it has seldom been revived or repeated since NBC, after one brief but shining season, sent it back to the drawing board.

Naked City, The. *1958–59, 1960–63, ABC. The Lone Ranger* has the most famous opening narration in the history of television, but *The Naked City* claims the most famous closing narration: "There are eight million stories in the Naked City. This has been one of them." The first such *Naked City* story was dramatized in a 1948 movie with the same title, which provided the blueprint (down to that final tag line) for the TV series that followed a decade later: New York cops chasing New York bad guys through New York buildings and streets. New York, New York, was a wonderful town for such purposes, and *The Naked City* became TV's first weekly drama series to shoot entirely on location—a concept so novel that, during the show's first season, the opening narration explained, and bragged, "This story was not photographed in a studio." The superb *East Side/West Side*, starring George C. Scott and Cicely Tyson as social workers, used city locations just as evocatively, but didn't premiere until 1963, the week before *The Naked City* was canceled. *N.Y.P.D.*, with its location filming, didn't come along until 1967; *The Naked City*, by contrast, had begun telling its stories back when the city's thin blue line was known as P.D.N.Y.C. (Police Department of New York City). In addition, *The Naked City* was one of the first shows to surprise viewers by killing off a leading character. Leading man John McIntire, who starred as Dan Muldoon, wanted out of the series, so producer Mark Hellinger obliged him—by staging a chase sequence in which his detective character died, spectacularly and unexpectedly, when his squad car smashed into an oil truck and erupted into flames. Pretty slick. The series, with scripts by such maverick writers as Roy Huggins (who wrote *Maverick)* and Gene Roddenberry (who wrote *Star Trek),* was unusual, and memorable, because it humanized its villains—and because, once it expanded to an hour in 1960 and began tapping the resources of the city's best young theatrical talent, *The Naked City* provided big breaks, and meaty roles, for such young performers as Dustin Hoffman, Robert Redford, Sandy Dennis, and Jon Voight. When the series left the air, 7,999,862 stories remained unaccounted for in the Naked City. In the nineties, the show had spiritual successors in *Law & Order*, which used New York's locations and actors to similar effect, and *NYPD Blue*, which took the *Naked City* title much more literally.

Name That Tune. *1953–54, NBC; 1954–59, CBS; 1970, 1974–80, 1984, syndicated; 1974–75, 1977, NBC.* This musical quiz show began as a radio program on NBC in 1952, and proved so popular that the network mounted a TV version the following year. A visual element was added for television, requiring contestants who thought they could identify a given song to run twenty-five feet and ring a bell before venturing their guess. On radio, the most a contestant could win was five hundred dollars; the final year the series was on TV, its title reflected the impact of inflation: *The $100,000 Name That Tune*. The *Name That Tune* title was one aspect of the show that made its way into popular culture's common vocabulary. The other was the phrase "I can name that tune in *x* notes," a familiar game of musical chicken which, surprisingly, didn't become part of the *Name That Tune* format until 1974.

National Geographic Specials. *1965–73, CBS; 1973–74, ABC; 1975–94, PBS; 1995– , NBC*. Here's an example of a network not knowing when to fold 'em and when to hold 'em. CBS ran these quarterly globe-trotting, nature-loving, culture-exploring specials for eight years, producing such quality and well-watched shows as *Miss Goodall and the Wild Chimpanzees* before deciding the audience base was dwindling. Third-rated ABC picked up the series and ran it for a while, adding such shows as *Bushmen of the Kalihari* to the list, then dumped the show in 1974. That same year, PBS inaugurated the similarly inclined series *Nova*, which is still running more than two decades later, and found the funding to back new episodes of *National Geographic Specials*, which returned in 1975 with a documentary using microphotography to examine the inner workings of the human body. Called *Man: The Incredible Machine*, it was the first *National Geographic Special* shown on public television, and remains one of the most acclaimed, popular, and repeated shows in the history of the network. Then, of course, there's the familiar *National Geographic* theme song, "Someone to Washoe-ver You" (just kidding about the title, but not about the widespread familiarity of Elmer Bernstein's instrumental). In 1994, two decades after moving to public television, *National Geographic Specials* continued to lead the list of top-rated PBS offerings—and proved popular enough for NBC to steal them away, beginning with a thirtieth-anniversary special in January 1995. The only difference in the NBC shows was the insertion of commercials, which had been an element of the first ten years' worth of the *National Geographic Specials* anyway. Obviously, the show's producers had learned a valuable lesson from the wild animals they had photographed for so long, a lesson that helped them survive in the ruthless jungles of prime-time television: adapt or die.

NBC Nightly News. *1970–85, NBC*. **NBC Nightly News with Tom Brokaw,** *1985– , NBC*. The day Chet Huntley retired in 1970, so did *The Huntley-Brinkley Report*, NBC's most successful news show. In its place came *NBC Nightly News*, with David Brinkley, John Chancellor, and Frank McGee sharing duties for one year. In 1971, Chancellor became solo anchor, and served in that capacity until 1976, when he and Brinkley teamed for another three years. Chancellor clocked more solo flying hours (on the air, that is) from 1979 to 1982, at which point NBC assigned Roger Mudd and Tom Brokaw as coanchors; Chancellor, like Brinkley before him, then took on the task of delivering commentaries. If the Mudd-Brokaw combo doesn't roll off the tongue as easily as does, say, Huntley-Brinkley, it's because this new NBC duo lasted only seventeen months, and was about as much of an oil-and-water mix as Connie Chung and Dan Rather would be for CBS a decade later. On September 5, 1983, Brokaw became solo anchor, and got his name in the title two years later. Chancellor, who had spent more than forty years at NBC, retired in July 1993, and was, for a while, the last commentator on a commercial broadcast network newscast. "It's not the end of an era," he said modestly on his final telecast, "just the end of my era." Chancellor wasn't unemployed for long; he served as narrator for *Baseball* the following year. What's more, Chancellor turned out to be right: the era of network news commentary soon was revived, with Bill Moyers providing personal remarks and reports for *NBC Nightly News* beginning in February of 1995. (Ill health, however, forced Moyers to step down after a few months, and made it a very short-lived feature.) Brokaw, whose tenure as solo anchor included impressive interviews with Mikhail Gorbachev, claims by far the longest stint as a solo anchor for NBC: his nearest challenger is John Cameron Swayze, who anchored the network's *Camel News Caravan* for seven years. Though Brokaw has spent many of his ten-plus solo seasons in third place, he was enjoying second-place status by the end of 1995, and remains, at this writing, firmly ensconced at *NBC Nightly News*. In other words, like Swayze's famous Timex watches, he takes a licking and keeps on ticking.

Newhart. *1982–90, CBS.* The premise of *Newhart* placed Bob Newhart as the manager of a rustic Vermont inn—a kind of Americanized *Fawlty Towers*, but with a major distinction. In *Fawlty Towers*, the acerbic attitude of John Cleese's Basil Fawlty drove the plots and the show; in *Newhart*, the star's Dick Loudon character was neither sour nor acerbic, but merely ineffective and flustered. Even more so than on *The Bob Newhart Show*, Newhart's comic persona was reactive, not active. It was not what his character did that generated the laughs. Instead, it was how he reacted to the actions of those around him—a group that included Tom Poston's daydreaming handyman George, Julia Duffy's pampered maid Stephanie, and that surrealistic trio of William Sanderson's Larry, who spoke, and his equally backwards, backwoods brothers Darryl (Tony Papenfuss) and Darryl (John Voldstad), who did not. Mary Frann played Loudon's wife, but her eight years with the show were overshadowed by the last scene in the final episode, in which Suzanne Pleshette, who played Newhart's wife on *The Bob Newhart Show*, made an unannounced appearance. After being hit on the head with a golf ball, Newhart's Dick Loudon passed out, but it was Newhart's Bob Hartley who awakened— in his old bed from *The Bob Newhart Show*, and next to his "former" wife, Pleshette's Emily. Bob then described to her the premise and characters of *Newhart*, effectively dismissing the entire run of that series as a bad dream. It was an ending that referred to both the dream season of *Dallas* and the daydream ending of *St. Elsewhere*, and provided viewers with one of the best, and most memorable, series finales in TV history.

Newlywed Game, The. *1966–74, 1984, ABC; 1977–80, 1985–90, syndicated.* This is another game show from Chuck Barris, who always found the losers more entertaining than the winners. The arguments sparked by the losing couples on this game show, like the painful looks of the rejected suitors on *The Dating Game* and the bufuddled misery of gonged contestants on *The Gong Show,* were the core of misery that kept a miserable series alive and thriving for years. Bob Eubanks presided over the vast majority of these network and syndicated versions, which, like their host, wallowed in double entendre and single-minded tastelessness. The only cynical opportunity missed by Barris was the launching of a *Celebrity Newlywed Game*—which, given the increasingly mercurial nature of today's celebrity marriages, could be paired with a sister series called *Celebrity Divorce Court.*

Nightline. *1980–   , ABC.* On November 4, 1979, militant Iranian students seized the American embassy in Tehran. ABC was the only network to dispatch a correspondent (Bob Dyk) before the borders were temporarily closed, and, like Cable News Network at the start of the Persian Gulf War, benefited greatly from its competitive advantage of having the sole continuing broadcasts emanating at the site of a major Middle East crisis. Evening news reports began counting the duration of the hostages' imprisonment ("Day 2," "Day 3"), and on the fourth day of the takeover, Frank Reynolds hosted a late-night ABC special called *The Iran Crisis: America Held Hostage.* One week later, it presented a second special, at which time Reynolds signed off by promising to return every weeknight with "a broadcast about the crisis in Iran as long as there *is* a crisis." *Day 26: America Held Hostage,* on November 29, also happened to be Reynolds's birthday, so he took the night off, and was replaced on the late-night program by diplomatic correspondent Ted Koppel. Four months later, on March 24, 1980, *America Held Hostage* officially became *ABC News Nightline,* vowing to follow the Iranian story while simultaneously giving similar in-depth treatment to other topics. Koppel was named solo anchor, and has held that post ever since—and has held audiences, too, to the point where, by the end of 1995, under the aggressive and intelligent stewardship of executive producer Tom Bettag, *Nightline* was the top-rated program in late-night TV, beating both *The Tonight Show with Jay Leno* on NBC and *Late Show with David Letterman* on CBS. Neither the technologies nor the formats utilized by *Nightline* were really that new. The interview-via-satellite idea had been honed by *The MacNeil/Lehrer Report,* and the occasional national "town meeting" specials, affording presidents, candidates, and other newsmakers the opportunity to discuss topics with average citizens and local experts, were prefigured as long ago as 1964, when CBS televised *Town Meeting of the World,* a special moderated by Eric Sevareid and featuring Richard Nixon, Harold Wilson, and others. But Koppel, with invaluable contributions by Jeff Greenfield and others, made *Nightline* his own, and became as credible and respected a TV news presence in his era as Walter Cronkite a generation earlier. Over the years, Koppel's late-night career highlights would include his groundbreaking reports from South Africa; his exclusive closed-door coverage of the final days of the Bill Clinton presidential campaign; his interviews with Jim and Tammy Faye Bakker, Gary Hart, Oliver North, and Los Angeles Dodgers Vice-President Al Campanis (who lost his job after unguardedly making racist remarks to Koppel about African-American athletes); and his invaluable, instructive, and often therapeutic "town meeting" *Nightline* and *Viewpoint* specials. Koppel, with *Nightline* and *Viewpoint*, traveled the country, and sometimes to other countries, to examine volatile issues, take the emotional temperature of newsmakers and ordinary citizens, and all but force people to explain their passions and positions thoroughly, and listen to their adversaries politely. Koppel was there to moderate discussions among American presidential candidates, and between President Clinton and some of his fellow Americans; to instigate frank and meaningful conversations between South African blacks and whites during and after the struggle over Apartheid; to listen to disenfranchised African-Americans after the initial Rodney King verdict, and to disenfranchised Midwesterners after the bombing in Oklahoma City; to tap the intensely varied reactions, among different ethnic groups, to both the O. J. Simpson verdict in the United States and the assassination of Israeli Prime Minister Yitzhak Rabin in Jerusalem. (Koppel canceled his own fifteenth-anniversary *Nightline* party to cover that last story, which is why he and his show are likely to be around to celebrate their twentieth.) Of all the nightly news programs on commercial network TV, *Nightline* continues to pander the least and impress the most.

Night Stalker, The. *1972, ABC.* Long before Anne Rice unearthed her literary vampires or *The X-Files* began playing with the paranormal, Carl Kolchak was on the case—and, in this stylish telemovie introducing Darren McGavin as the stubborn, disheveled newspaper reporter, staking a claim to a bit of TV history. At the time it was first broadcast, *The Night Stalker* drew the largest audience of any telemovie ever made—including the previous record-holder, the well-received *Brian's Song*, which ABC had televised two months earlier. *The Night Stalker*, based on the novel by Jeff Rice and adapted by Richard Matheson (author of *Duel*), was an engaging, alternately funny and frightening mystery about a serial killer, in modern-day Las Vegas, who turns out to be a vampire. The story unfolded not from the vampire's viewpoint, but from that of Kolchak, the rumpled reporter (think *Columbo* with a press pass) who was among the first to eliminate the impossible, accept the improbable, and treat the killer as an actual member of the undead. Simon Oakland costarred as Kolchak's eternally flustered editor, Tony Vincenzo, but it was McGavin's Kolchak who stole, and was, the show. Dan Curtis, who had produced daytime TV's vampire soap opera *Dark Shadows*, generated a much better product with *The Night Stalker*. Recognizing that, Curtis quickly produced and directed a sequel telemovie, 1973's *The Night Strangler*, reteaming McGavin and Oakland and transplanting their characters to a newspaper in Seattle, where Kolchak wound up pursuing another type of immortal murderer. *Kolchak: The Night Stalker*, the inevitable series spinoff with the same stars, lasted only one season (1974–75), but to many fans of the genre, it was a wonderful season indeed. Two of the shows, "Horror in the Heights" (about a sinister shape-shifter) and "Legacy of Terror" (with that ghastly image of Kolchak pouring salt in the mouth of a slumbering mummy, whose eyes suddenly and unexpectedly open), are little one-hour classics of both horror and humor, and held up well when rerun in 1995 by the Sci-Fi Channel. The writers for those twenty *Kolchak* episodes included Michael Kozoll, who went on to co-create *Hill Street Blues*, and Robert Zemeckis, who went on to direct *Back from the Future* and *Who Framed Roger Rabbit*. Still, it's the original *Night Stalker* telemovie that made the most lasting mark on TV history, even though *Kolchak: The Night Stalker*, with its weekly stories of an open-minded investigator puzzling over paranormal occurrences, is an obvious (and openly acknowledged) TV precursor to *The X-Files*.

Nixon Interviews with David Frost, The. *1977, syndicated.* The chronology goes like this: Watergate break-in, 1972. Reelection of Richard Nixon, same year. Congressional hearings into Watergate and its political cover-up, 1973. Impeachment proceedings begun against Nixon, 1974. Nixon resigns, and is granted a presidential pardon by Gerald Ford, same year. One year later, exactly to the day, Nixon signs a contract for six hundred thousand dollars, in exchange for which he agrees to be interviewed by David Frost for a series of four ninety-minute programs—one of which was earmarked specifically to deal with Watergate, and all of which would give Frost complete journalistic independence. Frost, without a network behind him, had outbid NBC, and his quite literal bid to end Nixon's electronic-media silence was both widely anticipated and warily regarded. Even though CBS previously had paid another former president, Lyndon B. Johnson, for exclusive TV interview rights regarding his years in office, Frost's deal with Nixon was the event that led to the entry of the phrase "checkbook journalism" into the common vernacular. Yet two years later, once the first of Frost's four syndicated interview programs was televised, the British interviewer was praised by many of the print and broadcast media that previously had attacked him. *The Nixon Interviews with David Frost* were low-key, low-budget affairs (you could hear planes flying overhead), yet the intimacy, and the impressive amount of research done by Frost and his staff, made for very compelling TV. Nixon's off-screen aides, at the time, included Diane Sawyer, but it was what happened on camera that made these interviews so unforgettable. It was here, and nowhere else, that Nixon said of Watergate and its aftermath, "I let the American people down. And I have to carry that burden with me for the rest of my life." And it was here, and only here, that Nixon said, during a discussion of his political and ideological opposition during the Watergate scandal, "I gave them a sword. And they stuck it in, and they twisted it with relish. And, I guess, if I'd been in their position, I'd have done the same thing." (Nixon also, with uncanny prescience and optimism, suggested that while he knew he would never again serve in any official government position, "Maybe I can give a little advice from time to time.") When Nixon died in April 1994, the PBS series *. . . talking with David Frost* marked the occasion by repeating portions of the syndicated Nixon-Frost interviews, and the Disney Channel, of all places, presented them later that year in their entirety, complemented by formerly unused and unseen outtakes. Those replays, seventeen years later, were just as riveting as the original broadcasts.

Northern Exposure. *1990–95, CBS.* Because of its remote rural setting and unusual characters, *Northern Exposure* often drew comparisons to *Twin*

Peaks, which had premiered earlier the same year. Its real template, though, was *Local Hero,* the 1983 British film about a young urban hotshot who grudgingly descends upon a Scottish fishing village, only to find himself slowly transfixed and transformed by the people and nature there. And where the soul of *Twin Peaks* gravitated toward the dark side, *Northern Exposure* was almost all sweetness and light. The fictional city of Cicely, Alaska, was the most tolerant town on TV. One classic episode flashed back to the town's origins, showing that Cicely's founding fathers actually were founding mothers—or, more precisely, lesbian lovers. In the present tense, *Northern Exposure* made room for two gay male characters who eventually got married; it also presented elderly characters normally overlooked by series TV, and spent most episodes exploring some aspect of spirituality. Chris Stevens, the town deejay/philosopher portrayed by John Corbett, presided over two of the show's most eclectic and exciting features: the constant references to literature and the arts, and the dazzling array of musical selections presented on the show's soundtrack, within and without Chris's radio show. The selections run from Louis Armstrong's "A Kiss to Build a Dream On" and Dean Martin's "That's Amore" to Vivaldi's "The Four Seasons" and Daniel Lanois's "Jolie Louise." Series creators Joshua Brand and John Falsey, whose credits include *St. Elsewhere,* concocted a strong string of supporting characters, including such favorites as John Cullum's gentle giant Holling, Barry Corbin's blustery ex-astronaut Maurice, Darren E. Burrows's Fellini–idolizing Ed, Peg Phillips's tender shopkeeper Ruth-Anne, Cynthia Geary's flighty Shelly, and Elaine Miles's charmingly calm Marilyn. The central characters, though, were Rob Morrow's Joel (the big-city fish in a small-town pond) and Janine Turner's Maggie, whose antagonistic sexual chemistry quickly elevated to volatile *Moonlighting* levels. They suffered the same type of implosion, too, because the long-awaited physical consummation of their relationship was one of the most anticlimactic climaxes since Maddie and David finally crossed the line on *Moonlighting.* After that, *Northern Exposure* got even less satisfying, struggling to find a way to write out Joel (prompted by Morrow's desire to pursue a film career, beginning with his role in *Quiz Show*), and fizzling completely with the 1994 arrival of Paul Provenza's Phillip Capra as the new doctor in town. During its first several seasons, though, *Northern Exposure* was a pleasure from start to finish, and a show that delighted in breaking barriers and ignoring boundaries. When the series was honored at the 1992 Emmy Awards as the Outstanding Dramatic Series, Brand said, with truthful irony, "Well, I guess we can reveal it to them now, that we really are a comedy."

Nova. *1974–   , PBS.* This science series premiered in 1974 by importing a behind-the-scenes BBC-TV documentary that remains one of the very best installments: *The Making of a Natural History Film,* which revealed all the complex tricks behind capturing animals and plants doing seemingly "natural" things. Unlike the *National Geographic Specials,* this series never got commercial network exposure, but the mass audience's loss was public television's gain. *Nova* introduced American viewers to such scientists as Carl Sagan (long before *Cosmos*) and Stephen Hawking (long before he became a best-selling author), and to such topics as recombinant DNA research and warm-blooded dinosaurs (long before *Jurassic Park*). Major highlights through the years have included 1974's *The First Signs of Washoe*, 1976's *The Race for the Double Helix*, 1977's *The Hot-Blooded Dinosaurs*, 1978's *The Case of the Ancient Astronauts* and *Still Life* (a year in the life of a beaver pond), 1983's *The Miracle of Life*—the most famous and remarkable *Nova* ever, in which Swedish filmmakers Lennart Nilsson and Bo Erikson used microphotography to capture the conception, development, and delivery of human life—and 1988's *Who Shot President Kennedy?*, which picked up where previous scientific analyses by CBS News had left off.

NYPD Blue. *1993–   , ABC*. Like *Homicide: Life on the Street* and the imported *Prime Suspect* miniseries, *NYPD Blue* hit the ground running as one of the most mature and satisfying cop shows of the nineties. Yet even had it not delivered the dramatic goods, it would have earned a spot in TV history because of all the controversy it generated prior to its premiere. Because co-creators Steven Bochco and David Milch had described and fashioned *NYPD Blue* as TV's first "R-rated" prime-time commercial network series, every epithet, and every exposed bit of epidermis, was scrutinized, cited, and debated. The occasional flashes of nudity and coarse language got *NYPD Blue* noticed, but the scripts, and the talented actors, are what made the show finish its freshman season as the top-rated new drama series of the year. The first season of *NYPD Blue* owed a great debt to *Hill Street Blues:* camerawork and editing were even more intentionally jerky, one prominent cop character was shot but not killed, and subsequent plots involved relationships with ex-wives, confessionals with a priest, secret office romances, and visits to an Alcoholics Anonymous meeting. Other direct *Hill Street* connections to *NYPD Blue* include director Gregory Hoblit, theme-song writer Mike Post (whose subway-drumbeat *NYPD Blue* opening sets the stage beautifully), and both of the new show's central stars. Dennis Franz, as Andy Sipowicz, previously played two different roles on *Hill Street Blues*, and David Caruso, whose portrayal of John Kelly made him a major sex symbol during the show's first season, had appeared in the second episode of *Hill Street* as the punk leader of an Irish street gang. That was in 1980. Thirteen years later, on the other side of the thin blue line, Caruso embodied a character that made him a star, while Franz got, and made the best of, the most challenging role of his career—winning a Best Actor Emmy after the first season. Caruso, less grateful and more ambitious, left *NYPD Blue* one month into the show's second season, with his character of Kelly resigning rather than accept a demotion. That year's clear winner of the McLean Stevenson Memorial "I'm Gonna Quit This Show and Become a Big Star" Award, Caruso went off and starred in two poorly received movies, *Kiss of Death* (which wasn't bad) and *Jade* (which was), rather than stay on *NYPD Blue* and embody a character much richer, and more challenging, than those or most other film scripts could provide. Franz knew better—and so did Jimmy Smits, who had made a similar move to Caruso's by leaving *L.A. Law* partway through that show's run in search of greater stardom. Given a second chance to embody and explore a series character on another quality drama series from Bochco's production company, Smits agreed immediately. At the end of the second season, *NYPD Blue* won an Emmy as Best Drama; midway through the show's third season, it was clear that Smits, as Detective Bobby Simone, had found his way, his character, and his place. Somewhere out in Hollywood, David Caruso was still searching.

Odd Couple, The. *1970–75, ABC.* Very early in their respective careers, decades before costarring in TV's *The Odd Couple*, both Jack Klugman and Tony Randall had appeared (though separately) on the same TV series: *Captain Video and His Video Rangers*. Randall went on to star in *Mr. Peepers*, and Klugman to perform in many of New York's live TV shows of the fifties, as well as on *The Twilight Zone*—while Neil Simon, one of many talented writers writing for Sid Caesar and company on *Your Show of Shows*, eventually struck out on his own, and struck gold, as a playwright. After *Barefoot in the Park* became a mammoth Broadway hit in 1963, Paramount Pictures offered Simon a deal he couldn't refuse. In exchange for movie and TV rights to Simon's next comedy play, the studio would pay him six hundred thousand dollars, plus a promise to match 10 percent of the box-office gross for the show's entire Broadway run. Simon agreed, and quickly provided Paramount with a thirty-nine-word outline: "Two men—one divorced and one estranged and neither quite sure why their marriages fell apart—move in together and save money for alimony and suddenly discover they're having the same conflicts and fights they had in their marriages." Two years later, *The Odd Couple* opened on Broadway, with Art Carney as fastidious Felix Unger and Walter Matthau as gruff Oscar Madison, and proved instantly the prescience and wisdom of that studio deal maker. Paramount mounted a movie version in 1968, with Jack Lemmon replacing Carney, then set about generating a TV spinoff, turning over the reins to executive producers Garry Marshall and Jerry Belson, a former scriptwriting team on *The Dick Van Dyke Show*. Marshall went after seasoned actors with direct *Odd Couple* experience—Randall had played Felix in Chicago, while Klugman had starred as Oscar in London. The show worked well, largely because of the leads; the writing wasn't as crisp as in Simon's play, but Klugman and Randall worked hilariously together, and the supporting cast, including Penny Marshall in her first sitcom role, was very likable. (Very best episode: "Password," with Felix getting the secret word *Bird* and feeding his one-word clue of *Aristophanes* to a still-clueless Oscar.) *The Odd Couple*, after five years on the air, became even more popular in reruns. Simon's original premise appeared foolproof, but over the years several fools proved that to be wrong. In the seventies, an animated ABC children's TV series called *The Oddball Couple,* about a fussy cat and a messy dog, proved to be a crass menagerie, while a live-action, African-American series revival, *The New Odd Couple,* came and went in one season in the eighties. After Klugman's bout with throat cancer, he and Randall reunited for a 1991 benefit stage performance of Simon's original play, teamed for a somewhat maudlin 1993 telemovie *Odd Couple* "sequel" (in which Oscar, like Klugman, dealt with the effects of throat cancer), and starred in a road-show tour of the original *Odd Couple* play in 1994. Such was the power of television that Randall and Klugman, not any of their stage or screen predecessors, had become most strongly identified as the "true" odd couple. And oddly enough, Randall and Klugman teamed one additional time in 1994—to cohost a TNT cable telecast of the Lemmon-Matthau *Odd Couple* film.

O. J. Simpson Low-Speed Chase, Murder Trial, and Verdict. See *Simpson, O. J.*

Olympic Games, The. *1960–   , various networks.* It's sad, but true, that the two most famous events associated with the television-era Olympic Games are acts neither of skill nor grace, but acts of violence: the terrorist attack on Israeli athletes in Munich during the 1972 Summer Games; and, much less tragically but no less reported, the kneecap attack on American ice skater Nancy Kerrigan that made her "showdown" appearance opposite Tonya Harding, an alleged co-conspirator in the attack, such an astounding media circus. Live coverage of the former story, with sports anchorman Jim McKay covering the unexpected and ultimately tragic events ("They're all gone," McKay said wearily, noting the deaths of the kidnapped athletes after a shootout between Arab terrorists and German police), was superb—network TV at its best. Live coverage of the latter story, with *CBS Evening News* coanchor Connie Chung following Harding around like a lapdog, was putrid—network TV at its worst—and undoubtedly played a part in her losing that coanchor job a year later. Yet on February 23, 1994, the day on which CBS presented prime-time coverage of the women's technical skating program with Harding and Kerrigan in direct competition, that program was viewed by so many people that it was ranked sixth on the list of all-time highest-rated TV events. Its 48.5 Nielsen rating was higher than all but two Super Bowls, and it easily eclipsed the audience figures for more deserving athletic displays that year, such as Dan Jansen's remarkable gold-medal speed-skating performance after a long string of personal tragedies and mishaps. (The white-hot media spotlight soon turned elsewhere, though, and less than a year later, Kerrigan was reduced to headlining a Walt Disney skating special on CBS, wearing a black-and-white fright wig and skating as Cruella de Vil.) In other Olympic years, memorable televised events and athletes include, but certainly are not limited to, eighteen-year-old light heavyweight boxer Cassius Clay's gold-medal performance in 1960 on CBS, years before he changed his name to Muhammad Ali; Jean-Claude Killy's thrilling performances on skis at Grenoble, France, in 1968 on ABC; Mark Spitz in the water, and Olga Korbut on the uneven parallel bars, in 1972 on ABC, in the days immediately prior to the massacre in Munich; Nadia Comaneci in 1976 on ABC, becoming the first female gymnast to earn a perfect "10" in Olympics history; and, in 1980 on ABC, the U.S. ice hockey team upsetting the Soviets in a thrilling victory capped by announcer Al Michaels screaming, "Do you believe in miracles?" Another potent Olympics moment involving American athletes on ABC took place on the winners' platform in Mexico City in 1968, when medalist black sprinters Tommie Smith and John Carlos protested minority conditions back in America by raising black-gloved fists during the national anthem. Their quiet salute enraged some, inspired others, but showed just how hot the spotlight of the Olympic Games had become—and this was a mere eight years after CBS had become the first American network to provide Olympics coverage (taped, not live), with Walter Cronkite taking a sort of *You Are There* approach. The very first Olympics to be televised elsewhere in the world, though, occurred much earlier—in Berlin in 1936, when experimental TV cameras and receivers were in place to catch Adolf Hitler as his German track and field athletes attempted to beat the competition in general and America's Jesse Owens in particular. The German TV experiments, like the German athletes and Hitler himself, failed. In America, for the record, here's which networks have covered the Olympics in the modern era. **Winter Games:** Squaw Valley, California, 1960, CBS; Innsbruck, Austria, 1964, ABC; Grenoble, France, 1968, ABC; Sapporo, Japan, 1972, NBC; Innsbruck, 1976, ABC; Moscow, 1980 (there was no coverage by NBC, due to President Jimmy Carter's imposed boycott protesting the Soviet invasion of Afghanistan); Sarajevo, 1984, ABC; Calgary, 1988, ABC; Albertville, France, 1992, CBS; Lillehammer, Norway, 1994, CBS (the year the Winter and Summer Games became staggered at two-year intervals, rather than occurring quadrennially in the same calendar years). **Summer Games:** Rome, 1960, CBS; Tokyo, 1964, NBC; Mexico City, 1968, ABC; Munich, 1972, ABC; Montreal, 1976, ABC; Lake Placid, 1980, ABC; Los Angeles, 1984, ABC; Seoul, Korea, 1988, NBC; Barcelona, 1992, NBC; scheduled for Atlanta, 1996, NBC. After that, rights go to CBS for the 1998 Winter Games in Nagano, Japan, then revert exclusively to NBC, thanks to a billions-dollar contract signed in late 1995, for all Olympic Games up to and including the year 2008.

Omnibus. *1952–56, CBS; 1956–57, ABC; 1957–59, NBC.* Lots of people still remember the name of this ambitious cultural-arts anthology series, but fewer remember the actual program itself. The host was Alistair Cooke, basically providing weekly on-air audition tapes for his eventual role as host of the equally highbrow PBS anthology series, *Masterpiece Theatre* (and making him, in the process, probably the only cultural host to preside over series on CBS, ABC, NBC, and PBS). What *Masterpiece Theatre* and cable services such as Bravo continue to do today, *Omnibus* did in the fifties: its aims were high, and its aim usually true. Its eclectic offerings included jazz concerts conducted by Leonard Bernstein, dramatic readings by Charles Laughton, undersea documentaries by Jacques Cousteau, interviews with Frank Lloyd Wright and Agnes DeMille, performances by the original cast of Broadway's *Oklahoma!*, and such dramatic offerings as a 1953 production of Shakespeare's

King Lear, starring Orson Welles in his dramatic TV debut. During its early CBS days, *Omnibus* also mounted what counts, at least to me, as one of the earliest miniseries ever presented on network television: a five-part version of James Agee's *The Birth and Death of Abraham Lincoln,* brief installments of which were presented over four months in 1952 and 1953. After NBC became the third network to broadcast and cancel *Omnibus,* the series was reincarnated as a number of specials on NBC in 1960, and again on ABC in 1980. Viewers recognized the name, but didn't sit still for the programs, and *Omnibus* was driven back to the *'bus* terminal.

One Day at a Time. *1975–84, CBS.* This Norman Lear series, starring Bonnie Franklin as a divorced woman trying to rear her two daughters, is too dominant as part of the seventies, and too prominent a step in the development of women on television (female empowerment and all that), to be forgotten or ignored. That's too bad, because I never liked it, and time certainly hasn't treated it well: *One Day at a Time* seems even more preachy and shrill now than it did then. Valerie Bertinelli grew up on this show, but, unlike her character of Barbara Cooper, never left home, and remains a telemovie and miniseries fixture well into the nineties. One decade at a time.

One Life to Live. *1968– , ABC.* This was the first soap opera created from scratch by Agnes Nixon, and it immediately established the veteran soap writer as a formidable production force in daytime TV. By mixing standard soap characters (multiple-personality heroines and gold-hearted prostitutes) with new relevant plots for the sixties (sexually transmitted diseases, child abuse, drug addiction), Nixon and *One Life to Live* went after, and captured, a new generation of daytime viewers. The acting helped, too, because this series had more than its share of talented players and future stars—especially in the seventies, when its casting directors showcased such talented male cast members as Tommy Lee Jones (Dr. Mark Toland, 1971–75), Laurence Fishburne (Joshua Hall, 1973–76), and Tom Berenger (Tim Siegel, 1975–76). Other future stars included Jeff Fahey (Gary Corelli, 1982–85), Phylicia Rashad (Courtney Wright, 1983–84), and Judith Light (1977–83), whose witness-stand histrionics as prostitute Karen Wolek propelled her into prime time on *Who's the Boss?* More recently, Blair Underwood and Richard Grieco have spent a *Life* time on this soap, and two talented regulars, Gerald Anthony as Marco Dane and Jessica Tuck as Megan Gordon, enlivened *Life* during its dull stretch in the late eighties.

On the Road with Charles Kuralt. *1983, CBS.* In half-hour series form, *On the Road with Charles Kuralt* lasted only three months, in the summer of 1983. But as a series of short reports on *The CBS Evening News,* beginning with the first report on October 26, 1967, Kuralt delighted American viewers by allowing them to view America. With cameraman Izzy Bleckman and soundman Larry Gianneschi, Jr., Kuralt did nice, modest stories about nice, modest people, and in the process provided some of the best-written TV poetry of the century. What Woody Guthrie did with a guitar, Kuralt did with a television crew. He traveled the back roads and visited the small towns, sending back dispatches brimming with optimism, decency, and good cheer. One prototypical example: Kuralt's *On the Road* profile of Jethro Mann, the Belmont, North Carolina, "bicycle man" who set up a "lending library" of bikes for underprivileged area kids, repairing and supplying the bicycles so long as they were returned at the end of the day. Kuralt sought out such decent folk and treated them decently—a recipe that, for all its simplicity, is all but absent from TV in the midnineties. After his *One for the Road with Charles Kuralt and Morley Safer* special in 1994, Kuralt retired from CBS and headed back on the road—to write a book, *Charles Kuralt's America*, in which he visited his favorite places at their respective optimal times of the year. On *Sunday Morning*, CBS replaced Kuralt, but regarding *On the Road*, the network didn't even try. "I hate seeing old institutions vanish," Kuralt complained to Safer on that *One for the Road* special. Then he, too, vanished, and TV is the poorer for it.

Oprah Winfrey Show, The. *1986– , syndicated.* Phil Donahue revolutionized and dominated the TV talk-show arena by getting the studio audience involved in the act. Then, in the eighties, Oprah Winfrey took Donahue's blueprint and ran with it—adding her own personal perspective, which was female and black to Donahue's male and white. Winfrey had cohosted a local show, *Baltimore Is Talking*, from 1977 to 1984, when she moved north to host *A.M. Chicago*, a low-rated local show emanating from Donahue's home turf. Three months later, her show was outperforming his in local ratings; Donahue moved his show to New York, but when the retitled *Oprah Winfrey Show* went national in 1986, she soon dominated him on that scale as well—and, a decade after her national launch, continues to draw more viewers than any other syndicated talk show. Like Donahue, she traffics in curiosity and empathy, and encourages the studio audience to speak its mind. In addition, Winfrey seems singularly unafraid to reveal her own opinions and insecurities. She speaks of her own faith in God, carts out a wheelbarrow full of fat to illustrate the results of one of her diets (her most famous stunt, the Winfrey equivalent to Donahue's donning of a skirt), and appears to take it personally when Tom Cruise, in the movie *Interview with the Vampire*, enacts something that offends her sensibilities. Detractors offended by Winfrey's approach—which seeks to understand, if not forgive, all aspects of human behavior, however aberrant—disparagingly bemoan "the Oprah-ization of America," one sure measure of her show's lasting sociological impact.

Original Amateur Hour, The. *1948–49, DuMont; 1949–54, NBC; 1955–1957, ABC; 1957–58, NBC; 1959, CBS; 1960, ABC; 1960–70, CBS.* The phrase "amateur hour" remains part of the language, and even the name of Ted Mack, this TV show's host, rings a bell all these decades later. So do things that have become part of the vernacular, even though *Amateur Hour* may no longer be remembered as their source—the show's Wheel of Fortune, for example, and even the phrase uttered whenever it was spun: "Round and round and round she goes, and where she stops, nobody knows!" The format, wheel, and slogan all came from radio, where, from 1934 to 1946, *Major Bowes and His Original Amateur Hour* trotted out hopeful performers and let them strut their amateur stuff. On radio, the most famous contestant was a very young Frank Sinatra; on TV, Pat Boone and Gladys Knight were among the then-unknown winners. Yet the most interesting fact about *Amateur Hour* is how it got on TV in the first place. The radio version left the air when Edward Bowes died in 1946. At the time, and until March 1948, the American Federation of Musicians refused to allow its members to perform live on television—but DuMont executives reasoned correctly that amateur music wouldn't fall under the ban. They went to Bowes's assistant, Ted Mack, who held the rights to the title, and rushed a TV version onto the air while all other networks were still hamstrung by the AFM boycott. DuMont had an instant hit on its hands, which NBC soon stole and CBS soon "borrowed": *Arthur Godfrey's Talent Scouts*, another amateur showcase and early TV hit, premiered on CBS almost a full year after DuMont's *Original Amateur Hour*. The DuMont show, in every way, lived up to its title.

Oscar Awards. See *Academy Awards, The*.

Oswald, Lee Harvey, murder. See *Kennedy, John F., Assassination and Funeral Coverage*.

Our Miss Brooks. *1952–56, CBS.* In 1948, the same year radio's *Original Amateur Hour* was adapted for TV, *Our Miss Brooks* began on radio, starring Eve Arden as schoolteacher Connie Brooks, Richard Crenna as geeky student Walter Denton, and, eventually, Gale Gordon as the stuffy principal, Osgood Conklin. Four years later, the same trio of characters and actors made their way to television—and surviving kinescopes attest to the gentle cleverness, and quiet intelligence, of this series. In its first season, *Our Miss Brooks* landed in the Top 25, where the only other women starring in hit sitcoms were portraying housewives: *I Love Lucy* and *Mama*. Give Arden and *Our Miss Brooks* credit for championing the working woman a generation before *That Girl* supposedly broke similar ground. Unfortunately, aside from its title and (to older viewers) its theme song, *Our Miss Brooks* is slip-sliding away from our cultural consciousness.

Our World. *1967, NET (pre-PBS public TV).* Look, I loved the *other* TV show called *Our World*—the 1986–87 history series written and hosted by Linda Ellerbee and Ray Gandolf on ABC—as much as you did. Maybe more, since most people never watched it when it was on, much less recall it fondly today. However, the *Our World* that's being noted here is much more famous, even though it's paradoxically even more obscure. This June 25, 1967, special was the first live worldwide TV broadcast in history, transmitted to thirty countries via a string of satellites. Still doesn't ring a bell? This'll help: it's the show on which the Beatles, appearing live from Studio One at Abbey Road, performed and premiered one of their best sixties anthems: "All You Need Is Love." And that, basically, is All You Need to Know.

Outer Limits, The. *1963–65, ABC.* *The Twilight Zone* and *Star Trek,* two other sixties series dealing with weekly explorations into unknown territory, had even more famous opening narrations, but *The Outer Limits* boasted a close third. The robotic announcer of this sci-fi anthology series, accompanied by an equally high-tech sine wave visual, delivered a memorably terse warning to viewers: "There is nothing wrong with your television set. Do not attempt to adjust the picture. We are controlling the transmission. . . . We will control the horizontal. We will control the vertical. . . . " The producers behind *The Outer Limits* were like the Ernie Kovacs of horror—always pushing the envelope of the technology for another clever visual effect. The show's premiere episode, "The Galaxy Being," presented what at the time was an unbelivably creepy-looking creature: humanoid in shape, yet almost translucent in appearance, glowing white with black spots and bright white eyes. (The effect, virtually synonymous with *The Outer Limits,* was achieved by dressing an actor in a smudged wet suit, then optically reversing the image on the negative and inserting it into the rest of the scene.) Other unforgettable episodes from the show's three-year run included "The Sixth Finger" (with David McCallum as a scientist experimentally progressing and regressing on the evolutionary scale); "Corpus Earthling" (a creepy variation on the *Invasion of the Body Snatchers* theme), "The Zanti Misfits" (memorable mostly for its ants-with-humanoid-faces aliens); "The Chameleon" (a thoughtful episode written by Robert Towne and starring Robert Duvall); and the most famous *Outer Limits* episode of all, with Robert Culp starring in "Demon with a Glass Hand"—a show written by Harlan Ellison, who also happened to contribute the most acclaimed episode of *Star Trek,* "City on the Edge of Forever." In 1995, thirty years after its cancellation, *The Outer Limits* was revived, with a series of all-new episodes, for the Showtime cable network on syndicated TV. In its first season, the new *Outer Limits* turned out a few shows that ranked among the best in the history of the franchise, including "Quality of Mercy" (with Robert Patrick and Nicole De Boer as tortured prisoners of alien invaders), "Valerie 23" (with Sofia Shinas as a beautiful but lethal android assigned to paraplegic scientist William Sadler), and "I, Robot" (with Leonard Nimoy, delivering one of his best performances in years, as an attorney defending a robot accused of murder). To fans of the old *Outer Limits* series, the "I, Robot" episode had special meaning. It was the only installment from the first season of the new series to be based on an episode from the old *Outer Limits;* moreover, that 1964 "I, Robot" featured, as a newspaper reporter, Leonard Nimoy, who was returning to *The Outer Limits* thirty-one years later to play a more central role in a remake of the same episode.

Partridge Family, The. *1970–74, ABC.* It's hard to imagine a seventies family series worse than *The Brady Bunch,* but this was it. Yet like *Gilligan's Island* in the sixties, its unwavering awfulness somehow made it popular with some, and unforgettable to the rest, with a theme song to match. Shirley Jones, David Cassidy, Danny Bonaduce, and Susan Dey played the most prominent members of a rock 'n' roll family act, although only Jones and Cassidy sang, and the rest of them made the Monkees look like Mozarts. Frighteningly, Dave Madden's Reuben Kincaid, as the group's manager, has emerged as some sort of mini–icon for the "X Generation," like some bell-bottomed Barney Fife. Even more frighteningly, the premiere episode of *The Partridge Family* involved the group's attempt to record a song in their garage and persuade a major label to release it. The song was "I Think I Love You"— and when it was released in real life, that first single by the Partridge Family became a painfully durable Number One hit two months later, duplicating an earlier life-imitates-TV feat by the Monkees. But I like the Monkees. The Partridge Family? I Think I Hate You.

Password. *1961–67, CBS; 1967–69, syndicated; 1971–74, ABC.* The password is . . . *teleliteracy.* Allen Ludden presided over this genial quiz show, handing out the secret word to contestants while their partners waited to receive synonymous clues. It was a simple show with a simple secret for its success: for the first time on a TV quiz show, everyday contestants were paired with celebrity partners, including frequent guest Betty White, Ludden's real-life wife. In 1974, the series changed its title and format to *Password Allstars,* eliminating the middleman—or, in this case, the everyman. Like later versions with and without Ludden, it lacked the innocent charm of the original format, which played like the simple parlor game it was.

Patty Duke Show, The. *1963–66, ABC.* "Meet Cathy, who's lived most every-where / from Zanzibar to Berk'ly Square," begin the famous lyrics to this sixties sitcom. "But Patty's only seen the sights / A girl can see from Brooklyn Heights / What a crazy pair! / But they're cousins, identical cousins. . . . " This preposterous, yet rather in-gene-ous TV premise of "identical cousins" was dreamed up by Sidney Sheldon—whose subsequent sitcom creation, *I Dream of Jeannie,* also explored the "dissimilar twin" theme on occasion by having Barbara Eden play both the title Jeannie and her evil twin sister. For that matter, a rival supernatural sitcom, *Bewitched,* sporadically gave Elizabeth Montgomery the opportunity to play not only good witch Samantha, but her mischievous relative Serena—another identical cousin. (Also, don't forget that other genetic rarity that appeared subsequent to *The Patty Duke Show,* Elvis Presley's dual role in the 1964 film *Kissin' Cousins.* On second thought, *do* forget that.) Patty Duke, fresh from her triumph in *The Miracle Worker*, was featured in *The Patty Duke Show* as a one-girl *Odd Couple*, as though fussy Felix and sloppy Oscar had emerged from opposite ends of the same gene pool (except, of course, that *The Patty Duke Show* predated the Broadway premiere of *The Odd Couple* by a few years, so no plagiarism was possible). The series episodes are much less memorable than the theme song, but one particular episode is worth saluting. In it, Patty fantasizes about herself as a mother and housewife, and is scared out of the prospect of marriage by a nightmare vision of a messy, rowdy home in which she gets no respect from either her spouse or her offspring. It was a far cry from the usual sixties sitcom, but inadvertently provided the blueprint for such "groundbreaking" eighties comedies as *Roseanne* and *Married . . . with Children*.

Pee-wee's Playhouse. *1986–91, CBS*. This Saturday morning children's series already had completed its successful and inventive five-year original run on CBS, and was showing summer reruns in July 1991, when *Playhouse* star Paul Reubens, a.k.a. Pee-wee Herman, was arrested in a Sarasota adult theater—to be precise, in *the* Sarasota adult theater—for violating Florida statute 300.08, "indecent exposure of a sexual organ." Charged with exposing himself and masturbating, Reubens pled "no contest" and, in 1992, paid his fifty-dollar fine, did his fifty hours of community service, and that was that. Except that CBS reacted to the arrest of Reubens by yanking the reruns of *Pee-wee's Playhouse* from its schedule (though perhaps, in this context, yanking isn't the best word), effectively ending the reign of Pee-wee Herman as a children's TV host. The good news is that his work stands on its own—five seasons' worth of a thoroughly delightful potpourri of animation, puppetry, songs, skits, big-headed salesmen, and the best living quarters this side of *Swiss Family Robinson*. Pee-wee would encourage viewers to "scream real loud" whenever they heard the day's secret word, and played host at a place that made Alice's Wonderland seem like a stable environment: ice cubes danced in the freezer, tiny dinosaurs lived in the mouse hole, and even the furniture and toys had lives of their own. The Sarasota "scandal" derailed the career of Reubens, who vowed to retire permanently the Pee-wee persona. Years later, Reubens returned to weekly series TV, quietly but triumphantly, by playing (and making the most of) a recurring role as a TV executive's ruthless relative on *Murphy Brown*. As for *Pee-wee's Playhouse*, it was a true TV original, with its bouncy Danny Elfman theme song, its featuring of Laurence Fishburne (or "Larry," as he was then credited) as Cowboy Curtis, and its laudable early sensitivity to abrasive salespeople. "*Saaaales-man!*," Pee-wee would scream, as a sort of early warning system, whenever he saw one coming, or heard one calling. Years later, due to the geometric increase in the frequency and rudeness of annoying telemarketers, I often find myself screaming the same thing.

Pennies from Heaven. See *Singing Detective, The*.

People's Court, The. *1981–   , syndicated*. All that needs to be said about the widespread popularity of this long-running courtroom "reality series" was relayed by the obsessive anticipation of Dustin Hoffman's autistic Raymond character in the 1988 movie *Rain Man:* "Ten minutes to Wapner! . . . Four minutes to Wapner! . . . One minute to Wapner!" Retired California Judge Joseph Wapner launched a new career at age sixty-one, settling the minor disputes of real-life litigants in a "binding" TV courtroom. The concept had been done before, but with actors re-creating courtroom conflicts, as far back as 1958, when *Divorce Court* tried to cash in (and did) on the *Perry Mason* craze. By allowing real people to vent their passions and prejudices, though, *The People's Court* tapped a whole new mother lode, one that a subsequent generation of daytime talk shows eagerly copied, using themselves as judges and their studio audiences as juries. (Picture Montel Williams or Ricki Lake in black robes, asking their studio "juries" to applaud or boo as relatives bicker and tempers flicker.) One thing that works for Wapner, though, is his overall crankiness—a formula that works just as well, come to think of it, for Ray Walston, in his portrayal of the fictional, equally frictional Judge Bone on *Picket Fences.* As for Wapner's on-air partner, host Doug Llewelyn, he ought to be hauled before Wapner and charged with the crime of coproducing Geraldo Rivera's *The Mystery of Al Capone's Vaults.* The verdict: Guilty! Guilty! Guilty!

Perry Como Show, The. *1950–55, CBS; 1955–63, NBC.* Perry Como was a crooner who got his first show on radio, *The Chesterfield Supper Club,* in 1944. His first TV series, for NBC in 1948, had the same title, and for the last few years of his weekly TV career, in the early sixties, the show he head-lined was called *The Kraft Music Hall.* In between, for the entire decade of the fifties, Como held court on *The Perry Como Show,* with a musical and conversational style so laid back it could almost be described as Como-tose. Dean Martin used a similarly loose approach in his TV variety show years later, but Como played it straight—without exaggeration, without any pre-tense of inebriation, and became and remained famous for it. Como was the bridge between Arthur Godfrey on the one hand and, say, Andy Williams on the other, and proved popular enough with viewers that, like Williams, he continued to host holiday specials on PBS well into the nineties.

Perry Mason. *1957–66, CBS.* This is the TV show, based on the novels of Erle Stanley Gardner (and the 1943–55 CBS *Perry Mason* radio series), that taught a generation of viewers about courtroom lingo and histrionics: "Objec-tion!" "Sustained!" "Your honor, I object!" "Overruled!" Fred Steiner's omi-nous opening theme music let you know from the start that this was serious business, and Raymond Burr, as attorney Perry Mason, let you know from his demeanor that he *meant* business. He was as good a defense lawyer as Marcus Welby was a doctor, and William Talman's poor Hamilton Burger, who prosecuted most of the cases, was little more than the Wile E. Coyote to Mason's Road Runner. (In the entire run of the original series, Mason lost only one case, and it was subsequently reversed.) The character of Burr's Perry Mason remains a resonant TV icon, right along with Peter Falk's Columbo—and, like Columbo, was revived and revisited by its leading man in the eighties. *The Return of Perry Mason*, in 1985, was the season's highest-rated telemovie, sparking a series of subsequent telemovies that, improbably, eventually outlived Burr and outlasted Mason. *Perry Mason: The Case of the Killer Kiss*, the 1993 telemovie featuring the final appearance by Burr (who died that year) in the title role, was the twenty-sixth *Perry Mason* telemovie, but not the last. After Burr's death, sporadic installments were billed as *A Perry Mason Mystery*, featuring "friends" of Mason's—attorney colleagues played by Hal Holbrook and Paul Sorvino. This unusual arrangement actually had a precedent during the original run of *Perry Mason* (and precedent, on a courtroom show, should count for something). In 1963, when Burr was recuperating from surgery and unable to film the series, "guest attorneys" appeared during a three-week period to pick up the slack. The most famous, and surprising, of the three? Bette Davis.

Persian Gulf War Coverage. *1991, CNN, CBS, NBC, ABC and occasionally PBS and C-SPAN.* The predecessor to this book, *Teleliteracy: Taking Television Seriously*, covered this event at great length, but a few years' distance allows for a quicker, if not clearer, recounting. As I write this, it is some six years since the Allied air strike known as Operation Desert Storm was launched on January 16, 1991. Except for those people whose loved ones fought or perished during that war, faces and events from that conflict that have truly "stuck" with the general populace are relatively few—and "general" is the key word. From the military side, there's General H. Norman Schwarzkopf, who, after his retirement, turned his bully-pulpit live press conferences and well-plotted military strategies into subsequent TV shots cohosting World War II documentaries on CBS with Charles Kuralt and Dan Rather, and even an impressive celebrity guest turn on *Jeopardy!* (At the end of 1995, Schwarzkopf joined NBC News as a national contributor and military analyst.) There's also General Colin L. Powell, chairman of the Joint Chiefs of Staff, who spent most of 1995 deciding whether to accept the conventional wisdom of political analysts and mount a campaign for the presidency. Ultimately, Powell decided against it, though public opinion polls certainly made it seem feasible. Finally, on the broadcast side, there's Peter Arnett, the veteran print reporter who, in his dogged reporting from Baghdad for CNN, managed to land several scoops, including an exclusive discussion with Iraqi President Saddam Hussein (the mother of all wartime interviews), while the whole world was watching. Or, at least, listening. Arnett scored his biggest scoop of all, that first night of the war, when he and colleagues John Holliman and Bernard Shaw were providing CNN (and much of the United States) with gripping audio but no video. The only network with a special four-wire phone line approved and installed in Baghdad, CNN was able to maintain communications with its reporters there, and vice versa, for the entire first night of the air strike, even though other networks were cut off almost immediately. Arnett's description of the incoming bombs and outgoing antiaircraft fire were gripping, and the lack of video images made them even more resonant. "There's no sense cowering from the comparison," I wrote at the time. "It was the most riveting eyewitness account of a war strike since Edward R.

Murrow intoned those famous words, 'This is London.' " The next day, an ABC camera operator's night-scope footage of what Arnett and company had described the night before was smuggled out and televised, and the sounds and images have been paired so relentlessly since then that "common memory" now recalls them as a unified event. At the time, though, the images were a day late in arriving, and the most potent coverage of the entire Gulf War were nothing more, and nothing less, than TV as radio. At the end of 1995, Bob Simon, the CBS reporter who had been held captive in Iraq for forty harrowing days, found himself once again held at gunpoint in the middle of a war zone—but this time in Bosnia, and only for thirty minutes before being released.

Person to Person. *1953–61, CBS.* More people recall the name of this series than the series itself, which is fortunate for admirers of Edward R. Murrow— because, despite occasional cerebral conversations with fascinating guests, this was far from the veteran CBS newsman's finest hour, or hours. Whereas his *See It Now* was a fabulous documentary series, *Person to Person* was, for the most part, a facile interview series, in which Murrow, usually from the safety of his TV studio, would toss puffball questions at celebrities in their cozy private habitats. Watching those shows today, with Murrow gently questioning an uncomfortable Marilyn Monroe, or a coy Lauren Bacall in tandem with a shy Humphrey Bogart, leaves you with the uncomfortable realization that among Murrow's many other, more laudable achievements, he also "pioneered" obsequious celebrity interviews as smarmy and fawning as anything seen on *Entertainment Tonight* or the E! Entertainment Network. For the record, Charles Collingswood hosted *Person to Person* for the show's final two years, but Murrow is the person invariably linked to *Person*.

Peter Gunn. *1958–60, NBC; 1960–61, ABC.* Perhaps it's unfair, because this Blake Edwards-produced series did add some wit and flair (more flair than wit, actually) to the TV detective genre of the period, but it's true and unavoidable: the only lasting imprint by this series, all these decades later, is the pulsating theme song by Henry Mancini. A few years later, when Mancini and Edwards were no longer under the *Gunn*, they would reteam for an even more durable collaboration, the *Pink Panther* movie series. Edwards went on to revive *Peter Gunn* as a one-shot telemovie with Peter Strauss in the title role, but that 1989 effort was so bad that almost no one remembers it— making it one *Gunn* that draws, not shoots, blanks.

Peter Pan. *1955, 1956, 1960, NBC.* This classic James M. Barrie story has been flying so high for so long, and in so many different media, that it's likely it will Never Never Land. The ageless *Peter Pan*, though, really came of age in the fifties, when it conquered, in successive years, screen, stage, and television. The Walt Disney animated version came in 1953, the Broadway production in 1954, and the first live TV version in 1955. That TV version, starring the original Broadway cast of Mary Martin as Peter Pan, Cyril Ritchard as Captain Hook, and a beam of light as Tinker Bell, was such a hit it was restaged, in another live presentation, in 1956. In 1960, the same stars teamed yet again, this time for a version captured on videotape and shown in living color. I was among the millions of wide-eyed viewers that night, because my diary entry for December 8 of that year, when I was seven years old, says, "Was Peter Pan good today!" That color version, with choreography by Jerome Robbins and music and lyrics by Carolyn Leigh, Moose Charlap, Jule Styne, Betty Comden, and Adolph Green, was shown three additional times between 1961 and 1973, then was retired until 1989, when it made a heartwarming, hand-clapping comeback. My own children, about the same age then as I was when I first saw Martin singing "I Won't Grow Up," were just as enchanted as I had been, exemplifying the true spirit of *Peter Pan*. At the end of that story, the ageless hero returns to visit his old friend Wendy, but discovers she's older than he thought—a whole generation older. So, while Wendy looks on with a mixture of affection and envy, Peter charms her child instead. That's precisely what happened with the next-generation 1989 telecast of *Peter Pan*, returning triumphantly after so many years of dormancy. In 1992, New York's Museum of Television & Radio called it "high on the list of the most memorable broadcasts in television history," a review that is accurate, affectionate, and anything but a *Pan*. Conversely, a 1976 TV version, with a totally different musical score by Anthony Newley and Leslie Bricusse, fared much less well, though it at least deserved credit for creative casting. Danny Kaye portrayed Captain Hook, and the part of Peter Pan was played by Mia Farrow.

Peyton Place. *1964–69, ABC.* And speaking of Mia Farrow. . . . She shot to stardom as the virginal Allison Mackenzie in this ABC serial, based on the Grace Metalious book and the 1957 Lana Turner movie. Allison was in love with wealthy Rodney Harrington, who was played by Ryan O'Neal—the other young performer to attain major fame as a result of this unexpected hit. Third-rated ABC, with lots of holes to fill in its prime-time schedule, slotted *Peyton Place* as a twice-weekly series (a strategy it would later repeat with *Batman*), and struck ratings gold. *Peyton Place II*, as the Thursday telecast was called for terms of differentiation, landed in the season's Top 10 that first year, while Tuesday's *Peyton Place I* made the Top 20. The following year, ABC launched a third weekly installment, but with less success. Nevertheless, *Peyton Place*, as a whole, was the first prime-time soap-opera hit in TV history—and the first prime-time soap, period, since the forties. The title became, and remains, synonymous with the concept of TV soap opera, and *Peyton Place* was the clear forerunner of such prime-time serialized dramas as *Knots Landing* and, yes, the similar-sounding *Melrose Place*. No plot line on *Peyton Place*, though, could match Farrow's real-life romantic entanglements, even back then. When she left the show abruptly for a few weeks to go sailing with Frank Sinatra, *Peyton Place* placed Allison in a temporary, off-camera coma; when Farrow married Sinatra in 1966 and left the series again, never to return, the writers explained Allison's absence by saying she had "mysteriously disappeared." Many years later, her body was found at the side of a river, wrapped in plastic. (Not really. That little digression is my idea, and my fault, alone. Mia culpa.)

Philco Television Playhouse. *1948–55, NBC.* **Goodyear TV Playhouse.** *1951–57, NBC.* The titles of these two anthology series often are intertwined in memory, because, for five years, they were intertwined in reality. From 1951 until 1955, *Philco Television Playhouse* and *Goodyear TV Playhouse* (in later years, known also as *Goodyear Playhouse* and *Goodyear Theatre)* took turns, on alternating weeks, in the same Sunday night time slot. But *Philco* came first, by several years. Both shows were overseen by the brilliant young producer, Fred Coe, whose ability to nurture writers and team them with the right directors and actors was truly impressive. Coe was adept at producing comedy and music as well as more serious fare (he was executive producer of the *Mr. Peepers* sitcom, and, on an installment of his 1954–57 anthology series *Producers' Showcase,* mounted the aforementioned live versions of *Peter Pan),* but live TV drama was the place he made his biggest mark—and with which, along with the likes of the subsequent *Playhouse 90,* he helped establish the period as TV's "Golden Age." Paddy Chayefsky's *Marty,* the single most famous live drama from the era (see separate listing), was a *Goodyear* presentation. *Philco,* however, could claim Horton Foote's *A Trip to Bountiful,* a 1953 drama starring Lillian Gish and Eva Marie Saint— a teleplay so successful it was transferred to Broadway later that year. (And, finally, made into a movie in 1985, with Geraldine Page winning a Best Actress Oscar for her touching performance.) Other classic presentations that later became Broadway plays and Hollywood films included Richard Nash's *The Rainmaker,* starring Darren McGavin for *Philco* in 1953, and Gore Vidal's satirical *Visit to a Small Planet,* starring Cyril Ritchard for *Goodyear* in 1955. With writers such as Chayefsky, Foote, Vidal, and JP Miller (whose 1955 *The Rabbit Trap* also was turned into a movie), and directors such as Delbert Mann and Arthur Penn, Coe could mix and match quality talents, and find casts to match. The presentations already mentioned are the most resonant today, but others in the canon are equally tantalizing. From *Goodyear,* who wouldn't want to see John Cassavetes and Gena Rowlands in 1955's *The Expendable House,* written by Reginald Rose? And from *Philco,* the long-dormant gems include Jose Ferrer as *Cyrano de Bergerac* in 1949, and these three productions from 1955: Paul Newman in Vidal's *The Death of Billy the Kid* (made into the film *The Left-Handed Gun* three years later, with Newman reprising his role and Penn making his directorial film debut, jumping from TV to Hollywood the way Mann had with *Marty);* Jessica Tandy and Hume Cronyn in Ernest Kinoy's *Christmas 'til Closing;* and Lee Meriwether portraying herself in 1955's *The Miss America Story,* perhaps TV's earliest "I Gotta Be Me" subject-as-star docudrama.

Phil Donahue Show, The. *1969–74, syndicated.* **Donahue.** *1974–96, syndicated.* I come not to bury Phil Donahue, but to praise him. Yes, he dressed in a skirt once during a show on transvestism (bad idea, good legs), and booked lesbian nightclub dancers in a show quickly dubbed "lesbo-a-go-go"—

and when the ratings chips were down, he was likely to return to Chippendale's for another examination of male strippers. But he's done many more sober programs than silly ones, and Donahue, like his studio audience, seems as interested in listening as in talking. Many of his next-generation imitators have allowed themselves and their audiences to become jury as well as judge, but Donahue always does, and always did, want to provide his guests with a full forum. Credit his pioneering talk show with many things, including the introduction of sensitive or challenging topics, guests, and lifestyles into millions of TV households that might otherwise avoid confronting or considering them. By bringing his microphone into the studio audience, and opening the phones to callers watching the live show at home ("Is the caller there?"), Donahue was an early champion of the "national town hall" concept, as well as one of the first coast-to-coast travelers on the interactive TV superhighway. Finally, Donahue also deserves a lot of credit for reconfiguring the relationship between TV and politics, which he helped transform during the 1992 presidential campaign by devoting entire programs to such informative, welcome, and unusual events as an unmoderated "debate" between candidates Jerry Brown and Bill Clinton. Like Larry King, who similarly impacted the 1992 presidential race, Donahue elicits great questions from the people who watch his show; unlike King, Donahue probably could conduct as good and informative a show without the interactive feature. *The Phil Donahue Show* began as a local series on WLWD-TV in Dayton, Ohio, in 1967, was syndicated nationally in 1969, and moved to Chicago in 1974, at which time its title was shortened to *Donahue*. Ten years later, just as Oprah Winfrey's new local talk show in Chicago began outperforming his in the ratings, Donahue moved to New York, where he and his syndicated series, and his wife Marlo Thomas (whom he met as a guest on his show in 1977), continued to reside.

Phil Silvers Show, The. *1955–59, CBS*. Although the character of the constantly conniving Ernie Bilko never became as widespread a TV icon as Ralph Kramden or Archie Bunker or Columbo, he deserved to, because Bilko was just as singular and savvy an archetype. He was the guy who always had a scam, and *McHale's Navy* was a paragon of military order when compared to Bilko's Army. *The Phil Silvers Show*, which was titled *You'll Never Get Rich* for its first two months before giving due credit to its central star, premiered the same season as *The Honeymooners*, and set almost as high a comedy standard. Nat Hiken, a former comedy writer for Fred Allen, created the series (he later did *Car 54, Where Are You?*), and gave the characters, from Silvers's Bilko on down, a lot more bite and oddball credibility than most series of the fifties. Most of the supporting players looked like regular army types, from tough-guy athletes (the show's casting director, believe it or not, was Rocky Graziano) to funny-looking sad sacks (Maurice Gosfield's Duane Doberman, Joe E. Ross's Rupert Ritzik). To its credit, *You'll Never Get Rich* matter-of-factly presented its Company B as racially integrated, and also gave early exposure to many guest stars who later carried their own sitcoms—Alan Alda, for example, and Dick Van Dyke, and Ross's future *Car 54* costar, Fred Gwynne. Julie Newmar was featured in the recurring role of the local waitress, the insensitively nicknamed "Stacked" Stacy, and among the sports stars making their sitcom TV debuts on *The Phil Silvers Show* were Whitey Ford and Yogi Berra. The fast-talking character of Bilko is more resonant today than any particular catch phrases, and this sitcom remains inexplicably underappreciated and undertelevised. Only in America. And I mean that literally, because in the United Kingdom, a *Times* magazine 1995 article exhaustively ranking the all-time Top 100 cult TV shows placed *The Phil Silvers Show* right at the top, standing alone as Number One. Rather amazing, really, when you consider that the next three series on the list were, in descending order, *The Prisoner, Star Trek,* and *Monty Python's Flying Circus.* In America, even the syndicated reruns, presented under the title *Sgt. Bilko,* are all but impossible to find—but perhaps that, along with the American lethargy concerning Ernie Bilko and company, will change if the announced 1996 *Sgt. Bilko* movie remake, starring Steve Martin, Dan Aykroyd, and Phil Hartman, hits the screens. (Then again, considering the low level of certain movie remakes of classic TV series, perhaps not.)

Picket Fences. *1992–   , CBS.* David E. Kelley, the gifted and prolific writer-producer who emerged from *L.A. Law* to strike out on his own, didn't actually strike out at all. Instead, he hit a home run with his first series, *Picket Fences,* and provided his own strong quality competition with 1994's *Chicago Hope.* Together, they make a strong case for ranking Kelley, as I do, right up there with Rod Serling, Paddy Chayefsky, Dennis Potter, and Reginald Rose, the best TV dramatists in the history of the medium—and of them all, only Kelley wrote for continuing characters on a weekly series. Several things make *Picket Fences,* despite its relative youth, so special, starting with its surprise but worthy acknowledgment as Best Drama, for two years running, by Emmy voters. In addition, there's the crisp and challenging writing by Kelley and the other producers, who use the fictional town of Rome, Wisconsin, and especially the courtroom of Judge Henry Bone (played perfectly by Ray Walston), to dissect and debate the day's hottest political, emotional, social, and moral issues. There's the singular pace and pattern of the show, which likes to cross-cut among several conversations and events in the same compact scenes. There's the sense of playfulness, embodied by the *St. Elsewhere*-like buried in-jokes and the initially outlandish subplots (a serial bather, a singing Frog Man, a modern-day immaculate conception, a string of dead mayors and frozen corpses). There's the strong sense of its own history, which too few TV series take pains to demonstrate: on *Picket Fences,* characters constantly refer, often obliquely, to events and conversations from previous episodes, rewarding loyal, long-time viewers. And finally, there's the acting, which in the show's first three seasons reaped well-earned Emmys for stars Kathy Baker and Tom Skerritt as Jill and Jimmy Brock, for Fyvush Finkel as the town's defense attorney, Joseph Wambaugh, and for Walston's Judge Bone. Other standouts have included Don Cheadle, who played District Attorney John Littleton for two seasons (1993–95); Lauren Holly as police officer Maxine Stewart; and Holly Marie Combs, one of the best young actresses on television, as daughter Kimberly Brock. Standout episodes are many, but any complete list would

LEFT: *Peter Pan*, with Mary Martin in full flight.
RIGHT: *Peyton Place*, with Mia Farrow, pre-haircut.

LEFT: *Picket Fences*, with Tom Skerritt and Kathy Baker.
RIGHT: *Prime Suspect*, with Helen Mirren as Jane Tennison.

have to begin with the one featuring Michael J. Anderson of *Twin Peaks* as an elephant trainer who ran away *from* the circus; the two-part episode in which TV violence and guns in the schools were debated more intelligently than on most of television's nonfiction talk and news shows; the stigmata episode, with Adam Wylie's Zach suddenly and inexplicably bleeding from his palms; and the disturbing episode in which Father Gary Barrett, the town priest played by Roy Dotrice, was killed in cold blood. The focus and overall quality of *Picket Fences* changed substantially, and not for the better, once Kelley walked away from the series in the fall of 1995; scripts began to focus more attention on characters and less on issues, and had many characters acting in unsatisfactory or contradictory ways. Kelley did return to provide one script that fall, though, and it was wonderful: in it, Pope John Paul II (played by an uncanny look-alike) paid an unexpected visit to this *other* Rome, and ended up being the sole witness to a murder.

Pink Lady. *1980, NBC.* Originally titled *Pink Lady & Jeff*, this famously miscast series was a variety show teaming American comic Jeff Altman with singer-dancers Mitsuyo (Mie) Nemoto and Keko (Kei) Masuda, stars of a hit TV variety series back in their native Japan. The problem, which somehow seemed to elude NBC President Fred Silverman before ordering this series, is that though the duo sang some of their songs in English, those lyrics were learned and sung phonetically. When speaking, once Mie and Kei opened the show and said "Hello, welcome to *Pink Lady & Jeff*," they basically had used up their entire non-native vocabulary, except for the word *good-bye*—which they uttered on American TV for the last time one month after the show's inexplicable premiere. "It was like Tony Orlando and Dawn," recalled TV executive Brandon Tartikoff, who joined NBC with the *Pink Lady & Jeff* deal already in place. "Except Dawn didn't speak English." Anyone today who knows the name *Pink Lady* remembers the series for how surrealistically awful it was, but here's something most people may have forgotten: Jim Varney was a regular member of the supporting cast, and in skits on three of the six shows, Mie and Kei were joined by Sid Caesar, who played their father. Caesar spoke in his patented nonsense Japanese, Mie and Kei followed his lead and responded in actual Japanese, and somehow they made their way through the skits. Caesar, by playing a recurring role on *Pink Lady* after his *Your Show of Shows* glory days, managed to figure in what arguably were the best *and* worst TV variety series ever made.

Playhouse 90. *1956–60, CBS.* The numeral 90 in the title of this unsurpassed anthology series is crucial, because it referred to the number of minutes allotted to its subject each week. Prior to *Playhouse 90*, the only network programs to occupy ninety minutes of prime time each week were sports shows, movies, the classic *Your Show of Shows*, and the short-lived *Ozark Jubilee*. *Playhouse 90* was the first drama anthology to go that distance, and the freedom and opportunity it provided resulted in the strongest such series in the history of television. At ninety minutes, what *Playhouse 90* really was doing each week, with its rotating roster of live, filmed, and eventually videotaped teleplays, was presenting TV movies before the term was coined, and mounting intimate Broadway-level plays to an audience so large no Broadway show could come near it. The second week on the air, *Playhouse 90* presented Rod Serling's *Requiem for a Heavyweight*, a drama sufficiently powerful, and durable, to deserve its own listing here; a subsequent *Playhouse 90* triumph, JP Miller's *The Days of Wine and Roses*, is similarly segregated. With its expanded canvas and its level of artistry, no other "Golden Age" drama came near it, and today, *Playhouse 90* is the one title most often and instantly recalled whenever the phrase "TV's Golden Age" is mentioned. The show's producers over the years included Martin Manulis, John Houseman, Herbert Brodkin, and Fred Coe; directors, later famous for their films, included John Frankenheimer and George Roy Hill. The writers were the very best, with adaptations of works by F. Scott Fitzgerald, William Faulkner, and Ernest Hemingway, and originals by Serling, Miller, Horton Foote, Reginald Rose, and others. Together, they arguably were responsible for more memorable productions than any other dramatic TV anthology series. *Playhouse 90* had clunkers, too, but the ratio of excellence was relatively, almost amazingly, high. Consider, from 1957 alone, *The Miracle Worker*, starring Patty McCormack in the original Helen Keller role that later would win Patty Duke an Oscar; Serling's potent adaptation of Ernest Lehman's *The Comedian*, starring Mickey Rooney in a strong dramatic role; and Art Carney in *Charley's Aunt*. Later seasons presented such tantalizing treats as Andy Griffith in an adaptation of the James Thurber-Elliott Nugent comedy *The Male Animal*; Robert Ryan and Jeanne Crain in a David Shaw adaptation of Fitzgerald's *The Great Gatsby*; Jackie Gleason in a triumphant dramatic performance as the star of a version of William Saroyan's *The Time of Your Life*; Horton Foote's adaptations of several Faulkner stories, including *Old Man* (with Sterling Hayden) and *Tomorrow* (with Richard Boone); Jason Robards heading a strong cast in A. E. Hotchner's version of Hemingway's *For Whom the Bell Tolls*; Abby Mann's *Judgment at Nuremberg*, starring Claude Rains and Maximilian Schell; and Roddy McDowall, Boris Karloff, and Eartha Kitt in a Stewart Stern adaptation of Joseph Conrad's *Heart of Darkness*. *Playhouse 90* was a class act, with classy actors and writers, to the very last: its final 1960 telecast, a production of Rod Serling's *In the Presence of Mine Enemies*, starred Robert Redford as a sympathetic Nazi soldier who saves a Jewish girl from the ghetto. It's a role Redford credited, nearly a quarter-century later, as his "first big break." *Playhouse 90* itself seemed to get a big break of its own, in 1991, when producer-director Francis Ford Coppola saluted the memory and legacy of *Playhouse 90* by announcing his plan to produce two or three annual live dramatic TV productions for CBS, under the clever banner title of *Playhouse 90's*. Great idea—but somewhere along the way, both Coppola and the live element became separated from the final concept. Even so, with the franchise in danger of being delayed to the point where it would have to be retitled *Playhouse 00's*, the network finally came through in 1995 with the first presentation under the banner of *CBS Playhouse '90s*. It was a telemovie version of Tennessee Williams's *A Streetcar Named Desire*, starring Jessica Lange as Blanche, Alec Baldwin as Stanley, Diane Lane as Stella, and John

Goodman as Mitch. The other 1995 production was Ernest Thompson's *The West Side Waltz*, starring Shirley MacLaine and Liza Minnelli. The *Playhouse 90's* legacy was continued into 1996 courtesy of two Neil Simon comedies: *Jake's Women*, starring Alan Alda, Anne Archer, and Mira Sorvino, and *The Sunshine Boys*, starring Woody Allen and Peter Falk.

Police Squad! *1982, ABC*. Surely you know that this daringly daffy little sitcom, despite presenting only six episodes in 1982, went on to inspire the successful series of *Naked Gun* movies. (Of course you do—and don't call me Shirley.) After mercilessly lampooning the disaster-movie genre in the 1980 film *Airplane!*, collaborators Jim Abrahams, David Zucker, and Jerry Zucker created this TV cop series that poked fun at *other* TV cop series. Leslie Nielsen starred as Frank Drebin, and *Police Squad!* was as crammed with visual and verbal humor—from the episode titles and closing credits to the bad puns and forced-perspective gunfights—as the subsequent, much more popular *Naked Gun* films. The movie versions recycled a lot of the jokes from *Police Squad!*, but the films had at least three things the TV series didn't: bigger budgets, Priscilla Presley, and, sigh, O. J. Simpson.

Political Conventions. *1948 and quadrennially, various networks.* Political conventions first were broadcast by radio in 1924, and television was there as far back as 1940, with that year's conventions in Philadelphia relayed by coaxial cable to NBC's experimental New York station, W2XBS. In 1948, both CBS and NBC offered their cable-linked east-coast stations partial coverage of the three Philadelphia conventions (Republican, Democratic, and Progressive), utilizing the services of TV newsmen whose pioneering network newscasts had premiered that very same year: Douglas Edwards on CBS and John Cameron Swayze on NBC. By 1952, the next time conventions rolled around, they were seen not only as political news, but as a valuable promotional opportunity. One reason the networks were so eager to provide convention coverage in 1952 was that television manufacturers, in turn, were equally eager to use advertising time to pitch TV sets to all the political junkies watching in bars and at the homes of friends. The lengthy, often gavel-to-gavel coverage on CBS and DuMont was fully sponsored by Westinghouse; Admiral did the same on ABC, and Philco on NBC. The networks, in turn, were able to showcase their TV news personnel as never before. It was during the 1952 conventions, in fact, that the term "anchorman" was coined, to describe the pivotal role played at the convention by Walter Cronkite of CBS. (It later, of course, came to refer to the central "host" of any TV newscast or newsmagazine.) By 1956, the role played by anchormen at conventions was so prominent that one new team of anchors emerged as genuine TV stars: Chet Huntley and David Brinkley of NBC. In later years, the memorable moments from these televised platforms (which, with the advent of cable, eventually saw gavel-to-gavel coverage relegated to C-SPAN) included the emotionally extended applause that greeted Robert F. Kennedy at the 1964 Democratic Convention, Mario Cuomo's stirring keynote address at the 1984 Democratic Convention, and HIV-positive Mary Fisher's plea for compassion at the 1992 Republican Convention. Nothing, though, was nearly so memorable as TV coverage of the 1968 Democratic Convention, where protesting Yippies and baton-swinging Chicago cops came to a head (and busted several), and where even reporters on the convention floor were fair game for foul actions by the local authorities. On CBS, Dan Rather got pushed around so much that anchorman Cronkite, from the safety of the broadcast booth, said, "I think we've got a bunch of thugs here, Dan, if I may be permitted to say so"—while John Chancellor of NBC, while being carted away by angry security forces, managed to conclude his report with one of the most famous, and funny, signoffs in TV history. "This is John Chancellor," he said, "somewhere in custody."

Presidential Debates. *1960, 1976, 1980, 1988, 1992, various networks.* The famous 1960 debates between Vice-President Richard M. Nixon and challenger John F. Kennedy, widely acknowledged to be the first televised presidential debates, actually were not. ABC had staked that claim back in May 1956, by televising the Democratic primary "discussion" between Adlai Stevenson and Estes Kefauver. However, the Nixon-Kennedy debates were the first general-election discussions to be televised, and their impact remains unmatched in modern political history. Directed by Don Hewitt, who later created *60 Minutes*, those debates generated an impression so strong and widespread it almost approaches folklore. Nixon's gaunt, stubbly, and sweaty appearance, especially the first night, is generally said to have cost him the debate, and perhaps the election: radio listeners ranked Nixon ahead of Kennedy, but Kennedy's ease in front of the cameras reflected a more comforting and commanding image, and TV viewers declared him the winner instead. When televised debates were resumed sixteen years later, after an understandable absence, the concept of "image" very quickly became what these showcases were all about. Consider that, of all the candidates' political comments in these debates, only one, arguably, has resonated after the fact: Ronald Reagan's pointed 1980 query of voters, asking, "Are you better off than you were four years ago?" Otherwise, the lasting moments have ranged from the casual to the comical. In that same 1980 debate, Reagan effortlessly deflected Jimmy Carter's verbal attack by shaking his head like a patient parent and saying, "There you go again." In 1984, the most durable remark came during a Democratic primary debate, and was a direct quotation from a Wendy's TV commercial: Walter Mondale's sarcastic complaint about Gary Hart's policies, "Where's the beef?" Similarly, in 1988, the most widely quoted phrase (during the second George Bush-Michael Dukakis debate) was a question—but not by a candidate. It was panelist Bernard Shaw's shockingly personal query of the Democratic candidate: "If Kitty Dukakis were raped and murdered, would you favor an irrevocable death penalty for the killer?" (That same year, during the vice-presidential debate, Democrat Lloyd Bentsen won the battle, though his ticket later lost the war, by telling Dan Quayle, "You're no Jack Kennedy.") In 1992, the feisty and interruptive style of independent candidate H. Ross Perot, though not the substance, made an impression in his debates with Bill Clinton and Bush—though in presidential debate history, not even Perot's sounds of protest could outdo the sounds of silence from 1976. That's when Carter and Gerald Ford, thrown by a malfunctioning sound system in the midst of a nationally televised debate, opted to stand stiffly at their respective podiums, stare straight ahead or at their notes, and wait silently for a signal to resume the debate. They waited, all right, on live TV—for twenty-seven astounding "silence is golden" minutes.

Presidential Speeches. *1939–   , various networks.* On radio, the first incumbent president to broadcast a political speech was Woodrow Wilson, in 1919. Yet it took Franklin Delano Roosevelt, with his enormously popular radio "fireside chats" beginning in 1933, to demonstrate the true potential of broadcasting. Consequently, it's hardly surprising that FDR also was the first to give a presidential speech on live television, on the experimental setup at the 1939 New York World's Fair. Since then, the rest is history—literally. And while entire books can be written, and have been, about the content and presentation of presidential addresses and speeches, a handful of phrases over the decades rise to the top as among the most memorable of the postwar era. My nominations, among those remarks broadcast live to American viewers, would include John F. Kennedy's 1961 inaugural address, "Ask not what your country can do for you; ask what you can do for your country," as well as his address to a joint session of Congress the same year: "I believe this nation should commit itself to achieving the goal, before this decade is out, of landing a man on the moon and returning him safely to the earth." And Lyndon B. Johnson's surprise speech in 1968, announcing, "I shall not seek, and I will not accept, the nomination of my party for another term as your president." And the ever-quotable Richard M. Nixon, who, among his many other presidential remarks, announced in 1973 that "I am not a crook," before resigning, on a live TV address the next year, witnessed by an estimated one hundred million people—leading to Gerald R. Ford's opening words as president in 1974, "Our long national nightmare is over." So is this entry.

Price Is Right, The. *1956–63, NBC; 1963–65, ABC; 1972–   , CBS.* At the end of 1995, *The Price Is Right* stood alone, for some reason, as the last surviving network quiz show. *The Price Is Right* began during the Eisenhower administration, and, except for a seven-season hiatus from 1965 to 1972, has been on network daytime TV ever since. Its prehiatus years were hosted by Bill Cullen, and a simultaneous 1994 syndicated version (which flopped quickly) was hosted by Doug Davidson, but from 1972 on, the sole host of the CBS series has been Bob Barker, who has made a name for himself on several levels. One is as host of the program that, under his reign, became TV's longest-running daily game show (and, as of 1995, remains daytime's top-rated one). The series has had several announcers over the years, including Don Pardo and Johnny Olsen, but one consistent clarion call: the announcer's frantic scream of "Come on down!," the words with which audience members were summoned as contestants, became and remains a national catch phrase. The game itself, in which contestants tried to guess the value of displayed items without exceeding that value, was a simple one: part blackjack, part consumer savvy. The contestants, on occasion, could be simple as well. One attractive young woman, pulled from the audience in 1980, was so smitten with her own image on the studio TV screens that she paid little attention to the game, or even to Barker. "You're so busy looking at yourself in the monitor," Barker said to her, chuckling, "you don't know what's going on." Two years later, that young woman, Vanna White, landed a full-time job on a rival game show, spinning letters on *Wheel of Fortune*. The simplicity of *The Price Is Right* served it well from the beginning, and turned out to be a virtue. Because it was almost too simple to be rigged, it was allowed to remain on the air while other, more challenging game shows were canceled after the quiz-show scandal of 1958. To the show's producers, Mark Goodson and Bill Todman, the other primary virtue of *The Price Is Right* was that items from sponsors were displayed almost throughout the show, making it a virtual, yet acceptable, wall-to-wall commercial. Backstage, though, things apparently were far less virtuous. In 1994, one of the show's veteran "spokesmodels," Dian Parkinson, filed a sexual-harassment lawsuit against the seventy-year-old Barker, accusing him of forcing her, under threat of dismissal, to (among other things) engage in "oral sex twice a week for three-and-a-half years." Barker insisted that all sex acts were consensual, and the matter went to court. Either way, under the circumstances, it lends an entirely different meaning, and a somewhat unsettling image, to the show's trademark phrase of "Come on down!"

Prime Suspect. *1992, 1993, 1994, 1995, 1996, PBS.* For three straight seasons, Helen Mirren, as detective chief inspector Jane Tennison, turned in a miniseries performance that rivaled no other. Her characterization was so rich, and the stories by series creator Lynda La Plante and others so complex and credible (devoting equal attention to intricate mysteries and oppressive interoffice politics), and the supporting cast so strong (Ralph Fiennes played a grieving boyfriend in the first *Prime Suspect* series), that these imported *Mystery!* mysteries equaled, if not outshone, the best American cop series of the same period—and since that period includes *Homicide: Life on the Street* and *NYPD Blue*, that's high praise indeed. (I also have the highest praise for film actress Mirren, whose previous, lesser-known TV triumphs include magnetic performances in several of the BBC's *The Shakespeare Plays*, including the cross-dressing Rosalind in *As You Like It* and the teasing Titania of *A Midsummer Night's Dream*.) In 1995, England's Granada TV shifted *Prime Suspect* from miniseries to telemovie form; there was an additional shift in America the same year, with the *Prime Suspect* franchise being transplanted whole from *Mystery!* to *Masterpiece Theatre*. With a movie version also in preproduction, the *Prime Suspect* series will get even higher exposure than it has thus far—though if Mirren is denied the opportunity to reprise her role for the large screen, the result is likely to be the most offensive movie adaptation of a terrific TV miniseries since the leading role in *Life and Loves of a She-Devil* was turned over to Roseanne.

Prisoner, The. *1968, CBS.* Perhaps the biggest and boldest "cult TV series" of them all, this allegorical Patrick McGoohan series arrived in the volatile

summer of 1968, looking like nothing that had come before—and, with the
arguable exception of *Twin Peaks* and the inferior but obvious variant *Nowhere Man*, like nothing that has come since. A summer replacement for
The Jackie Gleason Show, McGoohan's *Prisoner* was hardly as reassuring or
accessible as the series whose time slot it was temporarily occupying. The
bare-bones description is that McGoohan played a secret agent who resigned
for mysterious reasons, returned to his apartment, was overcome by knockout
gas, and woke up in a mysterious and isolated seaside community known as
The Village, where he had been sent, by person or persons unknown, to
ascertain the reason for his sudden resignation. Some of the lyrics to McGoohan's previous series, *Secret Agent*, became reality in *The Prisoner:* "They've
given you a number / And taken away your name." The prisoner was now
called Number Six, and each episode dealt with his efforts to resist the inter-
rogations and schemes of a succession of authority figures known as Number
Two (the most familiar of them played by *Rumpole of the Bailey* star Leo
McKern). The still-resonant phrases and images from *The Prisoner* include
the bouncing-balloon watchdog known as Rover; the ubiquitous "Be seeing
you" farewell salute; the strikingly and widely used symbol of the old-
fashioned penny-farthing bicycle; and the prisoner's shouted declarations of
independence, repeated during the memorable opening credits montage of
each show. "I will not be pushed, filed, stamped, indexed, briefed, debriefed,
or numbered," said the man known as Number Six, adding, even more famously and defiantly, "I am not a number! I am a free man!" *The Prisoner*
definitely was a series of its time, reflecting all the angst, rebellion, and
political pananoia of the summer of 1968, but it was far ahead of its time as
well. With its beginning, middle, and end, *The Prisoner* deserves credit as
one of television's first, and still best, long-form miniseries. In that genre, it
arrived one year before *The Forsyte Saga*, and eight years before *Rich Man,
Poor Man*. That's not to suggest that the interpretations of the beginning and
ending of *The Prisoner* are widely agreed upon; in fact, there are ongoing
debates among fans, and lots of messages on the Internet, about who the title
character was supposed to represent in each case. Before his arrival in the
Village, was the secret agent supposed to be John Drake, the British spy
played by McGoohan in *Secret Agent?* (My vote is yes.) And in the final
episode of *The Prisoner*, when Number Six finally confronts, and literally
unmasks, the Village leader known as Number One, how are viewers to inter-
pret the fact that both Number Six and Number One are played by McGoohan? I ascribe to the theory that Number One represents a darker side of
Number Six, and that, by allowing the tyranny of overzealous authority to
run unchecked, that side of Number Six effectively has built his own prison—
and found himself unable to escape it. My obscure corroboration for this
interpretation? In the final episode, when Number Six finally escapes the
Village, he returns to his London apartment, whereupon the series returns
to the beginning, like a never-ending dream. But this time, for the first (and
last) time, we get to see the street numeral on the once and future prisoner's
apartment door. It's the number one.

Queen Elizabeth II Coronation. *1953, CBS, NBC, ABC.* The success of the voluminous TV coverage of the presidential conventions of 1952 left the networks eager to find and present the "next big thing"—and especially eager, if possible, to present it ahead of the competition. The June 2, 1953, coronation of Elizabeth II was just such an opportunity, and both the limits and developments of new technologies made for a fascinating competition. Members of Parliament unanimously advised against allowing TV cameras access inside the Abbey, but the young future Queen insisted, and the resultant live coverage by BBC-TV, of the first British monarch to be crowned on television, marked the medium's coming of age in that country, in much the same way America's coverage of another solemn occasion, the funeral of John F. Kennedy, would mark the maturation of TV in the United States. (In England, it was the first time TV coverage of an event drew a larger audience than radio.) Yet because the coronation of Queen Elizabeth II took place in England in an era before communications satellites, American TV could provide no such live coverage to its own viewers. Instead, CBS and NBC planned to film the BBC coverage as it occurred, fly the kinescopes back to America, edit the footage, and rush to be first to show it domestically as a same-day "scoop." NBC got the inside track by inventing a new way to process and edit the film during the return flight, and indeed beat CBS to the punch—but lowly ABC, without even leaving home, won this particular battle. The Royal Air Force and the Royal Canadian Air Force, charged with providing footage of the coronation to Canadian citizens as quickly as possible, flew kinescopes of the BBC coverage on a high-priority basis. The first pictures arrived, and were televised by the Canadian Broadcasting Corporation, before NBC's plane had even landed—and ABC, merely by grabbing and relaying the CBC signal via a coaxial cable link, beat NBC and CBS to this particular TV crown jewel.

Queen for a Day. *1956–60, NBC; 1960–64, ABC.* In England, when you don the crown, you're queen for life. In the United States, on TV, it lasts a mere twenty-four hours. Basically, the title of this show, and host Jack Bailey's elongated opening query—"How would *yoooou* like to be Queen For a Day?"— are the sum total of what's commonly remembered today about this daytime game show. Just as well, really. Like the radio show that spawned it, TV's *Queen for a Day* could just as easily have been called *Begging for Dollars:* four contestants compared sob stories to compete for a day's worth of prizes and respect, and the one who most abjectly humiliated herself usually won. Syndicated versions tried to update the format every now and then, but by the seventies the entire concept was seen, quite rightly, as more insulting than inspiring.

Quick Draw McGraw. See *Huckleberry Hound.*

Quincy, M.E. *1976–1983, NBC.* This mystery series, starring Jack Klugman as a medical examiner for the Los Angeles County Coroner's office, wasn't very good—but the title of the show remains familiar today because of the protagonist's odd name and his even odder (at least for prime-time television) profession. A sort of Columbo with cadavers, the title character of *Quincy, M.E.,* so far as network TV was concerned, basically had the autopsy market coronered. Were Quincy still on the job in 1995, he could have been called as an expert witness during the O. J. Simpson trial—but Quincy's name was invoked then anyway. Judge Lance Ito casually, and respectfully, referred to forensic specialist Henry C. Lee in open-court conversation as "the Quincy of Connecticut." Some might consider it almost conspiratorially meaningful that the character of Sam Fujiyama, the coroner's loyal assistant on *Quincy, M.E.,* was played by another man named Ito—actor Robert Ito. Personally, though, I tend to dismiss that sort of thing as mere Quincydence.

Quiz Kids. *1949–52, NBC; 1953, 56, CBS.* The *Quiz Kids* radio show, which premiered in 1940, ran for a hugely successful thirteen years, with a TV version airing concurrently during the last four seasons. A forerunner to the likes of *Juvenile Jury* and *College Bowl,* both the radio and TV versions of *Quiz Kids* posed very tough questions to very smart little rascals—questions such as, "Define a dodo, a dido and a dado." At that age, my answer would likely have been limited to "I dunno," but these youngsters were brilliant, and made such a lasting impression that, even today, the term "quiz kid" sometimes surfaces as a term of admiration—or derision.

Rawhide. *1959–66, CBS.* The most famous and lasting elements of *Rawhide* are on display in the show's opening credits. There's that rollin', rollin', rollin' theme song sung by Frankie Laine (and revived by John Belushi and Dan Aykroyd in *The Blues Brothers* movie and by Billy Crystal in *City Slickers),* which makes up for in durability what it lacks in originality: "Keep movin', movin', movin' / Though they're disapprovin' / keep them doggies movin', Rawhide . . . / Move 'em on, head 'em up / Head 'em up, move 'em on / Move 'em on, head 'em up, Rawhiiiiide." Also on display in the opening credits: a bare-chested Clint Eastwood, who went straight from playing Rowdy Yates on this Western TV series to starring in a series of spaghetti Western movies by

Italian director Sergio Leone—and made a name for himself, paradoxically, as the Man With No Name. Supporting costar Sheb Wooley, who played Pete Nolan, had made a name for himself *before* appearing on *Rawhide*, as the vocalist of that goofy 1958 novelty hit "The Purple People Eater." The nomadic structure of *Rawhide* made it one of the better and more credible efforts during TV's boom Western years. Trail boss Gil Favor (Eric Fleming), weaving his crew and cattle around deep water, hostile Indians, and treacherous terrain, demonstrated each week that in the cattle-drive business, getting there wasn't half the fun. It was all the work.

Reagan, Ronald, Assassination Attempt. *1981, CBS, NBC, ABC, CNN.* Although no one was broadcasting live at the time, cameras were rolling, and footage was quickly relayed to the networks and televised, as John Hinckley stepped out of a crowd of reporters and shot President Ronald Reagan and three other men, including press secretary James Brady, after Reagan had attended a luncheon at the Washington Hilton on March 30, 1981. ABC broke the news at 2:42 P.M., and televised the unedited videotape less than ten minutes later; NBC and CBS soon followed. For a while, the footage was all the networks had. The source to whom they would normally turn for information, White House press secretary James Brady, had been shot in the head. At first, no one even knew that Reagan himself had been wounded, and misinformation ran rampant. (So did Secretary of State Alexander Haig, who responded to the confusion by screaming his infamous power-grab "I'm in charge here!" announcement to the astounded press corps.) All three broadcast networks confirmed Brady's death, then had to retract their statements. "If you're confused about whether Brady is alive or dead," said Dan Rather, in his first major test as an anchor after succeeding Walter Cronkite at CBS, "know that your confusion is matched by our own." At ABC, Frank Reynolds, a friend of Brady's, expressed both his personal and professional frustration by shaking visibly and announcing, to the nation as well as his own staff, "Let's get it nailed down, somebody! Let's get the word here and get it straight so that we can report this accurately." CNN, which had begun operation in June 1980, was not yet up to speed as a competitive news force, even though three high-profile shootings would take place during its first year of operation: the murder of John Lennon, and the attempted assassinations of Reagan and Pope John Paul II. Reagan survived to complete two terms as President; Brady recovered sufficiently to be an active, as well as symbolic, proponent of the anti-handgun legislation known as "the Brady bill," and was himself the subject of a 1991 HBO docudrama, *Without Warning: The James Brady Story,* with the title role going to Beau Bridges.

Real McCoys, The. *1957–62, ABC; 1962–63, CBS.* A family of hillbillies relocates to a less rural life, deciding that Californee is the place they oughta be. Five years before *The Beverly Hillbillies* struck black gold with that same premise, and three years before *The Andy Griffith Show* explored the charm, wisdom, and eccentricity of small-town folk, *The Real McCoys* established the franchise. This clever, funny series is one Nick at Nite run away from being discovered and embraced by a whole new generation, but even now, with the series basically lying dormant for three decades, Walter Brennan's crackly voice and sloppy limp as Grandpa Amos McCoy were kept alive for many years by impressionists and everyday conversationalists alike. Richard Crenna, as grandson Luke, turned in another of his solid and endearing performances, and the "jus' folks" folks behind *The Real McCoys* went on to spin even greater rural sitcom success elsewhere: executive producers Danny Thomas and Sheldon Leonard presented *The Andy Griffith Show,* and writer Paul Henning created *The Beverly Hillbillies.*

Red Skelton Show, The. *1951–53, NBC; 1953–68, CBS.* **The Red Skelton Hour.** *1968–70, CBS.* Although never as heralded as *Your Show of Shows, The Smothers Brothers Comedy Hour,* or *The Carol Burnett Show,* the TV variety series *The Red Skelton Show* lasted longer than all three of those other shows combined—and, amazingly, competed contemporaneously with all three. From the time *The Red Skelton Show* won TV's first Best Comedy Show Emmy in 1951 to its unexpected and unfair cancellation in 1970, Red Skelton's humor never changed, and never relied heavily on guest stars or costars to bolster his appeal. When you watched *The Red Skelton Show,* as tens of millions happily and regularly did, what you got was heaping helpings of Red Skelton: Red as the dopey Clem Kadiddlehopper, as the clownish Freddie the Freeloader, as the bratty "Mean Widdle Kid," and, perhaps most memorably and improbably, as seagulls Gertrude and Heathcliff (who had just flown in, no doubt, from wuthering heights). Most of the characters were holdovers from Skelton's top-rated radio show, which, when it began in 1941, featured Ozzie Nelson as bandleader and Ozzie's wife, Harriet, as a comedienne and vocalist. Equally durable on radio as on TV, Skelton continued doing double duty on his radio program for two years after he made the leap to television. Throughout the years, Skelton's gentle closing message remained constant and became a national catchphrase: "Good night, and may God bless"—a message he repeated on TV on the occasion of his eightieth birthday, while being inducted as a charter member of the Comedy Hall of Fame. In retrospect, a few other facts about *The Red Skelton Show* are worth repeating. When CBS canceled *The Red Skelton Hour* in 1970 as part of its programming purge to attract younger audiences, Skelton's show was ranked seventh for the season, with an average viewer age of thirty-five—numbers today's networks would kill to have. One of Skelton's original writers was a young man named Johnny Carson, who got a big early break by substituting for Skelton on his live show in 1954 after the star had collapsed during rehearsal. Later in the run of *The Red Skelton Show,* another of Skelton's writers to reach prominence on his own was Sherwood Schwartz, who, after moving on to write for Skelton's old bandleader on *The Adventures of Ozzie & Harriet,* would achieve major success, of a sort, by creating *Gilligan's Island* and *The Brady Bunch.*

Requiem for a Heavyweight. *1956, CBS.* Its second week on the air, the anthology series *Playhouse 90* showcased the strengths of its ninety-minute format, and one of TV's finest writers, by presenting Jack Palance, Keenan Wynn, and Ed Wynn in Rod Serling's *Requiem for a Heavyweight*. Serling already had made his reputation with another Emmy-winning teleplay, the *Kraft Television Theatre* production of *Patterns*, the year before, but *Requiem for a Heavyweight* put him over the top—and, like Paddy Chayefsky with *Marty*, established him for all time as one of TV's very finest dramatic writers. The 1962 movie version, starring Anthony Quinn, Jackie Gleason, and Mickey Rooney, was inferior to the live TV presentation, although the movie did have Cassius Clay (later known as Muhammad Ali) among its supporting players. On TV, Palance's literally brutal disappointment was haunting and unforgettable, and the elder Wynn, in his dramatic debut, succeeded admirably in a role many people, including Serling himself, thought he was incapable of portraying. Kinescopes of *Requiem for a Heavyweight* attest to its power over time, and John Crosby, TV critic of the *New York Herald Tribune*, was on duty to attest to its power overnight. "I remember walking into '21,' a fairly sophisticated [Manhattan] beanery . . . and finding the whole restaurant buzzing with talk about *Requiem for a Heavyweight*," Crosby later recalled. "The important thing was that *Requiem* set the whole town talking. . . . Television was *the* medium of the moment and it attracted all the brilliant young kids."

Rescue 911. *1989–95, 1996– , CBS*. The best thing about this series, in which host William Shatner introduced reenactments of emergency-line rescue operations, was how it educated viewers, especially young ones, about a method with which, in most cities, they could literally call for help: thanks to this series, "911" is a numeral synonymous with rescue efforts, even in communities where that number is not in service. The worst thing about this series was the method of dramatic reenactment, which ranged from the hokey to the needlessly horrific. When actual "911" calls were used, the dramatic credibility was enhanced substantially, but an editorial flaw existed even then. Calls in which rescues are botched or tragically unsuccessful, or in which dispatchers are inefficient or negligent, fail to make the cut, making emergency-team workers look like so many mobile Marcus Welbys. The creator of this series, Arnold Shapiro, also was responsible for another groundbreaking "reality TV" venture, the excellent 1978 syndicated *Scared Straight!* documentary special (see separate listing).

Rich Man, Poor Man. *1976, ABC*. The popularity of *The Forsyte Saga*, imported to America by public TV in 1969, led several commercial TV entrepreneurs to seek and develop their own "novels for television." The planning, and the race, began in 1970, with Barry Diller, then a young executive at ABC, interested in mounting long-form versions of both Irwin Shaw's *Rich Man, Poor Man* and the Leon Uris novel *QB VII*, and with executives at MCA/Universal looking at several properties, including *Rich Man, Poor Man*, Fletcher Knebel's *Vanished*, and Herman Wouk's *The Winds of War*. The first of these grand plans to be realized on the small screen, by far, was Universal's *Vanished*, adapted by Dean Reisner into a two-night, four-hour version that ran on NBC in 1971. Other two-part adaptations followed, but the next major step wasn't undertaken by the commercial networks until 1974 (the year of *Upstairs, Downstairs* on PBS), when ABC devoted two nights of its prime-time schedule to present a six-hour, fifteen-minute version of *QB VII*, starring Anthony Hopkins. That two-part drama (the term "miniseries" had yet to be coined), produced by Douglas S. Cramer for Screen Gems/Columbia Pictures Television, was a major success both critically and in the ratings. ABC was hungry for more, and Universal already had handed in a complete treatment of *Rich Man, Poor Man*, written by *Vanished* screenwriter Reisner. Incoming ABC executive Brandon Stoddard gave it the green light and increased the order to twelve hours, at which time rewrites and casting began. Finalists for the three *Rich Man, Poor Man* leading roles—responsible Rudy Jordache, impulsive brother Tom, and leading lady Julie—included Sam Waterston as Rudy, Jeff Bridges as Tom, and Lindsay Wagner as Julie. Good casting choices all, but ABC instead went with almost total unknowns: Peter Strauss as Rudy, Nick Nolte as Tom, and Susan Blakely as Julie. *Rich Man, Poor Man* premiered in February 1976 on a Sunday, then ran weekly installments on Monday, taking advantage of the vacancy created when *Monday Night Football* finished its season. By the time the drama presented its last installment in March, all three unknowns were stars; *Rich Man, Poor Man* was a hit; supporting actor Ed Asner, as the Jordache's violent immigrant father, was poised to win an Emmy (which he did); and the major strengths of "long-form TV" were demonstrated for all to see. A dozen hours of screen time allowed for a depth of character and plot development that no movie could equal. The self-contained story line allowed leading characters to be placed in true jeopardy, a dramatic asset few weekly series would consider—indeed, the climax of *Rich Man, Poor Man* was the death of the beloved character of Tom Jordache. The addictive popularity of the episodes proved that commercial networks, like public TV with its highbrow serials and documentaries, could successfully (very successfully) present what came to be known as "appointment television"—shows, in that pre-VCR era, that you stayed home to watch. And while many talents in Hollywood were hesitant to be tied to a potential seven-year commitment for a standard TV series, the prospect of working for a few months on a high-profile "mini" series, now known as *miniseries*, became much more attractive. Less than a year after *Rich Man, Poor Man*, ABC presented *Roots*, and the rest is miniseries history. Regarding *Rich Man, Poor Man*, though, there is one more bit of history to cover. Ratings for that long-form drama were so good that ABC couldn't resist mounting a weekly sequel, *Rich Man, Poor Man, Book II*, six months later. Strauss reprised his role as Rudy, but Blakely appeared only as a guest star in the series premiere, and Nolte balked entirely, even though ABC had offered to let him sign up with the series sequel by playing the late Tom's now-grown son. "I didn't think that idea carried much integrity," Nolte accurately noted at the time. The sequel series lasted only one season; the original version, in TV history, has cast a tall shadow for decades.

Ricki Lake. *1993–   , syndicated.* Lake, the hefty star of the 1988 John Waters cult film *Hairspray*, lost weight, launched a TV talk show aimed at a new

LEFT: *The Prisoner,* with Patrick McGoohan as Number Six.
RIGHT: *Rawhide,* with Eric Fleming and Clint Eastwood.

LEFT: *The Rockford Files,* with James Garner and guest star Tom Selleck, as Lance White.
RIGHT: *Roots,* with Chuck Connors as slave owner Tom Moore and Ben Vereen as Chicken George.

generation of viewers, and became a heavyweight of a different kind. By her second season on the air, Lake was ranked second among all syndicated talk shows, beaten only by Oprah Winfrey—and no less than Steve Friedman, savvy producer of the *Today* show in its Jane Pauley-Bryant Gumbel heydey, pegged Lake early as "the Oprah Winfrey of the nineties." Her major contributions to the genre? What she calls "the surprise element" (secreting someone backstage and having them come out after another guest has finished "like, dissing them"), and an increased desire for the studio audience to be vocally judgmental. If the goal of Phil Donahue and Oprah Winfrey was to bring people together, *Ricki Lake* seemed based on the opposite philosophy: to break up romantic couples whose relationships were faltering, to pit one family member against another, and to ambush guests with surprise confrontations that made for "exciting TV." Sample show topic titles included "You're the Rudest Thing Alive . . . and I'm Sick of Your Attitude" and "Get Real, Honey, Your Boyfriend Is a Dog." Like a younger, hipper *Morton Downey, Jr. Show,* this talk show had a mean-spirited core, but its rapid rise in the ratings prompted a rash of competitors—and subsequent talk shows aimed at the same young viewers—to follow suit. One of them, the syndicated *Jenny Jones* show, set up an "ambush" confrontation in March 1995 between a guest who was expecting to meet his "secret admirer," and that admirer, who was a gay male. The ambushed guest, who had expected the enamored person to be a woman, was outraged; three days after the show was taped, he tracked down his secret admirer and killed him. That particular *Jenny Jones* show never aired, and the homicide sparked some general (and perhaps even sincere) hand-wringing and soul-searching among TV's talk-show producers, but the genie was out of the bottle—and this was less of a dream-of genie than a nightmare. *Ricki Lake,* you're the rudest thing alive . . . and I'm sick of your attitude.

Rifleman, The. *1958–63, ABC.* To longtime fans of this Western series, the most resonant memory is from the opening credits sequence, with Chuck Connors's Lucas McCain living up to the show's title by brandishing, twirling, cocking, and firing his 44.40 Winchester rifle. There's also ex-Mouseketeer Johnny Crawford as son Mark, a frontier latchkey kid raised by McCain's sharpshooting single parent. *The Rifleman* was action-packed, relatively violent, and an immediate Top 10 hit, and boasted its share of noteworthy guest stars, including separate appearances by Michael Landon and Dan Blocker the year before they were teamed on *Bonanza.* Dennis Hopper, Robert Vaughn, Agnes Moorehead, Robert Culp, Martin Landau, Adam West, James Coburn, and Sammy Davis, Jr., also traded lines, if not gunfire, with the Rifleman, but the biggest surprise of all is the man who created the series, wrote the pilot, and directed several of its early episodes: Sam Peckinpah. The future director of *The Wild Bunch* already had gotten his start in TV by writing for such shows as *Gunsmoke, Broken Arrow* (where he got his first directing job), and *Have Gun, Will Travel.* When *Gunsmoke* rejected a Peckinpah script about a frontier rifleman and his impressionable young son, Peckinpah turned around and sold a revised version to *Dick Powell's Zane Grey*

Theater, which televised it in the spring of 1958 as a potential series pilot. It went to series that fall—and even though Peckinpah departed after one year, *The Rifleman* made his reputation as it had made Connors's. In 1991, Connors and Crawford reunited, reprising their respective characters, in the Kenny Rogers miniseries *The Gambler Returns: The Luck of the Draw*, appearing alongside other TV Western actors and characters of similar vintage.

Rockford Files, The. *1974–80, NBC.* Very few performers can claim to have embodied one durable TV icon, but James Garner has given shape to two: Bret Maverick of *Maverick* and Jim Rockford of *The Rockford Files*. Although they lived in different centuries, Bret and Jim had much in common, including a dislike of confrontation and violence, a strong moral code camouflaged by a seemingly selfish exterior, and a clear preference for brainpower over firepower. Another common thread was writer-producer Roy Huggins, who not only created *Maverick*, but, under the pen name John Thomas James, wrote the original story which Stephen J. Cannell turned into *The Rockford Files*. Clearly, Rockford was to the standard private eye what Maverick was to the standard Western hero (a lot more cowardly, conniving, and concerned with self-preservation), but Garner wasn't even initially intended to play Rockford. In fact, *The Rockford Files* wasn't initially intended as a series at all. Huggins and Cannell were working on the ABC cop series *Toma* when the 1973 writers' strike threw their production schedule behind, and it became clear that the show's fifth episode would not be ready in time. ABC refused to preempt the show or allow a repeat that early in the season (ah, for the good old days), so Huggins came up with the idea of having Toma, played by Tony Musante, "turn over" a case to a friend, therefore necessitating Musante's presence only in the opening and closing scenes. The rest of the hour would feature a private detective named Rockford, an anti-hero type who was somewhat cowardly, kept track of his expenses, and kept getting beaten up by bad guys. Cannell wrote the script in record time, but ABC executives hated the premise so much, they reversed their earlier decision and ran a *Toma* repeat instead. Undaunted, Cannell pitched the script, as a telemovie pilot, to Universal, who liked it, and suggested Robert Blake as Rockford. Huggins instead sent the script to his old *Maverick* pal Garner, who loved it and jumped aboard immediately. (Blake wound up working with Cannell anyway, starring in Cannell's quirky and exciting *Baretta* series, which was a reworked version of *Toma*—and, like *Rockford*, was infinitely superior to the series from which it sprang.) It's ironic that the genesis of Jim Rockford can be traced to a planned feature appearance on an existing cop show, because the finest episodes of *The Rockford Files* turned right around and showcased other oddball private eyes: Dennis Dugan as a wet-behind-the-ears detective eventually given his own short-lived 1978 spinoff series, *Richie Brockelman, Private Eye*, and Tom Selleck as Lance White, an astoundingly optimistic and strait-laced hero type who, to Rockford's seething astonishment, always found the clue, unmasked the villain, and got the girl. As for *The Rockford Files* itself, the most durable elements are the harmonica-heavy musical theme by Mike Post (the first big break for a composer whose classic TV works include the instrumental themes to *Hill Street Blues* and *NYPD Blue*), and the answering-machine message (still something of a novelty when the series began) that preceded the music each week: "This is Jim Rockford. At the tone, leave your name and message. I'll get back to you." And he did, too. In 1994, fourteen years after *The Rockford Files* went off the air, Garner reprised his role in *The Rockford Files: I Still Love L.A.*, the first in a series of CBS telemovie sequels. Attesting to Rockford's, and Garner's, continued popularity, that revival emerged as the highest-rated telemovie of the 1994–95 TV season. Naturally, other telemovies followed.

Rocky and Bullwinkle; Rocky and His Friends. See *The Bullwinkle Show.*

Romper Room. *1953–87, local TV.* Before *Sesame Street*, even before *Captain Kangaroo*, there was a preschool TV program that made an impact by trying to be different, and by giving small kids something worthwhile to watch. *Romper Room* began as a daily program on Baltimore's WBAL-TV, where producer Bert Claster had the simple yet ingenious idea of letting his wife, a nursery-school teacher, bring her class to the TV studio to play and work— letting young viewers at home in on the action. Nancy Claster became "Miss Nancy," slowly and lovingly showing kids how to use safety scissors and work with paste and construction paper, and teaching them the differences between desired and destructive behaviors (with help, of course, from that most positive of role models, the Good Do-Bee). Like *Bozo*, where each city had a different clown, *Romper Room* was franchised locally rather than syndicated nationally, and each TV market had its own home-grown hostess, hunting for kids in her local audience by peering into the camera and holding up the famous Magic Mirror. "Romper stomper bomber boo, tell me, tell me, tell me do," she would say. "Magic Mirror, Magic Mirror, tell me today, did all my friends have fun at play?" Then she would call out the randomly chosen names of some kids ("I see Bobby, I see Cindy . . . "), while those of us overlooked each day blamed ourselves for not waving or shouting frenetically enough to catch her eye. *Romper Room* became an international sensation, but *Captain Kangaroo*, as a nationally delivered network show, soon cut into its audience, and the combined forces of *Mister Rogers' Neighborhood* and *Sesame Street* all but obliterated it. America's last *Romper Room* TV show, on New York's WWOR-TV, ended in 1987; Canada produced its own version until 1992, and reruns in both countries vanished from the airwaves by 1994. The sixties, though, were when *Romper Room* made the most headlines. In 1964, Baltimore's Miss Nancy, the original host when the series began, was replaced by Miss Sally—Miss Nancy's real-life daughter. And in 1962, a Phoenix *Romper Room* hostess, Sherri Finkbine, became an inadvertent national celebrity after the media got wind of her intention to abort what had been diagnosed as a deformed thalidomide fetus. That dilemma was much more controversial and serious than anything Miss Sherri, or any other *Romper Room* hostess, presented to their innocent young audience members. For them, things were much more simple: Do-Bee or not Do-Bee, that was the question.

Rootie Kazootie. *1950–53, NBC (weekdays) and ABC (Saturdays).* Like the similarly titled, or at least similarly rhyming, *Howdy Doody,* this children's show from the early fifties was centered around a smart-aleck, and rather sinister-looking, marionette. These days, only the name of the series is likely to ring any bells among most viewers, although this series, which began on what then was New York's WNBT-TV, was far ahead of its time when it came to two things: cross-promotion and self-promotion. Regarding the former, *Rootie Kazootie* merchandise was cranked out and sold all over the place, and fan clubs—with dime dues—were all the rage. Regarding the latter, the weekday NBC versions of *Rootie Kazootie* used to end most shows with continuing story-line cliff-hangers, long before most "mature" TV series got into the act. And when Little Richard wrote and sang his 1956 hit "Tutti-Frutti," was there any question who—or what—had inspired his "Oh, Rootie" rejoinder?

Roots. *1977, ABC.* **Roots: The Next Generations.** *1979, ABC.* **Queen.** *CBS, 1993.* In the seventies, a TV miniseries dramatized slavery in very personal terms, causing an entire nation to reflect upon racial pride and prejudice and embrace or confront its own past. That was in 1974, the nation was England, and the miniseries was *The Fight against Slavery,* a six-part BBC and Time-Life TV dramatization that had a substantial impact in that country. In America, though, it was Alex Haley's *Roots,* broadcast three years later, that struck both a nerve and a vein. The story of Haley's purported family tree, beginning with the birth of African ancestor Kunta Kinte (played by LeVar Burton), was, at twelve hours, the first lengthy drama in American TV history to be televised on consecutive evenings. Broadcast in January, albeit against limited competition and with parts of the country in the grip of a sizable snowstorm, *Roots* nonetheless attracted and held viewers in record numbers. Not only does *Roots* remain, to this day, the highest-rated miniseries ever broadcast (a record likely to stand forever, given the increasing fragmentation of network TV audiences), but its final episode ranks third on the list of all-time top-rated network TV programs, behind only the finale of *M*A*S*H* and the resolution to the infamous "Who Shot J.R.?" mystery on *Dallas. Roots* was to television what, a century earlier, *Uncle Tom's Cabin* was to literature: it reached an impressively, almost amazingly large audience, sparking national discussion and reevaluation along racial lines. Within months of the telecast of *Roots,* Haley's TV account, like his best-selling print account, was attacked on several fronts for alleged inaccuracies and plagiarisms, including charges, by more than one history professor, that Haley's identification of Kunta Kinte as the renamed American slave "Toby" was, according to existing records, wholly erroneous. Whatever the reliability of Haley's story, its essence made viewers respond like never before—or since. A far more polished and dramatically effective televised sequel, *Roots: The Next Generations,* appeared in 1979, becoming the most popular miniseries that year. At this writing, it holds firm at the ninth spot among the genre's all-time Top 10. A third *Roots* miniseries, *Queen,* starring Halle Berry as Haley's maternal grandmother, was presented by CBS in 1993, and it, too, was the most popular miniseries of its year. The original *Roots* included standout performances by Ben Vereen as Chicken George and Louis Gossett, Jr., as Fiddler (not to mention a brief appearance by O. J. Simpson as Kadi Touray, except I just *did* mention it). The biggest *Roots* casting coup of all, though, was getting Marlon Brando to play George Lincoln Rockwell in *Roots: The Next Generations.* It was Brando's most famous TV appearance—unless you count the times, during televised prime-time interviews, he described watching ants in his sink to Connie Chung or kissed Larry King smack on the lips—but it wasn't his first. Back in 1949, after Brando's Broadway triumph in *A Streetcar Named Desire* but before his first movie, he starred in a live TV drama, *I'm No Hero,* for the *Actors Studio* anthology series.

Roseanne. *1988– , ABC.* Like *The Cosby Show,* this sitcom burst onto the scene with a fully realized comic sensibility, based on the point of view of the standup comic who was its star. With Cosby, the approach was something like *Father Knows Best, but Nobody Listens to Him.* With *Roseanne,* it was more like *Mom's Mad as Hell, and Not Gonna Take It Anymore.* In real life, Roseanne (a.k.a. Roseanne Barr and Roseanne Arnold) could be a royal pain in the tattooed butt, generating tabloid headlines for everything from butchering the national anthem to loving and leaving Tom Arnold with equal enthusiasm. On her TV series, though, she made sure the show's quality never faltered, and made *Roseanne* one of the smartest, funniest, and most realistic comedies of modern times. During the last of the Reagan-Bush years, it was *Roseanne* that complained most loudly and cleverly that no money was trickling down to the working class as a result of the trickle-down theory of economics. While the Conners tried hard, struggling with both unemployment and various types of employment, just meeting the bills and making the meals often seemed like Herculean labors. At the same time, Thanksgiving family gatherings were as much a cause for dread as cheer, and the older the kids got, the more troubles (and significant others) they brought home. John Goodman, Laurie Metcalf, and Sara Gilbert—as Roseanne's husband Dan, sister Jackie, and younger daughter Darlene, respectively—all portrayed strong, credible characters in their own right, making *Roseanne* even stronger as a result. The relationships depicted on *Roseanne* cover many generations, and lots of touchy issues. What's more, no other series on American television has presented gay characters, male and female, in as nonjudgmental a light. Sometimes that tolerance intentionally expanded into hotly promoted and widely covered "controversial" episodes, such as when guest star Mariel Hemingway, portraying a lesbian, planted a big kiss right on Roseanne in one show, or when Martin Mull and guest star Fred Willard (costars, a TV generation ago, on *Fernwood 2-Night*), portraying gay men, got married. Those episodes, though, tended to be less cleverly written than the rest; like its star, *Roseanne* the show was better when not calling attention to itself. What *Roseanne* is likely to be remembered for most, though, are the clever closing-credits sequences that step outside the show's self-imposed "reality," and the annual

Halloween episodes, my favorites, that get top grades each year for creative costuming and pranks. In terms of its place in TV history, *Roseanne* is like *The Honeymooners: The Next Generation*—after the honeymoon's over.

Route 66. *1960–64, CBS; 1993, NBC.* Like the 1961 Corvette convertible around which this series revolved, *Route 66* embodied male adolescent fantasies in almost undiluted form. Cool car. No job. Just a good buddy, an open road, and women and adventures down the road to nowhere. In the original series, the '61 Corvette was hot off the showroom floor, and the buddies were Tod Stiles (Martin Milner) and Buz Murdoch (George Maharis). The 1993 remake featured the same car—now a vintage 'vette—but a new owner: James Wilder's Nick Lewis, who inherited the car from Buz, the father he never knew. (Dan Cortese, as an endlessly prattling hitchhiker, completed this less than dynamic duo.) To fans of the original series, that inheritance was a little jarring, because the convertible in the old *Route 66* never belonged to Buz; it belonged to Tod. Not only that, but Maharis (and, thus, Buz) left the series midway through its run, leaving Glenn Corbett, as Linc Case (one of the first Vietnam vets depicted on prime-time TV), to drive around with Tod. So how did Buz end up with the car in *his* garage? Don't ask. There auto be a law against such lapses in continuity. At any rate, neither the original series nor the remake is as resonant as the music associated with the title: Nelson Riddle's piano-tinkling instrumental theme song, which came from the TV series, and Nat King Cole's hit jazz vocal of "(Get Your Kicks on) Route 66," which didn't. Cole and his trio recorded and released that Bobby Troup song in 1946, fourteen years before the TV series even existed. Obviously, Cole and company had taken an alternate *Route*. But the original series, at least, gave work to some directors who enjoyed the freedom of the open road, including Robert Altman and Sam Peckinpah.

Rowan & Martin's Laugh-In. *1968–73, NBC.* This seminal TV variety series is listed here, so you don't have to look it up in your *Funk and Wagnalls*. *Laugh-In* took the blackout formula from vaudeville and adapted it to television, using rapid edits, disorienting juxtapositions, and habit-forming repetitions to stampede from one punch line or sight gag to another. (Those who blame MTV for introducing "short attention span" entertainment to television forgot about the fast-paced barrages by Dan Rowan, Dick Martin, and company.) Such predecessors as *That Was the Week That Was* and *The Smothers Brothers Comedy Hour* get credit for clearing the antiestablishment TV field that *Laugh-In* was to plow, and Ernie Kovacs was another clear comic influence, but *Laugh-In*, in turn, gets credit for concentrating the formula later adapted, to great success, by *Saturday Night Live:* lots of repertory comics, an off-the-wall sensibility, and more catch phrases and repeating characters than you could shake a *shtick* at. No other series in the sixties generated so many memorable faces, images, and quotable punch lines. There was Arte Johnson, as the dirty old man, falling over on his tricycle or being beaten by an old woman (Ruth Buzzi) who wielded her purse like John Belushi, on *Saturday Night Live*, wielded his samurai sword. And Johnson, again, as the

"verrrr-ry interesting" German soldier. Lily Tomlin as Ernestine the telephone operator (a one-woman precursor of such modern horrors as voice
mail), or as little Edith Ann (" . . . and that's the truth!"). Henry Gibson with
his poetry corner. Gary Owens introducing the show "from beautiful down-
town Burbank." Goldie Hawn with her giggle, bikini, and body paint. There
were the hosts themselves, with Rowan closing each show by telling his partner (with apologies to George Burns and Gracie Allen) to "Say goodnight,
Dick"—after which Martin, of course, responded obediently, "Goodnight,
Dick." The joke wall, the Flying Fickle Finger of Fate Award, and even such
goofy phrases (some new, some appropriated) as "Here come de judge!" and
"Sock it to me." That latter phrase, when asked as an incredulous question
by presidential candidate Richard Nixon in 1968, may be the series' most
famous single moment, but *Laugh-In* also featured memorable guest cameos
by the likes of John Wayne, Sammy Davis, Jr., Jimmy Stewart, and ukelele-
strumming Tiny Tim. A series of specials in 1977 and 1978 revived the *Laugh-
In* name and style, but only one repertory comic, the then-unknown Robin
Williams, revived its spirit. Sad to say, but the rapid-paced presentation style
of the old *Laugh-In* is best represented on TV today by the scatter-shot,
anything-goes montages on, sigh, *America's Funniest Home Videos*. Tomlin's
Edith Ann lives on in a series of successful prime-time animated specials
begun in 1994, about the same time NBC began showing a series of *Laugh-
In* retrospective specials. Were some parts of the old series laughably dated,
and others laugh-out-loud funny, after all these years? You bet your sweet
bippy. And what *was* a "walnetto," exactly?

Royal Wedding, Prince Charles and Lady Diana Spencer. *1981, CBS, NBC,
ABC, CNN.* Nearly thirty years after the coronation of Queen Elizabeth II,
American television networks invaded England again to provide TV coverage
of another highly anticipated royal ceremony. This time the coverage was live,
and was preceded by a week's worth of build-up on the networks' respective
morning shows. The wedding itself was a long and sumptuous affair, and the
images were those of a storybook come to life: golden carriages, flowing
gowns, and a handsome young prince and his glowing bride, apparently destined to live happily ever after. Lady Di proved so popular in America that her
storybook romance and wedding were dramatized in two 1982 docudramas
broadcast within days of one another: ABC's *Charles & Diana: A Royal Love
Story* and CBS's *The Royal Romance of Charles and Diana*. (The latter production starred Catherine Oxenberg, later of *Dynasty*, as Diana, but the
other title roles went to unknowns, then and now.) When, in real life, "happily
ever after" turned into a royal romance that fizzled, there was another round
of competing dramatic accounts: ABC's 1992 *Charles & Diana: Unhappily
Ever After* (which, in an odd sort of symmetry, recast Oxenberg as a much
more morose Lady Di) and NBC's 1993 *Diana: Her True Story*, in which
Serena Scott Thomas portrayed the Princess of Wales. Neither of these TV
portraits, either, was to Di for: once you saw Lady Diana throwing up in a
toilet bowl, the rest of *Diana: Her True Story* was pretty much of a royal
flush. In 1995, the real Lady Di went on television herself, in a BBC special

Roseanne, with John Goodman and Roseanne in typically outrageous Halloween costumes.

Rowan & Martin's Laugh-In, with Dan Rowan and Dick Martin.

called *An Interview with H.R.H. the Princess of Wales*—and discussed, with quiet questioner Martin Bashir, not only her bulimia and depression, but her husband's mistress ("There were three of us in this marriage, so it was a bit crowded," Princess Diana said, in what proved to be the special's most famous quote) and her official separation from the Prince of Wales. "The fairy tale had come to an end," she said simply, in a TV moment as intimate as it was rare. Barbara Walters quickly grabbed exclusive first American rights to the interview, and broadcast portions of it on ABC's *20/20;* shortly thereafter, the A&E Network repeated the original BBC interview in its entirety. American viewers, increasingly in the past decade, have become used to seeing their leaders probed on TV about such intimate matters—but for a British princess to take such matters public was largely without precedent, in Great Britain or in America, and, in its way, was as hypnotic a TV event as the Royal Wedding had been. At this writing, the royal couple has yet to make its story truly final. It's a safe bet, though, that another round of royal docudramas is yet to come. Too bad the best title, *Di Hard,* is already taken.

Roy Rogers Show, The. *1951–57, NBC.* The most well-known legacy of this series, of course, is the theme song—in which Roy Rogers and his on-screen and off-screen partner Dale Evans sing "Happy trails to you, until we meet again. . . . " What's less well known is that the "Happy Trails" theme was written by Dale Evans herself. Like many TV Westerns at the time, *The Roy Rogers Show* featured an amiable, straight-shooting, highly moral cowboy, one who wasn't above (or beneath) singing songs around the campfire. It also generated enough offshoot merchandise to fill a toy store—or, at least, enough to fill twelve pages in the 1955 Sears, Roebuck catalogue. Unlike most TV Westerns at the time, *The Roy Rogers Show* was set in the twentieth century, so the Double R Bar ranch boasted such modern contraptions as a telephone and a horseless carriage. That car was so unreliable, though, it's no wonder Roy Rogers remained so Trigger-happy.

Rush Limbaugh, The Television Show. *1992–   , syndicated.* As that media rarity, a talk-show conservative with a sense of humor, Limbaugh climbed rather quickly through the ranks of radio and TV, ascending at just the right time to ride, then drive, the wave of "New Right" Republicanism sweeping across America. One irony, for those who decry Limbaugh's steamroller media tactics, is that he got his first big break in the Orwellian year of 1984, hosting a conservative California talk-radio show in Sacramento. An even richer irony is that Limbaugh was hired to replace Morton Downey, Jr., later an incendiary TV personality in his own right—make that *far* right—who had been fired for making a racist joke. In 1988, the year George Bush succeeded Ronald Reagan in the White House, Limbaugh succeeded in moving to New York for a nationally syndicated radio show. In 1992, as Bush lost power, Limbaugh gained his, by taking his radio act—and a hefty percentage of his twenty million radio listeners—to television, where he continued to refer to his loyal (as in unquestioning) fans as "dittoheads," his female detractors as "feminazis," and to push the sales of his books by, in an impressively blatant act of self-promotion, displaying them as the background set for his popular TV show. Limbaugh, like Downey before him, got to take his views to TV in relatively uncontested fashion because of the repeal of the Fairness Doctrine in the mideighties. Limbaugh, in turn, was instrumental in getting many freshmen Republicans elected to Congress in 1994. Like a right-wing Howard Beale from *Network*, Limbaugh used his own network of radio and TV outlets to act mad as hell and get his "dittoheads" to mobilize and vote accordingly. Less civil but more entertaining than TV's previous reigning conservative, William F. Buckley, Jr., Limbaugh enjoys more media fame and power than Buckley ever did—but fame is fickle and often fleeting. Just ask that other prominent conservative Jr., Morton Downey.

St. Elsewhere. *1982–88, NBC.* For what it did, when it did it, and even how it ended, *St. Elsewhere* gets my vote as the best dramatic series in the history of television. It was more ambitious, playful, intense, and unpredictable than anything else around, and even its most prominent characters could die suddenly or have their lives changed significantly. One doctor, Terence Knox's Peter White, degenerated into a serial rapist; another, David Morse's Jack "Boomer" Morrison, was a rape victim himself, having been taken hostage and brutalized while tending to male patients at a local prison. Regular characters died suddenly, committed suicide, became clinically depressed, lost their medical residencies, or suffered razor slashes to the face and gunshots to the groin. Compared to all that, even the night shift on *ER* was a relative breeze. One doctor at St. Eligius (the hospital disparagingly referred to as the *St. Elsewhere* of the title), Mark Harmon's Bobby Caldwell, became the first prominent TV character to contract AIDS—not the first time *St. Elsewhere* had explored that particular subject matter. A story line in 1983, involving a secretly gay politician who tested positive for HIV, was the first mention and depiction of the AIDS virus on prime-time dramatic television (two years before Rock Hudson went public with his condition). In addition to presenting these tense, often shocking stories about the staff and patients of Boston's rundown hospital, *St. Elsewhere* also deviated from its everyday "reality" to present episodes set in the past, in dream states, even in an imagined afterlife. And somehow, during all this dramatic turmoil and bold experimentation, the writer-producers of *St. Elsewhere* amused themselves, and their loyal viewers, by sprinkling most episodes with an impish succession of puns, allusions, and inside jokes. Some of these jokes were teleliterate, as when an amnesiac patient decided he was Mary Richards from *The Mary Tyler Moore Show* (which, like *St. Elsewhere*, emanated from MTM Productions), or when the hospital public-address system paged such familiar TV doctors as Casey,

Zorba, Welby, and Kildare. (One *St. Elsewhere* producer, Tom Fontana, continued that latter tradition in an episode of *Homicide: Life on the Street* by having a hospital loudspeaker announce the name of "Dr. Ehrlich," a reference to Ed Begley, Jr.'s, Victor Ehrlich from *St. Elsewhere.*) Other in-jokes involved playful echoes of song lyrics (one nurse is asked, "Have you seen polythene, Pam?"), sarcastic allusions to the show's behind-the-scenes problems with new NBC corporate owner General Electric (like David Letterman, the *St. Elsewhere* folks delighted in biting the hand that fed them), and purely gratuitous name-dropping (while some of the names announced on the St. Eligius loudspeaker were familiar from TV, others were culled from the eighth-grade class of executive producer Bruce Paltrow's daughter). Speaking of Paltrow, he and Steven Bochco teamed for an unsold MTM Productions hospital sitcom, *Operating Room*, in 1978. When that pilot didn't sell, Paltrow created *The White Shadow* (for which Bochco contributed scripts), and Bochco eventually moved on to *Hill Street Blues*, after which Paltrow and company generated *St. Elsewhere.* Therefore, while Bochco has gotten most of the credit for reformulating the TV drama series, Paltrow is, at the very least, an unindicted co-conspirator. Early *St. Elsewhere* collaborators Joshua Brand and John Falsey went on to create *Northern Exposure* and *I'll Fly Away*, while others, like Fontana, John Tinker and Mark Tinker, went on to such quality series as *Homicide: Life on the Street*, *L.A. Law*, and *NYPD Blue*. In front of the camera, Denzel Washington was there from start to finish as the intense Dr. Phillip Chandler, Norman Lloyd was a soothing presence as Daniel Auschlander, William Daniels was an abrasive yet lovable presence as Mark Craig, Howie Mandel was a pre-*ER* emergency-room hotshot as Wayne Fiscus, and Ed Flanders was the sensitive soul of the series as Dr. Donald Westphall (who, years before the butt-baring on Bochco's *NYPD Blue*, flashed a rather cheeky precedent in TV history by mooning his boss). Morse, Knox, Ellen Bry, Bonnie Bartlett, and Alfre Woodard also turned in terrific work as series regulars, and Dave Grusin contributed an equally terrific instrumental opening theme. From start to finish—and especially at the finish—*St. Elsewhere* was a classic. The last episode not only restaged, knowingly and fondly, the "mass hug" scene from the finale of *The Mary Tyler Moore Show*, but climaxed with a scene in which the exterior of St. Eligius hospital was shown inside a snow globe, shaken by a daydreaming, mentally challenged youth. That closing scene suggested that all the events dramatized on *St. Elsewhere* over the years were nothing more than the idle imaginings of an autistic child—a child who ended his reverie when his father returned the globe to its proper place atop the family television set. TV endings, and TV shows, don't get any better than that.

Sanford and Son. *1972–76, NBC.* This Americanized version of a British BBC-TV sitcom, *Steptoe and Son*, starred Redd Foxx as junk dealer Fred Sanford, a widower living with his adult son (Demond Wilson). Foxx previously had played a junk dealer in the 1970 movie *Cotton Comes to Harlem*, and further personalized his new role by changing the character's name from Steptoe to Sanford, his real last name before, because of his hair color, he

St. Elsewhere, with Denzel Washington (top left) and the rest of the final-season cast.

adopted the name "Chicago Red." (Under that name, he worked as a Harlem dishwasher in the same restaurant as another hot-hued young man, "Detroit Red"—later known as Malcolm X.) Like Dabney Coleman on *Buffalo Bill*, Redd Foxx on *Sanford and Son* played a lazy, sneaky curmudgeon, but the comedy roots here could be traced as far back as *Amos 'n' Andy* and, in terms of Fred's eternal yet unsuccessful get-rich-quick schemes, *The Honeymooners*. Garry Shandling broke into TV by selling a script to this series, but its most lasting contribution is the often-repeated gag in which Foxx's Fred Sanford would respond to bad news or a good insult by feigning a heart attack, clutching his chest, looking heavenward, and screaming to his late wife, "I'm comin' to join you, Elizabeth!" The sad irony is that in 1991, on the set of a new CBS sitcom called *The Royal Family*, Foxx clutched his chest and collapsed, Sanford-style—but this time he was the victim of an actual, and ultimately fatal, heart attack.

Saturday Night Live. *1975–   , NBC.* The curse of *Saturday Night Live* today is the success of *Saturday Night Live* in the past. When staking out its late-night TV territory in 1975, the *Saturday Night Live* repertory company billed itself as "The Not-Ready-for-Prime-Time Players." It was a demonstration not of lack of confidence, but of defiance: show biz, as defined by prime-time TV at the time, was everything series creator Lorne Michaels and company wanted to avoid. Yet by swimming against the tide, *Saturday Night Live* wound up not only tapping into a deep new talent pool, but diverting, and ultimately dominating, the entire pop-culture mainstream. Chevy Chase, with his "I'm Chevy Chase, and you're not" wise-guy "Weekend Update" newscaster, was the first to attain mass popularity and leave the show for greener show-business pastures, but it was John Belushi, with his buzzed-about appearance as Bluto in *National Lampoon's Animal House*, who proved instantly, and single-handedly, that a whole new generation was out there ready and willing to create and embrace a new generation of stars. Twenty years after it began, *Saturday Night Live* can no longer even pretend to adopt a counterculture stance, not when so many of its stars, skits, and featured performers have joined the new California Gold Rush by heading to Hollywood. If the adage is true that a conservative is nothing but an old liberal, then, regarding *Saturday Night Live*, an opportunist is nothing but an old satirist. The fact that lame *SNL* skits and characters, like Julia Sweeney's androgynous Pat or Al Franken's life-affirming Stuart Smalley, flop when turned into feature films is less surprising, and revealing, than the fact that they somehow got made as movies in the first place. For years, so many of the performers and writers on *Saturday Night Live* saw the show as a springboard, and used their first flush of celebrity to develop and juggle simultaneous solo showcases for other media, that on many weeks the actual live performance of *Saturday Night Live* seemed like an afterthought and a chore—whereas, back when "Saturday night live" meant ninety prime-time minutes of *Your Show of Shows*, the show indeed was the thing. Nevertheless, over its cyclical history of good and bad casts and seasons, *Saturday Night Live*, broadcast from the same facility as Arturo Toscanini's classic radio concerts, has contributed more catch phrases, characters, and entertainers to American pop culture, over a longer period, than any TV showcase since *The Ed Sullivan Show* and *The Tonight Show Starring Johnny Carson*. Its TV comedy lineage can be traced not only to *Your Show of Shows* and to Steve Allen, but also to *That Was the Week That Was*, *The Smothers Brothers Comedy Hour*, *Rowan & Martin's Laugh-In*, and, more immediately, *Monty Python's Flying Circus*. Irreverence, and an eagerness to poke fun at everyone up to and including themselves, was the key from the start. In the 1975 NBC press release announcing *Saturday Night Live*, Michaels was quoted as saying, "Our writing staff is made up of the best creative talents in the industry"— but quickly adding, "Unfortunately, the industry is tuna fishing." Perhaps so, because that initial group (1975–80) came up with an astounding number of hooks: the Coneheads; the Killer Bees; the Blues Brothers; Belushi's "But nooooooo!" complaint and his samurai warrior antics; Chase's land shark; Gilda Radner's editorializing Emily Litella ("never mind") and Roseanne Roseannadanna ("It just goes to show you: it's always somethin' "); Dan Aykroyd and guest host Steve Martin's Czech Brothers ("We are two wild and crazy guys!"); Aykroyd berating "Point-Counterpoint" partner Jane Curtin ("Jane, you ignorant slut") or bleeding to death as a woozy Julia Child; Garrett Morris's Chico Escuela ("baseball been berry, berry good to me"); and so on, up to and including the accident-prone, Gumbyish clay figure, Mr. Bill ("Ooooh, nooooo!"). And who can forget Belushi mimicking musical guest Joe Cocker during a "duet" on "Feelin' Alright"; Bill Murray crooning as a tacky lounge singer; Eddie Murphy (as convict-poet Tyrone Green) reciting "C-I-L-L My Landlord"; Steve Martin and Gilda Radner dancing *a la* Fred Astaire and Ginger Rogers; Martin singing "King Tut"; or Andy Kaufman lip-synching to the *Mighty Mouse* theme? Kaufman and Martin pioneered and popularized a new form of absurdist stand-up comedy on *Saturday Night Live*, and during the late seventies, *Saturday Night Live* was the hottest show on television (even though the syndicated *Second City TV*, running contemporaneously, often was much better). When the first of many "new" casts was introduced in 1980, the show suffered, and only Joe Piscopo and eventual film star Eddie Murphy kept it afloat until further help arrived. Since then, *Saturday Night Live* has attracted and showcased some wonderful comic talent (Billy Crystal, Martin Short, Jan Hooks, Dana Carvey, Phil Hartman, Mike Myers, Michael McKean, Chris Farley, the brilliant "Weekend Update" work of Dennis Miller, the goofy music of Adam Sandler, and, most recently, the antic characterizations of Cheri Oteri). The show also has wasted some wonderful comic talent over the years—Harry Shearer, Ben Stiller, Julia Louis-Dreyfus, Pamela Stephenson, Ellen Cleghorne, and Janeane Garofalo. (If you don't recognize a few of those names, that's precisely the point.) Durable catch phrases, in more recent years, have included "Yeah, that's the ticket" (by Jon Lovitz's Liar character), "Isn't that special?" (Carvey's Church Lady), "Wouldn't be prudent at this juncture" (Carvey's George Bush), "Not!" (like "schwing!" and other examples of teenspeak, from "Wayne's World," with Mike Myers and Carvey), and dozens of others, while movie offshoots have included the Broadway-to-film Gilda Radner showcase *Gilda Live*, two *Wayne's World* movies, and one each starring *The Blues Brothers*, *The Coneheads* and, courtesy of *Mr. Saturday Night*, Billy Crystal's Buddy Young, Jr. Guest hosts, like musical guest stars, ran the gamut. The former included such kindred comedy spirits as Richard Pryor, Lily Tomlin, Buck Henry, Peter Cook and Dudley Moore, Eric Idle, Michael Palin, Robin Williams, Sam Kinison, Garry Shandling, and The Smothers Brothers, as well as such veteran live-TV masters as Milton Berle and Sid Caesar. William Shatner also served as guest host, and made both *SNL* and *Star Trek* history by poking fun at overly fervent Trekkies by yelling at them, in a marvelously edgy skit, to "Get a life, people!" In the musical category, *Saturday Night Live* got most of the biggest names in the business, succeeded in temporarily reuniting Paul Simon and Art Garfunkel for one 1975 show, and, in 1976, nearly succeeded in sparking what easily would have been the show's most crowning moment: an impromptu mini-reunion of the Beatles. Lorne Michaels, appearing on camera from his office, offered the Beatles three thousand dollars (a laughably low sum, which was precisely the point) to come on the show and sing three songs. "This is made out to the Beatles," Michaels said. "You divide it up any way you want. If you want to give Ringo less, it's up to you." A few weeks later, Michaels repeated the offer, increasing it by fifty dollars per Beatle. That's the offer that very nearly paid off. Shortly before John Lennon died, he said that he and Paul McCartney were in New York watching *Saturday Night Live* at John and Yoko's Dakota apartment that night, and "almost went down to the studio just as a gag. We nearly got into a cab, but we were actually too tired." Sigh.

Saved by the Bell. *1989–93, NBC.* **Saved by the Bell: The College Years.** *1993–94, NBC.* **Saved by the Bell: The New Class.** *1993– , NBC.* This wretched show belongs here because, like it or not (and I'm firmly in the "not" camp), its syndicated reruns proved so popular among preteens that, like the equally insipid and inescapable *Full House*, *Saved by the Bell* is bound to be *The Brady Bunch* of tomorrow. This despite the fact that, by the time the cast members were ready for *The College Years*, they looked longer in the tooth than the overage high-schoolers of either *Welcome Back, Kotter* or *Beverly Hills, 90210*. And despite the fact that Dustin Diamond, as Screech, was so irritating he should have been called Scratch. And despite the fact that the adventures of Zack (Mark-Paul Gosselaar) and his buddies are so insufferably insane, they make the *Archie* comic books look like *Ulysses*. Except for *The College Years*, which bombed after a brief prime-time run, the other incarnations have been relegated to Saturday mornings. The only thing worth noting about the series, really, is that two of the original female cast members later "graduated" to much less wholesome assignments. Tiffani-Amber Thiessen, who portrayed highly moral cheerleader Kelly on *Saved by the Bell*, went on to play a vampy vixen on *Beverly Hills, 90210*. Elizabeth Berkley, whose intensely feminist character of Jessie on *Saved by the Bell* once wore an overcoat to a swimsuit beauty pageant rather than display her body, subsequently shed her coat, and inhibitions, to portray the lascivious lap-dancing leading lady in the controversial, and universally panned, 1995 film *Showgirls*.

Scared Straight! *1978, syndicated.* Arnold Shapiro, who later created *Rescue 911*, made this local nonfiction special for KTLA-Los Angeles, where it garnered such positive acclaim and large audiences that it soon was syndicated to local stations nationwide. Surprisingly, the Los Angeles documentary was about something happening on the other side of the country: an experimental New Jersey youth program in which juvenile delinquents were taken to prison—for a brief visit—to be lectured to by convicts about the realities of life behind bars. These "lectures" were riddled with obscenities as well as frank talk, which is why the networks never touched *Scared Straight!*—except, that is, in a dramatized and sanitized CBS telemovie, *Scared Straight! Another Story*, broadcast in 1980. In 1987, a nonfiction Shapiro follow-up, *Scared Straight: Ten Years Later*, revisited the seventeen young adults who had been flagged as problem youths a decade earlier. Fifteen had, at that time, indeed been "scared straight," one was behind bars, and one was somewhere in between. The title continues to resonate in popular culture, but perhaps the message has been diluted over time. A recent *Beavis and Butt-Head* cartoon (quite rightly) sent the two-dimensional delinquents into a *Scared Straight* program and isolated them in a cell with menacing, antisocial prisoners. What lessons were learned? By the end of the visit, the convicts and Beavis and Butt-Head had bonded behind bars, playing air guitar together while screaming a song by Iron Maiden.

Scooby-Doo, Where Are You? *1969–72, CBS.* Unfortunately, it's here—included because, in one incarnation or another, this animated not-so-Great Dane has been seen on TV from the sixties (with this original series) through the nineties (with revised versions and reruns), and Hollywood has set its sights on making a live-action *Scooby-Doo* movie. A better question, one for which I have no answer, is *Scooby-Doo, Why Are You?* And the only thing I find remotely interesting regarding this series is that Don Messick, who provided the voice of Scooby-Doo, also provided the voice for Boo-Boo Bear on *Yogi Bear*. Messick's partial résumé, then, would read, "Scooby Doo and Boo-Boo, too."

SCTV; SCTV Network 90. See *Second City TV*.

Sea Hunt. *1957–61, syndicated.* What can you say about this Lloyd Bridges underwater series? The best thing, I guess, is "tanks for the memories." Even though the original *Sea Hunt* was filmed in black-and-white, its underwater photography, in those pre-*Undersea World of Jacques Cousteau* days, made the series quite a hit—much more so than in 1987, when a full-color remake starring Ron Ely (already not-so-famous for a TV remake of *Tarzan*) fizzled and drowned. Even though Lloyd Bridges had little dialogue in the original series (unless you count bubbles), he did most of his own stunts, flipped off a boat backward with the best of them, and dove to the rescue without hesitation. He was, in other words, the strong, silent, and soggy type—like a Bridges under troubled water. And, in fitting fashion, *Sea Hunt* is surfacing again: a movie remake, written by Peter Benchley of *Jaws* fame, is just around the bends.

Search for Tomorrow. *1951–82, CBS; 1982–86, NBC.* The title has survived, even if the show itself hasn't. *Search for Tomorrow* lasted on television for thirty-five years, long enough so that it ranks, to this day, as the third longest-running serial in TV history (only the *Guiding Light* and *As the World Turns*, both of which are still around, proved more durable). *Search for Tomorrow*, created specifically for TV rather than adapted from radio, was television's first successful soap opera. Nearly a decade after its demise, though, only the announcer's deeply intoned recitation of the title remains truly familiar. That, of course, and the cast members who have since become much more familiar in the days after *Tomorrow*. Don Knotts, before winning all those Emmys as Barney Fife on *The Andy Griffith Show*, played Wilbury Peabody on *Search for Tomorrow* (1953–55). Hal Linden, before playing a different guy named Barney on *Barney Miller*, portrayed Larry Carter on *Search* in 1969. Wayne Rogers, pre-*M*A*S*H*, was cast as Slim Davis in 1959; Audra Lindley, pre-*Soap*, played Sue Knowles in 1962; and, more recently, *Search for Tomorrow* provided early breaks for Morgan Fairchild (as Jennifer Pace Phillips, 1973–77), Kevin Bacon (Tod Adamson, 1979), and Olympia Dukakis (Barbara Moreno, 1983). Also clocking time on the soap: Robby Benson, Melanie Chartoff, Barbara Babcock, and Susan Sarandon.

Second City TV. *1977–81, syndicated; 1981–83, NBC; 1983–84, Cinemax.* This series went under a number of names, at a number of different venues, with a number of different players—but wherever it played, with whatever players it used, and under whatever name it presented itself, *Second City TV* (a.k.a. *SCTV*, the common shorthand for the series also known as *SCTV Comedy Network*, *SCTV Network*, and *SCTV Channel*) was brilliantly, consistently funny. Its early history is interesting, because of how much it dovetails with the genesis of *Saturday Night Live*. The original Second City troupe was headquartered in Chicago, but a Canadian offshoot was created in Toronto in 1973, with an inaugural repertory company that included Dan Aykroyd, Gilda Radner, John Candy, Joe Flaherty, and Eugene Levy. When the first two were imported to New York for *Saturday Night Live*, the rest were joined in Toronto by Andrea Martin, Catherine O'Hara, Dave Thomas, and Harold Ramis. That left *SCTV* with a seven-person cast every bit as gifted as the performers of *Saturday Night Live*—and, despite an infinitely lower budget, *Second City TV* quickly proved it had even better writers. Ramis, in fact, was one of the cowriters of *National Lampoon's Animal House* as well as the costar and cowriter of *Stripes*, making him partly responsible for the big-screen breaks of TV rivals John Belushi and Bill Murray, respectively. And when Ramis left *Second City TV*, Rick Moranis came in, eventually followed by Martin Short. Not too shabby. The hilarious comedy and perfect parodies of *Second City TV* were presented under a brilliant comedy premise: the series was set at a low-rent TV operation in the fictional town of Melonville, and each episode presented not only the news, entertainment programming, and commercials from that TV station, but also the behind-the-scenes activities of its on-air personalities, station management, and janitorial help. It was a lot like a human version of *The Muppet Show,* which had premiered in syndication the year before; both series were about crazy characters struggling, on-stage and off, to put on a rather outrageous brand of entertainment. Most concepts worked on several levels at once, as when serious newscaster Floyd Robertson (Flaherty) augmented his meager salary by moonlighting, totally humiliated, as Count Floyd, host of "Monster Chiller Horror Theatre." (After screening some public-service industrial short or similarly inappropriate offering, he'd try to generate enthusiasm by howling, "Ooooh, wasn't *that* scary, boys and girls?") Flaherty, in another role, played Guy Caballero, who ran the station with Andrea Martin's gaudily dressed Edith Prickley. Edith, too, would occasionally perform on camera, as in a Melonville version of *Body Heat,* called "Prickley Heat." More obscure parodies ranged from an intentionally stupid melodrama called "Jane Eyrehead" to a sitcom teaming William Shakespeare and Francis Bacon (its title alone, "Shake and Bake," justified the concept). The *SCTV* players could do anything and imitate anyone—and just about did. The show's single best parody was "Play It Again, Bob," in which Rick Moranis, as Woody Allen, tried to persuade Bob Hope (Dave Thomas) to team for a new road picture. Filmed in the style of *Annie Hall,* with an ending echoing *Casablanca,* "Play It Again, Bob" was a sitcom-length TV masterpiece, down to its *Play It Again, Sam* homage in which Allen consulted the ghost of Bing Crosby (Flaherty). *SCTV,* though, was full of such dizzyingly ambitious and arcane delights. "The Great White North" segments, featuring Moranis and Thomas as beer-guzzling Canadians Bob and Doug McKenzie (think of them as the original Beavis and Butt-Head, or, even better, as Beavis and Moosehead), introduced the term "hoser"—which, like every other word in those skits, was totally improvised on the spot. (Unfortunately, a subsequent movie spinoff, *Strange Brew,* was not.) Flaherty's Sammy Maudlin, Candy's sycophantic William B., and Levy's Bobby Bittman skewered show-biz talk shows long before *The Larry Sanders Show* got around to it. Levy's "Perry Como: Still Alive!" parody was unforgettable, as were Levy and John Candy as the Leutonian polka-playing Schmenge Brothers, who eventually headlined a real toe-tapper of an HBO special, *The Schmenge Brothers: The Last Polka.* Other major memories: Flaherty and Candy hosting the "Farm Film Report," where all movies were rated based on the number of explosions and whether things "blowed up real good" (boy, given the way most action films are made today, were *they* ahead of their time). Thomas and Martin as the stiff proprietors of "Tex and Edna Boil's Prairie Warehouse and Curio Emporium." Candy and Levy, as bad genre actors Dr. Tongue and Woody Tobias, Jr., starring in and hosting "Dr. Tongue's 3-D House of Stewardesses," "3–D House of Pancakes," and "3–D House of Representatives." And the endless stream of fabulous characters, including Martin as immigrant cleaning woman Pirini Scleroso (the one who, when told to sit down, would reply, "See-a down?"), O'Hara as a perfect Katharine Hepburn and the imperfect Lola Heatherton,

Short as Jerry Lewis and Ed Grimley, Candy as underground transvestite superstar Divine, and so many more. With no studio audience, the cast members of *SCTV* were able to do sustained parodies and be concerned chiefly with amusing themselves, which made for a lot of brilliant comedy work. The down side, though, is that the immediate feedback available on a show like *Saturday Night Live* had its own rewards, which most cast members of *SCTV* had to leave the series to appreciate. Perhaps the best indication of the relationship between *Second City* and *Saturday Night Live* is that when Martin Short left the former and joined the latter, his very first *Saturday Night Live* appearance as the pointy-haired, totally bizarre Ed Grimley brought down the house and created a new string of pop-culture catch phrases, I must say—even though he'd been doing the character just as brilliantly, in relative anonymity, on *SCTV* for years, starring in such memorably cross-pollinated movie parodies as "Oliver Grimley" ("Well, that certainly wasn't much gruel, I *must* say; I mean, these portions are a joke"). Some of the other *SCTV* ideas and parodies were so uncannily on target, they later were realized in real life. A *Leave It to Beaver* reunion show, with John Candy as a grown-up Beaver, later was echoed by the original-cast reunion in the 1983 telemovie *Still the Beaver*. And in perhaps the spookiest example of life imitating art, one vintage *SCTV* ersatz commercial pitched a record album called "Stairways to Heaven," complete with musical parodies of popular singers (Rickie Lee Jones, Barry White, Luciano Pavarotti, Slim Whitman), all doing their own versions of Led Zeppelin's "Stairway to Heaven." In 1995, a real-life parody CD was released, in which the same song was interpreted by artists imitating the likes of the Beatles, Elvis Presley, and the B-52's. The title of the collection? *Stairways to Heaven*.

Secret Agent. *1965–66, CBS.* In the United States, this imported spy series, starring Patrick McGoohan as suave secret agent John Drake, was seen as a clear and quick response to the popularity of the James Bond films. In England, however, the TV series was viewed as a pioneer, not a follower: in that country, where the series was known as *Danger Man*, it had preceded that first 007 movie by 003 years. *Danger Man* was introduced there in 1959, and finished its run in 1962, the year Sean Connery was introduced as James Bond in *Dr. No*. In America, however, CBS waited until Bondmania was high to present a repackaged *Danger Man*, retitled *Secret Agent* for American audiences and given a new theme song, "Secret Agent Man," that became a still-memorable Top 10 hit for Johnny Rivers in 1966—these days, probably the most memorable thing about the entire series. That, and the fact that another McGoohan series, *The Prisoner*, is widely perceived as having been a direct (though subtle) sequel to this spy series. See also: *Prisoner, The*.

Secret Storm. *1954–74, CBS.* The biggest storm generated by this soap opera occurred in 1968, when Joan Crawford appeared for four days as self-obsessed Joan Borman—ludicrously serving as stand-in for her ailing adopted daughter, Christina, who normally played the role. This absurd attention-getting ploy got lots of publicity then—and later, too, as recounted by daughter Christina

Saturday Night Live, with the infamous 1980 cast: Denny Dillon, Charles Rocket, Ann Risley, Joe Piscopo, Gail Matthius, and Gilbert Gottfried.

Second City TV, with Joe Flaherty as Count Floyd and Andrea Martin as Edith Prickley.

in the book and movie versions of her savage memoir, *Mommie Dearest*. Except for that (and its familiar title), *Secret Storm* made little lasting impact with its twenty-year run. Its biggest claims to future fame included showcasing a very young Robert Morse (as teenager Jerry Ames, 1954), Roy Scheider (Bob Hill, 1967), and smaller roles for Troy Donahue and Donna Mills.

See It Now. *1951–55, CBS.* Television's all-time most important and impressive newsmagazine, more so even than *60 Minutes*, was also its first. It began in an almost hidden time slot—3:30 on a Sunday afternoon—with reporter Edward R. Murrow and director Don Hewitt broadcasting live from a cramped CBS News studio. "This is an old team," Murrow said on that initial installment, "trying to learn a new trade." The key components of that team, Murrow and producer Fred Friendly, had linked up four years earlier, when CBS Radio veteran reporter Murrow, of "This . . . is London" fame (it was with that phrase that Murrow opened his live reports from the city's rooftops, describing the bombing raids and burning buildings during World War II), agreed to narrate a series of spoken-word long-playing records presenting actual recordings of historic events and speeches since the development of recorded sound. Their first effort, a five-record set called *I Can Hear It Now, 1933–45,* became an instant hit in 1948, leading to LP sequels and, in 1950, a continuation of the partnership on the CBS Radio spinoff, *Hear It Now.* Almost instantly, *Hear It Now* went from recounting old news to seeking out "new" news: relaying the sound of artillery fire from ground level of the Korean War, or letting viewers listen as an atom smasher was switched on. A year later, Murrow and Friendly transplanted *Hear It Now* to television, with the obvious name change and an even more obvious affinity for the new medium. Throughout his radio career, Murrow was like an Ernie Kovacs of news, always eager to put new technologies to previously untapped uses, and he dove into television more eagerly than might be expected from a career radio reporter. On that very first *See It Now,* director Hewitt (who later created *60 Minutes)* opened the show by presenting, at Murrow's command, images on separate TV monitors—unprecedented simultaneous live views of the Brooklyn Bridge in the East and the Golden Gate Bridge in the West. In his now-famous, often-quoted narration, Murrow said, "We are impressed by a medium in which a man sitting in his living room has been able for the first time to look at two oceans at once." (Perhaps, on that inaugural occasion, the show should have been called *Sea It Now.)* The same program featured Eric Sevareid from Washington, Howard K. Smith from Paris, and Robert Pierpoint from Korea, a clear demonstration of the range, seriousness, and ambition of this new network program. Less than a year after its debut, *See It Now* moved into an early Sunday evening time slot, then, in 1953, into prime time. Not every week's show was a classic, but many classics were among them, including *The Case of Lieutenant Milo Radulovich* (the first *See It Now* to tackle the tactics used to identify, label, and punish "Communist sympathizers"), profiles of physicist J. Robert Oppenheimer and poet-historian Carl Sandburg, and *Christmas in Korea,* a 1952 *See It Now* special in which Murrow visited and interviewed frontline troops during the Korean

War. (That wartime documentary would be approximated years later in a very memorable episode of *M*A*S*H*, with Clete Roberts conducting interviews and basically playing the part of Murrow.) Yet no other report in the history of *See It Now*—or, arguably, in the history of television—was more important than the March 9, 1954, *Report on Senator Joseph R. McCarthy*. Afterward, *New York Times* critic Jack Gould called it "a foretaste to television's true glory." Sadly, as things turned out, it was less an appetizer than the main course. But what poetry and bravery! "The line between investigation and persecuting is a very fine one," Murrow said during that half-hour show, "and the Junior Senator from Wisconsin has stepped over it repeatedly. . . . We must not confuse dissent with disloyalty." At the program's climax, Murrow looked straight into the camera and said gravely, "We cannot defend freedom abroad by deserting it at home. The actions of the Junior Senator from Wisconsin have caused alarm and dismay among our allies abroad, and given considerable comfort to our enemies. And whose fault is that? Not really his. He didn't create this situation of fear; he merely exploited it, and rather successfully. Cassius was right. 'The fault, dear Brutus, is not in our stars, but in ourselves.' " Then, as always, Murrow signed off, "Good night, and good luck." Director Hewitt said later, quite accurately, "That night, television came of age." Unfortunately, TV soon "outgrew" *See It Now*, because game shows had proven more popular and lucrative. By 1955, *See It Now* was relegated to a series of specials; after its cancellation in 1958, Murrow reappeared on the show's spiritual successor, *CBS Reports*, doing such continued great work as *Harvest of Shame*. For CBS, and all of television, the real shame was that *See It Now* could not find a safe and perennial home. (In 1986, Bill Moyers tried to interest CBS in reviving the series with himself as host; the network, missing a golden opportunity, passed, and let Moyers go back to PBS.) Only in retrospect, it seems, is *See It Now* truly appreciated for what it was. Both PBS and CBS, in recent years, have produced in-depth, loving specials devoted to Murrow in general and the *See It Now* McCarthy broadcast in particular, and bemoaning the general demise of network news documentaries. How ironic: now that we love *See It Now*, we *can't* see it now.

Seinfeld. *1990–   , NBC.* When *Seinfeld* first appeared on NBC, as a one-shot pilot called *The Seinfeld Chronicles*, cowriters Jerry Seinfeld and Larry David already had the basic concept down: less is more. This was to be, in a phrase that came to summarize the show neatly if too simplistically, "a show about nothing." It was to be about the little things in life—the wait for a table at a restaurant, the search for the perfect piece of fruit, the fight for a free curbside parking space. Yet in the original pilot designed by Seinfeld and David, some now-familiar elements of *Seinfeld* were missing. There was no endearingly goofy segue music, no Elaine (Julia Louis-Dreyfus joined the cast a few episodes into the series), and a very different Kramer. In that protean *Seinfeld Chronicles* version, the character played by Michael Richards is not only a recluse ("You haven't been out of the building in ten years," Jerry tells him), but when Kramer enters a room, he knocks first, and waits for the door to be opened. Times changed, and when *Seinfeld* went to series a year later,

Kramer's high-energy entrances eventually became one of the show's many hallmarks—along with key phrases, recurring characters, and several defiantly unusual plot lines. The first great *Seinfeld* episode, the one that solidified the show's against-the-grain identity, was "The Chinese Restaurant," in which Jerry and friends spent the entire episode waiting to be seated for dinner. Then came "The Parking Garage" (a lost car leads to all sorts of trouble, including multiple arrests for public urination); "The Pick" (a show about, among other things, proper nose-cleaning etiquette); "The Outing" (the hilarious episode that introduced the disclaimer "Not that there's anything wrong with that," said by Jerry or Jason Alexander's George whenever they denied being gay); "The Implant" (the show that popularized both Teri Hatcher and the concept of "double dipping"); "The Junior Mint" (in which Jerry, remembering only that his date's name rhymes with a female body part, mistakenly comes up with "Mulva"—among other, less famous tries, like "Delores" and "Aretha"); "The Puffy Shirt" (a visual gag of unforgettably frilly proportions); "The Marine Biologist" (in which Kramer's oceanside golf game and George's occupational impersonation became amazingly and unforgettably intertwined); and "The Hamptons" (in which, discussing the condition of male genitalia after bathing, George uses the memorable term "shrinkage"). Most recently, *Seinfeld* added another classic episode of the mix by introducing "The Soup Nazi" (a man, based on a real cook in New York, whose love for making gourmet soups was matched only by his dislike for the people to whom he sold them). Other touchstones along the way include Cosmo (Kramer's more recently revealed first name), Cuban cigars, the Virgin, the Bubble Boy, the spot, the smelly car, subplots that intertwined like strands of DNA, and Jerry's nastily delivered greeting, "Hello, Newman!" However, the ultimate *Seinfeld*, and writer-producer Larry David's most brilliant triumph, was "The Contest," in which Jerry, George, Kramer, and Elaine placed bets on which of them could refrain the longest from masturbating—a word never once uttered in a show featuring a dazzlingly clever array of euphemisms, including that mother of all catch phrases, "Master of Your Domain," referring to successful abstention from self-abuse. Getting away with this sort of subject matter in prime time, and making it hilarious as well, qualifies the *Seinfeld* folks as Masters of Their Domain—as well as the inspiration for such other friendship-obsessed sitcoms as, well, *Friends*. Not that there's anything wrong with that. . . .

Selling of the Pentagon, The. *1971, CBS.* Along with Edward R. Murrow's *See It Now* McCarthy telecast and the *Harvest of Shame* documentary for *CBS Reports*, this program (also from *CBS Reports*) ranks as one of commercial network television's most famous nonfiction specials. Perhaps only the title is remembered today, but this study, written and produced by Peter Davis and reported by Roger Mudd, questioned the government's prowar stance, and specifically its public-relations budget and intense lobbying efforts, at a time predating the Pentagon Papers. Mudd accused the military of conducting a "propaganda barrage" aimed at its own citizens, occasionally misleading them and the media as part of a deliberate policy. *The Selling of* *the Pentagon* proved so controversial and popular that it was rebroadcast a month after its premiere, generating even higher ratings the second time around. (Try that with a lot of other documentaries, and see what happens.) Considering that 1996 marks the twenty-fifth anniversary of *The Selling of the Pentagon*, CBS could do a lot worse than to plan a next-generation sequel.

Sgt. Bilko. See *Phil Silvers Show, The.*

Sesame Street. *1969– , PBS.* PBS, the Public Broadcasting Service, was born on November 3, 1969, replacing National Educational Television (NET) as the service providing noncommercial programming for viewers nationwide. One week later, on November 10, PBS presented its first episode of *Sesame Street*, a series that still is on the air, and now ranks as one of the most important TV shows the medium has ever presented. It's the place where many of our children are first exposed to allusion and satire, and get to enjoy jokes based on their then-tiny body of stored knowledge: nursery rhymes, fairy tales, popular music, and other TV shows. What, on TV, counts more than a show that teaches preschoolers to count, and read, and develop both a sense of self and a sense of humor? *Sesame Street* has been around so long that viewers who watched it as toddlers have grown up to revisit it with their own children—and though both the neighborhood and the cast of characters have expanded, and (unfortunately) the long-running theme song and opening credits have been replaced, *Sesame Street* remains a familiar, friendly place to visit. The cultural touchstones here are many—and so durable that the Cookie Monster's "Me want cookie!" is one of only a handful of television-related quotes included in the most recent edition of *Bartlett's Familiar Quotations*. Despite the warmth and talent of the show's human cast members, from Bob McGrath's Bob (who has been with *Sesame Street* since its inception) to such recent additions as Ruth Buzzi's Ruthie, most of this show's best and most memorable moments come courtesy of Jim Henson's Muppets. Kermit the Frog has been there from the start, and 123 Sesame Street would be a much emptier address without Big Bird, the Cookie Monster, Oscar the Grouch, Elmo, Grover, Count von Count, Snuffleupagus, and especially Bert and Ernie (named after the affable policemen in *It's a Wonderful Life*) in residence. Everyone has different favorite *Sesame Street* segments and characters; mine would include "Monsterpiece Theatre," Oscar, Bert and Ernie, and the guest appearances by Muppet approximations of reigning pop-culture figures, from Meryl Sheep and H. Ross Parrot to Placido Flamingo. And, of course, there's the music, which over the years has included an infinite number of number songs, and at least twenty-six songs devoted to the alphabet. It also includes some occasional *Sesame Street* "standards," such as the 1970 Top 20 hit novelty song "Rubber Duckie" (sung by Henson as Ernie) and "Put Down the Duckie," sung on the show by, among others, Paul Simon, John Candy, and Madeline Kahn. For good reason, *Sesame Street* is the most widely viewed children's series in the world, with the American version shown in more than forty countries, and with many nations producing their own authorized local versions, such as Germany's *Sesamstrasse* and Norway's

Sesam Stasjon. In America, oddly, some educators and watchdog groups feel that *Sesame Street* is bad for kids, and that the quick pace of the show makes them bored by the time they get to school. To which I say: I doubt very much whether that's true, and even if it is, then it's the schools, not *Sesame Street*, that should adapt accordingly. This *Sesame Street* entry was brought to you by the letter S. . . .

700 Club, The. *1975–   , syndicated; 1977–   , Christian Broadcasting Network and the Family Channel.* The Reverend Pat Robertson, son of a Virginia senator, started his TV empire the same way as another privileged media visionary, Ted Turner—by buying a low-rated UHF television station and using it, and then satellite-delivered cable TV, to deliver his programming and expand his power base. Robertson acquired his first TV station, a nearly bankrupt facility in Portsmouth, Virginia, in 1961; two years later, he kept his religious programming afloat by asking for pledges of ten-dollar monthly donations from seven hundred viewers. In 1966, Robertson staffers Jim and Tammy Faye Bakker got their own talk show, styled after *The Tonight Show Starring Johnny Carson* and, in honor of Robertson's most loyal financial supporters, titled *The 700 Club*. After six years, the Bakkers left to establish *The P.T.L. Club* (and, even later, to embroil themselves in financial and sexual scandals), and Robertson took over as host, with Ben Kinchlow as second banana. Robertson stepped down from *The 700 Club* in 1986 to begin an unsuccessful yet significant run for the presidency of the United States, and resumed his hosting chores after leaving the race in 1988. *The 700 Club* now steals from David Letterman, not Johnny Carson (when Kinchlow wears a particularly garish tie, viewers are treated to a close-up shot from the show's "Tie-Cam"), but its news and features are presented in a polished, lengthy, and often incendiary fashion. (If you've never seen the show, imagine if Walter Cronkite gave his opinion after every story, then decided to run for office, and you'll get a basic idea of Robertson's approach.) In 1992, Robertson gave a speech at the Republican National Convention that was unsettlingly exclusionary, and surely hurt his party's chances for retaining presidential power that year. In 1995, with the Christian Coalition power base formed after his failed 1988 bid, Robertson exerted significant power and policy within the right wing of the Republican party, while still commenting on politics as well as religion on his *700 Club* bully pulpit.

77 Sunset Strip. *1958–64, ABC.* The finger-popping theme song is the best-remembered thing about this often silly private-eye series, which came from the prolific Roy Huggins, whose pre-77 credits (referring to the TV series, not the calendar year) include *Maverick*, and whose post-77 credits include *The Fugitive, The Rockford Files*, and *Baretta*. In all of those other series, it was the central hero who made the biggest impression. But on *77 Sunset Strip*, it was a supporting character who ran away with the show: Edd Byrnes as Cookie, the jive-talking, hair-combing parking-lot attendant who became a teen phenomenon (best explained, perhaps, as pre-Beatlemania hysteria). Cookie "dug" things, chased "dreamboats," and called his elders "daddy-o."

He at least seemed to be enjoying himself—unlike his stiff costars (especially Efrem Zimbalist, Jr., and Roger Smith), who, to use one of Cookie's terms, were "squaresville, man." Byrnes was such an instant hit that, before the first season was over, his 1959 recording (with Connie Stevens) of "Kookie, Kookie (Lend me Your Comb)" was a Top 10 hit. Today, most of 77 *Sunset Strip* looks about as tacky as that awning in the opening credits. Yet it was a genre pioneer—the first hour-long detective series on television—and, for at least a while, the popularity of Edd Byrnes made him a real Kookie monster.

Shakespeare Plays, The. *1979–85, PBS.* This six-year BBC presentation of all thirty-seven of William Shakespeare's plays was more ambitious than successful, with a few outright flops (especially *Romeo and Juliet*, done by performers who were the same ages as the youthful title characters, and acted like it) and only six unqualified successes. Even so, it ranks as one of the biggest single undertakings in TV history, and included such interesting casting choices as John Cleese in *Taming of the Shrew* and Ben Kingsley and Judy Davis in *The Merry Wives of Windsor.* The six truly triumphant productions, though, were *As You Like It*, starring Helen Mirren as a radiant Rosalind; *A Midsummer Night's Dream*, with Mirren again, this time as Titania; *Measure for Measure*, with Kate Nelligan as Isabel; *Hamlet*, starring Derek Jacobi; a controversial yet compelling *Othello*, with Bob Hoskins as Iago and Anthony Hopkins, Moor or less, in the title role; and *Titus Andronicus*, starring Eileen Atkins in the Shakespearean equivalent of a splatter film (severed tongues and limbs abound, with dead bodies all around). Unfortunately, these productions have not been repeated by PBS in the decade since their original presentation; even more unfortunately, the mere existence of an "official" TV canon has led to a predictable lack of subsequent Shakespearean TV productions, discouraging what should be a much more frequent source for adaptation and inspiration. There already has been one notable exception, however. A syndicated Mobil Showcase Network presentation of *King Lear*, televised in 1984 (two years after an inferior *Shakespeare Plays* version), offered a classic performance of a classic drama, with Laurence Olivier in the title role and Diana Rigg as Regan. That dazzling dramatization proved, quite convincingly, that *The Shakespeare Plays* had no meaningful monopoly on the playwright's works—but a decade after *The Shakespeare Plays* was first telecast, it has yet to be repeated as a full cycle. And while both Mel Gibson and Kenneth Branagh have mounted new movie versions of classic Shakespearean dramas and histories, distressingly few TV producers since *The Shakespeare Plays* have displayed any eagerness to belly up to the Bard.

Shari Lewis Show, The. *1960–63, NBC.* **Shariland.** *1957, NBC.* **The Shari Show.** *1975, syndicated.* **Lamb Chop's Play-Along!,** *1992– , PBS.* In 1952, when Shari Lewis was in her late teens, she took a ventriloquist's dummy named Samson and won first prize on TV's *Arthur Godfrey's Talent Scouts.* Four years later, after headlining a local New York children's show called *Facts 'n' Fun*, she was given a guest shot on *Captain Kangaroo*, and asked to bring along something "softer" than a typical wooden sidekick. Reaching into her sock drawer for inspiration, Lewis emerged with the idea for the sock-puppet character of Lamb Chop—and once Shari had a little lamb, stardom was right around the corner. Hush Puppy and Charlie Horse were the other major puppet characters given life by Lewis (who was a much better ventriloquist than Edgar Bergen), but Lamb Chop was the runaway star. That point was driven home, three decades after the original run of *The Shari Lewis Show,* when the puppet took top billing in the PBS series *Lamb Chop's Play-Along!* (and entertained a new generation of kids, while providing a new form of musical torture for parents, thanks to her frequent repetition of "The Song That Never Ends"). Also in the nineties, Lewis and Lamb Chop popped up on an episode of *The Nanny,* where viewers could be treated to the rather unsettling sight of Lamb Chop being carried around in the jaws of a dog (not to mention the sight of Lamb Chop flirting with a grown man, which was even more disturbing). Between her sixties showcase and her nineties come-back, how did Shari Lewis keep herself busy? For one thing, by cowriting "The Lights of Zetar," a 1969 episode of *Star Trek.*

Shelley Duvall's Faerie Tale Theatre. See *Faerie Tale Theatre.*

Shindig! *1964–66, ABC.* In the midsixties, *Hullabaloo* was the rock 'n' roll show with all the mod dancers. *Shindig!,* which predated *Hullabaloo,* had its own dance troupe, but they were less obtrusive: if you were more interested in the music than the go-go girls, *Shindig!* was the place you went-went. In those days, this prime-time showcase was the closest thing to MTV—a place where the newest songs and acts were presented by someone younger than Ed Sullivan and hipper than Dick Clark. Taking its cue from the musical diversity of the era, *Shindig!* was dazzlingly eclectic. Pioneer rockers (Chuck Berry, Jerry Lee Lewis) shared the bills with soul singers (Marvin Gaye, Aretha Franklin). Sonny & Cher and Neil Sedaka performed on *Shindig!,* and so did James Brown and the Who, Tina Turner and the Beach Boys, the Supremes and the Righteous Brothers. One special program, produced in England and broadcast in October 1964, showcased the Beatles. Most *Shindig!* shows were performed and presented live, disdaining the common practice of lip-synching to studio recordings. *Shindig!* came and went quickly, but had a lot of impact at the time: its second-season premiere in 1965 featured the Rolling Stones, the Byrds, the Kinks, and the Everly Brothers. In the nineties, some episodes of *Shindig!* finally resurfaced, presented in reruns on VH-1 (now VH1) and in half-hour compilations on Rhino Home Video. If you looked closely at the "Shindogs" house band, you could try and catch a glimpse of one of its occasional members, keyboard player Leon Russell.

Shogun. *1980, NBC.* This post-*Roots,* twelve-hour long-form drama is one of the highest-rated miniseries of all time (in fifth place, behind *Roots, The Thorn Birds, The Winds of War,* and 1976's *Helter Skelter,* a CBS dramatization of the Charles Manson murder trial). *Shogun* also is one of the very best, with an exotic setting (feudal Japan), an exciting story (the English pilot of a Dutch ship is captured in Japan), and an educational approach (we learn, as the pilot does, about Japanese language, customs, and beliefs). Richard Chamberlain, who would earn his "King of the Miniseries" title because of his work here (along with his roles in *Centennial* and *The Thorn Birds*), stars as pilot John Blackthorne, who eventually assimilates enough Japanese culture to become honored as a samurai. It's a wonderful performance by Chamberlain, and his work is matched by John-Rhys Davies as fellow pilot Rodrigues, Toshiro Mifune as the warlord Toranaga, and Yoko Shimada as interpreter Lady Mariko. *Shogun* author James Clavell had written the screenplays for *The Great Escape* and *The Fly*, and both written and directed *To Sir, with Love*, but the task of adapting *Shogun* for television fell to Eric Bercovici, who came up with the key—though risky—concept of showing everything only through Blackthorne's eyes. This meant many scenes of Japanese dialogue, untranslated and unsubtitled, as Blackthorne (and viewers) tried to make sense of what was happening. The approach worked so well that by the end of *Shogun*, most viewers were sufficiently educated and enthused to say *arigato* to NBC for presenting such a bold and distinctive miniseries. In 1993, NBC announced plans to turn another of Clavell's "Asian Saga" novels, *Gai-Jin*, into an eight-hour miniseries, but pulled up stakes and abandoned the *Gai-Jin* project one week after production had begun in Japan in 1995. NBC, frightened by escalating costs, obviously retreated because it was more concerned with saving money than with saving face.

Simpson, O. J., Low-Speed Chase. *1994, all networks.* Amazing but true: up to that point, no single event in the history of television was covered live by as many different networks as the June 17, 1994, "low-speed chase" in which police located, followed, and eventually apprehended O. J. Simpson, freshly named a murder suspect in the deaths of ex-wife Nicole Brown Simpson and Ron Goldman, who had been stabbed to death on June 12 outside of her home. Simpson's white Ford Bronco, driven by friend Al Cowlings, slowly negotiated the freeways of Southern California as Simpson sat in the back seat, a cellular phone in one hand and a revolver, pointed at his own chin, in the other. Because live televised car chases are something of a cottage industry in Southern California (go figure), each local station soon had its own airborne images to relay, and broadcast and cable networks scarfed them up in unprecedented fashion. Not only did CBS, ABC, and CNN run with live coverage from start to finish, but even NBC, which was televising the fifth game of the NBA Finals, preempted its sports coverage for a significant stretch to follow the Simpson story—and, literally, to follow Simpson. That's the typical sort of wall-to-wall competitive coverage TV provides in cases of hot breaking news, whether the story be a fiery showdown in Waco, a terrorist explosion in Oklahoma City, or devastating earthquakes in California. Because of Simpson's celebrity, though, the rest of TV's coverage was much less typical. Viewers could watch the low-speed chase unfold that night not only on the major broadcast networks and CNN, but also live on such cable networks as CNN Headline News, ESPN, E! Entertainment, and even, as a measure of Simpson's international celebrity status, the Spanish-language Univision network. Not even the Persian Gulf war got that sort of coverage. (The same networks all returned the following month, it should be noted, to provide live coverage as Simpson entered his plea of "absolutely, one hundred percent not guilty.") Networks began relaying pictures from Los Angeles shortly before 10 P.M. eastern time, and the amazement voiced by Larry King, whose *Larry King Live* talk show shifted into impromptu coverage of the "low-speed chase" between Simpson and police, was both typical and accurate: "There has never," he said simply, "been a story like this." Simpson's surreal road trip was accompanied by a bevy of squad cars at ground level, a swarm of news helicopters hovering above, and, inexplicably, impromptu roadside rows of onlookers cheering for Simpson as he eventually made his way back to his Brentwood home. News crews were parked alongside the street as the Bronco came to rest in Simpson's driveway, but it was KCBS-TV helicopter pilot Bob Tur, the same airborne reporter who shot the famous video of the Reginald Denny beating, who broke the story of Simpson's surrender, putting him way above his competitors in more ways than one. At ABC, the best information came from sportscaster Al Michaels, who, ironically, had replaced O. J. Simpson years earlier in the broadcast booth on *Monday Night Football*. And while the image of a slowly moving white Bronco is now part of our collective cultural memory, there's a grisly reason behind it. As many as ninety-five million viewers were estimated as having seen all or part of the live, low-speed Simpson chase, and surely some of that interest was due to the fact that Simpson, on that night, seemed headed for a fatal ending himself. Instead, he lived to "star" in another TV event, one even more improbable, incredible, unprecedented, and unforgettable. . . .

Simpson, O. J., Murder Trial, Verdict, and Aftermath. *1995, Court TV, CNN, E! Entertainment, occasional broadcast network coverage, various other cable networks.* On July 22, 1994, as he was arraigned on murder charges for the second time in five weeks, O. J. Simpson announced to the court, and the world, that he was "absolutely, one hundred percent not guilty." On October 3, 1995, the jury agreed with him, and set him free—free to return home in his white Bronco, with news helicopters hovering overhead and relaying live TV pictures of his uncannily familiar low-speed journey. What happened in between, in terms of both TV coverage and legal posturing, was almost beyond belief. Judge Lance A. Ito, on the day he was assigned to preside over the case, told the *Los Angeles Times*, "The sirens of mythology pale in comparison to the allure of seeing yourself on CNN. The results, however, can be about the same." Those sirens, and others, almost never stopped singing—and over on *The Tonight Show*, in the form of "The Dancing Itos," they danced, too. From start to finish, CNN covered an estimated six hundred hours of Simpson trial coverage. Court TV, which did the best job overall, provided some seven hundred hours, and the cable network offering the worst coverage of all, E! Entertainment Television, also offered the most: almost one thousand hours of Simpson-related stories. Because it seemed people couldn't get enough of this story, the media basically approached the story with the idea that nothing succeeds like excess. One TV low point occurred early, when, only one week after prosecutors Marcia Clark and

Christopher Darden presented their opening statements, the Fox television network presented *The O. J. Simpson Story*, starring Bobby Hosea in the title role, Jessica Tuck as Nicole Brown Simpson, and Bruce Weitz as Simpson attorney Robert Shapiro. At the beginning of the trial, Shapiro looked to be the star of the defense's "Dream Team"—but by the end, it was Johnnie Cochran who had stolen the spotlight and, during his closing argument on September 27, delivered the trial's most memorable sound bite. Referring to his client's struggling attempt to don leather gloves found at the crime scene (the trial's most potent, if silly, image), Cochran told the jury, "If it doesn't fit, you must acquit!" For a trial that consumed so much air time for so long, relatively little of it resonates after the fact, but certain things do, for a variety of reasons. There was the tearful testimony of Denise Brown, Nicole's sister, who attracted more CNN trial watchers than any other witness; the angry, impromptu press conference held by Fred Goldman, Ron's father; the puppylike Brian "Kato" Kaelin, whose Farrah Fawcett hair and eager-to-please manner made him seem almost like the court jester; the "race card" wild card of Detective Mark Fuhrman, who denied making racial epithets, but was caught on tape, tainting his entire testimony; the description of the "plaintive wail" of a neighborhood dog the night of the murder; and, most of all, the dramatic climax, with Cochran happily hugging Simpson from behind as the "not guilty" verdict was read. At 1 P.M. eastern time, on October 3, mere minutes before the verdict was to be read, channel-surfers could tune in and watch the proceedings not only on CBS, NBC, ABC, CNN, and Court TV, but on Fox, E!, CNN Headline News, ESPN, ESPN2, Univision, CNBC, and even MTV. Estimates on the viewing audience for the verdict went as high as 150 million, and CBS executive David Poltrack called it the "most-watched live event ever." There are many more people and televisions now than there were in the days of the moon landing and the John F. Kennedy funeral, he explained. And while its daytime aggregate Nielsen rating of 42.9 (with a whopping 91 percent share of the audience) is not in itself a record, the added viewership outside of the home that day—at work and elsewhere—pushed it over the top. In its end-of-1995 issue, *Time* ranked the O. J. Simpson trial as the Number One show of the year, and called the verdict "the single most suspenseful moment in television history." (Sorry, but I still think landing and walking on the moon ranks a little higher.) At any rate, after appearing in what *Time* called the Show of the Year, Simpson failed to appear in what could only be described as the No-Show of the Year: agreeing to be interviewed live on *Dateline NBC* by Katie Couric and Tom Brokaw, then backing out on the day of the scheduled prime-time interview (October 11, 1995). At the last minute, Simpson apparently began to suspect that the interview would be too adversarial, and would no longer fit with his post-trial image rehabilitation plans. And if it doesn't fit, you must, uh, quit.

Simpsons, The. *1990– , Fox.* Actually, the dysfunctional yet adorable Simpson family goes back a lot further than that. Matt Groening first created them as the protagonists of an "unpublishable" novel, "Mean Kids," he wrote in high school ("my version of *Catcher in the Rye*," he explained). Much later, when producer James L. Brooks asked cartoonist Groening to create characters for a series of thirty-second animated shorts on Fox's *The Tracey Ullman Show* in 1987, Groening revived the Simpson name, jettisoned the profanity but retained the edge, and somehow floated his wonderfully warped vision right into the cultural mainstream. The rest is history, even though history didn't really kick in until Homer, Marge, Bart, Lisa, and Maggie Simpson left the *Tracey Ullman Show* nest and got their own series. Bart Simpson, whom Groening once likened to "what would happen if Eddie Haskell got his own show," quickly became an international icon, with such oft-quoted catch phrases as "Don't have a cow, man," "Ay, carumba!" and "I'm Bart Simpson. Who the hell are you?" Merchandising overkill went into high gear, but *The Simpsons* outlasted it. One major miracle of *The Simpsons* is that, like *The Bullwinkle Show*, it entertains several generations simultaneously. Another is that, like very few comedy shows in the history of television, it began brilliantly and never flagged; each season packs as many ideas, laughs, and cultural cross-references as the ones before it, and the acting and writing rival that of any other modern sitcom. The theme song, by Danny Elfman, is a classic, and millions scour the opening sequences each week to see how the Simpsons will end up on the TV-room couch this time, or what new phrases Bart writes repeatedly on the blackboard in detention. (My favorite: "I will not waste chalk.") Best episodes? "Simpsons Roasting on an Open Fire," the 1989 Christmas special that served as a full-length introductory pilot, would have to be one. Others would include "Bart Gets at F" (after actually trying to study); "Bart's Dog Gets an F" (in which Tracey Ullman, who showcased *The Simpsons* in the first place, is showcased as a regimental dog trainer); "A Streetcar Named Marge" (in which Marge and meek neighbor Ned Flanders star in a musical community-theater production of *A Streetcar Named Desire)*; "Lisa's First Word" (in which baby Maggie says her first and only word, "Daddy," to end the episode, with a voice provided by Elizabeth Taylor); all the "Tree House of Horror" Halloween outings; and what is perhaps the most fabulous episode of all, "Itchy & Scratchy & Marge." In that 1990 installment, broadcast long before *Beavis and Butt-Head* became an issue, Marge launches a crusade against the ultraviolent children's cartoon "Itchy & Scratchy," which happens to be the favorite show of both Bart and Lisa. Like Terry Rakolta, a housewife whose letter-writing campaign in protest of *Married . . . with Children* gained her a degree of notoriety, Marge finds herself in demand as a TV talk-show guest—in Marge's case, appearing on *Smartline,* the local version (and cartoon spoof) of *Nightline.* "Are cartoons too violent for children?" anchor Kent Brockman asks to open the *Smartline* show. "Most people would say, 'No, of course not, what kind of *stupid* question is that?' But one woman would say yes, and she's with us tonight. . . . " Harry Shearer provides the voice of Kent Brockman and dozens of other *Simpsons* characters, including rich Montgomery Burns (who was shot, to end the 1994–95 season, in an extended "Who Shot J. R.?" lampoon) and his sycophant Smithers, neighbor Ned Flanders, bus driver Otto, and even Scratchy. The show's four primary cast members are equally gifted, if not equally prolific: Dan Castellaneta provides the voice of Homer, but also the voices of Krusty the Clown, Barney, groundskeeper Willy, Grandpa Simpson, and Itchy. Julie Kavner does Marge and her sisters, Patty and Selma. Yeardley Smith is the voice of Lisa, and Nancy Cartwright, a woman, is the voice of Bart. Hank Azaria, another important contributor, provides the voices of Moe the bartender, Apu the convenience-store owner, and police chief Wiggum. (Guest voices over the years have included, in addition to Elizabeth Taylor, such notables as Johnny Carson, Kelsey Grammer, Glenn Close, Leonard Nimoy, Dustin Hoffman, Tony Bennett, Jon Lovitz, Winona Ryder, Audrey Meadows, Danny DeVito, Michelle Pfeiffer, Patrick Stewart, Donald Sutherland, an uncredited Michael Jackson, and, on separate occasions, Paul McCartney, George Harrison, and Ringo Starr.) Not only do those involved with *The Simpsons* not get enough credit, but they often get too much blame. At a pep rally for the 1992 Republican National Convention, then-President George Bush spoke to the crowd and said, "We are going to keep on trying to strengthen the American family . . . to make American families a lot more like the Waltons and a lot less like the Simpsons." A few days later, a rush animation job allowed Bart Simpson to open that week's episode of *The Simpsons* by watching, and responding to, Bush's remarks. "Hey, we're just like the Waltons," Bart replied. "Both families spend a lot of time praying for the end of the depression." Bart got renewed that year; Bush didn't. In another typically devilish *Simpsons* response to a real-life inspiration, *The Simpsons* concluded that aforementioned "Who Shot Mr. Burns?" two-parter (a story line poking fun at the "Who Shot J. R.?" cliff-hanger on *Dallas*, with good-hearted jabs at *The Fugitive* and *Twin Peaks* along the way) by revealing that baby Maggie, the youngest Simpson, was the accidental culprit. How did Police Chief Wiggum prove it was her? By subjecting the crime scene to a series of lab tests—and uncovering "Simpson DNA."

Sing Along with Mitch. *1961–64, NBC*. Bandleader and record producer Mitch Miller took the old "follow the bouncing ball" gimmick from musical film shorts, took it to television, and emerged with a music series popular enough to last four full years. The title *Sing Along with Mitch* still is remembered today, even if, thank goodness, most of the show's musical renditions are forgotten. Songs like "I've Been Working on the Railroad" were performed, while anything remotely connected to the rising phenomenon called rock 'n' roll was strongly avoided. All group songs were televised with superimposed lyrics, making Miller the spiritual predecessor of a popular musical movement. Just as Neil Young is considered the godfather of grunge, Mitch Miller arguably deserves partial credit as the kreator of karaoke.

Singing Detective, The. *1988, public TV*. This Dennis Potter miniseries, produced for BBC-TV in 1986 and televised in America two years later, quite simply is the best dramatic work ever written specifically for television. Ever. No exceptions; no qualifiers. Scores of other outstanding TV specials, dramas, comedies, and miniseries didn't make the cut in this book—not because they were in any way inferior to those that did, but because they failed to register the widespread impact or recognition that, in my definition, makes them a candidate for teleliteracy. In the miniseries genre alone, that strict standard leads to the unfortunate omission of a number of brilliant, daring, yet largely unheralded works from all around the world: America's *Concealed Enemies* (about the Alger Hiss case); Canada's *Anne of Green Gables* (a perfect adaptation of the Ludy Maud Montgomery novels); Germany's *Das Boot* (a six-hour U-boat miniseries trimmed to movie length for American theatrical distribution) and *Berlin Alexanderplatz* (by Rainer Werner Fassbinder); Sweden's *Scenes from a Marriage* (by Ingmar Bergman); Australia's *Bangkok Hilton* (a harrowing prison drama starring, in one of her first and best roles, Nicole Kidman); and such pioneering British miniseries as *Edge of Darkness* (about nuclear terrorism), *Rock Follies* (an MTV-style drama long before MTV existed), and Dennis Potter's *Pennies from Heaven*, a "drama with music" that, with Bob Hoskins as a sheet-music salesman given to light daydreams and dark deeds, is dazzling in its originality and brilliance. All of these pale, though, beside this other, later Potter masterpiece. And if *The Singing Detective* remains, at this writing, largely unknown and appreciated, I firmly believe (and hope) that, like the novels of Herman Melville and the paintings of Vincent Van Gogh, it will be recognized, embraced, and valued as genius by future generations. Therefore, I proudly, and a bit stubbornly, make room for it here. Right now, curious and discerning TV viewers can't even seek out *The Singing Detective* on video, because, at this writing, the 1986 production has yet to be released for that market. Nor has it yet been given a single national telecast in the United States. Both *Masterpiece Theatre* and *Great Performances* passed on *The Singing Detective* because Potter's contract insisted the drama be presented unedited, and PBS was wary of the film's occasional sex, nudity, and obscenities. On cable, the Arts & Entertainment Network backed away for the same reason, and *The Singing Detective* finally was sold on an *ad hoc* basis to specific PBS-member stations and televised on a local, market-by-market basis in 1988; in some cities, the best television drama in the history of the medium has yet to be shown even once. A thumbnail description fails to do it justice, but Potter's *The Singing Detective* is about a pulp fiction author named Philip Marlow (played superbly by Michael Gambon) hospitalized with a severe, debilitating skin disease. His treatments range from the pharmacological (drugs which, along with his high fevers, make him hallucinate) to the psychological (a psychiatrist interrogating Marlow is certain the psoriasis is linked to a traumatic event from the author's youth). To defiantly combat both kinds of treatments, Marlow busies himself by mentally rewriting one of his pulp novels, *The Singing Detective*, into a screenplay, with a healthy version of himself as the leading man. But the memories and hallucinations keep percolating to the surface, leading to a stunning collision of past and present, fantasy and reality, trust and paranoia, and drama and music (lip-synched songs from the forties play a major part). Coproduced by Kenith Trodd (who also produced *Pennies from Heaven)* and John Harris, and directed by Jon Amiel, *The Singing Detective* uses images, music, overlapping dialogue, and its epic seven-and-a-half-hour length to create a work of art ideally suited for television, one clearly demonstrating the medium's full potential. It also contains one of TV's most memorable lines of

LEFT: *Sesame Street*, with Snuffleupagus and Big Bird.
RIGHT: *Shogun*, with Richard Chamberlain as Blackthorne.

The Simpsons, with a scene
from "Who Shot Mr. Burns?"

dialogue: the one in which Joanne Whalley-Kilmer, as the beautiful nurse applying salve to Marlow's hideously inflamed skin, politely tells him, "I'm sorry, but I shall have to lift your penis now to grease around it."

Siskel & Ebert. See *Sneak Previews.*

Six Million Dollar Man, The. *1974–78, ABC.* This stupid series starred Lee Majors as a cyborg superhero, with one bionic eye and arm and two bionic legs. Eventually, a spinoff series, starring Lindsay Wagner, showcased *The Bionic Woman,* who had one bionic ear and arm and two bionic legs. Both of these cyborgs, for the most part, left me cybord. One question never fully addressed, in either series or in several subsequent telemovies, was precisely what was between their respective bionic legs. Like *The Man from U.N.C.L.E.* and *The Girl from U.N.C.L.E.,* this series and its sister spinoff ran simultaneously on network television, with the same boss (in this case, Richard Anderson as Oscar) doling out their respective secret-agent assignments. The series and telemovies also introduced a bionic boy, girl, and dog, but the only things that really stuck in all these cyborg stories were the slow-motion action sequences and the accompanying twangy sound effects. It's worth noting, however, that the 1989 telemovie *The Bionic Showdown* featured, as the new bionic girl, a young actress named Sandra Bullock, who eventually would go from bionic slow-motion to bus-driving *Speed.*

$64,000 Question, The. *1955–58, CBS.* **The $64,000 Challenge.** *1956–58, CBS.* Back in the forties, a radio quiz show called *Take It or Leave It* gave winning contestants the opportunity to take the money and run, or either double or lose it by fielding another, even tougher question. Prize money started at one dollar and ended, if the contestant went all the way, with "the sixty-four-dollar question"—a phrase that not only became the show's eventual new title, but, when radio was king, became synonymous with a truly crucial query. Then television flexed its muscles, co-opted the concept, added three zeroes, and upped the stakes to *The $64,000 Question.* It was a gamble that, for a while, paid off big for CBS. In its first full season on the air, *The $64,000 Question* was TV's top-rated show, quickly spawning a spinoff series, *The $64,000 Challenge,* in much the same way Arthur Godfrey had spawned two quick hits, *Arthur Godfrey's Talent Scouts* and *Arthur Godfrey and His Friends,* a few years earlier. The cliff-hanger format of *The $64,000 Question,* with winners of each round returning the next week to announce whether they would continue, made it TV's first big-money, big-hit, prime-time quiz show. Many contestants became celebrities as a result of their impressive displays of specific-topic knowledge: Dr. Joyce Brothers won the top prize answering questions about boxing, and Barbara Feldon, long before becoming Agent 99 on *Get Smart,* proved she already *was* smart by correctly answering fourteen progressively difficult questions about William Shakespeare. After Charles Van Doren won all that money and acclaim on *Twenty-One,* one of this show's many imitators, *The $64,000 Question* lifted its self-imposed prize-money ceiling and allowed winners to keep piling up money; however, as Van

Doren and *Twenty-One* became embroiled in the quiz show scandal, both *$64,000* shows plummeted in the ratings and quickly were canceled. A syndicated revival version doubled the pot in 1976, but *The $128,000 Question* went nowhere, even though one of the show's two hosts was future *Jeopardy!* star Alex Trebek. When, if ever, will another knowledge-based quiz show appear in prime time and make the Top 10? That, of course, is the sixty-four-thousand-dollar question.

60 Minutes. *1968–   , CBS.* In a 1967 memo, Don Hewitt—the man who had directed, among other things, the premiere of *See It Now* and the first Nixon-Kennedy presidential debate—asked his CBS bosses, "Somewhere in all the minutes of make-believe . . . couldn't we make room for sixty minutes of reality?" The following year, a show called *60 Minutes,* created by Hewitt, made its debut. All these years later, *60 Minutes* still is running, and Hewitt still is running it. The show has not merely survived, but, until very recently, has thrived. It's been in the Top 10 every year from 1977 to 1995, and has finished the season as TV's top-rated show four different times—in three different decades. (Top honors were earned in 1979–80, 1982–83, 1991–92, and 1992–93.) No other prime-time TV series has had a Top 10 streak as long, or, for that matter, lasted as long, period. (According to TV historians Tim Brooks and Earle Marsh, *60 Minutes,* by dint of its popularity and durability, now ranks as the Number One TV series of all time.) And while *60 Minutes* had surprisingly few newsmagazine competitors and copycats its first decade on the air, since then there has been an absolute glut of *60 Minutes* wannabes—and some, like ABC's *20/20* and *Dateline NBC,* found and held their own audiences as well. At the beginning of 1996, for the first time in TV history, *20/20* actually (though only marginally) was outranking *60 Minutes* in the season-to-date Nielsen ratings. At the same time, *60 Minutes* was suffering not only from problems outside its control (the loss of its pro football lead-in and several key network affiliates), but from problems well within its control. Specifically, the program's largely untarnished reputation was hurt by some questionable journalistic actions regarding a tobacco-industry story. According to reports, *60 Minutes* had agreed not only to compensate an interview subject if his former tobacco-industry employers sued him for libel, but to give him veto power over whether the completed interview would run. It was, perhaps, the lowest hour in the history of *60 Minutes*—but if TV history is any indication, good newsmagazines have a way of learning from their most egregious mistakes (see also: *Dateline NBC* and *20/20*). As for the slight ratings decline, perhaps the real surprise there is that it took so long for it to happen. *60 Minutes* has stood firm for decades, with its ticking stopwatch becoming a TV icon, and with anchor Mike Wallace, like executive producer Hewitt, going the entire distance. The mixture of investigative and celebrity journalism on *60 Minutes* really was nothing more, and nothing less, than a one-stop blend of the two TV styles of Edward R. Murrow: part hard-hitting *See It Now,* part softball-lobbing *Person to Person).* Since *60 Minutes* began—back when Lyndon B. Johnson was still in the White House—certain of the show's segments and techniques have come and gone. The "Point/Counterpoint" debate format, later parodied by Jane Curtin and Dan Aykroyd on *Saturday Night Live*, was retired in favor of "A Few Minutes with Andy Rooney," while the hidden cameras and ambush interviews typifying early *60 Minutes* investigative pieces eventually fell by the wayside. Overall, though, the series has been a model of consistency. In its entire history to date, *60 Minutes* has had only nine primary correspondents: Wallace, Harry Reasoner, Morley Safer, Dan Rather, Ed Bradley, Diane Sawyer, Steve Kroft, Meredith Vieira, and Lesley Stahl. In 1993, *60 Minutes* celebrated its silver anniversary with a two-hour prime-time special hosted by Charles Kuralt, who, with typical poetic flair, described Wallace's grand inquisitor role on *60 Minutes* as that of "a national district attorney." The outstanding program's long-standing popularity is a credit not only to the people who make *60 Minutes*, but to those who so loyally continue to watch it. Its most memorable stories and profiles, over the years, are a matter of personal taste. My votes would include certain celebrity profiles (Bradley's interviews with Lena Horne and George Burns, Wallace's with Vladimir Horowitz, Kroft's with Woody Allen, Safer's with Jackie Gleason); soft features (Reasoner's lyrical homage to *Casablanca);* and hard-hitting newsmaker interviews (Wallace's with the Shah of Iran, Stahl's interview with H. Ross Perot, and especially Kroft's with Bill and Hillary Clinton, which aired after *Super Bowl XXVI* in 1992, openly discussed the issue of his marital fidelity, and may well have kept Clinton's political career alive in much the same way that Richard M. Nixon's "Checkers" speech prolonged his). Also worth remembering are the breaking news stories (Rather's report from war-torn Afghanistan, his native wardrobe during which briefly and unfairly earned him the nickname "Gunga Dan"); hidden-camera stories (the all-time best of which included Rather's dishonest meat-inspector exposé and the "Highway Robbery" piece on crooked service-station mechanics); and extraordinary profiles of ordinary people (including, among many, Safer's interview with Holocaust survivor Fania Fenelon and Wallace's interview with secret service agent Clint Hill, who was on duty when John F. Kennedy was assassinated). And, most recently, there's the outstanding May 1995 edition the Sunday after the terrorist bombing in Oklahoma City, keyed specifically to an examination and discussion of that tragedy. Those are the triumphs of *60 Minutes*. The question at the midpoint of the nineties, though, is whether it can take a licking and keep on ticking. And whether Hewitt and Wallace will successfully turn over their franchise, in time, to a strong new regime, or see the fruits of their labor wither on one of TV's longest vines. These stories and more, on *60 Minutes*. Tickticktick. . . .

Six Wives of Henry VIII, The. *1971, CBS; 1972, PBS.* This 1970 BBC-TV miniseries was imported to America very quickly by CBS, because network founder William S. Paley was eager to generate the kind of "highbrow" prestige and excitement public TV had experienced by televising *The Forsyte Saga* in 1969. During the summer of 1971, CBS presented *The Six Wives of Henry VIII* as its first official long-form drama. Starring Keith Michell as the fickle monarch, the drama did indeed generate a lot of buzz, and even won Michell an Emmy—against such high-profile competition as both James Caan and Billy Dee Williams of *Brian's Song*. *The Six Wives of Henry VIII* was repeated the following January—not by CBS, which was more interested in ratings than recognition, but by PBS. The miniseries was presented on the fledgling anthology series *Masterpiece Theatre*, immediately before the United States premiere of another well-received BBC costume drama, Glenda Jackson as *Elizabeth R*. Those two dramas, run consecutively, did more for the literary image of PBS than *Six Wives* alone had done for CBS the previous summer, but each six-part drama was impressive in its own way. *Elizabeth R* had a terrific star turn by Jackson, and *The Six Wives of Henry VIII* had one of the best natural story structures ever for a dramatic miniseries: one wife per week.

Smith, William Kennedy, Rape Trial. *1991, Court TV and CNN.* The Kennedy name, even as a middle name, was enough to propel this Palm Beach trial onto the front pages—and to entice Court TV and CNN into televising gavel-to-gavel coverage for the duration of the December 1991 trial. William Kennedy Smith, nephew of Massachusetts Senator Edward M. Kennedy, was accused of rape by a woman who, throughout the trial, requested her identity not be divulged. Smith admitted to having sex with the woman, but insisted it was consensual, and the stage was set for what Court TV anchor Cynthia McFadden called "a trial seen by more people than any other in history." (This was, of course, pre-O. J. Simpson, but the Smith trial's unusually high ratings on CNN were a harbinger of things to come.) After Smith was found not guilty, his accuser went public on ABC's *PrimeTime Live*, revealing (or, to some news organizations, confirming) her identity as Patricia Bowman. However, it was when her identity was hidden that the Smith trial made its bid for teleliteracy, by forcing the networks to obscure her features electronically as she testified. Court TV used the same electronic masking used by the reality series *COPS*, but CNN, more famously, superimposed a big blue dot over Bowman's face. It was a visual echo, of sorts, of a famous case forty years earlier, when the fidgeting hands of mob figure Frank Costello were all that were shown during the televised 1951 Kefauver hearings on organized crime.

Smothers Brothers Comedy Hour, The. *1967–69, CBS.* You can't truly comprehend the importance of *The Smothers Brothers Comedy Hour* without knowing how it began, why it ended, and the prime-time TV climate in which it existed. In that context, though, *The Smothers Brothers Comedy Hour* was a perfect microcosm of the artistic aspirations and generational conflicts of the sixties. It melded the clever sketches and parodies of *Your Show of Shows*, the musical variety of *The Ed Sullivan Show*, and the topicality of *That Was the Week That Was* into a show all its own, one that paved the way for a new generation of American TV comedy—most specifically, *Rowan & Martin's Laugh-In*, *All in the Family*, and *Saturday Night Live*. *The Smothers Brothers Comedy Hour* came about, and amassed its prime-time power base, almost by accident. By 1966, NBC's *Bonanza* had been the top-rated show on television for three straight years, and CBS had thrown everyone from Judy

Garland to Garry Moore in the time slot, but to no avail. CBS then went to Tom and Dick Smothers, with a midseason order for thirteen shows; the brothers Smothers, unhappy with their experiences on the same network's 1965 sitcom *The Smothers Brothers Show*, asked for creative control. CBS had nothing to lose (the CBS series then opposite *Bonanza*, *The Garry Moore Show*, was the lowest-rated show on TV), so its executives agreed, and *The Smothers Brothers Comedy Hour* went on the air in February 1967. Within two months, it was a Top 20 show, a surprise hit attracting thirty million viewers each week—and guaranteeing its return the following fall as a certified hit series. The summer hiatus following those initial thirteen episodes was very significant, because it was the summer of 1967, the "summer of love," the summer of our discontent, the summer during which the Beatles released *Sgt. Pepper's Lonely Hearts Club Band*. When the Beatles brought an advance tape of that album to America and played it for friends at a special preview party, Tom Smothers was one of those in attendance. When Tom and Dick resumed production in September, it was with the desire to shake things up a little, and with the creative control and popular clout to make it happen. For example, their special guest on that first fall show in 1967 was folksinger Pete Seeger, who had been blacklisted from prime-time TV ever since his name was listed as an alleged "Communist sympathizer" in *Red Channels* in 1950. When the show was taped, one of the songs Seeger performed was a new composition called "Waist Deep in the Big Muddy," the final verse of which was an indirect yet clear criticism of then-President Lyndon B. Johnson's military policy regarding the Vietnam War. CBS refused to broadcast the song. Later that same season, though, Seeger was invited back, sang the song again, and it got past the network's in-house censors. Those same censors, however, won as many times as they lost, and became locked in weekly, intense battles with the stars and writers of *The Smothers Brothers Comedy Hour*. (Early in 1968, Tom and Dick took tapes of some of the sketches rejected by CBS and, in a typical display of defiance, showed them on NBC during a guest appearance on *The Tonight Show*.) Just prior to the critically competitive November ratings sweeps in 1968, CBS instituted a new policy of requiring the Smothers Brothers to turn in episode tapes for preview by network affiliates two days in advance. Those backstage battles with CBS finally erupted volcanically when a show delivered for broadcast on April 6, 1969, was rejected outright by the network—allegedly because it had failed to be delivered in time for preview, but more likely because of political pressure (Richard M. Nixon had been inaugurated just ten weeks earlier) and because CBS objected to guest David Steinberg's comic "sermonette" in which he comically, yet very innocuously, retold some Old Testament stories. CBS fired the Smothers Brothers outright, replaced the episode with a rerun, dropped the series from its schedule, and effectively torpedoed the duo's career. Yet what *The Smothers Brothers Comedy Hour* had done, in its three years on the air, could not be so easily erased. Though CBS and the censors found the series a source of constant irritation, most viewers did not. *The Smothers Brothers Comedy Hour* was a hit not because it widened the generation gap and alienated certain viewers, but because it walked the precipice and appealed to young and old alike. The eclectic guest rosters each week made *The Ed Sullivan Show,* its lead-in on CBS, look exclusionary by comparison. Bette Davis and Mickey Rooney appeared on the same show as the Who. Another show made room for Kate Smith and Simon & Garfunkel. On others, Jimmy Durante shared the bill with Janis Ian, and Don Knotts costarred with Mel Torme and Ravi Shankar. The show evolved and became more outspoken and impish (with increased references to drugs, Nixon, and the censors themselves), but the studio audience evolved even more. In 1967, those in attendance to watch *The Smothers Brothers Comedy Hour* in person looked like holdover crowds from *The Garry Moore Show;* by 1969, the Smothers Brothers were doing entire shows in the round, with a hip, hippie audience singing along to the likes (and songs) of Donovan and Peter, Paul & Mary. Musically, the show made many stars, and made friends of others. The Beatles sent a music video of them performing "Hey Jude," and George Harrison, in November 1968, showed up as an unannounced studio guest merely to voice his support of the Smothers Brothers: "Whether you can say it or not," he told them, referring to their battles with CBS censors, "keep *trying* to say it." The Who did their famously explosive rendition of "My Generation" on *The Smothers Brothers Comedy Hour,* and other performers appearing on the show included the Doors, Joan Baez, Buffalo Springfield, Jefferson Airplane, Ray Charles, the Everly Brothers, Ike & Tina Turner, Dion, Sonny & Cher, and the West Coast cast of *Hair.* And perhaps more than any other show on prime-time TV, *The Smothers Brothers Comedy Hour* embraced the media's past stars while simultaneously creating stars of the future. Most of television's (and radio's, and Broadway's) great comedy performers and personalities showed up to play: Steve Allen, Jack Benny, Edgar Bergen, Carol Burnett, George Burns, Sid Caesar, George Gobel, Elaine May, Robert Morse, Anthony Newley, Tony Randall, Carl Reiner, Danny Thomas, Andy Williams, and Jonathan Winters. Comics showcased on *Comedy Hour* included not only Steinberg, but Mort Sahl, George Carlin, and David Frye—as well as occasional appearances by such staff writers as Steve Martin, Rob Reiner, and Bob Einstein. Most of what is remembered about *The Smothers Brothers Comedy Hour,* in fact, comes from the core company. There's the banter of Tom and Dick, the "Mom always liked you best" and "Oh, yeah?" catch phrases, and the trademark songs. And the deadpan comic presence of Pat Paulsen, who began as an ersatz editorialist ("The Bill of Rights says nothing about Freedom of Hearing," he said in one editorial sarcastically supporting network censorship, adding, "This, of course, takes a lot of the fun out of Freedom of Speech") and, in a brilliant comic concept, wound up running for the U.S. presidency in 1968. (Twenty years later, Garry Trudeau and Robert Altman would take the same idea and run, so to speak, with *Tanner '88.*) And Bob Einstein's straight-faced, strait-laced Officer Judy; Leigh French's totally unlaced "Have a little tea with Goldie" character; Chuck Braverman's *American Time Capsule* (a superb, subliminal, three-minute American history montage); frequent performers John Hartford and Glen Campbell; and, perhaps most significantly, the comedy, conscience, and music of Mason Williams. Williams not only wrote the show's musical theme (which, like the stained-glass stage on which the Smothers Brothers stood, became their personal trademarks), and gave himself a Top 10 hit in 1968 by appearing on the show to perform his instrumental composition "Classical Gas," but contributed many of the show's best comic bits. And, in the end, it was Williams who appeared before the Federal Communications Commission in July 1969, giving his opinion why *The Smothers Brothers Comedy Hour* was no more. "It was kicked off for not pacifying," he said. "It didn't divert your attention away from social problems; it called your attention to them. It's very hard to sell you something when you're thinking." That summer, *The Smothers Brothers Comedy Hour* was replaced by a new comedy-variety hour: *Hee Haw.* But the baton carried by Tom and Dick Smothers already had been picked up in prime time by Dan Rowan and Dick Martin, and soon would reach the finish line in late-night with *Saturday Night Live.* After a generation of dormancy, the original *Smothers Brothers Comedy Hour* episodes, including the censored ones, finally surfaced in 1993 on the E! Entertainment Network, with the brothers themselves providing new commentary regarding those old shows. In the interim, the Smothers Brothers themselves emerged victoriously in the courts, when a 1973 jury decided CBS had violated the terms of its contract, and awarded the Smothers Brothers a high six-figure settlement. Tom and Dick Smothers also emerged several times, and on several networks, with subsequent variety shows—including NBC's *The Smothers Brothers Show* in 1975 and a bury-the-hatchet reunion special and series for CBS in 1988—all of which contained occasional flashes of the old brilliance and artistic aspirations. The original *Smothers Brothers Comedy Hour,* though, shone the brightest and had the most impact. It was a beacon in and of its time, a show whose emotional residue runs a lot deeper than mere punch lines or comic characters. You had to be there—but if you were of that era, especially at the right age, it was as important as TV could get.

Sneak Previews. *1978–82, PBS.* Actually, this PBS movie-review series is still running, but only its first five years, the ones teaming Chicago's Gene Siskel and Roger Ebert (who themselves moved on to other, more lucrative shows), are worth discussing. Like a flesh-and-blood Statler and Waldorf from *The Muppet Show,* who also sat in the balcony and criticized, Siskel and Ebert turned movie reviewing into performance art, so much so that they became a successful show-biz duo in their own right, showing up to discuss movies, and themselves, on everything from *Saturday Night Live* to *Late Night with David Letterman*—while, at the same time, being widely lampooned as a pompous pop-culture critical team. Siskel and Ebert had come a very long way from *Opening Soon at a Theater Near You,* the 1975 low-budget local public TV show in Chicago from which *Sneak Previews* was spawned. The irony after more than twenty years of TV teamwork, though, is that the bigger Siskel and Ebert get, the less the content of their newspaper or TV reviews is quoted. Their insights often are as impressive as their on-air chemistry, but most of the time, all the movie studios care to repeat and reprint in their TV

LEFT: *The Singing Detective*, with Michael Gambon as a disfigured writer and his dashing alter ego.
RIGHT: *60 Minutes*, at a time when the team consisted of Morley Safer, Dan Rather, Harry Reasoner, and Mike Wallace.

The Smothers Brothers Comedy Hour, with Tom and Dick Smothers flanking George Harrison.

and newspaper ads is the team's famous, nearly illiterate minihaiku of praise: "Two thumbs up!"

Soap. 1977–81, ABC. Like *NYPD Blue* many years later, the Susan Harris sitcom *Soap* came under fire by pressure groups long before it reached the air, thanks to advance word that the show would attempt to challenge and redefine current network standards. Susan Harris created the show as a prime-time network answer to the syndicated *Mary Hartman, Mary Hartman,* and literally got into the act herself by appearing on several episodes as a prostitute named Babette. The best players in the ensemble cast, though, all went on to other prime-time venues: Robert Guillaume took his butler character into the successful spinoff series *Benson;* Richard Mulligan (whose befuddled Burt was abducted by aliens) wound up on *Empty Nest;* Robert Urich (as an oversexed tennis bum) went on to star in *Vega$* and countless other series; and Billy Crystal, as gay son Jodie, outlived the series' most controversial role. Religious groups were so angry to have an openly gay character on the series that Harris derailed her original plot line, which was to have Jodie get a sex change, and made him conflicted about his sexual orientation—which served only to upset many gay rights advocates. The truth, though, is that *Soap* was much ado about not very much: with this *Soap,* only the theme song leaves a familiar ring. When the series was repeated by Comedy Central in 1993, it looked about as outdated as Mike Brady's wardrobe on *The Brady Bunch.* The limitations of this particular genre, in the hands of Harris and company, was driven home all over again in 1981, when Harris created another prime-time soap opera satire, *Good & Evil,* starring Teri Garr. That series lasted all of one month, and even that was one month too long.

Sonny & Cher Comedy Hour, The. *1971–74, CBS.* Here's something that really surprised me when I went back and looked at the Nielsen ratings: *The Sonny & Cher Comedy Hour* is the only variety series in the last quarter-century to finish a season in the Top 10. The 1969–70 season had two series arguably qualifying in that genre, *Rowan & Martin's Laugh-In* and *The Red Skelton Hour,* but no other variety show finished in the Top 10 until *Sonny & Cher* did it in 1973–74—and, amazingly, no variety show has done it since. *Sonny & Cher* the series might have had an even longer run back then, except that Sonny and Cher the couple didn't. Sonny Bono and Cher separated in 1974, and went their separate TV ways—him with *The Sonny Comedy Revue* and her with *Cher,* neither of which lasted more than a season. Two seasons later, they reunited—professionally but not personally—for *The Sonny & Cher Show,* but the bickering banter that seemed funny before had a crueler edge, and they soon were free to explore other careers (Sonny in politics, and Cher in movies, rock videos, and infomercials). The key elements of *The Sonny & Cher Comedy Hour* were presented as early as 1967, when the pop stars headlined their first movie, a little-seen flop called *Good Times.* Director William Friedkin's first film, it had the duo fantasizing about the type of film they'd like to make, and covered everything from film noir to Westerns, with lots of costume changes. It also included their 1965 hit song, "I Got You Babe." Add the back-and-forth insults from Sonny & Cher's Las Vegas performing days, and you've got the recipe for *The Sonny & Cher Comedy Hour:* lots of wisecracks, costumes, and music, with a duet of "I Got You Babe" closing each show. Although the performance level of most sketches was fairly juvenile, the show featured some sharp writing (Steve Martin and Bob Einstein, as both writers and performers, wound up here a few years after working together on *The Smothers Brothers Comedy Hour*); one very funny repertory member (Teri Garr); imaginative set designs; decent music; and dazzling costumes. Fashion designer Bob Mackie, already known for his costumes on *The Carol Burnett Show*, became a star designer for how he (barely) clothed Cher, whether she was singing solo, standing next to Sonny, or performing in costume as one of the many historical temptresses she embodied in the show's memorable "Vamp" sketches. The pop-culture resonance of Sonny & Cher's "I Got You Babe" closing was demonstrated in 1987, when the host of *Late Night with David Letterman* persuaded them to perform the song, impromptu, for the first time in ten years. Like Dean Martin and Jerry Lewis being brought together amicably by Frank Sinatra during the 1967 *Muscular Dystrophy Telethon*, it made for a somewhat awkward, very temporary reunion indeed. And the beat goes on. . . .

Soul Train. *1970–   , syndicated.* This long-running syndicated music series is like a pop-culture sneak preview system: street attitudes, fashions, hair styles, and dances continue to be flashed here long before they're absorbed and relayed on the fashion runways and in department stores. *Soul Train* has long been described as the soul equivalent of *American Bandstand*, but calling Don Cornelius the black Dick Clark is like calling Pat Boone the white Little Richard. Something's definitely lost in the translation. True, *Soul Train* grew out of the Chicago streets the same way *American Bandstand* had emerged from Philadelphia, by capturing and disseminating the raw music, energy, and dance steps enjoyed by the youth of that city. Once *Soul Train* became a hit in syndication, Cornelius eventually made tracks for Los Angeles, the city from which *Soul Train* continues to emanate more than two decades later. The original announcer's "Sooooull train!" opening squeal has been used since the beginning, and, though once-frequent guests the Supremes have given way to the likes of En Vogue, a lot of *Soul Train* has remained constant throughout—including the segments where dancers still line up to form a human aisle and dance down "the Line." Rap videos shown on Black Entertainment Television and MTV now carry the same sort of street-level fashion, energy, and excitement, but throughout the seventies and most of the eighties, at least, *Soul Train* was the major African-American music and dance showcase on national television—and Cornelius deserves a lot of credit, or blame, for popularizing extra-wide ties and ultra-high Afros. In 1995, CBS devoted two hours of prime time to *The Soul Train 25th Anniversary Hall of Fame Special*; its host, making his first TV appearance since his own series left the air the year before, was Arsenio Hall.

Soupy Sales Show, The. *1955, 1959–61, ABC; 1965, syndicated.* Some TV children's show personalities were huge stars in local markets, others developed a major national following, and a few did both, turning local celebrity into national acclaim. It's doubtful, though, that any other performer in the history of TV did it the same way as Soupy Sales, by not only achieving success on network TV and in syndication, but by moving to several different local TV markets and conquering them individually. Milton Hines, a.k.a. Soupy Sales, began his TV career in 1950, as the amiable proprietor of *Soupy's Soda Shop* in Cincinnati. By 1953, he had moved up the TV ladder to Detroit, where he simultaneously hosted a daytime kids' show (*Lunch with Soupy Sales*) and a slightly more mature late-night effort (*Soupy's On*). The live daytime show, with its pie-in-the-face comedy style (in this case, that description is literal, not figurative) and Soupy-in-your-face visual style (the show relied heavily upon extreme close-ups), was a major hit in Detroit as well— so much so that ABC tapped the program, by then retitled *The Soupy Sales Show,* as the network's summer replacement for *Kukla, Fran & Ollie,* then carried it a few years later as a Saturday morning offering. Meanwhile, Soupy and his gang moved to Los Angeles in 1960, conquering that market so completely that Bob Hope, Burt Lancaster, Sammy Davis, Jr., Dean Martin, Jimmy Durante, and Frank Sinatra all lined up to get cream pies in the face. (Sinatra, Davis, and Trini Lopez once dropped by to stage a lengthy, messy pie fight at Soupy's "Chez Bippy," a use of the word *Bippy* that long predated *Rowan & Martin's Laugh-In.*) In September 1964, Soupy Sales and his on-camera furry friends—including the puppet Pookie the lion and the giant "dogs" White Fang and Black Tooth (who, except for their huge paws and arms, were heard but not seen)—moved to New York for a local show on WNEW-TV. It was there, a few months into his run, that the big-bow-tied comic made his big boo-boo. On New Year's Day, 1965, he told his young viewers not to wake up their parents (who, he said, may have been up very late the night before), but, instead, to tiptoe into their bedrooms, look in their pockets and purses, "take those green pieces of paper" with presidents' faces on them, and mail them to him. WNEW suspended him for the still-infamous ad lib, but New York fans picketed the station and launched protest campaigns until *The Soupy Sales Show* was reinstated—which it very quickly was, and soon was launched into syndication. (Ironically, Sales had used the same tossaway "green pieces of paper" joke while on TV in Detroit and Los Angeles, but nobody there seemed to mind.) Further evidence of popularity of *The Soupy Sales Show* during the New York years was that one of Soupy's many silly dances, "the Mouse," somehow became a minor novelty hit on the pop charts. As TV–inspired dances go, I prefer "the Batusi," as performed by Adam West on *Batman* and revived by John Travolta and Uma Thurman during their dance-contest sequence in *Pulp Fiction.* Finally, there's one other clear legacy of *The Soupy Sales Show:* the illegitimate son it left behind. I refer, of course, to the similarly attired, and similarly anarchistic, proprietor of *Pee-wee's Playhouse.*

Soviet Coup Attempt. *1991, various networks.* The unsuccessful attempt by Communist hard-liners to usurp then-Soviet Union President Mikhail Gorbachev (of the then-Soviet Union) was a turning point in terms of both global politics and the global village. On August 19, 1991, American TV viewers awakened to the news that Gorbachev had been displaced overnight by an "emergency committee" of Party officials and military leaders. Yet despite CNN's hasty initial labeling of the breaking news event as "The Fall of Gorbachev," TV images relayed live from Moscow suggested the coup was far from over. In the city streets, angry Soviet citizens overran tanks (and, in one grisly case, vice versa), and Russian Federation President Boris Yeltsin even stood defiantly atop one tank to call for help and reform, and for Gorbachev's safe return. For the next few days, as the world watched, Yeltsin managed to amass supporters and inform reporters without leaving the relative, though tenuous, safety of the Russian Parliament Building. In successfully turning back the military forces that had arrested Gorbachev and surrounded the Russian Parliament, Yeltsin's key weapons were not guns and tanks, but instead were phones, fax machines, ham radios, amateur camcorders, and access to foreign news broadcasts and broadcasters. By being and staying there, and covering the story so aggressively and impressively, television almost surely affected the path of history. "George Orwell was wrong," Ted Koppel had said in his *Television: Revolution in a Box* news special two years earlier, discussing Orwell's classic novel *1984*. "The media, which he predicted would become the instrument of totalitarian control, has become, instead, its nemesis." The Orwellian warning, "Big Brother Is Watching You," turned out in reality to be just the opposite. The 1991 Soviet coup failed because, thanks to television, we were watching Big Brother.

Space Exploration Coverage. *1961–   , various times and networks.* The space race between America and the Soviet Union was launched, so to speak, on October 4, 1957, when the Russians successfully placed Sputnik, the first man-made satellite, in orbit. The Soviets upstaged America again on April 12, 1961, by sending cosmonaut Yuri Gagarin into a brief but successful orbital flight around the planet and making him the first man in space. Less than a month later (May 5, 1961), America countered as best it could, by sending astronaut Alan Shepard on a fifteen-minute suborbital flight aboard a Mercury spacecraft—the first space launch to be broadcast live on American television. Before the month was out, President John F. Kennedy, in a nationally televised speech before a joint session of Congress, laid down the gauntlet: "I believe this nation should commit itself to achieving the goal, before this decade is out," he said, "of landing a man on the moon and returning him safely to the earth." On February 20, 1962, Mercury astronaut John Glenn became the first American to orbit the planet, and demonstrated just how big a draw this space race was: Glenn's aircraft-carrier rescue after his Atlantic Ocean splashdown was watched live on United States TV by an estimated one hundred million viewers. From then to now, the viewing patterns have pulsated to a similar ebb and flow: first-time excursions attract large viewerships, but repeat missions become downplayed as "routine," with reduced network and viewer interest until a new triumph or an unexpected tragedy shatters the country's space-age complacency. The first known casualties of the space race occurred on January 27, 1967, when an electrical fire in the cockpit during a simulated countdown claimed the lives of Apollo 1 astronauts Virgil "Gus" Grissom, Edward White, and Roger Chaffee while still on the launching pad. A few months later, on April 23, 1967, Soviet cosmonaut Vladimir Komarov crashed to the earth and died when the parachutes in his already malfunctioning Soyuz 1 spacecraft tangled upon deployment at reentry. Neither of those 1967 tragedies was televised (Apollo 1 because it was a practice training session, Soyuz 1 because of Iron Curtain constraints), but the January 28, 1986, Challenger disaster received wide and memorable TV coverage (see separate listing). The nearly disastrous flight of Apollo 13, on the other hand, received its share of live coverage and news updates on network TV, but only after an explosion left the spacecraft crippled in space the night of its April 13, 1970, launch. Prior to that point in the mission, network attitudes were so cavalier about space travel that a live one-hour TV transmission, hosted by astronaut Jim Lovell as he and fellow astronauts Fred Haise and Jack Swigert hurtled toward the moon, was rejected by CBS, NBC, and ABC as being too dull to preempt regular programming. That prime-time snub was dramatized in the outstanding 1995 film *Apollo 13*, which revealed the severity of the flight's problems more clearly and honestly than had either TV or the National Aeronautics and Space Administration at the time. (Ron Howard, director of the *Apollo 13* film, took a few liberties in restaging that Not-Ready-for-Prime-Time Mission—*I Dream of Jeannie*, among other series shown on TV that night in the film version, was not really on the schedule—but the point was valid nonetheless.) Another real-life NASA near-disaster, averted only when Neil Armstrong manually regained control of a wildly gyrating Gemini 8 in 1966, has yet to be given the *Apollo 13* or *The Right Stuff* big-screen treatment. As for triumphs and memorable televised images from space, they were numerous. TV news coverage relied, in part, upon animations, drawings, and scale models that were laughably crude by today's standards, but the real images captured and brought back from space were another matter entirely. They included the live, beautiful pictures of Earth from space, courtesy of Mercury astronaut Gordon Cooper in May 1963; Edward White's giddy Gemini 4 extra-vehicular activity in June 1965, as the first American to walk in space; the December 1965 rendezvous of Gemini 7 with Gemini 6, providing the first pictures of one manned spacecraft in orbit as seen from another; and the December 1968 Apollo 8 mission, which midway between Earth and the moon sent back humbling black-and-white live TV pictures of Earth as seen from that far out in space, and, from an even greater distance, relayed the first live close-up TV pictures of the moon. After the Apollo 11 moon landing on July 20, 1969 (see separate listing), visual highlights provided by subsequent lunar flights included the first color TV pictures from the moon (Apollo 14, January 1971), and live color footage, from a camera placed on the lunar surface in December 1972, of the Apollo 17 lunar module blasting off after completing what remains, to this writing, mankind's last visit to the moon. The orbiting space station Skylab was launched in 1973, American and Soviet spacecraft docked successfully in space during the joint Apollo-Soyuz mission (officially ending the space race) of 1975, and the first space shuttle, Discovery, was launched in 1981. Fourteen years later, in July 1995, Discovery released in space a replacement satellite for the one destroyed when Challenger exploded in 1986, and on the same mission tested a new camera called Hercules, which relayed astonishingly clear color images of Earth from space. Astronauts aboard noted the achievement by holding a live press conference in space—but, as with the out-of-this-world briefing by the Apollo 13 astronauts back in 1970, the major networks weren't at all interested; nor was CNN. The questions, answers, and pictures from space, though, were available to satellite dish owners tuned to NASA Select TV, a free, satellite-delivered network devoted entirely to live coverage of NASA activities. This example of high-tech narrowcasting is almost a world away, so to speak, from the time when Armstrong's first steps on the moon were viewed live by an estimated 94 percent of all homes equipped with television. That made Apollo 11 the space program's most-watched live TV event, which is hardly surprising. The event that ranked number two, though, *is* surprising: it occurred four years earlier, when White's Gemini 4 spacewalk was seen live by an estimated 91 percent of all TV homes. See also: *Challenger Disaster, Moon Landing*.

Star Search. *1983– , syndicated.* The name of this series, and its association with host Ed McMahon (who, as a result, has even more money to carry as he laughs all the way to the bank), are all that truly qualify *Star Search* for inclusion here. Yet though the series has clear ties to the past (specifically, to *Arthur Godfrey's Talent Scouts*), it also, over the years, has successfully conducted searches for at least a few future stars, including Martin Lawrence, Dennis Miller, Rosie O'Donnell, Sinbad, and Sharon Stone.

Starsky and Hutch. *1975–79, ABC.* In the midseventies, *Starsky and Hutch* was to television what disco was to music: it helped define the decade, thanks to its high energy and total vapidity. Kinetic cops, airborne autos, mindless mayhem—*Starsky and Hutch*, starring Paul Michael Glaser and David Soul, was a typical buddy-cop series in which car chases drove the show and wise-cracking characters drove the car (in this case, a flashy Ford Torino). In those largely dismal pre-*Hill Street Blues* days, that was enough to make *Starsky and Hutch* a Top 20 hit, and to lodge its title into pop-culture consciousness.

Star Trek. *1966–69, NBC.* Yeah, like America needs more words written about *Star Trek*. The veritable media industry this show has spawned—the movies, TV spinoffs, novelizations, fan clubs, Internet sites, the dozens of books written about it, the comics and cartoons and so on—becomes of paramount importance (especially to Paramount Studios, which controls the immensely lucrative franchise) when arguing the concept of teleliteracy. However, because anyone tackling the subject of *Star Trek* is going where so many have gone before, the only things seemingly worth including in this context are (a) the show's indelible catch phrases and (b) a fast, opinionated rundown of the very best episodes. From William Shatner's Captain James T. Kirk, there's the clipped cadence that makes him so universally imitable, as well as the variants on "Beam me up, Scotty" (which has come to be a shorthand synonym for anyone desiring to exit an uncomfortable social situation) and the classic captain's narration that opens each *Star Trek* episode: "Space, the final frontier. These are the voyages of the starship *Enterprise*. Its five-year mission: to explore strange new worlds, to seek out new life and new civilizations, to boldly go where no man has gone before." From DeForest Kelley's Dr. McCoy, there are the endless variations on "Damnit, Jim, I'm a doctor, not a ————," as well as the terse medical pronouncement, "He's dead, Jim." From Leonard Nimoy's Mr. Spock, there's the Vulcan blessing of "live long and prosper," as well as the puzzled dismissal of something as "illogical." And from James Doohan's perpetually frazzled Scotty, there's the basic "I canna do it, cap'n!," mimicked most recently by Jim Carrey in *Ace Ventura, Pet Detective*. As for best episodes from the original series, my votes go to "City on the Edge of Forever" (a time-travel episode written by Harlan Ellison and featuring Joan Collins); "Plato's Stepchildren" (Michael Dunn as the abused plaything of telekinetic sadists, with Barbara Babcock as one of the memorable meanies); "Mirror, Mirror" (an alternate-universe plot that allowed several *Enterprise* crew members to act decidedly unheroic); "Space Seed" (guest star Ricardo Montalban as Khan, the villain he later played in the second *Star Trek* movie); "The Cage" (a clever recycling of the original *Star Trek* pilot); "The Naked Time" (an episode in which a runaway virus affects the actions and emotions of the crew); "Whom Gods Destroy" (an episode that makes it, in my book, because of the green-skinned alien played by Yvonne Craig); and "A Piece of the Action" (a gangster-era fantasy that is amusing because of, rather than despite, its tongue-in-cheek tackiness). Gene Roddenberry's initial series gets the credit for going where no futuristic TV series had gone before, and for slipping allegorical pleas for racial harmony and planetary peace into prime time. With its optimistic vision of the future and premise of exploration, *Star Trek* also supported the space race at the very time it was happening in real life: *Star Trek* was launched in September 1966, while Gemini missions were still being flown, and the seventy-ninth and final episode of *Star Trek* was televised in June 1969—one month before Neil Armstrong landed on the moon. (Eventually, NASA returned the favor by succumbing to popular opinion and, in 1976, renaming the space shuttle *Constitution* as the *Enterprise*.) Back on Earth, though, *Star Trek* escaped cancellation once only after an extensive letter-writing campaign by fans, never ranked higher than fifty-second place for a single season, and achieved its seemingly eternal popularity only after lapsing into off-network syndication. Since then, the most visible offshoots of the series have included, to date, seven *Star Trek* movies (the best was *Star Trek IV: The Voyage Home;* the worst, *Star Trek V: The Final Frontier)* and the three spin-off live-action TV series attached to *Star Trek* prefixes, *The Next Generation, Deep Space Nine,* and *Voyager.* While the original *Star Trek* series did not live long, it certainly has prospered. And while Shatner's James T. Kirk, after a long life on the small and big screen, died while saving the universe in the 1994 film *Star Trek Generations,* nothing in the *Star Trek* universe is absolute. Except, that is, for the absolute certainty that one *Star Trek* franchise eventually will result in another. As in . . .

Star Trek: The Next Generation. *1987–94, syndicated.* **Star Trek: Deep Space Nine.** *1993– , syndicated.* **Star Trek: Voyager.** *1995– , UPN.* The

The Sonny & Cher Comedy Hour, with Cher and Sonny Bono flanking Raymond Burr on Halloween.

Star Trek: The Next Generation, with Patrick Stewart surrounded by the 1989 cast. Clockwise from lower left: Jonathan Frakes, LeVar Burton, Michael Dorn, Wil Wheaton, Brent Spiner, Gates McFadden, and Marina Sirtis.

first official plan for Gene Roddenberry to revive *Star Trek* involved a proposed theatrical film called *Star Trek II*, intended for release in 1975. That failed to materialize, so the project moved to television as a proposed 1977 series sequel that would serve as the cornerstone of a new Paramount TV network. A two-part script was written, all the original *Star Trek* regulars but Leonard Nimoy signed for the new series, and Stephen Collins and Persis Khambatta were cast as primary guest stars. Yet at the last minute, Paramount decided not to launch a fourth TV network after all, and the two-part script became the basis for 1979's *Star Trek—The Motion Picture*, with the same veteran cast members and guest stars, and with Nimoy reconsidering, and returning as Mr. Spock. Ten years after first planning to present a TV series sequel to *Star Trek*, Paramount tried again, with the syndicated *Star Trek: The Next Generation*, an instant and well-deserved success. The special effects were infinitely superior to those in the original *Star Trek*, and the stories and characters were both more logical (the captain didn't always throw himself in harm's way) and less sexist (even the show's opening narration was changed to the more inclusive "where no *one* has gone before"). Patrick Stewart, as Captain Jean-Luc Picard, makes the "Kirk vs. Picard" arguments no contest at all; whether you're judging acting talent or character strengths, Stewart and Picard win hands down. (Conversely, Nimoy's Spock wins over Brent Spiner's amiable android Data, though it's a much closer call.) LeVar Burton, coming from *Roots*, was one previously famous cast member, playing ship's engineer Geordi La Forge; another was recurring cast member Whoopi Goldberg, as mysterious bartender Guinan. The best guest star of all time, relatively speaking, was physicist Stephen Hawking, who made a cameo appearance in the ship's anything-goes virtual-reality "holodeck" suite. The only truly resonant catch phrase from *The Next Generation* is Picard's officious "make it so," but Roddenberry and his collaborators and successors left behind a lot of strong episodes. My subjective list this time would include the show's first episode, "Encounter at Farpoint," which not only triumphantly multiplied the *Star Trek* power base but introduced John de Lancie as "Q," the single best (and often revisited) "villain" in *Star Trek* history; its dazzling finale, "All Good Things," which ended the series with a Big Bang; and many clever shows in between. "Darmok," in which Picard spends the hour trying to understand Paul Winfield's metaphor-spouting alien, is one. Others include "The Best of Both Worlds," with Picard being turned into a metal-headed Borg; "Cause and Effect," a terrific time-loop episode; "Hollow Pursuits" and "Realm of Fear," two episodes featuring crewman Barkley (Dwight Schultz) and, respectively, his love of computer-generated fantasy and his fear of transporting; "Man of the People," in which empathic counselor Deanna Troi (Marina Sirtis) becomes older but not wiser; and "Yesterday's Enterprise," in which Denise Crosby's Tasha Yar, the security officer who remains the only regular *Star Trek* character to die on one of the TV series, is revived, briefly, in an alternate-universe scenario. As the *Next Generation* series ended, the cast members were graduated to feature-film status, starring in the seventh *Star Trek* film, *Generations*—the one that teamed Picard and Kirk in a time-warp setting, only to have Kirk die a hero so that the new captain of the

Enterprise could boldly go wherever he wanted without having to fight for the wheel. The crossover between the two shows was standard *Star Trek* operating procedure: McCoy, Scotty, and Spock all made appearances on TV's *Next Generation,* and that show's assistant engineer, Miles O'Brien (played by Colm Meaney), became a key cast member of a second spin-off series, *Star Trek: Deep Space Nine.* (Eventually, Michael Dorn, as Klingon security chief Worf, joined *Deep Space Nine* as well.) *Deep Space Nine,* which premiered in syndication in 1993, hasn't yet accomplished enough to earn its own listing here, but it's noteworthy for having the first black captain (Benjamin Sisko, played by Avery Brooks), and for a few strong episodes, including "Fascination" (crew members get virus-induced crushes on one another); "Heart of Stone" (shape-shifter Odo, played by Rene Auberjonois, has his loyalty tested while trying to save a rock-encased Kira, played by Nana Visitor); and "Crossover," in which Kira accidentally revisits the same evil mirror-image universe that Kirk and company stumbled into in "Mirror, Mirror" on the original *Star Trek,* with even more enticing results. In fact, *Deep Space Nine,* which has since returned to that same alternate world, would do itself a service by moving there permanently, since most of the characters (especially Kira, Sisko, and Terry Farrell's Dax) have a whole lot more vitality and sexuality on the other side of the mirror. Meanwhile, a third *Star Trek* spinoff series, *Star Trek: Voyager,* was launched in January 1995, finally realizing the vision originally set forth by Paramount eighteen years earlier: using the *Star Trek* name as the cornerstone of a new network. The United Paramount Network (UPN) presented several other new programs along with *Voyager* when it premiered, but only *Voyager,* predictably, earned high enough ratings and praise to be renewed for a second season. It also made some instant *Star Trek* history by casting Kate Mulgrew as Kathryn Janeway, the first female captain of a Federation starship to be showcased in a weekly series. (It made the second-season opener, in which Janeway came face to face—don't ask how—with Amelia Earhart, that much more interesting.) Mulgrew's Janeway character, and that equal-opportunity *Star Trek* honor, was offered first to actress Genevieve Bujold, but that actress quit the role, and *Star Trek: Voyager,* after the first two days of filming. Apparently, she was reluctant to Bujoldly go where no woman had gone before.

Steve Allen Show, The. *1950–52, CBS; 1953–54, New York's WNBT-TV; 1956–59, NBC; 1962–64, syndicated.* Jay Leno, current host of *The Tonight Show,* spoke for talk-show hosts everywhere—and spoke the truth—when he told *Newsweek* in 1995, "I think we all borrowed from Steve Allen." In the early fifties, Steve Allen was doing in New York, for CBS, what Ernie Kovacs was doing in Philadelphia on the local series *3 to Get Ready:* proving there was an appetite, and an audience, for an anything-goes daytime "talk" show. Kovacs was more intrigued by camera effects and blackout skits, while Allen preferred more spontaneous humor and events, but both men were TV pioneers, pulling the sort of stunts the best of today's talk-show hosts continue to present. On the first *Steve Allen Show,* the daytime CBS version, Allen did stuff that even now would make headlines if done by David Letterman or

Jay Leno. Once, when put off by the lack of responsiveness in that day's studio audience, Allen led them all on an impromptu conga line, led them outside, returned to the studios without them, locked the doors, and finished the live TV show by quietly playing poker with members of his crew. And for his final CBS show, Allen left enough time at the end to have the cameras rolling as he said good-bye to the regulars (who included Peggy Lee), dismantled the set, put on his hat and coat, exited the studio, and walked outside into the New York daylight, getting smaller and smaller as the theme music played for the last time. A year later, in 1953, a new *Steve Allen Show* appeared in New York, this time a local show on the rival NBC station. It was televised after prime time, as was a local variety show on the ABC-owned station, but Allen's show was more focused: comedy, music, and casual conversation were the dominant elements. Gene Rayburn was the announcer, and two very young singers, Steve Lawrence and Eydie Gorme, were featured regulars. That New York version of *The Steve Allen Show* vanished on September 27, 1954, but only because it went national under its new title: *Tonight!*, the first late-night network talk show. (See separate listing.) The *Tonight!* show, which later dropped the exclamation point, was so popular on NBC, and the network's *Colgate Comedy Hour* was slipping so dramatically against its prime-time CBS rival, *The Ed Sullivan Show*, that the network asked Allen to do double duty and host a prime-time variety series as well. In 1956, he complied, and yet another incarnation of *The Steve Allen Show* appeared on television. This is the series on which Allen had Elvis Presley sing "Hound Dog" to a real dog, and gave the Muppets their first network TV exposure, and presented a commendably wide range of guests (Lenny Bruce and the Three Stooges on one show, Wally Cox and Vincent Price on another, Johnny Carson and Zsa Zsa Gabor on a third, Jerry Lewis and Coleman Hawkins on a fourth). It's also the one with a heavyweight group of ad-lib comic regulars: Don Knotts, Louis Nye, Tom Poston, Bill Dana, Pat Harrington, Jr., and bandleader Skitch Henderson, all of whom worked hilariously with Allen. Allen's memorable bits included solemnly reading the "lyric poetry" of current rock songs such as "Be-Bop-a-Lula"; the prankish Funny Fone Calls; portraying "The Answer Man" (a direct antecedent of Carson's "Carnac the Magnificent"); presenting a news spoof called "The Nutley Hinkley Butley Winkley Report"; and the Man on the Street interviews, during which Knotts acted nervous, Poston acted befuddled, and Nye, as the gregarious Gordon Hathaway, greeted Allen with the still-famous "Hi-ho, Steverino!" Headlining both *The Steve Allen Show* and *Tonight* proved too much for Allen; eventually, he split the latter's hosting chores with, fittingly, Ernie Kovacs, then abdicated entirely, at which point Jack Paar soon took over. In prime time, Allen's show ultimately switched networks, and names, but still another *Steve Allen Show* showed up on TV—the 1962–64 syndicated version. This version is the one closest in spirit to Letterman's *Late Night* and *Late Show* antics. Allen mud-wrestled a lady wrestler on TV long before Andy Kaufman got into the act, jumped into a vat of Jell-O, turned himself into a human tea bag, and played the piano while he and his piano were suspended in midair (it was easier that way, one supposes, to hit the high notes). Photographing passersby and suddenly bursting into the street during a show were still a big part of Allen's routine, as was an eagerness to showcase new talent. In 1963, stand-up comic Woody Allen was a featured guest; in 1964, Bob Dylan made one of his earliest TV appearances, singing "The Lonesome Death of Hattie Carroll." Also in 1964, as he had in 1952, Allen ended the run of *The Steve Allen Show* with an intentionally dramatic finale. This time he reminisced about previous shows as stagehands dismantled the set around him. Johnny Carson was a special guest on that final show, joining Allen in placing an on-air surprise phone call to Jack Paar—thereby linking by telephone, and on television, the first three permanent hosts of the *Tonight* show. In addition to *Tonight!* and these groundbreaking series, all called *The Steve Allen Show*, Allen starred in many other noteworthy TV vehicles, including NBC's *The Steve Allen Plymouth Show* (1959–60, featuring Bill "My name Jose Jimenez" Dana), ABC's *The New Steve Allen Show* (which, in 1961, started several TV careers by hiring as regulars Buck Henry, Tim Conway, and the Smothers Brothers), and the PBS series *Meeting of Minds*, which earns its own separate listing in this book. In the nineties, Comedy Central added *The Steve Allen Show*—kinescopes of the classic 1956–59 NBC version—to its rotation, making it clear to a new generation of viewers just where Carson, Letterman, and Leno had gone for part of their inspiration. Hi-ho, Steverino!

Studio One. *1948–1958, CBS.* Even though I noted earlier in this book that *Kraft Television Theatre* deserves credit as television's first weekly anthology drama series, *Studio One* actually premiered first—on April 29, 1947, eight full days before the May 7 launch of the *Kraft* showcase. The problem was, just before *Kraft Television Theatre* premiered on NBC-TV, *Studio One* premiered on CBS Radio. It didn't move over to television until more than a year later, by which time *Kraft* had long established itself with TV tenure. Both shows, though, proved impressively durable, lasting more than a decade and presenting many ambitious and memorable hours of television. The most famous *Studio One* productions are by writer Reginald Rose: the 1954 *Twelve Angry Men*, which is detailed under that listing, and the 1957 two-part drama *The Defender*, which starred Ralph Bellamy, William Shatner, and Steve McQueen. The acclaim for *The Defender* led to a spin-off series, *The Defenders*, starring E. G. Marshall and Robert Reed. (It, too, is detailed under its own listing.) *Studio One* also presented *Thunder on Sycamore Street*, another well-received Rose drama, this one about an ex-convict moving into a suburban neighborhood bitterly opposed to his presence. Other writers contributing to *Studio One* included Rod Serling, Gore Vidal, Ernest Kinoy, Abby Mann, and Horton Foote; directors weren't very plentiful (Franklin Schaffner may be the most prominent), but performers included Charlton Heston (almost a repertory player here, especially in adaptations of Shakespeare plays), Yul Brynner, Jack Lemmon, Eva Marie Saint, James Dean, Nancy Marchand, Grace Kelly, Hume Cronyn, John Forsythe, Tom Poston, Lee Grant, Eddie Albert, Peter Falk, Leslie Nielsen, Art Carney, Jason Robards, Elizabeth Montgomery, Lloyd Bridges, Anthony Perkins, and, in a rare dramatic role in 1955, Mike Wallace. Among the more enticing little-known *Studio One* productions are these odd concoctions: future *Defenders* star E. G. Marshall, and Mary Wickes, in a 1949 version of *Mary Poppins;* Thomas Mitchell and Boris Karloff starring in a 1952 version of Mark Twain's *A Connecticut Yankee in King Arthur's Court;* a 1953 dramatization of George Orwell's *1984,* with Eddie Albert as Winston Smith and Lorne Greene in a supporting role; *Uncle Ed and Circumstances,* starring Jackie Gleason as a fictional contestant on *The $64,000 Question* (the 1955 teleplay, based on a short story by Gleason himself, was performed live one week after the premiere of Gleason's *Honey-mooners* series); and perhaps the most intriguing of all, *The Night America Trembled,* a 1957 docudrama reenactment of the 1938 *War of the Worlds* broadcast by Orson Welles, and the resultant panic that set in when listeners took news of the Martian invasion seriously. Edward R. Murrow, his *See It Now* series long since canceled, narrated *The Night America Trembled,* thereby making a connection between Murrow and Welles, two of the most famous radio voices in history. Meanwhile, on camera, the cast of *The Night America Trembled* wasn't too shabby, either: Warren Beatty starred, with Alexander Scourby among the costars. In terms of widely recalled teleliterate offerings, none of these intriguing productions makes the cut, but the commercial spokeswoman for all of them certainly does. For a full decade, Betty Furness appeared during commercial breaks on *Studio One,* providing live demonstrations of the sole sponsor's various household appliances—and always ending with the ultra-famous slogan, "You can be sure if it's Westing-house." The final irony, of course, is that nearly a half-century after Westinghouse sponsored this series on CBS, the company turned around and *bought* CBS.

Sunday Morning. *1979–   , CBS.* Since its premiere in 1979, this superb, leisurely presented CBS News show has been hosted by poets—first by Charles Kuralt, who anchored the show until his retirement in 1994, and then by Charles Osgood, who replaced Kuralt as well as anyone could. Osgood is famous for his rhymes; Kuralt dealt only in prose, but it was poetry nonethe-less, whether the subject under discussion was soft features or hard news. The Sunday after the 1994 southern California earthquake in Northridge, Kuralt began his report on the emotional aftereffects of the disaster by saying, "Tremors of the earth are aftershocks, of course. So are tremors of the soul." It's the sort of writing, and compassion, that was rare on television, and is even more rare now that Kuralt is gone from CBS. (Osgood, though, helps keep the compassion meter from plummeting completely.) *Sunday Morning* boasts some of the best arts coverage on television, and on the subject of television itself, has showcased the two best media critics ever to appear on TV, Jeff Greenfield and John Leonard. *Sunday Morning* has covered its share of breaking news—American embassy bombings, student uprisings in Beijing, summits between world superpowers—but the delight in nature and the arts is what makes *Sunday Morning* so singular and memorable. The closing segment each week, presenting beautiful scenery or animals in real time, is more poetic and informative, rather than less, by being shown without narrative accompaniment. And in the history of *Sunday Morning,* nothing ranks higher, or resonates more fully, than the 1986 show totally devoted to a solo concert by Vladimir Horowitz, broadcast live from the Soviet Union. The pianist, then eighty-two years old, was returning to Moscow for the first time in sixty-one years, and both he and his concert audience were visibly moved by the music and the reunion. Horowitz died three years later; the Soviet Union, five.

Super Bowl, The. *1967–   , variously presented by CBS, NBC, and ABC.* Here's something that says a lot about the perceived value of television history: even though the first Super Bowl was broadcast simultaneously by NBC and CBS in 1967, neither it nor the 1968 Super Bowl game televised by CBS was saved for posterity on videotape. The third annual Super Bowl, on NBC, fared better, and it's a good thing: that 1969 game, still the most famous of all Super Bowls, was the one in which New York Jets quarterback Joe Namath guaranteed a victory, then provided it, against the heavily favored Baltimore Colts. The championship game wasn't officially given the name *Super Bowl* for the first few years, and had no Roman numeral attached to it until *Super Bowl V* in 1971. By that time, ABC—which was locked out of the alternate-years Super Bowl broadcast arrangement between CBS and NBC—had brought football into prime time on a regular basis with *Monday Night Football,* and it wasn't long at all until Super Bowls, too, were played in prime time, which pushed the ratings even higher. Of the Top 20 highest-rated TV programs of all time, Super Bowls occupy fully half of those slots. (Not that the games lived up to the hype; with one or two exceptions, TV's Super Bowls have been Super Boring.) *Super Bowl XVI,* the 1982 game between the San Francisco 49ers and Cincinnati Bengals, earned a 49.1 rating for CBS; it remains the fourth highest-rated TV show in history, right behind the *M*A*S*H* finale, the resolution to the "Who Shot J.R.?" cliffhanger on *Dallas,* and the final episode of *Roots.* Yet with the advent of Nielsen's "People Meters," there are different ways of counting heads, and NBC insists that its 1993 *Super Bowl XXVII* game, in which the Dallas Cowboys massacred the Buffalo Bills 52–17, nonetheless is the most-watched Super Bowl game of all, with an estimated 133.4 million viewers. Even though the game's rating of 45.1 doesn't even place it among the ten highest-rated Super Bowls, the head count bolstered by its unusually popular halftime show—the one featuring a live performance by Michael Jackson—gives NBC's *Super Bowl XXVII* the alleged edge. The other most memorable non-game-related Super Bowl offering? A commercial shown for the first time, and the only time, during CBS's *Super Bowl XVIII* in 1984: a very Orwellian commercial for Apple's brand new personal computer, the Macintosh. The next year, in 1985, ABC finally joined the club and broadcast its first Super Bowl. By then, of course, there was plenty of videotape to go around.

Supertrain. *1979, NBC.* Like *My Mother the Car* in the sixties, this series, a short-lived, shockingly expensive *"Love Boat* on rails" concoction, is famous—make that infamous—as one of the all-time worst shows in the history of television. It's a bit unfair, because NBC, at this horrid point in its history, had several equally awful new shows on the air at about the same time. Re-member $weepstake$, *Sword of Justice,* or *Whodunnit?* Of course you don't. And shouldn't. Yet *Supertrain,* created by Dan Curtis, somehow rose above those other new NBC shows, or sank beneath them, to emerge as The Title That Wouldn't Die—a video embarrassment invoked so disparagingly and frequently, even all these years later, that it's one for the history books. *This* history book, anyway.

Sybil. *1976, NBC*. Sally Field overcame years of typecasting, and the goofball reputation that came from having starred on TV as *Gidget* and *The Flying Nun,* by portraying a woman with a multiple-personality disorder in this excel-lent four-hour miniseries. Joanne Woodward, who had portrayed a similarly afflicted woman in the 1957 film *The Three Faces of Eve,* played Sybil's psy-chiatrist, and both Woodward and Field were tremendous. Field won an Emmy for the convincing way in which she acted out sixteen distinct person-alities, and also won an invaluable amount of acclaim and respect. (We liked her; we really liked her.) In 1990, another sitcom graduate, Shelley Long, tried a similar tack by starring in *Voices Within: The Lives of Truddi Chase,* a miniseries in which she played a woman with even *more* distinct personali-ties. All Long did, though, was prove how difficult Field's job had been; *Voices Within* was laughable, whereas *Sybil* was mesmerizing. Twenty years later, I still rank *Sybil* as one of the best miniseries ever made. No, I don't. Yes, I do. No, I don't. Yes, I do. . . .

T

Tales from the Crypt. *1989–   , HBO*. Like *Alfred Hitchcock Presents* in the fifties and *Thriller* in the sixties, *Tales from the Crypt* was hosted by a per-son—or, in this case, by a cackling cadaver—with a penchant for scary tales, unsavory characters, trick endings, bad deeds, and worse puns. *Thriller* had Boris Karloff, and *Alfred Hitchcock Presents* had Hitchcock himself, but *Tales from the Crypt* has a computerized puppet called the Crypt-Keeper, who introduces and concludes his gruesome stories while adorned in a variety of ghoulish guises. In one episode, he's a political candidate who dismembers his own hand in order to make "a real stump speech"; in others, he's a deadly deep-sea diver named "Shock Cousteau" or a knife-wielding salesperson for the "Home Chopping Network." Yet despite the similarities to Hitchcock's TV series, *Tales from the Crypt* could not be accused of stealing the overall concept. The structure and style, as well as some of the puns, came straight from the original EC Comics of the fifties, which predate the Hitchcock series. The comic book *Tales from the Crypt* and its sister publication *Vault of Horror* appeared from 1950 to 1955; *Alfred Hitchcock Presents* premiered the year those cult comics folded. A pair of British horror movies based on those comics appeared in the early seventies (one, 1972's *Tales from the Crypt*, featured Joan Collins), but it wasn't until a group of producers and directors revived the concept in the late eighties that *Tales from the Crypt* realized its true live-action potential. The overseers of the HBO series included Robert Zemeckis, Joel Silver, Richard Donner, and Walter Hill, all of whom directed episodes. The freedom afforded by cable TV allowed them, and others (including directors William Friedkin, Todd Holland, Tobe Hooper, and Russell Mulcahy), to have fun in an intentionally cartoonish and garish genre. *Tales from the Crypt* was such a quick and easy romp that even high-profile actors took part, either as performers (Kirk Douglas, Roger Daltrey, Whoopi Goldberg, Isabella Rossellini) or as fledgling directors (Tom Hanks, Michael J. Fox, Arnold Schwarzenegger). Brad Pitt, before achieving superstar status, starred in one *Crypt* tale; other individual episodes featured Brooke Shields, John Lithgow, William Hickey, Don Rickles, Lea Thompson, Buck Henry, Carol Kane, Wayne Newton, Teri Hatcher, Tim Curry, and Traci Lords. Danny Elfman's musical theme was perfectly suited to *Tales from the Crypt*, as was John Kassir's voice, and laugh, as the Crypt-Keeper. The episodes most worth seeking out, for both their casts and stories: "Dead Right," with Demi Moore reluctantly marrying, for his alleged fortune, an obese and repugnant Jeffrey Tambor; "House of Horror," with Wil Wheaton falling for a sorority girl from Delta Omega Alpha (and they don't call it D.O.A. for nothing); "Loved to Death," with Mariel Hemingway swallowing a too-potent love potion; "And All through the House," with Larry Drake as a mad slasher in a Santa suit; "Let the Punishment Fit the Crime," with Catherine O'Hara and Peter MacNicol as hotshot city lawyers swallowed up by a strict small-town court system; "Abra Cadaver," with Beau Bridges as a doctor with a drop-dead sense of humor; "Well Cooked Hams," with Martin Sheen, Billy Zane, and Maryam D'Abo as rival magicians with malice up their sleeves; and "What's Cookin'?," a cannibalistic comedy starring Christopher Reeve and Bess Armstrong as owners of a diner featuring a very secret barbeque recipe. *Tales from the Crypt Presents Demon Knight*, the first of a series of all-new *Crypt* feature films, was released in 1995, the same year edited versions of the HBO series began showing up on Fox. The film put a little too much emphasis on rough gore and language, while the Fox rebroadcasts, conversely, were far too sanitary. Viewers who were turned off by those diluted TV versions, and turned them off in response, had reason to look back at the original HBO *Tales from the Crypt* even more fondly—as an uncensored representative of TV's Ghoulden Age.

Tanner '88. *1988, HBO.* At least every twenty years, it seems, American popular culture gets feisty enough to offer someone from its ranks as a presidential candidate—not in the actual, Ronald Reagan sense, but in a sarcastic, performance-art sense. It happened in 1928, when Will Rogers mounted a facetious yet wisdom-filled "run" for the White House. It happened again in 1948 when Howdy Doody announced his candidacy, and again in 1968 when Pat Paulsen, on *The Smothers Brothers Comedy Hour*, announced his. Then came 1988, when *Doonesbury* writer-cartoonist Garry Trudeau and director Robert Altman cast Michael Murphy as young, Democratic, Kennedyesque presidential aspirant Jack Tanner, and sent him out on the "real" campaign trail to create a brilliant satire in a persuasive mock-documentary format. (Tim Robbins's similarly themed 1992 *Bob Roberts* movie, with an ersatz conservative candidate, was nearly as clever, but *Tanner '88* beat it by a full four years.) Shot on hand-held video, written on the fly, and costarring Pamela Reed as Tanner's aggressive campaign manager, *Tanner '88* took a simultaneously destructive and instructive approach. It poked fun at politicians, reporters, campaign workers, and television on one hand, while exploring and explaining their symbiotic relationship on the other. The fictional characters of *Tanner '88* traveled the same campaign trail as the real candidates, and even interacted with them. During the series, Altman and Trudeau managed to position Murphy's Tanner so that he talked and shook hands with Gary Hart, Bob Dole, Pat Robertson, and, in an episode guest-starring Bruce Babbitt, got some advice from the former candidate about what message to give to the voters: "Talk about a little bit of sacrifice," Babbitt advised Tanner, "for the common good." The charismatic Jack Tanner and the brilliant *Tanner '88* ran from February to August 1988, then, like so many real-life Democratic aspirants that year, folded up stakes long before the November election. As Michael Dukakis emerged as the apparent Democratic favorite, Tanner considered running as an independent third-party candidate, but gave up and went fishing instead. However, the legacy of *Tanner '88* was far from forgotten. *Tanner '88* won at Cannes for the best TV series, reviving Altman's directorial career and giving him a blueprint for such fiction-and-reality mixtures as his subsequent films about show business (*The Player*) and the fashion industry (*Ready to Wear*). The series also is a clear forerunner of *The Larry Sanders Show*, which intermixes real celebrities and fictional characters to remark knowingly on the TV talk-show scene. In politics, Jack Tanner apparently was just one campaign ahead of his time: in 1992, not only did the Tanneresque Bill Clinton win the Democratic nomination and the presidency, but H. Ross Perot, taking Tanner's third-party option, made that a more viable route for future presidential aspirants. Some, but not all. In 1995, the satirical Fox series *TV Nation* (formerly on NBC) ignored the unofficial twenty-year waiting period by introducing its own candidate for president: former convict Louis Bruno, to whom series creator Michael Moore gave the memorable campaign slogan, "He's a pro; he's a con." Jack Tanner would have been proud.

Taxi. *1978–82, ABC; 1982–83, NBC*. *Taxi* was an amazingly funny, complex, and unconventional series, one that boasted as much talent behind the screen as in front of it. James L. Brooks, one of the show's creators, ranks it at the top of all the TV series on which he's worked—and since his other series include *The Mary Tyler Moore Show*, *The Simpsons*, and *The Tracey Ullman Show*, that about says it all. *Taxi* was a sitcom about cab drivers, one that showed them away from work, and waiting for work, as well as behind the wheel. That sounds simple enough, but *Taxi* was a show fluid and crazy enough to encompass the surrealistic antics of Andy Kaufman, the drug-culture haziness of Christopher Lloyd's Reverend Jim Ignatowski, the oddball "old country" customs and language of Kaufman's Latka and Carol Kane's Simka (his eventual bride), and the abrasive antics of Danny DeVito's Louie De Palma, along with Judd Hirsch's solidly centered Alex Reiger. (Tony Danza, Marilu Henner, and Jeff Conaway rounded out the cast.) And the show's writers and/or producers, in addition to series creators Brooks, Stan Daniels, David Davis, and Ed. Weinberger, included a virtual Who's Who, or Who's about to Be Who, of TV comedy. Writer-producers Glen and Les Charles and director Jim Burrows, all of whom collaborated on *Cheers*, worked here first. So did Glenn Gordon Caron of *Moonlighting*, Ken Estin of *Cheers*, Barry Kemp of *Newhart*, Sam Simon of *The Simpsons*, and many others. The Charles brothers wrote, and Burrows directed, the single best episode of *Taxi*, and one of the most perfectly written, directed, and performed scenes in sitcom history. The episode was "Reverend Jim: A Space Odyssey," the one in which Lloyd's Reverend Jim, in his second appearance on the show, is encouraged to get his driver's license and become a cabbie. Even the form to take the test is a daunting challenge for Jim, especially the question "Mental illness or narcotic addiction?" Jim thinks a moment and responds, "That's a tough choice"—but eventually, he gets the written test and tries his best. However, his best isn't nearly good enough, so he stage-whispers across the room for some help from Conaway's Bobby Wheeler. "What does a yellow light mean?" Jim asks. Bobby whispers back, "Slow down." Jim nods his head, then says, more loudly and more slowly, "What . . . does . . . a . . . yellow . . . light . . . mean?" Great, great stuff, and the sequence is repeated again, even more deliberately and hilariously, before switching to the next scene. The instrumental *Taxi* theme is well-remembered, as is Kaufman's "Ibeeda" nonsense word (actually, in context, it meant "please" or a form of agreement), and DeVito's shockingly funny first scene as Louie, when he berates and bullies the cab drivers from the safety of his dispatcher's cage, then descends the steps to get howls from the studio audience because of his unexpectedly small stature. In addition, *Taxi* fans would have good reason to have strong and fond memories of the following classic *Taxi* episodes: "Memories of Cab 804," featuring Mandy Patinkin as a frazzled father-to-be whose wife gives birth in Alex's cab, and Tom Selleck as a perfect gentleman courting Henner's Elaine Nardo; "The Wedding of Latka and Simka" and "Scenskees from a Marriage," two stories making brilliant use of Kaufman and Kane; "Mr. Personalities," in which Kaufman portrayed not only Latka and sleazy alter ego Vic Ferrari, but also did a deadpan, dead-on impersonation of Alex; "Jim Joins the Network," with guest star Martin Short as a TV executive soliciting programming advice from Jim; "Hollywood Calling," with guest star Martin Mull as a Hollywood director planning to make a film about the cabbies; "The Elegant Iggy," where Jim tickles the ivories at a formal party; and "The Unkindest Cut," in which guest star Ted Danson plays a very snippy hairdresser. Nick at Nite brought back all these, and more, by adding *Taxi* to its cable lineup in 1994—and that same year, *Frasier* slyly saluted *Taxi* by having Frasier, and his brother and father, riding in a cab whose driver suddenly stopped to have a baby. The cab number, not at all coincidentally, was "804."

Teddy. *1979, CBS.* The title of this particular *CBS Reports* may not ring any bells, but its content certainly will, at least to anyone alive and politically aware at the time. This one-hour special, broadcast on November 4, 1979, was the one in which Roger Mudd questioned, in two separate and challenging interviews, Massachusetts senator and presidential aspirant Ted Kennedy. Mudd asked Kennedy about everything from Chappaquiddick and his marriage to why he wanted to run for President, and Kennedy's answers were so inept, and subsequently reported and repeated so widely on other TV outlets, that *Teddy* effectively torpedoed Kennedy's candidacy at that early stage. As reporter Tom Pettit noted soon after on NBC, Kennedy, in that prime-time interview with Mudd, "revealed an inability to thoroughly explain Chappaquiddick, or anything." It was Mudd's toughest hour as a reporter, yet CBS didn't exactly reward him for it; when Walter Cronkite retired two years later, Mudd, Cronkite's regular substitute, was passed over as his successor in favor of Dan Rather. However, the behind-the-scenes men who teamed up for *Teddy,* producer Andy Lack and executive producer Howard Stringer, fared better politically. Both ended up running CBS News—and, in Stringer's case, eventually the entire network.

Teenage Mutant Ninja Turtles. *1988–92, syndicated; 1990– , CBS.* I don't mean to mock *Turtles,* but the only apt reaction to the phenomenal worldwide success of *Teenage Mutant Ninja Turtles* is to be totally shell-shocked. Based on an underground comic book, the adventures of Michaelangelo, Leonardo, Donatello, and Raphael began as a syndicated cartoon miniseries in 1987, a syndicated series the following year, and a CBS Saturday-morning series beginning in 1990. The toy merchandising was insanely popular, as was the first live-action *Teenage Mutant Ninja Turtles* movie, a 1990 phenomenon that still ranks as the most successful independent film in Hollywood history. Other live-action films followed, but eventually the teen turtles were replaced, briefly, by an even more baffling children's TV craze: *Mighty Morphin Power Rangers,* which premiered on Fox in 1993. By the time a movie version of that film was released in 1995, however, the *Mighty Morphin* phenomenon had peaked, the film flopped, and modern civilization eagerly awaited the Next Big Thing. Despite its stupidity and vapidity, though, *Teenage Mutant Ninja Turtles* made a big enough splash, for a long enough time, and in enough different media, to leave an imprint on the teleliterate of tomorrow. As someone way too old to enjoy the phenomenon, all that sticks with me regarding this series are its enjoyably silly theme song (especially the line, "Heroes in a half shell!") and the unsettling knowledge that Fred Wolf, who transplanted *Teenage Mutant Ninja Turtles* from comics to television, is the same animator who collaborated with Harry Nilsson in 1971, directing and animating that superb 1971 musical cartoon fable, *The Point* (the source for Nilsson's hit song "Me and My Arrow"). In less than twenty years, then, Wolf went from *Point* to pointless. It's a lucrative but unimpressive career move that can best be described as a major shell-out.

$10,000 Pyramid, The. *1973–74, CBS; 1974–76, ABC*. **$20,000 Pyramid, The.** *1974–1980, ABC*. **$25,000 Pyramid, The.** *1974–79, syndicated; 1982–88, CBS*. **$50,000 Pyramid, The.** *1981, syndicated*. **$100,000 Pyramid, The.** *1985, 1991, syndicated*. Except for the earliest and latest syndicated versions, all installments of this *Pyramid* scheme, regardless of their face value, were presided over by the same ubiquitous host. The gimmick of the game was, as with *Password*, to pair celebrities and "everyday" contestants, with one team member throwing fast-paced clues at the other in hopes of identifying the secret word—or, in this case, category, since most answers dealt with phrases beginning with "Things that are . . . " (the closest this series gets to a catch phrase). Given that, try finding the common element in these TV title clues: *TV's Bloopers and Practical Jokes, The $10,000 Pyramid, American Bandstand*. As Ed McMahon, the *Bloopers* cohost would say, "You are *correct*, sir!" The category is: "Things That Are Hosted by Dick Clark."

Texaco Star Theater. *1948–53, NBC*. As the host of this pioneering NBC variety series, Milton Berle earned two nicknames that stayed with him forever after: "Uncle Miltie" and "Mr. Television." The former was coined when, while ad-libbing a good-bye to the kids in the TV audience at the end of one show, he told them to "listen to your Uncle Miltie, and kiss Mommy and Daddy goodnight, and go straight upstairs like good little boys and girls." The latter nickname came about because, for a couple of years when TV was a very small and urban pond, Milton Berle was its very biggest fish. Texaco, which had sponsored a similarly titled radio series for the previous ten years, decided to attempt a TV version, and tapped the star of another radio show it sponsored, *The Milton Berle Show*, to guest-host a handful of summertime *Texaco Star Theater* installments for NBC-TV, beginning with its June 8, 1948, premiere show. One guest shot was all it took: Berle packed the show with everything he had developed, learned, or "borrowed" from his career in vaudeville, and made room for guest stars such as Pearl Bailey and Señor Wences. Days after Berle's network TV debut, *Variety* raved that Berle was "one of those naturals," credited him with "a performance that may well be remembered as a milestone in television," and described that first *Texaco Star Theater* TV outing as "Vaudeo," which *Variety* defined as "the adaptation of old-time vaudeville into the new video medium." The term Vaudeo soon was Deadeo, but Texaco wasted no time in springing to life: by that fall, *Texaco Star Theater* had a permanent host, and his name was Milton Berle. Within four months, by the end of 1948, Berle's show was seen each week by an estimated 80 percent of all TV owners. He was the primary reason many people purchased their first TV sets; Tuesday nights were his, and both *Time* and *Newsweek* put him on the cover in 1949, on the same week. Other networks and performers scurried to copy his formula, trade on his success, or simply to get into the TV act with their own "Vaudeo" efforts. *Toast of the Town*, later renamed *The Ed Sullivan Show*, was launched by CBS the same summer as Berle's 1948 debut. *Arthur Godfrey's Talent Scouts* was on CBS by the end of that year, and *Admiral Broadway Revue,* later renamed *Your Show of Shows,* premiered on both NBC and DuMont in January 1949. Berle not only paved the way, but took some of them along for the ride. Three months before starring on *Admiral Broadway Revue,* Sid Caesar had been a guest, making his TV debut, on Berle's show. One 1949 show featured Desi Arnaz in a South American production number, two years before he costarred on *I Love Lucy.* And though Sullivan eventually appropriated Señor Wences as his own, Berle and *Texaco Star Theater* were there first, hands down. Berle made fun of his own flat monologue jokes long before Johnny Carson did, and threw around dummies decades before *Second City TV* did, and did more for giant powder puffs and bow ties than any other clown inside or outside a circus tent. *Texaco Star Theater* topped the TV ratings for three straight seasons (the first season there *were* TV ratings), and NBC, in 1951, responded by signing Berle to a thirty-year contract. His costumed opening appearances each week, especially his cross-dressing stints wearing an ornate Carmen Miranda or Cleopatra headdress, are legendary. (Other things about Berle are legendary, too, but this isn't that sort of compendium.) What is most remarkable about the surviving kinescopes of old *Texaco Star Theater* shows is the same thing that's so striking about Caesar's TV work, and by the Dean Martin-Jerry Lewis outings on *The Colgate Comedy Hour* of the early fifties: the raw energy, and infectious comedic thrill, generated by these anything-goes headliners. And "anything goes," in this context, wasn't far from the truth. One *Texaco Star Theater* show featured Berle, along with guest stars Eva Gabor and Frank Sinatra, impersonating Kukla, Fran, and Ollie. Yet as TV sets spread across the nation, the popularity of Berle slowly decreased, and Texaco dropped its sponsorship in 1953. It was a sad day for both parties, because "Mr. Television" never again enjoyed the same sort of superstar status, and Texaco never again enjoyed the same sort of massive product-name recognition it had in those *Texaco Star Theater* days—when a quartet of singers, decked out in white Texaco uniforms, stepped forward each week and sang, "Oh, we're the men of Texaco / We work from Maine to Mexico. . . . " Both Berle and Texaco may be saddened by the news that, almost fifty years later, it's perhaps the most remembered *Texaco Star Theater* element of all. In 1982, NBC mounted a one-shot revival of *Texaco Star Theater,* a special headlined by Sammy Davis, Jr., Carol Burnett, and Ethel Merman—but, amazingly, without Milton Berle. Perhaps it was a purely financial consideration. After all, his thirty-year contract had run out the year before.

That Girl. *1966–71, ABC.* Like father, unlike daughter: even though Danny Thomas enjoyed a major Top 10 hit with his TV series *The Danny Thomas Show,* his daughter Marlo never achieved the same ratings success with her series, *That Girl.* But because it showed a single woman—Marlo Thomas as aspiring actress Ann Marie—on her own in the big city, this midsixties show scored lots of points, and is remembered today, for its neofeminist leanings and message. What else is remembered? The theme song and opening credits sequence, of course, and Thomas's ski-lift of a flip hairdo. What's probably forgotten, on the other hand, is that both George Carlin and Dabney Coleman were regulars on this series during its first season (playing an agent and a neighbor, respectively), and that Ted Bessell, as Ann's boyfriend Don Hollinger, actually was engaged to, and close to marrying, That Girl as the series came to an abrupt close. However, both of them continued to have good luck with future TV flirtations: Bessell, in a series of guest shots on *The Mary Tyler Moore Show*, portrayed a serious boyfriend of Moore's beloved Mary Richards, and Thomas, after one guest appearance on *Donahue*, eventually became the real-life wife of Phil Donahue.

That Was the Week That Was. *1964–65, NBC.* This was the classic that was. *That Was the Week That Was* (or *TW3*, as it often was sensibly abbreviated) brought sharp, intelligent satire to network television, paving the way for such later disciples of irreverence as *The Smothers Brothers Comedy Hour, Rowan & Martin's Laugh-In, Saturday Night Live, Not Necessarily the News,* and, most recently, *Dennis Miller Live, TV Nation,* and even *Politically Incorrect.* The show's format came from England, where *TW3* held court on BBC-TV from 1962–63 with David Frost as host, Roy Kinnear as one of the repertory players, Millicent Martin as the featured vocalist of memorably topical tunes, and John Cleese as one of the writers. Its reign was short but celebrated: even Dennis Potter, then a tough TV critic for the *Daily Herald*, noticed its singular wit and attitude from the very first show (and, after a positive review, eventually wound up contributing sketches to the series). A month before the final show was broadcast in England, NBC experimented with an Americanized special; that November 1963 show, hosted by Henry Fonda and featuring singer Nancy Ames, led to a full-fledged *TW3* series in America two months later. Elliott Reid hosted for the first season, but contributor Frost was in charge by the second. Regulars included Nancy Ames and Phyllis Newman (who shared singing duties), puppeteer Burr Tillstrom (creator of *Kukla, Fran & Ollie*), Buck Henry, and, for the second season, Tom Bosley and Alan Alda. Writers included Herb Sargent (who later became a key writer-producer on *Saturday Night Live*), Gloria Steinem, Calvin Trillin, and, though he never appeared on camera to sing the songs he composed for the series, Tom Lehrer. His contributions alone, still in circulation on such compact disc reissues as his *That Was the Year That Was*, make *TW3* a classic; the songs "Pollution" and "Vatican Rag," just to name two, show why pianist-satirist Mark Russell will never escape or outgrow Lehrer's looming shadow. Both the British and American versions of *TW3* were preempted several times, and drew considerable flak, during political election years, but both series held their ground and went out with a bang. In America, for example, even though a cigarette company was one of the show's few regular sponsors, its advertising revenue was withheld from the final episode of NBC's *TW3* so that the program could present a satirical set piece about the recently released health warnings linking cigarettes to lung cancer. To the tune of "Smoke Gets in Your Eyes," this last *TW3*—which, like all the others, was performed live from New York—presented a showstopper that had the studio audience roaring with laughter and, at the same time, gasping at the show's eagerness to totally devour the hand that, until very recently, had fed it. Close-ups of cancer-riddled chest X rays were shown to accompany the lyric "Something here inside cannot be denied," and scenes of smokers and cigarette commercials were intercut with scenes of patients being wheeled into operating rooms. (It's no wonder the series didn't last long.) That final *TW3* installment began with Frost holding up a *New York Times* headline about the show's impending demise, and ended with the entire company gathering to sing Lehrer's "We Will All Go Together When We Go" ("You will all go directly to your respective Valhallas / Go directly, do not pass go, do not collect two hundred dollahs"). The most telling blow, though, may have been struck during a solo by Phyllis Newman, who sang: "Big deal, this show, we're really not important at all / Tonight, we'll go, but look what you've got to look forward to for fall: / *Run for Your Life* and *My Mother the Car* / Sometimes you don't know how lucky you are. . . . " Indeed. Revival specials were presented by ABC in 1973 and 1985, but for all intents and purposes, that last show, during the first week of May in 1965, was the grand finale for *TW3*. After all, that was the week that *That Was the Week That Was* was canceled.

thirtysomething. *1987–1991, ABC.* When this series first came out, I hated it. The characters all seemed so self-absorbed, so utterly selfish, that it was impossible to connect with any of them. Ken Olin and Mel Harris, as Michael and Hope, were too nice, Timothy Busfield's Elliot was too irresponsible, Peter Horton's Gary was too flaky, and so on; it was like watching the days of whine and neuroses. The high caliber of the writing, directing, and acting kept luring me back, but every time I revisited, a line of dialogue, or a particularly smarmy fantasy sequence, would spoil the spell, and my mood. But *thirtysomething* matured, as did I, and once David Clennon joined the cast as tyrannical ad-agency executive Miles Drentell, *thirtysomething* found its best and most dramatic dynamic. Over the course of the series, three episodes stand out above all others. There's "The Mike Van Dyke Show," in which Michael confronts his ambivalent religious attitudes while imagining himself in a *Dick Van Dyke Show*-style sitcom universe; and "Second Look," the episode in which Patricia Wettig's Nancy survives her hospital visit but Gary doesn't; and, most memorably, "A Stop at Willoughby," whose title echoes an episode of *The Twilight Zone* and, in similar fashion, charts the nervous breakdown of its protagonist. In this case, it's Michael himself who was emotionally shattered—after his boss, Miles, refused to help an actor fired from the firm's ad campaign by their client, who resented the actor's attendance at a rally protesting American involvement in the Persian Gulf. The speech Miles gives in his defense to Michael, written by series producer Joseph Dougherty, is unforgettably potent—and, given its appearance on prime-time network TV, surprisingly daring. "He expressed an unpopular opinion," the ad-company executive says of the dismissed actor. "No one wants to be unpopular. That's why we're here. That's the dance of advertising. We help people become popular. . . . We calm and reassure. We embrace people with the message that we're all in it together, that our leaders are infallible, and that there is nothing, absolutely nothing wrong. That is what we do. It's what we've always done." Miles also tells Michael, "Do you know what I love about this country? Its amazingly short memory. We're a nation of amnesiacs. We forget everything—where we came from, what we did to get here. History is last week's *People* magazine, Michael." But with speeches like that to remember, *thirtysomething* just might stick. The series' final episode, broadcast just two weeks after "A Stop at Willoughby," was a half-hearted, inconclusive, confused mess, but *thirtysomething* quickly found a home in reruns on Lifetime cable, and series co-creators Marshall Herskovitz and Edward Zwick lost no time in jumping to feature films. If ever a series was ready-made for a reunion telemovie, though, this is it—although, if they wait much longer, they'll have to call it *fortysomething*. The legacy of *thirtysomething*, in addition to its wispy theme song, is its intentional and successful targeting and examination of the Baby Boomer generation. Its success paved the way, in a way, for *Seinfeld* and *Mad about You*—and how different, really, are the unshakeable friendships of *thirtysomething* from the similarly unshakeable twentysomething friendships shown on *Friends?*

This Is Your Life. *1952–61, NBC; 1970–72, 1983, syndicated.* There's no exclamation mark in the title of this "ambush reunion" series, but there ought to be, because the most resonant memory connected to the show is that of host Ralph Edwards sneaking up behind his subject of the week, saying their name, and shouting, "This is your life!" The surprised guest (usually, but not always, a celebrity) then stood or sat there, gamely trying to identify voices piped in by telephone or from behind the studio curtain—voices of old lovers, old teachers, and basically old people in general. Edwards had begun the practice, and the series, on radio in the late forties, and moved it to TV rather effortlessly; on TV, there was the added attraction of seeing the subjects' facial expressions, which was a big plus. On the NBC version, which was live, Edwards always had a standby kinescope ready in case something went wrong, but nothing ever did. Everyone from Gloria Swanson and Joe Louis to Stan Laurel and Oliver Hardy were happy to be the life of the party, and party to the *Life*. The subsequent syndicated versions of *This Is Your Life* were taped, not live, as were stand-alone NBC specials in 1981, 1987, and 1993. Good thing, too, because when Angie Dickinson was ambushed by new *This Is Your Life* host Pat Sajak in a taped segment for the 1993 NBC special, her response was to shout "Not on your life!" and immediately leave the studio to which she had been lured under false pretenses. One of the guests she left behind the curtain was Bob Hope—a special irony, since Dickinson basically *had* said "No thanks for the memories."

This Week With David Brinkley. *1981– , ABC.* It's hard to imagine, but easy to applaud, that after thirty-eight years with NBC, veteran newsman David Brinkley was just getting started. At age sixty-one, he switched networks to ABC, where they were so thrilled to have him they built a new type of Sunday public-affairs show around their crusty, crafty centerpiece. And not only does this series feature Brinkley's sharp wit, sharper cynicism, and excellent writing, but it boasts top newsmakers, probing interviews, and, perhaps best of all, a loose roundtable discussion featuring George Will, Sam Donaldson, Cokie Roberts, and others. ABC, as it did with *Nightline*, took an essentially empty time slot and turned it into a proud jewel in its ABC News crown. Like the CBS *Sunday Morning* show, it's a weekend program that both presumes and rewards intelligence.

Thomas, Clarence, Senate Confirmation Hearings. *1991, various networks.* The quest for Clarence Thomas to become the second African-American member of the U.S. Supreme Court hit a Supremely unusual snag on October 11, 1991, when his former colleague Anita Hill testified during the Senate Confirmation Hearings. She recounted several alleged instances of her former boss's misconduct, from boasts about the length of his penis and discussions of porn star "Long Dong Silver" to jokes about finding a female "pubic hair" on his can of Coke. Her Friday testimony proved so riveting, and the story so volatile and important, that daytime and prime-time coverage was provided not only by CBS (which, even when showing that night's major league baseball playoff game, often split the screen to follow the testimony), NBC, and ABC, but by PBS, CNN, C-SPAN, and Court TV. The networks didn't know quite how to cover this story; they merely knew that they had to. Jim Lehrer of PBS prefaced the "highlights" of that first day's testimony with an uncharacteristic disclaimer: "Please be advised," he warned, "that they include graphic descriptions that some people might find offensive." The next morning, as the networks preempted their Saturday morning children's schedules to continue coverage of the special weekend session, Peter Jennings of ABC commendably, and concisely, described the conflict and the stakes for the benefit of younger viewers—and, perhaps, for older ones as well. "Think how awful it would be," Jennings said of the dilemma facing the Senate committee members, "if they made the wrong decision, and the Supreme Court had a man on it who had been mean to a woman and lied about it, and was going to make a lot of decisions about the way other women are treated. Think how awful it would be if she were not telling the truth, and Senators believed her and told the judge he couldn't sit on the court." By Monday morning, the conflict had spread out from its epicenter on Capitol Hill and brought sexual harassment into the mainstream, and the forefront, as a hot national issue. Fourteen white men sitting in judgment of one black woman's sexual-harassment claims and her fears of career-stalling retribution didn't sit well with a lot of people—especially, but not exclusively, a lot of women. CBS *Morning* cohost Paula Zahn spoke for many when she said, "Men just don't get it." In terms of memorable TV images, the hearings and their aftermath provided plenty. There was Anita Hill, quietly but firmly relating, and sticking to, her story. There was Clarence Thomas, taking the offensive when he returned to the witness table by calling the Senate hearings "a circus, a national disgrace," and by describing the nationally televised confirmation process, in intentionally volatile language, as "a high-tech lynching for uppity blacks." There was Orrin G. Hatch, a Republican Senator from Utah, providing the most unforgettable—and laughable—visual image of the hearings, by brandishing a copy of *The Exorcist* and citing the book's "alien pubic hair" passage as a possible source for Hill's testimony. As even more comic relief, there was the astoundingly narcissistic and sexist testimony of John Doggett, one of Thomas's former classmates. Nina Totenberg of National Public Radio, one of two reporters who broke the Hill story, coanchored the PBS coverage and, not surprisingly, did the best job overall. By the most narrow of margins, Thomas was confirmed, with a Tuesday night vote carried live by all the networks. However, Thomas's seat on the Supreme Court was only one lasting legacy of the thirty-nine hours of those 1991 hearings. The other was a marked increase in the number of women seeking, and winning, political office, even in the Senate itself. As for my most vivid personal memory surrounding the case, it occurred on October 15, the day of the vote, when NBC—which, alone among the major networks, had stayed in the Senate chamber to eavesdrop—caught on live TV an exchange of dirty politics that no longer appears anywhere in the *Congressional Record*. Arlen Specter, a Republican Senator from Pennsylvania, had taken the podium to accuse Hill of "perjury" when testifying against Thomas; Massachusetts Senator Ted Kennedy, a Democrat, attacked Specter's "shameful" characterization; Specter returned to take a swipe at Kennedy, and Kennedy followed suit. Then came Orrin Hatch, the *Exorcist*-waving member of the committee, who took the podium to respond to the Specter-Kennedy cage-rattling, and to Democratic claims that the White House had a heavy hand in the way the Thomas hearings were conducted. If anyone believed that, Hatch said in the Senate chamber on live television, "I know a bridge up in Massachusetts that I'd be happy to sell to them, with the help of Senator Kennedy." That was at 3:10 P.M.—and before 4 P.M., Hatch apparently had taken enough heat for the thinly veiled Chappaquiddick reference to scamper back to the mike and say: "Mr. President, I am extremely mortified by the mix-up in words in my prior remarks. I ask unanimous consent that the word 'Massachusetts' be deleted, and the word 'Brooklyn' be substituted therefore, as originally intended. And I also want to apologize to my colleagues for this unfortunate and insensitive mistake. I'm just mortified by it, and I meant to say 'the senator from Massachusetts,' and that apparently got mixed up." (Yeah, right. And if anyone believes that, I know a little tabernacle in Utah. . . .) Then again, perhaps Hatch wasn't to blame after all. Maybe the devil made him do it.

Thorn Birds, The. *1983, ABC.* Of the five highest-rated miniseries in TV history, Richard Chamberlain is the only actor to have starred in two: 1980's *Shogun*, and this 1983 romantic drama, second only to *Roots* on the all-time list. Based on Colleen McCullough's sprawling novel, *The Thorn Birds* is less ambitious and satisfying than *Shogun*, but as major melodramas go, this ten-hour ABC drama contains some strong performances, especially by Chamberlain as Ralph de Bricassart (the priest torn between his religious vows and his life-long love for Meggie Cleary), by Barbara Stanwyck as the matriarch who tries to seduce him, and by supporting players Richard Kiley, Piper Laurie, Christopher Plummer, and, as young Meggie, Sydney Penny. (The "elder" Meggie, played by Rachel Ward, became a minor star as a result of her costarring role here, but barely earned it.) *The Thorn Birds* also boasted some strong set pieces, such as the sheepshearing race that, in more than one sense, qualified as shear entertainment. In addition to sheepshearing, the miniseries did a lot of leapfrogging, jumping from time frame to time frame so quickly that one unintentionally funny superimposed caption read, "Nineteen years later." That came in handy, though, when CBS began production in 1995 on a miniseries sequel dramatizing that neglected portion of the original story. Called *The Thorn Birds: The Missing Years*, it once again starred Chamberlain as Father Ralph, but this time gave the role of the adult Meggie to *L.A. Law* alumnus Amanda Donohoe. Ironically, Sydney Penny, the young actress who had portrayed the preteen Meggie in 1983, was by that time an adult actress, playing Julia on *All My Children*, and old enough to play opposite Chamberlain in the sequel. She was not, however, offered the part, which must have been a real *Thorn* in her side.

Three's Company. *1977–1984, ABC.* Actually, American TV has presented two series called *Three's Company.* The first was an otherwise forgettable music series on CBS in 1950, and the other is the unfortunately unforgettable sitcom on ABC for seven years beginning in 1977. Based on a British sitcom called *Man about the House*, it starred John Ritter as Jack Tripper, a heterosexual young man pretending to be gay so he could deceive the landlord and live, platonically, in the same apartment as two beautiful (and heterosexual) women. Joyce DeWitt played one of the roommates, but the female who drove this sitcom was Suzanne Somers, the same actress who had driven the mysterious white Thunderbird in *American Graffiti*. In an era that saw ABC shoot to popularity with a gaggle of so-called jiggle TV shows, Somers and *Three's Company* were jiggling at ground zero. She stayed with the series only until 1981, but it was long enough to make *Three's Company* one of the hottest series on television, and to establish her character of Chrissy as one of the most vapid, demeaning women's roles in modern TV history. Ritter took a long time to live down this series, but, like a male Sally Field, eventually did enough good work to be taken more seriously as a performer. Somers, who tried everything from other sitcoms to talk shows and exercise videos, was less fortunate—but also was less talented. That's what happens when, instead of developing as an actress, you leave it to cleavage.

Thriller. *1960–62, NBC.* Another underrated and short-lived TV series, this show, hosted by Boris Karloff, scared me half to death (okay, maybe 60 percent) when I was a kid. Apparently, I was not alone, because Stephen King, in his *Danse Macabre* collection, calls *Thriller* "probably the best horror series ever put on TV." He cites three of its episodes as among the most macabre dramas ever televised: "The Hungry Glass" (based on a Robert Bloch story and starring William Shatner), "Pigeons from Hell," and "A Wig for Miss DeVore." Other notable entries—in my opinion, not King's—include "The Watcher" (starring Richard Chamberlain), "Man of Mystery" (starring Mary Tyler Moore and William Windom), "La Strega" (starring Ursula Andress), and "The Premature Burial," starring Karloff himself in a TV adaptation of the Edgar Allan Poe classic. But also, for comic relief, there's

"Masquerade," a change-of-pace black comedy in which Elizabeth Montgomery and Tom Poston star as newlyweds forced to stay at a spooky old house hosted by an equally spooky old man (John Carradine). "Masquerade" was one of the first episodes offered when *Thriller* finally was released on home video in the midnineties, making the series available to a whole new generation of horror fans.

Tiananmen Square Student Uprising. *1989, various networks.* In May 1989, Chinese students set up a tent city in Beijing's Tiananmen Square to protest its repressive government. After a few weeks of posturing back and forth, with tens of thousands of young dissidents amassing in the square, the conservative Chinese rulers got tough, circled Tiananmen Square with troops and tanks, and shut down the local flow of information by forbidding Chinese television crews to transmit any live pictures from the center of Beijing. Prior to that, though, in the global village, pictures were relayed by international TV crews (who had gotten contractual permission to cover the summit visit by Soviet leader Mikhail Gorbachev) until the Chinese government shut them down as well. NBC and ABC weren't broadcasting live from Beijing on May 20, 1989—the night the Chinese pulled the plug on American network coverage—but CNN and CBS were, and relayed their reports and news footage during prime time (CBS even interrupted the season finale of *Dallas* to do so). CNN's Bernard Shaw, and then CBS's Dan Rather, were ordered by angry Chinese officials to stop broadcasting that night, in televised confrontations that were both riveting and frightening. CBS was the last to go dark that night, but in the weeks that followed, images kept finding their way out—including one, from the Tiananmen uprising, that ranks as one of the most remarkable and resonant images of the decade: a lone unarmed Chinese student, standing bravely and passively in front of a column of Chinese Army tanks as they bore down toward Tiananmen Square. A still photograph of the same confrontation became equally famous, but the moving image, with the turrets turning and the tanks alternately inching forward and stopping, was even more moving. The needlessly bloody confrontation between students and the military took place on June 3 and 4, 1989, and the true number of students killed will never be known—but that one brave student, emblematic of them all, will not soon be forgotten.

Time for Beany. See *Beany and Cecil*.

Toast of the Town. See *The Ed Sullivan Show*.

Today. *1952–   , NBC.* "Here it is, January 14, 1952, when NBC begins a new program called *Today*," said Dave Garroway, proudly but somewhat awkwardly rising from his desk and walking toward the camera—and, thus, getting even closer to the viewers watching the early-morning live telecast at home. "And if it doesn't sound too revolutionary, I really believe this begins a new kind of television." Broadcasting from a New York studio with a glass partition so passersby could peer in, Garroway the host, along with announcer and sidekick Jack Lescoulie and newsman Jim Fleming, did indeed begin a new kind of television: a program, designed by Sylvester "Pat" Weaver, that took the musical and chatty elements of Steve Allen's late-night New York TV show (a format Weaver would tap again, with Allen as co-conspirator, to create the *Tonight* show), and added them to news and feature elements common to sections of a daily newspaper. The format was a perfect one for early morning television, but at first, there were almost as many *Today* viewers outside the studio window as there were out there in TV land. To get more adults to watch, Weaver hired Estelle Winwood in 1952 as the first "*Today* girl," with duties that ranged from helping to report the weather to eventually conducting interviews and delivering "women's" features. To get kids to watch, while they still had control of the TV dials before heading to school, Weaver added a baby chimpanzee to the show in 1953—and that improbable bit of monkey business, courtesy of J. Fred Muggs, is what got *Today* the attention and viewers it needed to stay afloat. In 1954, CBS tried to counterprogram *Today* by presenting *The CBS Morning Show*, featuring Jack Paar as host and Walter Cronkite and Charles Collingswood as reporters. By then, though, *Today* already reigned supreme, and CBS turned over the time slot to *Captain Kangaroo* in 1955. Muggs was retired from *Today* after a four-year run, not because the show had outgrown him, but because he had outgrown the show, and become too large and unpredictable for the confines of the TV studio; a tiny replacement, Mr. Kokomo, was brought in for a while, but soon was deemed chimply unnecessary. *Today*, like J. Fred Muggs, was maturing as it went along, and that would also be the case for some of its famous graduates— especially Barbara Walters, who began as a writer and "*Today* girl" and wound up as an official cohost and celebrated interviewer, and Jane Pauley, who came to *Today* a few years out of college and basically grew up on the show. Actually, the format of *Today* has changed surprisingly little over the years. It did its first live remote broadcast in 1954, from Miami Beach, and still does special traveling shows forty years later; its 1992 trip to Africa was a particularly strong recent effort. And while *Today* stopped broadcasting from its "window" set in 1958, it tried again from 1962–65, and eventually resumed the practice in June 1994. It's stupid and distracting, but, I guess, it's also tradition. Just as traditionally, *Today* continues to present an affable mix of cohosts, contributors, and newspeople, currently represented by cohosts Bryant Gumbel and Katie Couric, weathermen Willard Scott and Al Roker, news anchor Matt Lauer, movie critic Gene Shalit, and lots of others. Over the years, *Today* has, understandably, taken on the tone of its respective hosts. Garroway, like Arthur Godfrey, had a gift for conversational gab, especially when "interacting" with the viewing audience at home by staring directly into the camera. Garroway and his quiet manner also gave *Today* its most famous and durable catch phrase: he ended each show, including his final appearance in 1961, by holding out an outstretched palm, like a cop stopping traffic, and saying, "Peace." John Chancellor was next, but hated the job and eagerly went back to news reporting; his lasting and important contribution to *Today* was refusing to read ad copy, as Garroway had done, thereby making *Today* a more "serious" news outlet. In 1962, Hugh Downs took over as host, displaying the affable anchor skills that would serve him well on *20/20*. Next came Frank McGee and Jim Hartz for short stints, during a period when Barbara Walters was promoted to coanchor, and basically carried the show until her departure in 1976. That's when Tom Brokaw took over as host of *Today;* he was joined later that year by Jane Pauley, and that's when, for the first time, a morning program had a male and female team that got along well and worked well together. From then on, *Today* has worked like a tag team, handling its changings of the guard, and retaining continuity and viewer loyalty, by replacing only one anchor at a time. The Brokaw-Pauley era lasted from 1976 until 1981, when Brokaw left to anchor the *NBC Nightly News;* Bryant Gumbel, smart and smooth, joined Pauley in 1982, and that team lasted until 1989, when Pauley retired temporarily; then, after a brief stint with Deborah Norville, Gumbel and *Today,* in 1991, brought in Katie Couric, who, like Pauley, is a charming and intelligent presence on camera. If the pattern holds, it will be Couric, rather than Gumbel, who stays put and coanchors *Today* tomorrow. As for the *Today* of yesterday, what else is worth mentioning? That Brokaw's space-shot coverage on *Today* was exemplary; that Joe Garagiola's folksy friendliness served the show well in three different decades; that the other "*Today* girl" alumni include Lee Meriwether, Betsy Palmer, and Florence Henderson; that Frank Blair, who succeeded Fleming as news anchor in 1953, was an authoritative *Today* regular until 1975; and, last but certainly not least, that Willard Scott, as the show's effervescent weatherman, has been announcing century-mark birthdays, sampling local cuisines, and basically serving as the show's traveling goodwill ambassador since 1980. Second only to Garroway's "Peace" sign, it is Scott, rather than any of the subsequent *Today* hosts, who has provided the show's next most memorable moment— the time he borrowed a page from the Milton Berle comedy handbook and delivered the weather dressed in drag as Carmen Miranda. Luckily, the trend stopped there, or else TV would have had to start issuing Miranda warnings.

Tomorrow. *1973–82, NBC.* Just as *Today* was the first network foray into early morning programming, *Tomorrow* was the first nightly network shot at a "late late show." It was a shot that hit the bull's-eye. Tom Snyder, the host of *Tomorrow* who had held a variety of broadcasting jobs since 1955, understood three things about TV—specifically, about TV at that late hour—which made his show a major success. He knew, from the start, that the untapped audience available at that hour was a little different, with a decidedly postmidnight mentality: loyal, leisurely, maybe even a little lonely. He also knew, or correctly guessed, that the show best suited to that late hour, at least best suited to his own strengths, was one that embraced and offered intimacy. And finally, he knew enough about himself to have the confidence to *be* himself—to be prepared, but also to be prepared to digress. Snyder talked to the camera lens as if he were confiding to a friend, and talked to guests the same way. The pace was intentionally slow, and Snyder opened each show with a casual commentary, mixing general news of the day with specific news of Snyder's day. It was an intentionally different show opening from Johnny Carson's joke-after-joke monologue on *Tonight,* which served as its late-night lead-in, and

Tomorrow looked different as well: more low-key, more low-budget. The entire show was conducted through the thickest haze of cigarette smoke since
Mike Wallace hosted New York's *Night Beat* in the fifties, but Snyder's style,
while just as smoky, was conversational rather than confrontational. Not that
he couldn't ask tough questions or do tough interviews. In 1973, his first year
at the helm of *Tomorrow*, Snyder visited Saigon to interview South Vietnamese officials about the status of the Vietnam War—filing the kind of story that
would have been right at home on ABC's *Nightline*, except that *Nightline*
wouldn't exist for another six years. And in 1981, shortly before the end
of Snyder's late-night reign, he presented that show's all-time most famous
installment: a taped-in-prison special show featuring the first network interview in thirteen years with convicted killer Charles Manson. In between those
powerful bookends were late-night conversations with everyone from Orson
Welles to Jimmy Carter. An interview with John Lennon did a lot to cement
the show's cult status on college campuses, even though, once *Saturday Night
Live* arrived in 1975, Dan Aykroyd got a lot of mileage out of poking fun
at Snyder's loud laughter, chain-smoking, geniality ("fair enough, sir"), and
tendency to stray from the chosen subject. But all that was part of the style
and the fun of *Tomorrow*—fun that was ruined when NBC executives forced
Rona Barrett onto the show as a gossip contributor, and renamed the show
Tomorrow Coast to Coast. In 1982, the late-night host of *Tomorrow* was
replaced by the late-night host of tomorrow: *Late Night with David Letterman*. In 1988, an even later series—fittingly titled *Later*—was presented
on NBC after Letterman, and the host, Bob Costas, conducted intimate and
in-depth interviews in a way that revived the spirit of *Tomorrow*. The real
revival, though, came when Letterman jumped ship to CBS, mounted *Late
Show with David Letterman*, and wisely hired Snyder to star in a show following his on CBS, just as Letterman had once been hired to replace Snyder in
the post-Carson slot on NBC. It was a wonderful, almost cyclical bit of TV
synergy, and paid off nicely: *The Late Late Show with Tom Snyder*, broadcast
live to the East Coast from California, premiered on January 9, 1995, and
immediately turned into another mesmerizing Snyder showcase, with only
one significant change: no smoking. Snyder's personality, however, remained
delightfully unfiltered.

Tonight Show, The. *1954–   , NBC.* Johnny Carson dominates any historical
appreciation of this landmark late-night NBC series, because of both his longevity and a tactical advantage. Many of Carson's best *Tonight Show* bits were
repeated regularly on anniversary shows, imprinting them into our national
memory banks with almost frightening effectiveness over the years. It's been
more than thirty years since Ed Ames, who played Mingo the Indian opposite
Fess Parker's *Daniel Boone*, demonstrated his tomahawk-throwing technique
to Carson on one live show in 1964—and yet, thanks to repeated anniversary-
show exposure to that kinescope, most of America has no problem remembering and envisioning just where that tomahawk landed. (For the rest of
America, Carson's well-timed ad-lib to Ames, "I didn't even know you were
Jewish," should answer the question nicely.) Many hosts and guest hosts took

The Steve Allen Show, with Steve Allen.

Tales From the Crypt, with Jeffrey Tambor and Demi Moore as a laughably mismatched pair.

The Tonight Show Starring Johnny Carson, with Carson hosting former host Jack Paar.

their places at the *Tonight* desk, but only a handful deserve singular mention—and of those, Carson overshadows them all by dint of his tour of duty. Johnny Carson hosted *The Tonight Show* for thirty years. By comparison, the combined reigns of Steve Allen, Jack Paar, and Jay Leno, as of 1996, add up to twelve. Put it this way: for Leno to match Carson's *Tonight* tenure, he'd have to hold his job until the year 2022. So if this entry is Carson-heavy, that's why. But to trace this NBC franchise to its beginnings, you have to go all the way back to *Cafe Television*, *Broadway Open House*, and *The Steve Allen Show*. In May 1943, when its network rivals were dark during wartime, DuMont's New York station presented an odd hybrid, a talk and variety special called *Cafe Television*, hosted by Jerry Lester. "This is a feature that has promise," noted *Variety*, "despite a number of rough edges." In 1950, NBC hired Lester as one of two hosts (Morey Amsterdam was the other) of *Broadway Open House*, a variety show that first tested the waters of network late-night TV. That same year, Steve Allen began strutting his stuff on local TV in New York, and NBC executive Sylvester "Pat" Weaver finally took notice and promoted Allen to a network position, renaming the new show *Tonight!* in the process. Allen's first NBC show, broadcast on September 27, 1954, launched *Tonight!* into orbit, and it hasn't returned since. Except for a few brief holding patterns between the show's major hosts, the history and legacy of *The Tonight Show* unfolds in four different major chapters.

Tonight! (1954–57). A separate entry in this book, under *The Steve Allen Show*, details many of Allen's attributes and comedy bits that also were in evidence on *Tonight!* But this late-night show is the place where Allen popularized some of his most famous routines, including his "Stump the Band" segments (showcasing Skitch Henderson and his orchestra), his "Answer Man" bits, his "Schmock! Schmock!" nonsense catch phrase, and his angry readings of actual letters from the *New York Daily News*. Allen gets credit for establishing the blueprint for most late-night TV talk shows: his *Tonight!* presented an opening monologue, a faithful announcer-sidekick (in this case, Gene Rayburn), a desk and living-room arrangement of furniture for guests, room for "real people" to participate via outdoor segments and (for those with strange talents, like one wood-crunching man billed as the "human termite") guest appearances, and a mix of sketch comedy, musical performances, and casual talk. It's tough to understand today, with the gruesome glut of TV talk shows, how rare it was then to see and hear celebrities and newsmakers in a relatively uncontrolled setting, but that was part of the joy of those early programs. One recently discovered early kinescope, of a special Halloween *Tonight!* show mounted a month after the series' premiere, demonstrates the giddy freedom of those early days. Allen opens the show dressed head to toe in a ghostly sheet, with his band wearing identical white robes ("This is not a Klan meeting," Allen says), and plays piano, leading the band on an improvised number. Then he introduces the show's regulars, all of whom—Andy Williams, Steve Lawrence, Eydie Gorme—are in costume, and invites them and the night's guests, including Jayne Meadows and Kim Novak, to engage in such old-fashioned holiday party games as a taffy pull and a no-hands-allowed pass-the-grapefruit contest. (Steve Lawrence, trying to get the grapefruit from under Novak's chin, was the one to envy that night.) On other shows, Allen's party atmosphere often carried out to the street, where he would dress up as a hot-dog vendor, point the TV cameras outside and act as a video voyeur, and generally go out of his way—or go anywhere—for a big laugh, a lively conversation, or a strong tune. Some were more serious than others; one extended show featured Richard Rodgers as the only guest ("Just ninety minutes with sheet music spread out on the piano top," Allen recalled recently), while another showcased Carl Sandburg. Near the end of his *Tonight!* reign, Allen went part-time at night in order to combat Ed Sullivan in prime time; the alternating host at that time (1956–57) was a former DuMont late-night rival and fellow TV pioneer, Ernie Kovacs (also covered in a separate listing, under *The Ernie Kovacs Show*). Allen's last first-run *Tonight!* performance was on January 25, 1957, after which he devoted all his attention to his prime-time *Steve Allen Show*. Because Allen's *Tonight!* show was performed entirely live, and so few tapes or kinescopes survived, most of the memories attached with that show are blurred with his work on subsequent talk and variety series, for which he recycled many of his most successful characters and bits—this time for posterity. Yet every incarnation of *The Tonight Show* since Steve Allen has borrowed from him to varying degrees, while making their own stamp on the show and on TV history. "Let me give you the bad news first," Allen had said as part of his opening remarks on that very first *Tonight!* episode more than forty years ago. "This program is going to go on *forever*." He meant until the wee hours of the morning—but was telling the truth in more ways than one.

Tonight; The Jack Paar Tonight Show (1957–62). After an abortive twenty-six-week experiment called *Tonight: America after Dark* (hosted by Jack Lescoulie, who left the morning comfort of *Today* for his brief shot in the dark), *Tonight* (when Allen left, so did the exclamation point) returned to strong form with Jack Paar as host. Paar's show, which premiered July 29, 1957, was more structured than Allen's, with a more formal monologue and a strong emphasis on conversation. However, within that structure was a lot of unpredictability, and nothing was more unpredictable than Paar himself. Like Arthur Godfrey, Paar spoke directly to the TV camera with ease—and, also like Godfrey, sometimes showed his temper on the air. Like Allen, Paar feuded with Ed Sullivan, at an even higher pitch and intensity. Hugh Downs was Paar's announcer and sidekick, and others featured on the show in various capacities included Dody Goodman, Peggy Cass, Cliff "Charley Weaver" Arquette, Joey Bishop, Florence Henderson, Hermione Gingold, Betty White, Buddy Hackett, and frequent guest Zsa Zsa Gabor. Yet under Paar's reign, what we remember most is Paar himself, talking in that hesitant yet winning manner about his personal life and the news of the day, and expecting each guest to converse, rather than merely perform or promote. In fact, Paar discouraged guests from plugging upcoming appearances or projects. Once, when he anticipated guest comic Jack E. Leonard would try to monopolize a sit-down conversation, and did, Paar blithely reached over, pulled out a pair of garden shears he had hidden for precisely that eventuality, and cut Leonard's microphone cord—effectively, and literally, cutting him off in midsentence. Paar and company were capable of generating popular catch phrases (Paar's "I kid you not" was one; Downs's "Well, Kemo Sabe" was another), but most often stepped back to allow guests to talk and shine. Richard Nixon, in a famous 1960 appearance while campaigning for the presidency, came on and played piano; John F. Kennedy appeared on a separate show during the same race, and *The Jack Paar Tonight Show* also accommodated Robert F. Kennedy, Judy Garland, and a young Barbra Streisand. A few years into his run, Paar began taping shows in advance (a practice eventually adopted by every subsequent *Tonight Show* host), which led to the most famous episode of Paar's *Tonight Show* era. On February 10, 1960, Paar told a "water closet" joke during his monologue, but NBC, concerned about the "risqué" material, cut it from that night's show—making Paar's alleged "sin" seem much worse than the rather tame story he actually had told. The next day, without warning anyone on his staff, Paar waited until that night's taping began, then shocked the studio audience, and sidekick Hugh Downs, by tearfully announcing he was quitting. "I'm leaving *The Tonight Show*," Paar said. "There must be a better way of making a living than this, a way of entertaining people without being constantly involved in some form of controversy. . . . I don't need it." He walked out, Downs ran the show—and, a few hours later, so did NBC, televising Paar's impromptu resignation to a stunned nation of viewers. Guest hosts filled Paar's chair until he finally returned on March 7, receiving a standing ovation and beginning his return show with the impish phrase, "As I was saying before I was interrupted. . . . " Paar then added, "When I walked off, I said there must be a better way of making a living. Well, I've looked, and there isn't." Be that as it may, Paar, like Allen, eventually walked away from his *Tonight Show* post, ending in 1962 with a run of shows in which celebrity guests came by for one last farewell chat with Paar. On March 29, 1962, *The Jack Paar Tonight Show* closed shop with a flashy finale: at the end of his last show, Paar was carried offstage by a team of celebrity "pallbearers," including Bobby Kennedy. *The Jack Paar Tonight Show* was dead; long live *The Tonight Show*.

The Tonight Show Starring Johnny Carson (1962–92). "This show is kind of like television roulette," Johnny Carson said during his opening-day monologue on October 1, 1962. "It should be fun. . . . We booked four or five guests, and hope that one of them shows up loaded." One thing Carson discovered on that first show, and repeated on every show thereafter, was his impromptu golf swing. Another thing he discovered was that replacing the king of late night TV was no easy task, at least not at first. Some of the critics who had loved Carson when he served as a guest host on Steve Allen's *Tonight!* show now thought he was a watered-down version of his former comedic self— ironically, the same sort of criticism Jay Leno would face when ultimately replacing Carson three decades later. "This audience-courting 'Johnny Carson' who is on TV now," asked *Village Voice* TV critic Martin Williams in 1963, "is he the same Johnny Carson who ran an impudently funny show from

Hollywood a few years ago and who took over *Tonight!* from time to time from Steve Allen with equally impudent wit? Sure, he *looks* like the same fellow. . . . " Carson not only persevered; he thrived, and ruled, and bested all pretenders to his late-night throne until his retirement on May 22, 1992. Much of what Carson presented on *The Tonight Show* was borrowed from either Allen or Paar (Carson's "Carnac the Magnificent," for example, was a close relative of Allen's "Answer Man," and "Stump the Band" returned, as did bandleader Skitch Henderson), but Carson's *Tonight Show,* in and of itself, churned out a stubbornly long-lived batch of TV memories, from both its 1962–72 New York days and its Hollywood era thereafter. Start with "Johnny's Theme," the show's big-band theme song, cowritten by Paul Anka and Carson himself, and go from there. There's announcer-sidekick Ed McMahon's "Heeeere's Johnny!" intro, and his "Hey-yo!" shout of conspiratorial approval; the aforementioned tomahawk toss; the audience's eagerness to shout "How hot was it?" whenever Carson begins a joke line with "It was so hot . . . "); the convoluted "fork in the road" directions of Carson's slick "Tea Time Movie" alter ego host, Art Fern (with Carol Wayne serving, for many of those Mighty Carson Art Players years, as a modern Dagmar); Carson's Carnac, ripping open the "hermetically sealed envelope" to read the questions to such divinely predicted answers as "Dippity Do" ("What forms on your Dippity early in the morning?"); Carson's "We'll be right back" commercial intro, and his constant jokes about McMahon's drinking and the wardrobe of Doc Severinsen, who had been promoted from trumpet player to bandleader in 1967 after Henderson's departure; Carson imitating Carl Sagan, talking about those "billions and billions" of stars; Carson unabashedly wiping away tears after guest Jimmy Stewart reads "A Dog Named Bo," a self-penned poem about his recently deceased pet; Carson and guest Jack Webb trading tongue teasers in a *Dragnet* spoof about the "copper clappers" caper; Carson watching with amusement as Dean Martin sneakily (and repeatedly) flicks cigarette ashes into George Gobel's drink; and Carson watching in amazement as Tiny Tim plays his ukelele and sings. On December 17, 1969, *The Tonight Show* pulled its biggest ratings stunt by devoting itself to Tiny Tim's wedding to "Miss Vicki"; as it turned out, *The Tonight Show* outlasted that marriage, and many of Carson's as well. No video copy of Carson's first *Tonight Show* is known to exist, and many of the first decade's shows were erased by asinine NBC engineers (most of Allen's shows had met the same fate). However, night after night, and year after year, Carson turned *The Tonight Show* into one of TV's most important cultural cornerstones. Carson dealt with topical events as reliably as Walter Cronkite, and the impact of his monologue made Carson the TV equivalent of Will Rogers: one joke could make all the difference in indicating whether someone (or something) was up or down, in or out. Some of Carson's frequent guests, such as Robert Blake and Burt Reynolds, were there not because they had projects to promote (a practice Carson reinstituted after Paar left), but merely because Carson loved their irreverence. Carson also loved young children, elderly adults, and animals of all ages, and specialized in showcasing them all. Joan Embrey and Jim Fowler of the San Diego Zoo kept Carson supplied with a steady stream of giant snakes and baby orangutans, and when a tiny marmoset nestled in Carson's silver hair and urinated there, it was a highlights entry that, forever after, was marmoset in stone. One element of *The Tonight Show* that retired when Carson did, and is unlikely ever to be duplicated in this fragmentary TV universe of the late nineties, is the reverence with which two generations of standup comics held a guest spot on Carson's *Tonight Show*. Appearing on *The Tonight Show* was every comic's dream and goal—and if Carson not only gave you that honor, but flashed a sign of approval or laughed or said something complimentary as you left, your career was made. It happened to Bill Cosby, to Roseanne Barr, and to literally hundreds of talented comics in between. That impact is no longer there, on *The Tonight Show* or any other single TV venue. For singers and actors as well as comics, Carson's *Tonight Show*, especially after the demise of *The Ed Sullivan Show*, was the biggest show in town. Fittingly, when Carson, like Paar before him, gave advance warning of his intention to retire, a virtual parade of celebrities lined up to thank the *Tonight Show* host and say good-bye. Carson himself, sitting alone on a stool after saying thanks to stalwart companions McMahon and Severinsen, said his own good-bye on May 22, 1992, ending his last show with a tearful "I bid you a very heartfelt good night." The ultimate farewell, however, actually occurred on the penultimate *Tonight Show* the previous evening, when Bette Midler, Carson's final guest, added new appropriate lyrics to "One More for My Baby (and One More for the Road)," and sang them, beautifully, straight at the retiring host of *The Tonight Show Starring Johnny Carson*. "Well, that's how it goes / And John, I know you're getting anxious to close . . . / For all of the years / For the laughs, for the tears / For the class that you showed / Make it one for my baby, and one more for the road / That long, long road." Midler's vocal was filled with emotion; as she finished singing, so was Carson. It was a perfect moment of television, a guaranteed tearjerker, and a fitting finale (even if it was a day early) to one of the most durable and impressive careers in show business. Carson, like Carnac, was magnificent.

The Tonight Show with Jay Leno (1992–). Johnny Carson said farewell on a Friday. The following Monday, on May 25, 1992, Jay Leno said hello, after a protracted behind-the-scenes tug-of-war that ultimately awarded him, rather than David Letterman, custody of *The Tonight Show*. (Letterman had the show following Carson's, while Leno had been exclusive *Tonight Show* guest host for the previous five years.) With more *Tonight Show* history from which to derive, *The Tonight Show with Jay Leno* at first seemed even more derivative. He bantered with bandleader Branford Marsalis (who left in 1995) just as often as Carson had kidded with Severinsen, did the same sort of monologue, and presented lots of deskside comedy bits (reading newspaper headlines, for example) that owed a very large debt to Allen. One year after taking over *The Tonight Show*, Leno held a special live edition to help the cast of *Cheers* celebrate its final show; they celebrated a bit too boisterously, and Leno essentially lost control of the show as the inebriated cast members threw insults and spitballs, but all the bad behavior was rewarded in the ratings. That rowdy 1993 installment wound up as the third highest-rated episode in the five-decade history of *Tonight*, behind only the Tiny Tim wedding of 1969 and Carson's farewell show in 1992. Eventually, Leno regained control of his own show and changed the look and feel of it for the better, moving the audience closer and extending the monologue to encompass several individual video clips and comedy bits as well. At first, Leno did his best work interacting with *NBC Nightly News* anchor Tom Brokaw, who "reported" from the 1992 presidential conventions for Leno and displayed a pleasantly irreverent side to his personality. Then, with the advent of the O. J. Simpson trial, came infrequent but attention-grabbing appearances by "the Dancing Itos," a group of dancers made up to look like Judge Lance Ito and the principal legal figures in the decade's most prominent murder case. Some thought that in questionable taste, but audiences liked it, much as they liked, and flocked to, Hugh Grant's post-prostitute *mea culpa* appearance in 1995. That interview, in fact, may be the precise moment when Leno hit his stride and emerged from the shadows of both Carson and Letterman to make his own mark on late-night TV. Not only did he get to Grant first when every other show wanted him, but with everyone waiting to see how Leno would handle the topic, Leno hit Grant with an opening question so perfectly phrased, and so energetically delivered, that no one could have done it better: "What the hell were you *thinking?*" Leno asked him. Grant smiled sheepishly, and another *Tonight Show* all-time highlight was ready to be placed in TV's time capsule. Leno was finding his own way, and, like a baseball player slowly but surely working his way up the statistics charts, is making his mark on *The Tonight Show* in several categories. In the ratings, Leno's tortoise actually overtook Letterman's hare at the end of 1995—and even though the ups and downs of their respective networks played a part in that power shift, another factor might (and should) be the marked improvement in *The Tonight Show* during Leno's third year on the job, and under his more direct influence. Job tenure is another area where Leno is advancing: already, at this writing, he's hosted the show longer than Allen did, and is fast approaching the five years clocked by Paar. Carson's thirty-year mark may be unassailable, but there's one category in which Leno, not Carson or any other host of *Tonight*, holds the all-time record. Jay Leno was forty-one years old when he got the job as permanent host, compared to thirty-nine for Jack Paar, thirty-six for Johnny Carson, and thirty-three for Steve Allen. Although Leno often is thought of as the new kid on the block, he's actually the *Tonight* shows' "old man."

Topper. *1953–55, CBS.* A decade before *Bewitched, I Dream of Jeannie,* and *My Favorite Martian* played around with magic on TV, *Topper* was doing it— and, considering the state of special-effects technology at the time, doing it very well. Based on the movie series from the late thirties, which in turn was inspired by the Thorne Smith novel, TV's *Topper* starred Leo G. Carroll (later the boss on *The Man from U.N.C.L.E.*) as stuffy Cosmo Topper, who found himself haunted by three very free spirits: the ghosts of George and Marion Kirby (played by Robert Sterling and Anne Jeffreys) and their St. Bernard, Neil. One small legacy of this genial sitcom could be found in a much later one: when *Seinfeld* finally revealed the first name of the "Kramer" character played by Michael Richards, that name turned out to be "Cosmo." Yet so far as this fifties series was concerned, here's the real Topper: during the show's inaugural 1953 season, eleven of those *Topper* scripts were written by recent college graduate Stephen Sondheim, years before he began writing lyrics and music for the Broadway stage. Even then, Sondheim's penchant for puzzles served him well. "The leading lady, Anne Jeffreys, had a sibilant problem," Sondheim recalled decades later. "The idea was to keep S's, the letter S, out of the scripts. That meant no plurals, and no present tense." Tougher than it thoundth.

To Tell the Truth. *1956–68, CBS; 1969–77, 1980, 1990, syndicated.* This quiz show outlasted most of the others of the period, especially after the 1958 scandal (see *Twenty-One* for details), partly because it had nothing to hide. After all, this was one game show where every contestant was *supposed* to be untrustworthy. The major memories from this quiz show are mostly visual, and come from the beginning and end of each game. At the start, there are the silhouettes of the three contestants, standing there like statues before the scrim curtain rises to reveal their faces. And at the end, after the panelists had recorded their guesses as to which of the three contestants was really the person described at the beginning, host Bud Collyer (or, in the long-running syndicated version, Garry Moore) asked the still-famous phrase "Will the real————please stand up?"—whereupon all three contestants teased the panel, and the viewers, by bobbing up and down randomly until one finally confessed and stood tall. Orson Bean, Peggy Cass, Tom Poston, and Kitty Carlisle were the core panelists on the CBS version, but, to tell the truth, those visual gimmicks, and that "stand up" query, are what really stand out today.

Truth or Consequences. *1950–51, CBS; 1952, 1954–65, NBC; 1966–74, syndicated.* This series had been an immense hit on radio since 1940 when its creator, Ralph Edwards, transferred it to CBS-TV with himself as host (on the NBC versions, Jack Bailey, then Bob Barker, took over). The radio version continued until 1957, yet the TV version was an instant success—except with critics, who generally loathed the lowbrow antics that had contestants performing outlandish, usually embarrassing stunts as penalties for incorrect answers. John Crosby, reviewing the premiere telecast in New York's *Herald-Tribune*, wrote, "It reminded me strongly of Bedlam, the first English lunatic asylum, whose inmates provided amusement to throngs of spectators." Nevertheless, the loud buzzer sound used by the show to indicate a wrong or tardy response has since entered our common playful vocabulary. One other claim to lasting fame: how many other TV game shows have had towns renamed in their honor? Though television's *Truth or Consequences* has been canceled, its namesake city still exists: Truth or Consequences, New Mexico.

Twelve Angry Men. *1954, CBS.* One of several classic dramas Reginald Rose provided for TV anthology series during the so-called Golden Age, this September 20, 1954, *Studio One* offering was perfectly suited to live TV. Its confined setting of a jury room, with one juror (Robert Cummings) arguing with the other eleven about the proper verdict in a murder case, made for great drama. Not only did Rose, who had just served as a juror before writing the teleplay, win an Emmy, but Hollywood made an equally strong movie version, starring Henry Fonda, three years later. Only two of the TV cast members got to repeat their roles for the film version—which, presumably, made for ten angry men.

$25,000 Pyramid, The. See *$10,000 Pyramid, The.*

Twenty-One. *1956–58, NBC.* This quiz show, hosted by Jack Barry, is most remembered for making a college professor very famous, then very infamous, and for bringing to a boil the quiz-show scandal of the late fifties. Rumors and accusations had swirled around other shows of the period, especially *Dotto* and *The $64,000 Question,* but it was the extended, escalating war of wits between defending champion Herb Stempel and charismatic challenger Charles Van Doren that caught the attention of America in a very big way. Set up like a TV wrestling match (and about as honest), *Twenty-One* pitted the dweeby Stempel against the suave Van Doren. Their contests ended in ties for a few weeks, then, on the December 5, 1956, installment, Van Doren beat Stempel and went on to an extended run of victories against other challengers. By the middle of 1957, he was a *Time* cover subject and a cultural correspondent on *Today,* where he remained employed, and celebrated, until a grand jury investigation and a congressional subcommittee eventually revealed Van Doren's entire *Twenty-One* triumph as an elaborate sham, with questions, point values, and even suggested dramatic gestures provided in advance. In November 1959, Van Doren took the stand and said, "I would give almost anything I have to reverse the course of my life in the last three years. . . . I was involved, deeply involved, in a deception." President Dwight D. Eisenhower likened the quiz show scandal to the 1919 Black Sox World Series baseball fix, and most quiz shows involving big prizes and tough questions were yanked off the air immediately—leaving lots of room for Westerns, which became the next big TV craze. Van Doren disappeared in disgrace, and that disgrace was compounded in 1994 when a Robert Redford-directed movie, *Quiz Show,* dramatized the *Twenty-One* scandal, with Ralph Fiennes starring as Charles Van Doren and John Turturro as Herb Stempel. Ironically, *Quiz Show,* like the quiz show, took certain artistic liberties to enhance the dramatic effect. In the movie, the three-year rise and fall of Van Doren was eclipsed into as many weeks, and the climactic contest between Van Doren and Stempel—in which the latter lost the game after failing to identify *Marty* as the Oscar-winning film of 1955—was not, in real life, the climax at all. Yes, Stempel took a dive by missing the *Marty* question as instructed, but rebounded, and the end of that game was merely another Stempel-Van Doren tie. The real ending came partway through the next game on that same December 5, 1956, show, when Stempel declined, but Van Doren exercised, the standard *Twenty-One* option to award the game to the contestant with the highest point total. Glass isolation booths supposedly prevented each contestant from knowing the score of the other, but it's pretty safe to say that Van Doren knew it was pretty safe to say "I'll stop." He did, and with an 18–to–10 lead in that game, was declared the big winner. Three years later, though, he was a much bigger loser.

20/20. *1978–   , ABC.* Two of ABC's most prominent newsmagazines, *20/20* and *PrimeTime Live,* survived remarkably inauspicious beginnings. *Prime-Time Live,* which started out in 1989 with Sam Donaldson and Diane Sawyer working in front of a live audience and going to such absurd "live" locations as the trunk of a giant dying tree, could have died in those early days, with Saywer and Donaldson at the elm. Without a doubt, though, ABC News executive Roone Arledge had learned his lesson with *20/20,* which had premiered in 1978 with a particularly awkward inaugural broadcast. Rather than cancel the show outright, Arledge dismissed the cohosts (Harold Hayes and Robert Hughes) and turned over the show to former *Tonight* sidekick and *Today* host Hugh Downs. In 1984, regular correspondent Barbara Walters was promoted to cohost, and *20/20* has thrived ever since, presenting a promotable mix of newsmaker interviews, celebrity stories, and often enterprising journalism. Memorable offerings include the imported BBC-TV interview with the Princess of Wales (see *Royal Wedding),* Walters's revelatory interview with Mike Tyson and Robin Givens, and Walters's emotional, exclusive conversation with paraplegic Christopher Reeve and family; Downs's trip to the South Pole; and well-crafted reports about conditions in Somalia and a touching reunion between a Vietnamese family and its raised-in-America children. For *20/20,* though, the biggest accolade is its longevity: it is the third oldest series currently on prime-time TV, behind only *60 Minutes* and *Monday Night Football.* And halfway through the 1995–96 TV season, *20/20* had a chance, for the first time ever, to outrank that "big brother" CBS newsmagazine in the end-of-season ratings.

Twilight Zone, The. *1959–65, 1985–87, CBS; 1987–88, syndicated.* Imagine, if you will, a more persuasive proof of the existence and impact of teleliteracy than *The Twilight Zone.* It's difficult to imagine, because Rod Serling's oddball anthology series has been absorbed, reflected, and perpetuated by our culture in ways too numerous to count. Movie offshoots, sequel series, annual marathons, and Serling imitators abound. Marius Constant's musical theme, especially its four-note introduction, serves as a shorthand synonym for surrealism. The show's opening images—disconnected eyeballs and doors and such—are truly classic, as is Serling's introductory narration, which evolved slightly over the years but is typified by this memorable version: "You're traveling through another dimension, a dimension not only of sight and sound, but of mind. . . . Next stop, the Twilight Zone!" Serling, like Alfred Hitchcock, became more famous for his TV anthology hosting chores than for the less glamorous behind-the-scenes creative work that landed him the job in the first place. When TV anthology series were televised live, Serling had written such superb dramas as *Requiem for a Heavyweight* (see separate listing) and *Patterns.* But those early Serling conquests were in the midfifties. Within a few years, live TV was succumbing to tape or film, and anthologies were succumbing to Westerns (eight prime-time anthology shows were canceled in an eighteen-month period). When *Studio One,* one of the best of them, was canceled, Westinghouse made a deal with Desi Arnaz to sponsor a new series called *Westinghouse Desilu Playhouse*—a series that, in two brief seasons before its own demise in 1960, presented separate installments serving as launching pads for two memorable series. One was a two-parter called *The Untouchables,* and the other was Serling's 1958 story called *The Time Element,* a time-travel fantasy that persuaded CBS to back *The Twilight Zone.* That's how Rod Serling arrived at *The Twilight Zone.* What he did when he got to that fifth dimension was, quite simply, to create, and collaborate in creating, one of the most singularly inventive TV series in history. "We want to prove," Serling wrote in *TV Guide* the month his *Twilight Zone* premiered, "that television, even in its half-hour form, can be both commercial and worthwhile." Commercial? Not entirely, because *The Twilight Zone,* like *Star Trek,* never ranked in the Top 25 for any given season. Worthwhile? Indisputably, because no other anthology series on television can claim to have produced so many episodes that have meant so much to so many for so long. Serling, Richard Matheson, Charles Beaumont, and the other writers let their imaginations fly, and took viewers along for the ride. Nine of the *Twilight Zone* installments, by my estimation, are so resonant they have to be listed here—yet, at the same time, so familiar that shorthand identifications will suffice. See how many you can replay in your mind after these briefest of mentions: "Nightmare at 20,000 Feet" (William Shatner with a fear of flying); "Time Enough at Last" (bookworm Burgess Meredith without his glasses); "The Eye of the Beholder" (cosmetic surgery fails to make Donna Douglas look "pretty"); "Number Twelve Looks Just Like You" (cosmetic surgery succeeds in making everyone equally beautiful); "To Serve Man" (aliens cook up a use for humanity); "The After Hours" (Anne Francis as a mannequin on her night off); "The Invaders" (Agnes Moorehead silently battling some tiny spacemen); "Stop at Willoughby" (James Daly takes a fast train to a slower lifestyle); and "Living Doll" (Telly Savalas is terrorized by a talking doll). There are other, less universally remembered episodes of *The Twilight Zone* that I particularly liked, and, from the 1985 sequel series, I also was quite impressed by "Shatterday" (an episode directed by Wes Craven and based on a Harlan Ellison story, starring Bruce Willis as an extreme victim of split personality), and by a remake of "Dead Man's Shoes" from the original *Twilight Zone* series, only this time with the sexual roles reversed and with Helen Mirren in the leading role. It was "Living Doll" from the original series, however, that frightened me the most as a kid, thanks to that squeaky doll-voice saying sinister, unforgettable things like, "My name is Talky Tina, and I'm going to *kill* you." As it turns out, that spooky Talky Tina voice was provided by June Foray, the same woman who, in another TV show from the same period, gave voice (a much happier one) to one of my favorite characters of all: Rocky the Flying Squirrel.

Twin Peaks. *1990–91, ABC.* It's fashionable, five years or so after its demise, to dump on *Twin Peaks* as having been an eccentric failure. It was eccentric, certainly, and its ratings fall was as swift as its rise, but *Twin Peaks* did as many things right as it did wrong. Ultimately, and regrettably, what it did wrong killed it: *Twin Peaks* dragged on the "Who killed Laura Palmer?" mystery long past acceptable limits (counting the loose ends, it consumed twenty hours of TV time, about the same as the entire season-long mystery on *Murder One*). After its bold and often brilliant initial season, *Twin Peaks* seemed to care less about continuity, coherence, and common sense than even its most fervent fans could accept. As the series progressed into a second season, subplots came and went with no rhyme or reason, and though the journey was intriguing to the very end (the very inconclusive end, that is), *Twin Peaks* wound up as a series that was headed nowhere fast, filling up space with digressions and distractions like a college student trying to fake his way through an essay test. The drawn-out chess game with Kenneth Welsh's demonic Windom Earle, for example, made little sense dramatically—and, after a few moves, made no sense at all as an actual chess game. But think, for a moment, about what *Twin Peaks* did right. The series, created by David Lynch and Mark Frost, introduced a murder mystery—the serial killing of Sheryl Lee's enigmatic Laura Palmer—that viewers and the media quickly inflated to "Who shot J.R.?" proportions. Its slightly (or, in some cases, wholly) surrealistic characters, led by Kyle MacLachlan's stoic and heroic Dale Cooper, made *Twin Peaks* the most unusual and puzzling TV series since *The Prisoner*, and its hefty helpings of intentional allusions, to everything from *Laura* and *Double Indemnity* to the lookalike-cousin concept from *The Patty Duke Show* and the one-armed man from *The Fugitive*, made it the subject of animated and lengthy scrutiny, everywhere from the lunch room to the classroom. Even when it lost its way in terms of plot, *Twin Peaks* tried harder, and did more, than most weekly series on television. It gave as much emphasis to visual images and lighting, and to the musical score and sound effects, as it did to the scripts and performances. Some sequences consisted of long, unbroken camera takes; others were subliminal montages, cut together a frame at a time. Several core scenes, such as the Tibetan rock-throwing experiment and the so-called Dancing Dwarf dream, stretched from one commercial break to the next without changing scenes. Conversely, in the series' final episode, as a doppelgänger Laura Palmer ran screaming toward a frightened Cooper, director Lynch increased the tension of the scene by inserting single-frame images of the villainous Windom Earle as she ran forward—close-ups alternating from a black-and-white negative image of Earle to a full-color positive image, then to a blending of the two, all shown too briefly for the naked eye to detect. Lynch directed only a handful of *Twin Peaks* episodes, but all of the show's most resonant, unforgettable set pieces—Cooper extracting a tiny letter 'R' from deep within one of the late Laura's fingernails, Cooper's Tibetan rock-throwing, the "Red Room" sequences featuring the tiny Man from Another Place (seen early in the series and again in its final episode), and the disturbing death of Laura's lookalike cousin, Madeleine, at the hands of Laura's father, Ray Wise's Leland Palmer—were directed by Lynch. They also were written or cowritten by Mark Frost, who, like Lynch, deserves credit for TV boldness on a very large scale. Elements of *Twin Peaks*

LEFT: *Twenty-One,* with infamous contestant Charles Van Doren in the isolation booth.
RIGHT: *The Untouchables,* with Robert Stack as Eliot Ness.

Twin Peaks, with Mädchen Amick, Peggy Lipton, Everett McGill, Wendy Robie, and Kyle MacLachlan at the front row of a graveside service for Laura Palmer.

that caught on quickly, and enjoyed a half-life after the series itself had vanished from ABC, included strange snippets of dialogue ("She's dead; wrapped in plastic," "The owls are not what they seem," "This must be where pies go when they die," "Diane, I'm holding in my hand a small box of chocolate bunnies," "She's filled with secrets"); seemingly benign yet complex images (stacks of doughnuts, a sensuously tied cherry stem, whirring ceiling fans, changing traffic lights); and Angelo Badalamenti's alternately eerie and playful music. *Twin Peaks* had an amazingly deep and talented cast, with terrific contributions by MacLachlan as Cooper, Michael Ontkean as Sheriff Harry Truman, Sheryl Lee as both Laura and Madeleine, Sherilyn Fenn as Audrey Horne, Ray Wise as Leland Palmer, Don S. Davis as Major Briggs, Jack Nance as Pete Martell, Piper Laurie as Catherine Martell (and the Japanese mystery man Tojimura), Joan Chen as Josie Packard, Miguel Ferrer as Albert Rosenfeld, and, in smaller roles, David Duchovny as Denise Bryson and Michael J. Anderson as the Man from Another Place. Even the underused regulars, like Peggy Lipton and Mädchen Amick, shone, and only the pressures of weekly production and a meandering series of plots dragged *Twin Peaks* from its pop-culture pedestal. Had it been a self-contained eight-hour miniseries, with the Laura Palmer murder resolved at the end, *Twin Peaks* would have come and gone quickly, been hailed as utterly brilliant, and left critics and audiences clamoring for more. As it was, *Peaks* lost its way, lapsed dangerously close to self-parody, and was further hurt by the merciless reaction to Lynch's feature-film prequel, 1992's *Twin Peaks: Fire Walk with Me*. Yet the Japanese embraced the series, Bravo repeated it on cable as "TV too good for TV," and the influence of *Twin Peaks* could be found in several ambitious subsequent series, from the oddball characters of *Northern Exposure* and *Picket Fences* to the sinister underpinnings and visual artistry of *VR.5* and *Wild Palms*. *Twin Peaks* peaked early—but it made a difference.

Uncounted Enemy, The: A Vietnam Deception. *1982, CBS.* This CBS documentary is remembered not because of its content—when it was televised, it finished dead last in the weekly ratings—but for what came afterward. General William C. Westmoreland, who in the documentary was accused of intentionally underestimating enemy strength in South Vietnam to paint a rosier wartime picture, sued CBS for libel. He also sued, as codefendants, narrator Mike Wallace, producer George Crile, and paid CBS consultant Samuel A. Adams. Westmoreland withdrew his suit just before the case went to the jury for deliberation, but an internal CBS study, while not invalidating the documentary's conclusions, found fault with the way it had been edited, researched, and presented. It was an embarrassing incident for CBS in general and Wallace in particular, though not ultimately fatal to the journalistic credibility of either. And, like the equally notorious exploding-truck story on *Dateline NBC*, it drove networks to think more carefully about how such exposés should be assembled and televised.

Underdog. *1964–66, 1968–73, NBC; 1966–67, CBS.* Wally Cox provided the voice of Shoeshine Boy (which should have been, in this case, Shoeshine Puppy) turned supercanine, and it's that voice that's remembered most—the one that opened the show each week with Cox's proud cry, "There's no need to fear! Underdog is here!" Slightly less familiar, but perhaps still stuck in many memories, is the bouncy chorus from that same theme song: "Speed of lightning, roar of thunder / Fighting all who rob or plunder. . . . / Underdog!" Ordinarily, those might be considered insufficient grounds for inclusion here, but I've always been one to root for the *Underdog*.

Undersea World of Jacques Cousteau, The. *1968–76, ABC.* This series of ABC nature specials made Jacques-Yves Cousteau the world's most famous oceanographer. Actually, it was Johnny Carson who did that, by making an endless series of "Jacques Cousteau" jokes on *The Tonight Show*, but these are the shows that got Carson's attention in the first place. Back in the forties, Cousteau, along with colleague Emile Gagnan, had invented the Aqua-Lung, opening up a wet new world for human exploration. In the sixties, armed with newly developed submersible craft and underwater cameras, Cousteau and company dove into television with a passion. They did (and, on the TBS series *National Geographic Explorer* and elsewhere, continue to do) fine work, and their exploration of the Great Barrier Reef, in particular, was breathtaking. *The Undersea World of Jacques Cousteau* may have been intellectually and photographically inferior to the underwater portions of David Attenborough's *Life on Earth*, *The Living Planet*, and *The Trials of Life* series, but Carson never made any David Attenborough jokes, so Jacques Cousteau is the man upon whom I bousteau a higher recognition factor—at least where the average viewer is concerned. In 1995, TBS celebrated the life and triumphs of Cousteau by presenting a birthday special, *Jacques-Yves Cousteau: My First 85 Years*.

Unplugged. *1989– , MTV.* On October 31, 1989, musician Jules Shear hosted the pilot of a new series called *Unplugged*, the highlight of which was an acoustic jam featuring Shear, Syd Straw, Elliot Easton, and Squeeze members Chris Difford and Glen Tilbrook performing the old Monkees hit "I'm a Believer." It was a fairly low-level highlight, but Shear had tapped into something big, even if he and MTV mutually agreed it was too big to require the services of a collaborative host. *Unplugged* did some wonderful shows in its first year of operation, showcasing the likes of 10,000 Maniacs, Sinead O'Connor, Stevie Ray Vaughan, Neil Young, and, in a 1990 solo piano concert, Elton John. But it was in April 1991, when Paul McCartney and his band appeared, that *Unplugged* moved to a higher level. McCartney so loved the loose feel of his acoustic set that he released a seventeen-song version of it on CD, called *Unplugged: The Official Bootleg* and limited to a pressing of five hundred thousand copies, after which, he vowed, no more would be available. It was a canny way for McCartney to avoid embarrassing comparisons if the informal album didn't sell, but not to worry: it quickly hit the Top 20, and, five years later, *The Official Bootleg* is an official collector's item. R.E.M. was next, with a stunning acoustic set that remains one of the series' best "unofficial" bootlegs, and Sting, L L Cool J, and Elvis Costello all followed with high-energy, high-artistry 1991 editions. But it took Eric Clapton, in 1992, to plug *Unplugged* into the apex of pop culture, with an *Unplugged* performance that took him back to his blues roots, launched him on an unexpected musical journey, and, when *Unplugged* was released on CD, rewarded him with his most popular album ever, an "Album of the Year" Grammy-winner with more than seven million copies sold. At that point, *Unplugged* became big business, appealed to all the big artists, and created a synergy between TV exposure and record sales that made *The Monkees* look like a warmup act. ("I'm a Believer," indeed.) Subsequent *Unplugged* CD releases, most of them selling several million copies apiece, have featured a rather eclectic roster of artists: Rod Stewart, Mariah Carey, Jimmy Page and Robert Plant, Tony Bennett (another Grammy-winning *Unplugged* artist), Nirvana, Bob Dylan, Bruce Springsteen (in a defiantly electrified *Unplugged* performance), and Neil Young. The Nirvana concert, capturing Kurt Cobain in a suitably soulful and an unusually intimate setting, was an artistic and emotional triumph on both CD and TV, as were the concerts by Clapton and Dylan (Clapton's acoustic *Unplugged* reworking of "Layla," and Nirvana's hauntingly stripped-down "All Apologies," became radio hits in their own right). Of the *Unplugged* performances officially available only on MTV, the best concerts include those by Paul Simon, k. d. lang, Elton John, Hole, and Melissa Etheridge, whose already strong solo showcase jumped a notch when Springsteen joined her on stage for an acoustic duet on "Thunder Road." With showstoppers like that, it's no wonder that, by the midnineties, the word "unplugged," at least among the MTV generation, had all but replaced that old-fashioned musical term, "acoustic."

Untouchables, The. *1959–63, ABC.* If *Westinghouse Desilu Playhouse* had a series spinoff in mind when it presented its two-part drama called *The Untouchables* in 1959, it achieved success in spite of itself. That inaugural *Untouchables* adventure, introducing Robert Stack as incorruptible treasury agent Eliot Ness, did a lot of things wrong. First, it ended with Ness and his task force arresting Al Capone, thus removing the major villain from center stage before a series could begin. Second, its shootouts were staged with little regard for credibility: one climactic battle took place in a Chicago bootlegging warehouse, with agents and the mob trading gunfire while standing ankle-deep in flammable alcohol. Third, Neville Brand's performance as Capone was so stiff that he'd only occasionally remember he was supposed to be playing an Italian gang leader, and at such times would a-throw in an extra 'a' for good a-measure. (You'd think studio executive Desi Arnaz, of all people, would-a be sensitive to such a-tacky accents.) But viewers loved it, and the unprecedented levels of televised violence made *The Untouchables* a steadily building hit when it went to series (by its second season, in more ways than one, it had shot into the Top 10). Walter Winchell provided the memorably no-nonsense narration, couching the series in a context of historical accuracy, but accuracy was hardly the show's strong point: The "Untouchables" unit assembled by Ness, in real life, had disbanded after nabbing Capone. But working under the dictum that Ness is more, *The Untouchables* sent him off after a succession of other bad guys (and gals), such as Bruce Gordon's Frank Nitti, Lloyd Nolan's George "Bugs" Moran, Peter Falk's Nate Selko, Claire Trevor's Ma Barker, and Elizabeth Montgomery's Rusty Heller. (Other guest stars included Robert Redford, Robert Duvall, Carroll O'Connor, and Telly Savalas.) Characters, good and bad, were dispatched by machine-gun fire, hit-and-run "accidents," stabbings, hangings, drownings, involuntary high dives from tall buildings, and so on—all staged almost cartoonishly, yet with such frequency and undisguised glee that *The Untouchables*, as it became more popular, also became a major target of antiviolence TV groups and congressional investigators, and was cited frequently and often contemptuously during Senator Thomas J. Dodd's 1961 Senate Subcommittee on Juvenile Delinquency hearings. That led to a temporary dilution of the show's violence quotient, but the biggest objections, and most drastic responses, revolved around the Federation of the Italian American Democratic Organizations of the State of New York. Its members showed their opposition to *The Untouchables*, and what they called its ethnic stereotyping, by boycotting Liggett & Myers, whose L&M cigarettes were advertised on the show. L&M dropped its sponsorship, Desi Arnaz panicked and relented, and from that point on *The Untouchables* chased a lot of crooks named "Smith" and "Jones"—and, in one laughable instance doubtlessly inspired by the Cold War, a villain named "Joe Vodka." Ratings plummeted, and Arnaz eventually returned *The Untouchables* to an approximation of its early years, but by then most viewers had declared it *Unwatchable*. The reputation of the series was enhanced greatly in 1987, when director Brian De Palma presented Kevin Costner as Eliot Ness, and Robert De Niro as Al Capone, in a big-budget movie remake of *The Untouchables*. Stack himself reprised the Ness role in a 1991 telemovie, *The Return of Eliot Ness*, while a new syndicated series, with Tom Amandes as Ness and William Forsythe as Capone, appeared the following year. The movie version was very entertaining, but neither of the *Untouchables* TV sequels was even remotely Ness-essary.

Upstairs, Downstairs. *1974, 1976, 1977, PBS. Masterpiece Theatre* had been up and running for three years when it finally imported its first major attention-getting "hit": *Upstairs, Downstairs*, a period piece covering the years 1900 to 1930 and examining a London household from the perspectives of both its residents and servants. The London Weekend Television miniseries had been "a national institution in Britain," according to one British critic, since its 1970 debut there—and even though PBS butchered the original sequencing of the series, dropping thirteen of the early episodes, *Upstairs, Downstairs* proved very popular here as well. The series had been concocted by actresses Jean Marsh and Eileen Atkins, both of whose parents had been in domestic service, but Atkins abdicated her intended costarring role to pursue other projects, leaving Marsh to star, and steal the show, as the sensible maid Rose. Other cast members who came to prominence in these serialized stories included Gordon Jackson as Hudson and Lesley-Anne Down as the stunning Georgina. The title is the most resonant reminder of this PBS soap opera, but that's to be expected. After all, it was lifted from a familiar nursery rhyme: "Goosey goosey gander, / Whither do you wander? / Upstairs, downstairs, / And in my lady's chamber."

U.S. Steel Hour, The. *1953–55, ABC; 1955–63, CBS. Theatre Guild on the Air,* an ambitious and popular radio series sponsored by U.S. Steel, ran from 1945 to 1949 on ABC radio, and from then until 1953 on NBC, sometimes under the title of *The United States Steel Hour.* In 1953, the production switched over to television, and for the next ten years presented live dramas from New York on a biweekly basis. The title *U.S. Steel* may not jar many memories, but some of the anthology series' individual productions certainly will—especially *No Time for Sergeants,* the 1955 program introducing Andy Griffith in the role he would re-create for Broadway and the movies, and *Bang the Drum Slowly,* the 1956 drama starring Paul Newman (see separate listing). Rod Serling wrote the intense wartime interrogation drama *The Rack* for *U.S. Steel* in 1955, the same year James Dean starred in a drama called *The Thief.* Cliff Robertson starred in a 1961 character study called *The Two Worlds of Charlie Gordon,* based on the *Flowers for Algernon* story by Daniel Keyes; seven years later, Robertson would repeat the role in a movie called *Charly,* and win a Best Actor Oscar for his efforts. Lesser-known but tantalizing productions from the more than two hundred *U.S. Steel Hour* installments include two *Wizard of Oz* alumni, Bert Lahr and Margaret Hamilton, reuniting for a 1957 show called *You Can't Win;* Gypsy Rose Lee and Rip Torn costarring in 1958's *The Charmer;* George C. Scott and Dick Van Dyke teaming for 1959's *Trap for a Stranger;* Sid Caesar, Audrey Meadows, and Tony Randall in a 1959 *Holiday on Wheels* special; Ernie Kovacs and Edie Adams teaming for a 1961 gumshoe spoof called *Private Eye, Private Eye;* and, on the very last *U.S. Steel Hour* in 1963, a production of *The Old Lady Shows Her Medals,* starring theatrical legends Alfred Lunt and Lynn Fontanne. Among the other noteworthy performers appearing on the TV version of *U.S. Steel* were, just to provide a representative sample, Helen Hayes, Steve McQueen, John Cassavetes, William Shatner, Jack Klugman, Richard Boone, Gene Hackman, Wally Cox, Martin Sheen, Piper Laurie, and, in a rare dramatic role, Johnny Carson. Though the common memories of this fine anthology series may be fading fast as the decades pass, I'm *Steel* crazy after all these years.

Victory at Sea. *1952–53, NBC*. Eight years after the end of World War II, NBC presented a Sunday afternoon documentary series—twenty-six episodes and thirteen hours long—devoted to retelling the story of that war. Richard Rodgers, who only three years previously had written the music for the Broadway hit *South Pacific*, returned to the South Pacific with a vengeance, writing virtually wall-to-wall music for the mammoth nonfiction series, and the music was a very big reason *Victory at Sea* was so warmly received from the start. Other elements, though, were equally important. *Victory at Sea* was the first lengthy TV study of its type, and hooked audiences just as miniseries of a less factual nature would do a generation later. It was a critical hit from the start, with even the *New Yorker* chiming in to dub it "certainly one of the most ambitious and successful ventures in the history of television." The skillfully edited images, taken from war footage and documentary films from ten different countries, told the story from all perspectives, and told it in a straightforward, intentionally simple manner. The opening words by narrator Leonard Graves established the program's bare-bones, telegram-type tone: "War has begun. Ships are sinking. Men are dying." *Victory at Sea* was such a hit that, after its initial TV run, it was shown theatrically in a New York art house, and has been available on TV or video ever since: in 1995, on the fiftieth anniversary of the end of the war in the Pacific, the entire series was rerun on cable's History Channel.

Voyage to the Bottom of the Sea. *1964–68, ABC*. Based on the 1961 movie, this underwater Irwin Allen action series got more absurd every year—as did its spiritual TV successor of the nineties, *seaQuest DSV* (and the newer, but not at all improved, *seaQuest 2032*). However, the pinging radar sounds from *Voyage to the Bottom of the Sea* are hard to forget, as are the tacky bathtub models used whenever audiences were given a sea view of the Seaview. The ultimate legacy of this show, though, is the way series stars David Hedison, Richard Basehart, and the rest of the crew would fling themselves from one side of the set to another as the TV camera tilted with them, giving the "illusion" of a ship in distress (and accompanied, always, by that "whee-oo!" warning signal). It was a maneuver gleefully imitated by most young fans of the series—and even before *Voyage to the Bottom of the Sea* sank to the bottom of the ratings and was jettisoned from the ABC schedule, the same maneuver was adopted by the far-flung crew of *Star Trek*. You'd think, after all those years of being human pinballs under the sea or out in space, someone would have thought to install seat belts on the bridge. . . .

Waco Showdown and Branch Davidian Fire. *1993, CNN and various networks.* The last time a religious compound burned to the ground and claimed many victims, including children, on live TV—as reporters and viewers watched in disbelief—was in 1985, when an incendiary device was dropped by police on the headquarters and living quarters of the MOVE organization in Philadelphia, with the resultant blaze and carnage relayed by local stations. But on April 19, 1993, as the Branch Davidian's Ranch Apocalypse compound near Waco, Texas, became engulfed in flames, the TV coverage was national—and as the fire spread, all the major networks preempted regular programming to join in. The standoff between cult leader David Koresh and his followers had reached deadly proportions fifty-one days earlier, when an unsuccessful February 28 raid had left four federal agents dead. TV news operations kept an eye on the story, and the compound, thereafter, but only CNN was televising live at 1:07 P.M. (EDT) as the first wisps of smoke began to waft from a compound window. Ironically, and ghoulishly, CNN was conducting a telephone interview at the time with Bonnie Haldeman, Koresh's mother, who was watching the standoff on live TV. Perhaps even more ghoulishly, she hung up at the first sight of flames—not because of grief or shock, which would have been perfectly understandable, but because a camera crew for *A Current Affair* was ready to record her previously arranged phone interview with anchorwoman Maureen O'Boyle. The attendant "How do you feel?" questions, as a mother watched her son burn to death on national TV, were reprehensible. So was the decision by NBC to rush-produce a telemovie, based on the initial February assault on Koresh headquarters, for broadcast during the May ratings sweeps. As it turned out, *In the Line of Duty: Ambush in Waco*, starring Timothy Daly as David Koresh, was filming the day the real compound went up in flames. Instead of a rush to judgment, it was a rush to dramatize—and a totally indefensible one, especially since no telemovie author, at that point in time, could know what happened behind those walls. In fact, it was more than two years later, in July 1995, before *Nightline* obtained and broadcast excerpts of government-recorded audiotapes, from phone taps and other sources, revealing the true nature of behind-closed-door conversations during the fifty-one-day standoff, including the shootout dramatized in the NBC telemovie. An equally impressive and informative *Frontline* edition, *Waco—The Inside Story*, was presented by PBS a few months later.

Wagon Train. *1957–62, NBC; 1962–65, ABC.* The year 1957 was a boom year for quality Westerns: *Maverick* started that year, and *Have Gun, Will Travel*, and so did *Wagon Train*. Based on a 1950 John Ford movie called *Wagonmaster*, the TV version starred the same actor, Ward Bond, who had held the reins in the original film. With Robert Horton as his costar, the two set out on a cross-country trek that, each week, focused on a guest star whose character was part of, or somehow affected by, the ongoing wagon train. This anthology-story approach explains how *Wagon Train*, which from 1958 to 1962 was one of TV's most popular series, kept going for years, *Law & Order*-like, after the departure of both of its original leading men (Bond died, Horton quit), and also explains the rather amazing list of guest stars during the Western's seven-year, two-network run. Bette Davis appeared in three separate episodes, playing a different character each time. Peter Fonda and Dennis Hopper, several years before *Easy Rider*, took to the open road here, though not together. Others hopping aboard *Wagon Train* over the years included Ronald Reagan, Peter Falk, Lee Marvin, Angie Dickinson, Rod Steiger, Martin Landau, James Caan, Barbara Stanwyck, Robert Culp, Robert Vaughn, Wally Cox, Katharine Ross, Art Linkletter, Suzanne Pleshette, Audrey Meadows, Mickey Rooney, Lou Costello, and Annette Funicello. That kind of *Train* passes this way but once.

Walt Disney's Wonderful World of Color. See *Disneyland*.

Walter Cronkite in Vietnam. See *CBS Evening News, The*.

Waltons, The. *1972–81, CBS.* If you count the first and most recent telemovies as well as the long-running CBS series, Earl Hamner, Jr.'s, story of *The Waltons* spans nearly a quarter-century on television, as well as more than thirty years in the dramatized life of the Walton clan. (Actually, its history runs even deeper: Hamner's original semiautobiographical novel first came to the screen as *Spencer's Mountain*, the 1963 film starring Henry Fonda.) For TV, Hamner first adapted his own story in the 1971 telemovie *The Homecoming*, which was set in 1931 and told its tale of a poor but proud Virginia mountain family, the Waltons, from the point of view of the eldest son, John-Boy. Richard Thomas reprised his John-Boy role when *The Waltons* was spun off as a TV series the following year, with Hamner himself providing the narration by the "adult" John-Boy. (Or is it John-Man?) After a slow start, *The Waltons* became one of TV's biggest hits of the early seventies, and its signature closing scene—a far shot of the Walton home at night, with the bedroom lights being turned off as we hear the family members deliver their traditional nocturnal exchanges—has been embraced, or parodied, far and wide ("Goodnight, John-Boy" remains the series' most famous catch phrase). CBS said goodnight to *The Waltons* for good in 1981, only to see them resurface on NBC in a trio of *Walton* telemovies the following year. They returned on CBS for a 1993 telemovie, *A Walton Thanksgiving Reunion*. In that particular production, John-Boy was a New York TV writer attending a holiday reunion in 1963, bringing home a young lady to meet the folks (Ralph Waite and Michael Learned)—just in time to witness, along with the rest of America that fateful November, TV coverage of the assassination of John F. Kennedy. Another CBS telemovie, *A Walton Wedding*, followed in 1995, marking a significant maturation in the central character's development: John-Boy proposed marriage. "I'd like that very much, John-Boy," says the bride-to-be, at which point the groom-to-be flashes a wry smile and says, "Why don't you call me John?"

Wanted: Dead or Alive. *1958–61, CBS*. Like Chuck Connors in *The Rifleman*, Steve McQueen in *Wanted: Dead or Alive* is remembered on his TV Western, if at all, for speaking softly and carrying a big gun. Actually, in McQueen's case, it was a sawed-off carbine—and *Wanted: Dead or Alive* makes the cut here merely because its star was a bigger screen idol, whatever the size of the screen. Simply put: more kids, indulging their imaginations, wanted to be McQueen for a day. And that day may not be over yet, because Universal recently acquired film rights to the story.

War and Remembrance. See *Winds of War*.

Watch Mr. Wizard. *1951–65, 1971–72, NBC*. The familiar cry of "Gee, Mr. Wizard!" is familiar for a good reason—and the reason is former public school science teacher Don Herbert, who, for the benefit of one young wide-eyed studio "assistant" and millions of children watching at home, conducted thousands of simple, easily duplicated scientific experiments using common household items and ingredients. How do you fully inflate a toy balloon inside a soda bottle, for example? Simple. Before you blow up the balloon, slip a soda straw into the bottle, so the air already inside the bottle can be pushed out through the straw as the balloon expands. Then remove the straw, show the bottled-up balloon to friends, and see if they can figure out how to duplicate the trick. Gee, no wonder Mr. Wizard lasted so long on TV. After an amazingly long run and a brief comeback on NBC, Herbert came back yet again, launching the similarly structured *Mr. Wizard's World* on Nickelodeon in 1983. By this time, Herbert was more or less an old dog teaching old tricks, but the concept, the experiments, and Herbert are as appealing and inspirational as ever: a dozen years after its Nickelodeon premiere, *Mr. Wizard's World* still is part of the cable network's daytime lineup.

Watergate Hearings. *1973, CBS, NBC, ABC, and PBS*. Television didn't really pick up the Watergate ball, carried chiefly by *Washington Post* print reporters Carl Bernstein and Bob Woodward, until October 1972, when *The CBS Evening News with Walter Cronkite* devoted nearly all of one newscast to a *Nightline*-like examination of the White House scandal and cover-up. Television, however, became the primary player the following summer, when Democratic Senator Sam Ervin of North Carolina hammered his gavel to open the Senate Select Committee on Presidential Campaign Activities— known more informally, and widely, as the Ervin Committee, or the Watergate hearings. The public hearings began on May 17, 1973, and TV was there, gavel to gavel, every weekday thereafter until the initial hearings concluded on August 7. Not every network was there every day: after the first full week of as-it-happened coverage, the commercial broadcast networks presented live daytime testimony on a rotating basis, with CBS, NBC, and ABC taking turns every third day. The option existed for networks to provide live coverage outside of their turn in the rotation, but that happened only once, during the week-long testimony of former White House counsel John Dean. That testimony was key, it was riveting, and it was responsible for the two most famous phrases from the Watergate hearings: Dean's recounting of his warning to Richard Nixon that Watergate was a cancer growing on the presidency, and Republican Tennessee Senator Howard Baker's simple yet crucial question to Dean: "What did the President know, and when did he know it?" The other major bombshell during those hearings came on July 16, when an unscheduled witness named Alexander Butterfield, a former Nixon aide in the White House, testified to the existence of a private taping system installed at the President's own request—a revelation that ultimately helped lead to Nixon's resignation. The televised Watergate hearings, pulling even larger audiences than the Estes Kefauver and Army-McCarthy hearings of the fifties, were a rare chance (in those days before C-SPAN) to see the government at work, in real time, on a truly crucial national issue. And for those who were unable to watch during the day, PBS presented a valuable service, gained millions of new viewers, and increased its own fund-raising coffers enormously, by televising delayed but unedited nightly coverage of each day's Watergate testimony—coverage hosted by a newly teamed pair of PBS anchors, Robert MacNeil and Jim Lehrer. In 1994, twenty years after Nixon's resignation, the Discovery Channel presented a five-part documentary, *Watergate* (coproduced with the BBC), which answered, more completely than any previous account, Baker's famous Watergate query about the President. The persuasive answer, bolstered by newly discovered evidence: he knew a lot, and he knew it early.

Welcome Back, Kotter. *1975–79, ABC*. In this frighteningly popular seventies sitcom, standup comic Gabe Kaplan starred as Gabe Kotter, the wisecracking high-school teacher of a bunch of slacker "sweathogs." The elements of the series that really caught on, though, had little to do with Kotter's central character. Instead, they were sex symbol John Travolta as Vinnie Barbarino, who catapulted from this series to movie stardom; Ron Palillo as Arnold Horshack, whose loud horse-laugh catapulted him to instant popularity and eventual anonymity; and the theme song, "Welcome Back," written and performed by John Sebastian, one of the dozen or so TV themes to go all the way to Number One. Today's young viewers might not have remembered much about the sweathogs, or realized how closely many of those characters resembled the classmates of *Saved by the Bell*, were it not for Travolta's latest comeback as one of the stars of the film *Pulp Fiction*. As a result of the widespread popularity of that movie, Nick at Nite began rerunning episodes of *Welcome Back, Kotter* in 1995, exposing a new generation to Barbarino, Horshack, and company. *Welcome Back* again? Not by me.

What's My Line? *1950–67, CBS; 1968–75, syndicated*. The longest-running prime-time TV game show in history, *What's My Line?* ran for seventeen years as a nighttime CBS fixture, then turned around and clocked another seven successful years in syndication. The syndicated series was much less intelligent and entertaining; the CBS version is the one worth remembering. It's the one in which moderator John Daly, who himself had been a panelist on the short-lived 1948 CBS game show *Riddle Me This,* hosted an amiable panel of witty urbanites whose collective task was to take turns guessing a contestant's occupation—or, in the case of the weekly "mystery guest," to don silly-looking blindfolds and ascertain the unseen celebrity's identity. (The very first mystery guest? New York Yankees shortstop Phil Rizzuto.) Panelists were restricted to asking yes or no questions, and any contestant drawing ten "no" answers before revealing his or her secret was proclaimed a winner and given the game's highest prize—fifty dollars in cash. (Partly because of this paltry payoff, *What's My Line?* comfortably rode out the quiz-show scandals that claimed so many other prime-time game shows in the fifties.) The *What's My Line?* practice of steering contestants toward a chalk board and asking them to "enter and sign in, please" was repeated so often, and for so many years, that it became a national catch phrase—as did frequent guest panelist Steve Allen's "Is it bigger than a breadbox?" query, a question so strange it managed to stick in pop-culture consciousness. Daly had the most polished TV grammar this side of Eric Sevareid, and his black-tie wardrobe and approach made *What's My Line?* much more conversational than confrontational. Dorothy Kilgallen, Bennett Cerf, and Arlene Francis quickly became the series' regular panelists, and guest panelists filling the fourth chair on the CBS version over the years included Fred Allen, Ronald Reagan, Groucho Marx, and three eventual hosts of the *Tonight* show: Ernie Kovacs, Johnny Carson, and the aforementioned Steve Allen. Gene Shalit was another guest panelist, and it was he who correctly identified contestant Jimmy Carter's then-current occupation as the governor of Georgia—although it took two rounds of questioning to do so. Finally, not only did *What's My Line?* last longer than its competitors, but it was directly or indirectly responsible for many of them, including such chief copycats as *To Tell the Truth* and *I've Got a Secret.* That's the truth, and it's no big secret.

Wheel of Fortune. *1975–89, 1991, NBC; 1989–91, CBS; 1983–   , syndicated.* The rules in *Wheel of Fortune* are easy: a good samaritan or hero is selected as a contestant, given the opportunity to spin a giant carnival-type wheel, then awarded the prize indicated on the spot where the wheel stops spinning. Doesn't sound familiar? Well, those were the rules of the original *Wheel of Fortune,* a prime-time game show that ran on CBS in the summer of 1953. That show, apparently, was under a major disadvantage: Vanna White, the young woman who turned wheel-spinning and letter-turning into some inexplicable sort of TV superstardom, wasn't born yet. The modern *Wheel of Fortune,* created by Merv Griffin (who also concocted *Jeopardy!*), was introduced as part of NBC's daytime lineup in 1975. For the first seven years, it was hosted by Chuck Woolery, with Susan Stafford as the letter-turner. They made little impression, but the game itself did: it was a supersimple mixture of dumb luck (spinning the wheel for prizes or penalties) and dumb rules (basically, a high-tech variation of "Hangman," with names and phrases deciphered one letter at a time). Yet in 1982, the year before *Wheel of Fortune* was offered in syndication, Pat Sajak replaced Woolery as host, and the totally unknown Vanna White became the show's new wheel-spinner, letter-turner, and applause-leader. From this, somehow, sprang major celebrity for them both, and a game-show series that, despite its eventual network cancellations, continues to rank among syndicated TV's most popular offerings. (The phrase "buy a vowel" became famous as a result, and led to the durable real-world variation in which one person sarcastically tells a confused acquaintance to "buy a clue.") Both Sajak and White, though, cashed in their celebrity chips rather unwisely in the late eighties. He flopped as a late-night talk-show host in *The Pat Sajak Show* on CBS in 1989, and she flopped as a prime-time actress, portraying a vapid Venus in the 1988 NBC telemovie *Goddess of Love*.

Wide World of Sports. *1961– , ABC*. From 1948 until 1960, the most durable and prominent sports showcase on TV was NBC's *The Gillette Cavalcade of Sports*, a Friday-night boxing showcase. When Gillette moved away from boxing and wanted to put its ad revenue elsewhere, ABC concocted a weekend afternoon show called *Wide World of Sports*, with an emphasis on amateur athletics and out-of-the-way contests—as far out of the way, in some instances, as cliff-diving in Acapulco. With Gillette and other sponsors in hand, and with ABC executive Edgar Scherick and protegé Roone Arledge at the helm, *Wide World of Sports* managed to build an amazingly successful sports franchise. *Wide World of Sports* also changed the way TV covered sports, with an emphasis on the visual (slow motion, splitscreen, freeze-frame) and the emotional (with what, in later Olympics coverage, would be dubbed "Up Close and Personal" athlete profiles). Jim McKay, who anchored the very first installment in 1961, has been there ever since—a phenomenally long run as a program's single host, easily outdoing even Johnny Carson's thirty-year streak—and anchored the coverage during ABC's glory years with the Olympics (see separate listing). For the first year, McKay's introduction to *Wide World of Sports* promised viewers a look at "sport in its unending variety"; in its second season, that slogan was changed to the famous refrain of "the thrill of victory, the agony of defeat." Howard Cosell and Frank Gifford are among those who contributed strong pieces to *Wide World of Sports* (Cosell brought with him one Muhammad Ali, who in 1972 playfully and famously picked at Cosell's toupee while both Ali and Cosell wore matching *Wide World of Sports* blazers), and the sports themselves have ranged from the Kentucky Derby and the Tour de France to the Little League World Series. Nothing, though, is quite in the same unforgettable league as ski jumper Vinko Bogataj, the Yugoslavian athlete whose astounding out-of-control fall was shown each week during the show's opening credits to exemplify "the agony of defeat." After a crash landing like that, I'll bet he also suffered a lot of agony in dehead, dehands, dearms, and delegs.

Wild Kingdom. See *Mutual of Omaha's Wild Kingdom*.

Wild Wild West, The. *1965–69, CBS*. In terms of TV history, this amiable Western series was a lot more important, or at least influential, than most people realize. Thirty years later, the most lasting elements of *The Wild Wild West* are Richard Markowitz's bass-heavy theme song; the frozen-action illustrations that punctuated the end of each act (appropriated, in the midnineties, by another TV Western, *Lonesome Dove: The Outlaw Years*); the genial byplay between Robert Conrad's James T. West and Ross Martin's Artemus Gordon; and the show's inventive fight and stunt scenes. *The Wild Wild West* was set in the post–Civil War era, with West and Gordon assigned as special secret agents working directly for President Ulysses S. Grant, roaming the country in a lushly appointed steam engine and passenger car. As a result, *The Wild Wild West*, with its period setting, wild plots, and wilder gadgetry, managed simultaneously to spoof Westerns, spy stories, and science-fiction fantasies— all served up with commercial-break cliff-hangers worthy of *Raiders of the Lost Ark*. *The Wild West West* spoofed spies and spy technology before *Get Smart* (only a day before, since both series premiered the same weekend, but it still counts). It showcased Martin's acting abilities by making Artemus a master of disguise and accents, a full season before *Mission: Impossible* did the same thing with Martin Landau's Rollin Hand (perhaps significantly, Landau had witnessed Martin's talents first-Hand by making a guest appearance on *The Wild Wild West* before accepting his *Mission: Impossible* role). And before *Batman* came along and made a cottage industry of it, *The Wild Wild West* was very successful offering up plum roles for the often outrageous villains of the week. Agnes Moorehead won an Emmy for her role as protofeminist Emma Valentine (making it, I guess, an Emma Emmy), and both Burgess Meredith and Victor Buono flexed their bad-guy muscles on *The Wild Wild West* before doing the same on *Batman*. Other *Wild Wild West* guest stars during its four seasons included some impressive and surprising performers: Richard Pryor, Pat Paulsen, Boris Karloff, Ray Walston, Robert Duvall, Harvey Korman, Katharine Ross, Sammy Davis, Jr., and even a post-*Bonanza* Pernell Roberts. The biggest *Wild Wild West* villain of all, though, also was the smallest: Michael Dunn's Miguelito Loveless, a brilliant but deviant dwarf whose quest for world domination was driven by a giant-sized inferiority complex. Dunn was such a good actor, and Loveless such a good character, that they deserve to be ranked right alongside such *Batman* TV pop icons as Frank Gorshin's Riddler and Julie Newmar's Catwoman. (One classic *Wild Wild West* Loveless episode, in which the twisted genius found a way to enter and live inside framed paintings, was titled, memorably, "The Night of the Surreal McCoy.") Although never as popular as *Batman*, *The Wild Wild West* outlasted it, and was still doing well in 1968 when Milton Eisenhower led hearings by the National Commission on the Causes and Prevention of Violence, the first major congressional examination of televised violence since the days of *The Untouchables*. The following year, to appease the committee and fulfill a promise to reduce the level of violence on its own network, CBS canceled *The Wild Wild West* outright, rather than make it less *Wild*. Reunion telemovies eventually appeared in 1979 and 1980, but they paled next to the original series episodes, which TNT finally brought back in marathon form in 1994.

Winds of War, The. *1983, ABC.* **War and Remembrance.** *1988–89, ABC.* With only *Roots* and *The Thorn Birds* drawing more viewers, *The Winds of*

Wheel of Fortune, with
Vanna White and Pat Sajak.

The Wild Wild West, with
Michael Dunn's memorable villain,
Dr. Miguelito Loveless.

War ranks in the Nielsen ratings as the third-highest miniseries in TV history—and, like those other ABC long-form dramas, eventually spawned a sequel, despite the fact that all three projects were envisioned as one-shot deals. (The sequel, in this case, came about because *Winds of War* had drawn a Nielsen rating of 38.6, a phenomenally high number.) And as with *Roots: The Next Generations*, which had a better cast and better script than the original, the *Winds of War* sequel, *War and Remembrance*, was a marked improvement on its more popular predecessor. The first *Winds of War* miniseries, based on the Herman Wouk novel, was tagged as a possible long-form TV contender as early as 1970, when the novel was still in galley form, but not until 1983 did it reach the small screen. TV's *Winds of War* starred Robert Mitchum as Navy Commander Victor "Pug" Henry, John Houseman as Jewish intellectual Aaron Jastrow, and Ali McGraw as Jastrow's niece, Natalie; their personal stories were played against the backdrop of historical events leading to World War II. Yet after eighteen hours of *Winds of War*, amazingly little had happened. The "conclusion" showed Mitchum's Henry staring out at the sad aftermath of the Japanese attack on Pearl Harbor—yet as a war drama, *Winds of War* had been positively pacifistic. None of the major characters had died, three hours went by before the first shot was fired, and party scenes outnumbered battle scenes by more than five to one. (It was so boring, I spent time counting.) Only David Dukes and Victoria Tennant, in supporting roles, delivered good performances—which is why, when ABC picked up the story with *War and Remembrance* in 1988, the major cast changes necessitated by the five-year delay reaped dividends rather than disappointments. When production resumed, John Gielgud had replaced Houseman, and Jane Seymour had replaced McGraw—good trades both. Since their characters' concentration-camp fates were the best part of the continued story, it was a key reason why *War and Remembrance* is worth remembering. All the romantic scenes were as junky as before, but the way director Dan Curtis re-created some of the atrocities of the Holocaust was excellent—better than even the best scenes in *Holocaust,* and as good as many of the scenes in Steven Spielberg's subsequent *Schindler's List*. ABC presented *War and Remembrance* in two major chunks, first in November 1988 and concluding in May 1989. By that time, from the first breeze of *Winds of War* to the last image of *War and Remembrance,* the ABC telecast of Wouk's World War II saga had taken six years to present (longer than the war it was dramatizing), consumed forty-seven total hours of TV time, and cost an estimated, unprecedented one-hundred-ten-million dollars. Yet though the quality of the mega-miniseries rose with every massive installment, its ratings declined just as measurably, and by the time *War and Remembrance* was over, so were the boom years for the TV miniseries.

Winky Dink and You. *1953–57, CBS.* This Saturday morning children's series is fast fading from common cultural memory, but nevertheless deserves credit as the first truly interactive show in TV history. The gimmick behind *Winky Dink and You* was a special "Winky Dink Kit" which young fans could order by mail—a kit consisting, basically, of a soft cloth, a crayon or two, and a large plastic overlay sheet, roughly the shape of a then-standard TV picture tube. When the show's live-action host, Jack Barry, introduced cartoons featuring Winky Dink and his dog, Woofer, viewers were instructed to spread the sheet over the TV screen, draw or trace whatever prop Winky Dink needed to complete his adventure, and thus become active rather than passive participants in the fun. (Completing secret codes was another regular use of the *Winky Dink* "technology.") The half-hour series was canceled by CBS after a four-year run, but the five-minute cartoons with Winky Dink and Woofer continued to appear in syndication throughout the sixties. Even before *Winky Dink and You* was canceled, however, Barry and his partner Dan Enright teamed up to produce *Twenty-One,* the quiz show which brought us the rise and fall of contestant Charles Van Doren. Barry hosted both series, but only one, decades later, has an unsullied reputation. Which one? Draw your own conclusions. Just be careful not to smudge the screen.

Wiseguy. *1987–90, CBS.* It's astounding, and a little frightening, to realize that Stephen J. Cannell and Frank Lupo, the same two men who concocted that execrable exercise in empty-headed entertainment known as *The A-Team,* turned around, a handful of years later, and co-created *Wiseguy,* one of the most interesting and innovative cop shows of the eighties. Ken Wahl starred as undercover cop Vinnie Terranova, who served more than a year in prison to solidify his cover as a low-level mobster, and it was totally appropriate that the name Terranova translated to "new ground." The new ground was the concept of the "story arc," which essentially was a middle ground between the miniseries and the weekly TV series. Like most miniseries, the "story arc" consumed somewhere between six and ten hours of screen time, allowed characters to develop fully and be placed in actual life-threatening jeopardy, and attracted to TV actors unwilling to make a multiyear series commitment; yet, like most episodic TV series, the same "story arc" concept offered the familiarity and attraction of continuing characters. Vinnie would be assigned to investigate someone, would take a few months of TV time to solve the case, then, after a brief breather, move on to the next case (until the final season, that is, when Wahl quit the series and it moved on without him). The show's first season, which introduced Wahl as Vinnie and Jonathan Banks as field director Frank McPike, not only established the "story arc" concept, but, with its first two extended story lines, presented the series' very best work. First came "the Steelgrave arc," with Ray Sharkey playing self-made mob figure Sonny Steelgrave; it took half a season for Vinnie to get close enough to Sonny to lead to a conviction, and by that time, their relationship was so multileveled that Sonny, tortured by Vinnie's betrayal, killed himself. (It's the most familiar episode in *Wiseguy,* as easily recalled by viewers of the show as is Mike Post's pounding theme song.) After the Sonny went down, the rest of the first season was consumed by "the Proffit arc," a wild TV ride in which Kevin Spacey (later to play the serial killer in the film *Seven)* and Joan Severance portrayed, with apparent delight, a rich, ruthless, glamorous, and totally twisted brother-sister crime duo, Mel and Susan Proffit. Within those two arcs, other actors got to shine as well: Annette Bening dominated one episode in the Steelgrave saga, playing an ill-fated undercover operative, and William Russ, as rogue agent Roger Loccoco, was so good that the series should have become his when Wahl left and his character of Vinnie was killed. Instead, the central role of the new *Wiseguy* operative went to Steven Bauer, who starred in the show's final, useless season. But before Bauer got there, other *Wiseguy* story arcs starred Jerry Lewis, Ron Silver, Tim Curry, and Paul Winfield, with delightful supporting performances by Stanley Tucci (who would resurface as the initial murder suspect in *Murder One*), Deborah Harry, David Strathairn, Glenn Frey, Joan Chen, Jon Polito, Diedre Hall, and Traci Lords. Yet though the casting was strong, the stories weakened with the passage of time, presenting more flashy moments than coherent plots—the same fate that befell *Twin Peaks*, one of the only post-*Wiseguy* series to attempt a modified, bloated "arc" format (Laura Palmer being one giant arc, Windom Earle being another). The latest TV series to set sail on the *Wiseguy*-inspired arc? The aforementioned *Murder One*, the latest engrossing courtroom drama series from Steven Bochco Productions.

Wizard of Oz, The. *1956, 1959–62, 1964–67, 1976–   , CBS; 1968–75, NBC.* How does a theatrical film that predates network television earn a spot, and a high one, in the annals of teleliteracy? Easy: the now-annual broadcast of *The Wizard of Oz* is one of the few family TV traditions to have endured in America. Despite the film's yearly exposure on network TV, as well as a plethora of versions released on videocassette and laserdisc, this 1939 movie musical, starring Judy Garland in her most famous role, continues to attract tens of millions of viewers each year when presented in prime time. In fact, it took television to turn the MGM musical into the accepted classic it is today. Critics were lukewarm to downright nasty when the film was first released, and neither the original L. Frank Baum books nor the theatrical reissues, which began in 1949, approached the popularity of the movie's national broadcasts. *The Wizard of Oz* was first shown by CBS on November 3, 1956, with Bert Lahr serving as host of the film and with Garland's daughter Liza Minnelli, then ten years old, as Lahr's special guest. The next *Wizard of Oz* telecast was three years later, with Red Skelton as host and his young daughter Valentina along for the fun. After that came Richard Boone in 1960, and Dick Van Dyke in 1961 and 1962. Finally, after a year off, *The Wizard of Oz* returned with its last and most widely recalled guest host: Danny Kaye, whose 1964 introductions and good-byes were replayed by CBS, along with the movie itself, for the next three years, at which time *Oz* moved to NBC for a lengthy stretch. Aside from some remarks by Gregory Peck in 1970, the year after Garland died, the movie was shown unhosted—but, for the first time, not unedited, as little snippets of footage began being trimmed to make room for more commercial time. Up to and including 1967, when CBS was showing the hosted versions of *The Wizard of Oz*, the film never drew less than half of the available viewing audience. NBC took over in 1968, doubtlessly because its parent company, RCA, was eager to sell color TV sets using the Yellow Brick Road as a lure. CBS regained control of *The Wizard of Oz* in 1976, and has shown it annually ever since. As recently as 1970, *The Wizard* *of Oz* accounted for half of the top-rated movies in television's all-time Top 10; soon thereafter, parents who had watched *The Wizard of Oz* on TV as kids began showing it to their own kids, and a multigenerational TV tradition was born. It was, and is, a very special case, one in which familiarity breeds contentment. Television proved so much more popular a venue than the theaters for showing *The Wizard of Oz* that, when it came time for audiences to choose a place to watch it, Dorothy's heel-clicking mantra rang true: "There's no place like home. There's no place like home. There's no place like home. . . . "

WKRP in Cincinnati. *1978–82, CBS.* This clever sitcom, created by Hugh Wilson, might have lasted a lot longer, but CBS scheduled it in twelve different time slots over a four-year period. Even so, a few of its characters and set pieces managed, like its hummable theme song, to make a lasting impact. The most durable characters were Howard Hesseman's Johnny Fever, an anti-establishment deejay who could have been the best friend of Christopher Lloyd's Jim Ignatowski on *Taxi;* Richard Sanders's Les Nessman, a dweeby newscaster; and Loni Anderson's Jennifer Marlowe, a sex symbol with brains and an agenda. Nessman's radio traffic report, in which he beat his chest loudly to fake the sound of a helicopter while describing the road conditions "below," was one classic moment. Ironically, the show's absolute high point also involved a helicopter: it was the unforgettable Thanksgiving show in which, as a promotion for the radio station, WKRP staffers rented a helicopter, hovered over an expectant crowd at a parking lot giveaway site, and tossed out live turkeys—only to learn, in an audio-only report intentionally reminiscent of Herbert Morrison's radio coverage of the Hindenberg disaster ("Oh, the humanity!"), that turkeys don't fly. Wilson insists the fowl deed was based on an actual radio stunt that backfired. *WKRP*, on the other hand, was no turkey. Its most distinguished alumnus, Tim Reid (who played late-night deejay Venus Flytrap), went on to star in an even better Wilson comedy, *Frank's Place*, but that show was treated even *more* shabbily by CBS. A revival series, *The New WKRP in Cincinnati*, appeared in 1991, but drew neither viewers nor acclaim, and vanished after two years.

Wonder Woman. *1976–77, ABC; 1977–79, CBS.* ABC first tried to launch this series with a 1974 telemovie starring Cathy Lee Crosby as the DC Comics heroine, but the casting, the tone, and the costume were all wrong. A 1975 telemovie starring 1973's Miss World-USA, Lynda Carter, was much more successful. Especially the comic-book authentic costume—an aerodynamic, low-cut marvel that, during the four-year run of *Wonder Woman* on TV, kept more than just this series afloat. ABC's version, originally titled *The New Original Wonder Woman,* actually predated its revamped CBS successor, which at first went under the title *The New Adventures of Wonder Woman.* Both series eventually went for the simpler *Wonder Woman,* and their major difference was that the ABC version was set during World War II, while the CBS version was updated to present times. (Lyle Waggoner costarred as Major Steve Trevor in the former and, in true comic-book fashion, as Steve Trevor,

Jr., in the latter.) This "super" example of the seventies phenomenon known as "jiggle TV" had few, if any, strong villains, scripts, or actors—unless you count Debra Winger, who appeared in three episodes as "Wonder Girl," the little sister to Carter's Diana Prince and her Amazonian alter ego. Carter's "spin move," when twirling like a top to transform from Diana to Wonder Woman or vice versa, is one laughingly lasting legacy of this silly series. Another, needless to say, is that breathtaking, breath-constricting costume—the original Wonder-bra. Nothing, though, beats the charmingly inane lyrics from the ABC version's theme song: "All the world is waiting for you / And the power you possess, / In your satin tights / Fighting for your rights / And the old red, white, and blue / Wonder Wommmannnn!"

Wonder Years, The. *1988–93, ABC*. This TV series, like *The Waltons*, was built around the concept of an adult narrator looking back at the days and loves and lessons of his youth—but with a slightly more modern focus. Daniel Stern provided the voice of the present-day Kevin Arnold, and Fred Savage, the star of the series, portrayed Kevin as a young kid. The series progressed in more or less real time, with the five seasons of *The Wonder Years* corresponding with five "wonder years" in the lives of the characters. The premiere episode began with Kevin's first day of junior high school in the fall of 1968, and the final episode concluded with him taking and leaving a summertime job in 1973. Yet as Kevin's voice got deeper, *The Wonder Years* got shallower, and what began as a superb series ended as merely a good one. As a kid growing up on TV, Savage matured as an actor with as much ease and effectiveness as had Jerry Mathers on *Leave It to Beaver* and Ron Howard on *The Andy Griffith Show*—high praise indeed. Savage's costars were wonderful, too, especially Dan Lauria as Kevin's gruff father, Josh Saviano as his geeky best friend, Jason Hervey as his bullying brother, and Robert Picardo as his equally bullying gym teacher. What went wrong, though, was that the show's creators, Neal Marlens and Carol Black, quit the series after the first six episodes, and the show very slowly, but just as surely, repeated and diluted itself after that. The most egregious offense is that the emotional kiss in the series premiere between Kevin and his first girlfriend, Danica McKellar's Winnie Cooper, was described by the adult narrator as their last—and yet this most basic and touching of plot guidelines was ignored by the series' subsequent writers, up to and including a very passionate love scene between Kevin and Winnie in the final episode. Even so, *The Wonder Years* left behind a lot of memorable scenes and episodes, made great use of period music (the show's theme song was the Joe Cocker rendition of "With a Little Help From My Friends"), and, even in its less stellar moments, cut against the grain of most family sitcoms by going for the unexpectedly realistic. Among the most memorable moments: Kevin accompanying his dad on a humiliating day at the office; a dead-on *Star Trek* parody with Kevin as Captain Kirk and Winnie as the leader of a mysterious race of short-skirted, incomprehensible females; and the clueless gym teacher's baffling "bovine" drawings during a school sex education lecture. Speaking of clueless: although Kevin carried a torch for Winnie for most of the series, he drifted in and out of other relationships, real and imagined. In one 1992 episode, his "dream date" was played by Alicia Silverstone, who would emerge from her own wonder years to star in the movie *Clueless*. And for one too-brief season of shows in 1994–95, the inner thoughts and private lives of high-schoolers would be dramatized superbly in ABC's *My So-Called Life*, with young actress Claire Danes devoting one of her own Wonder Years to the superb portrayal of "typical" teenager Angela Chase.

World Series, The. *1947– , various networks.* Unlike football's Super Bowl, a postseason sports contest originating during and largely because of the television era, major league baseball's World Series predated not only TV, but radio. Commercial radio began in 1920; the first "World's Series," as it was called then, was played in 1903. It didn't take radio long, though, to crash the postseason ballpark. Only one year after radio as we know it began, station WJZ in Newark, New Jersey, set up a relay system to provide radio's first live broadcast reports of a World Series—the 1921 contest between two New York teams, the Giants and the Yankees, with the action relayed by telephone from one reporter at the ballpark to another in the studio. The first televised World Series was in 1947, when another New York rivalry—the Yankees against the Brooklyn Dodgers—was available to viewers in four cities (New York, Philadelphia, Schenectady, and Washington, D.C.). A patchwork system of three networks—NBC, CBS, and DuMont—made the seven-game series available to an estimated 3.9 million people, of which fully 3.5 million were watching TV sets installed in neighborhood bars. After that first successful TV experiment, NBC and Gillette combined to lock up exclusive TV rights to future World Series games for *The Gillette Cavalcade of Sports*, the umbrella title under which games once were shown. *Cavalcade* ended in 1960, but NBC retained exclusive World Series coverage until 1977, when NBC and ABC began rotating coverage in alternating years (ABC took the odd-numbered years from 1977 to 1989, NBC the even-numbered ones). CBS took over from 1990–93, and NBC and ABC reteamed in 1995 for another rotating arrangement—but this time, instead of trading years, the networks traded games within the same series. The missing year, 1994, saw no televised World Series coverage because, thanks to an acrimonious battle between players and management, there *was* no World Series that year—the obvious lowlight of World Series history in the television era. (Another lowlight would be the 1971 Baltimore Orioles-Pittsburgh Pirates series, only because that was the first time a World Series game was played, and televised, at night. Still sinful after all these years.) As for the most memorable all-time televised World Series moments, I have two votes. One is for Game 5 of the 1956 World Series, when Don Larsen of the Yankees pitched a perfect game against the Dodgers (twenty-seven batters faced, twenty-seven batters out, a feat never accomplished before, or since, in postseason play), and catcher Yogi Berra punctuated the win by gleefully jumping into Larsen's arms. The other is for Game 6 of the 1975 World Series, when a seesaw battle between the Cincinnati Reds and Boston Red Sox was decided, in the bottom of the twelfth inning, by a home-run blast from Boston catcher Carlton Fisk. While running toward first, Fisk watched the ball sail down the third-base line right at the foul pole and, in a spontaneous reaction captured by an isolated camera, furiously and repeatedly waved his arms to help "will" the ball into fair territory. No less an authority than the Ken Burns-Geoffrey C. Ward documentary series *Baseball* called that one game, with its thrilling and very human climax, "the greatest game in World Series history—a game that rekindled the whole country's love of baseball." Apparently, though, viewers loved football a lot more. Not one World Series game ranks among television's all-time Top 40, even though the same list, through the end of 1995, includes sixteen different Super Bowl contests (the most popular of which drew a 49.1 Nielsen rating, accounting for nearly half of all TV homes in America) and one National Football Conference championship game. The highest Nielsen rating for a World Series, by comparison, is 32.8, and two postseason contests tied in achieving it: the 1978 World Series between the Yankees and Los Angeles Dodgers, and the 1980 World Series between the Philadelphia Phillies and Kansas City Royals. Yet the most earthshaking World Series ever televised, without a doubt, occurred on October 17, 1989, as ABC was just about to televise Game 3 of the World Series between the San Francisco Giants and Oakland Athletics. That was when the Bay Area earthquake rattled Candlestick Park, collapsing a stretch of Interstate 880 (the most potent and poignant image from TV coverage of the disaster) and putting ABC World Series sportscaster Al Michaels in the same hot-seat, hard-news position in which Jim McKay found himself after the terrorist attack on Israeli athletes in Munich during the 1972 Summer Olympics. (Michaels, like McKay, performed admirably.) The earthquake delayed the World Series for ten days; five years later, a players' strike proved much more devastating, obliterating it for the season. No wonder football gets bigger ratings.

X-Files, The. *1993–   , Fox.* Like *Kolchak: The Night Stalker,* a seventies series in which Darren McGavin played reporter Carl Kolchak, the original "ghostbuster" (and "vampirebuster," and "mummybuster," and so on), *The X-Files* revels in the paranormal—but with a parainvestigators instead of just one. David Duchovny plays Mulder the believer, and Gillian Anderson plays Scully the skeptic, and the two of them work for a division of the F.B.I., investigating mysterious parasites in the Arctic, human flukeworms in the sewers, alien abductors in the skies, beings that lurk in the shadows, and even shadows that lurk in the light. The level of the acting, scriptwriting, and direction of creator Chris Carter's *X-Files* series elevated it right to the top of the genre, sharing the same moody and impressive cult-status space as

The Twilight Zone—and, like *The Twilight Zone,* able to conjure up recollections of entire episodes by the merest mention of certain plot lines. From the first two seasons alone, there's "Ice," the episode about the Arctic parasite; "Beyond the Sea," in which Brad Dourif played a death-row inmate with alleged psychic powers; "One Breath," in which Scully returns from an apparent alien abduction and has a near-death experience; and "Humbug," an unusually lighthearted episode about circus people, cannibalism, and a strange guy called the Conundrum. The high regard with which *The X-Files* was received, in the TV industry as well as by viewers, was reflected by the fact that, during its second season, it was nominated for an Emmy as Best Dramatic Series. (Only a handful of other genre shows have received that honor: *Alfred Hitchcock Presents, The Twilight Zone, The Avengers, Star Trek,* and *Quantum Leap.* None has ever won—and in 1995, *The X-Files* didn't win, either.) *The X-Files* is an ambitious, sometimes excellent series, and is sure to be treasured, and remembered, long after its original run has ended. Also likely to be remembered: the creepy, ethereal, whistly instrumental opening music, one of the best TV themes of the nineties.

Yogi Bear. See *Huckleberry Hound.*

You Are There. *1953–57, CBS.* Long before the term "docudrama" was coined, this TV series—and the radio series that preceded it—made a practice, and a very successful one, of dramatizing fact-based stories, and of using actual CBS News reporters as co-conspirators. The project began on radio in 1947 as *CBS Is There,* changed its name to *You Are There* in 1948, and continued until 1950. Don Hollenbeck anchored the show, which offered dramatized "field reports" from actual CBS newsmen, broadcasting "from the scene" of famous incidents in history: reporter John Daly, for example, witnessed the assassination of Abraham Lincoln and interviewed front-line Yankee troops during the Civil War. When a TV version was mounted in 1953, it was equally noteworthy for who was in front of and behind the camera. For television, the *You Are There* correspondent was Walter Cronkite, long before he got the job reporting much fresher history on *The CBS Evening News.* The actors portraying historical figures were no slouches, either. The second show of the series, "The Capture of Jesse James," featured James Dean in the title role; subsequent installments starred, just to name a few, Paul Newman as Nathan Hale (an episode directed by Sidney Lumet), E. G. Marshall as Alexander the Great, Beatrice Straight as Anne Boleyn, DeForest Kelley in "The Surrender of Corregidor," and Lorne Greene as Ludwig van Beethoven. (Reportedly, whenever Greene was asked to comment about this particular

TV role, he would take the Fifth.) On television, especially, *You Are There* was a hotbed for controversial opinions in the fifties, doing an unusual amount of shows about free-speech issues, the Alien and Sedition acts, and the Salem witch trials—at a time when a witch-hunt of another kind, the McCarthy-era blacklisting of alleged Communists, was in full swing. The reason for the program's almost radical focus is both simple and astounding: producer Charles Russell, who hated the blacklist, intentionally and bravely hired a team of three blacklisted writers (Abraham Polonsky, Arnold Manoff, and Walter Bernstein) to write all the *You Are There* shows under assumed names, their identities concealed with help from various "front" men. The ruse worked for most of the show's run, thus allowing *You Are There* to make a little TV history in more ways than one. (Notably, one of those writers, Bernstein, went on to write *The Front.*) Today, the most memorable aspects of *You Are There* are the title and the closing narration: "What sort of a day was it? A day like all days, filled with those events that alter and illuminate our times . . . and you were there." In 1971, a jazzed-up sequel series was presented on Saturday afternoons by CBS, with Cronkite reviving his historical anchor role, but the revived *You Are There* fizzled quickly . . . because viewers weren't there.

You Bet Your Life. *1950–61, NBC.* Groucho Marx, who already had succeeded wildly on stage and screen as a young man, triumphed later in life on radio, and eventually on television, as a quiz-show host on *You Bet Your Life.* The format was simple and, for Groucho, relatively sedate: Groucho introduced and chatted playfully with a pair of contestants, then gave them a small sum of money and let them bet all or part of it on a series of questions. At the end of the show, the most successful team got a shot at a big-money jackpot question; a smaller jackpot could be had at any point during the show, merely by having a contestant stumble upon the day's chosen secret word: "Say the secret word," Groucho would explain, "and the duck will come down and pay you one hundred dollars." Even on radio, where *You Bet Your Life* began in 1947, that silly sight gag, that daffy duck, dropped from the ceiling to signify a secret-word winner. (Why a duck? Best not to ask—unless, in true Marx Brothers fashion, you ask "Viaduct?" instead.) The draw of radio's *You Bet Your Life* was the conversational banter between Groucho and the contestants, and it was quite a draw: by 1950, *You Bet Your Life* had worked its way into radio's Top 10 and won a Peabody Award. After originating on ABC and moving to CBS two years later, radio's *You Bet Your Life* moved to NBC—but this time, with a simultaneous leap to television. Groucho hedged his media bets by presenting the audio of each new show on NBC Radio every Wednesday, then showing the same program, with pictures, on NBC-TV the following night. It was a brilliant bit of fence-straddling, because the television audience grew exponentially as the audience for radio dwindled, and *You Bet Your Life* was poised to go either way. Did this simple quiz show translate its success to the new medium? You bet your life. The TV version was in the Top 20 during its first season, and firmly in the Top 10 for the next five. Groucho Marx won an Emmy to go with his Peabody, and *You Bet*

Your Life added some stubbornly lasting catch phrases to the language, from announcer George Fenneman's introduction of the host as "The one—the only—Groucho!" to one of Groucho's laughably easy consolation-prize questions, "Who is buried in Grant's tomb?" With Groucho at the helm, television's *You Bet Your Life* lasted for eleven years, much longer than either of the subsequent syndicated TV revivals. Buddy Hackett, woefully ill-cast, hosted an understandably brief version of *You Bet Your Life* in 1980, and Bill Cosby, a much better fit, tried again in 1992, coming off the phenomenal success of *The Cosby Show.* Except for some very minor alterations (such as changing the duck to a black goose), Cosby's *You Bet Your Life* was much the same as Groucho's, with an unrushed feel, a genial tone, and a good-natured sense of humor. However, in the frenetic, highly competitive environment of syndicated TV in the nineties, the secret word was "demographics," and *You Bet Your Life* didn't attract enough of the key ones to survive. Yet the original *You Bet Your Life* survived intact, and remains visible in filmed reruns on local and cable TV.

You'll Never Get Rich. See *The Phil Silvers Show.*

Young and the Restless, The. *1973–   , CBS.* This durable CBS soap has been around long enough for its original characters to be renamed *The Middle-Aged and the Resting,* but it hasn't withered with age. In fact, *The Young and the Restless* was the dominant soap of the first half of the nineties, thanks to its continued reliance on topical and controversial themes (a practice established by series creators William J. and Lee Phillip Bell). Everything from alcoholism to lesbianism, from euthanasia to child abuse, was and is grist for the *Young and the Restless* mill—and though the writing often is stilted and preachy when dealing with such subjects, the cast list is deeper and stronger than most, and the alumni list is particularly impressive. Two of the biggest male sex symbols in TV history, Tom Selleck of *Magnum, p.i.* and David Hasselhoff of *Baywatch,* were regulars during this daytime soap opera's early years: Selleck played Jed Andrews from 1974 to 1975, and Hasselhoff played Dr. "Snapper" Foster from 1975 to 1982. Performers who became stars later on other soaps included Diedre Hall (as Barbara Anderson, 1973–75) and Anthony Geary (who, as George Curtis in 1973, raped a young woman—as a sort of warm-up act to his Luke and Laura story line on *General Hospital*). Nothing, though, is as famous as the show's instrumental theme song, which was lifted intact from the 1971 film *Bless the Beasts and Children.* In 1976, after Olympic gynmast Nadia Comaneci used it as part of her performance music, the song—newly released under the title "Nadia's Theme"—became an international sensation.

Young People's Concerts. *1958–72, CBS.* Leonard Bernstein and television first found one another in 1954, when the young conductor appeared on the stellar CBS arts series *Omnibus.* A few years later, CBS founder William S. Paley persuaded Bernstein to concoct a series of educational music specials aimed at young viewers, and the *Young People's Concerts,* initially broadcast live on Saturday afternoons, was born. They were intelligent, mesmerizing, thoroughly inspirational programs, with Bernstein leading the New York Philharmonic while simultaneously serving as one of television's all-time most charismatic hosts. The subject matter ranged from uncovering hidden jokes in classical music to analyzing the Beatles' "And I Love Her" as an example of the three-part sonata form. The series premiered in 1958, the year after Bernstein's triumph as the composer of *West Side Story*, and was highly acclaimed from the start. Somewhat ironically and fortuitously, *Young People's Concerts* got an unexpected boost in 1961, courtesy of Federal Communications Commission head Newton Minow and his blistering "vast wasteland" speech. Months later, CBS responded by moving Bernstein's classy classical showcase into prime time, where it earned an even larger loyal viewership. There were fifty-three separate *Young People's Concert* specials over a fourteen-year period, including one featuring Aaron Copland as guest conductor, and another in which Stephen Sondheim, who wrote the lyrics to Bernstein's *West Side Story* music, reteamed with Bernstein by providing challenging questions for a special "classical-music quiz show" installment of *Young People's Concert* in 1968. Nearly half of those *Young People's Concert* shows were packaged, in the nineties, as a special home-video collector's item—an acknowledgment of this series' lasting legacy that is music to any true music lover's ears. And in 1995, the spirit of Bernstein's joy of teaching in *Young People's Concerts* was carried on by Wynton Marsalis, who presided over a four-part PBS *Marsalis on Music* series aimed at explaining the intricacies of music to children and adults alike.

You're in the Picture. *1961, CBS.* In and of itself, Jackie Gleason's monumental game-show bomb, which was televised for the first and last time on January 20, 1961, may not have earned an entry in this collection. After all, other one-shot failures, from *Turn-On* to *South of Sunset*, didn't make the cut. But not only was *You're in the Picture* a monumentally stupid idea for a TV game show—celebrity contestants, including Keenan Wynn and Arthur Treacher, stuck their heads into Coney Island-style cartoon cutouts, then tried to guess, from host Gleason's clues and jokes, who and what they were supposed to represent—but it was unprecedented in one important respect. The week after *You're in the Picture* premiered and was canceled, Gleason returned to the same time slot to spend the entire half hour apologizing. "We had a show last week that laid the biggest bomb," Gleason told what few viewers were left seven days later. "I've seen bombs in my day, but this one made the H-bomb look like a two-inch salute." In other words: baby, it wasn't the greatest.

Your Hit Parade. *1950–58, NBC; 1958–59, CBS.* On NBC Radio, *Your Hit Parade* began all the way back in 1935, with a simple but surefire formula that remained essentially the same over the next quarter-century: the top songs of the week were identified, ranked, and performed, with a suspenseful countdown leading to the Number One song of the week. The most famous featured vocalist on the radio version was Frank Sinatra, who Paraded his singing talent from 1943 to 1945; others, over the years, included Doris Day and Dinah Shore. When NBC adapted *Your Hit Parade* to television in 1950, it needed visuals as well as vocals, and choreographers and set designers worked hard to make each week's *Hit Parade* a treat for the eye as well as the ear (one featured dancer, as it happens, was Bob Fosse). Dorothy Collins and Snooky Lanson were among the biggest stars of the TV version, which is remembered, or ought to be, as a very early forerunner of the music video in general and MTV in particular.

Your Show of Shows. *1950–54, NBC.* **Admiral Broadway Revue.** *1949, NBC and DuMont.* **Caesar's Hour.** *1954–57, NBC.* (Be forewarned. Included in this entry is the debunking of one of the most persistent myths in TV history: that Woody Allen wrote for *Your Show of Shows.* Keep reading.) The Sid Caesar showcase *Your Show of Shows,* and the two other series in which he starred before and after that landmark show, constitute one of the most innovative and important creative bursts in TV history. Thanks to the 1973 release of the film compilation *Ten from Your Show of Shows,* both the *Your Show of Shows* title and some of its classic skits have remained familiar to subsequent generations of comedy fans, and the astoundingly deep pool of writing talent that worked for Caesar and company has attained almost legendary status. Actually, "legendary" is a good description, because a lot of it is myth, at least who did what, and when, during that golden age of televised comedy. One common mistake is that skits performed for *Caesar's Hour,* the comedian's successor to *Your Show of Shows,* are wrongly attributed to *Your Show of Shows* instead. The most widespread error, though, is crediting Woody Allen as one of the *Your Show of Shows* writers. He wasn't. Neither was Larry Gelbart, although he and Allen worked for Caesar later—much later. Because all three of these variety series were so crucial to the development of televised comedy, and because so much misinformation has been spread about them over the decades, consider this an effort to set the facts straight and to give each series its individual due. I come not to bury Caesar, but to praise him—highly.

Admiral Broadway Revue (1949). Every word in this show's title turns out to have special significance. Its sponsor was Admiral, which underwrote the series in hopes of selling more of its TV sets; it was telecast live from a Broadway theater; and, as a revue, it was decidedly different from anything else on the air. *Admiral Broadway Revue* premiered on January 28, 1949, only four months after Milton Berle had been designated as permanent host of *Texaco Star Theater*—and almost immediately, *Admiral Broadway Revue* began dominating Friday nights on TV just as Berle was dominating Tuesdays. Yet the two shows, while similarly exciting, were quite different. Berle basically transplanted vaudeville routines and jokes to television, while *Admiral Broadway Revue* presented extended character-driven and satirical sketches, along with ballet, opera, and solo comedy and pantomime spots. The concept for the show had been transplanted virtually intact from Pennsylvania's Pocono Mountains, where, from 1934–40 and again in 1948, writer-producer

Max Liebman had created a weekly stage show for the Tamiment adult summer camp. Danny Kaye had been discovered during the early years at Tamiment, and a young comedienne named Imogene Coca became a star of the 1948 version. Six months later, Liebman took the Tamiment stage-revue concept, and Coca, and another comic named Sid Caesar (for whom Liebman had provided comic material on several occasions), and sold them to Sylvester "Pat" Weaver, who in turn sold them to NBC. (DuMont also bought the show, running it simultaneously on Friday nights as one of the few instances of a dual-network series simulcast.) *Admiral Broadway Revue* was an immediate hit, featuring guest stars such as Rex Harrison, choreography by James Starbuck (with Marge and Gower Champion and Bob Fosse among the featured dancers), and such popular sketches as "Nonentities in the News," in which regular cast member Tom Avera played the straight-man interviewer to such crazy characters as Caesar's humorously ignorant "know-it-all" professor. Coca shared leading lady status with Mary McCarthy, and the writers on *Admiral Broadway Revue* were Liebman, Lucille Kallen, and Mel Tolkin; Mel Brooks hung around and contributed, but received little money and even less credit. The series ran for only nineteen weeks, from January to June, and was such a big hit that the sales of Admiral TV sets, over the same period, went from eight hundred per week to ten thousand. Ironically, in a stunning case of corporate shortsightedness, Admiral executives decided to take the money they were spending to sponsor *Admiral Broadway Revue* and earmark it for factory production instead, to help meet the demand for TV sets that the program had created. A victim of its own success, *Admiral Broadway Revue* was canceled by the sponsor. But Liebman, Caesar, Coca, and NBC all wanted to keep going, so *Your Show of Shows* was born.

Your Show of Shows (1950–54). This series was NBC's, and television's, original *Saturday Night Live*. It was ninety minutes of live comedy and variety on Saturday nights, with a weekly guest host (for the first two weeks of *Your Show of Shows*, it was Burgess Meredith) and a heavy emphasis on satire. Caesar, like most of the others on or behind the show, was in his twenties, making it a young person's game and an irreverent, no-rules TV sandbox. On camera, Tom Avera was replaced by Carl Reiner the first season, and Howard Morris joined a year later (in 1951), completing the comedy quartet that made *Your Show of Shows* so famous: Sid Caesar, Imogene Coca, Carl Reiner, and Howard Morris. Robert Merrill was a featured singer the first season, James Starbuck stayed for the duration as choreographer (and, with Coca, starred in a series of memorable ballet spoofs), guest stars were plentiful and talented (the series was commendably color-blind when it came to presenting musical talent, offering early showcases for Pearl Bailey, Nat "King" Cole, and Lena Horne), and the writing staff was incredible. Mel Brooks didn't get full credit as a writer, or get put on the regular payroll, for two years, but was there from the start. So were Caesar, Max Liebman, Mel Tolkin, and Lucille Kallen, all from *Admiral Broadway Revue*. (All of whom, unlike Brooks, were duly credited and handsomely salaried.) Shortly after *Your Show of Shows* started, Reiner worked his way into the writers' room, and another permanent staff

Your Show of Shows, with Sid Caesar and Imogene Coca.

writer joining early was Tony Webster, who had written for Bob Elliott and Ray Goulding (and who later would write for *The Phil Silvers Show*). Joe Stein was added to the show near the end of its run, and when Kallen took maternity leave for a season in 1952, her substitutes for that year, and that year only, were Danny Simon and his little brother, Neil. Together, these writers created, and the performers embodied, sheer comic brilliance. Watching a full ninety-minute show was like watching a marathon, and the participants looked nearly as weary as if they'd run one. One running sketch, so to speak, was called "The Hickenloopers," and starred Caesar and Coca as the invariably feuding married couple Charlie and Doris. It was a *Your Show of Shows* staple that predated even Jackie Gleason's earliest "Honeymooners" sketches on Du-Mont's *Cavalcade of Stars;* the first time Gleason stepped into the role of Ralph Kramden was on October 5, 1951, more than a year after *Your Show of Shows* and "The Hickenloopers" were up and running. (A sample exchange: When Doris Hickenlooper plaintively asks, "Where did our romance disappear?," her weary husband Charlie grumbles, "How do I know where you put things? I can't even find my shirts.") Caesar's "Professor" character, in the "Nonentities in the News" interviews (with Reiner taking over the straight-man chores), was another classic element, and *Your Show of Shows* was rightly renowned, and widely remembered, for its extended satires of hit movies, foreign films, Broadway plays, other television series, and even ballets and operas. "From Here to Obscurity" had Caesar and Coca embracing on the beach while being buffeted by buckets of water; "A Trolleycar Named Desire" featured Caesar doing a Marlon Brando impersonation that hinted at the madness in Brando's method acting. *The Blue Angel, Shane,* and *The Bicycle Thief* were other memorable parodies, and perhaps the most famous of all is Caesar's hilariously reluctant turn as Al Duncey, Reiner's biographical subject in a *This Is Your Life* satire called "This is Your Story." That last sketch is on view in *Ten from Your Show of Shows,* as is my personal favorite famous sequence, when Caesar, Coca, Reiner, and Morris, dressed as life-sized Bavarian action figures, portrayed malfunctioning mechanisms in a town belfry—hammering and otherwise abusing each other like a clockwork quartet equivalent of Ernie Kovacs's Nairobi Trio. How Caesar and company ever got through that extended sequence on live TV without cracking each other up is a major media mystery. (I also confess a pronounced fondness for one of Caesar's oddball doctor characters, who prescribed near-drowning as a cure for amnesia—the reasoning being that as the forgetful patient approached death, his whole life would flash before his eyes.) The core company of *Your Show of Shows* worked brilliantly together, and just as brilliantly apart: most shows featured one solo segment each by Coca and Caesar. Perhaps that, as much as NBC's desire to spread the show's success around the schedule, led to the dissolution and fragmentation of *Your Show of Shows* while the series still was at the top of its game. Caesar went one way, Coca another, and everyone else had to decide where, and with whom, to go next. The final installment of *Your Show of Shows,* on June 5, 1954, ended with guest hostess Faye Emerson and the regular cast standing downstage, holding hands, and saying good-bye, much as the *Saturday Night Live* company still does today. For *Your Show of Shows*, however, it was the final curtain call.

Caesar's Hour (1954–57). Both Caesar and Coca returned to NBC with new series in the fall of 1954. In the custody battle for writers from *Your Show of Shows*, Coca got Lucille Kallen, Mel Brooks, and Tony Webster, and soon added Ernest Kinoy. Yet *The Imogene Coca Show* was revamped three times during its one season on the air, going from sitcom to variety series and back again, never quite clicking creatively or with an audience. *Caesar's Hour*, however, was a different story. Caesar, Reiner, and Morris all continued their association as costars, adding Nanette Fabray and other regulars to the mix— including, in the show's final season, Bea Arthur and an announcer named Hugh Downs. In the writers' room, *Caesar's Hour* was an embarrassment of riches. In addition to Caesar and Reiner, it boasted Mel Tolkin, Danny and Neil Simon, Selma Diamond, and, for the first two years, Larry Gelbart. After Coca's show folded, Mel Brooks returned to the fold; another writing addition was Mike Stewart, who later wrote *Hello, Dolly* and *Bye, Bye Birdie*. Guest stars often appeared (Gina Lollobrigida appeared in the opening show), and *Caesar's Hour* created many classic comedy segments in its own right. These included "The Three Haircuts," in which a bewigged Caesar, Reiner, and Morris lampooned, yet oddly presaged, the anything-goes rock movement; "The Commuters," which established a group of characters as familiar and entertaining as "The Hickenloopers" from *Your Show of Shows*; and, as another favorite example of ambitious TV comedy, "A Drunk There Was," a forty-three-minute silent-movie skit built around "the shot heard round the world" (and a very sober comment on Caesar's problems with alcohol at the time). *Caesar's Hour* lasted for three very strong years, after which Caesar mounted two noteworthy 1958 ventures before slipping out of the spotlight. One was a fifteen-episode summer series, *The Sid Caesar Show*, produced and presented in England for the BBC (where Caesar's mostly recycled routines were received quite warmly). The other, back in America on NBC, was an all-new variety special called *The Chevy Show*, presented on November 2, 1958, and teaming star Caesar and writer Gelbart, for the first time, with a young writer named Woody Allen.

To give Caesar all that is due Caesar is to credit him not only with providing a nurturing ground for an entire generation of comedy writers, producers, directors, and performers, but with proving that satire could live and thrive on commercial network television. *That Was the Week That Was, The Smothers Brothers Comedy Hour, Rowan & Martin's Laugh-In, Saturday Night Live,* and *Second City TV* all have Caesar and company to thank. As do we all. And for what it was like to work in the writers' rooms, look no further than the movie *My Favorite Year,* or to Neil Simon's own Broadway staging of those silly salad days, *Laughter on the 23rd Floor.* They, too, are part of the valuable legacy of *Your Show of Shows* and its sister series.

Z

. . . .

Zorro. *1957–59, ABC*. "Out of the night / When the full moon is bright /
Comes a horseman known as Zorro . . . / Zorro, the fox so cunning and free /
Zorro, who makes the sign of the Z!" That great theme song, and that famous
scene of Zorro astride a rearing horse (like *The Lone Ranger*, except in silhouette against a dark and stormy night), each week opened Walt Disney's *Zorro*
series, the studio's most famous TV do-gooder after *Davy Crockett*. Based on
a character first introduced by Johnston McCulley in a 1919 magazine serial,
ABC's *Zorro* had been preceded by a phenomenally popular series of novels,
and by Hollywood films starring some of the most athletic and dashing leading
men of their day (Douglas Fairbanks in the twenties, Tyrone Power in the
forties). Walt Disney decided the story, set in the eighteen-twenties and telling of a "foppish" aristocrat by day who doubled as a costumed avenger at
night, was perfect for TV. (And why not, since the basic concept long predated
the similar comic-book origin of Batman?). Disney, as it turned out, was crazy
like a *Zorro*—which is the Spanish word for "fox." So Disney, looking for a
suitable actor to play Don Diego de la Vega, a.k.a. Zorro, castanet and found
Armando Catalano, who a few years before had changed his name to Guy
Williams. *Zorro's* basic adversaries throughout the series were the equally
inept Captain Monastario (Britt Lomond) and his lazy and corpulent Sergeant
García (Henry Calvin), essentially the Spanish precursors of Colonel Klink
and Sergeant Schultz on *Hogan's Heroes*. Gene Sheldon, as Don Diego's mute
servant Bernardo, was the show's best actor, even though he had the fewest
lines. In 1960, the year after *Zorro* was canceled, a few episodes were cobbled
together into a feature film, *The Sign of Zorro*, employing a trick Disney had
used earlier with *Davy Crockett*. After that, the *Zorro* name (and cape, and
mask, and zigzagging sword) were resurrected several times, but never with
much respect or effectiveness. Frank Langella and Ricardo Montalban starred
in a 1975 ABC telemovie called *The Mark of Zorro*, and Duncan Regehr and
Efrem Zimbalist, Jr., starred in a TV series *Zorro* revival for The Family
Channel in 1990, the only times American pop culture revisited the *Zorro*
character in a serious vein. Otherwise, Henry Darrow played an aging Don
Diego de la Vega, and Paul Regina played his similarly swashbuckling offspring, in the 1983 CBS sitcom *Zorro and Son;* and George Hamilton played
Don Diego's twin sons, one of which took "foppishness" to a whole new level,
in the 1981 movie comedy *Zorro, The Gay Blade*. But it was the original
Disney series that counts in teleliteracy terms—especially since that show's
prominent guest stars included *The Mickey Mouse Club* Mouseketeer Annette Funicello (as a singing señorita), Neil Hamilton (who later worked alongside another caped crusader by playing Commissioner Gordon on *Batman*),

and Jonathan Harris (who subsequently teamed with the star of *Zorro* on another series, playing Dr. Zachary Smith to Williams's John Robinson on *Lost in Space*). And now that this final entry is over and the *Dictionary of Teleliteracy* completed, I'm going to emulate *Zorro*—and make the sign of the z-z-z-z-z-z-z. . . .

BIBLIOGRAPHY

Aldrin, Buzz, and Malcolm McConnell. *Men from Earth*. New York: Bantam Books, 1989.

Allen, Steve. *Mark It and Strike It*. New York: Holt, Rinehart and Winston, 1960.

———. *Meeting of Minds*. Los Angeles: Hubris House, 1978.

———. *Meeting of Minds: Second Series*. New York: Crown Publishers, 1979.

Allen, William Rodney. *Conversations with Kurt Vonnegut*. Jackson, Mississippi: University Press of Mississippi, 1988.

Alley, Robert S. and Irby B. Brown. *Love Is All Around: The Making of The Mary Tyler Moore Show*. New York: Delta, 1989.

Andacht, Sandra. *Joe Franklin's Show Biz Memorabilia*. Lombard, Illinois: Wallace-Homestead Book Company, 1985.

Anderson, Jack. "Jerry's Telethon under Fire," *New York Post* (June 27, 1981), p. 9.

Andrews, Bart. *The "I Love Lucy" Book*. Garden City, New York: Dolphin Books, 1985.

Anobile, Richard. *The Making of Rich Man, Poor Man*. New York: Berkeley Medallion Books, 1976.

Applebaum, Irwyn. *The World According to Beaver*. New York: Bantam Books, 1984.

Asherman, Allan. *The Star Trek Compendium*. New York: Pocket Books, 1986.

Aylesworth, Thomas G. *Great Moments of Television*. New York: Exeter Books, 1987.

Barnouw, Erik. *Documentary*. Revised edition. New York: Oxford University Press, 1983.

———. *The Image Empire: A History of Broadcasting in the United States, Volume III—From 1953*. New York: Oxford University Press, 1970.

———. *Tube of Plenty*. 2nd revised edition. New York: Oxford University Press, 1990.

Bartlett, John, edited by Justin Kaplan. *Bartlett's Familiar Quotations*, sixteenth edition. Boston: Little, Brown and Co., 1992.

BBC Television: Fifty Years. New York: Museum of Broadcasting, 1986.

Beatts, Anne, and John Head, eds. *Saturday Night Live*. New York: Avon Books, 1977.

Bergan, Ronald, Graham Fuller, and David Malcolm. *Academy Award Winners*. New York: Crescent Books, 1986.

Beck, Ken, and Jim Clark. *The Andy Griffith Show Book*. New York: St. Martin's Press, 1985.

Bianculli, David. "Laugh-Track Record," *New York Daily News* (May 16, 1993), "City Lights," pp. 16–17.

———. "Networks Turn into Instant Rumor Mills," *Akron Beacon Journal* (March 30, 1981), p. C5.

———. "Still Flying High," *New York Post* (March 23, 1989), p. 124.

———. "The Subject Executives Shun for TV," *Philadelphia Inquirer* (February 5, 1984), pp. M1, M10.

———. *Teleliteracy: Taking Television Seriously*. New York: Continuum, 1992.

BIB Television Programming Source Books: Series, 1992–93. Philadelphia: North American Publishing Co., 1992.

Bleum, A. William. *Documentary in American Television*. New York: Hastings House, 1965.

Bliss, Edward, Jr. *Now the News*. New York: Columbia University Press, 1991.

Block, Alex Ben. *Outfoxed*. New York: St. Martin's Press, 1990.

Boddy, William. *Fifties Television*. Urbana, Illinois: University of Illinois Press, 1990.

Bogle, Donald. *Blacks in American Films and Television: An Illustrated Encyclopedia*. New York: Fireside Books, 1989.

Bordman, Gerald. *The Concise Oxford Companion to American Theatre*. New York: Oxford University Press, 1987.

Breslin, Jack. *America's Most Wanted: How Television Catches Crooks*. New York: Harper & Row, 1990.

Briggs, Asa. *The BBC: The First Fifty Years*. Oxford: Oxford University Press, 1985.

Bronson, Fred. *The Billboard Book of Number One Hits*. Revised and enlarged edition. New York: Billboard Publications, 1988.

Brooks, Tim. *The Complete Directory to Prime Time TV Stars*. New York: Ballantine Books, 1987.

Brooks, Tim, and Earle Marsh. *The Complete Directory to Prime Time Network TV Shows, 1946–Present*. 5th edition. New York: Ballantine Books, 1992.

Brown, Les. *Les Brown's Encyclopedia of Television*. 3rd edition. Detroit: Visible Ink Press, 1992.

Burke, James. *Connections*. Boston: Little, Brown & Company, 1978.

Burros, Marian. "For Julia Child, an Intimate Dinner for 500," *New York Times* (February 10, 1993), pp. C1, C6.

Caesar, Sid, with Bill Davidson. *Where Have I Been?: An Autobiography*. New York: Crown Publishing, 1983.

Campbell, Joseph. *The Power of Myth, with Bill Moyers*. New York: Doubleday, 1988.

Canton, Maj. *Maj Canton's Complete Reference Guide to Movies and Miniseries, Made for TV and Cable, 1984–1994*. Fair Oaks, California: Adams-Blake Publishing, 1994.

Castleman, Harry, and Walter J. Podrazik. *Harry and Wally's Favorite TV Shows*. New York: Prentice Hall Press, 1989.

Cavett, Dick, and Christopher Porterfield. *Cavett*. New York: Bantam Books, 1974.

Chaikin, Andrew. *A Man on the Moon: The Voyages of the Apollo Astronauts*. New York: Penguin Books, 1994.

Chunovic, Louis. *The Northern Exposure Book*. New York: Citadel Press, 1993.

Cleese, John, and Connie Booth. *The Complete Fawlty Towers*. New York: Pantheon Books, 1988.

Coe, Sebastian, with David Teasdale and David Wickham. *More Than a Game: Sport in Our Time*. London: BBC Books, 1992.

Coffey, Frank. *60 Minutes: 25 Years of Television's Finest Hour*. Los Angeles: General Publishing Group, 1993.

Collins, Ace. *Lassie: A Dog's Life*. New York: Cader Books, 1993.

Cooke, Alistair. *Masterpieces: A Decade of Masterpiece Theatre*. New York: VNU Books International, 1981.

Copeland, Mary Ann, contributing author. *Soap Opera History*. Lincolnwood, Illinois: Mallard Press, 1991.

Coupland, Douglas. *Generation X: Tales for an Accelerated Culture*. New York: St. Martin's Press, 1991.

Cowan, Geoffrey. *See No Evil*. New York: Simon and Schuster, 1979.

Cox, Stephen. *The Hooterville Handbook: A Viewer's Guide to Green Acres*. New York: St. Martin's Press, 1993.

Crescenti, Peter, and Bob Columbe. *The Official Honeymooners Treasury*. Expanded edition. New York: Perigee Books, 1990.

David, Nina. *TV Season 74–75*. Phoenix, Arizona: Oryx Press, 1976.

Davis, Gerry. *The Today Show: An Anecdotal History of the First Thirty-Five Years*. New York: William Morrow and Company, 1987.

Davis, Stephen. *Say Kids! What Time Is It?* Boston: Little, Brown & Company, 1987.

Dawidziak, Mark. *The Columbo Phile*. New York: Mysterious Press, 1988.

———. *Night Stalking: A 20th Anniversary Kolchak Companion*. New York: Image Publishing, 1991.

Dayan, Daniel, and Elihu Katz. *Media Events: The Live Broadcasting of History*. Cambridge, Massachusetts: Harvard University Press, 1992.

DeLong, *Quiz Craze: America's Infatuation With Quiz Shows*. New York: Praeger, 1991.

Denis, Christopher Paul, and Michael Denis. *Favorite Families of TV*. New York: Citadel Press, 1992.

DeRosa, Robin. "Taking up Mason's Crusade for Justice," *USA Today* (December 17, 1993), p. 3D.

Douglas, Mike. *Mike Douglas: My Story*. New York: G. P. Putnam's Sons, 1978.

Dunning, John. *Tune in Yesterday: The Ultimate Encyclopedia of Old-Time Radio, 1925–1976*. Englewood Cliffs, New Jersey: Prentice-Hall, 1976.

Eisner, Joel. *The Official Batman Batbook*. Chicago: Contemporary Books, 1986.

————, and Barry Magen. *Lost in Space Forever*. Staunton, Virginia: Windsong Publishing, 1992.

Ely, Melvin Patrick. *The Adventures of Amos 'n' Andy: A Social History of an American Phenomenon*. New York: The Free Press, 1991.

Emery, Fred. *Watergate: The Corruption of American Politics and the Fall of Richard Nixon*. New York: Times Books, 1994.

Erickson, Hal. *Syndicated Television: The First Forty Years, 1947–1987*. Jefferson, North Carolina: McFarland & Company, 1989.

Essoe, Gabe. *The Book of TV Lists*. Westport, Connecticut: Arlington House, 1981.

Feuer, Jane, Paul Kerr, and Tise Vahimagi. *MTM: Quality Television*. London: British Film Institute, 1984.

Finch, Christopher. *Of Muppets and Men: The Making of The Muppet Show*. New York: Alfred A. Knopf, 1981.

Fischer, Stuart. *Kids' TV: The First 25 Years*. New York: Facts on File Publications, 1983.

Fishbein, Leslie. " 'Roots': Docudrama and the Interpretation of History," *American History/American Television*, John E. O'Connor, ed. New York: Frederick Ungar Publishing, 1985.

Fisher, David J. *The Music of Disney: A Legacy in Song*, CD booklet. Burbank, California: Walt Disney Records, 1992.

Floyd, Patty Lou. *Backstairs with Upstairs, Downstairs*. New York: St. Martin's Press, 1988.

Franklin, Joe. *Joe Franklin's Movie Trivia*. Mamaroneck, New York: Hastings House, 1992.

Fretts, Bruce. *The Entertainment Weekly Seinfeld Companion*. New York: Warner Books, 1993.

Fricke, John, Jay Scarfone, and William Stillman. *The Wizard of Oz: The Official 50th Anniversary Pictorial History*. New York: Warner Books, 1989.

Frost, David. *An Autobiography*. London: HarperCollins, 1993.

————. *"I Gave Them a Sword": Behind the Scenes of the Nixon Interviews*. New York: William Morrow, 1978.

Garay, Ronald. *Congressional Television: A Legislative History*. Westport, Connecticut: Greenwood Press, 1984.

George, Nelson. *In Living Color: The Authorized Companion to the Fox TV Series*. New York: Warner Books, 1991.

Gianakos, Larry James. *Television Drama Series Programming: A Comprehensive Chronicle, 1947–1959*. Metuchen, New Jersey: Scarecrow Press, 1980.

————. *Television Drama Series Programming: A Comprehensive Chronicle, 1959–1975*. Metuchen, New Jersey: Scarecrow Press, 1980.

Goldberg, Lee. *Television Series Revivals: Sequels or Remakes of Cancelled Shows*. Jefferson, North Carolina: McFarland & Co., 1993.

Goldstein, Fred, and Stan Goldstein. *Prime-Time Televison: A Pictorial History from Milton Berle to "Falcon Crest."* New York: Crown Publishers, 1983.

Graham, Jefferson. "Part 2 of a 'Peanuts' Christmas," *USA Today* (November 27, 1992), p. D3.

Greenfield, Jeff. *Television: The First Fifty Years*. New York: Crescent Books, 1981.

Green, Joey. *The Unofficial Gilligan's Island Handbook*. New York: Warner Books, 1988.

Green, Stanley. *The Great Clowns of Broadway*. New York: Oxford University Press, 1984.

Gross, Ben. *I Looked and I Listened: Informal Recollections of Radio and TV*. New York: Random House, 1954.

Gross, Edward. *The Unofficial Story of the Making of a Wiseguy*. Las Vegas: Pioneer Books, 1990.

Gross, Larry. *The L. A. Law Book*. Las Vegas: Pioneer Books, 1991.

Grossman, Gary H. *Saturday Morning TV*. New York: Dell, 1981.

Gunther, Marc. *The House That Roone Built*. Boston: Little, Brown and Co., 1994.

————, and Bill Carter. *Monday Night Mayhem: The Inside Story of ABC's Monday Night Football*. New York: Beech Tree Books, 1988.

Halberstam, David. *The Powers That Be*. New York: Dell Publishing, 1986.

Hall, Bruce Edward. " 'Romper Room' Signs off for Good," *New York Times* (July 31, 1994), p. H28.

Halliwell, Leslie. *Halliwell's Film Guide*. Sixth edition. New York: Charles Scribner's Sons, 1987.

————, with Philip Purser. *Halliwell's Television Companion*. Second edition. London: Granada Publishing, 1982.

Hansen, Barry. CD liner notes, *Dr. Demento 20th Anniversary Collection: The Greatest Novelty Records of All Time*. Santa Monica, California: Rhino Records, 1991.

Harris, Jay S., editor and compiler. *TV Guide: The First 25 Years*. New York: Simon and Schuster, 1978.

Harmetz, Aljean. *The Making of the Wizard of Oz*. New York: Limelight Editions, 1984.

Hawes, William. *American Television Drama: the Experimental Years*. University, Alabama: The University of Alabama Press, 1986.

Heldenfels, R. D. *Television's Greatest Year: 1954*. New York: Continuum, 1994.

Henry, William A. III. *The Great One: The Life and Legend of Jackie Gleason*. New York: Doubleday, 1992.

Hill, Doug, and Jeff Weingrad. *Saturday Night: A Backstage History of Saturday Night Live*. New York: Birch Tree Books, 1986.

Hirsch, E. D., Jr., Joseph F. Kett, and James Trefil. *The Dictionary of Cultural Literacy*. Boston: Houghton Mifflin, 1988.

Holbrook, Hal. *Mark Twain Tonight!* New York: Ives Washburn Inc., 1959.

Jack Benny: The Radio and Television Work. New York: HarperPerennial, 1991.

Jacobs, Norman, and Kerry O'Quinn. *Starlog Photo Guidebook of TV Episode Guides*, Volume 1. New York: Starlog Press, 1981.

Jamieson, Kathleen Hall. *Eloquence in an Electronic Age*. New York: Oxford University Press, 1988.

————. *Packaging the Presidency*. Oxford: Oxford University Press, 1984.

————, and David S. Birdsell. *Presidential Debates*. New York: Oxford University Press, 1988.

Javna, John. *Cult TV: A Viewer's Guide to the Shows America Can't Do Without!!* New York: St. Martin's Press, 1985.

————. *The TV Theme Song Sing Along Song Book, Volume 2*. New York: St. Martin's Press, 1985.

Jim Henson's World of Television. New York: Museum of Television & Radio, 1993.

Johnson, Kim "Howard." *The First 200 Years of Monty Python*. New York: St. Martin's Press, 1989.

Jones, Gerard. *Honey, I'm Home!: Sitcoms, Selling the American Dream*. New York: St. Martin's Press, 1992.

Katler, Suzy. *The Complete Book of Dallas*. New York: Harry N. Abrams, Inc., 1986.

Kass, Judith M. *Robert Altman: American Innovator*. New York: Popular Library, 1978.

King, Larry, with Mark Stencel. *On the Line: The New Road to the White House*. New York: Harcourt Brace & Company, 1993.

Kisseloff, Jeff. *The Box: An Oral History of Television, 1920–1961*. New York: Viking, 1995.

Klatell, David A., and Norman Marcus. *Sports for Sale: Television, Money, and the Fans*. New York: Oxford University Press, 1988.

Kuralt, Charles. *On the Road with Charles Kuralt*. New York: Random House, 1985.

Lackmann, Ron. *Remember Television*. New York: G. P. Putnam's Sons, 1971.

LaGuardia, Robert. *Soap World*. New York: Arbor House, 1983.

Lang, Kurt, and Gladys Engel Lang. *Politics and Television*. Chicago: Quadrangle Books, 1968.

Lathan, Caroline. *The David Letterman Story: An Unauthorized Biography*. New York: Franklin Watts, 1987.

Lavery, David. *Full of Secrets: Critical Approaches to Twin Peaks*. Detroit: Wayne State University Press, 1995.

Lefcowitz, Eric. *The Monkees Tale*. San Francisco: Last Gasp, 1985.

Lenburg, Jeff. *The Encyclopedia of Animated Cartoon Series*. New York: De Capo Press, 1983.

Leonard Bernstein: The Television Work. New York: The Museum of Broadcasting, 1985.

Lewis, Jon E., and Penny Stempel. *Cult TV*. London: Pavilion Books, 1993.

Lewisohn, Mark. *The Beatles Recording Sessions*. New York: Harmony Books, 1990.

Lovece, Frank. *The Television Yearbook*. New York: Perigee Books, 1992.

————, and Jules Franco. *Hailing Taxi*. New York: Prentice Hall Press, 1988.

MacDonald, J. Fred. *Blacks and White TV: Afro-Americans in Television Since 1948*. Chicago: Nelson-Hall Publishers, 1983.

McCarty, John, and Brian Kelleher. *Alfred Hitchcock Presents*. New York: St. Martin's Press, 1985.

McCrohan, Donna. *The Life and Times of Maxwell Smart*. New York: St. Martin's Press, 1988.

————. *The Second City*. New York: Perigee Books, 1987.

————, and Peter Crescenti. *The Honeymooners Lost Episodes*. New York: Workman Publishing, 1986.

McMurtry, Larry. *Film Flam*. New York: Touchstone Books, 1987.

McNeil, Alex. *Total Television: A Comprehensive Guide to Programming from 1948 to the Present*. 3rd edition. New York: Penguin Books, 1991.

Making of James Clavell's Shogun, The. New York: Dell Publishing Co., 1980.

Making of The Jewel in the Crown, The. New York: St. Martin's Press, 1983.

Maksian, George. "Jerry Lewis Lines up a 'King,' " *New York Daily News* (August 19, 1977), p. 61.

Maltin, Leonard. *Leonard Maltin's TV Movies and Video Guide*. 1993 Edition. New York: Signet, 1993.

Marc, David. *Comic Visions: Television Comedy and American Culture*. Boston: Unwin Hyman, 1989.

————, and Robert J. Thompson. *Prime Time, Prime Movers*. Boston: Little, Brown and Company, 1992.

Marill, Alvin H. *Movies Made for Television: The Telefeature and the Mini-Series, 1964–1986*. New York: Zoetrope Press, 1987.

Martin, Rick. "Dave vs. Jay, CBS, Oscar . . . ," *Newsweek* (July 10, 1995), pp. 52–53.

Markoe, Merrill, editor. *Late Night With David Letterman: The Book*. New York: Villard Books, 1985.

Martindale, David. *The Rockford Phile*. Las Vegas: Pioneer Books, 1991.

Meyers, Richard. *TV Detectives*. San Diego, California: A. S. Barnes & Co., 1981.

Miller, Arthur. *Death of a Salesman*. New York: Viking Press, 1949.

Milton Berle: Mr. Television. New York: The Museum of Broadcasting, 1985.

Mitz, Rick. *The Great TV Sitcom Book*. New York: Richard Marek Publishers, 1980.

Montgomery, Kathryn C. *Target: Prime Time: Advocacy Groups and the Struggle over Entertainment Television*. New York: Oxford University Press, 1989.

Morrow, Lance. "But Seriously, Folks . . . ," *Time* (June 1, 1992), pp. 29–31.

Murrow, Edward R., and Fred W. Friendly. *See It Now*. New York: Simon & Schuster, 1955.

Nalven, Nancy. *The Famous Mister Ed*. New York: Warner Books, 1991.

Niccoli, Christopher. CD liner notes, *Original Music From the Addams Family*, Vic Mizzy, composer. New York: RCA Victor, 1991.

O'Neil. *The Emmys: Star Wars, Showdowns, and the Supreme Test of TV's Best*. New York: Penguin Books, 1992.

Paar, Jack. *I Kid You Not*. Boston: Little, Brown and Company, 1960.

Parish, James Robert. *Let's Talk! America's Favorite Talk Show Hosts*. Las Vegas: Pioneer Books, 1993.

Perry, George. *Life of Python*. Boston: Little, Brown and Co., 1983.

Perry, Jeb H. *Universal Television: The Studio and Its Programs, 1950–1980*. Metuchen, New Jersey: Scarecrow Press, 1983.

Potter, Dennis. *The Singing Detective*. New York: Vintage Books, 1988.

Powers, Ron. *Supertube: The Rise of Television Sports*. New York: Coward-McCann, 1984.

Quinlan, Sterling. *Inside ABC: American Broadcasting Company's Rise to Power*. New York: Hastings House, 1979.

Rader, Benjamin G. *In Its Own Image: How Television Has Transformed Sports*. New York: Free Press, 1984.

Rico, Diana. *Kovacsland: A Biography of Ernie Kovacs*. San Diego, California: Harcourt Brace Jovanovich, 1990.

Ritchie, Michael. *Please Stand By: A Prehistory of Television*. Woodstock, New York: Overlook Press, 1994.

Rogers, Dave. *The Complete Avengers*. New York: St. Martin's Press, 1989.

Rolling Stone Rock Almanac. New York: Collier, 1983.

Rubin, Leon. *The Nicholas Nickleby Story*. Middlesex, England: Penguin Books, 1981.

Sackett, Susan. *Prime Time-Hits: Television's Most Popular Network Programs, 1950 to the Present*. New York: Billboard Books, 1993.

————, and Cheryl Blythe. *Say Good-Night, Gracie!* New York: E. P. Dutton, 1986.

Sandahl, Linda J. *Rock Films*. New York: Facts on File Publications, 1987.

Sander, Gordon F. *Serling: the Rise and Twilight of Television's Last Angry Man*. New York: Dutton, 1992.

Sandoval, Andrew. CD liner notes, *The Monkees: Listen to the Band*. Santa Monica, California: Rhino Records, 1991.

Sanford, Herb. *Ladies and Gentlemen, The Garry Moore Show*. New York: Stein and Day, 1976.

Schemering, Christopher. *The Soap Opera Encyclopedia*. New York: Ballantine Books, 1985.

Schickel, Richard. *The Disney Version*. New York: Avon Books, 1969.

Schmertz, Herb. Interview with author, 1983.

Schow, David J., and Jeffrey Frentzen. *The Outer Limits: The Official Companion*. New York: Ace Science Fiction Books, 1986.

Schumer, Arlen. *Visions from the Twilight Zone*. San Francisco: Chronicle Books, 1990.

Seminars at the Museum of Broadcasting: Larry Gelbart. Museum of Broadcasting, October 1984.

Sennett, Ted. *Your Show of Shows*. New York: Collier Books, 1977.

Settel, Irving. *A Pictorial History of Radio*. New York: Grosset & Dunlap, 1971.

———, editor. *Top TV Shows of the Year, 1954–55*. New York: Hastings House, 1955.

Shapiro, Mitchell E. *Television Network Daytime and Late-Night Programming, 1959–1989*. Jefferson, North Carolina: McFarland & Company, 1990.

Shapiro, Walter. "What Debates Don't Tell Us," *Time* (October 19, 1992), pp. 32–33.

Shepard, Alan, and Deke Slayton. *Moon Shot: The Inside Story of America's Race to the Moon*. Atlanta: Turner Publishing, 1994.

Shulman, Arthur, and Roger Youman. *How Sweet It Was*. New York: Bonanza Books, 1966.

Simmons, Garner. *Peckinpah: A Portrait in Montage*. Austin, Texas: University of Texas Press, 1982.

Slide, Anthony. *Selected Radio and Television Criticism*. Metuchen, New Jersey: Scarecrow Press, 1987.

Spector, Bert. "A Clash of Cultures: The Smothers Brothers vs. CBS Television," *America History/American Television*, John E. O'Connor, ed. New York: Frederick Ungar Publishing, 1985.

Sperber, A. M. *Murrow: His Life and Times*. New York: Freundlich Books, 1986.

Stein, Ben. *Fernwood, U.S.A.* New York: Simon & Schuster, 1977.

Stempel, Tom. *Storytellers to the Nation: A History of American Television Writing*. New York: Continuum, 1992.

Stern, Jane, and Michael Stern. *Jane & Michael Stern's Encyclopedia of Pop Culture*. New York: HarperCollins, 1992.

Stock, Rip. *Odd Couple Mania*. New York: Ballantine Books, 1983.

Story, David. *America on the Rerun*. New York: Citadel Press, 1993.

Sturcken, Frank. *Live Television: The Golden Age of 1946–1958 in New York*. Jefferson, North Carolina: McFarland & Company, 1990.

Taylor, Philip M. *Steven Spielberg: The Man, His Movies, and Their Meaning*. New York: Continuum, 1992.

Teddy, Danny, with Bill Davidson. *Make Room for Danny*. New York: G. P. Putnam's Sons, 1991.

Terrace, Vincent. *Encyclopedia of Television: Series, Pilots and Specials, 1937–73*. New York: Zoetrope, 1986.

———. *Radio's Golden Years*. San Diego, California: A. S. Barnes, 1981.

———. *Television Character and Story Facts*. Jefferson, North Carolina: McFarland & Company, 1993.

———. *Television 1970–1980*. San Diego, California: A. S. Barnes, 1981.

Trebek, Alex, and Peter Barsocchini. *The Jeopardy! Book*. New York: HarperPerennial, 1990.

Truffaut, Francois. *Hitchcock/Truffaut*. Revised edition. New York: Touchstone Books, 1985.

Twenty Seasons of Mobil Masterpiece Theatre, 1971–1991. New York: Mobil Corporation, 1991.

Variety Television Reviews, Volume 4: 1951–53. New York: Garland Publishing, 1989.

Variety Television Reviews, Volume 5: 1954–56. New York: Garland Publishing, 1989.

Wallechinsky, David, and Irving Wallace. *The People's Almanac*. New York: Doubleday, 1975.

Walley, David G. *The Ernie Kovacs Phile*. New York: Bolder Books, 1975.

Walley, Wayne. "Super Bowl: Most-Watched TV Show Ever," *Electronic Media* (February 8, 1993), pp. 4, 23.

Ward, Geoffrey C., with Ric Burns and Ken Burns. *The Civil War: An Illustrated History*. New York: Alfred A. Knopf, 1990.

Weiner, Ed, and the editors of *TV Guide*. *The TV Guide TV Book*. New York: HarperPerennial, 1992.

Wertheim, Arthur Frank. "The Rise and Fall of Milton Berle," *American History/American Television*, John E. O'Connor, ed. New York: Frederick Ungar Publishing, 1985.

Wetterau, Bruce. *The New York Public Library Book of Chronologies*. New York: Prentice Hall, 1990.

Whitburn, Joel. *The Billboard Book of Top 40 Hits*. 4th edition. New York: Billboard Books, 1989.

White, Matthew, and Jaffer Ali. *The Official Prisoner Companion*. New York: Warner Books, 1988.

White, Patrick J. *The Complete Mission: Impossible Dossier*. New York: Avon Books, 1991.

Whittemore, Hank. *CNN: the Inside Story*. Boston: Little, Brown, 1990.

Who's Who on Television: A Fully Illustrated Guide to a Thousand of the Best Known Faces on British Television. London: Independent Television Books, 1980.

Wicking, Christopher and Tise Vahimagi. *The American Vein*. New York: E. P. Dutton, 1979.

Wilford, John Noble. "When We Were Racing with the Moon," *New York Times* (June 25, 1995), pp. H1, H22.

Williams, Martin. *TV: The Casual Art*. New York: Oxford University Press, 1982.

Willis, John. *Screen World 1979*. New York: Crown, 1979.

Willis, Susan. *The BBC Shakespeare Plays*. Chapel Hill, North Carolina: University of North Carolina Press, 1991.

Wilmut, Roger. *From Fringe to Flying Circus*. London: Methuen London Ltd., 1987.

Winship, Michael. *Television*. New York: Random House, 1988.

Wolper, David, and Quincy Troupe. *The Inside Story of T.V.'s 'Roots.'* New York: Warner Books, 1978.

Yagoda, Ben. *Will Rogers: A Biography*. New York: Alfred A. Knopf, 1993.

Zicree, Marc Scott. *The Twilight Zone Companion*. 2nd edition. Los Angeles: Silman-James Press, 1992.

Zoglin, Richard. "Talking Trash," *Time* (January 30, 1995), pp. 77–78.

ACKNOWLEDGMENTS

· ·

Evander Lomke, the managing editor of Continuum and the person who steered me through both this book and its *teleliteracy* predecessor, gets top billing this time around. Wrestling with a project that turned out to be years overdue and more than twice its original length, he dealt with all the delays, details, and extra work with not only infinite patience, but welcome enthusiasm. Had he not known and cared so much about television, this book not only would not exist in its present form, but would not exist, period.

Bruce Cassiday, like Evander, was masochistic enough to handle editing chores again this time around—and this time, in addition to catching a wide variety of errors large and small, he gets due credit, and my thanks, for educating me about the literary origins of *The Cisco Kid*.

In addition to Evander and Bruce, three others whose TV and writing opinions I value highly did me the favor of reading the manuscript in rough form, and their aggregate comments improved virtually every entry. Mark Dawidziak of the *Akron Beacon Journal*, Mike Naidus of CBS, and Ron Simon of the Museum of Television & Radio, thank you. (Many of the pictures in this book are from the archive of Mark Dawidziak.)

As a personal challenge and point of pride, I tried—but failed—to compile this book without any direct assistance. Not only did the people already named above contribute valuable thoughts and pose persuasive arguments, but invaluable outside help on specific entries, when all other sources ran dry, was provided by Ann Elliott of A. C. Nielsen and Glen Macnow (on the World Series); R. D. Heldenfels (on *Marty*); Jonathan Rosenthal, research services at New York's Museum of Television & Radio (on both *Marty* and Martin Luther King, Jr.); and Eric Luskin of New Jersey Network (on *Doctor Who*).

As with the first *Teleliteracy* book, I'd like, once again, to acknowledge the chain of people who encouraged me to keep pursuing this particular avenue of criticism. Mark Woodruff and Cathy Cook were the editors at *Taxi* magazine, now defunct, who ran my full-length "Teleliteracy" quiz and article in November 1989. Michael Leach, then president of Crossroad/Continuum, saw that article and thought there was a book in it. Six years later, it turns out there were two.

On the office front, I have to thank Jeff Weingrad, my TV editor at the *New York Daily News*, for cutting me slack when I most needed it. On the home office front, I have to thank Chris Sandell, my part-time assistant who helped me organize and deal with a full-time mess; without her to organize my tapes, files, and life, I'd still be on the letter "D."

Finally, on the home front, there are three people who deserve the most thanks of all. To Kathy, my wife, and Kristin and Mark, our children, I apologize for another three years of delayed promises, and thank you all, with lots of love, for being there—even when I wasn't.

Index of Names

Index of Titles